From Coast to Coast, Canada to Florida, New York to Hawaii, Italy to Japan . . . Here's What People are Saying About

THE EARTHQUAKE AMERICA FORGOT

Fascinating. Gripping. Incredible. Brilliant. Suspenseful. Vivid. Great. One of a Kind. Fantastic. Educational. Entertaining. A Masterpiece. A book with Heart. Like a Stephen King Novel. Like a James Michener Novel. Like a Steven Spielberg Movie. Informative. Scientifically correct. Easy readability. Impressive. Comprehensive. Exhaustive. Encyclopedic. Colorful. Tantalizing. Terrific. Engaging. Spell-binding. Must reading. Good work. Unforgettable. Melodramatic. Nicely done. A gold mine. Rewarding. A great read. A feast of fat things. Splendid. Remarkable. Extraordinary.

Absolutely marvelous. Exciting. Wonderful. A real pleasure. Enjoyable. A great resource. Well documented. Excellent. Entrancing. Profound. Insightful. Dramatic. Jam packed. An experience. Would make a great movie. Fun to read. Enough material for a TV mini-series. Honest. Scary. Uplifting. Captivating. A real page-turner. Important. Enlightening. Reads like a techno-thriller. Rich. Fabulous. Masterful. Intriguing. Painstaking research. Outstanding. Eloquent. Useful. Practical. Helpful. Extremely valuable. A must book. Beautifully written. The best book I have ever read on the New Madrid earthquakes.

What People Say about this book . . .

"A terrific account of this earthquake and period of time—both scientific and historical. With all the emphasis today on inter-disciplinary studies—Stewart and Knox have really hit it with this book. Very well done. Vivid images. Most enjoyable. A must reading for all earth science teachers. Good Work!"

Leonard Sharp, President
National Earth Science Teachers Assoc.
Cornelius, New York

"Great style! It flows well. Would make a good movie—like a James Michener novel.

"I started reading it on a Saturday. Once I got into it, I was hooked. I spent the whole day reading. Really enjoyable!

"It literally lifted the hair on the back of my neck when I read how the quakes rang church bells in Boston and woke President Madison in Washington.

"The experience of the steamboat on the Mississippi River was a totally new perspective for me. I had never realized how devastating a quake could be on the water.

"I also did not know that the Midwest has small quakes every year that do considerable damage, sometimes even at great distances. I found this very interesting.

"Overall, a fantastic book!"

Jack Wright, Engineer
Chino, California

"If you think you have heard all there is to hear about 'The Big One,' you are wrong. Dr. Stewart and Dr. Knox have unturned every stone in their research of the great New Madrid catastrophe of 1811-12 and then allow you to soak up all this information in a very enjoyable way, taking you back to the days of our ancestors and letting you relive their nightmare in your mind.

"For those of you thirsty for the facts, history and folklore of the New Madrid earthquakes, this book will quench that thirst. I was short on time the day I received the book, but as I attempted to skim through, I was unable to put it down. The fascinating tales made me keep turning 'just one more page,' . . .

"The book also gives you everything you need to know in the event of an earthquake today. That information, alone, is well worth the price. An excellent job of telling the story. This book is a must for earthquake buffs."

Clement Cravens, Editor
THE WEEKLY RECORD
New Madrid, Missouri

What People Say about this book . . .

"Fascinating. Gripping. Incredible. Suspenseful. Useful. Plunges you into the actual experience of a major Midwestern earthquake. I will never think of an earthquake in the same way again.

"So vivid. I could actually see what was happening—like I was there. I could just feel it. There are images I'll never forget. I loved the drama. I loved the first-person accounts. I kept catching my breath with each story. I just wanted to keep reading.

"I had no idea how a Midwestern earthquake is so different from a California earthquake. Good information on what to expect. Prepares you for a real one. Now I am anxious to visit New Madrid.

"The experience of reading this will always stay with me. The only book like this. One of a kind. Extremely Important! This book will save lives."

Marian Tompson
Former President, LLL International
Evanston, Illinois

"My words cannot do justice to this book. It is a masterpiece! The only work I have ever read that accounts for geological changes, political changes, physical changes and historical changes all at once.

"A history lesson with emotion! A socio-economic lesson with heart! The story of an earthquake wrapped up in the lives of people! Interesting. Alive with the happenings and lives around the globe in that time. An education in itself.

"Thank you for the privilege of reading this book."

Dr. Gennaro Costantini, Optometrist
San Pedro, California

"Great! Educational, yet very entertaining."
Morgaine Madrona, Midwife
Lewis Mehl Madrona, M.D., Ph.D.
Burlington, Vermont

"I was thrilled. Incredible as reading a Steven King novel. Keeps you on the edge of your seat. The suspense of what was going to happen in the next chapter kept me going to the end."

Cheryl Meachan, Student
Cape Girardeau, Missouri

"I read the book with both great scientific interest and human emotion. The New Madrid area is, in fact, a 'compendium of the universe.' Its fascinating and tragic history speaks to all people faced with earthquakes.

"For earthquake researchers, I believe New Madrid is the major laboratory in the world. The information in this book is precious. Drs. Stewart and Knox have increased earthquake knowledge for the world.

"I particularly appreciate the form in which the authors have chosen: Science presented in the style of fiction. These are the two most effective ways that humanity has always followed for assessing reality and for teaching. In a technological society, these ways are rigorously separated, but is it possible to separate mind and earth, rationality and love? Are not they complementary?

"This book is a happy marriage between the rigors of science and the dramatic style of a novel. It is a marriage between information, knowledge, and wisdom— between attention to nature and interest in humanity and its history. I believe and hope that this good marriage will help many to become newly conscious of earthquake risks and to be able to cope with nature when it behaves as a bad stepmother.

"Thank you for the memory."

Professor Teresa Crespellani
Specialist in Earthquake Soil Dynamics
Universita Degli Studi di Firenze
Department of Civil Engineering
Florence, Italy

"The book is appropriately titled. I had never heard of earthquakes in the Midwest before. Very interesting, especially the eye-witness accounts.

"The duration of these earthquakes was impressive. We live in a seismic risk zone IV. So everything built here is reinforced. I am used to quakes that stop shaking in seconds. These lasted for months!

"It seems like Native Americans are always the last to be counted. This book has given them the recognition they should have received and never did before."

Mark Lewis, Building Contractor
Salmon, Idaho

What People Say about this book . . .

"Fascinating, Fact-filled book. I never thought I could enjoy a book so much.

"An extraordinary work about an extraordinary event. A book that will interest the scientist, housewife, historian, traveler, theologian, animal lover, futurist, city planner, environmentalist—practically everyone—with its fascinating, easy-to-read approach from the point of view of the real persons who experienced it. Some of these were famous people like Audubon, Jefferson, Tecumseh, Harrison, Boone, Lincoln's Parents, Lewis and Clark.

"A book of immense interest and practical advice for protection from the inevitable 'Big One' that is bound to occur.

"I can't imagine how the authors could have made something so interesting and brought so many different subjects together in one book. A real pleasure. I was thrilled."

John A. Brunsman, M.D.
Family Physician
Cincinnati, Ohio

"Wonderful! Absolutely marvelous! What a great book! A thrill! We were hardly able to put it down. It's a rare book that everyone in the family wants to hear out. We have been entranced.

"I don't remember when we have read a book that appeals so much to all ages, from eleven to fifty-five. My eleven-year-old. My teenager. My husband. We read it in the yard. In the bathroom. In the car. We carry it around everywhere. Every minute we had we grabbed another paragraph till we were through. We all loved it.

"The diversity of the subject matter is amazing. Some of the passages we went back to re-read, some parts several times. Sometimes we just had to stop and think a while about what we had just read. The book contains many profound incites.

"The favorite book of everyone in the family. Immeasurably popular in this house. You see it sitting closed and you yearn to pick it up and read some more. We have all had a great time with this book.

"The authors are truly gifted writers."
Kathleen G. Lewis, R.N.
Lynch Station, Virginia

"Four thumbs up! Five stars! What can I say! The best New Madrid earthquake book I have ever read—and I have probably read them all.

"*The Earthquake America Forgot* stands alone among all others. Much more in depth than any other. Never has a book actually dealt with what was going on in people's lives at that time. This book brings those people back to life—as if you knew some of them. Makes you realize how bad it was. Other books generalize the experiences of these pioneers. This book makes them personal.

"The first time the earthquakes of 1811-12 have ever been put into this kind of historical perspective. This is the book people have been waiting for—for a long time.

"Dr. Stewart and Dr. Knox have put it all together. An important book. Exciting! I didn't want it to end!
Glenda Hunter, Director
New Madrid Historical Museum
New Madrid, Missouri

"A great resource for home schoolers. In fact, an excellent text for any school. Geology, Religion, Social studies, History, Genetics, Genealogy, Native American Culture, Geography—I was impressed with the many subjects included.

"I knew there had been a big earthquake in that area a long time ago, but I never realized how big it really was! Yet there was no panic in the book. Very matter of fact. It did not try to raise the emotion of the reader, yet I could feel what it must have been like to have been there—like an eye witness.

"The book pointed out that quakes can be good. I never thought of that before. Gave me a lot of food for thought. It also kindled an interest in me to learn more about our history, like the War of 1812. I also got satisfaction from the perfect justice received by the brothers who killed the black man.

"If only I would have had a book like this when I was in grade school. It sure would have made things more interesting. This is the way the social sciences should be taught."
Nancy B. Perry, R.N.
Home School Teacher
Marlboro, Massachusetts

What People Say about this book . . .

"A gripping drama. Entertaining, Educational, Very Readable, A good combination of science and history. Clever subtitles which keep you going on and on to the next section. Nicely done.

"I enjoyed both the geologic and the human interest sides. Islands disappearing. The Mississippi River running backwards. Pirates, Indians, politics, adventure, romance—A real melodrama, yet very useful.

"Gives you a sense of mental preparedness because of the way it is written. You feel as if you've been thru an earthquake, first hand, and survived. Very instructive.

"I was impressed with how much history could be woven around the theme of an earthquake. This was learning made easy because it was so enjoyable. You find yourself remembering numerous facts without even trying. An unforgettable work.

"You'll want to read this book more than once. It's a classic. Like a good piece of music you want to hear again and again— each time discovering another twist, another nuance. This book is a gold mine of spellbinding tales and nuggets of little known facts."

Professor Lawson Inada
Department of English
Southern Oregon State College
Ashland, Oregon

"Reads like a novel. I couldn't put it down. My friends all said the same thing."

Don Greenwood, Artist
Cape Girardeau, Missouri

It is very important for engineers to study both present practice and past history. A big earthquake of magnitude 8.1 has just hit our country at Hokkaido on October 4, 1994, the third big one in two years. There was a lot of liquefaction damage, such as occurred in New Madrid in 1811-12. Many sand boils, fissures, and collapsed areas.

"Your book contains very significant information for earthquake engineers that we can use today."

Kazuo Saito, Earthquake Engineer
Kiso-Jiban Consultants Company
Sapporo, Japan

"A feast of fat things! A remarkable learning experience for me since I'm not American-born, and I was absolutely ignorant of the subject. All I've ever known of the hazards of the Midwest are tornados and cold winters. The book opened the door to me for a lot of geography also. There's much of this great land I've not seen.

"The book opens with Dr. Iben Browning from New Mexico, a prophet that makes the truth speak to us, to combat the mental laziness that makes some say maybe the earthquakes never happened. (Some say that also about the holocaust!)

"Chapter One—The Jefferson Connection— is pure gold to a historian. The information is dazzling. And Chapter Two— Tecumseh yet, and the Roosevelts afloat. And Daniel Boone, too!

And now, as a climax, Chapters Three and Four—'The Siege,' not of the War of 1812, but of the terror of nature. Then the lesson driven home by Chapters Five and Six—'Aftershocks' and 'Futureshocks.'

"Gentlemen authors, you have given us a Splendid Book!"

Rev. Bill Goddard, Episcopal Priest
Minneapolis, Minnesota

"I was fascinated by how much history could be told around a physical event like an earthquake. I really enjoyed it. This is the way to learn history. A great home schooling resource. Ties so much together in one book. I knew nothing about earthquakes before and even now I can't even imagine the magnitude of such a disaster as took place then. A Great Read!"

Mary W. Bell, Registered Nurse
Springfield, Virginia

"I really liked the book. I was pleased with the depth of research and the documentation of the sources. A good weld between history and the present. A good "what to do" book. I liked best your coverage of the people who were there, what happened to them and how they reacted. A good addition to this genre of history. Fascinating."

James M. Jenkins, Computer Science
Olive Branch, Mississippi

Dedication

This book is dedicated to the memory of the thousands who suffered from the New Madrid Earthquakes of 1811–12. Many were injured and many died while most of those who survived lost everything—their homes, their possessions, and even their land. Some of their tragic and brave stories are told here. But the vast majority of those who endured the pain, the fear and the devastating losses of these cataclysms shall remain forever nameless and unrecorded—their heroic and desperate struggles unnumbered, unknown, and untold. It is hoped that this book will resurrect, in part, the legacy of this forgotten history that we of today may gain inspiration, insight, and wisdom from the experiences of these pioneers of our past.

Cover & Title Page Artwork by **Don Greenwood**
Illustrations by **Anthony Stewart**

THE EARTHQUAKE AMERICA FORGOT

2,000 Temblors in Five Months . . .

And it Will Happen Again

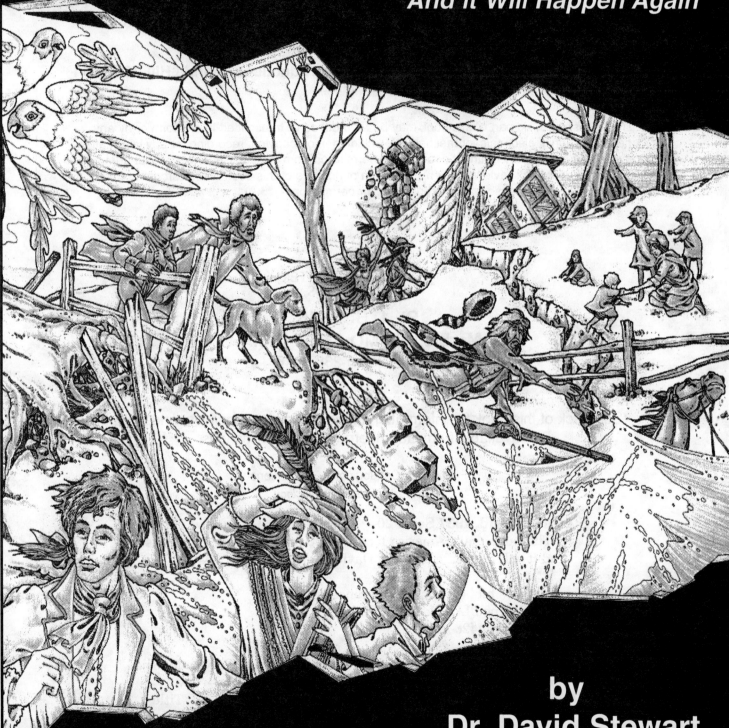

by
Dr. David Stewart
and Dr. Ray Knox

GUTENBERG-RICHTER
PUBLICATIONS

THE EARTHQUAKE AMERICA FORGOT   **by David Stewart & Ray Knox**
Cover Design and Artwork by Don Greenwood
Illustrations by Anthony Stewart
Figures and Maps by David Stewart and Kate Schaefer
Lilbourn Lewis Geneaology Chart by David Stewart
Photographs by David Stewart

Copyright © 1995 by GUTENBERG-RICHTER PUBLICATIONS,
a Division of Napsac Reproductions, Marble Hill, Missouri

GR
GUTENBERG-RICHTER
PUBLICATIONS
Rt. 1, Box 646
Marble Hill, MO 63764 U.S.A.
Phone: (314) 238-4846

*See back of this book for information on books, slides, services, and literature available from Gutenberg-Richter Publications.

Publisher's Cataloging in Publications
(Prepared by Quality Books Inc.)

Stewart, David, 1937 Sept. 20–
    The earthquake America forgot: 2000 temblors in five months—
and it will happen again / by David Stewart and Ray Knox.
    p. cm
    Includes bibliographical references and index.
    Preassigned LCCN: 91-91492
    ISBN 0-934426-45-7

    1. Earthquakes--Missouri--New Madrid Region. 2. New Madrid
(Mo.)--History. 3. Indians of North America--Missouri--New
Madrid Region--History. I. Knox, Ray, 1931 March 29- II. Title

QE535.2.U6S74 1995   551.2'2'09778985
                                                      QBI94-2113

viii

Other Books by Dr. David Stewart

God's Existence: Can Science Prove It?
Safe Alternatives in Chidbirth (with Lee Stewart)
Good Fathering & A Successful Career: Can a Man Do Both?
Twenty-First Century Obstetrics Now! in 2 vols. (with Lee Stewart)
Compulsory Hospitalization or Freedom of Choice in Childbirth
in 3 vols. (with Lee Stewart)
Five Standards for Safe Childbearing
The Childbirth Activists' Handbook (with Lee Stewart)
Field Guide to Representative Earthquake Features in the
New Madrid Seismic Zone (with Ray Knox)
Damages & Losses from Future New Madrid Earthquakes
The Earthquake that Never Went Away (with Ray Knox)
The New Madrid Fault Finder's Guide (with Ray Knox)

For Information on the availability of the above titles, contact Gutenberg-Richter Publications
Or write: Napsac Reproductions, Rt. 1, Box 646, Marble Hill, MO 63764
(314) 238-4273

THE EARTHQUAKE AMERICA FORGOT
Two Thousand Temblors in Five Months . . . And It Will Happen Again
Dr. David Stewart & Dr. Ray Knox

Cover Design by Don Greenwood • Illustrations by Anthony Stewart
Figures by David Stewart & Kate Schaefer • Photographs by David Stewart

TABLE OF CONTENTS

What People Say About this Book	i
Dedication	v
Other Books by David Stewart	viii
List of Maps, Photos, Figures, Illustrations, Charts & Tables	xiv
Acknowledgements	xvii
Introduction: AMNESIA AND RECALL	1
WWII & Loss of Cultural Memory	2
Enter Dr. Browning	4
State of the Art in Earthquake Prediction	6
Maybe the Earthquakes Never Happaned	8
Nineteenth Century Communication	11
The New Madrid Earthquake Experience	13
A Buster of Myths	16
Earthquake Demographics	17
For Further Facts	18
A Trilogy of Books	20
Visit New Madrid Museum & Scenic Overlook	20
New Madrid, History, and the World	23
Chapter One: THE JEFFERSON CONNECTION	25
Jefferson's Vision	25
Tom's Relatives Go West	26
The Lewis Clan Reaches Kentucky	27
Tragedy on Rocky Hill	28
Indicted by an Earthquake	29
Nature Was Hard and So Were the People	31
Kentucky: Supplier of Slaves	32
The Rise & Fall of the Lewis Empire	33
The Dangers of 19th Century Medicine	34
The Grim Reaper	36
Lilbourn's Luck	38
The Ghost of Lilbourn	39
How Descendants of Kings Came to New Madrid	46
The Consequences of Consanguinity	48
Visit New Madrid & Visit Royalty	50
Jefferson & the New Madrid Earthquakes	51

Contents Cont'd

Chapter Two: **PROPHECIES AND PRECURSORS** 55

The Great Comet of 1811 55
Tecumseh and His Brothers 58
Pukeshinwa's Death and Methoataske's Vision 59
Orphans 61
Noisemaker Meets Master of Life 63
A New Religion is Born 65
Indian Witch Trials 66
God's Chosen People 67
Harrison Puzzles Over the Prophet 67
Tecumseh Rises to Power 69
Tecumseh's First Prophecy 74
Paddle-Wheelers Enter the Midwest 74
The Roosevelts Leave Pittsburgh 80
Louisville and the Birth of Henry 81
The Falls of the Ohio 81
Shippingport 84
Yellow Bank 85
Rumors of War 86
Forerunners of World War 87
The Sensibilities of Animals 90
Daniel Boone Leads the Way 92
The Lincolns Move to Kentucky 93
The Boones Move to Missouri 95
Cape Girardeau and the Indians 98
"Savages" 100
Midwest Infrastructure Then and Now 101
Some Indians were "Civilized" 102
The Home of the Braves, The Land of the Free 103
Europeans Come to the Mississippi Valley 106
Morgan's Scheme to Get Rich Quick 109
What George Morgan Didn't Know 112
People Choose to Live Where Earthquakes Happen 114
Earthquakes are Not All Bad 116
George Morgan: Urban Planner Ahead of His Time 118
Morgan Switches Countries Again 119
Let's Make a Deal 120
Fort Osage 122
The State of the Union in 1811-12 127
It Could Have Been a Major Metropolis 130

Contents Cont'd

Chapter Three THE SIEGE BEGINS   133

    Dancing Houses   134
    One Family's Ordeal   136
    And This Was Only the First Day   137
    Mr. Cagle and His Indian Mound   139
    Pirates   141
    Big Prairie Disappears   143
    Escape from Little Prairie   144
    The Little Ice Age   147
    Meanwhile, Back at Little Prairie   150
    The Case of the Missing Smokehouse   152
    Field Report from New Madrid   155
    "Up to the Belly of My Horse"   156
    Chaos at Island #13   158
    The Davis Party   161
    Steamboat on Trial   162
    The Story of Cave-In-Rock   163
    Chased by Indians   166
    Fire On Board   170
    Roosevelt's Steamboat Reaches New Madrid   171
    Logjam in Long Reach   173
    Tied Up on Island #32   174
    On to Natchez   178
    The Unpleasant Fate of Point Pleasant   179
    Death Strikes the Crist Family   181
    John Audubon & the Birth of Reelfoot   181
    Zadoc Cramer Reports from Natchez   183
    Eastern Quakes are More Destructive   186

Chapter Four: THE BIG ONE   189

    The Ripples Sweep the Country   191
    The "Hard Shock"   199
    The River Runs Backwards   200
    Waterfalls on the Mississippi   201
    More Perils Downstream   205
    How Many Died?   207
    The River of Death   208
    The End of Old New Madrid   209
    The Land, Itself, Was Destroyed   214
    Disruption of Transportation   215
    Another Town's Future Destroyed   218
    Redeeming Ruined Real Estate   225

Contents Cont'd

The Fear of Being Swallowed Alive   226
How the Bootheel Was Formed   230
Night Lights   232
Warm Water   233
Friction, Geothermal Energy or Light?   235
Earthquake Smog   237
Seismic Tar Balls   238
Not a Simple Earthquake   240
The Final Tally   240

Chapter Five: AFTERSHOCKS   243
The Elder Wilson Thompson   245
Earthquake Christians   250
Government Relief and Fraud   251
Bankruptcy and Counterfeiting   253
All the Way to the Supreme Court   254
How Many Aftershocks?   255
The Crist Family in Indiana   256
Massacre at Pigeon Roost   257
George Junior Visits His Parents   260
Where Did the New Madrid Refugees Go?   260
The Year Without a Summer   262
Tecumseh's Second Prophecy   263
Tenskwatawa and the Earthquakes   265
The New Madrid Quakes in World Perspective   266
December 16, 1812   267
History Changed for Red Men and White   268
Reelfoot and The Legend of Kalopin   268
Dying Comets   269
Tecumseh's Last Prophecy   271
Tenskwatawa Fades Away   272
Tecumseh's Sister   274
The Last of the Shawnees   275
An Arch with a Double Meaning   278

Chapter Six: FUTURESHOCKS   281
Understanding the Richter Scale   281
Basic Truths About Earthquakes   283
Repeat Times for Midwestern Earthquakes   284
What to Expect in Future Earthquakes   285
Earthquake Probabilities for the Midwest   286
The Big Bang Balloon Theory   288

xiii

Contents Cont'd

What do Probabilities Mean? 292
Your Risk May Not Be What You Think 293
Serious Damages From Small Quakes 295
The Lawrenceville Earthquake 298
The Case of the Broken Basement 299
The New Hamburg Earthquake 302
Remote Damages from Light Quakes 304
Your Soil Type May Increase Your Risk 304
The Risco Earthquake 305
Liquefaction from a Light Earthquake 306
Insurance Company Reluctant to Pay 309
Earthquake at Rover 310
Earthquake at Lick Creek 311
Septic System Slope Failure 312
Big Damage from Really Small Tremors 315
When the Big One Hits What'll Happen Where You Live? 317
How to Use CUSEIS 317
Understanding Earthquake Forces 318
Estimation Formulas When Only Population is Known 320
Impact of a Major Quake at Jonesboro, Arkansas 320
Earthquake Mitigation Doesn't Cost, It Pays 322

Chapter Seven: PROTECTING SELF AND FAMILY 331
The Four Phases of Earthquake Preparation 331
Before the Quake 332
During the Shaking 333
Your First Response 334
A Family Reunion Plan 334
Long Term Recovery 335
Sources of Earthquake Information 335
Specific Sources 336
General Sources 337
Conclusion 338

Bibliography 339
Index 345
Books, Slides & Other Items Available from Gutenberg-Richter 361
Ordering & Shipping Information 367
About the Authors 368
What People Say About this Book 370
The Exclusive GR Earthquake Hazard Warranty 374
Order Form for Gutenberg-Richter Publications 376

MAPS, FIGURES, PHOTOS, ILLUSTRATIONS, TABLES AND CHARTS

Introduction: AMNESIA AND RECALL

Seismic Sand Fissures & Sand Boils Near New Madrid	10
Largest Sand Boil in New Madrid	11
Seismic Features on New Madrid Golf Course	12
New Madrid Quake Burgers	14
New Madrid County Health Department	15
New Madrid Historical Museum	21
Mississippi River Observation Deck	21
Seismic Retrofitting at New Madrid	22

Chapter One: THE JEFFERSON CONNECTION

Jefferson and Monticello	24
Jefferson National Expansion Memorial, St. Louis	26
Three Views of Lilbourn, Missouri	39
Lilbourn Lewis Hunter Crisler	41
Immaculate Conception Church, New Madrid	42
Lewis Family Plot, Evergreen Cemetery, New Madrid	43
Tombstone Inscriptions	44
Genealoby Chart & Origin of Name: "Lilbourn Lewis"	45
Virginia LaValle Carlson	51
Fort Jefferson, Kentucky	52

Chapter Two: PROPHESIES & PRECURSORS

Map of The Most Active Portion of the New Madrid Seismic Zone	54
The Great Comet of 1811 as seen over Daniel Boone's House	56
The Temple of Ramses II at Abu Simbel	57
Tenskwatawa as a Youthful Shawnee Prophet	64
William Henry Harrison	67
Tecumseh as a Youthful Shawnee Chief	71
Map of American Rivers, Towns and Cities, 1811-12	75
Lydia & Nicholas Roosevelt	77
Robert Fulton	77
Robert Livingston	77
The *New Orleans*, First Steamboat on the Mississippi	79
Title Page of *The Navigator*, 1818 Edition	82
Map of the Falls of the Ohio, from *The Navigator*	83
Daniel Boone	93
Abraham Lincoln, Age 3, in Front of his Childhood Cabin	95
Home of Daniel and Rebecca Boone, Defiance, Missouri	97
Tomb of Daniel Boone, Marthasville, Missouri	98
Indian Park, Cape Girardeau, Missouri	101
El Camino Real, Old Kingshighway, New Madrid	102
The Lilbourn Indian Mound	108

Maps, Figures, Photos, Tables, etc. Cont'd

Jean Bequette House (1778), Ste. Genevieve, Missouri	110
Louis Bolduc House (1770), Ste. Genevieve, Missouri	111
Map of Greasy Bent, Bessie Bend, Kentucky Bend, New Madrid Bend	113
Reelfoot Lake, Tennessee	117
Colonal George Morgan	118
Meriwether Lewis	122
William Clark	122
Fort Osage	124
Eckert's Tavern & Millington House, St. Charles, Missouri	125
Millington House, St. Charles Post Office & Castor Oil Factory	126
Map of American States and Territories in 1811-12	128
Map of Territorial Counties of Missouri, 1810-1816	130

Chapter Three: The Siege Begins

Map of Epicentral Locations for the New Madrid Earthquakes	132
Big Lake, Arkansas, Epicenter of the First Great Earthquake	138
Native American Graves Disturbed by Earthquakes	140
"Escape From Little Prarie"	146
Little Prairie Today	153
Pemiscot River & the Culbertson's Smokehouse	154
"Up to the Belly of my Horse"	157
Seismic Explosion Craters Along Interstate Highway 55	158
Map of Mississippi River Islands #1 - #60	168
Map of Mississippi River Islands #60 - #117	169
Map of Maiden Voyage of the *New Orleans*	176
Key to Map of *New Orleans* Voyage	177
Point Pleasant Today	180
View from Chicken Point in Hickman, Kentucky	182
Aerial View of Reelfoot Lake Visitors Center	184
Sand Boils on South End of Reelfoot Lake	184
Ground Waves in Mississippi County	185

Chapter Four: The Big One

Map of New Madrid Earthquake Intensities	188
Tywappity Hill Today	190
Ste. Genevieve Houses that Survived the Earthquakes	193
Earthquake Damage at Boone's House, Defiance, Missouri	194
Earthquake Damage at Boone's House, cont'd	195
Earthquake Damage to Kibby House, St. Charles, Missouri	196
Epicentral Area of Largest Earthquake in American History	199
Stumps of Trees Broken by Quakes of 1811-12	203
Pages 156-157 from *The Navigator* by Cramer	204
Maps of New Madrid Bend 1810 & 1905	210
Maps of New Madrid Bend 1990 & Superposed Views since 1810	211
Map of New Madrid Area Today (A.D. 1994)	212
Cushion Lake Today	217
Portage Open Bay Today	218

Maps, Figures, Photos, Tables, etc. Cont'd

Spanish Mill Today   220
Big Lake, Missouri, Today   221
Pemiscot Bayou and Culbertson's Farm Today   222
Cagle Lake and Epicentral Area of December 16 Quake Today   223
The Bootheel Fault and World's Largest Sand Boil—Aerial View   224
Earthquake Fissures from 1811-12   228
Dry Bayou, Earthquake Fissure from 1811-12   229
Map of the Missouri Bootheel   231
World's Largest Sand Boil—Ground View   239
Earthquake Obituary Chart   242

Chapter Five: Aftershocks
The Elder Wilson Thompson   245
Bethel Baptist Church and Cemetery   248
Tecumseh as British Officer in War of 1812   270
Tenskwatawa in Exile   273
Indian Thong Tree, Jackson, Missouri   276
Jefferson National Expansion Memorial, Gateway Arch at Sunset   279

Chapter Six: Futureshocks
Modern Map of the Central United States   280
Table One: Repeat Intervals for Earthquakes on New Madrid Fault   282
Table Two: Time Dependent Probabilities for Central U.S. Quakes   287
Table Three: Time Independent Probabilities for Central U.S. Quakes   287
Types of Faults   290
Map of The New Madrid Rift Complex   291
How Liquefaction at Depth Causes Damage   308
Septic System Slope Failure   314
Definitions to be Used with CUSEIS Charts   323
CUSEIS Chart One: People and Land Effects   324
CUSEIS Chart Two: Building Effects   325
CUSEIS Chart Three: Bridge and Utility Effects   326
Central U.S. Major Quake Intensity Map One   327
Central U.S. Major Quake Intensity Map Two   328
Central U.S. Major Quake Intensity Map Three   329
Central U.S. Major Quake Intensity Map Four   330

Author Biographies
Photo of Dr. David Stewart   362
Photo of Dr. Ray Knox   363

ACKNOWLEDGEMENTS

A work of this magnitude is not possible without the cooperation and assistance of many. Librarians, museum personnel, city and county employees, property owners, historians, and people everywhere were universally helpful. During the half-decade it took to write this book, many people provided important leads and key bits of information. It would truly be impossible to remember and acknowledge you all. We wish to express our appreciation to the following for contributing information, aiding us in our research, providing encouragement, and for helping in other important ways:

The New Madrid Historical Museum; Virginia Carlson, the immediate past Curator; Glenda Hunter, the present Curator; the Museum Board of Directors; Friends of the Museum; and everyone who works there whose dedication, cordiality and enthusiasm have always been an inspiration to us.

The Center for Earthquake Studies at Southeast Missouri State University; Linda Dillman, Associate Director; and Mark Winkler, Southeast Missouri Area Coordinator for the State Emergency Management Agency who have assisted in innumerable ways, including the locating of many facts and references.

KFVS Channel 12 TV in Cape Girardeau, Missouri; News Director, Mike Beacher; Evening News Anchorman, Mike Shain; Suzanna Baylon, Mike Wright, Mary Ann Maloney, Ron Wilson, Harold Bollinger, and all the staff who have always been so supportive and encouraging in this endeavor.

We also want to thank Charles Baker, James Baker, Norma Bagnall, Debbie Beasley, Jim Beavers, Jim Blacklock, Lynn and Marian Bock, Riley Bock, John and Sue Bormuth, Jim Bradley, Norman Brown, Iben Browning, Dan Cicirello, Katherine Cochran, Clement Cravens, Ed and Jacquelyn Close, Libba Crisler, Marshall Dial, Frances Dyhrkopp, Bill Emerson, Arzine French, Don Froemsdorf, Evelyn Browning Garris, Ed Gray, Charles Hatley, Grant and Marcella Hedgepeth, Dave Hoffman, Angie Holzhouser, Father David Hulshof, Martha Hunter, Sam Hunter, Lawson Inada, DeAnn Kincey, Eva Kirkpatrick, Ed LaValle, Lora Lee Manikam, Mark Meatte, Yvonne Morgan, Frank Nickell, Eloyce Noel, Steve Owen, Bob Parkinson, Shamsher Prakash, Don Rhodes, Steve and Mary Robertson, Larry Rost, Vonnie Snelling, Lorraine Stange, Phyllis Steckel, Keith Stewart, Jim and Helen Thogmorton, Sharon Tricamo, Gregory White, Ed Williams, Les Youd, and just about everybody living in and around New Madrid. Some of you did not directly contribute to the content of this book, but your encouragement and support during the five-year process of writing it has helped see it through.

We particularly want to thank Linda Dillman, Karen Knox, Steve Owen, Lee Stewart, and Ed Williams who helped edit the manuscript. They not only corrected typographical, grammatical, and syntactical errors but made many suggestions of content and clarity that have greatly improved this work.

And finally, we want to thank our wives, Lee Stewart and Karen Knox. Writing a book can be an all-consuming activity. We apologize for being distracted and inattentive at times and appreciate their patience and support.

Introduction

AMNESIA AND RECALL

According to Mike Shain, anchorman for the evening news on KFVS-TV, Channel 12 in Cape Girardeau, Missouri, his parents and grandparents were well aware of the history of the New Madrid earthquakes. It was a common topic of conversation throughout southeast Missouri. Natives of the area all had their tall tales to share on the earthquakes of 1811-12.. Some were true, some not so true, but all were fantastic and guaranteed to keep a visiting stranger spellbound.

Mike remembers the kitchen cabinets of his childhood home in Sikeston, Missouri. As a small boy, he had difficulty in opening them. When he asked why the latches were so strong, his mother's reply was, "That's to keep the doors from flying open with an earthquake." His grandmother never stored plates on edge, but always laid them flat to prevent their breakage during an earthquake. All of their whatnot shelves had lips to prevent things from falling off should a shake occur.

His father hung his tools on the basement wall at an angle and used bent nails to keep them secure. "There," he said to young Michael, "that'll keep them from falling on your head in an earthquake."

Mike's grandparents had moved into the area around 1870 and vividly remembered the strong earthquake on Halloween night of 1895 centered only 25 miles east of Sikeston between Charleston, Missouri, and Cairo, Illinois. The quake measured 6.5 on the Richter scale and caused extensive damage over a multistate area. There was only one recorded mortality. A mule was killed at Piedmont, Missouri, when a barn collapsed. Mike's father was a young boy at the time.

As an impressionable lad, six or seven years of age, Mike recalls a trip he made with his Uncle Fred Cole to Reelfoot Lake. After arriving there and being told that "the lake bottom had once been a 'high hill' that had collapsed during the earthquakes, filling with the rushing waters from a rampaging Mississippi and taking with it a tribe of Indians," little Michael was terrified. All he could think of for the rest of the day was, "When are we going to get out of here?"

To get to the lake, Mike and his Uncle had taken the ferry over the Mississippi between Portageville, Missouri, and Tiptonville, Tennessee. Michael had enjoyed the trip on the water that morning. But on the return voyage back, his vivid imagination could see "the river running backwards with towering waves" and "heaps of trees floating down" to crash into their boat.

"For years afterward," Mike said, "I was afraid of earthquakes."

The Portageville-Tiptonville ferry stopped operating in the 1980's, but Reelfoot Lake is still there—a tourist attraction visited by thousands every year. And, no, it was not a "high hill" before the quake, and, no, the Mississippi did not rush in to fill the void. at least not quite like Uncle Fred described it. But the earthquake did create the lake. It had been a mature forest of cypress and deciduous timber before the quakes. It is now permanently flooded and the site of a huge lake from the earthquakes of 1811–12. In fact, fallen cypress logs from the earthquakes were still being harvested from Reelfoot Lake as late as1900. There's a lot more to say about Reelfoot, but that story will be told later in this book.

WWII and the Loss of Cultural Memory

Natives of northeast Arkansas, southern Illinois, southeast Missouri, western Kentucky and Tennessee, remembered the New Madrid earthquakes well into the twentieth century. Through the early 1900's many people could still recall first hand the stories of grandparents who had survived the events. Then came World War II. Following the war there was a great influx of newcomers into the Midwest, and amnesia began to set in.

By the 1960's and 1970's thousands of people had moved in and around the New Madrid Fault Zone who had never heard of the great quakes of 1811–12. Even after many of these immigrants from elsewhere had lived in the area long enough to have felt a few of the light to moderate quakes the fault continues to produce today, they still were unfamiliar with the historic quakes that had given the fault its name. It was simply not a common topic of conversation any more.

And then there was also the influence of the business community that discouraged such conversation. To let it be known that this was "earthquake country" would be bad for commerce and industrial development, they thought. And so, there came to be a sort of unwritten code of silence about the New Madrid Fault, its past and its potential.

As for New Madrid, the few people living there whose ancestors survived the quakes had not entirely forgotten, of course. But until the late 1980's, the very town whose name had been given to the disturbances housed residents who did not know they were on top of one of the world's most active faults and the source of this nation's greatest earthquakes back in 1811–12.

Virginia LaValle Carlson is a New Madrid native and a descendent of some of the original settlers of the town. She was Director of the New Madrid Historical Museum until 1992. "When the Museum first opened in 1974 there was nothing whatsoever on earthquakes," she said. "In all the years I went to school here and lived here, nobody ever told me that there was a possibility of another earthquake. Even the big one back in 1811–12 was never talked about. For a long time, there was not one single item at the Museum about earthquakes. All the displays had to do with Indians, the Civil War, life on the Mississippi River, and early American history," she said. "We were amazed when people from outside the area came to visit and asked about earthquakes. We couldn't figure out why anyone would be so interested in something like an earthquake that happened so long ago. The people around New Madrid sure weren't interested," she said. "No one seemed to know much about it, or cared."

Thus, it was the curiosity of visitors from afar that prompted the officials of the Museum to begin digging into the history of the New Madrid quakes and include earthquake information in their exhibits. But most of that did not happen until the Museum was ten or fifteen years old, at least. Earthquakes did not become a primary focus for the town or the Museum until 1990 and since.

The town's leaders, who did know about the history of New Madrid and the great earthquakes, were proud of the unique geologic heritage they had inherited from the past but were not ready to admit that it could happen in the present or the future. History was okay, but to suggest that the town could be shaken again was a taboo not to be spoken. The "E-word" was to be used guardedly and only in the past tense. State Emergency Management Agency officials visiting the town in the late 1970's and 1980's were asked not to talk about earthquake preparation.

As for the United States at large,

very few living outside the immediate vicinity of the New Madrid fault zone knew anything about the history of these events until recently. It was common for people to move to southeast Missouri, northeastern Arkansas, southern Illinois, or western Kentucky and Tennessee and never know that they were moving into an active seismic zone that had produced the largest earthquakes in American History. In fact, it was not uncommon for people to move to this area from California, "in order to get away from earthquakes," only to learn that they had moved into a zone of equal, if not higher, seismic risk.

Stewart remembers talking with the director of an earthquake preparedness project in southern California in 1988 whose entire professional career had concerned earthquakes. Yet, he had never heard of the New Madrid Fault or of the New Madrid earthquakes of 1811–12.

It is our hope that this book will be of sufficient interest to Americans throughout the country that these historic events will no longer be forgotten. This book was not written for Midwesterners only. It was written with readers throughout the whole North American continent in mind.

These events disturbed two-thirds of the continental United States, from the Rocky Mountains to the Eastern Seaboard. At least minor damage was experienced in every state and territory comprising the United States in that day, touching every American living at the time. These earthquakes were not just local events. They were beyond even regional.

The New Madrid Earthquakes of 1811–12 were national events. They were covered in every newspaper in the country, not because the editors "heard" about the quakes, but because all of them "felt" them, wherever they were, be that St. Louis, Philadelphia, New Orleans, Boston, New York, Montreal, Washington, Savannah, Georgia, or Charleston, South Carolina. The New Madrid earthquakes were so huge that they did not need radio waves transmitted through the air to make themselves known throughout the country. The announcement of their release was by seismic waves transmitted directly through the ground to every news source on the continent at the time.

Even so, except in the immediate area of the disturbances, the great earthquakes of 1811–12 were virtually forgotten for several generations. There were a few who remembered, but for many decades the general American public was unaware that a monster sleeps beneath the Central Valley of the Mississippi and could awake and rise up at any time, sending shock waves across the nation again. We can no longer afford to be unaware.

Enter Dr. Browning

The level of awareness increased dramatically in 1990 when a climatologist from New Mexico, Dr. Iben Browning, stated that according to a theory he had devised, there would be "an enhanced probability of a major earthquake on the New Madrid fault on or about December the 3rd." He then added that in his opinion "there would be a 50-50 chance of a major earthquake on the New Madrid fault on or around that date."

Browning's theory was based on the fact that the gravitational forces of the sun and moon, which visibly lift the oceans up and down in their tides, also exert forces on the rocks of the earth's crust in such a manner that when these forces are at a maximum, earthquakes could be triggered from faults whose levels of strain were close to the breaking point. He knew that the New Madrid fault was overdue for a strong earthquake. Seismologists had been warning the public about that possibility since the late 1970's at least. Browning had used of a sophisticated computer program he had developed with the U.S. Naval Observatory in Washington, DC, to determine that the gravitational forces of sun and moon were to be uniquely aligned on December 3, 1990, to produce a maximum force at the latitude of the New Madrid fault. According to his calculations, which were later verified by geophysicists at St. Louis University, Memphis State University, and the U.S. Geological Survey, such a maximum at this latitude had not occurred for 180 years, since mid-December of 1811.

The theory was a new twist on an old idea and had not been proven. The vast majority of seismologists rejected it summarily without investigatigation. The media hyped it to the extreme. The publicity was global, from Europe to Hong Kong. Every newspaper, radio and television network in the world, it seemed, broadcast Browning's projection. When a 4.6 magnitude earthquake actually did occur in the New Madrid Fault Zone on September 26, 1990, the public concluded that it was a foreshock of a larger event to come in December.

Millions of Midwesterners had developed a concern over the potential for earthquakes by late 1990. Prior to Browning, most Midwesterners had not even heard of the New Madrid Fault and only a small fraction of those who did know of the fault realized that it posed a current threat. This abysmal level of awareness in the central U.S. was dramatically changed in 1990 due to the publicity given by the media to Browning's projection. A survey taken near the end of 1990 showed that, at that time, at least 98% of Midwesterners had not only heard of the fault, but most believed it could produce a major earthquake in the near future. For those who had been engaged in earthquake education efforts during the decade of the 1980's, Browning's forecast was a boon. It stimulated more beneficial public awareness and preparedness than in all previous history.

The anticipated earthquake never occurred. In fact, the whole month of December, 1990, passed without even a small tremor on the New Madrid fault. But the earthquake education, mitigation, planning, and enactment of building code legislation stimulated by this scare still remains and will some day pay off.

The Earthquake Engineering Research Institute (EERI) held its fifth national conference in July, 1994, in Chicago. A panel of seven experts discussed the Browning incident for two hours. Several of the panelists were sociologists who had studied the public's response to Browning. They unanimously concluded that a lot of good things happened because of Browning—things that would never have happened without him. The panel pointed out that four years after 1990, the level of earthquake awareness and preparation still remained higher than it was before. Jeanne Millin, an earthquake mitigation/education specialist with the Federal Emergency Management Agency (FEMA), commented that there has been a very heightened level of earthquake awareness since 1990. "Browning definitely contributed to that awareness," she said, "and from a long range point of view, things look darn good compared to fifteen years ago. Browning has helped."

As examples of the lasting benefits of Browning, consider the following facts mentioned by the EERI panel: Tens of thousands of water heaters are now secured against earthquake shaking in the Midwest. Hospitals have upgraded their emergency generators. Many buildings have been retrofitted to resist seismic forces. Seismic building codes were legislated in five of the seven states closest to the New Madrid Fault: Arkansas, Kentucky, Missouri, Indiana, and Tennessee. Eight new states joined the Central U.S. Earthquake Consortium (CUSEC) in reponse to Browning. Thousands of people bought earthquake insurance, and still have it four years later. Schools, hospitals, the American Red Cross, Salvation Army, National Guard Units, County Emergency Response officials, and numerous other organizations have formed networks that did not exist before Browning and now have coordinated disaster plans which they have not only written, but have exercised. Furthermore, for the first time, the state geologists of the central U.S. have formed an interstate organization to coordinate earthquake information and research. Because of the increased readiness for earthquakes, the states of the Midwest are now better prepared for disasters of all kinds, not just earthquakes.

Millions living within the reach of the New Madrid fault now know how to protect themselves when the next major earthquake hits. 1990 marks the year when the lost memory of the New Madrid earthquakes was lifted back to consciousness in the public mind.

Some day in the not too distant future there will be a major earthquake in the central United States. When it happens many lives will be saved, and millions in potential property damage will have been prevented because a man named Browning expressed his concern and stated what he believed, in spite of his critics. Browning passed away following a prolonged illness in July of 1991.

State of the Art of Earthquake Prediction

Browning's theory may have been flawed, but it did contain a kernal of validity. At least a dozen other scientists from several countries have also noted a connection between earthquake timing and the positions of the sun and moon. Some day, when earthquake prediction becomes a

reliable science, Browning's hypothesis will fill a necessary niche in the final formula.

So far, American seismologists have not been able to develop a viable method for predicting earthquakes. It is an extremely complex business. It may even turn out that each seismically active fault will require an individual methodology applicable only to the personality of that fault, thus requiring that there be many prediction methods. The United States Geological Survey (USGS) has had an ongoing prediction research program since the late 1960's—as yet without a successful earthquake prediction. But they continue to try.

Six years before Brownings projection, the USGS publicly predicted that an earthquake between 5.0 and 6.0 would occur near Parkfield, California, during the eight years between 1984 and 1992. It never happened. Browning's projection tried to hit a five day window. The government scientists gave themselves an eight year window, and still missed. Tens of millions of tax dollars have been spent on this project, as yet without an earthquake.

China, Japan, and the Soviet Union have been more successful. The Japanese have actually predicted some earthquakes with such precision that they had video cameras set up in the epicentral region to record the event when it happened. The authors have in their possession one of those tapes.

As for the Chinese, they have successfully predicted at least eighteen earthquakes with significant savings of lives. For example, on February 4,

1975, Chinese officials concluded that the evidence was sufficient for them to issue a warning that a major earthquake would occur within twenty-four hours in Liaoning Province. Several hundred thousand people were evacuated from their homes in Haicheng, Yingkow, and nearby towns. At 7:36 p.m., that same day, less than ten hours after the announcement had been made, a magnitude 7.3 earfthquake occurred.

According to a report released by the Chinese government, "Most of the population had left their houses, big domestic animals had been moved out of their stables, trucks and cars did not remain in their garages, and important objects were not in their warehouses. Therefore, despite the collapse of most of the hosues and structures during the big shock, losses of human and animal lives were greatly reduced. Within the most destructive area, in some portions more than 90 percent of the houses collapsed, but many agricultural production brigades did not suffer even a single casualty."

One of the signs correctly interpreted by the Chinese that indicated the coming of the Haicheng earthquake was strange animal behavior, some of which had begun to occur at least two months ahead of time. An excellent book on the subject of animals and earthquakes is entitled, *When the Snakes Awake*, by Helmut Tributsch. Another excellent introductory book on earthquakes in general with a good chapter on earthquake prediction is simply entitled *Earthquakes* by Bruce Bolt. Both are listed in the bibliography at the end of this book.

The Chinese seismologists have had their share of false alarms, too, along with their successes. They have also not predicted some destructive quakes that have occurred with considerable loss of life.

One of these missed events was the devastating Tangshan earthquake of July 27, 1975, only five months after the successful prediction at Haichung that saved so many lives. The magnitude of the quake was 7.8. It struck during the dark morning hours at 3:42 a.m. Seconds before, lightening flashed across the sky followed by a deafening rumble like thunder. Then the convulsions began. At least 240,000 people perished. Another 500,000 were seriously injured. 7,000 entire families were obliterated without a single surviving member. At one university in the city, 80% of the students and faculty were killed, including twenty-four of the twenty-eight members of the earth sciences department. How could the Chinese have been so successful a few months before and yet suffer such an apparent failure at Tangshan?

It turns out that this may have been a political failure, not a scientific one. Anomalous animal behavior was being reported to authorities for months before. Scientists had noted a variety of other signs, as well, including magnetic disturbances, tilting of portions of the land surface, and changes in water well levels and water quality. However, because of some political unrest at the time, appropriate actions were delayed. Finally, a panel of experts assembled in the city to set up additional instruments and evaluate the data. Their task was to decide if a warning should be issued. They never got the opportunity. They were all killed in the Tangshan temblor. We shall never know if they were about to issue a prediction or not. (For more information, see the book, *The Great Tangshan Earthquake of 1975*, by Chen Yong listed in the bibliography.)

Such is the state of the art of earthquake prediction today. No country has a fool-proof method as yet. It seems that no one but the Chinese, the Japanese and the Russians, have had any success at all—unless you count the American Indians, whom you will read about later in this book.

Maybe The Earthquakes Never Happened

During the decades following World War II, people forgot the New Madrid earthquakes. It was no longer a frequent topic of conversation. And when it was mentioned, it was always in vague terms, an event in the distant past about which little was known except that "the Mississippi River ran backwards." That much was fairly common knowledge, but not much else.

There were even those who said the earthquake never actually happened—that it was just a legend. This notion was not new. James MacFarlane, a nineteenth-century scientist and resident of Union City, in western Tennessee, insisted that the earthquakes never occurred. He presented a celebrated paper at the 1883 meeting of the American Association for the Advancement of Science. It was entitled, "*The 'Earthquake' at New Madrid, Missouri, in 1811—Probably Not an Earthquake.*"

MacFarlane argued that the "sunk lands" and other features attributed to the earthquakes were actually nothing more than a form of normal subsidence, the settling of land surface due to the dissolving of limestone strata that underlie the region. His argument centered on Reelfoot Lake, located near Union City. Most people believed that the lake with its thousands of submerged trees was created by the earthquakes of 1811–12. MacFarlane's theory suggested that the forest that had once existed there had been located over the roof of a large limestone cavern which collapsed in 1811, creating the lake. The rumble of this collapsing cavern had been mistaken for an earthquake, according to MacFarlane.

The idea that large areas of the Central Mississippi River region are underlain by vast caverns has been a popular one. In MacFarlane's time, trains passing a few miles to the west of his home in Union City caused the ground to vibrate, inducing the widely held belief that caverns must lie beneath. Even to the present day, there is a story told by residents of Caruthersville, Missouri, that the whole town is underlain by a cavern which could cause it to collapse at any time.

There is no cavern under Caruthersville, of course, and no scientist today believes that collapsing caverns were the cause of the New Madrid earthquakes or of the permanent landforms they produced.

Four Aerial Photos of New Madrid taken in 1990. The light colored spots are sand boils from the earthquakes of 1811-12. Sand boils form when the vibrations of an earthquake cause a temporary quicksand condition in the soil called "liquefaction." Thousands of these seismic liquefaction features can still be seen throughout the 5,000 square mile area of the New Madrid Seismic Zone. Areas liquefied in an earthquake can potentially boil or liquefy again and again in future earthquakes.

Photos #1 (upper left) and #3 (lower left) are looking toward the east. Photo #2 (upper right) is looking south. Photo #4 (lower right) is looking west. Highway 61 crosses Photos #1, #3, and #4 while it extends from the lower left corner to the upper right corner of Photo #2. The building with five wings in the center of Photo #1 is the New Madrid Nursing Center. The same facility can be seen on all four photos: At the center of Photo #2; At the right edge of Photo #3; and just right of the center of Photo #4. The building in the upper left corner of Photo #3 and at the left edge of Photo #2 is the New Madrid Elementary School. The top of New Madrid Bend on the Mississippi River is seen in Photo #2. It flows from left to right. New Madrid Island which was formed during the flood of 1927 is visible in this picture.

While it would be hard to find disbelievers in the New Madrid earthquakes today, there are still those who don't believe they were as severe as they were reported to have been. Edison Shrum, a resident of Scott City, Missouri, compiled and wrote a book entitled, *The Real New Madrid Earthquakes*, published by the Scott County Historical Society in 1989. "We know that the accounts written or told by local people differ as to what happened during these earthquakes, and that there are exaggera-

Seismic Sand Fissures and Sand Boils Near New Madrid. The view from inside the cockpit of the airplane (upper left) shows seismic sand fissures from 1811-12 at the end of the runway of the New Madrid airport. In the upper right photo we a bare patch where the wheat isn't growing very well. This is an earthquake sand boil. The building complex on the horizon in the distance is New Madrid Central High School. At the lower left we have an aerial view of the New Madrid-Marston Rest Stop on Interstate Highway 55. The streaks and light colored patches are all seismic liquefaction features from 1811-12. In the lower right photo we have a light stripe in the center of the picture. This is a fragment of what used to be a stream channel (Gut Ste. Anne) before the earthquakes. French, Spanish, and Indian boats used to travel this channel going from the Mississippi River over to the Little River before 1812. The earthquakes destroyed the stream, breaking it up into disconnected pieces. This portion was filled with quicksand from the earthquakes. This seismic sand deposit passes beneath Interstate Highway 55, a railroad, and a levee. In some future major earthquake this sand-filled channel could liquefy and destroy the highway, railroad, and levee all at once. The large light patch in the upper right corner of this photo is a giant 25 acre sand boil.

tions in most of them," Shrum writes. "But to make matters still worse, some of the eastern newspapers picked up these local exaggerations and exaggerated them still further. Later on, people such as Timothy Flint, came into the area

and swallowed everything he heard, both fact and fiction, apparently without much effort to discriminate between the two," says Shrum.

Actually, Mr. Shrum is right, and his book contains much valuable material. There are contradictory

Largest Sand Boil in New Madrid. This is the "Sinclair Sand Boil," a 500 foot diameter earthquake feature bigger than a football field. From the air it is seen as an almost perfect circle of sand. The road slicing off the edge of the boil is Highway 61. The building across the road is a Sinclair Station and Restaurant after which the boil has been named. The right-hand photo taken at the station shows the boil as a light streak completely across the picture. A black man is thought to have been caught in the quicksand and drowned in this boil in December of 1811. Many Native American artifacts have been found here. The dark lower left corner of the photo on the left is a "seismic sunk land"—a subsided area from 1811-12.

accounts, and there were many exaggerations about the earthquakes, including those of Mr. Flint, as he points out. But all things considered, it seems to the authors of this book that these events may have been, in fact, the most extraordinary sequence of seismic events, not only in North American history, but in the history of the world for at least the last 2,000 years. In this we feel there is no exaggeration. You, the reader, can decide for yourself when you consider the extraordinary narratives that follow. We have made every effort to base them on the most reliable accounts.

It must also be said that eyewitness acounts, of which we have quoted many in this book, are at the same time the most reliable and the least reliable of sources for any event. Interview ten witnesses to any crime and you will have ten versions. Sorting out these kinds of contradi-

tions has been a major task for the authors of this book

Nineteenth Century Communication

One of the handicaps to learning about the New Madrid earthquakes is the fact that they happened before railroads, before radio, before television, before the telegraph, before photography, and even before standards of good journalism had been well established for accurate reporting of the news. It was also a time when frontier Americans were only semi-literate.

The first American railroad was not inaugurated until July 4, 1828, the B & O Railroad with a terminal at Baltimore, Maryland. Its first trains were drawn by horses. The first steam locomotives did not come until 1834 between Philadelphia and Columbia, Pennsylvania. It carried horses just in case the engine broke

Seismic Features on the New Madrid Golf Course. The New Madrid Golf Course may be the only one in the world with seismic sand traps. The caretakers have fertilized the turf considerably to keep it green, which obscures most of the sand boils on these fairways most of the time. Even so, they still show through after prolonged periods of dry weather. A circular patch of dead grass reveals an underlying sand boil in the photo on the right. On the left, we see a golf cart gliding across the links. In the foreground of this photo we see a low area between a pair of tall cypress trees. This is a portion of an old stream channel called "Des Cyprie." This stream used to flow westward away from New Madrid and into the Little River five or six miles away. The earthquakes of 1811-12 so disrupted the drainage patterns in the region that most of the time this channel doesn't flow at all any more. It is broken up into discontinuous pieces. However, water still flows through here during heavy rains, but in the opposite direction from what it did before the quakes. This portion used to be swampy most of the year but was drained in 1991 and partially filled in. Two miles further up this channel the stream flows the other way, when it flows at all, but it no longer empties into the Little River. Since the quakes the west end flows into a huge sand deposit—mysteriously disappearing into the ground north of Lilbourn, Missouri. Des Cyprie is a seismically altered stream channel that now flows in both directions, depending on rainfall patterns and groundwater conditions, and has no surface outlet on either end—the result of the earthquakes of 1811-12.

down. The first transcontinental railroad would not be completed until 1869.

Photography, invented by the Frenchman, Jaques Maude Daguerre, did not come until 1839 when the art was confined to fixing images onto a silver coated copper or ceramic plate. The picture was called "a daguerreotype."

The first mature newspaper coverage did not really evolve until the founding of the *New York Tribune* by Horace Greeley in 1841. Samuel Morse did not develop the telegraph until 1844.

A Federal Postal Service was formalized by the U.S. Congress in 1792, but it was not very fast. The Pony Express, the fastest mail service in the land, was not established until 1860 and which, by the way, was not a part of the government postal service, but a private enterprise. Cost to deliver a letter from Missouri to California was $5.00 per half ounce.

Alexander Graham Bell did not patent a practical telephone until 1876. Guglielmo Marconi did not form the Wireless Telegraph and Signal Company until 1897 when his maximum broadcast distance was only seventeen miles. The first television transmissions did not take place until 1933, broadcast by the Radio Corporation of America (RCA) in New York and Philadelphia.

If the New Madrid earthquakes would have happened today, they would probably be broadcast in real time, as they happen. The Loma Prieta Earthquake that struck during the Baseball World Series in California on October 17, 1989, was watched by most Americans on national television as it occured—from the first temblor that shook Candlestick Park at San Francisco to the last aftershock in Santa Cruz.

But the New Madrid quakes of 1811–12 didn't happen in modern times, and we have to rely on the accounts, such as they are, reliable or not. This includes, also, the stories preserved in the soils and rocks that geologists read—circumstantial evidence, such as sand boils, landslides, faults and fissures still visible today. The New Madrid Seismic Zone contains more than 5,000 square miles of scars and gashes, craters and crevasses, earthquake lakes and ponds still seen today, irrefutable proof of the colossal cataclysms that shattered the country in 1811–12. The authors have written two other books that specifically deal with the stories told by the landscape. (See "Trilogy of Books" later in this introduction.)

The New Madrid Earthquake Experience

Understanding comes by the mind, but belief comes by feeling. The history of the great New Madrid earthquakes is easy to understand but hard to believe. When you read the stories recounted in this book we want you to have more than a mere encounter of the mind and intellect, although we want you to have that, too. Mostly, we want you to feel like you lived in the early 1800's—personally, politically, socially, and spiritually. We want you to sense, to hear, to taste, to smell, and to appreciate the terrifying and awesome experiences of those who lived there and then. We want you to feel as if you may have known them and, perhaps, been one of their neighbors or relatives. As you absorb the vital history of these pages, you will find yourself admiring those hardy pioneers whose hardships are almost unimaginable to those of us today who live in so much safety, convenience, and comfort.

The saga of the New Madrid earthquakes embraces every aspect of the human condition. It has all the ingredients of a spellbinding drama. Its rich source materials provide the basis for a documentary mini-series for TV or a great movie. There are adventure and romance, politics and conspiracy, Indians and pirates, racial pride and racial prejudice, science and superstition, treachery and tragedy, crime and punishment, war and peace, honor and dishonor, birth and death, heroes and villains, humor and pathos, religion and debauchery, midwifery and medical malpractice, prophecy and doom—even sex scandal, murder, and suicide, all played out against the backdrop of one of nature's most awesome displays of power ever in the history of human-

New Madrid Quake Burgers. Back in 1990 when tens of thousands of people flocked to New Madrid from all over the world to wait for the major earthquake that Dr. Iben Browning said might occur on December 3, Tom's Grill introduced a special: "The Quake Burger." The current owner, Donette Clark, is seen above holding a sample of the specialty of the house. A close-up view reveals a major fault running through the center of the bun and even down into the meat! The burger comes in only one Richter magnitude: "Great!" Tom's Grill is on Main Street a few blocks from the New Madrid Museum and across the street from the County Court House. Tom Hunter, the original owner, founded the restaurant during the depression in the 1930's. It has changed hands several times since then but has kept the name. It has been in business for more than sixty years now, and, so long as New Madrid has earthquakes, it will probably stay in business.

kind. There's a good historical novel to be written from the kaleidoscope of facts assembled in this book. Maybe several novels.

Hollywood's special effects would find plenty of challenge in recreating the unbelievable phenomena the earthquakes produced. The Mississippi River forming water falls and running backwards. The ground opening up to swallow people, cattle, and houses. The creation of new large lakes. Forests snapped into splinters. Hundreds of landslides sweeping from the bluffs and hills. Eerie flashing lights, rumbling noises, strange odors, and thick vapors emanating from the ground as it convulsed. Quicksand and dark fluids oozing from the soils. Explosions in the subsurface, blasting over tall tree tops, leaving huge craters in the

The New Madrid County Health Department. This 100-year-old mansion has a grand staircase inside and stained glass windows, an example of several historic and beautiful homes in New Madrid. Standing at the front steps are Dr. Charles Baker, Public Health Director, and his assistant, James Bradley.

landscape. Fires, floods, crashing cabins, boats hurled up onto dry land, whole towns disappearing. No exaggeration would be necessary. The straight facts would be dramatic enough. And all of this was preceded by comets, eclipses, ghostly lights, and bizarre animal behavior against a world tapestry of wars, romance and politics.

This book is much more than an earthquake story. It is a complete slice of history, cut from some of the world's most dramatic decades and served within the context of one of the most terrible bursts of natural energy ever unleashed upon this planet. While you experience the turmoil of the earthquakes through the words of this book, you will also find yourself immersed in the turmoil of the times. Mother nature wasn't the only one going through unsettling times. The political and social structures of the whole world were also quivering with instability and change.

Historians would not use the term "World War" until the twentieth cen-

tury, but the western hemisphere was perilously close to global warfare in 1811–12. While the British provoked the War of 1812, while Chief Tecumseh organized warriors to stop white men from moving west, while the first steamboats were launched onto American rivers, and while General Napoleon plotted his Russian campaign in Europe, the population of the United States was shaken by more than 2,000 earthquakes in five months!

Scientists agree that at least three, and perhaps five, of the quakes had surface wave magnitudes of 8.0 or greater. The biggest was probably a magnitude 8.8, the largest in the history of the lower 48 states, larger than any quake yet experienced by California. In the aggregate, these five months of almost continuous ground shaking represent the greatest outburst of seismic energy in American history. In fact, according to an article in the March 1990 issue of *The Scientific American*, a survey of the great seismic events of history does not reveal a series of earthquakes of such major magnitudes anywhere else in the world for at least the last 2,000 years.

It reads like a fiction novel or a set of short stories, but it is not fiction. It is all true. You will feel like you know these people, like you lived with them and went through the great New Madrid earthquakes of 1811–12 with them—and survived.

Earthquake survival is a skill you can use and, this book can help you. This work is not only an account of the past but a warning for the future. The first portions of this book tell you what did happen. The last portions tell you what will happen and how to prepare for it.

A Buster of Myths

This book destroys some of the common cliches about the New Madrid earthquakes. One of them is that "very few people died." Another commonly heard statement is that "the ground opened up in numerous large huge cracks, but nobody was killed in them." Yet another popularly held notion is that "the New Madrid Fault holds the greatest threat for major earthquakes in the Midwest in the near future." This book provides documentation that suggests that all of these statements are probably untrue, even though they have been published repeatedly in a variety of places for many decades. This book presents a new and different perspective on the historical quakes of 1811–12, as well as some new insights on their implications for the future.

The Earthquake America Forgot is a departure from past and present paradigms. If you have read other books on the New Madrid earthquakes, you will find this one to be uniquely different. We have done our research and drawn our conclusions without regard to whether or not they agree with previous sources. While this book will entertain you, it will also instruct and educate. It is meant to be an enjoyable work and a serious one, too.

We have probably tresspassed on sacred ground and stepped on sensitive toes in several places in this book. We have challenged more than a few scientific and historical dogmas. We hope our new paradigms will all be taken, as we have written them, in good faith and good humor.

Good research and great discoveries are not made by concensus. Truth is not determined by majority vote. New ideas are always minority ideas. Science and society make no progress ouside of controversy. We hope this work will be a stimulus to many productive discussions.

This book is a "before, during, and after" account. It is the first treatment of the New Madrid earthquakes that leads up to them in a historic and global sense, moves through them in real time, and then follows with the ultimate fates of those who experienced them.

This is the first book to deal with the profound impact of these earthquakes on Native Americans, who outnumbered the settlers more than two to one in the vicinity of the fault zone. This is the first book to discuss the plight of African American slaves in the area at the time. This is also the first published attempt to determine a true estimate of the number of people killed.

Many things that people (including ourselves) have believed, said and taught for years about the New Madrid earthquakes have turned out to be untrue. In light of the extensive research conducted to produce this book, many former statements thought to have been "facts" turned out to be "factoids," statements commonly believed and quoted to be true, but aren't true. If you are already familiar with the history of the New Madrid earthquakes as presented in previous publications, you will find many facts and conclusions in this book that you have never read nor heard of before. We would value your feedback

Earthquake Demographics

At least eighteen of the New Madrid quakes were felt as far away as the East Coast. Several of the greatest ones were felt by every person living in the United States at the time! No other earthquakes have touched so many or were felt so far. Compare this to California, where even the largest quakes are scarcely noticed beyond state boundaries.

At the time of the quakes in 1811–12, the United States census estimated that there were approximately 7,500,000 citizens. Add to this another 700,000 African American slaves and at least 10,000,000 Native Americans, who were not counted in the census, and we calculate approximately 18 million people living in North America between the Rocky Mountains and the Atlantic Ocean. This was the felt area of the largest temblors of the sequence, an area of about 1.7 million square miles. The mean population density was just over 10 people per square mile, Indians included. The Pacific coast and southwestern portions of the United States were still Mexican or Spanish at that time. It wasn't until after the Mexican War in 1848 that these lands became part of the country.

While the whites lived mostly in the East and the blacks in the south, the redskins lived mostly in the western territories which, in that day, was the region between the Appalachian and Rocky Mountains. Today we call that the Midwest.

Most of these tribes had lived along the east coast a century before but had been forced westward by the intrusions of foreign settlers who had come in boats across the Atlantic. Having been dislodged from their ancestral homes, many Indian tribes resettled along the Mississippi River where fish and game were abundant and white settlers were sparse.

Between St. Louis and Memphis the red men outnumbered the whites and the blacks at least two to one when the earthquakes hit. Hence the impact on Native Americans of these massive shocks was much greater than formerly recognized.

Considering the present population in these same regions, what would be the impact of a magnitude 8.6 earthquake today? The demographics have changed considerably since then. The population center of the United States was probably not far west of Philadelphia in 1811–12— almost 1,000 miles from New Madrid. Today the center of population is in Missouri, near Steeleville, only 100 miles from the fault zone.

Even so, not every American citizen would feel such an earthquake this time because those west of the Rocky Mountains would be shielded from the tremors. But everyone east of the Rockies would experience them, just as they did in 1811–12. Such a quake would be experienced by over half the people in the country.

From a population east of the Rockies of 18 million in 1811–12, the number had grown five fold by 1940 to 90 million. Today, in the 1990's, it has doubled again to about 180 million. That is ten times the population of 1812, The implications of this for future earthquake losses are discussed later in this book.

For Further Facts

For those who desire more meticulously footnoted and technical works on the New Madrid Fault, a bibliography is provided. These references, plus many old newspaper articles and several encyclopedias, are the main sources upon which the historical and scientific accounts of this book are primarily based. Some of the references in the bibliography are specifically noted as "recommended for further reading."

The narrative history of the earthquakes and their precursors is based upon published accounts, but is not intended to be a complete scholarly presentation that acknowledges every source and every discrepancy in the historical records. Its purpose is to tell a story that moves and enables the reader to experience some of the feelings and reactions of these brave pioneers. A more academic history would have to acknowledge the many contradictory accounts which would break the momentum of a good narrative. The letters, journals, news articles, and other accounts still available are incomplete and often contradictory, even from eyewitnesses in the same vicinity at the same time. When several versions exist, we have chosen the one we think is most plausible and woven it into our narrative without mentioning the others.

We have also taken the liberty and license of a good storyteller. To interrupt the flow of the narrative with too many footnotes, qualifications, disclaimers, and acknowledgements of alternative accounts would defeat the purpose of this book. For an excellent and scholarly history of the quakes that cites the various sources and their disagreements, read James Penick's book, *The New Madrid Earthquakes*, listed in the bibliography.

We will never know for sure exactly what happened in all its detail. Even the number of the largest earthquakes is not known for certain. Most seismologists count at least three main events greater than 8.0 in Richter magnitude: One on December 16, 1811, one on January 23, 1812, and one on February 7. But the December event was accompanied by two other great shocks around 8.0 in magnitude—all within a few hours on the same day. Some seismologists count the three events of December 16 as a single earthquake with two major aftershocks. Others count them as two events with aftershocks while some count them as three separate events. We count them as three in this book. It is hard for us to consider a magnitude 8.0 earthquake as an after-shock. So in our account of the quakes you will read of five quakes of magnitude 8.0 or greater in the New Madrid sequence—three on the first day. For a discussion of how the earthquakes were counted and how Richter magnitudes were assigned when the seismograph had not yet been invented at the time, see Nuttli (1973 and 1990) in the bibliography.

Authorities also disagree as to some of the times and dates of the main events. People did not have good clocks. Calendars were not easily obtained. Even dates and days of the week were not always known to the people on frontiers like those in Illinois, Missouri, and Arkansas. Many existing accounts were written down years after the quakes from the recollections of those who experienced them. Memory is fallible, especially when it comes to emotionally charged experiences filled with horror and confusion. This book adheres to historically documentable detail as much as possible .

Chapters One and Two help establish the flavor of the historical and cultural milieu in which these great natural events occurred. An appropriate understanding of these cataclysms is as much an historical endeavor as it is geologic. Every effort was made to render a historically rigorous, geologically sound, and genealogically accurate account, insofar as is possible. If you discover any errors, we would be grateful for the information in order to make corrections in future editions. For an excellent and scholarly history of the "Jefferson Connection," as related in Chapter One, read Boynton Merrill's book, *Jefferson's Nephews*, also listed in the bibliography.

Our attention to detail has been carried into the illustrations. The artists, Don Greenwood and Anthony Stewart, researched the clothing, dress and architecture of the times to make sure everything is authentic. For example, the back cover includes drawings of the Carolina parrot (or paroquet), a beautiful bird that was very common in the Midwest during the time of the earthquakes but which is now extinct. The model for Don Greenwood's drawing was taken from the colored sketches of John James Audubon who was living in the region during the time of the quakes and who meticulously documented the appearance of virtually every species of bird then extant. The picture of the *New Orleans*, the first steamboat to navigate the Ohio and Mississippi Rivers, is as authentic as we could make it. Anthony Stewart has drawn it as a single-decked, double side-wheeler with a single smoke stack in the midsection and two masts, fore and aft. Some books show the *New Orleans* as a multi-decked, stern-wheeler with two stacks, and no masts, which is not correct.

Every notable person whose portrait has been sketched here, such as Chief Tecumseh, the Shawnee Prophet, Tenskwatawa, Thomas Jefferson, John James Audubon, Lydia Roosevelt, William Henry Harrison, Colonel George Morgan, Daniel Boone, etc., is, insofar as it was possible, a faithful reproduction of the person's actual appearance, based on the best sources we could find. We have also produced, for the first time, a map of the states and territories of the United States as things actually were in 1811–12.

We hope that history professors, geographers, earth science teachers, geologists, engineers, seismologists, sociologists, journalists, and even psychologists will all find this book to be of value in their teaching, research, consulting, and field work. Although written for the public at large, this is also a professional work. While the subject matter is physical science, the perspective is on people, history and the social sciences. Who says history and science can't be combined, presented in an interesting and colorful way, and made relevant to present human activity? However, for a more matter-of-fact geologic treatment of the subject, we recommend Myron Fuller's classic book, *The New Madrid Earthquake*, published in 1912 and listed in the bibliography.

As for scholarly works on Chief Tecumseh and his brother, Tenskwatawa, the Shawnee Prophet, see the two books by R.D. Edmonds listed in the bibliography.

A Trilogy of Books

This book, *THE EARTHQUAKE AMERICA FORGOT*, is one of a three volume set by the same authors, each with different perspectives on the New Madrid earthquakes.

THE EARTHQUAKE THAT NEVER WENT AWAY, published in 1993, is subtitled, "The Shaking Stopped in 1812, but the Impact Goes On." This unique publication of original research by the authors contains more than 150 figures, photographs, and tables showing hundreds of landforms still visible today from the earthquakes of 1811–12. This book emphasizes the impact of the landslides, sand boils, surface faults, and other seismic features left by the New Madrid earthquakes on life there today. You will read how farmers lose their tractors in sand boils, how trains are derailed by liquefaction of old sand fissures, and how streets and buildings are crumbling and breaking apart because they were built over old earthquake landslides. A set of 150 colored slides is also available to accompany this book.

The trilogy also includes a book containing a set of self-guided tours of the New Madrid Seismic Zone, complete with maps, road logs, directions, narratives, and photographs so that you can make your own tour of this fascinating region. Also included is a commentary on the local restaurants of the area, whose cuisine was sampled during the many weeks of field work by the authors. The title is *THE NEW MADRID FAULT FINDERS GUIDE*.

See the end of this book for more on these and other publications .

Visit New Madrid Museum and Scenic River Overlook

You'll definitely want to visit the New Madrid Museum sometime and enjoy the hospitality of the town. The Museum's newest two-story addition, dedicated December 3, 1991, is seismically designed. You'll be safe there if an earthquake occurs. Amidst their displays you can glimpse the rich history of the area, including battles of the Civil War and the culture of the Native Americans who

New Madrid Historical Museum. The photo on the left was taken in 1988 looking north from the levee down Main Street. The five flags flying are indicative of the rich history of New Madrid which has been governed at various times by Spain, France, the "CSA," Confederate States of America, and the "USA," United States of America, as well as the State of Missouri. The picture on the right was taken after 1991 when a new annex was added on December 3rd. The left portion of the Museum was built in the 1880's and was a tavern, "The First and Last Chance Saloon." The newly added portion is seismically designed to resist earthquakes.

Mississippi River Observation Deck at New Madrid. The view on the left is from the levee just outside the New Madrid Historical Museum. Visitors watch a large barge moving upstream. Just beyond the barge, under the water, is the original site of Old New Madrid before it was destroyed by the earthquakes and swept away by the river. In the distance two smoke stacks can be seen at the Associated Electric Power Plant six miles away. Built in 1968, the 812 foot tall stack and power plant are located in the epicentral area of the largest earthquake in American history—a magnitude 8.8 on February 7, 1812.

The photo on the right, taken from the observation deck itself, is a view upstream at New Madrid. The land on the other side is Kentucky. Around the clump of trees on the left is the mouth of St. John's Bayou where a huge wave threw dozens of boats upon land during the dark morning hours of February 7, 1812, killing an untold number of people. The barge moving to the left in the distance is approaching the place in the Mississippi River where a temporary waterfall was caused by the earthquake of February 7. The falls lasted until February 10. Many passengers and boatmen perished during those three days as they came around the bend, got caught, and capsized in the raging waters of the cascade. New Madrid residents could only stand by and watch helplessly as they heard the cries of the drowning people.

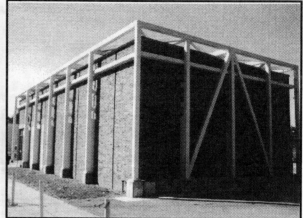

Seismic Retrofitting at New Madrid. The building on the left is the Immaculate Conception Elementary School. Before 1990 was an unreinforced brick building that could easily collapse in a strong earthquake. It is now safe. Large steel diagonal braces can now be seen inside the rooms which are visible through the windows in the picture. Strong steel rods also pass through the floors and roof in both directions. The bricks may still fall away in an earthquake, but the building cannot collapse any more. The school was able to do this at a cost of about $500 per child.

The building on the right was also an unreinforced masonry structure before 1990. It houses a telephone switching terminal owned by Southwestern Bell. While Immaculate Conception School was reinforced from the inside, this building has been reinforced from the outside by huge nine-inch square beams and braces. Southwestern Bell has reinforced every switching facility in southwest Missouri and northeast Arkansas in the same fashion so that telecommunications will be interrupted to the minimum in the event of a major earthquake on the New Madrid Fault.

occupied the region for thousands of years before the European and African Americans arrived.

In addition to checking out the Museum seismograph, you will also want to browse through their books, T-shirts, and other goods. You may want to visit their display on "Damages and Losses from Future New Madrid Earthquakes" to see how a large quake from New Madrid would affect your hometown. A strong magnitude 6.0 earthquake would reach out and touch at least twenty five states of the Midwest and the eastern seaboard.

Don't miss the Mississippi River Observation Deck just outside the Museum. It provides a photogenic panorama in 360 degrees for river and town alike. There you can look down Main Street of the town on one side of the levee and turn about face to view the site where the old town was drowned beneath the river. As you watch the boats and barges pass by, in the distance, six miles to the south of the deck, the Associated Electric stack can be seen, marker of where the nation's largest earthquake was centered.

The Immaculate Conception School, a few blocks from the Museum, is an excellent example of the seismic retrofitting of an unreinforced masonry building. Aesthetically engineered with structural steel, accomplished for about $500 per child, the building is now safe from earthquakes. If your school at home is not appropriately designed for earthquakes, a visit to Immaculate Conception by your school authorities would be beneficial.

And while you're in town, you might as well drive by the New Madrid Country Club, which is only a few blocks west of the museum. It has the only golf course in the world with seismic sand traps—sand boils from the earthquakes of 1811–12.

New Madrid, History, and the World

This book is for your enjoyment and for the enrichment of your appreciation of the past in an especially unique and exciting part of the planet. The New Madrid earthquakes of 1811–12 were world-shaking events of unparalleled magnitude. Their impact was not just local in a geographic sense. Neither was their impact limited in time to the early 19th century. Their influence continued into the present. These natural events changed the course of history for the midwestern United States.

Scientists and engineers from all over the world make special trips to visit and to study the New Madrid Seismic Zone. Dr. Teresa Crespellani, a professor of civil engineering at the University of Florence, Italy, is author of a book on earthquake-induced liquefaction. She was a participant on an international tour of the New Madrid Fault Zone conducted by the authors in 1991. "The New Madrid area is a compendium of the universe," she said. "Its fascinating and tragic history speaks to everyone faced with earthquakes. For earthquake researchers, New Madrid is the major laboratory in the world."

With hundreds of small tremors measured in the New Madrid Fault Zone every year and with the growing interest in preparation for future big shocks on the fault, the "aftershocks" of the Great New Madrid Earthquakes, both seismic and sociologic, still continue today.

There is a greater than 90% chance of a strong earthquake, magnitude 6.0 or greater, by the year 2,040 A.D. If you live within 600 miles of the fault, chances are you will at least feel such a quake. If you live within 200 miles, you can expect at least minor damage in your lifetime. The New Madrid Fault is more than a local phenomenon. It is also more than something of the past. It is ongoing and ever active. Every day is one day closer to the next "Big One."

We had more than Midwesterners in mind when we conceived this work. The New Madrid earthquakes are an historical heritage of the nation as a whole. An "All American Earthquake." You don't have to live near New Madrid to benefit from this book. It has been the authors' hope that if people will remember the earthquake that America forgot, they will be considerably better prepared to cope with earthquakes when they happen again, regardless of where they may occur.

David Mack Stewart
Marble Hill, Missouri

Burnal Ray Knox
Cape Girardeau, Missouri

December 3, 1994

Thomas Jefferson (1743-1826) in front of his home, Monticello, which he designed and began construction of in 1770. He was author of the Declaration of Independence (1776) and writer of the Northwest Ordinance (1784) which detailed America's plan for western expansion. He was the third President of the United States (1801-1809). His Monticello estate is three miles east of Charlottesville, Virginia, and 115 miles southwest of Washington, D.C. Jefferson was at Monticello during the New Madrid earthquakes in 1811-12.

Illustration by Anthony Stewart

Chapter One

THE JEFFERSON CONNECTION

Lilbourn and Isham Lewis rounded up their slaves and assembled them in the kitchen cabin, a small building separate from and just behind the main house. Normally this was a festive place filled with the savory aromas of southern cooking and the lighthearted chatter of pleasant social exchange among servants and masters alike. Not so tonight. The Lewis brothers had decided to deliver a grim object lesson.

It was Sunday at Rocky Hill Plantation, December 15, 1811, the day before the first great New Madrid earthquake.

Jefferson's Vision

Thomas Jefferson had a dream. When the British signed the Treaty of Paris in 1783, the Revolutionary War officially ended, and the United States became a free and recognized nation. The western boundary of the new country was the Mississippi River. Spain controlled the western lands, including the west bank of the river and both sides of its mouth at New Orleans. When Jefferson looked into America's future, he saw a land expanded westward all the way to the Pacific. The magnificent silver archway, now reflected in the waters of the Mississippi against the St. Louis skyline, is a symbol of the "Gateway to the West" that fulfilled that vision. The 630 foot high steel structure is the tallest historical monument in the world. It is named "The Jefferson National Expansion Memorial" and is now a national park. To most of us today that archway stands for the realization of the dream held by the early pioneers. But to Native Americans, that arch symbolizes something else—the end of a dream in which an earthquake played a part.

In Jefferson's day, even the east bank of the Mississippi was not securely possessed by the United States. It was a primitive frontier. Indians controlled much of it. Spain wanted it, too, and tried to persuade settlers in the territories adjacent to the east bank to take allegiance with Spain instead of the United States. In 1792 Kentucky became the first territory touching the Mississippi to become a state. It had barely received statehood when some of its leaders seriously considered Spain's proposal for secession from the union.

To counter such wavering allegiances, many American leaders encouraged U.S. loyalists to settle the "western frontier" right up to the banks of the Mississippi. Thus came

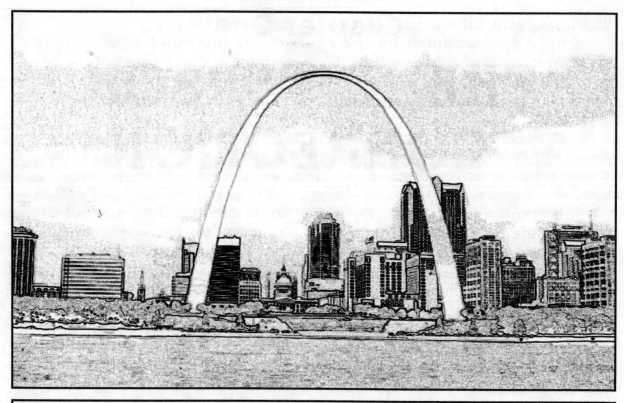

Jefferson National Expansion Memorial, Gateway Arch, St. Louis, Missouri

the establishment of several fortifications on the east bank—including Fort Pickering, where Memphis, Tennessee, would later be located.

Another of these outposts was established by George Rogers Clark in 1780. George was an Indian fighter and revolutionary war hero. He was the older brother of William Clark who would later explore the West with Meriwether Lewis and establish another outpost on the Missouri River at Fort Osage. George's settlement was named Fort Jefferson. It was located on a bluff where Mayfield Creek enters the Mississippi River, two miles below the Ohio River junction and about one mile upstream from Island #1. The city limits of Wickliffe, Kentucky, include the site of old Fort Jefferson today, but Wickliffe was not founded until after 1820. At the time the Fort was established, Kentucky was not a state. It actually comprised the western half of the state of Virginia of which Thomas Jefferson was governor from 1879 to 1881. Hence, the Fort was not named for the President Jefferson, but for the Governor Jefferson.

Tom's Relatives Go West

Several of Thomas Jefferson's relatives chose to migrate westward. These included his sister, Lucy, and her husband, Charles Lilbourn Lewis. Charles L. was not only Tom's brother-in-law, but was a first cousin as well. Marriage among cousins was common in those days.

Accompanying Charles L. and Lucy were their three youngest daughters and their two oldest sons,

Randolph and Lilbourn. The two sons were accompanied by their wives and children, including Lilbourn's oldest son, Lilbourn Livingston Lewis, then only five years old. In all there were twenty one Jefferson relatives—six adults and fifteen children . . . plus one more. Jefferson had a black niece.

The Lewises left Albemarle County, Virginia, in December of 1807, purchased a flatboat in Pittsburgh, and floated down a cold, icy, treacherous, Ohio River. In addition to the Lewises there were 15-20 slaves. One was Matilda, a young mulatto girl, about three years old at the time. Her father was Charles Lewis, Jr., the third son of Charles L. and Lucy. Charles Jr. never married. He died of a sickness in April of 1806 while serving in the U.S. military.

Although half black, Matilda was a blood relative of Thomas Jefferson. Thomas' sister, Lucy, was her grandmother. This made Thomas' father, Peter Jefferson, Matilda's great grandfather. It made Thomas Matilda's great uncle.

Matilda was raised as a servant girl in the Randolph Lewis household. In 1815 she was sold to Aaron Threlkeld, taking Threlkeld as her last name. She spent most of her life as a slave, rented out by the Threlkelds as a house servant. But "Aunt Matilda" was destined to die a free woman. She survived all of the Lewises who came to Kentucky with her and even ultimately survived the Civil War. She lived to celebrate her 80th birthday at her home in Crittenden County, Kentucky. The following excerpt is from the December 22, 1880, issue of *The*

Crittenden Press:

"In the quiet little village of Marion, where the eyes of the people have never fallen upon a President from father Washington down to James A. Garfield and where the visage of the lineage of either of the illustrious has never been knowingly looked upon, the discovery of a descendant of the "Sage of Monticello" might awaken a riffle of astonishment. Yet within the walls of a poorly chinked, ill-constructed log cabin in the suburbs of our out-of-the-way village may be found an ancient woman through whose veins the blood of Thos. Jefferson is slowly ebbing. "Aunt" Matilda Threlkeld is verging upon the age of four scores. And old Time has pressed his blighting fingers upon her, until the aged woman can no more leave the miserable hovel she calls home. According to her own statement she was born in Albemarle County, Virginia, and is a daughter of Charles Lewis whose mother was a sister of Thomas Jefferson."

The Lewis Clan Reaches Kentucky

Approximately forty people traveled on the Lewis flatboat. Also packed on that crowded vessel was their furniture and other belongings, including a few cattle, chickens, sheep, horses, and other livestock. It must have been like a miniature Noah's Ark! They reached their Kentucky destination in February of 1808. (See River Map on page 75)

Randolph and Lilbourn established two plantations in Livingston County overlooking the Ohio and across the river from Illinois. They were only a few miles upstream from the mouth of the Cumberland River. As the crow flies, the Lewis plantations would have been about seventy miles northeast of New Madrid. They were about eighteen miles upstream from where Paducah would be established in 1830. Today, the small town of Birdsville is located near the site of the old Randolph plantation.

Smithland, Kentucky, founded in 1796, was just below the mouth of the Cumberland River. The town was incorporated at its present position on a bluff overlooking the Ohio River in 1805, shortly before the Lewis's arrival. Smithland was only two miles downstream from Lilbourn's land. In fact, the Lewis plantations and those of their neighbors were referred to as "The Smithland Neighborhood."

The county had been named in 1798 after Robert R. Livingston (1746–1813), a member of the committee who drafted the Declaration of Independence and the man who, as Chancellor of New York, administered the first Presidential Oath of Office to George Washington on April 30, 1789. He was personally acquainted with all of the first seven presidents. He was a good friend of Thomas Jefferson.

Eddyville, the county seat at that time, was twenty miles up the Cumberland from Smithland. Until 1800, when the first county road between Smithland and Eddyville was commissioned, the only transportation link between the two towns was the river. In 1842 Crittenden, Lyon, and Caldwell Counties were formed out of Livingston County. Smithland was then designated as the seat of the remaining portion of

Livingston County, which it remains today.

The elderly Charles L. and wife, Lucy Jefferson Lewis, lived on the Randolph plantation with their oldest son. Lilbourn and his wife, Elizabeth ("Betsy"), named their property "Rocky Hill," which was only about a mile-and-a-half downstream from Randolph's farm. The hills of one farm were visible from the hills of the other. Lilbourn's holdings at Rocky Hill were about 1000 acres in extent. Later he acquired another 500-acre tract about two miles up the Ohio opposite from Stewart Island and on the other side of Randolph's estate.

Isham was the youngest brother of Randolph and Lilbourn. In 1809, when he was eighteen years old, he moved to Rocky Hill, also. Earlier that year Isham had spent several weeks at his uncle's Monticello estate in Virginia. Thomas Jefferson was training his young nephew in the art and science of surveying.

Tragedy on Rocky Hill

Meanwhile, back in the kitchen, Lilbourn and Isham counted heads. When they were satisfied that all of their slaves were present, they locked the doors to the cook house. With the forced assistance of their slaves, they built up an unusually large fire. The flickering flames cast ominous shadows. Filled with dread, fearing what was to come, the slaves stood around nervously. In the center, spread and bound, face to the floor, was seventeen-year-old George, a habitual runaway.

While Isham held a gun on the terrified slaves, Lilbourn raised a broadax and with one blow partially severed George's neck. Lilbourn then handed the blade to one of the blacks and ordered him to hack the body into pieces. To add to the horror, the brothers forced the rest to participate by pitching bloody body parts, piece by piece, into the fire. Meanwhile, Lilbourn lectured to the remaining slaves that this would also be their fate if any of them ever "disobeyed orders" or "ever tried to run away."

The grisly deed completed, the servants were conscripted to clean up the gory mess. It was after midnight when they finished—December 16, 1811.

It was a dark night—a new moon. But the sky was clear and the stars could be seen peering down through the tree limbs.

Through the half-lit darkness, intimidated witnesses stumbled to their shacks. The fire smoldered into the night. But before it could consume the evidence, a violent earthquake shook down the stones of the fireplace, smothering the flames.

During the next day not one hour went by without aftershocks, some of them almost as hard as the first. Against the unsettling background of a trembling earth, the brothers and their slaves hastily rebuilt the fireplace. The incriminating bones were hidden in the masonry.

There had been no legal witnesses to the crime. Lilbourn's family, including his pregnant wife, Letitia, had spent the night in the main house, unaware of the atrocity that had transpired. All of Lilbourn's servants had witnessed the horror, but in Kentucky a Negro could not lawfully testify against a white. As long as the evidence was hidden, the Lewis brothers had little to fear.

One would think that news of such a gross crime would quickly leak out, but apparently it did not. Lilbourn is said to have kept Letitia confined and under close watch during the weeks that followed. As for the slaves, their fears continued to grow as they considered what might happen to them if Lilbourn were tried and taken away—especially if they had been the ones to tell on their master. After December 16, Lilbourn kept them in strict isolation on the plantation.

Indicted by an Earthquake

As if burdened by a secret too horrible to hold, the unsettled earth was not ready to rest in silence. Throughout the rest of December, all of January, and into February, tremors continued to shake the plantation daily. Some strong. Some weak. The shocks were accompanied by a grotesque symphony of disturbing sounds and phenomena so strange they seemed unreal. Some tremors hissed and swished like the sounds of rushing waters. Some quakes rumbled and exploded with noises like gunfire or distant cannon. Some of the quakes caused the ground to give off vapors and foul odors. Some were sudden, short, and startling. Some were long, rolling, and nauseating, like the pitching of a ship on a sick sea.

The Lewises and their servants also witnessed the phenomenon of seismoluminescence, but they did not know what it was, and it frightened them. When temblors struck during the dark hours, they sometimes saw an eerie glow flickering and flashing from the ground and reflecting from the clouds, casting the leafless trees in ghostly silhouettes against shades of pastel pink, blue, green, and yellow. Amidst this surrealistic background the boundary between the natural and the supernatural was becoming a blur. No one was resting well in the Lewis household. Rude seismic visitors shook their beds nightly. The children were afraid to go to sleep. They were living in a nightmare that went on for weeks and weeks, as if it would never end. But the nocturnal peace of Lilbourn and Isham was to be disturbed by more than just earthquakes.

On February 7, 1812, at about 3:15 a.m., a great shock emanating from New Madrid released a sequence of seismic waves so strong that they cracked foundations and caused brick buildings to fall in Louisville, more than 200 miles east of Rocky Hill. That shock also caused the kitchen fireplace at Lilbourn's manor to collapse again, spilling its grisly secrets.

This time a neighbor's dog, sniffing amid the rubble, discovered a charred head and carried it off. Jonah Hibbs, Lilbourn's closest neighbor and a justice of the peace, whose property adjoined Rocky Hill, was on his way to Smithland that morning. His attention was caught by a dog along the roadside gnawing on a strange looking object about the size and shape of a large cabbage. He dismounted his horse to get a better look. It was a human skull with much of its skin and features still intact. As Jonah was pondering what to do, Dickson Hurley, another neighbor, came down the road also on his way to Smithland. Inspecting the mutilated head, Dickson noted a peculiar scar on the face which he recognized as an identifying mark of George, one of Lilbourn's slaves. Wrapping the head in a cloth, Dickson carried it to Smithland where he and Jonah both reported what they had found to the authorities.

Lilbourn and Isham were charged with murder. No human witnesses were necessary. Their dreadful deed had been made public by the discovery of a dog and the testimony of an earthquake. The disgraced Lilbourn committed suicide. Isham broke jail and disappeared.

Isham is said to have adopted an alias, moved south, and entered the military under the command of Andrew Jackson (Also called "Old Hickory," he was later to become the seventh President, 1829-1837.) The war of 1812 had been in progress. The Battle of New Orleans, January 8, 1815, lasted only 25 minutes, yet the British lost 2,600 men. The Americans, under Jackson, suffered only light casualties. By one account, there were only thirteen Americans wounded. Only seven died. One of those reported as dead was Isham Lewis. The whereabouts of his body remains unknown.

Isham's unlikely death was even more ironic when one considers that the War of 1812 had already been officially ended before the Battle of New Orleans. The Treaty of Ghent had been signed in Belgium two weeks earlier on December 24, 1814.

Because communications were so slow in those days, neither the British nor the Americans at New Orleans were to know until late January that official hostilities had ended weeks before and a ceasefire declared.

One of the American soldiers who fought with Isham Lewis in the Battle of New Orleans was Edward Livingston (1764-1836), the youngest brother of Robert R. Livingston for whom Isham's home county in Kentucky had been named. Edward later became Secretary of State and U.S. Minister to France under President Andrew Jackson, following in the footsteps of his older brother who had served similar offices under President Jefferson.

As for Lilbourn, he lies in the Rocky Hill Cemetery in Livingston County where he killed himself. Lying beside him is his first wife, Elizabeth Jane Woodson (Betsy) Lewis. Some local legends have it that Lucy Lewis, his mother, is buried there also. But this is not so.

Lucy Jefferson is buried on the Randolph farm about one and a half miles away on a prominent hilltop overlooking the Ohio near Birdsville. A twelve-foot-tall obelisk was placed in the Rocky Hill Cemetery in 1924 by the Lucy Jefferson Lewis Chapter of the Daughters of the American Revolution (D.A.R.). The location of Lucy's grave is described on the south side of the monument as being on "a mountain which can be seen in the distance." Directions are given on how to get there. The graves of Lilbourn, his wife Betsy, and the monument to Lucy Jefferson can be visited today. They can be found two miles north of the bridge across the Cumberland River at Smithland, Kentucky. The bridge is named the "Lucy Jefferson Lewis Memorial Bridge."

Nature was Hard and So Were the People

Lilbourn and Isham had their faults, but there were some extenuating circumstances. Before we judge them too harshly, we must consider the harshness of the frontier in that day. It was not uncommon for masters to whip and beat their slaves. It was a violent culture. Kentucky, at the time, did have some statutes to protect slaves, including a law against "inhumane" treatment. However, the perception of what was "inhumane" was much different in 1811 than it is today. Parents beat children and husbands abused wives with impunity. Whites beat blacks. Whites killed Indians. Indians killed whites and blacks, as well as each other. And whites beat and killed each other, as well.

Many Kentucky settlements, including Smithland, had a pillory— a whipping post in the town square where corporal punishment was delivered to offenders of all races as a public display. Even women were whipped. The maximum penalty was 39 lashes, the same limitation as ancient Rome. (Forty Lashes was considered tantamount to a death sentence.) It was a brutal time.

Livingston County records describe many incidents of assault at that time—usually involving alcohol, and often resulting in permanent injury, disfigurement, and sometimes death. It was not unusual to see a man missing an eye or an ear, a lip or his nose, bitten off in a bar-room brawl. Smithland, not far from Lilbourn's plantation, had an especially notorious reputation for lust and drunkenness. Virtually every building lining Front Street, along the river, held a liquor license and served as a tavern. Smithland also harbored the unsavory and the unscrupulous who haunted the billiard halls to tempt boatmen into gambling away their hard-earned money.

Dueling was still legal. By subscribing to a specified setting and set of protocols, one man could legally kill another. Aaron Burr, a United States Vice President, had shot and killed Alexander Hamilton in a duel in 1804. Burr had been a United States Senator and had unsuccessfully run for President against Jefferson. Hamilton was America's first Secretary of the Treasury. In 1806, Burr moved west to Natchez, Mississippi, a city known for its lawlessness. There he was ultimately arrested by federal officers—not for murder, but for treason. He had been accused by President Jefferson of plotting to separate the western states from the Union.

Even as late as 1816, Thomas Hart Benton, who was to become Missouri's first and most famous U.S. Senator, shot and killed a U.S. District Attorney in St. Louis in a duel. It was not unusual for legislators to carry concealed pistols or knives into the very halls of Congress. Attitudes toward violence were different then. It was an accepted way of life, within limits.

Kentucky: Supplier of Slaves

Kentucky also became known as the state where slaves received the worst treatment. George wasn't the only slave to die at the hands of his masters in Kentucky. Many did. And even when charged with murder (which wasn't often), guilty slave owners always got off lightly. The abuse of slaves in this state is said to have become even worse as the Civil War years approached.

The hilly land of Kentucky was not as suitable for large plantation farming as were other parts of the south where slaves could be employed profitably. Most Kentucky slaves were kept for domestic service, not farm labor.

On March 2, 1807, President Thomas Jefferson signed into law a federal prohibition against further importation of black slaves from Africa. Since the external supply of slaves to America had been cut off, Kentuckians found that they could make a business of breeding slaves and selling them down the river for a profit.

During the fifty years prior to the Civil War, Kentucky bred and sold more than 80,000 slaves to other states. At the time of the earthquakes, prices ranged from $400 to $600 per slave depending on their potential for working in the cotton and sugar cane fields of the deep south.

It is a curious twist of fate that the same state that had made a brutal business of supplying slaves to the plantations of the South also gave birth to the very man who was destined to free them. Thomas and Nancy Lincoln and their two-year-old daughter, Sarah, lived on a 348-acre farm on the South Fork of Nolin Creek, eighteen miles southeast of Elizabethtown and forty-five miles south of Louisville, Kentucky. The Lewis Plantations were another 150 miles further to the west.

On a Sunday morning, February 12, 1809, Tom Lincoln asked his neighbor to go get "the granny woman." That same day, in a rough-hewn cabin built by his father, with a packed-dirt floor, only one window, and one door with leather hinges, Abraham Lincoln, future President and author of the Emancipation Proclamation, was born.

In the Spring of 1811 the Lincolns moved to another farm on Knob Creek, ten miles away on the Cumberland Trail, where the soil was a little richer and the neighbors more numerous. It is here that the Lincoln family experienced the New Madrid earthquakes.

The number of slaves were growing in Hardin County, and Tom Lincoln didn't like it. In 1816, when Abe was seven, his father decided to move to Pigeon Creek, Indiana, eighty miles west. Indiana was a free state. Tom could no longer bear to witness the cruelty of slavery as it had become in Kentucky.

The actions of Lilbourn and Isham on the night of December 15, 1811, were depraved, to be sure, but must be considered in the context of the culture of which they were a part.

The 1811 murder of George was also preceded by a long succession of failures and disappointments for the Lewis family.

The Rise and Fall of the Lewis Empire

The Lewis name is an ancient one, with its origin in Norway. Norsemen immigrating to France spelled it "Louis."

Freedom of thought, religious conviction, and courage of action had always been Louis traits. During the sixteenth century, the Louises became some of the first protestants in France. They were Huguenots. Their religious persuasions placed them on the opposite side of the French throne, a position that could result in one's arrest, torture, and execution.

In 1685, with the revocation of the Edict of Nantes, several members of the Louis family fled across the English Channel for their lives. Safely landed on British soil, they changed the spelling of their name to "Lewis."

The Lewises were among the very first to migrate from England to America. When Col. Charles "Byrd" Lewis established his plantation in Albemarle County, the Lewises had been one of the most respected and influential families in Virginia for more than a hundred years.

General Robert Lewis (1609-1655) was an attorney and a Jamestown settler. His grandson, John Lewis II (1669-1725) was known as "the wealthiest man in Virginia." John's mother, Isabella Warner, and his wife, Elizabeth Warner, were both descended from three different royal lines of England and France.

Charles Lilbourn Lewis (1747-1831) was the great-grandson of John Lewis II. Charles Lilbourn Lewis fought in the Revolutionary

War. Their Virginia estate, Monteagle, was adjoined to the Jefferson estate, Monticello. The Lewises and the Jeffersons had lived close by as neighbors for a long time.

But they were more than neighbors. The Jeffersons and the Lewises had also intermarried for generations.

After 1800 the income from the Monteagle farm began to decline. Charles L. and Lucy sank hopelessly into debt. In fact, Thomas Jefferson was among their creditors. Before they left Virginia they had lost all of their slaves, all of their horses, and all of their most fertile land, holding only a few hundred acres of spent soil that would no longer grow crops.

The sons, Randolph and Lilbourn, were also experiencing financial decline. By selling their remaining Virginia properties for about $18 per acre, they could purchase land on the Kentucky frontier for $2.00-$5.00 an acre. In this way, they could move and get a fresh start.

Lilbourn and his brother, Randolph, were the oldest sons, the most able, and the ones who assumed family leadership, even over their parents who were virtually destitute by then.

Their monetary situation began to improve in Kentucky. Randolph was appointed as a local magistrate, which netted an income. Lilbourn was commissioned as a captain in the Kentucky Militia. He was also appointed (and paid) to poll the county for the 1810 census.

But tragedy continued to pursue the Lewises.

The Dangers of 19th Century Medicine

1809 was a bad year. Almost all of the Lewises got sick. Most suffered from malaria. But worms, smallpox, whooping cough, cholera, and various "fevers" also took their toll. The treatments of Dr. Arthur Campbell, their family physician, did not help.

By nineteenth century standards, Dr. Campbell was no quack. He was well trained in the medical and surgical practices of the day. The customary therapies were laxatives, purgatives and blood letting. The physicians of the time were so convinced of the benefits of bleeding they even prescribed the application of leeches as a therapy for hemorrhage. We now know such practices can dehydrate and weaken the patient even to the point of death.

The logic of medical thinking in the early 1800's was based on the theory that illness was usually due to something in the body fluids that needed to be removed. Hence, it made perfect sense to prescribe every possible means to remove fluids by stimulating diarrhea, vomiting, and blood loss. If a patient continued to get worse, that could only mean that not enough fluids had been removed. Therefore, a good physician would redouble the therapies—increase the dosages of laxatives, administer more emetics, or take another pint of blood. If the patient died, the surviving family members could be assured that "everything that medical science could possibly have done, was done."

The germ theory had not yet made its debut. A lack of understanding of even the basics of sterile technique led to many infections, illnesses and deaths, including unnecessary mortalities in childbirth. No one knows how many mothers died of "childbed fever" by the unwitting hands of well-meaning physicians who attended healthy women with unwashed hands and let blood at the first signs of postpartum hemorrhage. Fortunately, this was mostly a problem in cities where women sought doctors instead of midwives and went to hospitals to "lie in and be delivered." In frontier towns and rural areas, virtually all women gave birth at home with the assistance of a midwife and with only a fraction of the mortalities experienced from the hands of doctors in city hospitals.

Dr. Campbell and his colleagues also prescribed medications such as camphor, castor oil, paregoric, opium, quinine, and toxic compounds, such as antimony, "spirits of niter," and calomel—a mercury poison we now know to be more harmful than beneficial. Sickness, death, or injury caused by the prescriptions or procedures of a physician are called "iatrogenic." One of the most famous victims of standard medical practice was George Washington who died from his doctors' treatments in 1799. Suffering from a simple case of the flu, he was bled to death by his physicians. No one realized that our first President had died from iatrogenic causes until more than a century later as medicine became more enlightened.

According to the meticulous records kept by Dr. Campbell, he regularly visited the Lewises. He charged $2.00 for a daytime house call at Rocky Hill and $3.00 for a night call, which was his compensation for the two-mile horseback ride from Smithland. The medicines and ointments he carried to the Lewis household cost extra, ranging from 25 cents to a dollar per dose. He charged 50 cents for a bleeding. A typical visit, with medicine, would run between three to six dollars. Dr. Campbell bled them, purged them, lanced boils, and prescribed a variety of strong medicines, all in the faith that the Lewises were receiving "the best that nineteenth century medicine had to offer."

Sometimes the Lewises or their slaves were bled or laxatives prescribed even when they were not sick. This was considered to be "preventive medicine." The therapies were the same for both the blacks and whites, but their prescription was not equal. Although the number of slaves at the Lewis plantations was about the same as the number of white folks, Dr. Campbell's accounting shows that for every dollar spent on medical care for the slaves, $5.00 was spent on the families of their masters. Lilbourn's health care costs averaged between $60 and $70 per year.

Considering the serious, and sometimes lethal, iatrogenic dangers of medical treatment in those days, one has to wonder how many members of the Lewis family who died in Kentucky were actually victims of the medical practices of their times. Perhaps one of the reasons Matilda Lewis Threlkeld outlived all of her slavemasters was that she could not afford, and did not receive, any health care and, thus, was better off for the lack of it.

The Grim Reaper

On April 25, 1809, Lilbourn's wife died. His "beloved Betsy" was the first to be buried in the family cemetery on Rocky Hill. She was only 27. Her death appears to have been a consequence of complications in childbirth. She had already borne five children during their twelve-year marriage. The tragedy was at the end of her sixth and final pregnancy, from which neither baby nor mother was to survive. The details of how the labor and delivery were handled were not recorded, but we do know that the good Dr. Campbell was on hand. Lilbourn now had to assume full responsibility for their five children.

One month later, May 26, 1809, Lilbourn's mother died. She was 58. Lucy Jefferson Lewis was the first to be buried in the family plot on Randolph's farm. By the time of the earthquakes, Lilbourn's mother and first wife had both been laid to rest and, thus, never had to experience the terror of the temblors nor the horror of Lilbourn's later deeds.

Lilbourn's little brother, Isham, arrived in August, 1809, but soon took ill, along with most of the Lewis children. Dr. Campbell was a regular visitor to both Rocky Hill and to the home of Randolph that year.

By the end of September of 1809 Lilbourn's ailing family had run up so many medical bills that they could not pay them. He still prevailed upon the good Dr. Campbell, who continued to make house calls to Rocky Hill and provide them with medicines for a time on credit. Eventually, the doctor discontinued his services to the Lewises and filed a suit for payment of his fees.

So here was the family of Lilbourn Lewis: Receiving medical care they couldn't afford which, unknown to them or their doctor, probably made them sicker, not better, and then, as if that were not bad enough—they were being sued to pay for the iatrogenic insult.

Then the Lewis clan suffered another loss. In October of 1809 the famous explorer and statesman, Meriwether Lewis died on a trip between St. Louis and Washington, DC. Apparently it was a suicide. His close friend, Thomas Jefferson, who knew him well, later wrote that Meriwether had long suffered from periods of depression, which "was a constitutional disposition in all the nearer branches of the family of the Lewis name." Jefferson attributed Lewis' suicide to be the result of one of those periods of melancholy brought on by the burdens of his heavy responsibilities as Governor of the Missouri (Upper Louisiana) Territory. The year before, Isham had visited Meriwether in St. Louis and had carried a message from him to Jefferson at Monticello. Lilbourn, Isham, and Randolph were all cousins to Meriwether. Meriwether is buried where he died—in Lewis County, Tennessee.

The year 1810 was better, but the fortunes of the Lewis family were, as yet, still unstable and insecure. Financially, the Lewises had the appearances of wealth, but they were, in fact, land poor. They had put all of their money into Kentucky real estate, but their speculated profits for the resale of some of that property never materialized.

Lilbourn's total income for 1810 was $350, which had to support approximately twenty-five people, counting slaves. That was not as bad as it sounds, however. At that time a man's wages ranged from a nickel to to 50 cents a day. A night's lodging at a hotel could be had for 12-15 cents. A cow could be bought for $5.00 and a sheep for $2.00. Eggs were 6 cents a dozen and milk was 6 cents a quart. Turkeys were relatively expensive. A small one could be bought for 25 cents, while a really big one might go for 50 cents.

The year 1810 held an especially happy note for Lilbourn. A widower for a year and a half, he married Letitia Griffen Rutter on November 22, 1810. Letitia was said to be "the belle of the county, . . .bright eyed, accomplished and beautiful," according to one source. She came from one of the most prominent and influential families of the area. This made Lilbourn an in-law to the powerful elite. Things had begun to look good for Lilbourn's future.

In January, 1811, Lilbourn's brother, Randolph, wrote his will for no apparent reason. He seemed to be in adequate health. Normally, wills were only made when one was old, seriously ill, or in a situation of imminent danger, such as military action. Randolph must have sensed something. In February he died. He was only thirty-seven. The cause of death is unknown. Some said it was a poisonous snake bite, but this would have been unlikely in a cold January when snakes hibernate and become immobile.

Randolph had held a paid position as a county magistrate. It was recommended to the governor that Lilbourn be appointed to fill his deceased brother's position. Instead, the governor passed him over for another, giving no reason. This was another disappointment for Lilbourn after a decade of many.

In May of 1811, Lilbourn's bride of six months, Letitia, became pregnant. That was followed by a wet spring and a dry, hot summer which did not do well for the crops that year. Lilbourn's responsibilities to family were mounting. In addition to the expectation of another child, he now had to look after two sets of children—his and his brother's. He was also responsible for the care of his aging father. Debts began to mount. Two lawsuits were filed against him for unpaid bills. He began to drink.

The end of the previous year, 1810, had been a happy one. His marriage to Letitia had been a real joy. But the honeymoon was destined to be short. One year, three weeks, and two days after their wedding, the fortunes of the Lewis family were to collide with another reversal. This time it could not be blamed on fickleness of the economy, acts of nature, accidental fate, nor chance misfortune. This time Lilbourn's undoing would be by his own intemperate hand, with the help of his youngest brother, Isham.

They were said to have been drunk on the night of December 15, 1811. And they were angry at George. Earlier in the day Lilbourn had asked him to go down to the spring for some water. George had sulked away in a show of resentment, which irritated his master.

And then, on the way back up the hill, he had broken a favorite pitcher, one that had been brought all the way from Virginia. It had belonged to Lilbourn and Isham's mother, Lucy.

Lilbourn's Luck

These are the circumstances that led up to the murder. Lilbourn was, of course, wrong for what he did. But, for the majority of his life, he could have been characterized as a good citizen, a servant to the community, and a dutiful husband and father. He was a faithful member of the Presbyterian church. His ancestors were upright people, members of a fine Virginia family. His children and grandchildren are said to have all led exemplary lives, some achieving prominence in their chosen fields. But Lilbourn was prone to bad luck. Some of it was of his own doing, but some was not.

His second wife, Letitia, gave birth to her first child, James Randolph Lewis, on January 31, 1812, during the siege of the New Madrid earthquakes, six weeks after George's murder. The evidence of the homicide was still securely hidden behind the masonry of the kitchen fireplace at this time. It is not clear how much Letitia knew. Then on February 7, only a week after his son's birth, came the quake that shook down the stones and exposed his crime.

A week later Mary Howell Lewis, Lilbourn's sister-in-law and widow of Randolph, became seriously ill. She died on February 19.

In March, his wife, Letitia left him, taking their newborn son with her. They had been married for less than sixteen months. He never saw them again.

Even Lilbourn's suicide did not go as planned. Lilbourn and Isham had made a pact after their indictment for the murder of George. On April 10, 1812, while out on bail, they went to the cemetery where Betsy was buried on Rocky Hill. Each had a loaded long rifle. Lilbourn wrote his will and laid it in the grave yard. Then they were to step a few paces apart, face each other, and fire at chest level on the count of three.

Isham had a question. What if one of the flintlocks did not fire, as was frequently the case? Lilbourn explained that in that event the surviving brother would simply shoot himself. "How am I supposed to do that?" inquired Isham. "These rifles are so long I can't put the muzzle on my chest and still reach the trigger."

Lilbourn had an answer which he demonstrated. He placed the butt of the rifle on the ground and leaned it toward him so that its muzzle was touching his chest near the heart. He took a stick about two feet long to show how to reach the trigger. Forgetting it was loaded, he accidentally tripped the hammer and killed himself before Isham's horrified eyes.

Isham fled the scene and went to report the accident. Already under indictment for one murder, he was then arrested under suspicion of contributing to his brother's death as well. Three weeks later, on May 5, Isham escaped from the Livingston County jail and never came back. Three years later he, too, was dead, killed in a futile battle at New Orleans.

Thus, within the short span of six

years, 1809-1815, five of the six adults who had come from Virginia were dead. Only the patriarch, Charles Lilbourn Lewis, was still alive. He died of natural causes in 1831 at the age of 84.

One would think that the name of Lilbourn Lewis would quietly disappear into obscurity after such an infamous deed and ignoble demise. That was not to be the case.

The Ghost of Lilbourn

Four miles west of New Madrid is the small Missouri town of Lilbourn in Lewis Township. It was founded in 1908 at a crossroads formerly known as "Paw Paw Junction." Its current name comes from the donor of an acre of land given to the city for the Frisco Railway depot. That donor was Lilbourn Anexamander Lewis (1843-1934), grandson of the infamous Lilbourn Lewis (1776-1812).

Lilbourn Livingston Lewis (1801-1876) was born to Lilbourn and Betsy two years before they left Virginia and moved to Kentucky. His namesake was Robert Livingston, a politician, financier, and friend of Thomas Jefferson's after whom Livingston County had been named. Lilbourn Livingston was about ten years old when orphaned by his father's suicide in 1812. He was raised by the Phillips family of Livingston County. In 1827, when he was twenty-five, he moved to New Madrid, Missouri, accompanied by his sister, Elizabeth, and her husband, Richard Phillips. Lilbourn Livingston married Hannah Ramsey Hayden of New Madrid that same year. They settled about four miles west of New Madrid, building a log

Three Views of Lilbourn, Missouri. (1) Lilbourn City Limits, Population 1,378; (2) Lilbourn City Water Tower; and (3) Welcome to the Village of North Lilbourn.

cabin, which was still standing as of the 1930's. They called their farm, "Lewis Prairie." They had ten children—five girls and five boys.

Lilbourn Anexamander Lewis was their sixth child and third son. It was he who would later organize the town of Lilbourn on the old Lewis estate. He fought for the South during the Civil War, was captured, and imprisoned in St. Louis. His father, Lilbourn Livingston, paid $500 for his release, which, in those times, was a considerable sum, almost enough to purchase a small house. Lilbourn Anexamander usually went by the "Lilbourn A." or simply "L.A." His nickname was "Billy Goat."

There are other Lilbourn Lewises. Randolph and Mary, who had died in Kentucky, had named their first son, Charles Lilbourn Lewis, Jr. He died without heirs. Randolph and Mary had another son, Warner Lewis, born in Kentucky in 1810. As a young man he moved to New Madrid to live with his cousin, Lilbourn L. and his sister, Elizabeth Lewis Phillips. He was described as a noble and honest man whose seven children left many descendants in the New Madrid area. One of his grandsons was Lilbourn Mitchell Lewis, born in New Madrid in 1899.

Lilbourn A. and his first wife, Sarah C. Meriwether (1843-1871), had a son, Lilbourn G. (1866-1889). Lilbourn G. left no heirs, having died at age 23. Another son of Lilbourn A. and Sarah was Winston P. (1872-1949) who had a son, Lilbourn Alexander Lewis (1900-1974). He is also known as "Lilbourn A. Lewis, Jr.," or "L.A. Lewis, Jr." He moved to Texas and died there.

Another grandson of Lilbourn A. is Lilbourn Lewis "Pud" Riley, born in 1908, the same year the town of Lilbourn was named. Pud is the son of Charlotte Lewis and Howard Edwin Riley. Pud still lives in New Madrid in the very home built by his grandparents, Emma and Lilbourn, over one hundred years ago.

As a name, Lilbourn is not reserved for men only. In fact, the first to bear it in the Lewis family lineage was a woman: Jane Lilbourn Rogers Randolph, a grandmother to both Thomas Jefferson and Charles Lilbourn Lewis. That was over 300 years ago. More recently, there is Lilbourn Lewis Hunter Crisler, a gracious lady born in 1913 and still living in New Madrid today. Her grandmother was Lilbourn Lewis Broughton Hunter. Both of these women are known by the name of "Libba." Libba Crisler is descended from two of the five daughters of Lilbourn Livingston and Hannah R. Lewis. Their oldest daughter, Mary Ann, born 1833, married a Hunter while their second oldest daughter, Elizabeth Ann, born 1835, married a Broughton. Her grandfather Hunter and grandmother Broughton were first cousins. Libba Crisler lives in a picturesque white frame house with a red brick foundation on Water Street. It is more than a hundred years old, built by her grandfather. It is directly in front of the New Madrid Museum.

The name Lilbourn comes from England and Wales. It means "little brook." (By coincidence the town of Lilbourn, Missouri, is located on the east bank of the "Little River," which became a little brook after the earth-

Lilbourn Lewis Hunter Crisler is better known as "Libba." She is a direct descendant of Lilbourn Lewis of Rocky Hill and Lucy Jefferson, sister to Thomas Jefferson. Her ancestors also include some of the earliest settlers of New Madrid where she lives in a house more than 100 years old built by her grandfather . Two views of the house are shown below..

quakes.) The name was originally spelled Lilburne or Lilburn. All three ways of spelling can be found on the records in Kentucky and Virginia. Since Lilbourn Livingston Lewis moved to New Madrid the spelling has consistently been "Lilbourn," although it is also occasionally seen spelled with an "e" as "Lilbourne." In any case, we have chosen to use the spelling of "Lilbourn" throughout this book to avoid confusion. It is enough to have many Lilbourns without adding several ways to spell the name.

When you drive through New Madrid you cross Lewis Street a few blocks before you reach Main Street. The Immaculate Conception Catholic Church in New Madrid has a window on the east side dedicated to L.A. and Emma Lewis. This would be Lilbourn Anexamander and his second wife, Emma C. LaForge (1854-1948). There is a small community just north of New Madrid called LaForge.

On the west side of the church is a window dedicated to Lilbourn Lewis and another to Mary Lewis. It is not clear which Lilbourn and which Mary this would be.

The New Madrid Cemetery (also called Evergreen Cemetery) has stones marking at least four Lilbourn Lewises, along with many of their children and wives. The harshness of the living conditions in that time is well documented by the number of infant graves and stones of mothers who died following childbirth. The stone of Sarah C. Meriwether, first wife of Lilbourn Anexamander, bears the sad statistics of her death at age twenty-seven years, seven months, and fifteen days. She died only nine days after the birth of son, Carol C., who followed his mother in death eleven days later at the age of three weeks. Lilbourn Anexamander, founder of the town of Lilbourn, is buried nearby with his second wife, Emma LaForge.

Around New Madrid there is obvious pride in the name of Lilbourn Lewis. Why?

Immaculate Conception Catholic Church in New Madrid (upper left);

Lewis Street, in New Madrid;

Lilbourn Lewis stained glass window in I.C. Church (left);

L.A. & Emma Lewis stained glass window in the I.C. Church. (right) L.A. (Lilbourn Anexamander) is the founder of Lilbourn, Missouri.

The Lewis Family Plot at Evergreen Cemetery in New Madrid. The plot is seen in the upper left. The small stones are all children, most of whom died in infancy. The two larger stones in the foreground of the top left photo are Lilbourn Livingston Lewis (1802-1876) and his wife, Hannah Ramsey Hayden (1811-1854), whose stones are also seen side by side in closeup in the next photo below. Hannah was born and raised in New Madrid and was less than a year old when the earthquakes hit. The tall stone in the background of this photo (also visible with a cross on top in the upper left picture) is that of Lilbourn G. Lewis (1866-1889), son of Lilbourn Anexamander Lewis (1843-1934) and Sarah C. Meriwether (1846-1874) who died a few days following the birth of her son, Carol C. Lewis, who only lived three weeks. Carol and his mother are buried side by side. Emma C. (LaForge) Lewis was the second wife of Lilbourn Anexamander ("L.A."). L.A. Lewis was the founder of Lilbourn, Missouri.

Tombstone Inscriptions, Evergreen Cemetery, New Madrid. (upper left) LILBOURN G., Son of L.A. & S.C. LEWIS, BORN DEC. 12, 1866, DIED MAR. 4, 1889; (upper right) SARAH C. Wife of L.A. LEWIS, DIED Mar. 18th, 1871, AGED 27 Y's, 7 M's, 15 D's; (lower left) OUR FATHER, LILBOURN LEWIS, DIED Feb. 28, 1876, AGED About 75 Years; HANNAH R., Wife of LILBOURN LEWIS, BORN May 15, 1811; *DIED* Nov. 16, 1854, Aged 43 Yrs, 6 m's & 5 d's.

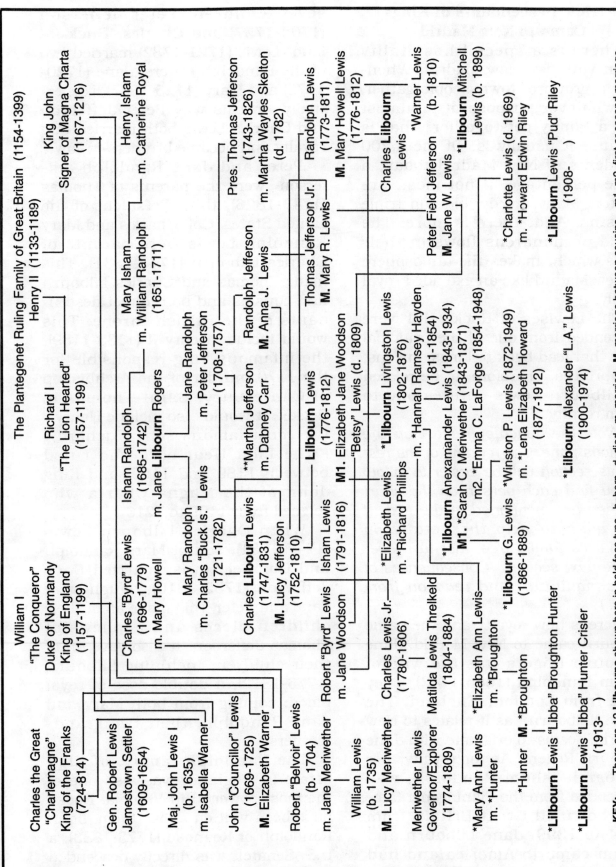

The Plantegenet Ruling Family of Great Britain (1154-1399)

William I
"The Conqueror"
Duke of Normandy
King of England
(1157-1199)

Richard I
"The Lion Hearted"
(1157-1199)

Henry II (1133-1189)

King John
(1167-1216)
Signer of Magna Charta

Henry Isham
m. Catherine Royal

Mary Isham
m. William Randolph
(1651-1711)

Charles the Great
"Charlemagne"
King of the Franks
(724-814)

Gen. Robert Lewis
Jamestown Settler
(1609-1654)

Maj. John Lewis I
(b. 1635)
m. Isabella Warner

John "Councillor" Lewis
(1669-1725)
M. Elizabeth Warner

Robert "Belvoir" Lewis
(b. 1704)
m. Jane Meriwether

William Lewis
(b. 1735)
M. Lucy Meriwether

Meriwether Lewis
Governor/Explorer
(1774-1809)

Charles "Byrd" Lewis
(1696-1779)
m. Mary Howell

Isham Randolph
(1685-1742)
m. Jane Lilbourn Rogers

Jane Randolph
m. Peter Jefferson
(1708-1757)

Pres. Thomas Jefferson
(1743-1826)
m. Martha Wayles Skelton
(d. 1782)

Mary Randolph
m. Charles "Buck Is." Lewis
(1721-1782)

Charles Lilbourn Lewis
(1747-1831)
M. Lucy Jefferson
(1752-1810)

**Martha Jefferson
m. Dabney Carr

Randolph Jefferson
M. Anna J. Lewis

Randolph Lewis
(1773-1811)

Thomas Jefferson Jr.
M. Mary R. Lewis

M. Mary Howell Lewis
(1776-1812)

Charles Lilbourn
Lewis

*Warner Lewis
(b. 1810)

Peter Field Jefferson
M. Jane W. Lewis

*Lilbourn Mitchell
Lewis (b. 1899)

Robert "Byrd" Lewis
m. Jane Woodson

Lilbourn Lewis
(1776-1812)
M1. Elizabeth Jane Woodson
"Betsy" Lewis (d. 1809)

Isham Lewis
(1791-1816)

*Lilbourn Livingston Lewis
(1802-1876)

*Charlotte Lewis (d. 1969)
m. *Howard Edwin Riley

*Lilbourn Lewis "Pud" Riley
(1908-   )

Charles Lewis Jr.
(1780-1806)

*Elizabeth Lewis
m. *Richard Phillips

m. *Hannah Ramsey Hayden
(1811-1854)

*Lilbourn Anexamander Lewis (1843-1934)
M1. *Sarah C. Meriwether (1843-1871)
m2. *Emma C. LaForge (1854-1948)

*Winston P. Lewis (1872-1949)
m. *Lena Elizabeth Howard
(1877-1912)

*Lilbourn Alexander "L.A." Lewis
(1900-1974)

Matilda Lewis Threlkeld
(1804-1884)

*Mary Ann Lewis
m. *Hunter

*Elizabeth Ann Lewis
m. *Broughton

*Hunter M. *Broughton

*Lilbourn G. Lewis
(1866-1889)

*Lilbourn Lewis "Libba" Broughton Hunter

*Lilbourn Lewis "Libba" Hunter Crisler
(1913-   )

KEY: There are 12 Lilbourns shown here in bold face type.   b=born   d=died   m=married   M=marriage between cousins   m1, m2=first or second marriage
* Residents of New Madrid are indicated by asterisks.   **Martha Jefferson's descendants also moved to New Madrid, thus giving rise to two Jefferson lines there.

Origin of the Name: "Lilbourn Lewis"

Its Descent from Royalty, Relationship to President Thomas Jefferson, and the Town of New Madrid

How Descendants of Kings Came to New Madrid

There is a special hospitality when you visit New Madrid. Whenever a group of townspeople gather, for whatever purpose, it is almost like a family get-together. That is because it usually is. Of the 3,200 residents of New Madrid today, a large percentage, if not most, are related. Many are double and triple cousins. And, there is more: The blood of monarchs flows in their veins which, makes the atmosphere at New Madrid like an extended royal family.

The Lewises of Rocky Hill were descended from one of the principal lines that lead back to kings, queens, and princes. Therefore, to be related to Lilbourn Lewis entitles one to claim royalty.

(Note the genealogy chart on the previous page. The reading of the rest of this section will be easier to follow if you find each person on the chart as they are mentioned in the text. If you wish to skip the details on Lilbourn's family tree, just turn over to the next section, "Consequences of Consanguinity," and read on from there.)

Here is how royalty and the name Lilbourn came to New Madrid. Jane Lilbourn Rogers was the wife of Isham Randolph (1685-1742). They were from London, England. The name "Lilbourn," as it relates to New Madrid, seems to originate with Jane Lilbourn Rogers. As for royalty, her husband, Isham Randolph, was descended from the Plantagenet family who ruled Great Britain from 1154 to 1399. Jane Lilbourn and Isham came to America and had seven children. Peter Jefferson (1708-1757) and Charles "Buck Island" Lewis (1721-1782) married two of the Randolph sisters, Jane (1720-1776) and Mary (1725-1803), respectively. In this way Peter Jefferson and Charles Lewis both married into royalty and became brothers-in-law.

Peter and Jane Randolph Jefferson were the parents of Thomas (1743-1826), third President of the United States. Col. Charles and Mary Randolph Lewis were parents of Charles Lilbourn (1747-1831). This made Thomas and Charles Lilbourn first cousins and both direct descendants of the British throne. This would include Henry II (1133-1189), the infamous king responsible for the 1170 murder of the Archbishop of Canterbury, Saint Thomas a' Becket. It would also include Henry's two most famous sons, Richard I ("The Lion Hearted") who ruled between 1189 and 1199, and King John of the Magna Charta who reigned from 1199 to 1216.

When Charles Lilbourn Lewis (1747-1731), son of Mary Randolph and Colonel Lewis, married Lucy Jefferson (1752-1810), daughter of Jane and Peter, this made all of their children nieces and nephews of Thomas Jefferson. It also gave all of their children, including Lilbourn (1776-1812), a double dose of royal blood, coming from both Mary and Jane Randolph, their two grandmothers.

The Randolph family, of high estate in England, was also one of the most powerful in Virginia. Books have been written about them. John Randolph of Roanoke (1773-1833), a U.S. Senator, was directly descended from John Rolfe (1585-1622) and his famous wife, the Indian Princess Pocahontas, who went to England, was treated as royalty by the British, and died there in 1614. The father of Pocahontas was Chief Powhatan. Hence, there is a good chance that the people of New Madrid can even trace their lineage through the Randolphs to a royal line of Native Americans.

The Lewis line has another direct connection with royal blood. Robert Lewis (1609-1654), a young lawyer, came to America from Wales. He was a settler of Jamestown, the first British colony in America. His son, Major John Lewis I, married Isabella Warner. Isabella's family connects not only with the Plantegenent Kings but also with William I of England, known as "The Conqueror" (1028-1087). Isabella's line also connects with French kings, including Charles the Great, "King of the Franks, better known as "Charlemagne" (724-814).

John and Isabella Lewis had a son, John Lewis II (1669-1725) who was said to be "the richest man in Virginia" and became known as "The Councillor." John the Councillor married his first cousin, Elizabeth Warner, which gave another link to royalty to the Lewis line. Col. Charles "Byrd" Lewis (1696-1779) was the oldest son of John Lewis II. Charles Byrd was father of Charles Lilbourn Lewis (1747-1831) and a grandfather to the Lilbourn of Rocky Hill.

Charles Lilbourn, his father, his cousins, his brothers, and many other Lewises fought in the Revolutionary War. They were also courageous in their opposition to the King of England prior to America's declaration of freedom, signing a number of petitions against the throne. Such defiance placed their lives and fortunes at considerable risk. Francis Lewis, a first cousin to Charles Lilbourn Lewis, was a signer of the Declaration of Independence. As a consequence of his endorsement of that document, all of his property was confiscated by the British, and his wife was thrown into prison, where she died.

The Lewises were courageous in other ways. The were also staunch Presbyterians and leaders for religious freedom at a time when only the Anglican Church of England was legal in the colonies, and one could be imprisoned for espousing another faith.

Charles Lilbourn Lewis (1747-1831) was father of Lilbourn (1776-1812), who was father of Lilbourn Livingston (1806-1876), who moved to New Madrid, had ten children, and whose son, Lilbourn Anexamander or "Billy Goat" (1843-1934) founded the town of Lilbourn in 1908. You can see that the Lilbourn who slew George is an essential link in the lineage to royalty for many residents of New Madrid.

Another famous and related Lewis was Meriwether (1774-1809). Going back to John I and Isabella, in addition to John II, they had another son, Robert "Belvoir" Lewis, born in 1704. Robert was Meriwether's grandfather. This made John I and Isabella great grandparents of Meriwether as well as to Randolph, Isham, and Lilbourn. During his short life Meriwether not only held positions as Thomas Jefferson's personal secretary, but also as Governor of the Northern Louisiana Territory and leader (with William Clark) of the famous "Lewis and Clark" expedition to the headwaters of the Missouri River and the Pacific Northwest. Meriwether's farm in Virginia was close enough to Monticello that when Thomas Jefferson needed Meriwether's assistance, he could signal him by sunlight with a mirror.

Hence, the Lilbourn Lewis connection is one that links the blood lines of his descendants with the gentry of colonial America, soldiers of the American revolution, defenders of religious freedom, one of the great explorers of the frontier west, one of America's greatest presidents, as well as with the ruling families of England and France. There is even the possibility of Native American royalty in the Lewis line.

The Consequences of Consanguinity

The Jefferson family and the Lewis family lived on adjacent plantations in Virginia and intermarried (cousin to cousin) for at least three generations. The Randolph family, to which both the Jefferson and Lewis lines can be traced (through Mary and Jane), were also a thoroughly intermarried clan and had been for more than a hundred years, even before immigrating to the New World.

Thomas Jefferson's brother, Randolph, married a cousin, Anna J. Lewis. Their son, Thomas Jefferson, Jr., also married a first cousin, Mary R. Lewis. In turn, their son, Peter Field Jefferson, married a first cousin, Jane W. Lewis. The tradition was continued when Thomas Jefferson's daughter, Martha, married a

relative, Thomas Mann Randolph.

The extent of these intermarriages is graphically displayed by the genealogical chart found on page 45 of this chapter. If there are no unions between blood relatives, the lines on a family tree do not cross. The maze of crossed ties in this chart is testimony to the frequent consanguinity that characterized the marriage preferences of these families. One wonders if the combination and repeated recombination of chromosomes among the Lewis, Jefferson, and Randolph families might have had some genetically ill consequences.

Thomas Mann Randolph was kin to and a son-in-law of President Jefferson. He was said to have been an intelligent young man of promise but who was also observed to have grown increasingly temperamental with age. He was eventually adjudged insane.

Thomas Jefferson's daughter, Martha, was to be the unfortunate observer of another tragedy through her marriage into the Randolph name. Her husband's cousin, Richard Randolph, married one of Thomas Mann Randolph's sisters. This led to an incestuous affair with another of Thomas's sisters, resulting in an illegitimate child. The baby is thought to have been murdered by the two adulterous parents. Richard, Martha's brother-in-law by marriage, was then found dead of poisoning—by suicide or homicide. Martha had to testify in the ensuing trials.

In addition to intermarriage between Lewises, Jeffersons, and Randolphs, there were also intramarriage relationships within the Lewis family. Elizabeth (Betsy), the wife of Lilbourn Lewis who died at Rocky Hill, and Mary Howell, the wife of Randolph Lewis, were actually sisters, both Lewises, the daughters of Robert "Byrd" Lewis, an uncle of both Lilbourn and Randolph. Hence, Elizabeth and Mary were Lewises both before and after their marriages. Sisters had married brothers of the same family.

There are many accounts of brilliance bordering on genius, as well as psychological aberration and mental disease, among these families. Thomas Jefferson, himself, suffered from severe headaches throughout his life. Among his siblings, only he was exceptional. He had one brother and seven sisters, two of whom died as infants. None of the other Jefferson children approached Thomas' level of intelligence except, possibly, his sister Jane, who died in her mid-twenties. Randolph, his brother, was said to be "simple-minded" while Randolph's twin sister, Anna Scott Jefferson, was characterized as "deficient in intellect." One sister, Elizabeth Jefferson, was noticeably retarded.

Of the five children born to Thomas Jefferson and his wife, Martha Wayles Skelton, three died in infancy, very possibly of lethal genetic abnormalities. One of his grandsons, Francis W. Eppes, suffered from the grand mal seizures of epilepsy.

Similar genetic maladies can be found in the Lewis branches of the family as well. According to Jefferson, states of depression and hypochondria were prevalent mental illnesses "in all branches of the Lewis side of the family."

Consider the case of Governor Meriwether Lewis who committed suicide in West Tennessee while enroute to Washington from St. Louis. His action was a shock, not only to the Lewis family, but to the nation at large by whom he was highly esteemed. However, even the news accounts of the time had noted his lapses into depression and mental disorder prior to his self-imposed death. In the contemporary reports of his demise we find reference to Meriwether's prior "uneasiness of mind."

The newspaper at Russelville, Kentucky (*The Farmer's Friend*) published a report on October 20, 1809, that quoted Meriwether's traveling companion as saying that during their trip "the governor had appeared at times considerably deranged."

On the day of the tragedy they had lost two horses. While Meriwether's friend went to find them, the governor went to rest in the nearby home of a Mr. Grinder. No one was home but a servant woman who became alarmed when Meriwether came to the door. "There was something wild in his appearance," she said. In fear she fled to the nearby servants' quarters, leaving Meriwether alone in the Grinder house. "About three o'clock," the woman said, "I heard the report of two pistols, which immediately awakened the servants, who rushed into the house, but too late. He had shot himself in the head and just below the breast," she said. He was not yet dead, but "was in the act of cutting himself with a knife." The only words he uttered were, "It is done, my good servant. Give me some water." A few moments later he expired.

Perhaps there was a genetic predisposition in the Lewis brothers, Lilbourn and Isham, that contributed to their vile and violent deed in the Rocky Hill cook house on the eve of the New Madrid earthquakes. Since Lilbourn's marriage to Letitia, things had not gone well family-wise, health-wise, financially, legally, nor conjugally. He was under stress from all sides. Even an emotionally strong and mentally healthy individual would have had difficulty coping with Lilbourn's avalanche of trials.

Acquaintances and relatives noted some distressing changes in his personality after 1810. Normally a kind, fair, and considerate master to his slaves, he was becoming more and more ill-tempered, impatient, and oppressive. As December of 1811 approached, he had begun to show signs of depression and character disintegration.

His self-confidence and positive outlook on life had been undermined by his numerous misfortunes. With a life of continuing disappointment and mounting difficulties that seemed impossible to resolve, combined with a history of mental imbalance within the family blood-line, perhaps Lilbourn reached his breaking point. George's impudence on that fateful December Sunday, insignificant in and of itself, could have been the final straw that caused Lilbourn's mind to crack.

In today's courts a murderous, rash, irrational act like that committed by Lilbourn and his brother could probably find a viable defense in a plea of " temporary insanity."

Visit New Madrid
And Visit Royalty

There is lot of traceable royal ancestry in New Madrid. But, not all of it is through Lilbourn Lewis of Livingston County. Many New Madrid residents with royal blood and connections to Jefferson can be traced through another line. Martha Jefferson Carr was another sister of Thomas. Several of her descendants also moved to New Madrid. The Newsum family is a branch descended from Martha Jefferson that still resides in New Madrid. Kathleen Newsum Bock is one of them. Another descendant of the Newsum line is Virginia LaValle Carlson, former Curator of the New Madrid Historical Museum. Virginia is also a direct descendent of Jean Baptiste LaVallee (spelled with two "e's" at that time) who was the Commandant at the New Madrid Garrison in 1804 when the French and Spanish flags were retired and the Stars and Stripes raised. You will find Virginia's name on the bronze dedication plaque of the New Madrid Museum Annex which opened on December 3, 1991.

Martha Jefferson was the wife of Dabney Carr, Thomas' boyhood best friend. When Dabney died at an early age, Thomas took his sister, Martha, and her children to live with him at Monticello, Virginia. Dabney Carr was the first to be buried at the Monticello Cemetery, later to be followed by his brother-in-law, the President, in 1826.

The last child of Lilbourn of Rocky Hill, James R. Lewis, was his only child by second wife, Letitia. The boy and his mother moved to

Virginia L. Carlson—a descendant of Martha Jefferson, sister to Thos. Jefferson.

Scott County, Missouri, around 1830, a few miles north of New Madrid. This gave rise to yet another line of Lewises in the area, all tracing back to the State of Virginia and the aristocracy of the Old World.

This is how hundreds, even thousands, of people in Missouri and Kentucky, and specifically in the New Madrid area, came to be kinfolk with connections to the Jefferson and/or Lewis families who lived in Virginia at the time of America's birth. This explains why so many sons and daughters of the American Revolution came to reside around New Madrid.

Hence, the towns of Lilbourn and New Madrid, Missouri, can trace their roots to noted patriots, monarchs, and at least one great president, author of the Declaration of Independence. Descendants of this lineage living today act as many of the current city and county leaders, including the former mayor of New Madrid, Mr. Dick Phillips. Mayor Phillips is a direct descendant of Richard and Elizabeth Lewis Phillips, a daughter of the infamous Lilbourn interred at Rocky Hill Cemetery. Until his retirement from office in 1993, if you ate lunch at Rosie's Diner in New Madrid, on most week days you could find Mayor Phillips conducting the affairs of the town over a piece of peach or blackberry cobbler.

Jefferson and the New Madrid Earthquakes

Many of the shocks that originated from the New Madrid Fault during 1811-12 were felt throughout all of the Eastern United States. No series of earthquakes in American history has ever reached so far nor affected such a large proportion of the population, before or since. Everyone east of the Rocky Mountains at least felt the tremors, regardless of where they were at the time, from New York to New Orleans, from Georgia to the Wyoming Territory.

At Monticello, Thomas Jefferson was 700 miles away from the epicenters. Yet in nearby Charlottesville, at his plantation, and throughout the whole state of Virginia, there were at least minor damages. People were frightened everywhere. Many ran out of doors when the ground shook and found walking difficult. Windows cracked. Glassware broke. Books and vases toppled from shelves. Pictures fell from walls. Furniture moved and overturned. Plaster and masonry cracked. The sounds of birds were hushed as the trees and bushes waved their branches with eerie rustling sounds at the passing

Fort Jefferson, Kentucky. The historical marker above is along Hwy 51 in Wickliffe where Ft. Jefferson was relocated after the earthquakes. The plaque says: "Fort Jefferson erected here in 1780 by General George Rogers Clark to protect claim of the infant United States to a western boundary on the Mississippi River." The middle photo on the left is an old earthquake landslide covered with trees where a bluff had overlooked the river before 1811-12. The bottom left photo is from an overpass looking north up Hwy 51 toward Wickliffe. The truck full of logs is turning into the Westvaco Paper Plant. The trees to the left cover an old earthquake landslide that continues beyond the photo toward the river out of view on the left. On the right we have three views of the Mississippi River from Ft. Jefferson. The top view is looking south (downstream) toward Island #1. The middle view is looking west to the bank on the Missouri side. The bottom view is looking north toward the mouth of the Ohio of each event. Such tremors visited Virginia and the East more than a dozen times during the weeks following that fateful December. But the damages east of the Appalachians were nothing compared to the utter devastation and havoc wrought to the states and territories bordering the Mississippi River.

Thomas Jefferson felt the ground repeatedly ripple across his Monticello estate. But he had no idea of the far-reaching connections the quakes and their namesake would make with his family for centuries to come, nor the heritage his good name would permanently bring to the community and countryside around New Madrid.

As for Thomas Jefferson's namesake— Fort Jefferson, Kentucky—the site did not survive the earthquakes. Destroyed by landslides, no trace of the original settlement can be seen today. Fortunately, the Fort was unoccupied at the time of the quakes. When it was established in 1780 the Chickasaw Indians were in control of the territory. The military troops that built the heavy log stockade were accompanied by a sizeable group of settlers who started homesteads and cleared land for farming around the Fort.

The Indians did not appreciate the occupation of their land without their consent. Late in 1781 the Chickasaws began a campaign that killed many of the new settlers and ended with a seige of the fort, itself, which lasted five days. The surviving people inside the wooden walls of the stockade were saved only when General George Rogers Clark came down the river from Kaskaskia, Illinois, with reinforcements.

The fort was then abandoned until the Jackson Purchase of 1818, which settled the claims of the Indians. By then, most of the Chickasaws had actually left the area because of the earthquakes— driven out by the forces of nature.

The bluff and hilltop which had been the site of Fort Jefferson was destroycd by carthquake landslides and, thus, became unstable and unuseable land after 1812. Fort Jefferson was reinstated after 1818, but it was rebuilt on a location about a mile to the north and east, away from the falling bluff and failing edges of the hillside.

A large paper company, Westvaco, Inc., now owns the site of old Fort Jefferson. U.S. Highway 51, which connects Memphis and Dyersburg, Tennessee, passes through Kentucky and into southern Illinois, and crosses the Westvaco property. When approaching Wickliffe from the south and passing the paper plant on the right (east side), look forward and to the left. There the highway ascends the scarp of an old earthquake landslide from 1811-12. The slump is now stabilized with trees but can still be followed visually as it wraps around the hillside toward the west to the Mississippi River where the fort used to be.

Remember the lost Fort Jefferson, when driving through here. And remember a historic president's Kentucky nephews whose crime was so dramatically exposed by an earthquake and whose descendants and relatives found themselves strangely drawn to live in the very town that gave the earthquake its name.

Approximate Boundaries
of the Most Active Portion of the
NEW MADRID SEISMIC ZONE
With Recent Epicenters, 1974-1987

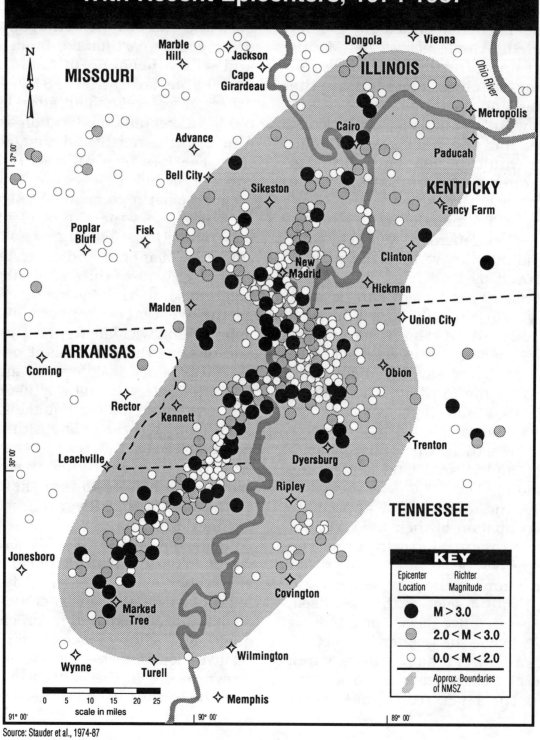

KEY

Epicenter Location	Richter Magnitude
●	M > 3.0
(shaded)	2.0 < M < 3.0
○	0.0 < M < 2.0
(shape)	Approx. Boundaries of NMSZ

scale in miles
0 5 10 15 20 25

Source: Stauder et al., 1974-87

Chapter Two
PROPHECIES AND PRECURSORS

The Year of Wonders, "Annus Mirabilis," that's what the year 1811 eventually came to be called. Comets, eclipses, record floods, droughts, Indian uprisings, provocations by the British, Napoleonic War in Europe, revolutions in Mexico and South America, volcanic eruptions, strange animal happenings, electricity in the atmosphere, and then, to finish out the year, there were the earthquakes. It was to be a time like no other, before or since.

The new year had been swept in by a destructive hurricane during December of 1810 that devastated the east coast from Cape Hatteras to Newfoundland. While the tempest was raging, a tragic fire blazed through a theater in Richmond, Virginia, killing seventy people, including the governor of the state.

Eliza Bryan was a school teacher who lived just outside the town of New Madrid before, during, and after the quakes. Following the disturbances she wrote down her recollections of the events and had this to say about the year 1811:

"There is one circumstance worthy of remark. This country is subject to very hard thunder. But for twelve months before the earthquakes, there was none at all."

The Great Comet of 1811

A faint streak in the sky appeared on March 26, first sighted at Viviers, France. The streak grew in size and intensity. It had a head and a double tail. The comet remained visible for seventeen months, attaining its peak brightness during the great New Madrid earthquakes. It was last seen On August 17, 1812, at Neu Tscherkask in Southern Russia.

The British astronomer, William Herschel (1728-1822), who discovered the planet Uranus, estimated the diameter of the comet's head to be 428 miles and the length of its tail to be at least 100 million miles with a breadth of 15 million. Astronomers have calculated that it orbits the sun with a return period of 3,065 years.

The last time it had been seen was around the year 1254 B.C. Ramses II had assumed the Egyptian throne about 1290 B.C. He ruled for 67 years. At the time of the comet, he had just completed one of the most incredible Egyptian temples ever. Located in the valley of the upper Nile, the Temple at Abu Simbel was situated on the face of a red granite mountain in a cliff that commanded a view of the upper Nile Valley. Earlier in his reign he had finished another colossal colonnaded

The Great Comet of 1811 as seen over Daniel Boone's Chimney near St. Charles, MO

structure at Karnak, begun by his predecessors, Ramses I and Sethi I. The temple at Karnak was the largest Egyptian temple ever built. Earthquakes were to eventually topple this temple, but the one at Abu Simbel was virtually earthquake-proof. It had been hewn 200 feet into solid rock. The sculptured chambers inside the mountain still stand, unshaken today, as strong and intact as they were when created over 3,000 years ago at an earlier time of the great comet.

The temple facade in the face of the bluff is adorned by four immense statues of the seated pharaoh. After surviving centuries of vandals and more than 3,000 years of earthquakes, the temple and sitting pharaohs could have been lost to the rising waters behind Aswan Dam, built in 1960–65. Fortunately this megalith of the ancient world is preserved today behind a special levee that holds back the waters of the great Aswan Lake. Inside the sanctuary and temple anterooms are more than 100 statues of Ramses' children, his mother, his father, Sethi I, and his wife, Nefertari. Most Westerners don't remember Ramses

Temple at Abu Simbel completed by Ramses II when Comet of 1811 last appeared.

Illustration by Anthony Stewart

II for his architectural feats, but for his confrontation and showdown with one of the greatest prophets of the Old Testament.

It was approximately 1285 B.C. when Moses led the Israelites out of their slavery in Egypt. Ramses II was the ruling monarch. The great comet that accompanied the earthquakes of 1811–12 would have also appeared during the wanderings of the Israelites from Egypt, across the Sinai, and into the Land of Caanan. The author of Exodus 13:21 noted that "The Lord went before them . . . in a pillar of fire by night, to give

them light." Could the "pillar of fire" have been this same comet?

It was probably near the very end of their journey when the Comet, seen in 1811–12, was witnessed by the Israelites. This would have been while they were camped on the plains of Moab. It was from there that Moses climbed to the top of Mount Nebo to view the promised land. (See Deuteronomy, Chapter 34.) Thus, the comet's appearance in 1254 B.C. would have corresponded closely with the death of Moses, which marked the end of a major transition in the history of Judaism and of the Holy Land.

Prior to the exodus from Egypt, Judaism, as we know it, did not yet exist. The Israelites were a loose confederation of Semitic people who considered themselves as descendants of Abraham. But after they had wetted their feet in the Red Sea, danced at the foot of Mount Sinai, eaten manna, and wandered the searing deserts for forty years, they had been purified and remolded into a new race. They had been forged into a new religion and a new force that would reach down through the ages, give birth to two other world religions (Islam and Christianity), and carry its ancient roots into the present.

These were the history-transforming events observed from outer space by the Comet of 1811 when it visited earth in 1254 B.C. The comet's last terrestrial bypass before that one had been in 4319 B.C. when the roots of the civilizations of Mesopotamia, Egypt, Asia and the Mediterranean were being established, and at the same time that early Native Americans were establishing their cultures throughout North, Central, and South America. A lot of changes had taken place between visits.

Now it was A.D. 1811, and the same outer-space traveler and extraterrestrial eavesdropper was back again, checking up on the earth once more. What would it find people doing this time? What wonders would it witness during this pass? How would human history be shaken during this visit?

The comet won't return for another close-up view of earthlings until the year 4876 A.D. What new customs and institutions will the comet discover then? Will democracy and the United States still exist, as we know it? Who can say? We only know that neither nature nor homo sapiens stand still.

The appearance of the comet in 1811 prompted many to prophesy an impending, imminent doom. There was a popular concern that the comet would collide with the earth, causing "great earthquakes." A feeling of fear and fatalism seemed to settle upon people around the world. That feeling increased as the year wore on. A singular sequence of events, both natural and political, was in the process of unfolding. Only the hindsight of history would be able to assemble it and sort it out.

Tecumseh and His Brothers

Puckeshinwa ("something that drops") was a member of the Kiskopoke clan of the Shawnee Confederacy. He was born in Florida on the Suwanee (or Swanee) River, later to be imortalized by Stephen Foster's famous song. The stream's name is a corrupted form of the word "Shawnee," the tribe that occupied northern Florida and southern Georgia at that time.

Puckeshinwa's wife, Methoataske ("turtle laying eggs"), was part Creek and part Muscogee, born and raised in the large Creek Indian town of Tuckhabatchee, Alabama. When first married, they lived in the Creek town of Sauvanogee on the Tallapoosa River, not far from its junction with the Coosa River. That would be fifteen miles east of present-day Montgomery, Alabama. Chiksika, their first child and son, was born there in

1760.

Soon after Chiksika's birth, the nomadic Shawnees began to move northward to resettle in Ohio. Puckeshinwa and Methoataske joined in the great migration across Tennessee and Kentucky, which took several years. On their way they had a daughter, Tecumpease, born in 1762, and another son, Sauwau-seekau, born in 1764. They finally settled at Old Piqua, a Native American city twenty-one miles east of Greenville, Ohio.

Old Piqua was one of the largest Indian settlements in the midwest. In fact, at that time, no white settlements west of the Appalachians were as big. Over 4,000 people lived there. Indian towns were usually not compact and concentrated like white towns. Old Piqua was strung out for miles along the bluffs of the west bank of the Mad River. Tecumseh, the third son and fourth child of Puckeshinwa and Methoataske, was born there in 1768.

Tecumseh's name comes from a Shawnee phrase meaning, "I cross somebody's path." It can also be taken to mean, "panther ready to spring on its prey." The panther (also puma or mountain lion) was the totem symbol of the Kiskopoke tribe. Years later, when Tecumseh had risen to the status of a respected chief, the whites translated "panther" as "celestial tiger" and eventually interpreted the name to mean "meteor," "comet," or "shooting star." The Comet of 1811, which appeared when Tecumseh was forty-three, became known in North America, among both whites and reds, as "Tecumseh's Comet." Thus, the interpretation of the meaning of his name took on special significance that year.

During the next four years after Tecumseh's birth, Methoataske bore two more daughters, Nehaaeemo, born in 1770, and Teceikeapease, born in 1772.

In 1773, when Tecumseh was five years old, his father, Puckeshinwa, kidnapped a white boy named Richard Sparks who was only four at the time. He adopted the child and gave him a Shawnee name—Shaw-tunte. Thus, Tecumseh came to grow up with a white brother only a year's difference in age.

Puckeshinwa's Death and Methoataske's Vision

During this period of American history, the Indians were locked in a desperate battle to stop the westward migration of colonial settlers, whom they referred to as "The Long Knives," so-called for their long rifles to which bayonets were sometimes attached. At that time, "the western frontier" was mainly in Ohio and Kentucky, but pushing further every day. The combined troops of the British and the Colonists were continually engaged in military actions to protect the migrating settlers and to keep the French from gaining a foothold as well.

Chief Puckeshinwa was killed after one of those battles. He had experienced a premonition about his imminent death. His sixth sense was inherited also by his sons. Before entering the Battle of Point Pleasant, he instructed his oldest son, Chiksika, who was only 14 at the time, to rear his younger brothers as fearless fighters and magnanimous victors. Both father and son fought in that battle and both survived. Soon after returning to Old Piqua, Puckeshinwa was hunting one day when he was accosted by a band of whites. After a heated verbal exchange, one of the whites pulled a pistol and shot "the insolent savage" in the chest.

When Puckeshinwa did not return to his wigwam that afternoon, Methoataske and her young son, Tecumseh, went searching. They found the chief dying by the side of the trail a mile or two from town. As he passed into the spirit world with his squaw and his son by his side, Methoataske poured out her lamentations.

"Tecumseh, you must be endowed with the soul of a warrior. You must be a whirlwind and a storm that will scatter desolation and death to the white man. You must become a fire spreading over the hill and the valley, consuming a race of dark souls."

Puckeshinwa was buried near his home beside the Mad River. His squaw delivered a requiem that was directed toward Tecumseh. He was just a boy, barely six at the time, but his mother already had a vision for his future:

"Tecumseh," she said, "you shall avenge the death of your father and appease the spirits of his slaughtered brethren. Already you are elected chief of many tribes. Your feet shall be swift as the forked lightning, your arm shall be as the thunderbolt, and your soul fearless as the cataract that dashes from the mountain precipice."

Tecumseh's poetic eloquence that would later stir the nationalism of his fellow Native Americans and captivate the admiration of his white enemies, was the gift of his mother.

The death of Tecumseh's father occurred in 1774, two years before the United States was to declare its independence from England. Methoataske, who already had three sons, three daughters, and an adopted son, was pregnant with triplets at the time.

In early 1775, the widow of Puckeshinwa gave birth to three sons. One lived only a short time and died from a lethal birth defect. The other two lived into adulthood. One was named Kumskaukau. The other became known as Lalawethika, which means "rattle" or "noisemaker." Methoataske sank into a deep postpartum depression, unable to cope with the loss of her husband and the added responsibilities of a large family with two infant sons. She slowly recovered.

Shortly after Puckeshinwa's death, the family moved to Chillicothe, a large Shawnee town further up the Mad River. During the next four years Methoataske imbued her son, Tecumseh, with the mission of a warrior and her son, Lalawethika, with the vision of a mystic. During this same time, when Tecumseh was between the ages of six and ten, the great warrior chief, Blackfish, took an interest in the boy and adopted him as a son. Tecumseh's time was, thus, divided between his mother and his adopted father.

When the Revolutionary War began in 1776, the Indians tried to stay neutral, considering this to be a battle between two groups of whites.

But this did not work. Like it or not, the Indians became involved. Without taking sides, they found themselves vulnerable to attack by both British and American troops. When Indians were killed in Ohio, the tribesmen would retaliate by crossing into Kentucky. There they burned farms, laid seige to towns, and then retreated back into Ohio. Angry white settlers would then mount their horses, cross the Ohio River, and raid the Indian villages, killing many. In May of 1779, Colonel John Bowman led an attack on Chillicothe. The battle was a draw. More whites were killed than reds and the Americans had to retreat, but the raid proved that the Shawnee towns were vulnerable.

Following Bowman's battle, approximately 1,000 Indians, representing one-third of the population of Chillicothe, picked up and moved in canoes down the Ohio River. Passing Indiana and Illinois, they eventually settled in southeast Missouri. Several Shawnee villages were already there, including one just north of Cape Girardeau of the same name, Chillicothe, like the hometown they had fled in Ohio.

Methoataske and her young children were especially frightened by Bowman's attack. In response to her fear, Methoataske did a strange thing. She joined the mass exodus and went to Missouri, never to return to Ohio again. Like a mother turtle who abandons her offspring after laying her eggs, Methoataske abandoned her children—all of them, that is, but one. For some reason, she chose to take her youngest daughter with her. Teciekeapease

was seven at the time. They resettled in Chillicothe, Missouri, safe and far away from entanglements in the Revolutionary War. In Missouri, they were in neither American nor British territory. In 1779 the lands west of the Mississippi River were still Spanish.

At the time they were orphaned, Chiksika, the oldest, was barely nineteen. Sauwauseekau was fifteen. Tecumseh was eleven. Shawtunte was ten. Nehaaeemo was nine. The surviving triplets, Lalawethika and Kumskaukau were four. And as for Tecumpease, she was seventeen and married.

Orphans

The deserted children were taken in by Tecumseh's oldest sister, Tecumpease. She and her husband, Wasabogoa ("stand firm") accepted the young Shawnees into their wigwam and raised them. Tecumseh was the favorite of both foster parents, as well as the favorite of his eldest brother, Chiksika. Lalawethika was generally ignored. Although he was sheltered, fed, and cared for, he never received the attention nor developed the relationship with Tecumpease and Wasabogoa that Tecumseh did. There may have been some sibling jealousy.

During this time Tecumseh was thoroughly trained in the skills of hunting and warfare by his older brother, Chiksika, his stepfather, Wasabogoa, and his adoptive father, Blackfish. Meanwhile, Lalawethika stayed around the bark hut, that was his sister's home, and played. In his insecurity he compensated by becoming boastful and obnoxious.

While toying with a bow and some iron-tipped arrows one day, Lalawethica accidentally stabbed himself in the right eye, destroying its sight and giving him a pitiful, if not hideous, appearance for life. As he entered his teen years, Lalawethika also developed a taste for the white man's firewater. His addiction increased his braggadocio and decreased his popularity at the same time. His name, "noisemaker," given to him in his infancy, took on new meaning.

While it may seem strange that Lalawethica was treated so differently from his older brothers, such seeming discrimination was actually rooted in Indian tradition. In actuality, he was not being neglected nor ignored. He was receiving special treatment in deference to the special circumstances of his birth.

According to Indian beliefs survivors of multiple births were imbued with special mystical powers and were usually assigned to serve as priests or medicine men. That's why Lalawethika was not schooled in the arts of hunting and warfare like his brothers, Chiksika, Sauwauseekau, and Tecumseh. He was not expected to become a warrior. Furthermore, because he was a "twin" he did not have to earn respect. He was automatically awarded a certain amount of esteem, and even reverence, even if he did not manifest the wisdom of a prophet. Tribes were tolerant of their twins, even when they did not measure up to the priesthood for which they were born.

Chiksika was killed in an assault on a frontier outpost in 1788. On August 20, 1794, Sauwauseekau was killed near Fort Miamis. A tornado had recently felled a grove of trees where the battle took place which caused the engagement to be called "The Battle of the Fallen Timbers." Tecumseh and Lalawethika also fought in this encounter and witnessed their older brother's death. It was a major defeat for the Shawnees.

On August 3, 1795, the Shawnees signed the Treaty of Greenville, which ceded all of the holdings of the tribe east of the Mississippi, except for a small sector in northwestern Ohio.

At that point, Kumskaukau appears to have migrated west with a band of Shawnees and disappeared into obscurity. Shawtunte, then a young man of twenty-five, escaped back into white society and returned to his life as Richard Sparks. As the turn of the century approached, from an orphaned family of six sons, only two of the Shawnee brothers remained in Ohio.

Tecumseh and Lalawethika both married and had children. Tecumseh had actually not been inclined to matrimony, preferring the independence of bachelorhood. He was twenty-eight when tribal customs finally prevailed upon him to find a wife. He could have had his pick of the Shawnee maidens, but, instead, he chose a homely halfbreed called Manete or "old woman." She was about forty, but not too old to conceive. She bore him one child in 1797, a son. They named the boy Pugeshashenwa.

During the next few years Tecumseh and Lalawethika lived in a variety of locations in northwestern Ohio, hunting and fishing. While

Tecumseh continued to sharpen his skills as a warrior, Lalawethika spent time with the medicine men learning the magical arts of the tribe. Their wives plowed the fertile bottoms with the shoulder blades of bison, raising corn, beans, and a few squash. When Ohio became a state, in 1803, the brothers and their families migrated to the northeastern corner of the Indiana Territory.

Noisemaker Meets Master of Life

Lalawethika's reputation, which was already not good, continued to grow worse. He was a drunkard and a do-nothing. Were it not for his hard-working wife, his family would have starved. He neither helped with the farming, gathered wild fruit, fished, nor hunted for game. And, as for being a protector, he was no warrior. He refused to bear arms. Drinking, smoking and bragging were his pastimes.

The winter of 1804-05 was long, icy, and cold. The Shawnees and the Delawares had both suffered from the weather but even more so from the paleface diseases. This year it was "the coughing disease," probably a form of influenza, or the flu. White folks survived it, but red folks died, often in less than three days. Whole villages had almost disappeared, annihilated by the sickness.

One evening in April of 1805 Lalawethika was sitting crosslegged by the fire in his wigwam when he pulled out a flaming stick to light the tobacco in his pipe. Suddenly he keeled over on his side. Unable to arouse him, his wife summoned help. Various means to revive him were applied, but to no avail. His eyes were closed. There was no heartbeat and no breath. He was pronounced dead, apparently another victim of a white man's disease.

The neighbors led the grieving wife from the hut and made plans to wash the body in preparation for burial, which was to take place in two days. As they were preparing the corpse, suddenly Lalawethika stirred, took a deep breath, awakened, and sat up.

To the amazed, if not horrified, villagers standing around, Lalawethika told of his near-death experience. The Master of Life had sent two handsome young men to carry his soul to the spirit world where he had been shown the past and the future. He was not allowed to enter heaven, but was given a glimpse of paradise which he described as "a rich fertile country, abounding in game, fish, pleasant hunting grounds, and fine corn fields" where virtuous Shawnees could hunt, live, or play in whatever ways they chose. It was a perfect description of the "happy hunting ground" that every Indian dreamed of.

But, not all Shawnee spirits proceeded directly to heaven, he said. Sinful tribesmen were led to the entrance of heaven, but after seeing the promised land, they were then ushered into a large lodge where a fire burned continually, and where sinners were subjected to torture in accordance with their wickedness. Finally, however, when their sins were expiated, they could enter paradise but never on the same level of pleasure as their more virtuous tribesmen.

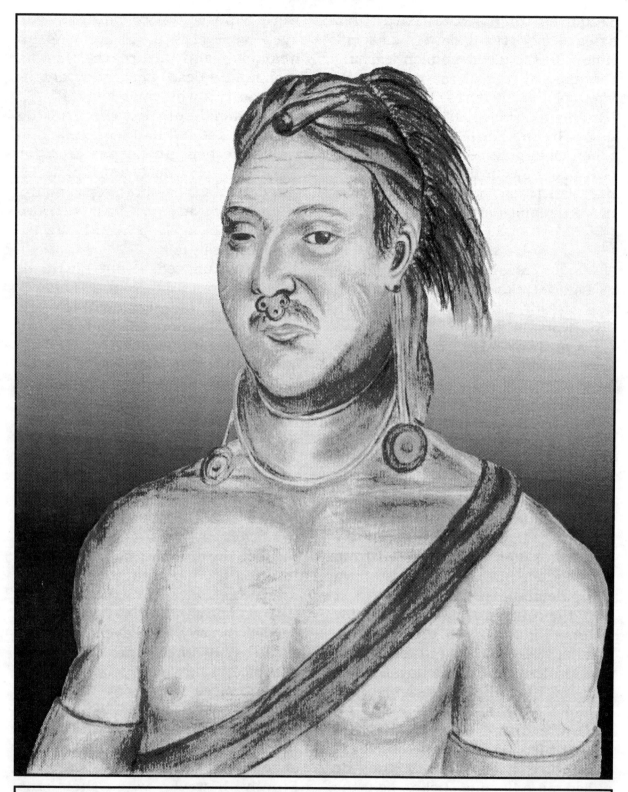

Tenskwatawa as the Younthful Shawnee Prophet. Based on a painting by J.O. Lewis at the Amon Carter Museum, Fort Worth Texas, Tenskwatawa is seen here with ear bobs, scalplock tube, wide metal arm bands and nose ring, items he customarily wore when performing his duties as a priest and a prophet. He also wore a mustasche throughout his adult life, something rare among Native Americans. His right eye, seen half closed, was injured while playing with arrows as a child.

Illustration by Anthony Stewart

A New Religion is Born

At age 30 Lalawethika was a changed man. He publicly confessed his sins and swore that he would never again drink the white man's whiskey. He took a new name, Tenskwatawa, meaning: "The One Who Opens the Door." According to his testimony Wakonda, the Master of Life, had appointed him to bring forth a new faith that would revitalize and save his people. Tenskwatawa continued to have visions and continued to deliver his messages from God.

Soon thousands of Indians from tribes everywhere were coming to seek a blessing from this man who had risen from the dead and who talked intimately with the Great Spirit himself, face to face. Tenskwatawa asserted that his "sole object was to reclaim the Indians from bad habits and to cause them to live in peace with all mankind." This Prophet of God had a simple set of rules for his followers:

• Give up alcohol.
• Treat tribal elders with respect.
• Provide for kinsmen who are injured, diseased, or incapable of caring for themselves.
• Refrain from intertribal violence, and treat each other as brothers.
• Stop quarreling.
• Never steal the belongings of another Indian.
• Always be truthful.
• Men were never to strike their wives or children.
• There was to be no adultery or infidelity.
• Young men should stop chasing women and get married instead.

He also said that polygamy was wrong and that, in the future, Shawnee warriors were to take only one wife. He went on to say that if a man already had more than one wife, he should keep them, but they should realize that such a union displeased the Master of Life. If a Shawnee woman had taken a white man for a husband, she should desert him, leave whatever children she had with him, and return to the tribe.

He also prescribed certain rituals that would please the Great Spirit. This included keeping fires continually burning in their camps, which had been the traditional Indian way, instead of using the white man's flint and steel to rekindle a new fire every day. He also forbade the wearing of white man's clothing and ordered a return to traditional tribal wear, including the shaving of the men's heads, leaving only the traditional lock of hair. They were also to return to the tribal practice of nakedness—except for a loin cloth and except in the coldest weather.

He also required that prayers be offered to Wakonda twice daily, morning and evening. For this he provided "prayer sticks" with words inscribed on them, as well as prayer beads (actually strings of beans) for the repetition of certain prayers.

The Prophet's ban on alcohol was a boon and a blessing to the Indians. While almost every other civilization in the world, from Africa, Europe and the far East, had discovered how to brew alcoholic beverages, the Native Americans had not. The Egyptians and the Babylonians had been drinking beer, malt liquor, and wine for thousands of years B.C. Wine was a daily staple in both the Old and the New Testaments.

The Indians of both North and South America had raised corn for thousands of years and had introduced it to the rest of the world, but they saw corn only as food. It did not take the Europeans long to figure out how to make corn into whiskey, something the Indians had never done. Thus, one of the most wholesome mainstays of Indian diet, a staple that had sustained their race for more than 10,000 years, was turned into their worst enemy.

At the time Tenskwatawa rose to power, tribes were purchasing corn liquor by the barrel and engaging in drunken orgies that lasted days, until the firewater ran out. Being descended from a race that had never ingested alcohol, the Indians had no genetic tolerence, no bodily resistance to the mind-altering substance. Total abstinence from the white man's liquor, as required by the Prophet's religion, had a positive and strengthening effect on the tribes, which helped make it possible for Tecumseh to unify and discipline them later for military service.

In addition to renouncing the white man's whiskey, the Prophet required that neither were his followers to eat the food of the paleface settlers. This meant no bread or wheat products. It also meant no beef, no pork, no chicken, no lamb, and no honey. They were to eat the traditional Indian foods of corn, beans, potatoes, squash, wild berries, fish, and wild game. According to the Prophet, maple sugar was an especially spiritual

food, a gift to the Native Americans from the Master of Life.

Strangely, he also taught peace with the settlers, urging his followers to not only give up the white man's implements, such as the plow and the wagon, but also the rifle. Traditional tomahawks, bows, and arrows were to be their sufficient defense since they now had the Master of Life on their side.

Indian Witch Trials

Many of Tenskwatawa's teachings were admirable and even "Christian." But his dogmas also had a dark side. If you did not agree to follow all of his rules, if you seemed to favor the white man, if you opposed Tenskwatawa, who was the appointed spokesperson for the Master of Life, then you were an enemy of God's people. You were a child of the Evil One. You were a witch.

The Prophet's prescription for alleged witchcraft was to bind up the accused, bring them before a fire, and ask them to "surrender their poison and give up their bad art" so they could be pardoned. If not, they would be bludgeoned to death by tomahawk and their bodies thrown into the fire.

Several men and women died in this manner. Tenskwatawa usually personally participated in the ceremonies and made the judgments as to who was a witch and who was not. Even the Delawares, who were followers of Christianity and who formerly had close relationships with the white community, succumbed to the practice.

Appalled at the deadly ritual, Governor William Henry Harrison sent messengers to try to dissuade the Delawares from such barbary. When asked why they did it, their answer was simple. "You white people also try your criminals, and when they are found guilty, you hang them or kill them, and we do the same among ourselves."

God's Chosen People

Tenskwatawa also taught that Native Americans were superior over all other races. "We are the chosen people of the Great Spirit," he said, "and this is our promised land." The Master of Life had assured him that "the Americans I did not make. They are not my children, but the children of the Evil Spirit." One of his visions revealed to him that the Long Knives came to North America in the form of a great ugly crab that had crawled from the sea with its claws full of mud and seaweed, the spawn of the great serpent of evil that inhabits the Atlantic Ocean. "The Americans," according to the Prophet, "grew from the scum of the great Water, and the froth was driven into the Woods by a strong east wind. They are numerous, and I hate them. They are unjust. They have taken away your lands that were not made for them," he said. "If you live a pious life and do everything I tell you, the Master of Life will drive the Long Knives away, and you, alone, shall inhabit the land."

These were words the beleaguered Indians wanted to hear. Here was what they wanted to see happen— the Long Knives driven out by the Great, and their lands restored. And all they had to do to achieve this was to follow this man who was obviously a Prophet. Why, he had conquered death, itself, had he not?

Tenskwatawa then set out upon a missionary endeavor that would rival the efforts of even the most ardent Christians. In fact, the Moldavians, the Quakers, and the Shakers began losing ground with the Indians after the Shawnee Prophet began his proselytizing campaign. The Prophet drew followers by the thousands.

Harrison Puzzles
Over the Prophet

William Henry Harrison (1773-1841) was one of the extraordinary leaders of his time. He came from a family of notables that both preceeded and followed his long life of accomplishments. His father, Benjamin Harrison, was a signer of the Declaration of Independence. William Henry, himself, was ultimately destined to become the ninth

William Henry Harrison (1773-1841)

Illustration by Anthony Stewart

President of the United States. His grandson, another Benjamin Harrison (1811-1901), was destined to become the 23rd President. William had originally studied medicine but traded that for a life in the military. Early in his career he was assigned to Fort Washington, later to become Cincinnati, Ohio. He fought in the Battle of the Fallen Timbers. He was governor of the Northwest Territory, which included what would eventually become the states of Ohio, Indiana, Illinois, Michigan, and Wisconsin. One of the main charges of his office was to keep peace between the citizens of the United States and the Nations of Native Americans. It was a difficult, if not impossible, assignment.

Harrison's tactic of "divide and conquer" had worked well in keeping the Indians under control, preventing them from becoming a major threat to the proliferating settlements of the Americans. All Harrison had to do was to foster the natural enemy and distrust between tribes that had always divided Native Americans. Then came this drunkard, a good-for-nothing who had declared himself a Prophet, and, amazingly, he had followers! And what was worse, the tribes were giving up their animosity toward each other, living in mutual peace and uniting behind this "charlatan." How could this be? Harrison never figured it out. But he knew he had a problem.

During the next five years Tenskwatawa was able to forge a confederation of Native Americans that constituted the greatest unity ever achieved in the history of the Indian nations. In addition to the Shawnee, these included segments of the tribes of the Assiniboine, Cherokee, Chippewa, Cree, Delaware, Fox, Huron, Illinois, Iowa, Iroquois, Kaskaskia, Kickapoo, Menominee, Miami, Mingo, Mohawk, Onondaga, Oneida, Piankashaw, Potawatomi, Sac, Sauk, Seneca, Wea, Westoe, Winnebago, and Wyandot. During this time, Tecumseh was Tenskwatawa's closest advisor as well as the Prophet's most widely traveled missionary. But the confederacy was a religious alliance, not a military one. At least not yet.

Tenskwatawa's credibility as a prophet was supported by the fact that he was a "twin," (actually one of a set of triplets). Native Americans believed that twins were supposed to be religious leaders and have prophetic powers. However, the peculiar circumstances of Tenskwatawa's birth were not sufficient to bring him recognition as a prophet, although they helped establish his authenticity in the minds of the Indians. Surviving native twins were rare enough to command a certain amount of respect and awe even if they did have character flaws. To be a surviving triplet was unheard of and something to be revered, indeed. But Tenskwatawa was much more than a prophet by birth.

In addition to his resurrection from the dead, Tenskwatawa had also accomplished one other notable feat that furthered his reputation among Native Americans. Governor Harrison had tried to discredit the "One-Eyed Priest" early on. In 1806, he circulated a notice to as many Indian villages as he could denouncing Tenskwatawa as "a fraud, an imposter, and a pretended prophet."

"Drive him from your towns," Harrison admonished the tribes, "he is leading you down a dark, crooked, and thorny road to endless woe and misery. Why would the Great Spirit have selected such a charlatan to deliver his message to his Indian children?" queried Harrison. He proposed that the Delawares and other tribes demand miracles, that the Shawnee should prove his powers. "If he is really a prophet, ask of him to cause the sun to stand still, the moon to alter its course, the rivers to cease to flow, or the dead to rise from their graves. If he does these things, you may then believe that he has been sent from God."

Harrison had unwittingly played into the Prophet's plan. During the spring of 1806 several teams of astronomers had traveled over Indiana, Kentucky, and Illinois to establish observation stations to study an eclipse of the sun calculated to occur on June 16. If Harrison knew about this, he had forgotten or did not believe that Tenskwatawa would find out.

The Prophet knew about the scientists' activities. He also knew that a "Black Sun," or Muykutaaweethee Keesohtoa, was an event filled with dread and warning of future war for Native Americans. If his detractors wanted proof of his divinity, he would provide it.

Early in June, Tenskwatawa gathered his followers at Greenville. He declared that he would use his powers to darken the midday sun. He instructed them to spread the word and directed them to reassemble at Greenville on June 16th. "The Master of Life will send a Black Sun," he told them.

When the appointed day arrived, Tenskwatawa stayed in his wood bark lodge throughout the morning while hundreds of Indians milled around outside, waiting. Then as the noon sun faded into a strange twilight, the holy man suddenly appeared shouting, "Did I not speak the truth? See, the sun is dark!" The Prophet then tried to calm his frightened audience by assuring them that just as he had taken the sun away, he would also bring it back as brilliant as it was before.

Even his worst doubters became converts after that. Harrison's ploy had been turned into an effective power play by the shrewd and clever Tenskwatawa. The Prophet's influence grew even faster and farther after that. It seemed as if there were no stopping the growth of his popularity and of his new religion.

Tecumseh Rises to Power

In 1808, Tecumseh and his brother established Prophet's Town near the junction of the Tippecanoe and Wabash Rivers 12 miles northeast of the present city of Lafayette, Indiana. Hundreds of pilgrims came to pay homage to the Prophet. Indians arrived from Ohio, Indiana, Illinois, Michigan, Wisconsin, Kentucky, Missouri, and even Canada. Prophet's Town had become an Indian Mecca. Many moved and lived there. Others returned to their homelands and recruited even more followers to this new religion that was going to save the red men from the Long Knives.

However, by this time it was becoming clear that peace with the Long Knives would only lead to the extinction of the red men. Even Tenskwatawa's powerful medicine had not stopped the inexorable wave of paleface pioneers moving westward. What had been a native movement of the ideal was becoming one of the pragmatic. Gradually, what had been a religious alliance was becoming a military one. Prophet's Town was the headquarters. This was where they were being assembled to combine their forces against their common enemy.

Tenskwatawa was a charismatic religious leader who could work up his followers to a fever pitch with his words. But he was no military leader. He did not even have the simple skills of a hunter, much less those of a warrior. His vision was not of this world. The Indians needed a pragmatist. It was time to take the metal of a religious movement and forge it into an army of steel that could take on the Long Knives. The time had come for Tecumseh to exhibit his genius.

Tecumseh had traveled to every tribe that had chosen to follow his brother. He had all the necessary contacts. And he also had the skills of a politician, a diplomat, and a brilliant military strategist. While Tenskwatawa continued to be underestimated, ridiculed, and called "a charlatan" by the Americans, for some inexplicable reason, Tecumseh was highly regarded—even feared— by his white foes. The fact remains, however, that without the incredible leadership and organizational skills of Tenskwatawa in uniting the tribes,

Tecumseh's talents may never have been given an opportunity for display. Without Tenskwatawa's accomplishments, Tecumseh would not have had the foundation upon which to build his own.

Tecumseh had seen his people lose their homes and hunting grounds to the Long Knives. He had seen his native brothers weakened and demoralized by the liquor sold by white traders. He had seen prejudice, abuse, assault, and death dealt to his people at the hands of the settlers. He had seen his friends, relatives, and tribesmen die from measles, influenza, smallpox, and consumption, all curses the Indians had never known until the intrusion of the white man. He was angry. He had vowed never to surrender except to death while fighting for his land and his people. Tecumseh was a man of his word.

As a warrior, political organizer, and a leader of the Confederacy of American Indians, Tecumseh was opposed to savage acts such as scalping. He had a reputation for frankness, for honesty and for keeping his part of any agreement, even when the other side reneged on theirs.

In August of 1810, Chief Tecumseh traveled down the Wabash from Prophet's Town to Vincennes, Indiana, to meet William Henry Harrison, who was now Governor of the Indiana Territory. He wore war paint and was accompanied with about three hundred of his most fierce warriors. He came in peace but wanted to make an impression on Harrison—which he did.

When the meeting between

Tecumseh as A Youthful Shawnee Chief. Based on an authentic portrait originally owned by the families of William Clark and George Rogers Clark—brothers who were both explorers and who both fought against the Shawnee. The portrait is now owned by the Chicago Museum of Natural History. The only other time Tecumseh allowed himself to be sketched was in 1808—five years before his death. (See Chapter Five)

Illustration by Anthony Stewart.

Harrison and Tecumseh began, one of the Governor's aides beckoned to the Chieftain saying, "Your Father (i.e. Harrison) wants you to come sit by him." Tecumseh drew his blanket about him with an air of offended dignity and replied, "The Great Spirit is my Father. I will rest upon the bosom of my Mother," whereupon he took a seat, Indian-fashion, upon the ground. He then bluntly informed the governor that he intended to wage battle if the lands of his ancestors were not restored to the Indians. "I am authorized by all the tribes to do so," Tecumseh announced, "I am the head of them all,"

At another point in the negotiations, which took several days, Tecumseh and Harrison were sitting on a long bench talking together side by side. Tecumseh kept crowding the Governor and the Governor kept politely moving over, an inch at a time, as they continued their conversation. Finally, Harrison found himself at the end of the bench and the end of his patience with Tecumseh who was still moving in, too close for comfort. Harrison then expressed his annoyance to Tecumseh who replied, "This is exactly what you are doing to us." Harrison got the point and was impressed. For the time being, he would back off and give in to the requests Tecumseh had made. But not for long.

Throughout 1810 and 1811, the eloquent and resourceful Tecumseh traveled extensively throughout the South and the Midwest trying to unify the various tribes to fight against white settlers while they still had the advantage of greater numbers. While the success of the Shawnee brothers in unifying the nations of Native Americans was truly remarkable, it was not perfect.

The Creek, the Choctaw, the Osage, the Chickasaw, the Objibway, and the Susquehannock had all rejected Tenskwatawa's leadership and religion. Even where tribal units had accepted the religious authority of the Prophet, many individuals within the tribes did not. Hence, there were leading Iroquois, Senecas, and even Shawnees who opposed the Prophet and his brother.

One major opponent of Tenskwatawa and Tecumseh was Black Hoof, a powerful Shawnee Chief. Black Hoof had many followers and lived in northwestern Ohio. Black Hoof, like many Indians, believed that the best interest of their people lay in compromise and cooperation with the white man. They adopted white man dress, white man housing, white man farming practices, and white man business methods. They did not want war.

There was also a legend about George Washington that entered here. The young Washington had successfully led the first battle of the so-called "French and Indian War" in May of 1754. He was twenty-two at the time. In this, and other battles, Indians, aiming their bows at the young officer, reported seeing the arrows bend around his body—as if he were invulnerable and immortal. Indians predicted that this man was special and had been chosen by the Great Spirit to lead the nation and that, therefore, it was the will of Wakonda that the white-faced foreigners settle and eventually rule this land.

Many Americans, including Thomas Jefferson, believed in the principle of "Manifest Destiny,"—the idea that God had ordained for the United States to become a great country from sea to sea, ruled by the descendants of the European settlers. Oddly, there were also thousands of Indians who believed the same idea, even though they did not like it. Accepting this premise, they concluded that it was better to join the Americans than to fight them. To fight them would, in their view, be an act against the Great Spirit.

This legend caused the Osage to decide, early on, that they would befriend the Americans, which they did. It was an important alliance which greatly accelerated the settlement of the lands west of the Mississippi.

The Osage were a tribe of "giants." Osage warriors were well over six feet tall, when most Indians were nearly a foot shorter. Other tribes were intimidated by their size.

During the Lewis and Clark expeditions between 1803 and 1806, the Osage accompanied them and protected them, even though they knew that this venture was the beginning of the end for Native control of their homeland. They understood well that they were aiding in the ultimate conquest of the continent by the white man, but they believed it was destiny, the will of the Great Father.

When Fort Osage was established on the Missouri River near the boundary of the Kansas Territory in 1808, it was completely surrounded and outnumbered by hostile Indians. However, this was not a problem. The Osage came with the Americans to build villages of their own around the Fort to protect the white man from other tribes. In fact, by the time of the earthquakes in 1811–12, Fort Osage, which never contained more than 100 whites, was guarded by as many as 5,000 friendly Indians of the Osage Nation who had encamped there.

As a further example of the divisions within the Shawnees, one of Tecumseh's own sisters, Nehaaeemo, married a Scotch trader, George Ironsides, and went to live the life of a white woman with her husband.

Furthermore, while visiting New Madrid, the youngest sister of Tecumseh, Teceikeapease, fell in love with a Canadian named Francois Maisonville. The beautiful Indian bride and handsome Frenchman were married in 1808 according to Indian custom and lived for a time in Chillicothe, a large Shawnee city a few miles north of Cape Girardeau, Missouri.

Her brothers were incensed. Tecumseh came to Chillicothe and prevailed upon her to return to "her people" at Prophet's Town. She did come "home," but not willingly and not for long. After a few months, she returned to her husband in Missouri who had moved back to New Madrid. Having left her tribal life as a Shawnee, Teceikeapease then took a French name, Genevieve Marie Maisonville. Genevieve and Francois were in New Madrid during the earthquakes.

Meanwhile, Methoataske, the mother, moved back to Tuckhabatchee, Alabama, and died shortly thereafter to be buried in the soil where she had been born.

Tecumseh's First Prophecy

Tecumseh's charisma and extraordinary leadership were recognized and feared by the leaders in Washington. The government had dispatched reporters to follow the Chief and write down his speeches, so that his plans might be known by Congress. By this time Tecumseh's name had been translated to mean "comet" or "shooting star." Some Native Americans took the arrival of the Comet of 1811 to be an anointment of Tecumseh by the Great Spirit. About the time of the great comet's first appearance, Tecumseh gave a well-publicized plea to the Osage tribes of Missouri and Arkansas. The speech was recorded by the title, "We Must Smoke the Same Pipe." It was delivered somewhere west of New Madrid in the region between present-day Poplar Bluff, Missouri, and Pocahontas, Arkansas.

"The white men are not friends to the Indians," he said. "My people wish for peace. The red men all wish for peace. But where the white people are, there is no peace. . . . Brothers, The Great Spirit is angry with our enemies. He speaks in thunder, and the earth swallows up their villages, and drinks up the Mississippi. The great waters will cover their lowlands, and their corn cannot grow."

The uncanny precision with which these last two sentences were to come true began to unfold within a few months. Before the year was over, Tecumseh's words were to be fulfilled in their entirety.

The spring of 1811 brought bigger floods on the Ohio and Mississippi Rivers than even the Indians could remember. "The Year of Waters," they called it. The Lexington, Kentucky, newspaper reported, in 1811, that "during the summer months the heat was, in many places, the most intense that was ever known." While many crops were destroyed by the extent and duration of the spring floods, others later succumbed to the summer drought.

In October of 1811 Tecumseh was to utter another prophecy in Alabama much more specific to the earthquakes which, unknown to the rest of the world at that time, were only two months away.

Paddle-Wheelers
Enter the Midwest

Among the assortment of wonders that year, one was man-made. The *New Orleans*, the very first steamboat to float the Ohio and Mississippi Rivers, was launched from Pittsburgh on October 20, 1811. The choice of a late fall embarcation was a result of the same reasoning that had been applied by Charles and Lucy Lewis, who had made their one-way voyage down the Ohio and settled in Kentucky a few years earlier. The idea was to arrange one's passage below Louisville at a time when the river stages were high enough to clear the rocky falls of the Ohio, which threatened most boats in the summer months.

The steamboat had been under construction for more than a year and-a-half and had become the curiosity of everyone in Pittsburgh. The enterprise was financed by three notable men.

Robert Fulton (1765-1815) was the engineer and inventor who designed and built the world's first

AMERICAN RIVERS, TOWNS AND CITIES IN 1811-12

CANADA

Lake Superior

St. Croix

Ottawa River

St. Lawrence River

Montreal

Ottawa

Montpelier

Portland

Concord

Lake Huron

Toronto

Lake Ontario

Albany

Hudson River

Boston

Hartford

Mississippi

Lake Michigan

Thames R.

Susque-

Detroit

Lake Erie

New York

Fort Dearborn

Allegheny

henna R.

Delaware

Trenton

River

Tippecanoe R.

Greenville

Philadelphia

Prophet's Town

River

Old Piqua

River

Pittsburgh

Monongahela

Baltimore

Missouri

R.

Illinois R.

Cincinnati

Washing-ton D.C.

Vincennes

Richmond

Cheaseapeake Bay

St. Charles

Wabash

Ohio

Louisville

Chillicothe

River

St. Louis

Roanoke

River

Fort Osage

Osage River

Henderson

Boonesboro

Raleigh

Ste. Genevieve

Smithland

Cumberland River

Pee

Cape Girardeau

New Madrid

St. Francis

Little Prairie

Nashille

Catawba R.

Dee

River

Arkansas

Fort Pickering

Tennessee River

Cooper R.

Red

River

Big Prairie

Coosa R.

Chatahoochee

Savannah River

Charleston

ATLANTIC

Pearl R.

Atlanta

Savannah

OCEAN

River

Alabama R.

Tuck-habatchee

Nacodoches

Sabine R.

Natchez

Swanee River

New Orleans

St. Augustine

GULF OF

St. Petersburg

MEXICO

steamboat. Dubbed as "Fulton's Folly," *The Clermont* had been launched in New England on the Hudson River in 1807. The launching of the *New Orleans* was an expansion of his steamboat business into the West.

Robert R. Livingston was a wealthy businessman from New York, Secretary of Foreign Affairs and Minister to France under President Thomas Jefferson. Livingston County, Kentucky, was his namesake. When Fulton built his first full-sized steamboat, Livingston financed it and named it the *"Clermont"* after his family estate on the Hudson River. Robert's younger brother was Edward Livingston, who was to hold positions under President Andrew Jackson similar to those held by Robert under Jefferson.

Nicholas J. Roosevelt was a builder of boats and steam engines. A friend of President John Adams, his experience included the design and construction of boats for the United States Navy. He was also the experienced navigator of some of Fulton's earlier experiments on the Hudson. He had been designated by his other two partners to be the supervising construction engineer at Pittsburgh. He had also been designated to be commander of the *New Orleans* on its maiden voyage to the destination for which it was named.

If the first voyage of the *New Orleans* was a success, the Mississippi Steamboat Navigation Company, a partnership of Fulton, Livingston, and Roosevelt, could become wealthy. The potential for profit was enormous. It was their hope that the steamboat could average eight

miles per hour downstream and at least four upstream. With such speed, the transportation times up and down the waterways would be reduced by more than half, and the steamboats could carry more cargo with only a fraction of the necessary crew. Nicholas' task, as charged by his partners, was not only to reach New Orleans, but to do so in record time while visiting every notable town along the way to promote the venture, persuade investors, and drum up business for future voyages. It was exactly the kind of assignment Nicholas and his wife loved—a combination of engineering, adventure, business, and politics.

Nicholas was descended from one of America's first settlers, a Dutchman named Klaes Martensen van Roosevelt who came to Manhattan Island in 1613. Van Roosevelt was one of the organizers of the Colony of New Netherland. In 1626 the Dutch formally purchased Manhattan Island from the Indians for a pile of beads and blankets valued at 60 guilders ($24). In that year, New Amsterdam was designated as the government seat. In 1664, when the island was taken by the British, the name was changed to New York City. In the century that followed, the Roosevelts were to amass a considerable fortune and to hold many high offices in both the city and state of New York.

In his forties at the time, Nicholas was accompanied by his twenty-year old wife, Lydia Latrobe Roosevelt. She was eight months pregnant with their second child when they embarked from Pittsburgh. Because of the large age difference, one might

Lydia Latrobe Roosvelt (1791–1878)

Nicholas Roosevelt (1767–1854)

Robert R. Livinston (1746–1813)

Robert Fulton (1765–1815)

Illustrations by Anthony Stewart

mistake them as father and daughter, but even so, one would have to say that Nicholas and Lydia were a handsome couple by any standard.

Lydia was the eldest daughter of the distinguished architect, Benjamin Latrobe, Surveyor General of the United States. Nicholas had been a family friend of the Latrobes since before Lydia's birth. "Uncle Nick," as he was called, had literally watched his future wife grow from infancy to womanhood. They married when he was thirty-eight and she was only fifteen.

The Roosevelts and the Latrobes ran in social circles that included the following Presidents: Washington, Adams, Jefferson, Madison, Monroe, and Jackson. Dolly Madison, the First Lady from 1809 to 1817, was a close friend of Lydia's stepmother, Mary Hazelhurst Latrobe.

Not far from the boatyard where the *New Orleans* was being built was the Bakewell Glassworks. Benjamin Bakewell, its owner, was an uncle to one of Lydia's best friends, Lucy Bakewell—wife of a young French woodsman and artist by the name of John James Audubon. John and Lucy lived in Henderson, Kentucky, where they kept a store. Henderson is located on the Ohio River, 150 miles downstream from Louisville and about 100 miles upstream from Smithland and Rocky Hill.

Lydia and Nicholas became friends with the Audubons during their first trip down the river in 1809-10. For more than six months they floated on a flatboat from Pittsburgh to New Orleans, stopping often to interview townspeople and boatmen along the way. They were surveying the river's course in anticipation of their next trip, which would be aboard something new and different—a boat that needed no oarsmen and could power itself against the current.

Nicholas and Lydia Roosevelt were also to be remembered in history in association with two U.S. Presidents, Theodore and Franklin Roosevelt. In a speech given in Memphis on October 4, 1907, Teddy Roosevelt commented: "Early in our industrial history this valley was the seat of the largest development of inland navigation in the United States; and perhaps you will pardon my mentioning that the first steamboat west of the Alleghenies was built by a Roosevelt, my great-grandfather's brother, in 1811, for the New Orleans trade, and in that year made the trip from Pittsburgh to New Orleans."

In March of 1905, during his term as the 26th President of the United States, Theodore, a Republican, attended the wedding of Anna Eleanor Roosevelt, his niece. The groom was Theodore's fifth cousin, Franklin Delano Roosevelt, a Democrat, who was destined to become the 32nd President. Eleanor and Franklin were sixth cousins.

During its construction and voyage, the *New Orleans* was frequently referred to as "Mr. Roosevelt's Steamboat." Fulton, who had designed the boat and who had a reputation for pride bordering on arrogance, was extremely annoyed by this. The designation also irked Livingston, who had financed a major portion of the venture.

Pittsburgh is located at the confluence of two great rivers, the

| The *New Orleans*, First Steamboat to Navigate the Ohio and Mississippi Rivers |

Illustration by Anthony Stewart

Allegheny and the Monongehela, which join to form the Ohio. Its location on these major waterways was ideal for the building and launching of boats headed west. Here, eight years earlier in 1803, Meriwether Lewis and William Clark had commissioned a large custom-built keelboat which was to take them on their great expedition West to discover the headwaters of the Missouri and other wonders of the nation's newly acquired territory.

The *New Orleans* was a wonder to behold, especially to a generation accustomed to seeing only flatboats, keel boats, barges, and canoes. The vessel was 26 feet wide and 148 feet long (half the length of a football field) with a sky-blue hull, a molded depth of twelve feet, and a peculiar pair of paddle wheels—one poked out on each side. A single smoke stack towered two stories above the deck belching black soot from her midsection while fore and aft stood two tapered masts, taller than the stack, just in case they should have an engine breakdown or run out of fuel and needed sails. From one of the masts flew a large American flag with seventeen stars and seventeen stripes. It weighed 410 tons and was driven by a thirty-four cylinder, 160 horse-power engine designed by Roosevelt, himself. Living quarters were in a long cabin above deck while the pilot house was mounted on top in the forward section. Heaps of firewood were stored on deck in the rear. The huge hulk looked more like a big ark than like the multi-decked sternwheelers that came later which we associate with Tom Sawyer and Huckleberry Finn. It was an experimental design. No steamboat has looked quite like the *New Orleans* before or since.

The *New Orleans* was the most curious, if not frightening, apparition that had ever come down the river. The deafening noise of clattering pistons and puffing steam valves could be heard for miles downstream as it neared a port. Many people fled in fear before the ship even came into sight—terrified by the mere sound of its approach. Since there were no radios or telephones, the people who lived along the banks were not forewarned of its coming. When they saw it for the first time, they could not comprehend how such a giant vessel could travel with such "fearful rapidity," snorting and whistling with sounds "never before heard by man nor beast."

The Roosevelts Leave Pittsburgh

When the boat left Pittsburgh on October 20, 1811, there were fifteen people aboard: Captain Nicholas Roosevelt; Pilot Andrew Jack; Engineer Nicholas Baker; six "Kaintucks and Creoles" (professional oarsmen who were hired as deckhands, not to man oars, but to cut wood and stoke fires). Also on board were a cook, a messboy, and two female maidservants to attend to Miss Lydia and her three-year-old daughter, Rosetta. Nicholas was a family man and would not think of taking such a trip without his family. In his design of the vessel he had not neglected to build comfortable, attractively finished captain's quarters for his wife, daughter, and their maids. In addition to the Roosevelts and their crew, the family dog was also aboard—a Great Labrador named Tiger.

The Roosevelts endured some criticism for taking such a risk with their daughter, Rosetta, and with their child-to-be, who would be born during the trip. They were also warned about departing on a Sunday. "You may provoke the wrath of God," they were told, "for starting a business trip on the Sabbath." But they had waited long enough, in Nicholas' judgement. The autumn rise had come, the water level was right, the weather was good, and they needed to get started. What they did not know was that a true encounter with an "Act of God" awaited them during that voyage, but it was to have nothing to do with their Sunday departure.

Cutting timber for fuel each evening as they went, they passed Cincinnati a week later on October 27. Much to Nicholas' satisfaction, their downstream speed was 14-16 miles per hour, considerably faster than he had anticipated. As a young boy saw them rapidly rounding the bend billowing clouds of black soot and heading for the Cincinnati shore, he raced home shouting, "The British are coming!" The entire town of 2,000 residents came down to the river to greet the strange vessel. The next day they departed.

Nicholas was in no hurry and wanted to make another stop at General William Henry Harrison's farm near Fort Washington, just below Cincinnati. There he had planned to stock up on beer and other supplies. But Lydia was heavy with child and feeling a bit cranky. She was anxious to get to Louisville where she was planning to engage a midwife and have her baby. They went on without making the stop and without the beer.

Louisville and the Birth of Henry

Around midnight on October 29, the *New Orleans* arrived at Louisville in a shower of red sparks, clanking engines, hissing steam, and loud explosions blasting from her stack. The whole town of 1,500 people was awakened. Many thought that the comet had fallen into the river.

Among the first to greet them were their friends, Lucy and John Audubon, and their two-year-old son, Victor. They just happened to be in Louisville. They had come from their home at Henderson, Kentucky, 150 miles down the river. They could have traveled by wagon, but they had come on horseback, instead, so that John would not miss seeing any of the birds along the way. Lucy and John had formerly lived in Louisville, so when Lydia arrived ready to give birth, Lucy brought her the same midwife who had attended the birth of little Victor.

The midwife boarded the *New Orleans* none too soon. On October 30, less than twenty-four hours after their arrival, little Henry Latrobe Roosevelt was born—the first birth aboard a steamboat, ever. Nicholas and Lydia decided to stay at Louisville for awhile. They had a newborn baby to care for, now, and the river stage was not quite high enough for them to attempt to shoot the falls.

The Falls of the Ohio

The "Falls of the Ohio" are caused by a resistant limestone outcrop. The cataract is two miles long with about twenty-two feet of drop. They descend between rocky Islands #61 and #64 at a velocity of 14-16 miles per hour. For water, that is extremely swift. In order to keep control, the velocity of the boat had to be faster than the water, which meant that relative to the stationary bank and rocky bottom the boat would need to be moving 25-30 miles per hour. That is about 40 feet per second. If an obstacle, like a submerged rock, were seen even 200 feet ahead, the boat's pilot would have less than five seconds to respond and take action to avoid a crash. One mistake, and all could be killed. Only those with years of experience—who knew every rock and shallow place, every twist and undertow of the current—could safely navigate these straits.

More of a rapids than a falls, it was only passable for large craft during high water at certain times of the year. Boats returning upstream had to be hauled by men pulling ropes from the bank. The cascades were referred to as "The Corpse Maker." Many had been wrecked, and many had died in these treacherous waters.

The barrier of the falls acted as a dam which created a deep natural harbor at Louisville. A whole cadre of men lived there whose sole occupation was to steer boats through the rapids and haul travelers upstream through those straits to the safety of Louisville. Today's boats navigate these falls the year round by a system of locks.

THE

NAVIGATOR,

CONTAINING

DIRECTIONS FOR NAVIGATING THE

MONONGAHELA, ALLEGHENY,

OHIO, AND MISSISSIPPI RIVERS;

WITH AN AMPLE ACCOUNT

OF THESE MUCH ADMIRED WATERS,

FROM THE HEAD OF THE FORMER

TO THE MOUTH OF THE LATTER;

AND A CONCISE

DESCRIPTION OF THEIR TOWNS, VILLAGES,

HARBORS, SETTLEMENTS, &c.

WITH MAPS OF THE OHIO AND MISSISSIPPI

TO WHICH IS ADDED

AN APPENDIX,

CONTAINING

AN ACCOUNT OF LOUISIANA,

AND OF

THE MISSOURI AND COLUMBIA RIVERS,

AS DISCOVERED BY THE VOYAGE UNDER

CAPTS. LEWIS AND CLARK.

TENTH EDITION.

———————

PITTSBURGH,

PRINTED AND PUBLISHED BY CRAMER & SPEAR,

FRANKLIN HEAD, WOOD STREET.

1818

A
Reproduction
of the
Title Page

to

THE
NAVIGATOR
BY
ZADOC CRAMER

10th Edition

**Published in 1818
in Pittsburgh**

This manual, whose
first edition was
published in 1801,
was the principal
guide used by boat-
men in the early 19th
century. The 9th edi-
tion was published in
1811, just before the
earthquakes.

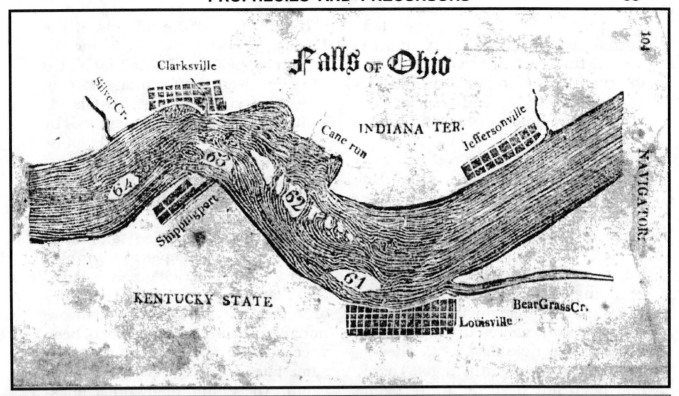

Clarksville

Falls of Ohio

INDIANA TER.

Silver Cr.

Cane run

Jeffersonville

64

63

62

Shippingport

61

KENTUCKY STATE

BearGrassCr.

Louisville

NAVIGATOR:

104

FALLS OF THE OHIO

Photocopy of Page 104 of *The Navigator* by Zadoc Cramer, 10th Edition, 1818.

Andrew Jack, pilot of the *New Orleans*, was glad to let another boatman take the helm for this ride. Chosen by Nicholas as an experienced river pilot who had passed this way many times, Jack had never steered a vessel over these cataracts, himself. He was quite willing to let someone else pilot the first steamboat over these perils.

The river was rising, and Nicholas consulted with the experienced boatmen on what stage the river would have to reach before it would be safe for him to take the *New Orleans* over the falls. His new son was a month old now, and he was growing impatient to continue. All he wanted was a few inches of freeboard. He was willing to take a chance, but not much of a chance, with his wife and two young children aboard.

A Sunday embarcation had worked well for them in Pittsburgh so far, despite the criticisms of their religious friends. So why not another Sabbath day farewell from Louisville? If the "Wrath of God" were to be the consequence, they had certainly not experienced any of it yet. On December 8th, while faithful Louisvillians went to church (mostly Presbyterians), Baker and his crew fired up the *New Orleans* for maximum steam and top speed. They would have to maintain a relative velocity faster than the water, or the raging rapids would take possession of the boat and toss it helplessly into the merciless rocks. Such a velocity would test the power of the *New Orleans* to the limit.

Nicholas and Andrew had engaged an experienced pilot, the

best they could find. They then left Louisville, chugging away at full steam, threaded their way between the islands, shot through the chutes, skirted the rocks, and cleared the falls of the Ohio. As rapids roared and pistons pounded, Lydia, who wanted to watch, stood out on deck grasping Tiger's thick hair. She held her breath most of the way.

Shippingport

At the foot of the falls on the Kentucky side lay the town of Shippingport where several barges and keelboats were anchored. As the *New Orleans* steamed toward the dock, it was welcomed amid cheers and shouts of congratulations. There had been much speculation, even some bets taken. But the very first steamboat had made it!

They were to stay at Shippingport several days to refuel, take on supplies, and, most importantly, to inspect the steamboat for any damages that might have resulted from that strenuous passage. The crew was kept busy cleaning, oiling, and tightening up every bolt or loosened joint.

Meanwhile, Nicholas and Andrew Jack interviewed the rivermen arriving from downstream so they could revise their charts to current conditions.

Their principal guide, in addition to their experience, was Zadoc Cramer's ninth edition of "*The Navigator*," which had been published in Pittsburgh only a few months before, in February of 1811. Cramer, a retired boatman living in Natchez, Mississippi, had numbered the islands of the Ohio, starting at Pittsburgh, and the islands of the Mississippi, starting just below the mouth of the Ohio. He had tabulated 98 islands on the Ohio and 127 on the Mississippi. These 225 Islands would be the principal landmarks by which the *New Orleans* would plot its progress along the voyage. But most useful were Cramer's comments as to which side of each island, left or right, was the safest.

Where are the hidden sand bars? Where are the deepest channels? Where have former channels silted in and new ones formed? What chutes are blocked with snags? Which are not? Where have previous boats been wrecked and how does one avoid the same fate? Where do hostile Indians camp? These, and many other questions, were asked by Nicholas and Andrew as they prepared to depart. Not all of the answers they received were satisfactory.

For several weeks, now, reports had been drifting into Shippingport, told by travelers from the lower waters about strange happenings downstream and a growing feeling of apprehension among the settlers around and below the mouth of the Ohio. Many feared increased Indian attacks. There had been floods and sickness. People were imagining portents of disaster in everything, including the weather.

According to one tale, the region around the confluence of the Ohio and Mississippi, which was used to frequent thunderstorms, had not experienced a single storm in over a year. Even more astonishing were the reports of woodsmen seeing deer suddenly bold or standing immobile and unafraid before the hunter. The birds were also acting strangely. Flocks of water fowl in that area were said to have been acting confused, taking to the air in disarrayed flights of frenzy instead of taking wing in ordered patterns of coordinated group motion as they always had before. Some boatmen reported seeing numerous bodies of dead squirrels floating in the lower reaches of the Ohio.

Nicholas and Andrew took note of these unsettling stories, as did Lydia, but it did not affect their resolve to continue. After all, they had just made a successful passage through what they believed was the most hazardous obstacle on the whole journey. Nothing downstream could match the challenge of the Falls of the Ohio. Or so they thought.

In Pittsburgh they had been 2,500 river miles from their final destination on the Gulf of Mexico. It was now only 1,400 miles to New Orleans. Only 500 to New Madrid.

Yellow Bank

A day or two after leaving Shippingport they pulled up to Yellow Bank, Indiana, where Nicholas had invested in two coal mines. Since the steamboat could be fueled by anything that burned, Nicholas was planning to experiment with coal for this portion of their journey.

They could only take on so much fuel at a time because the extra weight increased the risk of dragging, endangering the boat. When they could, the wood was purchased. But as they moved further and further downstream, settlements became smaller and fewer, and they would have to rely on their own axe-

menship more and more. About two or three days' supply of wood is all they could safely carry.

The *New Orleans* was a fuel hog. Under full power it consumed six cords of wood every day. One cord occupies a volume of 128 cubic feet, a stack of wood four feet wide, four feet tall, and eight feet long. Six cords would be a huge heap twelve feet square and five feet high. Visualize a sizeable room stacked wall to wall and head high with firewood. Most of the energy was wasted, lost in steam and unburned soot escaping through the smoke stack. Nicholas thought coal would burn hotter and more efficiently. For two days they lay at anchor at Yellow Bank, loading coal, enjoying a little time on land, and attending to other matters.

Lydia had noticed that the Engineer, Nicholas Baker, was giving more than the usual attention to one of her maids. The maid liked it. They were both single. "Could this be the beginning of something?" she thought. It was too soon to tell.

When they were ready to leave, it was Sunday evening, December 15, 1811. They decided to get a good night's rest before continuing their voyage, free from the deafening beats of boat machinery. They would depart at daylight. They hoped to make a brief stop a few miles downstream at Henderson, Kentucky, to visit with Lucy and John Audubon the next morning. But uninterrupted sleep was not to be their lot that fateful night. New Madrid was 350 river miles away, but in a straight line, as the crow flies, it was only 160.

Rumors of War

Since March the appearance of the Great Comet of 1811 had continuously grown brighter and larger. Then, on September 17, there was an eclipse of the sun. It was witnessed throughout the Midwest. The *Lexington Gazette* reported that "the day was remarkably serene, and the skies entirely clear of clouds, so that its appearance was the most solemn and impressive that we could conceive." The eclipse prompted newspapers to editorialize and others to prophesy of dire events soon to come.

One of those, of course, was Tecumseh's brother, the Prophet Tenskwatawa, who had been left in charge at Prophet's Town. Tecumseh was in Alabama rallying support for his cause among the Creeks. A few weeks before the eclipse, Tenskwatawa predicted to his followers that the sun would be darkened on September 17th as a divine sign. White reporters claimed that he had merely obtained foreknowledge of the event from an astronomical almanac published the year before. But Tenskwatawa's Native American brothers did not agree. "The Prophet had made the noonday sun turn black once before on June 16, 1806," they remembered, "and he could surely do it again."

The people at Prophet's Town believed that his correct foretelling of the September eclipse to be but another manifestation of his spiritual powers. Tenskwatawa claimed it had been a sign revealed to him by The Great Spirit that wars with the white men were inevitable and that the Native American brothers should unite under his brother's leadership before it was too late.

In Europe, the Emperor Louis Napoleon Bonaparte had taken the appearance of the Great Comet personally as a good omen. After all, its first sighting had been in France. To him, his astrologers and advisors, it was a sign to invade Russia. While the Comet of 1811 was known as "Tecumseh's Comet" in America, it was known as "Napoleon's Comet" in Europe.

To this point in time, Napoleon's military conquests had largely been quite successful. From 1808 to 1812, the French Empire he had forged was geographically greater than even that of his role model and predecessor, Charlemagne, King of the Franks a thousand years before. Those European states not directly annexed into the French Empire were either bound by treaties of submission or treaties of alliance. His political power umbrella shaded all of continental Europe, including France, Spain, Portugal, Belgium, Holland, Denmark, Italy, Switzerland, Prussia, Austria, the Confederation of the Rhine (West Germany), and the Duchy of Warsaw (East Germany and Poland). Sweden and Norway were also a part of his empire, as well as parts of Greece, Turkey, Syria and northern Egypt. Even Russia was in alliance with the French Emperor, but their divided loyalty, which included Napoleon's arch enemy, the British, troubled him.

His lust for new lands to rule had not been sated, and he longed for greater control over what he already had. Blinded by his ambition for a universal monarchy and encouraged by the sign of The Comet, he decided to strike Russia. In late 1811, he began to assemble more than half a million troops along the Neiman River on the Russian border in order to march against the Muscovites. To oppose this "mighty host of twenty nations," the Russians could only muster a small defensive force. When the fighting would actually begin a few months later, the French and their allies would outnumber the Russians three to one. Napoleon was confident that he would achieve a quick and complete victory.

Forerunners of World War

Meanwhile, throughout the year 1811, Americans suffered many indignities from the British, both on land and at sea. These actions were an overture to the War of 1812. In the last two years of his presidency, 1806-1808, Thomas Jefferson had tried to prepare Americans for what he saw as an inevitable war with the British. He also anticipated a war with the Indians whom the British were arming to aid them in their aggression against the United States.

The English had lost the thirteen original colonies, but they still had control of Canada where the boundaries, especially around the western Great Lakes, had not been firmly established. If the British could have their way, the "Northwest Territories" at the headwaters of the Mississippi would be theirs. This would have included the land that comprises today's states of Michigan and Wisconsin, as well as parts of Minnesota, Indiana, and Illinois. Great Britain had been forced to con-

cede American independence following the Revolutionary War, but it was not ready to accept America's apparent destiny as a world power without another fight.

During the years 1808-1812, the country was divided over the British question. Many leaders, including the powerful Henry Clay, argued for war with England. But Senator John Randolph of Roanoke was of the opinion that military involvement with England would draw the United States into the war in Europe, which was caught up in the Napoleonic campaigns. Randolph was afraid of igniting a world war.

Attempting to argue that it would be contrary to God's will for America to declare war against Britain, he warned that Divine Providence would "inflict dire consequences upon any nation" that would "venture to intermingle" in such a war. A few weeks prior to the earthquakes Randolph argued against conflict with Britain on the grounds that such an action would bring upon this country "a dreadful scourge, some great desolation, some awful visitation."

Whether the Senator from Virginia had in mind the possibility of "a dreadful, great, and awful earthquake," we do not know. In any case, his words, uttered shortly before the fact, did turn out to be an apt description of the aftermath of those great quakes.

On November 5, 1811, President James Madison called Congress into an emergency session to "prepare for hostilities." On November 7, 1811, the Battle of Tippecanoe took place on the upper Wabash in what is now the State of Indiana. The victor was

General William Henry Harrison.

The vanquished were followers of Tenskwatawa and Chief Tecumseh whose headquarters at Prophet's Town on the upper Wabash fell to Harrison's troops that day. Tecumseh was not there during the battle. He was campaigning in Tennessee and Kentucky to enlist the support of the Chickasaws and Choctaws against the white men. When he heard the news almost two months later, he decided to take sides with the British and fight with them against the American settlers, as the red man's only hope of stopping the westward migration.

Despite the impassioned objections of Senator John Randolph and others, the passing of the month of November, 1811, found the country much closer to another war with England. The Battle of Tippecanoe was actually a preliminary to the War of 1812—part of the United States strategy to weaken the strength of the British, who intended to use the Indians against the States should hostilities be declared.

Meanwhile, as Europe was at war, and North America was on the brink of it, things were happening in Mexico and South America. The American revolution, begun in 1776, and the French revolution, initiated in 1789, had impacted the thinking people throughout all of Latin America. In 1808, when Napoleon deposed Ferdinand VII, the rightful king of Spain, and replaced him with his brother, Joseph Bonaparte, Latin Americans saw their opportunity.

The Mexicans were first. They declared their independence on September 16, 1810, which began a long war with Spain. Some of the most intense fighting took place during the earthquakes, between December 1811 and May 1812, when General Jose Maria Morelos successfully defended the city of Cuautla against greatly superior royalist forces. Mexico was not to win its freedom easily. Morelos was captured in 1815 and executed. The Mexican war for independence would continue another six years. They would finally become free of Spain on September 27, 1821.

George Washington, "Father of our Country," was a hero and role model for Simon Bolivar (1783-1830). If Washington fathered one country, Bolivar fathered six—but not because of his physical stature. Washington was over six feet tall while Bolivar was less than five. On July 5, 1811, Bolivar was the first to sign a Declaration of Independence that started the war that would eventually lead to the freedom of Venezuela from Spain. During 1811–12 no less than five other South American countries were to declare their independence, as well, thus initiating wars on many fronts against Spain. Besides Venezuela, Bolivar was the military and political leader who would eventually liberate Colombia, Ecuador, Panama, Peru, and Bolivia.

While battles raged in Europe, North America, and South America, the rest of the world had its wars, too. At no previous time in history were more nations engaged in military combat than during the same period of time that North America was under attack from the New Madrid earthquakes. While the

United States was under seige by a series of national earthquakes, warfare, in one form or another, had encircled the globe.

In the Middle East there was civil war throughout the Arabian Peninsula with the holy Muslim cities of Mecca and Medina taken by siege in 1802 and 1804. That was followed by war between Arabia, Egypt, Turkey (which includes modern Iraq) and Persia (now Iran), which lasted until 1815. During the same time Egypt was at war with Arabia, it was also being torn by civil war within its own borders.

The nation of Palestine (now Israel and Lebanon) had been invaded by Napoleon in 1799-1800 and left in economic and political ruins. During this time Palestine was in worse condition than it had been in almost 2,000 years, since the Romans had pillaged its cities, plundered its resources, and killed its leaders. Palestine was not to begin recovery from this depression until well after 1813.

Persia, in addition to its war with Arabia, was also at war with Russia over the Territory of Georgia. Persia was decisively beaten in 1812, just before Napoleon invaded Russia from the west. Following its defeat by Russia, Persia then turned its army on its neighbor, Afganistan, in a war that was to continue several years.

In India scattered skirmishes and bloody battles took place throughout the country between Indian nationalists, Dutch, French, Persian, and British troops from 1799 to 1813 when the British finally gained military control over the nation. Then from 1813 to 1815 war was declared and fought between India and Nepal with the British in command of Indian soldiers.

In South Africa, in 1811, the British and Dutch Boer Commandos began their conquest of the African Tribes. These wars were to last until 1819.

Meanwhile, China had been at peace with the world and had suffered no internal uprisings for more than a hundred years until 1796. Then the White Lotus Rebellion broke out under the Manchu Dynasty. When that rebellion was suppressed by armed force and wholesale massacre in 1803, the Tai Ping Rebellion erupted and continued through 1813 and several years beyond.

When President James Madison signed the declaration of war against Great Britain on June 18, 1812, and Napoleon started his invasion of Russia six days later on June 24 more than forty countries of the world were simultaneously at war on four continents, including the Indians of North America. Battles were engaged around the globe on both land and on sea.

World Wars I and II were not to come until a hundred years later, but the War of 1812, the Latin American wars for liberation, the civil uprisings in Asia, the struggles for control of India and South Africa, the battles over religion and territory in the Middle East, and the Napoleonic campaigns—all raging simultaneously—were the forerunners of global warfare. The only thing that prevented an escalation of these multiple military conflicts into 20th century-type World Wars was the absence of 20th century technology. Early 19th century commanders simply did not have the means to rapidly transport large numbers of troops and their armaments great distances. Railroads, motorized vehicles, disel-powered boats, airplanes and the fuels to propel them had not yet been developed.

Even so, it has been said that the "Real First World War" took place in the nineteenth century (not the twentieth) between 1810 and 1815. It is a curious coincidence that the times of the great American earthquakes of unprecedented fury fall in the middle of this period of unprecedented global conflict.

The Sensibilities of Animals

The fall of 1811 was said to have been accompanied by strange animal behavior throughout the Mississippi and Ohio River Valleys around New Madrid. According to one report, hoards of squirrels were seen migrating out of western Kentucky, many drowning in the Ohio River as they tried to cross over into Illinois.

At the same time, millions of passenger pigeons invaded the Ohio River valley, consuming uncountable tons of seeds, berries, beechnuts, pecans, acorns, and other natural foods. Like a voracious tornado, they could sweep in and consume an entire field of carefully tended crop in minutes. They would swoop in and stay for several weeks—stripping the forest and lands clean until the food was gone—and then move on. Throughout the lower Ohio Valley, including Livingston County, thousands of the birds were killed during the nighttime when they could be

easily knocked down from the trees with poles. Some were eaten by people. Many were fed to hogs. The appearance of such masses of birds in the region of the earthquakes prior to their occurrence was unusual enough to provoke considerable speculation.

Another pest that seemed more aggravating than usual that year was the Carolina paroquet or parrot. They were of great beauty—emerald green in color with heads and necks of brilliant scarlet and yellow. About fourteen inches in length, their wing span was just under two feet. But, they were destructive. During the fall of 1811, thousands of parrots gathered in the valleys of the Ohio and Mississippi, stripping fruit from the trees and devastating fields of wheat. The only thing they did not eat, it seemed, was corn. They would flock so thickly that a shotgun could bring down as many as fifteen or twenty in a single blast.

The physical appearance of the passenger pigeon and Carolina paroquet have been preserved by the great artist and naturalist, John Audubon, whose detailed drawings served as models for the parrots sketched on the back cover of this book. Audubon was in Western Kentucky, not far across the river from New Madrid, when the quakes occurred. Carolina parrots and passenger pigeons are no longer a nuisance to farmers of the Midwest. Exterminated by man, they have been extinct since the late 1800's.

Allen Holloman, born in 1806, was raised in New Madrid. He was five years old at the time of the earthquakes. His great grand-daughter, K.J.H. Cochran, published an article in the *Southeast Missourian* of Cape Girardeau quoting from her family records: "The cats were so nervous all day, and so were the dogs. The cows stood in groups huddled and lowing. Horses ran wildly up and down the field; even birds acted strangely, and snakes came out of hibernation and laid on the ground in such numbers it was frightening." According to Cochran, these incidents of strange animal behavior occurred the day before the quakes began and have been a topic of conversation in her family for almost 200 years—an oral tradition handed down to the present through her grandparents. According to Helmut Tributsch in his book, *When the Snakes Awake*, for centuries the Chinese have recognized swarms of snakes emerging from the ground during winter as a warning sign of an impending major earthquake.

There were other accounts of bizarre animal behavior preceding the quakes. Some reported wolves, panthers, bears, foxes, rabbits, raccoons and deer seen together near their cabins, "with their red tongues hanging out of their mouths," acting like domestic animals without fear of each other nor of man. Others testified of wild ducks and geese migrating along the Mississippi waterway that landed, unafraid, near people and even upon some people's heads. Thousands of accounts of animal behavior for many centuries from all over the world lead one to generalize that it is not unusual prior to earthquakes for wild animals to act tame or for tame animals to act wild.

On November 30, 1811, about two weeks before the quakes began, William Leigh Pierce, a young man of twenty-one, reported what he later considered to be a precursor to the quakes. Pierce was in the New Madrid region on a boat tour from Pittsburgh to New Orleans. At sunrise on that day he witnessed "two vast electrical columns" that shot up from the horizon, passing very rapidly, and leaving a diffuse light in the sky. According to Pierce, "from that time until the 16th of December there was a continued want of perfect transparency in the atmosphere, and wherever the sun was even partially visible, it exhibited a dull and fiery redness."

Others reported magnetic compass needles refusing to point north for several minutes prior to some of largest of the New Madrid shocks. Twentieth century scientists now know that electromagnetic anomalies do precede many earthquakes and can make themselves manifest by visible signs in the atmosphere, including lightening bolts that strike from the ground up. In modern times, such phenomena have also been known to disrupt radio transmissions prior to strong earthquakes.

When December, 1811, arrived the peoples of the Midwest were apprehensive of some great calamity about to occur, but they were not thinking of earthquakes. Perhaps some Native Americans had a premonition of what was about to occur, but those of European descent were unable to recognize a single clue. They were more occupied with fears of war with the British and concerns over conflict with the Indians. They were also preoccupied with surviving what promised to be a hard winter after a bad summer when many crops had failed and the fall harvest had been less than previous years.

Daniel Boone Leads the Way

Daniel Boone was born in 1734 in Bucks County, Pennsylvania—the son of Quaker parents. Moving and living in a number of places in east Tennessee, North Carolina and Virginia, he developed his skills as a hunter, trapper, trailblazer, surveyor, blacksmith, and frontiersman. In 1769 he and a friend, John Stuart, headed west through the Cumberland Gap into the wild Territory of Kentucky. They were twice captured by Shawnee Indians but, after periods of detention, were released both times. Boone and Stuart blazed the beginnings of what was to be called "The Wilderness Trail," later known as the "Cumberland Trail "

In 1775 Boone returned to Kentucky and established a fortified settlement which he called "Boonesboro." He then returned to North Carolina to bring his wife, Rebecca Bryan, and his daughter Jemima, who were the first white women in Kentucky. He also brought two sons.

The daughter was kidnapped by a group of five Indians and forced to walk some 35 miles. But Jemima had been taught what to do. She tore off leaves and pieces of her clothing, leaving a trail. Her father was able to follow the marked path with a posse and rescue her within a few days.

Boone's first two sons were less fortunate. One, who was sent on an errand to obtain some supplies, was captured, tortured, and killed by Indians. On January 1, 1778, his second son was killed by Chief Blackfish and his Indian warriors in the Battle of Blue Lick.

A month later, on February 7, 1778, Boone had just shot a buffalo and was carrying the best cuts back to his camp when he was confronted with four Shawnee warriors. Their chief was Blackfish, who had led the attack at Blue Lick. Blackfish, like Boone, had also lost a son in that battle and had attributed the death personally to Boone. When Boone was brought before Blackfish, he was forced to ride to Old Chillicothe, a large Shawnee settlement in Ohio, where he remained a prisoner. Blackfish admired and respected Boone and in April of 1778 formally adopted him as a son to replace the one he had lost to Boone's marksmanship a few months before. The Shawnee name given to Boone meant "Big Turtle," the slowest of animals. The name reflected a bit of Shawnee humor. In actuality, the Indians held Boone's quickness of wit and physical dexterity in high esteem.

As it turned out, back in 1775, after Tecumseh's father had been killed and before his mother left him, Blackfish had adopted Tecumseh as a foster son and had given him much attention and training. Hence, it came to happen that from April to June, 1778, Daniel Boone, age 44, lived with Tecumseh, a young boy age 10. The two leaders, one red and one white, had become sons and brothers of the same adoptive father.

Tecumseh was never to forget the experience, considering Boone to be "the leading figure of the white race and the greatest of the Long Knives."

Daniel Boone (1731-1820) Based on portrait by John James Audubon at Boone's Home.

Illustration by Anthony Stewart

In June Boone escaped back to his family in Kentucky. After that the Shawnees bothered him and his family no more.

Daniel Boone led hundreds of pioneers through the mountains to settle in Kentucky and thousands of others came on their own, following the trail he had established.

The Lincolns Move to Kentucky

Among Boone's friends were Abraham Lincoln and his wife, Bathsheba. They had three sons. Mordecai, Josiah, and Thomas, and two daughters, Mary and Nancy. For years their friend Daniel, had told them about valleys with rich black soil, blue grass, tall timber, and clear running waters. In 1782, Abraham and his family left Virginia for the country Boone had described, where land was only 40 cents an acre and where fish and game could be had without limit.

One day, in 1784, Abraham was working in a field with his three sons when they heard the shot of a rifle and the whine of a bullet. Abraham suddenly fell to the ground with a grimace of pain. Indians! Mordecai ran to the cabin, Josiah raced into the woods to get help, while Tom, the youngest, crouched over his father's bleeding body. A large red man came up from behind. As Tom turned around, he saw a shining bangle hanging over the Indian's shoulder near the heart. As the Indian raised his tomahawk to strike, he suddenly doubled over with a groan. Mordecai had fired a rifle from a peephole in the cabin, aligning his sights on the silver bangle. The redskin was dead. But so was Abraham.

Tom grew up in Kentucky and stayed there. On June 12, 1806 he and Nancy Hanks were married at Beechland, Kentucky. The newly-weds settled some forty miles south of Louisville.

The Boone and Lincoln families actually intermarried for several generations, thus creating a blood relationship between Daniel Boone and Abraham Lincoln, the grandfather, as well as Abraham Lincoln, the President of the United States.

Another family to move into Kentucky by Boone's influence was that of Samuel and Jane Cook Davis. They left New Jersey in 1796 and settled in Todd County. That would be near present-day Hopkinsville, 120 miles due east of New Madrid and 50 miles southwest of the Lewis Plantations in Livingston County.

On June 3, 1808, their tenth and last child was born whom they named after President Thomas Jefferson. In 1810, when Jefferson Davis was two, he and his family moved to Wilkinson County, Mississippi, 20 miles south of Natchez.

Thus, it came to be that half a century later, when the country was divided by the Civil War, the Presidents of both sides were Kentuckians by birth—both born on a primitive frontier. There were only eight months difference in their ages.

During the earthquakes of 1811–12, the young Jefferson Davis, age three, felt the tremors in southern Mississippi, but he and his family escaped their damage.

Not so with the Lincoln family. Young Abraham Lincoln, who turned three during the earthquakes, also witnessed the repairs his father had

Abraham Lincoln, Age 3, in front of the cabin with the "stick and clay" chimney where he experienced the earthquakes of 1811-12 with his parents, Tom and Nancy, and sister, Sarah.

Illustration by Anthony Stewart

to make to their simple cabin in central Kentucky after the tremors had taken their toll.

Another notable couple who had emigrated to Kentucky as friends of Daniel Boone were John and Lucy Audubon. A portrait of Daniel Boone still hangs over the living room mantle in the Boone Mansion near Defiance, Missouri, a gift painted by John and presented to the Boones when their house was new.

When the earthquakes hit, the Audubons were living at Henderson —only 120 miles from New Madrid and the the epicenters.

The Boones Move to Missouri

Daniel and Rebecca moved many times and eventually bore a total of ten children. In 1798 they moved to Missouri to a place on Femme Osage Creek, just west of St. Louis, in what is, today, St. Charles County. Boone had left Kentucky after having been cheated out of much of his property. Daniel was a highly intelligent man, though uneducated. He could read some but wrote very little. In his numerous land dealings, he did not keep adequate paperwork and, thus, became vulnerable to unscrupulous land dealers. When he moved to Missouri, he was quoted as saying, "I don't care if I ever see Kentucky again."

Missouri was Spanish at the time Boone settled there. He and his family were all required to pledge their allegiance to the Spanish crown as well as to proclaim themselves Catholics, which they did. He was then appointed as a royal magistrate with full civil and military authority and for which he received an income. Later, when the Upper Louisiana Territory become part of the United States, he was appointed as Commandant of the Femme Osage District of Missouri.

His justice was dispensed beneath a large American elm tree, just west of his house, and was based more on truth than on the law. He also believed in "the use of the lash, well applied." He became a highly respected magistrate. He also maintained a good alliance with the Osage Indians who protected his family from tribes that were less friendly than they.

After losing his first fortune and living the life of a nomad with his wife and children, Daniel and Rebecca, now in their sixties, finally found themselves in a financially secure place and position to build their "dream home." A beautiful four-story mansion of stone and oak timbers, it stands in an enchanting setting on a hillside overlooking the Femme Osage bottom land where they farmed. The top floor is a ballroom where a hundred guests could dance and be entertained. A craftsman in every way, Daniel was a skilled mason, carpenter, wood carver, architect, and blacksmith. He even made his own glass for his windows. His wife, Rebecca, was also talented in weaving, needlework, and other crafts of that time.

Construction of the Boone house began in 1803. It was completed in 1810. With walls two feet thick and huge solid oak beams throughout, they thought the house would stand forever and that their troubles were over. They did not know about the New Madrid Fault 180 miles to the south. Neither they, nor anyone else, knew that one year after their mansion was finished it would be put to the test by a terrible temblor. Boone's survival skills were legendary. He had experienced almost every hardship known to man, and had made it through alive and well. But could he and his house survive a major earthquake?

When it comes to the subject of survival, Daniel Boone has attained immortality in at least one way—that of his progeny. Of the ten Boone children, seven lived to adulthood and bore, among themselves, a total of seventy grandchildren. From these came more than 250 great-grandchildren. Today, thousands can trace their ancestry to Daniel and Rebecca Boone.

There is an interesting postscript to be inserted here. When Daniel Boone died in 1820 he was buried in his wife's family plot near Marthasville, Missouri. His wife, Rebecca Bryan Boone, had died in 1813, shortly after the earthquakes. She was buried next to her sister and mother. When Daniel died, so many people came to his funeral it had to be held in a barn on his farm near Defiance, Missouri. His body lay in state in a cherrywood casket he had made himself and which he had stored under his bed for more than ten years. When his body was taken to the Bryan Cemetery, they tried to lay him beside his wife, only to discover that another body was already there. A black man-servant of the Bryan family had died several years before and, as was the custom, was buried in the plot of the family whom

Home of Daniel & Rebecca Boone near Defiance, Missouri, completed in 1810. From left to right, top to bottom: Front view; Front door; Rear view; Rear doors into kitchen; Elm tree; and Livingroom fireplace. Seven years to complete (1803-1810) it is of extremely rugged construction with solid walls of native limestone, two feet thick (see front & rear doorways). The chimneys on both ends are built into the walls for maximum strength. Thus, the chimnies don't project from the outside walls nor do the fireplaces protrude into the rooms inside (see living room photo). The window to the right of the front door is the bedroom where Daniel died. The huge trunk of a dead Ameican Elm seen here in 1994 lies just west of the Boone house (visible in the background). This is the "Judgement Tree" beneath which Daniel Boone dispensed justice in the early 19th century. Living for more than 200 years it finally succumbed to Dutch elm disease in 1990. The picture over the mantle is an original portrait of Daniel by his friend, John Audubon—a gift when the home was completed.

Tomb of Daniel Boone near Marthasville, Missouri. The photo on the left shows the walkway up the hill to the Bryan Family Cemetery and Daniel's grave, whose headstone is a boulder of Missouri granite. Rebecca was originally buried just to the right of the walkway at the foot of Daniel's grave. The bronze plaque, imbedded in the granite, shown on the right, says: "DANIEL BOONE, Born in Bucks County PA, February 11, 1735, Died in St. Charles County MO, September 26, 1820; and Wife, REBECCA BRYAN, Born 1737, Died March 18, 1813. Removed to Frankfort KY 1845; Erected by their descendants, Warren County, and the Missouri Daughters of the American Revolution, 1915." It wasn't until more than 30 years after the plaque was installed that it was discovered that only Rebecca's body had been removed to Kentucky—that Daniel's body was still in Missouri at the foot of this memorial stone,

he had served. Daniel was then buried just to the west of Rebecca, at her head.

In 1845 authorities from Kentucky sought to bring their "native son and his wife" back to Kentucky. They dug up what they thought were the graves of Daniel and Rebecca and reinterred the remains on the campus of the University of Kentucky at the State Capital in Frankfort.

Almost a century later a question arose as to whether the real bones of Daniel Boone were actually in Kentucky or, perhaps, still in Missouri. When the bodies had been taken to Kentucky, it was noted that the casket of Rebecca was of cherrywood, but that of the body they had thought was Daniel's was not. The grave at Frankfort was opened, and the skull in the tomb was deter-

mined to be that of a black male.

So Daniel Boone got his way and still has it to this day. When he said back in 1798, "I don't care if I ever see Kentucky again," his wish has held true even beyond the grave. It is a special irony that Kentucky, a state that dealt so much abuse to the slaves, has actually laid the body of a black man in the tomb of their greatest honor.

Cape Girardeau and the Indians

In 1811 the west bank of the Mississippi had only recently become a part of the United States. There were only a few towns and settlements by the American settlers. Even so, there were approximately 5,000 settlers of European and African descent living in and around the periphery of the region we now call "The New Madrid Seismic Zone."

At least another ten to fifteen thousand Native Americans also occupied the region in and around the fault zone at that time. They lived in hundreds of villages, towns, and hunting camps ranging in size from a dozen to 400 or more.

The zone of active faulting and recurrent seismicity that defines the New Madrid Seismic Zone includes western Kentucky, western Tennessee, northeastern Arkansas, southeastern Missouri, and southern Illinois. Cape Girardeau, Missouri; Carbondale, Illinois; Paducah, Kentucky; Memphis, Tennessee; and Little Rock, Arkansas, circumscribe the fracture zone on the north, east, south, and west.

Of these five cities, only Cape Girardeau existed in 1811–12. A small village of 200 at the time, it is now the largest metropolitan area on the river between St. Louis and Memphis. According to the 1990 census, the population of Cape Girardeau and surrounding county is about 60,000. Its French history dates back to the 1720's when Jean Baptiste Girardeau (also spelled Girardot and Girardo) moved from the Illinois side of the river at Kaskaskia to the Missouri side. At a scenic rocky prominence that extended into the swirling waters of the Mississippi, he established a trading post between Indians and French boatmen. It became known as "Cape Girardeau." Later, in 1793, Louis Lorimier, a French fur trader from St. Louis, landed just downstream from Cape Rock and established a town which he named "Cape Girardeau," after the trading post that preceded him. Although bearing a French name, the town was Spanish. Lorimier was 65 at the time, a devout Catholic and a faithful subject of the King of Spain. He did not believe in democracies. To him, a monarchy was the only "divinely approved" form of government.

Lorimier was able to maintain a friendly trading relationship with the Indians of the area. In the years prior to his landing, there had been wars between the Shawnees, the Delawares, the Osage, and other tribes that passed through. Intertribal warfare had always been a feature of Native Indian culture. The lack of unity among themselves was a form of protection enjoyed by the early pioneers intruding into Indian territory. The white settlers did not have to "divide" the Native Americans in order to "conquer" them. They were already divided. It was Tecumseh's purpose in life to change this if he could.

Today more than two million people live in the area within and around the New Madrid Seismic Zone with all the infrastructure of modern society, but in 1811 the world as we know it did not exist.

"El Camino Real," the King's Highway, was first marked out by Spaniards in 1789, the year New Madrid adopted its present name. It followed a series of old Indian trails known as the "Shawnee Path" which passed near the now-extinct Indian city of Chillicothe located north of Cape Girardeau. Chillicothe was one of the regional capitals of the Shawnee Nation.

The Shawnee phrase, "Chil-li-co-a-thee," means "big town where we live." Some of Tecumseh's family were among the 500 residents of Chilicothe, Missouri, including his mother and his sister, Teceikeapease. It was a town visited many times by Tecumseh. It was really quite a sizeable settlement for its day. In fact, in 1811 it was more than twice the population of Cape Girardeau.

At the same time there was also a Chillicothe, Ohio, where Tecumseh had lived as a young boy and from where his mother and sister had moved to Missouri back in 1779. Later there was to be another Chillicothe at another location in Missouri, but at this time in our story that town had not yet been founded. You will learn about that in a later chapter of this book.

Another village of the Shawnees at the time of the earthquakes was a few miles due east of Chillicothe at the site of present-day Shawneetown, Missouri, 20 miles north of Cape Girardeau. While this town was also large for its time, about the same size as Cape, it was called, by the French, "le Lesser Village de Suavage," or "The Smaller Village of the Savages."

"Savages"

The designation "Savage" had its basis in some body of fact. Tecumseh deplored such "savage" acts as scalping and mutilation of the dead following battle, but he encouraged and approved of other customs we would cringe to imagine.

For example, during the 45-year span that the Shawnees occupied the site at Chillicothe near Cape, a brand of witchcraft was practiced. Tecumseh's priestly brother, Tenskwatawa, was never in Missouri before the earthquakes, but Tecumseh visited many times. Apparently it was he who introduced Tenskwatawa's new religion to the Shawnees at Chillicothe. The teachings contained provisions for trying and executing witches. The practice resulted in at least 58 women being tied to the "death tree" at the edge of town where they were burned alive.

In 1811, numerous Indian villages speckled the area of the New Madrid Seismic Zone in Arkansas, Missouri, Tennessee, Kentucky, and Illinois. There were several large Indian settlements in the Blytheville, Arkansas, area as well as further south, near Lepanto and Marked Tree, Arkansas. There were also a number of villages of the Shawnees and Delawares that encircled Cape Girardeau on the north, west, and south, as well as throughout the county.

Several Indian villages were within the present city limits of Cape Girardeau. One of these was near Lorimier's original settlement at the intersection of Frederick and William Streets in a shaded glen with a spring. It is now known as "Indian Park." No trace of the village can be found there today, only a few picnic tables and some playground equipment. The Indians who lived there met and traded frequently with Lorimier. If you visit the park you will find a granite boulder engraved as a monument to Louis Lorimier and to the Native Americans with whom he did business. The stone monument bears the date the village was abandoned. The year was 1812.

It was not safe for white settlers

Indian Park at the Corner of Frederick & William Streets, Cape Girardeau, Missouri.
The site of this picnic spot, playground and outdoor basketball court used to be a trading village of the Delaware Indians. It was established in 1793, the same year Cape Girardeau was permanently settled. The village was abandoned in 1812 because the Indians were frightened away by the earthquakes. A natural granite boulder stands as a monument to that era. The engraving, as seen in the photo on the right, states as follows: "INDIAN PARK, Indian tribes often came here 1793-1812 to meet Don Louis Lorimier—their friend and leader."

to venture far from their towns in 1811 without some means of protection. The numbers of Native Americans in the Central Mississippi Valley were far greater than the numbers of American settlers. But this was soon to reverse itself.

Midwest Infrastructure: Then and Now

A spur of "El Camino Real" passed along Spanish Street in Cape Girardeau, one block east of Indian Park. It was unpaved and just wide enough for a coach to travel from New Madrid through Cape and Ste. Genevieve and on to St. Louis, a trip that could take as many as ten days to complete. Today, New Madrid and St. Louis are connected by Interstate Highway 55 which puts them only 2.5 hours apart by automobile. A portion of El Camino Real that passes through Cape Girardeau is still named "Kingshighway" and is now part of Highway 61 and Business

Interstate 55 on the west side of town.

In 1807 improvements were made in the El Camino dirt road, elevating it to the status of being "the first north-south highway in the Missouri Territory." However, at that time there were still no railroads, no large bridges, no high rise buildings, no electric power plants, no storage tanks of hazardous materials, no gas or petroleum pipelines, no nuclear reactors, no big dams, no major highways, no airports, no telephones, no radios—none of the things considered essential to modern living.

At the same time, the technologic sources of our comfort and high standards of living are also the sources of earthquake-induced hazards that did not exist in 1811–12. The most common risks of earthquakes are usually not natural but consist of the failure of human constructions. Collapsed buildings.

> **El Camino Real Today in New Madrid, Missouri.** El Camino Real, "The King's Highway," was first marked out by the Spaniards in 1789. It went from New Madrid, through Cape Girardeau and Ste. Genevieve, to St. Louis—a distance of approximately 180 miles. The town of New Madrid has still preserved the English name of the old road—identified by the sign in the photo above. The photo on the right shows a sign along Old Kingshighway, in New Madrid, that reads "El Camino Trailer Park." A United Parcel Service (UPS) van is seen approaching down the street to the right. Cape Girardeau, 50 miles to the north, has also preserved the name of the old highway where it passes through the city limits. Old Kingshighway has the appearance of an ordinary city street today, but it is no ordinary street. An incredible history once moved along this route, including Spaniards, French, and Americans—not to mention the Indians had who established and used the trail long before before white settlers came to claim it for their own.

Broken dams. Fallen bridges. Flying glass. Toxic fumes. Fires sparked by electricity and fueled by gas or oil. A repeat of the New Madrid earthquakes today would be a thousand times more destructive than what took place in 1811–12 because of the vulnerability of our built environment. However, even though the midwestern world of 1811 was unsophisticated, undeveloped, and relatively unpopulated, the devastation of the earthquakes, even in a primitive, non-technological environment, was almost unbelievable.

Most of the cities within the New Madrid fault zone we know today were not there in 1811. Cairo and Carbondale, Illinois. Paducah and Hickman, Kentucky. Dyersburg, Union City, and Reelfoot Lake, Tennessee. Charleston, Sikeston, Dexter, Malden, Poplar Bluff and East Prairie, Missouri. Blytheville, Paragould, Piggot, Pocahontas, Marked Tree and Jonesboro, Arkansas. There was no Memphis, Tennessee— only a small military post called Fort Pickering. None of these towns, and hundreds more we know today, were in existence in during the great earthquakes.

Some Indians were "Civilized"

One should not get the impression that all Indians of that era lived primitive lifestyles. Not all tribes were nomads, existing by hunting, fishing, gathering wild nuts and berries, and engaging in small-scale subsistence farming. There were some tribes in the East whose lifestyles were almost indistinguishable from those of the European settlers.

These included the so-called "Five Civilized Tribes"—Cherokee, Chickasaw, Choctaw, Creek, and Seminole. Many of them lived in sophisticated towns complete with well laid-out streets and public buildings. Many also lived on farms or plantations. They even bought and sold black slaves. Some were educated in law or the arts, owned businesses, dressed in western clothes and lived in houses or cabins much the same as their white neighbors. The main difference was their allegiance to a political authority different from the U.S. Constitution. They had their own instruments of government, including constitutions and laws which they enforced in their own ways.

These tribes made treaties with the United States in the same fashion as countries located on foreign soil. Hence, in the years preceding and during the great earthquakes, there were actually two nations occupying the eastern United States, from the Great Lakes to the tip of Florida—the United States of America and the Confederation of the Five Civilized Tribes.

But the relationship was never comfortable. Many U.S. leaders, including Thomas Jefferson, desired to see all Native Americans deported to the far West. It wasn't until the 1830's, however, that Congress began to take serious steps to accomplish this. These steps culminated in the infamous compulsory marches, the "Trail of Tears," between 1837 and 1840, when these civilized and sophisticated tribes were driven out of their houses and towns, stripped of their belongings and businesses, and herded to Oklahoma. Thousands died.

The Shawnees, however, were not considered to be "civilized," even though Tecumseh, their leader, was highly regarded for his intelligence, education, and articulate speech. The Shawnees were never made party to a mandatory march, but they still migrated to the West in response to other forces.

The Home of the Braves And the Land of the Free

The New Madrid Seismic Zone has been the homeland to humans for many thousands of years. The fault zone and its surrounding regions have always served as an important crossroads and mixing point for many cultures—including the French, the Spanish, the British, the early American settlers, as well as Native Americans of many tribes. This was true largely because of its location along the North American continent's greatest waterway—the Mississippi-Missouri-Ohio River system, a watershed that drains almost two-thirds of the United States.

The earliest evidence of human inhabitants along the central Mississippi Valley dates back to at least 12,000 years ago. The aboriginals were nomads subsisting on hunting and foraging. 10,000 years ago these wanderers began to establish more stable communities and develop the characteristics of recent Native American culture that archaeologists study today.

The river's name comes from the Objibway Tribe who inhabited the headwaters of the Mississippi southwest of Lake Superior. "Misi Sipi" are Objibway words that mean "Great

Water." Early French maps spelled the name of the river "Mechasebe," while the Spaniards spelled it "Misisipy." The English version was finally to prevail.

The most sophisticated cultural developments were made by the so-called Mississippian Indians after 900 A.D. They flourished from St. Louis to Memphis, building cities and large pyramidal mounds that have survived even to the present. For almost 600 years they thrived along the banks of the Mississippi. But after 1492 A.D., they declined rapidly due to the discovery of the New World by Europeans whose subsequent contact brought death—not by the sword, but by disease. By the time the French arrived a century later, the Mississippian Indians had been replaced by the Missouri and Osage Tribes.

Fifteen miles to the northeast of New Madrid is the Towosaghy Indian Mound and site of a Native American Mississippian city. They flourished there between 1000 and 1400 A.D. Another large Indian Mound, known as the "Lilbourn Site," is only a mile west of New Madrid.

A superficial review of the modern world does not seem to reflect much impact from these native civilizations that flourished throughout North and South America for so many milennia. When Columbus landed in 1492, the Indians were all still in the stone age. They did not know how to make implements of iron, and still transported their goods without the benefit of the wheel. Few tribes had any form of written language. None had an alphabet.

Modern society seems to be composed entirely of artifacts and inventions rooted in the languages, mathematics, and sciences of Europe, Asia, the Middle East, and North Africa. But look again. It was Thomas Jefferson who said: "The greatest service which can be rendered any country is to add a useful plant to its culture." Native Americans have influenced the cultures of the world in ways both profound and subtle. But in one way their impact is major, if not revolutionary. And that has to do with agricultural produce and diet.

Through the centuries the original inhabitants of North, South, and Central America cultivated and developed a variety of foods that have become so fundamental to the world's eating habits it would be impossible for us to imagine life without them. The Incas of South America were, perhaps, the greatest agricultural engineers of all time. Scientists still study and learn from their methods today. The cornucopia of plants, fruits, and vegetables the Native Americans farmed before the rest of the world ever heard of them is astonishing.

Before Columbus discovered the lands west of the Atlantic, no one in Europe, Asia, Africa, or Australia, had ever tasted corn, tomatoes, potatoes, yams, cucumbers, squash, pumpkin, cantelope, watermelon, pinto beans, kidney beans, lima beans, jalapeno peppers, bananas, maple sugar, cranberries, strawberries, pineapple, chocolate, or vanilla. No one outside of America had ever smoked tobacco. And no one but certain Indian tribes had ever worn cotton clothing.

There is probably not a day in our lives when we do not enjoy one or more of these commodities. Subtract these items from our lives and how impoverished we would be!

What would pizza be without tomato sauce? What would ice cream be without strawberry, chocolate, and vanilla? What would roast beef and gravy be like without mashed potatoes? Can you imagine life without banana splits, corn on the cob, potato chips, taco shells, tomato catsup, chili, refried beans, cranberry sauce, pumpkin pie, maple syrup, popcorn or blue denim jeans?

When we think of Italian food, we think of tomato sauces, but the Indians had them first. When we think of potatoes, we think of the Irish or the Germans, but the Indians had them first. When we eat Chinese food with those little ears of corn, we should remember that maize was first an Indian food. When you think of pickles, Poland comes to mind, but the little green vegetables from which they are made were borrowed from the Indians. When we enjoy Swiss cocoa or French vanilla ice cream, remember that Native Americans enjoyed these flavors first. Regardless of the color of the skin—be it black, white, yellow, or brown—the the tastes preferred the world over are those of the red skins.

Every time you sit down to eat, you can thank the Native Americans for your food, if not for the shirt upon your back. And if you have a headache, you can thank them again.

The most popular pain pescription in the world, is a gift from the Indians. Early settlers noticed natives chewing willow leaves or willow bark to ease their aches and fevers. In the late ninteenth century, the active ingredient, *acetyl salicylic acid*, was isolated from the willow and compounded into tablets we call "aspirin." What had been an ancient herbal remedy for Native Americans has now become an an over-the-counter medicine available everywhere—even gas stations.

But food, clothing, and medicine aren't the only riches we have inherited from the Indians. If you are an American descended from immigrants, you can thank them for the land in which you live, as well.

Because the Indians did not take the path of technologic development, as did Europe, we who inhabit the Americas today have been the benefactors and heirs of continents that were virtually virgin less than 300 years ago. Long before that, when the last cedar of Lebanon had been cut, when the great forests of Greece and Italy had been reduced to rocky hills, when the woodlands of North Africa had been changed into desert, and when the tree-covered highlands of Scotland had been reduced to grassy moors, the lands of the Indians were still close to a natural state—plenteous, clean, and bountiful. Seeking the soft and easy life was never their purpose. In their sacrifice, they preserved two whole continents such that every native generation after theirs would have the same beauties and resources as they had enjoyed.

In 1820 Major George Sibley, business manager of the Government Trading Post at Fort Osage, talked at length to an old Osage

Chief about the white man and his ways. The Old Chief had twice visited Washington, D.C. where he had received medals of friendship from the President. He admired the technical progress of white society but considered such a lifestyle to be a burden—like chains that chaffed and bound.

"Talk to my sons," he said. "Perhaps they may be persuaded to adopt your fashions or at least to recommend them to their sons. But for myself, I was born free, was raised free, and wish to die free."

Responsibility for conserving and preserving the Americas no longer rests with the natives who kept that task so well for so many millennia. The stewardship of these resources has been passed to other tribes, other races. The first of these were the Spanish.

Europeans Come To the Mississippi Valley

Hernando Desoto explored central North America in 1541–42. He was the first European to behold the Mississippi River. He called it "El Rio del Espirito Santo" (The River of the Holy Spirit). He claimed its watershed for his country and called it "New Spain." It is said that when Desoto came near the site where New Madrid would later be founded, he erected a large cross of cypress on a mound near the river. On this spot Desoto, his men, and his Indian guides celebrated the first Catholic Mass west of the Mississippi. According to the traditions of New Madrid residents, the location of this cross was on the Lilbourn Mound, a mile west of town—heart of an ancient

Mississippian Indian settlement abandoned before Desoto's time.

That was 270 years before the earthquakes that would catapult this region of planet earth into geologic history. But even then, as Desoto and his companions peacefully worshiped in the sunlight along that scenic river, deep beneath them a catastrophe was already building up in the dark recesses of the earth. The New Madrid Fault was alive, like a giant cocoon, seemingly dormant but silently undergoing a deadly metamorphosis—slowly storing up the energy that would some day burst into the daylight of the world above.

The Spaniards carried out trading expeditions along the river but made no permanent settlements and initiated no significant immigrations into the territory. The tales of gold and great wealth that drew the conquistadors to the New World centered more to the west and to the south, to Mexico, Central and South America.

In 1673 Louis Jolliet, a French-Canadian explorer, entered the Mississippi River from the north and came into Missouri, landing at the present site of St. Louis. He was accompanied by Father Jacques Marquette, a Jesuit priest. Two-hundred years later, Jesuit priests at St. Louis University were the first to install seismographs in the central United States to study the New Madrid Fault. In fact, Jesuit geophysicists dominated the field of earthquake seismology in the Midwest in the late nineteenth and early twentieth centuries. They even formed a Jesuit Seismological Society with its own technical journal and earthquake catalog.

Jolliet and Father Marquette continued their exploration of the Mississippi downstream through the New Madrid Seismic Zone all the way to the mouth of the Arkansas River. There they turned back for fear of encroaching on Spanish territory near the Gulf of Mexico. They knew that if they were caught, they would be killed. Besides, they had found out what they wanted to know. The Mississippi that flowed away from the Great Lakes did not flow into the Pacific Ocean, as they had hoped it would. It was definitely the same river that entered the Gulf at New Orleans—a fact no European knew for certain when they had started their trip from the north.

In 1682, Robert Cavalier de La Salle led an expedition from the north that reached the mouth of the Mississippi, whereupon he claimed the entire watershed of the Mississippi for France. Unlike the Spaniards, the French immediately sent Frenchmen to establish villages and trading posts. Their aim was not gold but a lucrative fur business which they built from the mouth of the Mississippi to the Great Lakes and the St. Lawrence River. It was La Salle who gave the territory its name, "Louisiana," after King Louis XIV.

The first permanent French settlement west of the Mississippi did not come until half a century later. It was at Ste. Genevieve, founded between 1732 and 1735. Unbeknownst to the founders, the settlement was located near a major tectonic feature—the Ste. Genevieve fault—which spans a hundred miles and connects with the New Madrid fault in southern Illinois, near Metropolis.

Earthquakes, including those of 1811–12, have caused damages in Ste. Genevieve from time to time. But terrestrial temblors are not the town's greatest natural hazard. Floods are. Its site was chosen because of a large expanse of fertile bottom land along the Mississippi, which they called "le Gran Champ," or "the Big Field." The town was destroyed by a flood in 1785, but that did not drive the people from the area. They did, however, move the town to higher ground in 1785, though apparently not high enough. In 1993, a levee-breaking flood again assailed the city limits. Some of the Ste. Genevieve houses that survived the earthquakes of 1811–12 were standing in water in 1993. But the damaging inundation did not dampen the spirits of the residents. It only caused the people of Ste. Genevieve to reaffirm their vow to stay.

In 1760, at the close of the French and Indian War (which was really between France and England), portions of Louisiana east of the Mississippi were ceded to Great Britain. This included the strategic Ohio River valley and the Great Lakes.

Two years later, in 1762, the Spanish again gained control of the lands west of the Mississippi via the Treaty of Fontainbleau. This time they did send Spaniards for the purpose of governing, controling, and collecting taxes and river-use fees for Spain. However, the French continued to migrate and settle in the territory, as did the British on the east side of the river. Hence, the Louisiana Territory was to remain predominantly French though gov-

The Lilbourn Indian Mound. Located between New Madrid and Howardville, Missouri, this is one of the largest of the Mississippian Indian mounds in the area. It was already abandoned by the Indians when the first European, Hernando Desoto, visited the site around 1542 and is thought to have held the first Catholic Mass there west of the Mississippi. To get an idea of its size, note the person standing on top of the Mound in the three photos on the left. Today the mound is surrounded by a cemetery and by the grounds of New Madrid Central High School. When excavating and landscaping for the new school back in the 1970's numerous Native American skeletons and artifacts were found, some of which are on display in the New Madrid Historical Museum. The two top right photos show views from the top of the mound where an Indian city once flourished but where . . . *(cont'd on next page)*

erned by a minority from Spain.

In 1783, the same year the United States achieved its final freedom from Great Britain, the first European settlement was established at the site that was to be New Madrid. Francois and Joseph LeSieur, two French-Canadian fur trappers set up a trading post there. It may have been Spanish territory, but the settlement's original name was French: "L'Anse a la Graisse," or "The Cove of Grease." Boatmen plying the river could stop at the trading post there and purchase bear and buffalo meat—of which there was an abundant supply. It is probably good that the name was changed to "New Madrid" or today's Americanized version would probably be "Greaseport."

Even though most of the residents of L'Anse a la Graisse were French, to have a French name in a Spanish territory was not pleasing to Spain. Six years after its founding, the name was to change.

Morgan's Scheme to Get Rich

Colonel George Morgan, an officer of the Revolutionary War, was a disgruntled man. After fighting for America's freedom, he felt as though he had not been justly rewarded. A native of Pennsylvania and resident of New Jersey, he had also spent considerable time in Louisville, Kentucky. He had many friends there.

Spain controlled the west bank and the mouth of the Mississippi at New Orleans, but wanted even more control so it could exact greater taxes from the passage of boats. Some leading Kentuckians, having been approached by a representative of Spain, were toying with the idea of their State seceding from the fledgling United States to take league with Spain. After all, they were west of the Appalachians and isolated from the rest of the country. They sometimes felt neglected by the government in Washington.

George Morgan was an entrepreneur and an opportunist. He made a deal with Spain. He led Spanish representatives to believe he could help persuade Kentucky to join with Spain. He was to become governor of a large territory of twelve million acres, including all of Arkansas and the adjacent part of Missouri from an east-west line just south of Cape Girardeau. Colonel Morgan had, thus, become a traitor to his country, pledging his allegiance to the Spanish monarchy, breaching his loyalty to the United States.

Because of its unusually high

The Lilbourn Mound, cont'd . . . a bustling school complex now functions. $5,000,000 were spent on the concrete frame building, but it was not designed to resist earthquakes. Such was the lack of earthquake awareness in 1975. The bottom right photo is a view from the top of the mound looking south toward a clump of willow trees. This is Lake Ste. Anne—a creation of the earthquakes of 1811–12. It is a fragment of an old stream channel (Gut Ste. Anne) that used to carry Indian canoes, French pirogues, and Spanish keelboats between the Mississippi and Little Rivers. The Mississippi was about two miles to the east at the time and the Little River was about three miles to the west. Thus, the Indians had placed their city in an ideal location with access to two river systems. Early settlers used to operate a ferry across Gut Ste. Anne here at the mound before the earthquakes destroyed the stream.

The Jean Baptiste Bequette House, built in 1778, Ste. Genevieve, Missouri. The first settlement west of the Mississippi was actually the one-man trading post of Jean Baptiste Girardeau at Cape Rock in 1720, but a permanent settlement was not established there until 1793 by Don Louis Lorimier who named it Cape Girardeau. The first permanent settlement west of the river was Ste. Genevieve, founded about 1735. New Madrid was founded in 1783, but no houses can be seen today in New Madrid or Cape Girardeau that survived the earthquakes of 1811–12. Many houses were also damaged in Ste. Genevieve, but surprisingly about a dozen still stand. The secret was in their incredibly strong construction—eight-inch-square vertical cedar columns imbedded in the ground, fastened at the top, with diagonal bracing at the corners, filled in between with stones and clay, and covered with plaster. This creates a building that is very strong, but still able to flex. After the earthquakes, the plaster had to be repaired, but the structure of the house remained intact. Bequette's house is shown in the three photos on the left. An out-building behind the house is shown on the right whose exposed walls show the inner construction. The bottom left photo is a view under Bequette's porch showing the imbedded posts. The missing plaster shows the water level of the record flood that innundated the lower portion of this house in 1993.

The Louis Bolduc House, built in 1770, Ste. Genevieve, Missouri. Designated as a National Historic Landmark by the U.S. National Park Service, the Bolduc House is the first instance of an authentic French colonial home on the Mississippi restored to its original form. It survived the earthquakes of 1811–12 while many other Ste. Genevieve homes did not—a tribute to its massive construction. The huge home is 82 feet long, built of solid oak timbers placed vertically on a stone foundation, diagonally braced, with clay and straw filling the gaps and covered with plaster. Heavy oak trusses and beams support the roof and large upstairs attic. The floors are of solid oak—six inches thick! Details of the construction can be seen in the views above. The top left shows the back of the house with a kitchen attached on the far corner which has a stone floor, to reduce fire hazard. The photo in the upper right is of the front porch where visitors begin their tours of the house and property. The lower right photo shows the six-inch-square planks that make up the floor around a stone hearth before a fireplace. The flood of 1993 was the highest suffered by Ste. Genevieve since 1785. While the Bequette House was standing in water in 1993, the Bolduc House was spared—partly because it is on slightly higher ground but also because it was inside of the temporary sand bag levee the townspeople built. This house is definitely worth a stop if you visit Ste. Genevieve.

ground and commanding view of the river, Morgan chose the site of L'Anse a la Graisse for the capital of his territory. The territory was "Louisiana" to the French, but "New Spain" to the Spanish. Morgan knew that a French name for his settlement would not please the King so he dubbed it "New Madrid," after the capital of Spain, which is "Madrid." Morgan hoped that some day New Madrid would be the capital of New Spain. We Americans never learned how to pronounce it correctly. In Spanish it should be pronounced Ma-dreed' with the emphasis on the last syllable. In American it was to be pronounced Mad'-rid, with the emphasis on the first syllable, which is pronounced like the word, "mad." That's the way natives there say it to this day.

Embarking from Pittsburgh with four large boats and seventy men, including his sons, Morgan landed there to take charge in 1789. He had a grand plan. He would advertise, promote, and develop his lands, selling it off in pieces. He would become rich and powerful. He would be Governor of a small kingdom.

"Come live in New Madrid. Queen City of the Mississippi. Center of Commerce and Trade in the New World. Beautiful Scenery. Abundant Wild Game. Fertile Soils. Clear Water. Stately Forests of Cypress and Oak. A Major Port on the Greatest River in the Land. Situated on High Ground, Above the Reach of Floods. A City with an Unequaled View of the River and a Vision of the Future."

Morgan's promotional handbills were spread throughout the East. Many came.

What George Morgan Didn't Know

George Morgan was unaware that his choice of location for his capital was a perfect bull's eye for one of the most active fault zones in the world. Positioned at the northern apex of the largest bend on the entire Mississippi, the location of New Madrid seemed ideal. Facing scenically southward on the outside of the bend, the currents would easily bring the river traffic to the shores of town and into the natural harbor of St. John's Bayou on the east side.

The bend begins about ten miles south of New Madrid near Island #10 where the river turns 180 degrees around Donaldson Point from south to north. As viewed from New Madrid the river flows northward toward town, turning gently toward the west in front of the city, and continuing a broad 180 degree bend until it flows out of sight to the south. It's the only place on the river one can see such a grand panorama. About ten miles downstream the river passes less than a mile from itself across a narrow isthmus of land known today as Bessie's Neck.

On an English map published in 1765, this river bend was labeled as "Greasy Bent." Today it is variously named, depending on what state publishes the map. Missourians call it "New Madrid Bend." Kentuckians call it "Kentucky Bend" since the little balloon-shaped piece of land it encircles is part of that state. Tennesseans call it "Bessie Bend" after a little town that used to exist just north of the narrowest part of the neck on the Tennessee-Kentucky line.

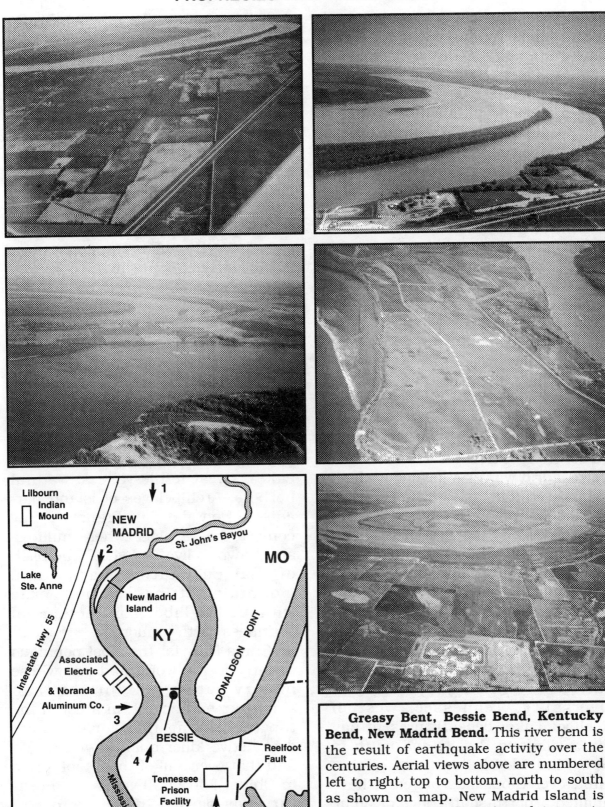

Greasy Bent, Bessie Bend, Kentucky Bend, New Madrid Bend. This river bend is the result of earthquake activity over the centuries. Aerial views above are numbered left to right, top to bottom, north to south as shown on map. New Madrid Island is seen in Photos 1-2. Bessie's neck is seen in photos 3-4. Donaldson Point, Reelfoot Fault and prison are seen in photo 5. Light patches are sand boils from quakes of 1811–12.

In the late 1800's and early 1900's boats coming down the river would stop at Bessie. Passengers from St. Louis, weary from the confinement of the boat, would disembark and spend the night on land at the Bessie Hotel. Meanwhile, their boat would continue northward and around the bend at New Madrid. The next day the passengers would be transported across the narrow neck of land to meet their boat and continue. It was only a short journey across the isthmus, about a mile, while the river route, from where passengers were dropped off to where they were picked up again, was twenty miles. Today you can stand on the levee at Bessie's Neck and see the Mississippi River in front of you and in back of you running in opposite directions.

In addition to its scenic and strategic location for river traffic, New Madrid was also located on high ground. To the east and to the west of New Madrid were lowlands, regularly flooded by the river. The site of the town was 15-20 feet higher and rarely flooded. What George Morgan and the early settlers did not know was that the reason the high ground is there is because of the tectonic forces from below. An active thrust fault several miles below the land surface stretches from present-day Dyersburg, Tennessee, west of Reelfoot Lake; beneath present-day Tiptonville and Bessie; and north to New Madrid. The motions of this fault, over thousands of years, have uplifted a north-south ridge or dome such that when the Mississippi River reaches a point south of Donaldson's Point, west of Reelfoot, it cannot get over the hump in the topography. So it turns north at Bessie's neck and finally cuts through and around this structure at New Madrid, where it turns southward back to the west side of Bessie's neck.

This bend is an earthquake feature. The high ground is the product of tectonic activity. But how could George Morgan have known that?

People Choose to Live Where Earthquakes Happen

Actually, people love to live in active earthquake zones. 80% of the population of the world lives where 80% of the world's earthquakes occur. This is between the latitudes of 10 and 45 degrees north. Why?

The reason is that earthquake activity and the associated faulting of the earth's crust produces attractive places to live. Scenic mountains. Flowing springs. High ground. Placid Lakes. Great fertile valleys. Natural harbors. Archipelagos of island paradises. How did San Francisco Bay come to be—a place where millions are drawn to live and visit? The birth of that enchanting marine and mountain setting was not borne without the labor contractions of countless earth tremors.

China is by far the most populous country in the world and one whose history dates back further than almost any other. Yet, in a list of the top ten among the world's most destructive killer quakes, you would find that over half of them took place in China. For 2,000 years not a century has passed in the history of China without at least one earthquake killing 100,000 people or more. Yet its people flourish, and its population grows despite such natural hazards.

Consider Japan. It is one of the most earthquake-prone countries of the world yet has thirty times the population density of the United States. Tokyo, with more than twenty million people, is the largest city in the world. Most of Japan is of mountainous, rugged topography. Tokyo is spread over a large natural lowland, the Kanto Plain, that projects into the sea. Its topography is ideal for the expansion and growth of a world center for commerce. What created this plain? Earthquakes. In fact, three plates of the earth's restless crust converge there. Most of Japan is seismically active, but the Kanto Plain is the most seismically active region of the whole country.

Take Greece and the Aegean Sea. Western civilization was cradled there. Most of the lands that border the Mediterranean are seismically active. And yet, from Italy, to Spain, to Egypt, to Israel and Turkey, all of which have a history of strong earthquakes, no portion of the Mediterranean has more or larger earthquakes than Greece and the Aegean.

Consider Iraq, host country to ancient Babylon, the original home of Abraham and Sarah, location of the Fertile Crescent, the valleys of the Tigris and Euphrates Rivers, birthplace of world religions and many civilizations. The productive valley and river systems that gave this region its early advantages is bounded and sliced through by many major faults. The very features that had most attracted the ancestors of Abraham to settle there are creations of tectonic activity and

numerous earthquakes.

Consider Jericho of the Old Testament. It is thought to be the oldest continuously inhabited city in the world. Yet the town sits in one of the world's great fault zones, the Dead Sea Rift, which divides the Arabian plate from the Sinai plate. For 10,000 years archeological remains document the repeated destruction of this site. The walls came tumbling down for Joshua. But the evidence shows that throughout history they fell repeatedly, over and over, from earthquakes. The last time was in 1927. Yet people come back again and again to live there. Why? It is one of the few places in the Palestinian Desert where vegetation is lush and springs perennially flow. And why are the springs and the oasis there? Because earthquakes and their associated faulting created the geologic circumstances for their existence.

Consider Utah. The Wasatch Fault slices the state in half, north to south, with a range of mountains on the east, the Great Salt Lake basin on the west. The Wasatch Fault is active. A major earthquake, magnitude 7.0 or greater, has a high probability on that fault during the next fifty years. And yet 75% of the population of Utah lives on that fault. Provo, Salt Lake City, most of the large cities of Utah are there. Why? Because it is scenic for one thing. And because there is where fresh water is most easily obtained, for another. People can build on the western flanks of the mountains where streams deliver the sparkling, clear waters from snow melt the year round while viewing gorgeous sunsets every day across the salty plains. And what made the mountains and the plains? Earthquakes.

We scarcely need to mention California and all of its natural beauty and mineral resources, the most populous state in the union, yet the one with the most earthquakes.

You don't have to live in earthquake country if you don't want to. Some regions of the world have an occassional small quake, but never have large ones. Other places are almost, if not totally, earthquake free. There are some whole countries with virtually no active faults at all. Among these faultless countries are Brazil, Paraguay, Argentina, Norway, Sweden, Finland, Estonia, Latvia, Lithuania, Poland, Germany, Libya, Ireland and Great Britain. Now, of course, all countries have their faults, but in those listed above, the faults they have simply do not produce major earthquakes.

In the United States you could live in Texas or Florida. They don't have earthquakes. But, then, they have hurricanes. Some choice. Right? It seems that no region is completely free of natural hazards of some kind.

If you really want to get away from earthquakes here are some other suggestions. Move to the Sahara Desert, Central Australia, Antarctica, Siberia, Northern Canada, Greenland, the Amazon River Basin, or Equatorial Africa. The Rub Al Kahli is another earthquake–free zone. The name means "the land of nothing" of "the empty quarter." It is a vast wasteland comprising the interior parts of Arabia where temperatures get up to 150 degees and it

never rains. No one lives there. Or here's another possibility. You could live on a seagoing vessel. Most areas of open ocean are quake free zones.

It's up to you. Most people of the world have decided that the benefits of living with earthquakes outweigh their risks and that living in zones of active faulting is definitely better than moving to the poles or to the equator.

No place is perfect. Every place on earth has its faults. It is just that some faults cause earthquakes while others lead to different problems. You have to take the good with the bad no matter where you live. And as for earthquakes, you can live with them. Chapters Six and Seven address this option.

Earthquakes are Not All Bad

Earthquakes have a worse reputation than they deserve. While destroying the old, they also create anew. Sometimes their changes, though wrought by violence, turn out to be improvements on the landscape and are ultimately beneficial to humankind.

Earthquakes create landscapes that attract us and provide us with many advantages. In fact, even the fertile soils of southeast Missouri and northeastern Arkansas can give at least some of the credit to earthquakes. Because of the periodic sand boiling and liquefaction of soils, along with subsidence, earthquake-induced flooding, and other changes caused by quakes, the trace elements and other nutrients are regularly replenished in the New Madrid Seismic Zone. The Bootheel of Missouri contains only 19% of the

Two Scenes on Reelfoot Lake, Tennessee, Created by the Earthquakes of 1811–12

farmland of Missouri, but produces 40% of its crops. Farmers there should thank an earthquake the next time they have a good crop of corn, cotton, rice, milo, soy beans or watermelons.

Areas such as central Australia which are seismically inactive have barren soils—an old erosion surface long depleted of certain essential minerals. In regions such as these with no geologic processes, such as periodic flooding or seismicity, to renew and maintain soil fertility, even with irrigation, crops are poor.

Faulting, and the earthquakes associated with active fault movement, is responsible for creating some of the richest mineral and oil environments in the world. Many ore deposits are associated with fault zones. Some of the largest oil fields are also in fault zones. Without the heat, the friction, the pressures, and the tectonic forces that cause earthquakes, many of our most valuable natural resources would not have come into being.

One of the most enduring and endearing of the products of the New Madrid earthquakes is Reelfoot Lake. This unique resort area is a haven for fishermen, tourists and vacationers. Here one can relax and enjoy a special serenity amidst one of nature's rare beauties. The peace that permeates the forests of centuried cypress in and about the lake offer no hint of the colossal contractions that gave it birth. After a day-long field trip in 1991 visiting landslides, sand boils, explosion craters, earthquake crevasses, broken forests, and other signs of cataclysm from the New Madrid earthquakes,

we stopped at Reelfoot Lake. While contemplating the calm beauty of this watery retreat, one of the participants commented that "Reelfoot Lake is nature's apology for the violence of the quakes."

George Morgan: Urban Planner Ahead of His Time

Morgan was an exceptional individual in many ways and whose plans for New Madrid were laid out on a grand scale with a farsighted view of the future. He was one of the country's first environmentalists and conservationists. He was a religious liberal and liked Indians. He was also a city planner with progressive, creative ideas that regional planners could well emulate today.

There were to be game preserves where no white men could hunt but where exceptions were to be made for the Indians. There were to be ten streets parallel to the river, each 60

Colonel George Morgan (c.1750-1810)

Illustration by Anthony Stewart

feet wide. There would also be eighteen streets perpendicular to the river, each to be 45 feet wide. There were to be six public squares. Every so many blocks there would be land left in forest for city parks. Trees were not to be cut down without Morgan's permission. There were to be plots of ground set aside in each neighborhood for public schools. There were to be properties set aside for the founding of churches "of such religious denominations as shall settle."

Morgan offered one-half acre lots to the first 600 settlers, and five-acre lots to those wishing to settle just outside the city limits. Government buildings and a fort were to line the waterfront. There was also to be a conveniently located market square, a central warehouse, and a plot of acreage set aside for newcomers to grow their first produce.

Morgan promoted his new development and people came from New England, Kentucky, Illinois, Ohio, and many other states of the East and the South. Several bands of Indians also came, refugees from Ohio and Indiana.

Morgan was unable to persuade the Spanish to allow freedom of religous practice. So long as New Madrid was Spanish territory, only Catholics (or those who professed to be so) were supposed to emigrate to Morgan's new province. But later, when the territory became part of the United States, Protestants came, too. The first Methodist congregation west of the Mississippi was formed there in 1809 and is still active today.

Morgan Switches Countries Again

Morgan's scheme would have made him wealthy to an extreme except for one thing. He had proceeded without formal approval from the King. When the King heard that Morgan wanted to sell pieces of his territory, he refused to allow it. The King's representatives informed Morgan, "You can be governor, you can collect taxes, but the land you cannot sell. The land you must give to people in grants, just as we have given it to you." Morgan was to have 1,000 acres for himself and for each of his sons, with which they could do as they pleased. But that was not good enough for Morgan.

Frustrated in his plan, Morgan left a few years after the town was founded and had began to flourish. From his home in New Jersey, he then turned to Canada where, again, he offered his allegiance to another country, and tried to made a deal with the British. Morgan died before the earthquakes.

Had he lived a few years longer, he would have felt the tremors in his secure Canadian estate and, perhaps, congratulated himself for his foresight in getting out of New Madrid when he did.

The town of New Madrid grew despite Morgan's absence. His flyers were still being passed around, attracting settlers by the hundreds. The people came, built houses on their half-acre plots, opened the marketplace, built the storehouse, and prepared the common field for newcomers. The first school started operating in New Madrid by 1793. Morgan's plan was working. It is truly a tribute to one's foresight and skill when their plan works even after they leave.

The territorial officers at New Madrid collected taxes for Spain, stopping all river traffic to levy payments for passage. Furthermore, the Spaniards controlled both banks of the mouth at New Orleans, often detaining and blocking the passage of American vessels.

The United States was unhappy with this. These extorted tributes to a European monarchy were an obstruction to commerce and to the development of America's frontier. There were no railways and no commercial highways. The early settlers of the Ohio and Mississippi Valleys maintained communication with the Atlantic Coast only by long, tedious overland journeys. The only outlet for their marketable produce was by river. If America was to grow and make progress, the waterways of the western frontier had to be accessible for free trade.

In 1800, during the Napoleonic conquest then in progress in Europe, France acquired the Spanish holdings in the New World by way of a secret agreement, the Treaty of San Ildefonso. Americans procured certain restricted rights from the Spanish by an earlier treaty in 1795. The Treaty of San Ildefonso ceded the territory to France without reserving to the United States any right to navigate the Mississippi or to deposit their vessels or their contents at New Orleans. Americans had been secretly robbed.

The discovery of the terms of this agreement by American intelligence in 1802 caused great excitement and concern in this country. The right to use the Mississippi River and trade at New Orleans were indispensable to the prosperity of the nation.

The success in gaining rights of river passage from Spain had been a qualified one. Spain's permission had been at a price since they collected heavy duties from American merchant vessels and inhibited American trade in other ways. Perhaps Napoleon and the French would be different.

Let's Make a Deal

With the west bank of the Mississippi now in French hands, President Thomas Jefferson saw his chance. Robert R. Livingston was America's Minister to France at the time. Jefferson sent instructions to Livingston via a special envoy, James Monroe, whom he named as "Minister Plenipotentiary." Monroe arrived in Paris on the 12th of April, 1803. Livingston and Monroe were authorized to purchase the site of the city of New Orleans, if possible, as well as a strip of the west bank of the river from the mouth to Tennessee.

"I can do better than that," was Napoleon's reply. "I need money now." Napoleon was planning an invasion of England, modeling after his great prototype, Julius Caesar, who had conquered England for Rome centuries before. "You can have the whole territory," he said, "all of it, from the river's mouth at New Orleans to the headwaters of the uppermost tributary. I could use $20,000,000 or so. How does that sound? Can your country handle that?"

Another factor in Napoleon's readiness to sell the Louisiana Territory had to do with Yellow fever. In 1801 an outbreak at New Orleans had decimated the French troops there and had killed his brother-in-law.

Monroe and Livingston were not prepared for such an offer. Congress had only authorized them to buy certain rights and had put a limit on the transaction of $5,000,000. Monroe and Livingston did not mention this to Napoleon, however. They wasted no time. They began working out a deal with Napoleon's representatives. Before the month was over, less than three weeks after Monroe had arrived, the terms of the treaty were finalized on April 30, 1803. Four days later it was signed by Livingston, Monroe, and the French authorities. The price was to be $11,250,000 plus another $3,750,000 in forgiven debts against France held by United States citizens, which would bring the effective purchase price to $15,000,000. In addition, there was to be a time payment plan. If paid off according to schedule, France would net another $12,267,622 in interest, thus raising the true cost to $27,267,622.

When Livingston and Monroe returned to Washington, Thomas Jefferson was anxiously waiting to hear the outcome. They gave him the good news first: "We now have possession of New Orleans, the entire west bank of the Mississippi and the watersheds of all of its tributaries. The bad news," they continued, "is that we agreed to pay several million more than Congress authorized."

"How much more?" Jefferson queried. "Only $10,000,000, if you don't count the interest," Monroe said.

Jefferson was ridiculed for spending "so much good money for such worthless land." At that time, no one knew exactly how much land was there. It had never been fully charted. Years later it was measured to be 828,000 square miles or 530 million acres. At 15 million dollars the price was less than three cents an acre. Yet many members of Congress declared that "Louisiana would never be worth a dollar to the American Union." New England representatives, who could see no direct benefit to their states, cried out that "the Louisiana Purchase stinks!" They threatened to secede from the Union.

The actual take-over of Louisiana was another comedy. It turned out that Spain had not actually formally transferred the land to France in 1800. Within a three-week interval arrangements were made for a quick double transfer from Spain to France and from France to the United States. On March 9th and 10th in St. Louis, the American Interim Governor, Amos Stoddard, ended up representing both the United States and France during the ceremonies.

Congress did eventually agree to pay the amount, but one can understand the resistance to such a sum. At that time there were only 7.5 million registered citizens of the United States. The purchase price of $15,000,000 amounted to a two dollar tax on every American. However, its value has long been verified by the existence of the thirteen states carved from its area. One of those states, of course, was Missouri,

Meriwether Lewis (1774-1809) and William Clark (1770-1838)

Illustrations by Anthony Stewart

including the town of New Madrid. Hence, also thrown into the deal (at no extra charge) was the purchase of the New Madrid Fault Zone.

Neither the Spanish, the French, nor the Americans knew exactly how much land was included in "Louisiana." That's why, in 1803, when the purchase was completed, Thomas Jefferson deployed his personal secretary and friend, Meriwether Lewis, to explore all the way to the headwaters of the Missouri River and to look for a northwest passage to the Pacific. Meriwether then invited his friend, Captain William C. Clark, to join him as co-leader for the expedition. William was the younger brother of George Rogers Clark, a Revolutionary War hero and friend of Washingtons. Jefferson felt an urgent need to find out just how much real estate the union had acquired and to quickly lay a firm claim to all of it.

Fort Osage

The effort to secure the territorial rights of the United States in the West caused Fort Osage to be established. On June 23, 1804, Lewis and Clark and their party of 45 men in keelboats and dug-out canoes stopped to rest on the north bank of the Missouri River, 30 miles east of what would someday be downtown Kansas City. The temperature was 90 degrees, and the wind was blowing so strongly that they had only made three miles progress against the current that day. Their attention was drawn to a hill on the other side of the river.

Clark wrote in his journal: "Directly opposite, on the south, is a high commanding position, more than 70 feet above high-water mark, and oerlooking the river, which is here of but little width. This spot has many advantages for a fort and trading house with the Indians." Clark marked the site on his map as "Fort Point."

After their successful expedition, completed in 1806, William Clark was appointed as Superintendent of Indian Affairs by President Jefferson. In August of 1808 a party of 81 soldiers, commanded by Captain Eli B. Clemson, set off from St. Charles, on a 330 miles voyage up the Missouri River to establish a western outpost for trade with the Osage Nation of Native Americans. William Clark was their guide. Also accompanying the expedition was George C. Sibley, then 26 years old, who would be the man in charge of the merchandise and of keeping all the records of the trading transactions. The Osage were granted a monopoly among tribes in return for which they would protect the outpost against all invaders, which they faithfully did.

When the U.S. expedition arrived at Clark's "Fort Point," they constructed a wooden stockade and several buildings, including a large store for doing business. They named it Fort Osage. The Osage Indians immediately set up villages and lived there in peace with the white settlers for as long as the fort was occupied.

Fort Osage was the westernmost settlement of the United States during the New Madrid earthquakes. By the time of the disturbances in 1811–12, thousands of Osage Indians came to live around the Fort. The fact that they had been given exclusive rights to trade with the government at that facility gave the Osage tremendous power over all other tribes. They, alone, could purchase guns, ammunition, metal knives, hatchets, pots, pans, glass-

ware, and other items the Indians could not produce for themselves. If a member of another tribe wanted a rifle, they had to trade for it from an Osage.

Hence, when the Osage protected the Fort and the passage of boats up and down the Missouri River for the white government, they were also protecting their own interests. It was an arrangement between red men and white that was mutually beneficial for many years. It is also one of the few U.S. Government enterprises that actually made a profit—thanks to the skills of George Sibley, chief trading agent and business manager.

Sibley was later to marry the daughter of the postmaster of St. Louis, Mary Easton. Years later George and Mary moved back to St. Charles and founded Lindenwood College, which still flourishes today. Some of the buildings in St. Charles, that the Sibleys knew and which predate 1811, are still standing today, despite their damages from the earthquakes of 1811–12.

Fort Osage was shut down in 1813 because the government needed the soldiers to return back east and fight in the War of 1812. It was briefly reopened in 1815 after the war but was abandoned as a military post in 1819. George Sibley was promoted to a rank of Major and continued to operate the government trading post with the Osage until 1822 when Congress abolished the system for such trade. Actually, by the early 1820's most Indians had left the area and traded there no more. Strangely, it was not military force that drove the Osage and other tribes west, but smallpox. Fort Osage was deserted for more than a hundred years and fell into ruins, but it has now been faithfully reconstructed as it was from 1808 to 1813.

As for Major Sibley, he was com-missioned in 1825 to lay out a road from Fort Osage to New Mexico which he did with the help of his Osage guides. That road would be-come known as the Sante Fe Trail.

Fort Osage—Westernmost U.S. Settlement During the New Madrid Earthquakes. The Fort has been restored to the way it was in 1808-1813. Photo 1 (upper left) is from outside the stockade The Missouri River is behind it from this angle. Photo 2 is from the inside across the courtyard toward the officer's quarters. Photo 3 is across the courtyard toward the enlisted men's quarters. The cannon in photo 4 is aimed through a gunport toward the river. Photo 5 is the trading post, itself, just outside the stockade. The righthand section of this building was the residence of George Sibley, the man in charge of the trading post. Photo 6 is a view of the kitchen in Sibley's quarters. Visitors are welcome.

Eckert's Tavern and Dr. Seth Millington's House in St. Charles, Missouri. Eckert's Tavern (515 South Main—left) was built in the early 1800's and is now the Cafe Beignet. George Sibley used to frequent this place. After he returned from his trip west in 1824-27, he and his collaborators, Benjamin Reeves and Thomas Mather, spent many hours at Eckert's Tavern to draw the maps and write the reports for the Santa Fe Trail which they had just established. Eckert's was a two story building and was not seriously damaged by the earthquakes; however, a tornado in 1876 blew off the second floor, which was never replaced. The home of Dr. Seth Millington (301 South Main—right) was built in 1808 and survived the earthquakes, too, although the chimnneys probably had to be replaced. Today it houses Goellner Printing. Millington's nephew, Dr. Elijah Lovejoy, was a minister, a St. Louis newspaper man, and an outspoken opponent of slavery. On October 1, 1837, Lovejoy was attacked at this building and almost lynched by a mob. He escaped to Alton, Illinois, but was murdered there—the first martyr of the free press in the U.S.

Home of Dr. Jeremiah Millington, St. Charles Post Office and Castor Oil Factory.
The rear portion was built in 1811—just before the earthquakes. It was probably damaged and repaired. The front portion was added in 1820. The two bottom photos are close-ups of the south wall of the house seen in the upper right. Notice how uneven the bricks are. The wall is very rough, with bricks sticking out and courses unlevel. The mortar joints have been extensively patched and repaired. Jeremiah and Seth were brothers, both from New York, and both physicians. They were two of the first doctors to settle in St. Charles. Together they owned 50 acres of castor beans, which they pressed into oil. They were the first to commercially produce castor oil which they shipped all over the world. They supplied the medicine for the Lewis and Clark expedition in 1804. Jeremiah also served as the St. Charles postmaster during the time that St. Charles was the Missouri State Capital. His postal duties were carried out in this building—along with his medical practice and castor oil business.

The State of the Union in 1811–12

When Francis Scott Key wrote the words that were to become America's national anthem, he was on a British boat in Chesapeake Bay during the bombardment of Fort McHenry in the War of 1812. The flag waving over the Fort that inspired his verses had fifteen stars and fifteen stripes. But this was an error. When the earthquakes struck in 1811–12, the United States was known to the Indians as "The Land of the Seventeen Fires."

The thirteen original colonies that became the first states were, in order of their ratification, Delaware, Pennsylvania, New Jersey, Georgia, Connecticut, Massachusetts, Maryland, South Carolina, New Hampshire, Virginia, New York, North Carolina, and Rhode Island. As for West Virginia, it was originally a part of Virginia and remained so until it split over the slavery issue in 1861. West Virginia was ratified as a separate state in 1863 and fought with the Union during the Civil War.

By 1803, when the United States acquired the west bank of the Mississippi, only four more states had been added to the original thirteen. They were Vermont, Kentucky, Tennessee, and Ohio, in that order. There were to be no more new states until after the earthquakes in 1811–12.

The rest of what was then the United States consisted of districts or territories, as follows: Maine, Michigan, Indiana, Illinois, Mississippi, Missouri, Orleans, and West Florida. Florida had been divided into two parts under Spanish rule: East Florida (the peninsula) and West Florida (the panhandle). West Florida was taken by American military conquest in 1810 and became a Territory. East Florida was still a Spanish colony in 1811–12 that would not be ceded to the United States until 1819. Texas and the lands to the west were also governed by Spain as part of Mexico. The Mexican Revolution had already begun in 1810, however, and was to rage sporadically for eleven years, both before and after the series of great earthquakes

Thus, at the time of the quakes, the United States of America consisted of seventeen states and eight territories, with East Florida, Texas, and the lands of the far west yet to be added.

As for New Madrid—between 1541 and 1801—the territory in which it was located changed hands six times in less than 300 years. Originally Native American, the land was then claimed by Spain, then France, then Great Britain, then Spain again, then France again, and finally the United States. New Madrid had only been a part of the United States for eight years when the earthquakes hit.

The Louisiana Purchase, in which the town was located, was divided in 1804 at the 33rd parallel into "Upper" and "Lower" Territories. That latitude corresponds to the southern boundary of present-day Arkansas. Lower Louisiana was also called the Territory of Orleans. New Madrid was in Upper Louisiana, which was also called the Missouri Territory, which included not only present-day Missouri, but all of Arkansas, Iowa

Canada

(GREAT BRITAIN)

District of Maine

VT

NH

New York

MA

CT

RI

Michigan Territory

Territory of Illinois

Upper

Louisiana

Or

Missouri

Territory

Indiana

Territory

Ohio

Pennsylvania

NJ

MD

DE

Virginia

Kentucky

North Carolina

Tennessee

South Carolina

Mississippi Territory

Georgia

Mexico (SPAIN)

Territory of Orleans

Territory of West Florida

East

Florida

(SPAIN)

American State

U.S. Territory

Other Country

AMERICAN STATES & TERRITORIES
IN 1811-1812

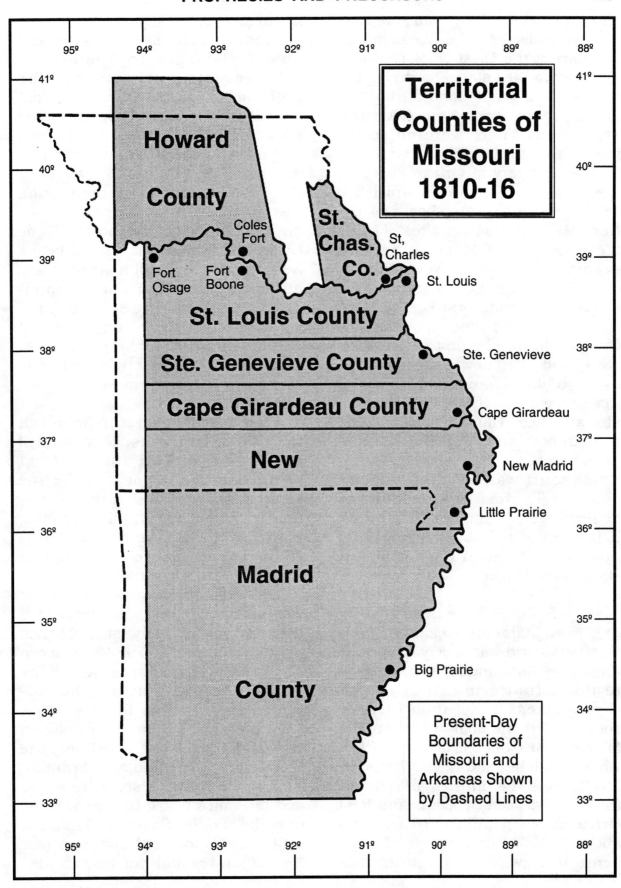

Territorial
Counties of
Missouri
1810-16

Howard County

Coles Fort

St. Chas. Co.

St, Charles

Fort Osage

Fort Boone

St. Louis

St. Louis County

Ste. Genevieve

Ste. Genevieve County

Cape Girardeau County

Cape Girardeau

New

New Madrid

Little Prairie

Madrid

County

Big Prairie

Present-Day
Boundaries of
Missouri and
Arkansas Shown
by Dashed Lines

and Minnesota. Wisconsin was part of the Illinois Territory. Alabama was still part of the Mississippi Territory. The only ratified states bordering the New Madrid Fault Zone during the earthquakes were Kentucky and Tennessee. There were no states west of the Mississippi.

The Territory of Orleans became the eighteenth state on April 30, 1812, during the aftershocks of the New Madrid earthquakes. Minor tremors were felt morning and evening that day in New Madrid, Cape Girardeau, Ste. Genevieve, St. Louis, Cincinnati, and Louisville. A few also noticed the shakes in New Orleans during the first day of their statehood. The new state took the name of Louisiana to which the western portion of West Florida was also attached. Thus, Louisiana came to span both sides of the Mississippi at its mouth.

Missouri was the first territory completely west of the River to achieve statehood, but that didn't happen until 1820. At the time of its ratification, Missouri was the largest state in the Union.

It Could Have Been a Major Metropolis

New Madrid was a very important town from its founding in the 1780's to its virtual demise during the earthquakes. Its location literally commanded the boat traffic on the Mississippi from the mouth of the Ohio to Natchez and New Orleans. In 1811 it was the third largest city on the river between St. Louis and New Orleans. Its population then was about 1,000. The number of residents in New Madrid County was

about 3,200, mostly families living on isolated homesteads or old Spanish land grants. The town of Ste. Genevieve, Missouri, 115 miles to the north, was slightly larger than New Madrid, with a population of around 1,200. Natchez, Mississippi, 400 miles to the south, was the oldest city on the entire river, even older than New Orleans. Its population was about 3,000. At the same time, only 60 miles to the north, Cape Girardeau, which was settled before New Madrid, was still a small village of 200, surrounded and outnumbered by Indians. In 1811, the number of residents in St. Louis was only 1,800 while those who lived in St. Charles, on the north side of the Missouri River, numbered about 1,100.

From a population more than half the size of St. Louis, New Madrid might have grown into a great metropolis had it not been for the earthquakes. It was in a prime location for commerce in all directions, north, south, east and west. These events forever changed the future of this portion of the world.

Zadoc Cramer, a pilot whose life was spent mapping and describing the rivers of the Midwest, published his ninth edition of *The Navigator* in 1811, only ten months before the earthquakes. At that time he described the town as follows: "New Madrid occupies a handsome site on the right or west bank of the Mississippi, commanding a beautiful view of the river for six miles above and ten miles below the town, being near the middle of a bend 25 miles in length. . .The original plan was that New Madrid would not be exceeded in size and in manner by many cities in the world. . . There were to be streets 120 feet wide and roads planted with trees for the health of the citizens. . . While still a Spanish territory (prior to 1800) "one lot of twelve acres" had been set aside "for the king's use" which is now "in the middle of the city, ornamented with trees, and preserved for public walks." New Madrid is "a considerable town, the inhabitants being chiefly French and Spaniards, and a few trading Americans," Cramer said. That was before the earthquakes.

The tenth edition of *The Navigator* was published in 1818, after the quakes. Cramer's description of New Madrid was changed as follows: "The terrific effects of the earthquake, which commenced on December 16, 1811, seems to have alarmed the inhabitants to that degree that few have had the hardihood to remain in or near the town since. . . It threw down the brick chimneys, shattered the houses, threw up the earth in some places, while it sunk in others. Water spouted up through cracks and holes of the earth in all directions. Trees lashed their tops together, while others were split, twisted and torn from their roots. The river itself appeared equally convulsed with the land. . . No wonder, indeed, that a people, accustomed to the quiet of a forest and the pacific rolling of the Mississippi, should, on this occasion of one of nature's greatest concussions of matter, feel terror and alarm to a degree little short of madness.

"There are still a few families, and a court is held here for a district of the Missouri Territory. The town has two badly supplied stores, a tavern and a post office, and from the number of old shattered vacant houses, the place, indeed, looks like "departing greatness."

Cramer ended his post-earthquake commentary with a note of optimism. "Time may yet revive New Madrid," he said, "and 100 years, nay 50, make it what it was intended to be by its original projector, a great and magnificent city."

Immediately following the earthquakes, the population of New Madrid and the surrounding territory west of the river fell from over 3,200 to less than a hundred. Eventually, some who fled came back. By 1820, the population of New Madrid County had been restored to 2,296, about two thirds of its former occupancy. It would not be until 1835, twenty-three years after the last of the big quakes, that it would again attain its former population. By 1840, the county numbered 4,554 residents, an increase in residents which corresponded with a decrease in the frequency of the aftershakes.

Today the small village of Cape Girardeau has grown to a population of 36,000, more than ten times the size of New Madrid, which has about 3,200 people. Were it not for the quakes, New Madrid might have rivaled St. Louis, Paducah and Memphis as a modern urban giant. But nature was not to have it so.

And what about the Native Americans? They far outnumbered the white pioneers and had occupied the region for thousands of years. What impact did the earthquakes have on them?

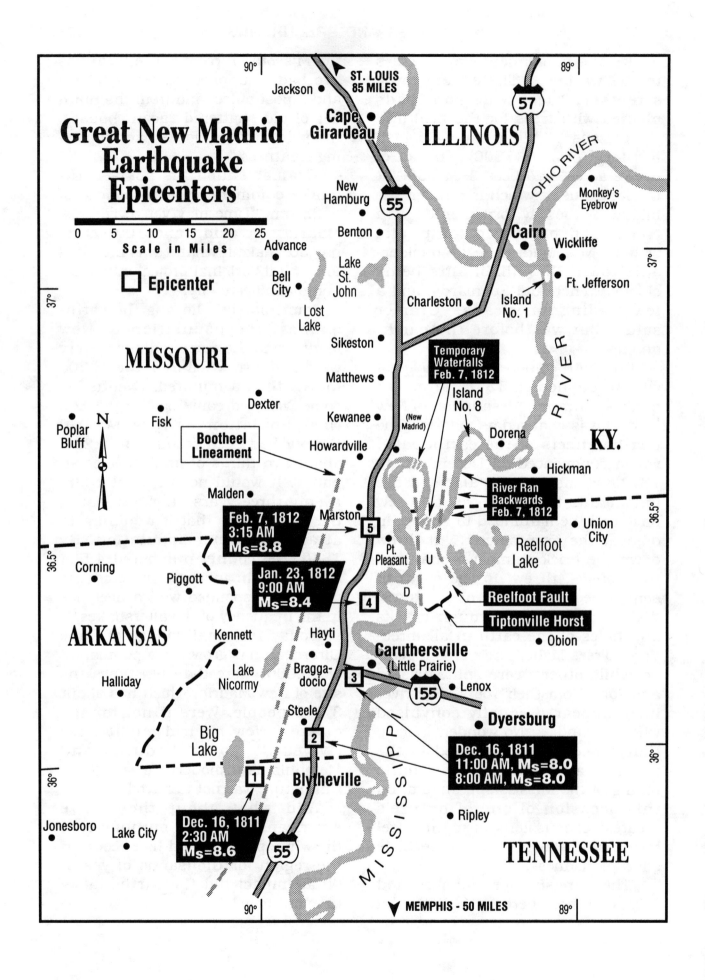

Chapter Three

THE SIEGE BEGINS

Friday the thirteenth is supposed to be an unlucky day, so some people say. December the thirteenth, 1811, was a Friday. There were no signs recognizable to the residents of New Madrid that this Friday was different than any other.

Unknown to those hapless inhabitants, millions of microfractures were already beginning to shatter the bedrock miles below ground surface. As the newly-formed cracks in the earth's crust split and multiplied, superheated, salt-saturated groundwater, under incredible pressures, seeped in to fill the voids. These stresses of the plutonic underworld coming into culmination during this New Madrid weekend had begun their buildup five centuries before in silence and in secret, hidden within the dark depths of the earth. Now the fault was fully set, like the spring of a steel wolf trap ready to snap. Even the tiniest trifle could trip the trigger and set it off.

Meanwhile, at ground surface, people moved, worked, ate, slept, and carried out their normal routines, oblivious to the fact that the foundations of the earth were rapidly crumbling to a climax beneath their very feet. It would soon reach the breaking point. Greater than a million atom bombs, armed and ready, it could

detonate at any instant. Fathomless forces, built up over aeons, were about to be released in seconds. While Indians danced and Frenchmen drank, the people of New Madrid went about their usual ways that Friday—unaware of the fury brewing below that would soon change their lives forever.

Saturday was quiet and normal. Farmers and their families came to town to shop and trade. Some walked. Some rode wooden carts. Others came on horseback. More than a dozen boats had come and gone that day, purchasing supplies and unloading their cargos. Some boatmen had come to spend the weekend, planning to disembark on Monday after some rest and recreation. The saloons conducted their usual Saturday night celebrations with the liquor and the gambling that were normal fare for a busy river city on the farthest frontier.

Sunday arrived—for some a day for worship, for others a day to sober up. Most went to church—Catholics, Baptists, and Methodists. Many crewmen stayed in their boats anchored safely in the harbor of St. John's Bayou, sleeping off the excesses of the night before, resting and preparing for another leg of their voyage on the restless river. Nothing particularly unusual had been noted. There were no foreshocks. No warnings. At least there were none that they had understood as a sign for what was so soon to come.

Then evening came and the first stars. There was a new moon. It had been overcast the last few days, but tonight the sky was clear. The great comet had been visible for nine months now, with its shimmering white head and spectacular split tail. With no moonlight to compete, it seemed unusually bright this cool winter night. Nature, it seemed, was at peace. All was calm. The people of New Madrid went to bed and slept with no fear, no special concern, and with no inkling of what was about to begin. It was December 15, 1811.

About 2:30 A.M. on Monday, December 16, 1811, during the dark hours of early morning, a great shock occurred. Centered just south and west of the future site of Blytheville, Arkansas, (which was not yet founded at that time) it is thought that it would have measured 8.6 on the Richter scale.

About 8:15 A.M. the same day another great shock occurred, centered east of present day Steele, Missouri, in the neighborhood of where the town of Cooter is today. Scientists believe it probably would have measured 8.0 Richter.

Numerous small tremors and several strong ones occurred throughout the morning. Some may have been magnitudes of 6.0 to 7.0 in size. Some sources report another powerful shock late in the morning equal in size to the 8:15 A.M. event. This would have been another Richter 8.0 earthquake. Its epicenter is thought to have been near present-day Caruthersville, Missouri.

Let us tell you how extraordinary this was. Eight point magnitude earthquakes are very rare. Out of hundreds of thousands of earthquakes of various sizes that occur globally every year, on an average there will only be one that tops 8.0. It is not unusual for a year to pass without a single event that large any place on the planet. In the 1950's there was a period of more than four years without a single quake anywhere in the world bigger than 7.6. So you can immediately appreciate that something truly out of the ordinary was happening in the New Madrid area. Already three earthquakes 8.0 or more on the Richter scale had occurred within a few hours in the same region on the same fault.

Dancing Houses

One New Madrid resident, whose name has been lost, took the time to write a letter to a friend in Lexington, Kentucky dated December 16, 1811. The letter was published on February 12, 1812, in the *Philadelphia Gazette*. Following are some extracts:

"About 2 o'clock this morning we were awakened by a most tremendous noise, while the house danced about and seemed as if it would fall on our heads. I soon conjectured the cause of our troubles and cried out it was an earthquake, and for the family to leave the house, which we found very difficult to do, owing to its rolling and jostling about. The shock was soon over and no injury was sustained, except the loss of the chimney and the exposure of my family to the cold of the night.

"At the time of this shock, the heavens were very clear and serene, not a breath of air stirring; but in five minutes it became very dark, and a vapour appeared which seemed to impregnate the atmosphere, had a disagreeable smell, and produced a difficulty of respiration. I knew not how to account for this at the time, but when I saw, in the morning, the situation of my neighbors' houses, all of them more or less injured, I attributed it to the dust . . . The darkness continued till daybreak. During this time we had eight more shocks, none of them so violent as the first.

"At half past 6 o'clock in the morning it cleared up and, believing the danger over, I left home, to see what injury my neighbors had sustained. A few minutes after my departure there was another shock, extremely violent. I hurried home as fast as I could, but the agitation of the earth was so great that it was with much difficulty I kept my balance.

"The motion of the earth was about twelve inches to and fro. I cannot give you an accurate description of this moment. The earth seemed convulsed—the houses shook very much—chimneys falling in every direction. The loud, hoarse roaring which attended the earthquake, together with the cries, screams, and yells of the people, seems still ringing in my ears.

"Fifteen minutes after 7 o'clock we had another shock. This one was the most severe one we have yet had. The darkness returned, the noise was remarkably loud. The first motions of the earth were similar to the preceding shocks, but before they ceased, we rebounded up and down, and it was with difficulty we kept our seats.

"At this instant I expected a dreadful catastrophe. The uproar among the people strengthened the colouring of the picture. The screams and yells were heard at a great distance."

Eliza Bryan was a young woman at the time. She lived with her parents, her three brothers, and her two sisters about two miles from the New Madrid settlement. In 1815 she wrote her recollections, saying, "I have put down precisely what I saw and felt back in 1811-12, as it was burned into my memory everything that happened." Her account of the night of December 15 and the morning that followed is reproduced below:

"We had been in bed about four hours. About 2 o'clock we were visited by a violent shock of an earthquake accompanied by a terrible noise. Maw tried to light the lamps, but the darkness was so dense they didn't help at all. The noise sounded like thunder. The house shook and seemed to tilt. So we all ran outside. From then on until dawn we stayed in a lean-to, and a number of lighter shocks occured, at which time one more violent than the first took place. We did not live in our house for twelve to eighteen months after the first big shock."

Col. John Shaw, a traveler from Wisconsin, had been put up for the night of December 15 just north of present-day Sikeston, 30 miles from New Madrid. His description of the opening night of the seige is as follows: "The house where I stayed was partly of wood and partly of brick structure," he wrote. "At 2 o'clock in the morning occurred a heavy shock of an earthquake. The brick portion of the house all fell down, but I and the family all fortunately escaped unhurt."

Shaw continued his journey to New Madrid the next day and was to remain in the area until after February 7th.

The letter from New Madrid to Lexington excerpted above contained another page dated December 17, 1811:

"I never before thought the passion of fear so strong as I find it here among the people. It is really diverting, or would be so, to a disinterested observer, to see the rueful faces of the different persons that present themselves at my tent, some so agitated that they cannot speak, others cannot hold their tongues. Some cannot sit still, but must be in constant motion, while others cannot walk. Several men, I am informed, on the night of the first shock deserted their families and have not been heard of since."

It was clear from this and other reports that many of those in the areas most affected by the New Madrid earthquakes would suffer more than bodily injury or property loss. Many also suffered emotional trauma and various post-disaster psychological disorders from which they would never fully recover.

The Lexington letter concluded by reporting that the residents of New Madrid who chose to remain in the area had set up encampments of fifty to one hundred persons each in the open fields outside of town.

One Family's Ordeal

George Heinrich Crist, Sr. and his wife, Besy, lived in Livingston County, Kentucky. All of their children and grandchildren were native-born Kentuckians. In December, 1811, they had three sons and three daughters living with them on the family farm: Henry Philip, age 22, Nicholas George, age 21, Rachel, age 19, Catherine, age 17, and Amandy Jane, age 15.

The oldest son, George Heinrich Crist, Jr., and his wife, Elizabeth Gerard, lived and worked on the same plantation. At the time of the first great New Madrid earthquake they had seven of their own children living with them: Hanna, age 17, Elizabeth, age 15, Stephen, age 12, Reason, age 10, Sarah, age 7, Benjamin, age 5, and James Martin, age 4. James Martin had been a twin, but his sister, Elizabeth Gerard, had died on the day of their birth, November 10, 1807.

Nicholaus Heinrich Crist was George Heinrich Sr.'s father. Nicholas had immigrated from Rotterdam, Holland, in 1738. The Crist family had kept an ongoing account of their life and experiences ever since that time, passed on from generation to generation. Keeper of that diary today is Eloyce Noel of Wright City, Missouri, a great great granddaughter of Nicholas George Crist, a young man at the time of the great New Madrid quakes. On pages 173-174 of that journal, dated 16 December 1811, George Heinrich Crist Sr. writes the following: (Note: The language, grammer, and spellings as used by Crist have been preserved in the quotes that follow.)

"There was a great shaking of the earth this morning. Tables and chairs turned over and knocked around—all of us knocked out of bed. The roar I thought would leave us deaf if we lived. It was not a storm. When you could hear, all you could hear was screams from people and animals. It was the worst thing that I have ever witnessed. It was still dark and you could not see nothing. I thought the shaking and the loud roaring sound would never stop. You could not hold onto nothing. Neither man or woman was strong enough— the shaking would knock you lose like knocking hickory nuts out of a tree. I do not know how we lived through it. None of us was killed—we was all banged up and some of us knocked out for awhile and blood was everywhere.

"When it got day break you could see the damage done all around. We still had our home. It was some damage. Some people that the home was not built too strong did not have a home no more. We will have to hunt our animals. Everybody is scared to death. We still don't know if anybody was killed.

"I made my mind up to one thing. If this earth quake or what ever it was did not happen in the Territory of Indiana then me and my family is moving to Pigeon Roost as soon as I can get things together."

And This was Only the First Day

The people of the area thought things were bad that day. What they did not know yet was that December 16, 1811, was just the beginning. It was only the first day of what would eventually become a series of more than 2,000 earthquakes in five months. Aftershocks would then follow on a regular basis for more than ten years.

But the first day was a big one. President James Madison and his wife, First Lady Dolly Madison, were awakened in the White House by the first shock, nearly 800 miles away. Only then it wasn't a "white house." It was a "grey house," built in 1792, fashioned of grey sandstone. At that time it was called "The President's Palace." It did not receive its distinctive coat of white paint until after it had been blackened by British soldiers who tried to burn it during the War of 1812. While shaken repeatedly, "The President's Palace" was not damaged by the New Madrid quakes.

However, the earthquakes did trigger landslides in the mountains of North Carolina, which caused the people there to think the epicenter was nearby, and for a while some Eastern newspapers reported it as a Carolina quake. It was several days before the Atlantic states were to realize from whence these ground motions had originated.

Near the epicentral region a permanent lake formed on December 16, 1811—ten miles long and four miles wide. It can still be seen today. This is Big Lake on the Arkansas-Missouri state line between Blytheville and Leacheville, Arkansas, west of Steele and east of Hornersville, Missouri. None of these towns existed in 1811. Today the Arkansas portion is known for its good fishing and its growing population of American bald eagles. Big Lake is a wild game preserve.

Another huge lake was created when the St. Francis River was tem-

Big Lake, Arkansas, Epicenter of the First Great Earthquake of December 16, 1811.
Although born in violence, Big Lake today is a peaceful fishing spot and wild game preserve. The two top views both show stumps of dead trees in shallow water—trees drowned in 1811 when the lake was formed by the earthquake. A man and his boy can be seen fishing at top left. The third photo shows 250-year-old cypress trees in deep water that survived the inundation. In the top of the cypress on the left of this photo are two bald eagles. Photo #4 looks more like an aerial view of a flooded forest than of a lake. Actually, it is a flooded forest, only the flood happened on December 16, 1811, and never went away. The bottom left photo is an aerial view from near Leachville, Arkansas, with a portion of Big Lake in the distance and a complex pattern of earthquake fissures in the foreground—still visible 200 years after the quakes that created them. Photo #6 is a view of Manila, Arkansas, with Big Lake in the distance and numerous sand boils within the city limits of the town—seismic remnants of 1811-12. The northern part of Big Lake is in Missouri which was drained in the 1920's and was renamed as the Hornersville Swampland and Wildlife Preserve.

porarily dammed up near present-day Marked Tree, Arkansas, forming an enormous body of water forty miles long that extended northward beyond Senath, Missouri, nearly to Kennett. None of these towns were there at the time. The lake lasted for nearly a hundred years. After the water was drained, Lake City, Arkansas, was established near the center of where this large lake had been.

Before the disturbances were over at least ten earthquake lakes would be formed—several of which were born on December 16, 1811, and lived for more than a hundred years thereafter.

Mr. Cagle and His Indian Mound

Another large body of water created that first day was witnessed by Mr. Cagle—a homesteader and one of the first settlers in his area. Cagle had built his house on an Indian mound in the center of what had been a large forty-acre settlement of Mississippian Natives centuries before. Archeologists digging in the twentieth century have named this "the Campbell site," after more recent landowners. The site is located in southeast Pemiscot County one-half mile east of Cooter, Missouri, three miles north of the Arkansas-Missouri State Line, five miles west of the Mississippi River, and two miles east of Interstate Highway 55 near Steele.

Prior to the earthquakes, the land around Mr. Cagle's house was a favorite hunting ground for both Indians and early settlers. Deer, bear, buffalo, as well as panthers, were plentiful. While there were a few clearings, and several small bayous

filled with clear water, most of the area was covered by heavy hardwood forest full of tall tupelo, oak, maple and walnut.

During the early morning daylight of December 16, after the shocks had begun, Mr. Cagle stood on his mound of high ground and watched the gyrations of the woods and fields around his cabin. During the most violent shaking, trees toppled, limbs lashed, branches broke, and trunks split. Then the land around him began to sink. Slowly over the next few hours, as the shocks continued, he watched his homestead become innundated by water forming a new lake—a mile wide, several miles long and eight feet deep. Cagle's cabin was in a shambles from the shaking, but was spared from the flooding. Cagle's Indian Mound remained an island of dry land on the edge of the lake.

It was known as Cagle Lake for the next eighty-eight years. In 1900 a man by the name of Franklin attempted to drain it and failed, at which time it became known as Franklin Lake. Ten years later the Martin family acquired the property and, again, tried to drain the lake, but without success. The publicity of their failed attempt caused it to become known as Martin Lake. Finally, with the organization of the Little River Drainage District in the 1920's, it was permanently drained. The fertile soils of the lake bottom have produced bumper crops ever since.

Some of the fish taken when the lake was drained were described as "unbelievable in size." A vast quantity of black walnut logs were also found on the old lake bed. Since wal-

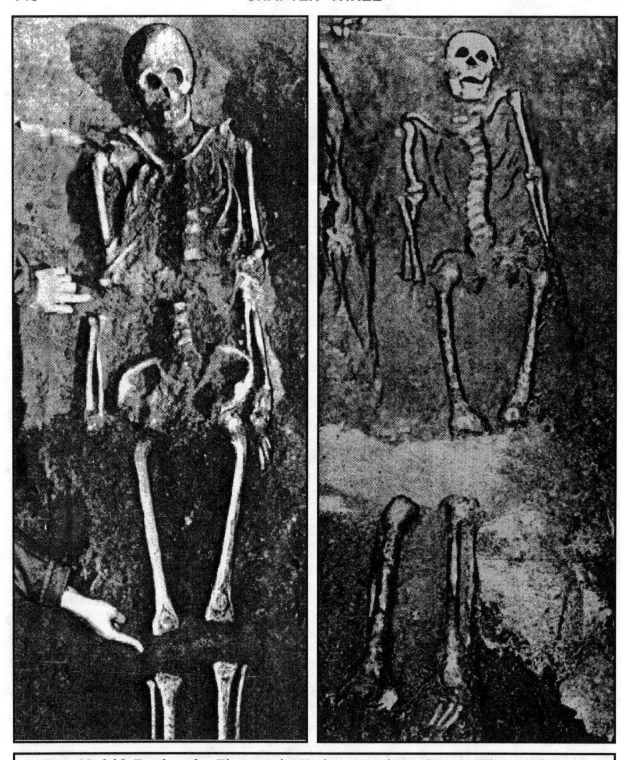

New Madrid Earthquake Fissures in Native American Graves. These Indians were buried several centuries before the New Madrid earthquakes. During the disturbances in 1811-12 cracks opened in the ground and quicksand was intruded to form seismic sand fissures which cut across these bodies at right angles. These photos are from Chapman, et al.,(1955) and are identified as Burial #16 (left) and Burial #19 (right) at the Campbell Site near Cooter, Missouri. In Burial #16 fissures have displaced the bones at the neck, at the midsection (including vertebrae and elbows), and at the knees. In Burial #19 a fissure has separated the legs at the knees, raising the lower legs 8 inches higher than the thigh bones as well as displacing them eight inches to the left.

nut will not grow on marshy or submerged land, this was confirming evidence of dry land conditions prior to the earthquakes. Through the 1920's and 30's it was common to see black walnut rail fences in this area—split from the logs found on the floor of Old Cagle Lake.

There is an interesting article in *The Missouri Archeologist* by Chapman, Anderson, and Spier describing their findings at the Campbell Site and the effects of the New Madrid earthquakes. A number of Native American graves were found with complete skeletons intact. Two graves were different, however—those of Burial #16 and Burial #19.

According to Chapman, et al., the skeletal remains of "Burial #16 were fully extended and supine lying in a north-south direction with head to the north. It lay 30 to 36 inches beneath the surface. A series of cracks in the earth filled with a light-colored sand had cut across the body at right angles and had displaced the bones and burial offerings. One of these cracks cut across the body at the neck and had disturbed the effigy bowl which had been placed as an offering at the left side of the skull. Another crack cut across the elbows and had separated the arm bones and the vertebrae by about one inch and had displaced the entier lower body two inches to the west and downward three inches. Still another crack cut across at the knees and had separated the thigh bones from the shinbones by two and a quarter inches."

Chapman et al. continue, "Burial #19 was the most unusual of all those found. It lay southeast of the other burials and within the area considered to be the village plaza. It was fully extended north-south, head to south, with arms at the sides, and the skull was upright and face up. The mouth was slightly open. The upper right arm was deformed and was noticeably shorter than the left. The vertebrae were twisted to one side and probably had been deformed when the individual was alive. The right shoulder was much lower than the left. The top of the skull was only twenty-two inches beneath the surface, but the pelvis lay thirty inches beneath the surface. A large crack in the earth occurred between the lower legs and the upper legs. This was filled with light-colored sand. The legs were separated by seven inches of this sand. Although the lower ends of the thigh bones appeared to have been smashed at the time this crack appeared, the tops of the lower leg bones were intact and had the knee caps in place on them. The lower legs were approximately eight inches higher and lay eight inches east of the upper legs. . . . Probably caused by the New Madrid earthquake."

Thus, the New Madrid earthquakes disturbed both the living and the dead.

Pirates

The islands of the Mississippi were first numbered during a French survey published in 1765. Later, Zadoc Cramer, a retired boatman living in Natchez, Mississippi, compiled a guide called *The Navigator* which included the islands of the Mississippi and also numbered the islands of the Ohio. The first edition of *The Navigator* was published in 1801. The ninth edition came out in February of 1811, just before the earthquakes.

Cramer's numbering system starts at Pittsburgh for the islands of the Ohio River. Island #98 is near the Ohio-Mississippi junction For the Mississippi River there are 68 numbered islands from St. Louis, just below the mouth of the Missouri, to Bird's Point, Missouri, just above the junction with the Ohio. Just below the mouth of the Ohio the islands of the Mississippi start numbering again from #1 to #127.

Island #1 is just south of Cairo, Illinois and Wickliffe, Kentucky, and was visible from the bluff where old Fort Jefferson used to be. Island #6 today provides a stillwater harbor for Hickman, Kentucky. Island #8 is located on a major bend of the river and is quite large. As the crow flies it is only ten miles east of New Madrid but is more than twenty miles upstream if you take the river. Island #10 is ten miles south and upstream from New Madrid. Today it is no longer an island but has merged with the mainland to become the tip of Donaldson Point. However, modern maps still label this land as "Island #10." Island #127 is just above New Orleans.

One hundred miles south of the epicenter of the first great 8.6 quake was Island #94. Vicksburg, Mississippi, is near that location today. It was known as "Stack Island" but also as "Crow's Nest" and "Rogue's Rest." It was inhabited by pirates. Crow's Nest was well suited for staging an ambush on boats that could be spotted approaching the island several miles away in both directions and because boats had to thread a long

narrow channel called "Nine-Mile Reach" on one side of the island.

It just so happened that on Sunday night, December 15, a Captain Paul Sarpy from St. Louis had tied up his boat for the night on the north end of Island #94. He was accompanied by his crew and family.

In those days the river was too treacherous to ply by night. There were shifting sand bars and many snags and stumps that could damage, sink or capsize a boat. There was no U.S. Army Corps of Engineers, as we have today, to dredge the river, mark it with buoys and stabilize the channel with jetties and dikes. Neither were there any lights on the banks for pilots to sight in making their turns through the many bends of the river. River maps were also poor and unreliable. Zadok Cramer's *Navigator* was the newest and the best, but it was only updated every year or two, while the river changed constantly. Therefore, it was the custom for boatmen to tie up at night and travel only by daylight.

Captain Sarpy didn't know about the pirates. When he landed, he and several crew members went ashore to get some exercise and stretch their legs. As they strolled through the trees, they came upon an encampment of pirates. They had not been seen. Hiding where they stood, they listened, overhearing the pirates' plans to ambush a boat with a valuable cargo and "a considerable sum of money" that was supposed to pass by any day, now, on its way from St. Louis to New Orleans. As they eavesdropped with intense concentration, crouching behind the bushes, they overheard a name. "Sarpy." It was

Sarpy's boat they were after!

Slipping away without being discovered, Sarpy and his men went back to their boat. Late that night, under cover of darkness, they drifted around the island undetected by the pirates. They tied up downstream just far enough to make a quick getaway when daylight came.

During the night strong vibrations shook their boat. At first they were afraid the pirates had found them and were boarding for plunder. But no one came aboard. The tremors continued, accompanied with the agitation of large waves that rocked their boat.

That morning, in the dim dawn light as the fog and mist began to clear, Sarpy's sailors looked upstream. Island #94 had completely disappeared—pirates and all!

For a hundred years there was no Stack Island, no Island #94. Since then the river has redeposited another body of sand in that location which carries the same name and number today. But it is not the same isle where Captain Sarpy so narrowly escaped a brutal ambush and was saved by an earthquake.

Further to the north, at the end of Long Reach, near the present-day town of Osceola, was Island #32. You won't find it on any modern navigation maps. There is an Island #31 and an Island #33 but no Island #32. It, too, was to disappear in the darkness of an early December morning— but not yet. As of December 16, 1811, Island #32 was still there, but its days were numbered. In less than a week, it, too, would follow the fate of Island #94.

Big Prairie Disappears

The St. Francis River forms the western boundary of the Missouri Bootheel. It leaves Missouri at the inner point of the "heel" between present-day Cardwell, Missouri, and Brighton, Arkansas. From that point it flows through Arkansas, where it eventually reaches the Mississippi fifty miles below Memphis near Helena, Arkansas, and Island #60.

But Helena wasn't there then. Another town preceded it. Big Prairie was its name, founded in 1797. It was a small village of approximately twenty families, around 100 people in all. When the great quakes of December 16 hit Big Prairie the sandy sediments upon which it stood began to liquefy and sink. Everyone successfully escaped, but the town of Big Prairie was never seen again. Its former site is now occupied by the river. Helena was established in 1820 on another site nearby.

John Bradbury was an English naturalist studying American flora and fauna along the Mississippi River at the time. His barge was carrying a load of lead from Herculaneum. On the night of December 15th he was tied up on Island #35 just above the entrance to a swift stretch of river known as "The Devil's Channel" with a treacherous bend called "The Devil's Elbow." His journal contains the following notes for December 16, 1811:

"2:00 A.M. Violent shock.

"2:30 or after, Terrible, but not equal to the first. 27 shocks before daylight at intervals of 6 to 10 minutes.

"Daylight. Violent shock. Equal to

the first. Same phenomena.

"Breakfast. Very severe; nearly thrown down.

"After breakfast. Man nearly thrown into river.

"11:00 A.M. Violent; trees shaken; banks fell; river agitated. So violent an agitation of the boat that it appeared in danger of upsetting. I could distinctly see the river agitated as if by a storm. Immediately the perpendicular surfaces of the banks, both above and below us, began to fall into the river in such vast masses as nearly to sink our boat by the swell they occasioned. The river was covered with foam and drift timber and had risen considerably. Two canoes floated down the river. We considered this as a melancholy proof that some of the boats we passed on the preceding day had perished. Our conjectures were afterwards confirmed."

The *National Intelligencer* was a newspaper published three times a week in Washington, DC. The February 29, 1812, issue contained this account of the area near Big Prairie, Arkansas: "A gentleman who was near the Arkansas River at the time of the first shocks in December last states that certain Indians had arrived near the mouth of the river who had seen a large lake, or sea, where many of their brothers had resided and had perished in the general wreck; that to escape a similar fate, they had traveled three days up the river, but finding the dangers increase as they progressed, frequently having to cut down large trees to cross the chasms in the earth, they had returned to the mouth of the river."

Today, in the vicinity of where Big Prairie used to be, you can still see "lakes" or "swamplands" around Helena, Arkansas, which are probably the remnants of sunklands from these earthquakes and which may well be the sites where Indians drowned during the quakes in 1811.

Escape from Little Prairie

Further to the north near present-day Caruthersville, another drama unfolded that day. Little Prairie was a small river town a day's float downstream from New Madrid and a mile upstream from Island #16. It had been founded around 1800 by Francois LeSeiur—a co-founder of New Madrid seventeen years before. There were between 100 and 200 inhabitants.

The day had been calm, clear and cool. Several of the townspeople had been duck hunting on Hog Lake that Sunday afternoon—including young Ben Chartier and his uncle Printerboyer. Others had caught some fish in a nearby bayou. The village was resting peacefully in the night under a canopy of bright stars in the dark of a new moon. Then it happened.

Sometime between 2:00 and 2:30 A.M. they were violently thrown from their beds. Within minutes vapors rising from the ground had produced a thick blanket of fog blotting out the stars. It became pitch black. Some were injured. Some were bleeding. Some were even knocked unconscious. Darkness was total, except for the glowing embers of fireplaces whose coals had been strewn about cabin floors. Some fires broke out. The ground roared, moaned, and rumbled. Strange lights flashed and glowed from the ground, providing an intermittent erie luminescence in the darkness. Lesser tremors rattled the residents almost continuously, it seemed, interspersed with occasional harder shocks.

Shortly after daylight another great earthquake struck—a magnitude 8.0 at least. To the residents of Little Prairie, it sccmcd stronger than the first. Unknown to them, the epicenters were moving closer as the fault rupture propagated to the northeast from its origin in Arkansas toward their town in Missouri. The ground quivered and writhed. The earth began to split open. Cracks and fissures were everywhere. "It seemed like you couldn't walk in any direction without stepping into a crevasse," remarked one witness. There were hissing sounds, like serpents. Blowing noises. The smell of sulfur, methane, and rotting vegetation. Steamy vapors and warm water "at blood temperature" issued from the cracks, along with quantities of liquid sand and mud. Sometimes, they said, the ground would open and then suddenly slam shut spouting groundwater over the tops of tall trees. Sometimes the ground would crack open beneath a big oak or cottonwood, splitting their trunks from bottom to top, exploding with a loud report.

Still later that morning a yawning chasm formed in the middle of town, more than twenty feet wide. The people stood around the brim, gazing into the gaping abyss—as groundwater and quicksand gurgled upwards to fill the void mingled with a foul warm mist that carried the smell of brimstone. It crossed the minds of many of those terrified observers that the gates of Hell, itself, may be opening from below.

Sometime late in the morning another tremendous earthquake occurred—another magnitude 8.0. This one seemed to originate directly beneath the town, lifting and heaving for more than a minute, tossing objects into the air and pounding houses into the ground. According to James Fletcher, a Little Prairie resident, the shock was accompanied "with a perpendicular bouncing that caused the earth to open in many places—some eight and ten feet wide, others of less width, and some of considerable length. Some parts of the settlement have sunk," Fletcher continued, ". . . some more, some less. But the deepest I saw was about twelve feet. The earth was, in the course of fifteen minutes after the shock in the morning, entirely inundated with water. The pressing of the earth caused the water to spout out of the pores of the ground to the height of eight or ten feet!" Believing that the whole country was sinking, Fletcher turned and fled from the river in horror. "The agitation of the earth was so great," Fletcher said, "it was with difficulty that any could stand on their feet, and some could not." The town, already a shambles, actually began to sink, while a dark liquid oozed from the sandy soil, flooding the village from beneath. Later Fletcher recalled, "Two dwelling houses, a granary, and a smoke house were sunk. One of the houses was sunk twelve feet below the surface of the earth. With the other dwelling, the top was even with the

"Escape from Little Prairie"

Illustration by Mark Farmer

surface. The granary and smoke-house were entirely out of sight, we supposed sunk and the earth closed over them."

Ben Chartier, who was sixteen years old at the time, had this recollection of the earthquake at Little Prarie on December 16, 1811: "Our house was made out of logs covered with cypress bark and had a puncheon floor (i.e. rough logs with the top sides hewn flat). We lived a quar-ter of a mile from Hog Lake where ducks were very thick. . . My cousins, John Detie and John Charlemine, were in the house, and my mother was sitting in the door smoking. Just then we felt a little earthquake. The sky turned green, and then it shook hard. My father and my cousins ran and turned the hogs out. The ground burst wide open and peach and apple trees were knocked down and then blowed up."

George Roddell, one of the town leaders of Little Prairie, tells this story: "When the tenth shock occurred, I was standing on the bank of the bayou when the bank gave way and sunk down about 30 yards from the water's edge, as far as I could see up and down the stream. It upset my mill, and one end of my dwelling house sunk down considerably." His family had scattered in terror, running for the woods. When they finally reassembled near their sinking, collapsing house, "the eleventh shock came on," after which Roddell reported that the ground was cracked and broken everywhere. About fifteen minutes after the shock the water rose around them waist deep, and they had to flee for their lives.

With George Roddell as their leader, the residents of Little Prairie headed west toward the high ground that holds present-day Hayti. For eight miles they waded through knee to waist-deep water, carrying small children on their shoulders, holding on to what few belongings they could, never knowing from one step to the next if they were going to trip over a submerged stump or "be precipitated headlong into one of those cracks in the earth," concealed by the dark murky waters through which they were wading. Meanwhile, all about them were snakes, wolves, possums, racoons, coyotes, and other creatures swimming for their own lives, too.

Imagine the fear and the misery of their trek. Before them, to the west, was water to the horizon as far as they could see. They could not be sure they would ever get out of there alive nor that they would even survive the day. And as they walked, they felt the ground ripple repeatedly under the soles their feet. Several times, as the earth shook, the waters around them would boil with sand, sometimes spouting geysers of mud and bituminous matter high into the air, spraying in their faces and raining upon their heads. Sometimes they found themselves wading over soft ground. Quicksand. If they didn't drown in the water, they could be swallowed up by the earth. All they could do was to keep trudging forward and pray.

And it was cold.

The Little Ice Age

To fully appreciate the misery of the Little Prairie refugees, one has to know how cold it was back then. The 400-year period from the early 1400's to the middle 1800's is called "The Little Ice Age" by geologists. The 19th century climate of the Mississippi-Ohio Valleys was cooler than that of today. In January of 1812, temperatures had fallen and remained so low for so long that most of the streams had completely frozen over in the New Madrid area. Even the mighty Mississippi used to freeze regularly, completely across, from Herculaneum, Missouri, northward. Herculaneum is about thirty miles south of St. Louis. (Chimneys fell and brick houses split there during the New Madrid earthquakes.) Winters in St. Louis used to be so frigid that, even as late as the early 1920's, automobiles could drive over river ice from Missouri to Illinois. During the last century it was not uncommon for the Mississippi River to freeze all the way across as far south as Cape Girardeau and even to Cairo at the junction of the Ohio. One hundred years after the earthquakes, Oscar T. Coil was a student at Missouri's Third District Normal School (now known as Southeast Missouri State University). In his autobiography he describes an "incredibly cold winter in 1911-12" and how he and many other students walked to Illinois and back over the ice on the Mississippi at Cape Girardeau. The climate of the Midwest has not been cold enough to do that for many years.

To get an even better idea of the harshness of the times, consider the account of Elder Wilson Thompson, a Baptist minister who rode from a point ten miles north of Cape Girardeau to New Madrid and back during the last week of December, 1811, and the first week of January, 1812. He was 24 years old at the time, accompanied by two older men.

"It was extremely cold," he wrote in his autobiography. "We had about ten miles of open prairie to ride, facing the wind. (This would probably have been near present-day Charleston, Missouri.) We pursued our way until we reached a large bayou, about half a mile wide. The road crossed it but was now frozen over with a slick hard ice, strong enough to bear a horse. On each side of the road was a thick growth of flags (cat tails or wild iris) as high as a horse's back. We tried to lead our horses on the ice, but mine was barefooted, and the other two were smooth-shod. They fell and could not get up until we slid them to the shore. After trying every plan, to no purpose, I told the old men if they would stay on the shore I would mount my little horse and try to find a way through the tall flags,

and if I were successful, I would return and help them over, for the flags were so thick, and the ice was so rough, the horses would not fall. I mounted into my saddle, and proceeded, perhaps, about twenty or thirty rods, when suddenly my horse broke through the ice. I sprang from my saddle, and lit into the water about waist deep, by the side of my horse, which was plunging, and could get no foothold that would bear him up. My feet seemed to be on a mat of the flag roots. The water being put in motion by the plunging of my horse showed that the ice continued no farther. All around shook like a quagmire and seemed as if it were soft mud that was under the mat of flag roots. I was afraid to move my feet lest I should loose my sod.

"My horse would plunge sometimes nearly under the water, and then he would rise again," Thompson continued. "I finally got him in a favorable position, and then I placed both arms under his breast. I made one mighty effort to lift him, just as he plunged forward, and succeeded in throwing him backward on the ice, with his head toward the shore. The ice bore him up, and he lay sprawling upon it. I sprang on the ice again and caught the bridle just as my horse was rising to his feet. I then got back to shore.

"We had no means of making a fire, and there was no house for ten miles back," Thompson continued. "I told them I should freeze before I could get half-way there for I was as wet as I could be. My boots were full of water, and I was covered with ice. I left my friends and took my horse by the bridle and, walking on the edge of the flags, along the smooth ice in the road where my horse could keep his foothold, I succeeded in getting over. I then left my horse, ran back, and finally got both the others over. We then traveled on about a mile when we came to another such lake. I went across on foot and examined the sides but found no chance of leading the horses over. I found a large hand-spike with which I broke the ice from one side to the other, and we led our horses over. It was four miles to the first house, and two of these were through a swamp. The rain had filled every low place, and the road was mostly covered with smooth ice, and on each side was a thick underbrush, matted with raspberry briers."

The thorny underbrush compelled Thompson and his companions to stay on the trace of the icy road, difficult as it was. Meanwhile, during their trek, tremors occasionally startled their steeds, causing them to spook or balk. When they got to within two miles of a house up the road they had remembered, Thompson, who was "literally shielded over with ice," left his friends and began to gallop ahead through the dark forest toward shelter. When he reached the gate he saw a bright light shining inside the cabin. When he dismounted he found that he could not walk. His limbs were too cold, and his pants were frozen solid. By holding onto his horse and hobbling toward the cabin, working his knees and legs as best he could, he arrived at the front doorstep.

"When I reached the door, I knocked," says Thompson, "but I did not wait for a reply. I rushed in. I then saw at a glance that I had intruded too abruptly." Before him was a woman in labor surrounded by neighbor ladies. The mistress of the house was, at that very moment, in the act of giving birth.

Instantly recognizing his pitiful state, covered with ice and nearly frozen to death, one of the midwives immediately took him in. There in the kitchen he took a seat to thaw by the fire. He then emptied the water out of his boots and, as best he could, wrung out his socks and pants.

He then got dressed again, bid the ladies and the new baby good evening, and went to his horse outside just as his two fellow travelers were drawing up. Thompson's boots and clothing were still damp, but he survived. That night they built a fire and slept on the ground next to it.

The next day, as they were passing along the river, not far from where Commerce and Scott City are today, Thompson wrote: "A severe shock came on. We sought as open a place as possible in the timber and dismounted from our staggering horses, who could scarcely stand up, and we, ourselves, found it difficult to stand. We could hear the screams of the people near the river and the falling of houses. Large trees were snapped off, and the boughs of others were lashing each other with fury, and old mossy logs were rolled out of their beds. All this was from the great agitation of the earth, but not a breeze of wind could be perceived. These heavy shocks were often introduced by a sound like distant thunder and then a roaring like heavy wind would come through the air. With this would come the shaking and convulsive surges of the earth. After the earthquake had ceased, we traveled on. The temperature was a little moderated, but still it was very cold," wrote Thompson.

The trio and their horses picked their way through the ice with much difficulty, but at last, cold and fatigued, they reached their homes that evening (1.5 miles south of present-day Jackson, Missouri) and found their families well. But the earthquakes were not yet over for the Thompsons.

Meanwhile, Back at Little Prairie

Everyone who could walk in Little Prairie had left town on that drear December day. Imagine how it must have been for those settlers slogging through frigid waters with wet clothes for miles and miles, seeking an escape from their plight and with no prospect of an opportunity to dry off or to find a warm place to spend the night—that is, if they would even survive to see the night.

Finally, by late afternoon on December 16, the people of Little Prairie reached high ground and tried to get some sleep, shivering through the night. They were near the present location of Hayti, Missouri. The next day they decided to head for New Madrid for refuge. They had no way of knowing the condition of that town. There were no phones. No radios. No evening news on television to brief them and help them to understand what was happening.

Little by little, camping and foraging as they went, they traversed the twenty six miles to New Madrid. The going was difficult. Quakes continued to agitate the wilderness throughout the days as they went. Trees were

fallen everywhere. Limbs covered the ground. New swamps had formed across former trails. The ground was broken, uneven, pitted with craters, and full of crevasses and soft places—bogs of quicksand from seismic liquefaction.

Old Jake, a negro slave belonging to Francois LeSier, had been assigned to carry little Auguste Chartier on the trek to New Madrid. Auguste was about two or three years old at the time. He was accompanied by his parents and sixteen-year-old brother, Ben. According to Ben, "The earth broke open, and trees fell across" so we had to shinny across logs like a coon. We had to make our way "through the woods and over big cracks in the ground, which were usually north and south." On the way "Old Jake fell down and mashed my brother's nose. The earth shook constantly."

On Christmas Eve, Tuesday, December 24, George Roddell and his pathetic band of a hundred refugees stumbled into New Madrid, cold and hungry. What they found was a town destroyed and a people as shaken as they, ill prepared to help. Miraculously, everyone from Little Prairie survived. One elderly black man had been left behind, too feeble to come with the rest. But he had been rescued the next day by a passing boat. There were no serious injuries other than Auguste's broken nose. Some suffered from exposure, deprivation, and fatigue. But there were no deaths.

In Washington, D.C., the February 29, 1812, issue of the *National Intelligencer* contained the following note: "We have just received authentic information from some places where this desolating concussion of nature had its direful effects. At a place called the Little Prairie, on the other side of the Mississippi, about 30 miles from New Madrid, immediately after the shock on the 16th last month, the inundation of water was so great as to compel the inhabitants to seek instantaneous refuge for the preservation of life. Some houses were engulfed in the chasms but no lives lost as we have yet heard of. Small lakes and rivers were converted into sand eminences, and fish common to the country were very plenty (sic) on the surface."

Three months after Little Prairie had been evacuated, in March of 1812, a merchant, James McBride, came down the river with two flatboats heavily laden with flour, whiskey, and pork. He tied up on the Missouri side a mile or two above Island #16, only to realize that he was moored over part of what had been a portion of Little Prairie—"now the bed of the Mississippi River." He observed coffins projecting from an adjacent bank, the remains of a graveyard carried off by the flood. Not all of the town was under water. McBride counted three French trappers who had made their way to Little Prairie after surviving the earthquakes in the wilderness. They had hoped to find help and company at Little Prairie where they had been accustomed to trading, but they had found neither. McBride found them sheltered in a rickety shanty they had thrown together from boards borrowed from collapsed houses. Of those that had not disappeared completely, not a single house remained standing.

According to McBride's journal, it was drizzling rain when he was there, and the day was dark and gloomy. A constant noise rumbled ominously from deep within the earth as he walked over the desolate acres that had once been a thriving settlement. "The surface of the ground was cracked in almost every direction," he recounts. "But what particularly attracted my attention were circular holes in the earth from five or six to thirty feet in diameter, the depth corresponding with the diameter so as to be about half as deep as wide, and surrounded with a circle of sand two or three feet deep and a black substance like stone coal . . . All nature appeared in ruins," he continued, "and seemed to mourn in solitude over her melancholy fate. . . Suddenly," he said, "I was overcome with dread and hastily returned to my boat."

Within and around the city limits of Caruthersville, Missouri, you can find sand boils and explosion craters even today, as described by James McBride 200 years ago.

A year after the earthquakes some of the people of Little Prairie, including Col. John H. Walker, went back to the few surviving ruins of their settlement. Some rebuilt and stayed for a few years, calling their establishment by a new name: "Lost Village." By the time Missouri was ratified as a State in 1821, Lost Village had become a ghost town, abandoned to the encroachment of the river which eventually overtook and occupied the site completely.

In 1846, thirty-four years after the earthquakes, Timothy Flint, an American geographer, and Sir

Charles Lyell, a famous British geologist, revisited the scenes of the disturbances. At the time of their visit, no trace of Little Prairie could be seen. The river was flowing over the site of where the town had been. A decade later, in 1857, the town of Caruthersville was founded, where Flint and Lyell had come to visit.

As of today, the river has migrated southward over the original site of Little Prarie by nearly a mile since 1812. The Bunge grain elevator at Caruthersville is ten stories high and can be seen for miles in every direction. It marks the 8.0 magnitude epicenter of the midday quake of December 16, 1811, that destroyed Little Prairie. Go to the Bunge elevator on the banks of the river and look straight across to the Tennessee side. From about halfway to the shores of Tennessee is where Little Prairie used to be. Not a trace of the town exists today. The riverfront of docks, shops, homes, and trading establishments that used to be Little Prairie is now a willow bank in Tennessee on the opposite side of the river from where it used to be.

Caruthersville is the county seat of Pemiscot County. "Pemiscot" is an Indian word. It means "liquid mud." Do you think the Native Americans may have known something about the liquefaction-prone soils of that area that the white men did not?

The Case of the Missing Smokehouse

Ten miles southwest of Little Prairie lived the Culbertson family. Their homestead was in an elbow of the Pemiscot River. They called their farm "Terra Rouge" because of the red-colored soil. Their cabin was located inside the bend of the river, but close to the neck. Not far behind their house, near the inside apex of the bend and encircled by the bayou on three sides, was their well and smokehouse.

During the dark morning hours of December 16 they felt a terrible shock, followed by several more. They remained huddled in the house until daylight, fearful of what greater risks might lurk in the darkness outside. At one point they had the disorienting sensation that the whole house was actually moving many feet. Fortunately, their well built cabin did not collapse although the kitchen was in a shambles.

Sometime after sunrise and after the vibrations of the second severe shock had subsided, Mrs. Culbertson left the house to draw some water from the well and get some meat for breakfast from the smokehouse. To her great astonishment, she found no well and no smokehouse.

Instead, not far from the back of the cabin, was a new channel filled with the water flowing where the river had never flowed before. Across the newly-formed stretch of stream, on the opposite bank, stood the missing smokehouse.

During the night a huge fissure over 100 feet wide and more than a mile long had formed across the neck of the river bend between the cabin and the smokehouse. The Pemiscot River now had a shorter, channel in which to flow. What had been the apex of the bend behind the smokehouse had been moved and filled with caved banks and sand boil deposits such as to close off the former chan-

Little Prairie Today. Looking through the Caruthersville welcome sign on the Mississippi River, one sees Tennessee on the opposite side. Where you see the tow boat passing in the photo above is approximately where the town of Little Prairie used to be before the earthquakes. The ten-story grain elevator in the photos on the right is on the water's edge at Caruthersville overlooking the former site of Little Prairie, now under the river. In the lower right photo, you can see the other side of Caruthersville Bend which flows east to west in the distance and west to east at Caruthersville. The lower left picture is a seismic feature in the city limits of Caruthersville—a place where the earthquakes of 1811-12 left a permanent depression. This intermittent body of water has no surface outlet or inlet. It is filled from the bottom up when the water table is high and becomes dry when the water table is low. Caruthersville was not founded until 45 years after the earthquakes. It is the seat of Pemiscot County. "Pemiscot" is an old Indian name for this area. The word means "liquid mud." Could it be that the Indians knew how prone to liqufaction this area becomes during large earthquakes? Caruthersville is located directly over the New Madrid Fault. What will happen to Caruthersville during the next major earthquake?

nel, blocking any flow on the far side. With the well and smokehouse now on the other side of the river from their house, Mrs. Culbertson and her husband had to use a canoe to fetch their meat and water. They considered themselves lucky. Had the fissure located itself a few feet closer in the direction of the house, the entire Culbertson family could have been swallowed alive—cabin and all.

The Pemiscot River was destroyed. Its channel was broken into discontinuous parts causing its waters to spread over the land creating new swamps. These were not drained until the 1920's. Traces of the river can still be seen today by the name of Pemiscot Bayou, about three miles west of Steele, Missouri.

PEMISCOT RIVER &
THE CULBERTSON'S SMOKEHOUSE

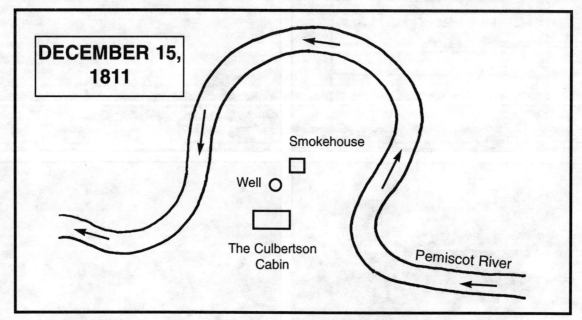

DECEMBER 15, 1811

Smokehouse

Well

The Culbertson Cabin

Pemiscot River

• It used to be a short walk from the Culbertson Family Cabin back to their smokehouse and water well. After the earthquakes of December 16, 1811, it was no longer a short walk. In fact, it wasn't a walk any more. It took a boat to get their morning bacon and day's water supply. The earthquakes had opened a crevasse over 100 feet wide and more than a mile long between their house and the smokehouse through which the Pemiscot River then flowed. They were lucky. These fissures, some of them miles long, opened by the thousands during the earthquakes. Had this one opened a few feet south, it would have swallowed their entire cabin, including the Culbertsons.

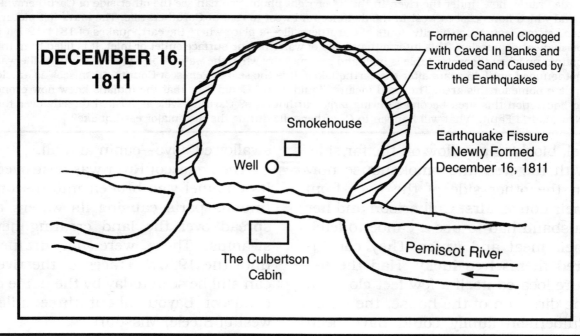

DECEMBER 16, 1811

Former Channel Clogged with Caved In Banks and Extruded Sand Caused by the Earthquakes

Smokehouse

Well

Earthquake Fissure Newly Formed December 16, 1811

The Culbertson Cabin

Pemiscot River

Field Report From New Madrid

Not understanding the ways of earthquakes, the residents of New Madrid had temporarily abandoned town. They were all camping out two or three miles to the north where they thought the quakes would be less severe. They had mistakenly thought the quakes to be centered within their city limits.

The townsfolk of New Madrid reported ten deaths on December 16, including one on a boat:

Six Indians near the river that night had drowned when a massive cave-in of the banks threw them into the swirling waters of the Mississippi.

One woman, a Mrs. Jarvis, refused to leave her cabin after the first great shock at 2:30 A.M. She was killed when it collapsed during another strong shock later that day.

Another woman, a Mrs. Lafont, panicked, ran screaming into the street, and died from fright of a heart attack.

One man fell into a sand blow crater and drowned, engulfed by quicksand and groundwater. For decades afterwards, an earthquake pond remained to be seen on that spot west of town. For many years residents would show visitors "the place where the negro drowned."

Firmin LaRoche was a captain of three barges that had tied up on a steep bank above Island #10, about eight miles south of New Madrid. He carried a load of furs and nine passengers from St. Louis. Among those aboard were Father Joseph, a French missionary to the Osage Indians, and a black deck hand—a slave called Ben. During the violence of the first great earthquake a large tree toppled from the tall bank onto one of the barges—killing Ben and breaking LaRoche's arm.

A few days after the shocks began, another New Madrid resident succumbed to the elements. Antoine LaForge had been ill for some time before December 16. When the quakes began and the townsfolk began to evacuate, he was carried from his warm cottage to a tent. Exposed to the discomforts of the days and the chilling dampness of the nights, he contracted pneumonia and died.

Betsy Masters, a seventeen-year-old girl, had her leg broken just below the knee from a fallen beam in her cabin. The terror and confusion of the townspeople were so great that she was abandoned—even by her parents and family—who feared that more quakes would come and kill them all if they stayed in town. They thought, erroneously, that if the quakes continued to visit, the shaking would be less outside of the city. A kind stranger passing through, Col. John Shaw, took pity on the girl's pathetic plight and bravely went back a day or two later to bring water, cook her some food, and cover her with a blanket. After that he, too, returned to the grand encampment of townsfolk—fearing to be caught by an earthquake within the city limits.

It didn't take too many days before the people there realized that the earthquakes had not just hit New Madrid. The refuges from Little Prairie could testify to that.

A boatman coming down the river later in the day on December 16 had noted in his log that much of the town of New Madrid appeared to be on fire. Even a simple pile of burning logs in a fireplace is a hazard in an earthquake. Today we have gas and fuel lines that can be ignited with sparks from broken electric wires. The fire hazard of earthquakes, present in 1811, is even greater today.

December 16 was the first day. By the New Year, with tremors almost daily, the residents of the area realized that it was not over yet. What they did not know was that the biggest quakes were yet to come.

"Up to the Belly of My Horse"

Several strong shocks, and numerous small ones, occurred during January, 1812, which seemed to increase in intensity with time. Louis Bringier was an engineer from New Orleans who, among other things, had spent many years living with the Indians who adopted him. It was said that he had even been elevated to the status of a "Chief," although to which tribe it was not known. During one of the larger events he was on horseback near New Madrid. His first person account was published in 1821 in the *American Journal of Science and Arts* (Vol. 3, pp. 15-46) As a scientist, his attention to detail is particularly valuable.

What he described here is the formation of an explosion sand blow crater. When a water table aquifer in the earth is successively squeezed by the vibrations of seismic waves over a period of time, groundwater can rapidly rise toward the surface pushing up a layer of air with such force that the sediments, themselves, are temporarily suspended by rushing air (air liquefaction). During this process, huge bubbles of air are blasted up into the atmosphere, raining soil and debris over a large area. The explosion creates a conical crater that may quickly fill with the rising groundwater which can flood the local area to a depth of several feet.

It was Tuesday, January 7, 1812, when these notes were recorded by Bringier: "It (gases from the ground) rushed out in all quarters, bringing with it carbonized wood, reduced to dust, which was ejected to the height of from ten to fifteen feet, and fell in a black shower, mixed with the sand which its rapid motion had forced along," wrote Bringier. "At the same time, the roaring and whistling produced by the impetuosity of the air escaping from its confinement seemed to increase the horrible disorder of the trees which everywhere encountered each other, being blown up, cracking and splitting, and falling by thousands at a time. In the meantime, the surface was sinking, and a black liquid was rising up to the belly of my horse, who stood motionless, struck with terror."

Bringier continues, "These occurrences occupied nearly two minutes. The trees kept falling here and there, and the whole surface of the country remained covered with holes, which resembled so many craters of volcanoes, surrounded with a ring of carbonized wood and sand, which rose to the height of about seven feet."

Seven months later Bringier measured the dimensions of some of these explosion sand blow craters. They varied from less than ten feet in diameter to more than fifty. Their depths were about half their diameters. Most were full of clear groundwater at a level of five to ten feet

"Up to the Belly of my Horse"

Illustration by Roberto Acuna

below their rims. Some were found to be as much as twenty feet deep— large enough to swallow a house. At the time Bringier measured them, much of the rim of sand about the craters had already washed into the center, partially filling them up.

Bringier described the appearance of the region prior to the earthquakes as being comprised of small prairies, or meadows, interspersed with patches of woods,. Afterwards, he said the area was covered with "slatches and sand hills" (earthquake ponds and sand boils). It must have looked like a moonscape.

Hundreds of these morphoseismic features, though modified in time, are still visible today. These seismic scars in the landscape, as they can be seen today, are documented in the two books, *The Earthquake that Never Went Away* and *The New Madrid Fault Finders Guide*.

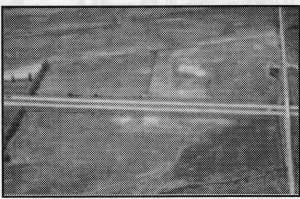

Seismic Explosion Craters Along Interstate Highway 55. In 1811-12 when the earthquakes blasted these craters in the ground, they were much deeper and had a rim around the edge, as described by Louis Bringier. These examples vary in size from 30 to 100 feet in diameter. The crater in the top photos is between New Madrid and Kewanee. The aerial photo shows three craters on either side of I-55 near Sikeston—one of which is shown in a ground view with two men. To the left is a soil-filled crater where water stands most of the year. The truck reflected there was speeding south on I-55.

Chaos at Island #13

Daniel Bedinger and his friend, Dr. Foster, were passengers on a barge, *The Louisville*, on its way to New Orleans when the earthquakes began. Excerpts from Bedinger's Journal were published in the March 14, 1812, issue of the *National Intelligencer* in Washington:

"December 13th, 1811: We arrived at the mouth of the Ohio, where she (the barge *Louisville*) fell in with the barges *Venus* and *Ohio*, whose captains were Hedington and Becktie. The Mississippi, it was observed, was lower than usual, though not so low as it has been. The banks presented an elevation, on an average, of about 20 feet above the surface of the river. The winds were light and the weather gloomy.

"December 14th. The temperature was 29 degrees Fahrenheit at sunrise and 46 degrees at three o'clock P.M. In the evening we came to at the

Island #8, as designated by the 'Navigator.'

"December 15th. . . . Got under way and touched at New Madrid, a fine handsome bank, but the place little improved. Descended the river to the Island #13. . . .The weather was very dark all day."

This would have placed the barge *Louisville* about ten river miles downstream from Point Pleasant and ten river miles upstream from Little Prairie. At the time, Daniel Bedinger and Dr. Foster would have been about 40 miles northeast of the first great shock of December 16. Today Island #13 no longer exists as an island but has merged with the Tennessee bank opposite Stewart Towhead on the Missouri side. That location would be about 12 miles southeast of Portageville, Missouri, and 8 miles southwest of Tiptonville, Tennessee, today.

Bedinger's journal continues: "December 16th. About 2 o'clock in the morning were alarmed by an unusual noise seemingly under the bottom of the barge, attended with a violent trembling and shaking of the vessel and, as all the boats in the company were, at the time, equally affected, all were soon convinced that the cause was no other than a violent shock of an earthquake which lasted (without intermission) about 40 seconds. Immediately after which the boats rolled considerably (though there was no wind).

"The river appeared to be much agitated. It was suddenly covered with a thick froth. It rose about 18 inches in a few minutes time and became very rapid where the vessels lay. But about two hours after, it sub-sided, and the current again became gentle. The froth, too, had passed down the stream and entirely disappeared before the day.

"In the meantime, the confusion that seemed to reign on all sides, was awfully alarming. Many acres of land in a body (as was discovered on the approach of day) had sunk to a surface level with the river, and some much lower, leaving only the tops of trees above water. Where the banks did not immediately tumble in, vast rents, or fissures, were made in the earth to an extent unknown. Some of these fissures received the waters of the river while others let out those of the neighboring lakes and ponds, with no inconsiderable roarings.

"Frequent rumbling sounds were heard, resembling distant thunder, and numerous heavy reports, indicative of explosions, seemingly from the bottom of the river and the lowlands adjacent, together with the crashing and falling of many large and heavy trees, at the same moment, seemed to threaten universal destruction.

"About 30 minutes after the first shock a second was felt. It was less violent and of shorter duration than the first. Two hours after (4:30-5:00 A.M.) another came on but was milder than either of the other two. From this time until day light nothing material occurred, except repeated rumbling sounds, seemingly, at a distance, and a continual falling in of the banks of the river.

"The boats now all got under way and moved in a line down the river. About half past 7 o'clock A.M. there was another shock, which for violence (it was agreed by all on board) exceeded the first, but it lasted only about 20 seconds. Soon after was seen (a short distance from the headmost boat) a large spout or body of water rising from the river to the height of about 18 or 20 feet, when it seemed to burst, and was instantaneously followed by a loud report. Similar reports were heard from the neighboring low grounds at various distances from the river."

Meanwhile, thousands of birds had taken to the air, alighting on the boats, and literally covering the canopies of the barges. The course of the Mississippi River is a major flight path for migratory water fowl from the north. The lower Mississippi Valley is the winter nesting grounds for millions of birds of all types. Countless numbers and species of wild birds were in the New Madrid Seismic Zone during the earthquakes. Bedinger and Foster reported seeing ducks, geese, egrets, cranes, terns, and dozens of varieties they had never seen before, flying in confusion and landing in large masses on the boats during the shocks that December morning. The frightened feathered flocks seemed less afraid of their natural enemies, the men on the boats, than of nature, herself. The squawking, screeching, cackling babel of the birds combined with the fluttering roar of thousands of wings created quite a din. The tumult only added to the confusion and the chaos of the turbulent river and the continuing turmoil of the tremors.

"A great number of old logs and trees of an enormous size were cast up to the surface from the bottom of the channel," Bedinger continued, "which caused the navigation (always difficult here) to be still more danger-

ous. The mischief done by these logs cannot be ascertained, but a Mr. Atwell of Salt River, Kentucky, lost two boats with their cargoes by the rising of one of them. His first boat was bilged [broken through on the bottom] and the other, being lashed to her, they both went down together. The people were saved,"

Bedinger's journal continues, referring to himself and his friend in third person. "The boats now were within a short distance of the village at the Little Prairie. Desirous of knowing what effects had been produced by the repeated shocks above mentioned, at and near that place, Dr. F. and D.B. got into the skiff and went ahead of the larger vessels. When they approached the town, they found it altogether unsafe to attempt a landing as the banks were all broken to pieces, and huge masses were, at short intervals, tumbling into the river. They, however, called aloud and were answered by a black man who shewed himself at some distance off. From him they understood that all the inhabitants but himself had, that morning, in the utmost consternation, fled into the country to the westward of the village. That the earth was broken up in many places and the openings filled with water. That the houses had all been much injured. That the only brick chimney in the place was entirely demolished, and that the shock at half past seven had been much more violent, terrible, and destructive than the first.

"As no further information could be obtained, Dr. F. and D.B. returned to the barges which, by this time, had passed the village. Below this place the country is an uninhabited wilderness for several hundred miles. They continued their course down the river. At 11 o'clock they felt another considerable shock, and 20 minutes after, another, not so severe."

The convoy of barges reached Island #23 that evening and made a landing there. This would have been just below the point where the Missouri and Arkansas State lines meet the river today. Bedinger and Foster made an excursion to the island and "found that every part of the beach, as well as the high land, had been much rent and torn to pieces. Numerous springs or holes remained which all had the appearance of having discharged large quantities of water, sand, mud, and pieces of wood which, in color and weight, greatly resembled mineral coal."

The convoy continued down the river the next day. On December 19 Bedinger noted that the temperature was a brisk 25 degrees at sunrise and only warmed up to 36 degrees by 3:00 P.M.

On December 21 they "anchored off of Fort Pickering at the fourth Chickasaw Bluff," the site that was later to become Memphis. They were told by the trading agency that "the earthquake had been felt there and also at the distance of 40 miles to the eastward but no damage done." This report, it turned out, was incomplete and premature. There had been considerable damage to the few settlements surrounding Fort Pickering for 100 miles in every direction.

The Louisville barge and its companion vessels continued downstream toward their destination, New Orleans. In that day, New Orleans was the giant of the southwest with a transient population in excess of 20,000 representing tongues and cultures from all over the world. The passengers and crew of the Louisville continued to feel shocks from time to time, but it was becoming clear that now they had passed the zone of greatest intensity. During the first week of January, 1812, they reached New Orleans in safety to tell their story and to hear from the residents of that city that they, too, had felt some of the shocks but had suffered no damage.

The Davis Party

Captain John Davis, a boatman with many years experience on the river, was guiding a party of forty boats down the Mississippi River in December of 1811. Some contained commercial cargo while others were family boats carrying immigrants to the west. He wrote a letter from Natchez to a friend in Sweet Springs, Virginia, dated January 5, 1812. The following are extracts from that letter:

"We arrived at night on the 15th of December at the 25th Island. On the 16th at 10 minutes past 2 o'clock we were surprised by the greatest commotion that can possibly be supposed of the boat, which I could compare to nothing more picturesque than that of a team of horses running away with a wagon over the most rocky road in our part of the country.

"There were about 40 boats in our company, and each thought his boat had broken adrift and was running over sawyers. An old navigator of the river just above our boat hailed us and said the disturbance was caused by the banks falling in. But a man on board of a boat lashed to us hinted it to be an earthquake.

"We were near a bluff bank which then suddenly cast off and fell in for about a quarter of a mile, which drew us into the current on the right side of the island where the water was shallow. We staid there till day.

"In the intermediate time, we experienced about 50 shocks which shook our boats with great agitation. At about 12 minutes after 7, we heard a tremendous distant noise, and in a few seconds the boats, island and mainland became perfectly convulsed. The trees twisted and lashed together. The earth in all quarters was sinking. And water issued from the centre of the 25th Isle just on our left and came rushing down its side in torrents. On our right there fell at once about 30 or 40 acres of land, I would say, although some say 300 acres."

"The shocks, by this time, became frequent at about every 15 minutes. The river rose from the first shock till about 8 o'clock, a total of 7 or 8 feet perpendicular and the current ran from 7 to 8 miles per hour. We ran from Island #25 and landed on Flour Island, a distance of 35 miles, in five hours and 25 minutes.

"The logs, which had sprung up from the bottom of the river, were so thick that it appeared almost impossible for a boat to find a passage. Three boats were sunk, two of which belonged to Mr. James Atwell, in value about $3000. The other was a family boat. The people were all saved except one man who belonged to the family boat. Another man was nearly lost from one of the boats that was

stove. He jumped on the sawyer that had bilged the boat and hung there for about four hours. Fortunately, he was taken into another boat."

Davis said that The Long Reach was so full of floating logs and roots it "gave the appearance of timbered fields." With the banks now under water and the surface of the river covered with timber, Davis said "it appeared as if the order of nature had been reversed," or that former water had become land and former land had become water.

Steamboat on Trial

The Roosevelt children, Rosetta and baby Henry, were both asleep now as the *New Orleans* lay quietly, anchored in the Territory of Indiana near Yellow Bank on the Ohio. Owensboro, Kentucky, is situated near there today. The crew was also resting, knowing that early tomorrow morning they would have to crank up the engine and feed the fire boxes for another leg of their journey. Henderson, Kentucky, was only 85 miles downstream, the half-way point of their 2,500 mile Odyssey. If they started early enough, they could be there before noon. Henderson, today, is located across the river from Evansville, Indiana, a town that had not yet been formed at the time of the quakes.

As the Roosevelts were preparing to turn in for the night, Lydia couldn't help noticing that Tiger seemed disturbed. The Great Labrador was afraid of something. As she tried to put him out, he refused to sleep in his accustomed place on the deck but insisted on staying in the cabin with the family. That was okay with the

Roosevelts, but Tiger had to understand that this was an exceptional night.

And an exceptional night it was. In the dark morning hours of December 16, the first of the great New Madrid earthquakes struck. To the occupants of the *New Orleans*, it was as if the boat had broken loose and suddenly run aground. When the vessel lurched, jerked by its anchor, everyone on board was awakened. "What was that?" they all wondered. By the first light of dawn they could see squatters gathered on the shore, shouting in fear and confusion. Some wanted to get aboard. Others blamed the monstrous hulk for the earthquake.

The fireboxes were already hot, building up a head of steam. Hastily, they pulled anchor and drifted away. Not yet realizing the cause of the disturbance, they thought, perhaps, that whatever it could be was probably coming from the direction of Louisville and that they were, therefore, going away from the disturbances by moving downstream. But, as they traveled, they began to notice huge chunks of freshly fallen bank along the river. Around 8 A.M. they noticed the trees on shore waving violently, but there was no wind. Occasional pieces of river bank fell into the turbid waters as they passed by, pulling trees and shrubbery with them. Andrew Jack steered to the middle, fearing the force of falling earth and the swells they created. Although they could not feel the shocks with their boat freely floating on the water, they could see that the land, itself, was periodically convulsing. It was then that they realized

they were experiencing earthquakes.

When they arrived at Henderson, the first thing that struck them was the absence of chimneys. It appeared as if the earthquakes had toppled every one. People were wandering about in a daze.

When the puffing blue hulk chugged toward land many thought that the devil incarnate had actually arrived and was shaking the earth with his great wheel. Some took to the woods, while others stood as if frozen, in a motionless stupor—victims of absolute fright.

Nicholas had hoped that stopping at the towns along the river to show off his steamboat would help sell merchants on the idea of using the boat for river commerce and, perhaps, entice more investors for their company. Now that the earthquakes had begun, his boat was being blamed for the disturbances. This was not good for business.

John and Lucy Audubon had no fears of the boat. They had already seen it and had come aboard in Louisville, six weeks before. They came out to greet Nicholas and Lydia and to see little Henry again, now a month-and-a-half old. The Audubons had spent most of the day cleaning up and trying to put things back on the shelves in their store—items shaken down by the earthquakes which had occurred repeatedly since early morning.

The Story of Cave-In-Rock

The next day *The New Orleans* passed Cave-In-Rock in the Illinois Territory. The wide entrance to this enormous system of caverns is high up in a bluff on the Illinois shore. For thousands of years it had sheltered Native Americans whose hieroglyphics painted the walls and whose artifacts were scattered throughout the chambers of the cave within. Around 1800 it was occupied by a marauding band of the Illinois Tribe.

In former centuries, the Illinois had been a proud race of highly sophisticated people who built giant pyramids of earth and administrated cities—some as populous as London and the urban giants of Europe at the same time. The word "Illinois" was an Indian word for "The Superior People." However, even before Columbus landed and Desoto crossed over the Mississippi, their civilization had already declined considerably from its former glory. With the encroachment of the white settlers, many of their numbers had been reduced to bitter bands, seeking revenge for the confiscation of their homeland.

The Illinois who lived at Cave-In-Rock at the turn of the century attacked river travelers as they passed—usually killing everyone, confiscating the cargo, and burning the boat. They also occasionally crossed over the Ohio and raided the homesteads of settlers on the Kentucky side—escaping to the security of their natural fortress in the Illinois bluff.

About 1803 a posse of Kentuckians crossed the river to deal with the Indian bandits and put an end to their attacks. But when the heavily armed platoon of pioneers arrived, they found the cave empty. The Indians in their cave camp were nowhere to be seen.

Suddenly a large group of red warriors appeared from the trees sur-rounding the mouth of the cave, overwhelming the white men and trapping them inside the caverns. They then built up a huge fire in the entrance with green wood, which suffocated most of the occupants. Those who survived the toxic smoke were bludgeoned to death with tomahawks, hacked to pieces and strewn over the floor of the cave. The Indians allowed only one survivor whom they instructed to return to his people and deliver this message:

"Tell your wise men that the Illinois have glutted their vengeance and that their spirit is satisfied and appeased. On the borders of the lake [Ohio River] we will bury the hatchet. Woe to those who make us take it from the ground."

Following the massacre at Cave-In-Rock, the Illinois fled the area, never to be seen nor heard of again. When the gruesome remains of the posse were discovered, they were all gathered up at one end of the cave's entrance and buried with a marker to attest to the tragedy. For the next year or so, it became a custom for curious river navigators to stop and view the makeshift monument.

A couple of years later, around 1805, the cave became possessed by a party of Kentuckians called "The Wilson Gang." First settling in with his family, Wilson fitted it up as a spacious dwelling. A sign was posted on the riverside that said: "Wilson's Liquor Vault and House for Entertainment."

According to Thomas Ashe, a British explorer who came down the Ohio River in 1806, "The novelty of such a tavern induced most all boats descending the river to call and stop for refreshment and amusement. Attracted by these circumstances, several idle characters took up their abode at the cave, after which it continually resounded with the shouts of the licentious, the clamor of riot, and the blasphemy of gamblers. Out of such customers as these Wilson found no difficulty in forming a band of robbers, with whom he formed the plan of murdering the crews of every boat that stopped at his tavern and sending the boats, manned by some of his party, to New Orleans and there selling their lading for cash—which was to be conveyed back to the cave by land through the states of Tennessee and Kentucky."

The reckless scheme worked for awhile. Wilson and his band of about 45 men did, in fact, confiscate a number of boats. They were actually able to find willing agents at Natchez and New Orleans to dispose of their ill-gotten contraband and who paid them cash. The people of the region soon became alarmed at the numbers of boats and crews that disappeared downriver, never to return. Wilson and his pirates at Cave-In-Rock were eventually identified as the cause of these crimes, and a price was put on Wilson's head. The ruthless band dispersed. Some were taken prisoners while others became fugitives on the frontier. As for Wilson, himself, he was killed by one of his associates who was tempted by the reward.

The Roosevelts knew the infamous history of this cave but also knew that it no longer harbored the threat to river traffic that it once had. Two years before, on their first trip, they had stopped to explore the fascinating caverns. The cave had been quite

visible from the river through the leaves of the catalpa trees that shaded its mouth. But today, as they passed again, the huge opening was only partially visible. A large landslide from above had partially blocked the entrance, the result of the earthquake the day before. For the next 100 years, it would be nicknamed "Rocking Cave."

Fearful that high banks could collapse onto their boat and bury them in the night should the earth move again, Captain Nicholas decided to tie up on islands in the middle of the river whenever possible. It was getting late, and they needed to stop. So they tied up on the downstream toe of Hurricane Island, just below Cave-In-Rock and only thirty-five miles above Smithland and the Lewis Plantations.

Early on December 18, 1811, they churned past the farms of Lilbourn and Randolph Lewis and past Smithland, Kentucky. Several times a day they could see trees swaying along the banks in response to earth movements. During the strongest shocks, taller trees would sometimes interlock their branches and remain frozen in an unnatural embrace. The caving banks and other signs of earthquake activity, visible from the *New Orleans*, seemed to be increasing in size and number. It was becoming evident to the crew and passengers that they were moving closer to the source of the disturbances, not further. Even more disturbing was the fact that the river that now lay before them had been changed by the quakes and was being changed even more by every passing tremor. Zadoc Cramer's carefully constructed maps and notes were becoming more and more useless as they progressed downriver. They were now plying uncharted waters that were changing almost daily.

Chased by Indians

On December 18 the Roosevelts traversed the last few miles of the Ohio before meeting the Mississippi. Once they had passed Smithland they knew they were in Indian Territory and would be, for the most part, until they got to New Madrid. Nicholas was hoping they would not have to go ashore for fuel.

"Penelore" is what the Indians called it. "Fire canoe." While the redskins upstream had retreated in fear or stood paralyzed in awe, these Indians were different. They had already connected the fiery sparks issuing from the stack of the steamboat with the blazing train of the comet in the sky. Like some of the squatters at Yellow Bank and some of the residents of Henderson, these Indians held the strange, blustering, fire-breathing hulk responsible for the earthquakes. If only they could kill the monster, the quakes would stop. But who would be brave enough for that?

Lydia was remembering when two Indian intruders boarded their flatboat two years ago, how afraid she was then, and how Nicholas had driven them off. Several canoes full of Indians were now rowing rapidly, approaching the steamboat. Who were they? Were they the same Illinois Tribesmen who had pirated boats at Cave-In-Rock a few years earlier? Those Indians left no survivors! If these warriors managed to get on board, what would they do?

"More wood!" shouted Andrew Jack to the engineer and his Creole firemen. Furiously they threw the logs into the fire. As the boat suddenly belched with additional steam and smoke and picked up speed, several of the canoes fell back.

But then ahead of them they saw the biggest canoe of all. Speeding along the water's edge it contained more Indians than there were people on the *New Orleans*. No signs of peace did they show. It was clear that they were steering for a confrontation course with the steamboat. It was also clear that the anticipated encounter would not be friendly. Did they have rifles? Would they shoot arrows? Would they try to jam the great paddle wheels and cripple their means of locomotion? Would they attempt to board? Was this a suicide mission? Would they try to ram the steamer and crack its hull?

"More wood! More steam!" Andrew screamed again. Baker and his crew redoubled their labors. Fires blazing, stacks puffing, steam sissing, safety valves straining, pistons beating, tempos accelerating, picking up the pitch, the *New Orleans* was in a grim race with the giant death canoe. Parallel, and along side, they raced. Closer and closer the red man's vessel slid toward the side of the steamboat. They were in a dead heat, the treacherous river for their track. Unlike the massive hulk of the steamer, the canoe could maneuver into the current and out. Would it be the river to make the final determination? Which craft would it favor?

Suddenly the steamboat jerked, lurched and shuddered as if it were breaking apart. Unable to steer clear at such speed, they had just clamored over a large floating log, the paddle wheels walking right over the obstacle as it lay emersed just beneath the waves.

Then slowly, the dreaded dugout began to drift backwards relative to the speeding steamboat. With one final burst of power, the *New Orleans* pulled decisively ahead. They had done it! The pilot, the engineer, and the crew all broke into cheers!

Nicholas was jubilant. The steamboat had proven itself. The engine had performed wonderfully under the utmost conditions of stress. Congratulating the crew, he grabbed two and three of them at once in an embrace of relief and gratitude. Engineer Baker, sweaty and smudged with soot, emerged from below deck to find out if "Missy" was okay. She was standing with Lydia, holding little Henry. She blushed and nodded. Everyone was safe. Penelore had beaten the Indians this time, but what about the next time?

There would be other Indians along the way. Would word about the "devil boat" be passed on ahead of them? What would the red men say? Perhaps it would be said that the magic of Penelore was mightier than the magic of all the medicine men and that the great fire canoe should be allowed to pass, unmolested, for the rest of their journey.

Soon after the chase, they came to the end of the Ohio and entered that vast expanse where two mighty rivers merge and mingle their waters from there to the Gulf of Mexico. Only 80 miles from New Madrid, they planned to make a stop there the next day to rest and to take on some food staples.

As they approached Island #1 in the Mississippi, they could see the bluff where Fort Jefferson had been. Only now it wasn't much of a bluff anymore. Unstead they saw a tangled slope of fallen trees, twisted vines, and blocks of broken rock and soil. Where the Fort had been was now the tumbled scarp of a fresh landslide. They didn't stop. They were anxious to make a few more miles toward New Madrid.

Evening was approaching, and they needed a safe place to tie up for the night. Would Indians come again? Would they use stealth this time, gliding silently through the waters to board under cover of darkness and take them in their sleep?

Nicholas and Andrew consulted their copy of Zadoc Cramer's *Navigator.* They had counted the islands since entering the Ohio and figured they were just passing Island #4. The next island, which was a couple of miles ahead, was already well in view. It was one of the largest on the river, 15,000 acres in size, and nearly ten miles long on its western side—the shoreline facing the main channel. Also known as "Wolf Island," Mr. James Hunter lived there with his family—raising pigs, cattle, and domestic geese which he supplied to passing boats and barges. They thought about entering the chute on the east side where they could, perhaps, obtain some meat from Mr. Hunter, but they decided to stay in the main channel since they would soon be stopping at New Madrid where they could get everything they needed. There were no Indians on this Island. Cramer's notes indicated the presence of a sand bar at the

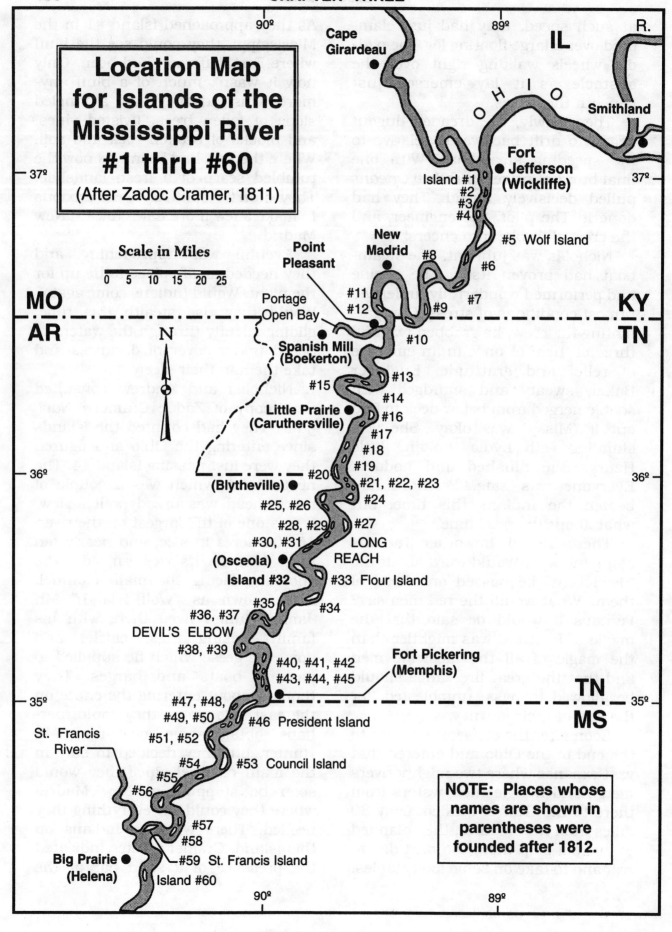

**Location Map
for Islands of the
Mississippi River
#1 thru #60**
(After Zadoc Cramer, 1811)

Scale in Miles
0 5 10 15 20 25

N

MO
AR

KY
TN

TN
MS

IL

O H I O   R.

Cape Girardeau

Smithland

Fort Jefferson (Wickliffe)

Island #1
#2
#3
#4
#5 Wolf Island
#6
#7
#8
#9
#10
New Madrid

Point Pleasant

Portage Open Bay

#11
#12

Spanish Mill (Boekerton)

#13
#14
#15
#16
#17
#18
#19
#20
#21, #22, #23
#24
#25, #26
#27
#28, #29
#30, #31
LONG REACH
#33 Flour Island

Little Prairie (Caruthersville)

(Blytheville)

(Osceola)

Island #32

#34
#35
#36, #37
DEVIL'S ELBOW
#38, #39
#40, #41, #42
#43, #44, #45
Fort Pickering (Memphis)

#47, #48, #49, #50
#46 President Island

St. Francis River

#51, #52
#53 Council Island
#54
#55
#56
#57
#58
#59 St. Francis Island
Island #60

Big Prairie (Helena)

NOTE: Places whose names are shown in parentheses were founded after 1812.

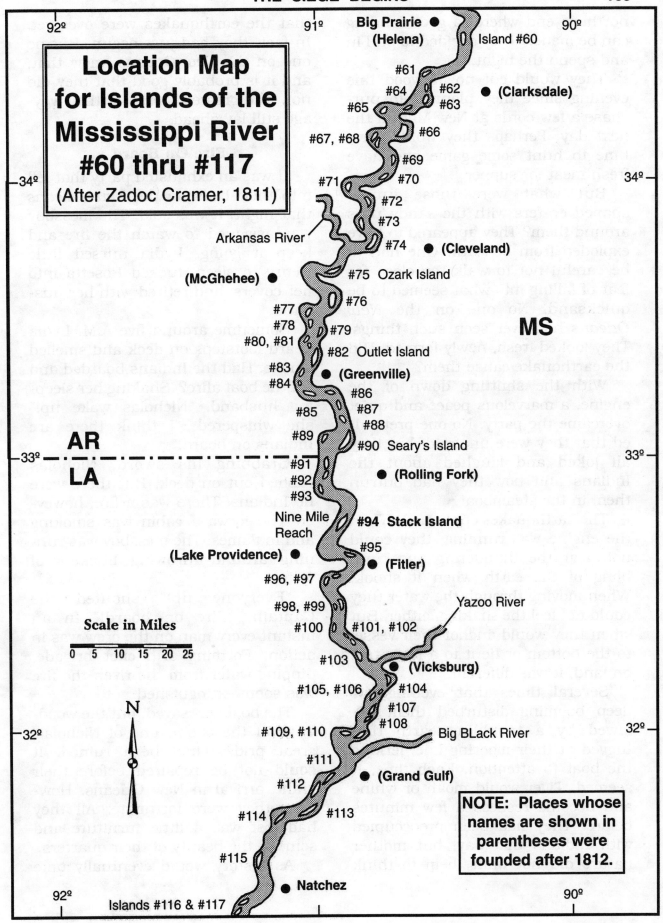

Big Prairie
(Helena)

Island #60

#61

#64   #62
             #63
#65

             #66
#67, #68

             #69
             #70
#71
             #72
             #73
Arkansas River
             #74   (Cleveland)

(McGhehee)   #75   Ozark Island

             #76
#77
#78   #79
#80, #81
             #82   Outlet Island
#83
#84   (Greenville)
             #86
             #87
#85   #88
#89
             #90   Seary's Island

#91
#92   (Rolling Fork)
#93
Nine Mile   #94   Stack Island
Reach
             #95
(Lake Providence)   (Fitler)

#96, #97   Yazoo River
#98, #99
#100   #101, #102

             #103   (Vicksburg)
#105, #106   #104
                  #107
                  #108
#109, #110   Big BLack River
             #111
             #112   (Grand Gulf)
#114   #113

#115

Natchez
Islands #116 & #117

**Location Map
for Islands of the
Mississippi River
#60 thru #117**

(After Zadoc Cramer, 1811)

AR
LA

MS

Scale in Miles
0   5   10   15   20   25

N

NOTE: Places whose
names are shown in
parentheses were
founded after 1812.

92°   91°   90°
34°   34°
33°   33°
32°   32°
92°   90°

northern end where "a good landing can be made." They decided to pull in and spend the night.

They would cut no firewood this evening since they planned to purchase a few cords at New Madrid the next day. Perhaps they would have time to hunt some game and have fresh meat for supper.

But what were those funnel shaped craters with the sandy rims around them? They appeared to have exploded from beneath. One had to be careful not to walk too close for fear of falling into what seemed to be quicksand. No one on the *New Orleans* had ever seen such things. They looked fresh, newly formed. Did the earthquake cause them?

With the shutting down of the engine, a marvelous peace and quiet overcame the party. No one pretended that they were unafraid, but they all joked and laughed about the Indians and how they had outrun them in the steamboat.

The earthquakes continued. When the engine was running, they could not hear the thundering and rumbling of the earth when it shook. When moving through the water they could not feel the shaking, either. But when they would anchor their vessel to the bottom or tie it to a large tree on land, it was different.

Several times that evening the deep booming disturbed them followed by a trembling earth that tugged at their mooring line, jerking the boat to attention. Each time, it seemed, Tiger would moan or whine and become restless a few minutes before. They had been preoccupied with Indians that day, but mother nature did not want them to think

that the earthquakes were over yet. In fact, they had just begun. But no one on the *New Orleans* knew that, and it is probably good that they did not. The greatest perils of their voyage still lay ahead.

Fire On Board

It was an exhausted party that fell into their beds on the *New Orleans* that night. It was cold. The messboy was assigned to watch the fire and keep it going. Lydia nursed little Henry to sleep, tucked Rosetta into her covers, and retired with her husband.

Sometime around five A.M. Lydia heard footsteps on deck and smelled smoke. Had the Indians boarded and set the boat afire? Shaking her sleeping husband, "Nicholas wake up!" she whispered, "I think there are Indians on board."

Grabbing his sword, Nicholas rushed out on deck. But there were no Indians. There was a fire, however. The forward cabin was smoking and in flames. The messboy was running around throwing buckets of water.

"Everyone up!" shouted the Captain, "Fire on board!" In an instant every man on the crew was in action. Forming a bucket brigade, dipping water from the river, the fire was soon extinguished.

The boat was saved, but the woodwork of the cabin, one of Nicholas' great prides, had been ruined. It could not be repaired before their grand arrival in New Orleans. However, they were fortunate. All they had lost was a little furniture and some of the beauty of their quarters.

As history would eventually take

tragic note that the greatest enemy of the steamboat was neither Indian, nor river, nor earthquake. It was fire—the very element that gave them their edge. For the next one hundred years the victory of steam over man-power would exact a terrible toll in human life in horrible explosions, floating conflagrations, and scalding steam baths that killed more than statisticians ever counted.

The cause of the fire, it appeared, was a bit of negligence on the part of the messboy. Some of the wood was damp, and he had leaned a few logs against the hot stove to dry them out. He had then fallen asleep, and they caught fire. After a serious scolding from Captain Roosevelt, he let up on the boy. After all, they were all exhausted and under great tension. It could have happened to any one of them. No one was hard on him. No one had wanted a fire. But, then, who had signed up for an Indian attack or an earthquake either?

Although there were many triumphs, it was beginning to seem as if this boat and this voyage were cursed. Perhaps the church ladies in Pittsburgh were right. Maybe Sunday was not a good day to start a business trip after all.

On their way to New Madrid, several strong tremors shook the trees on the banks while huge boils welled up in the river. As they passed Islands #8 and #9, about 20 miles above New Madrid, the troubled waters became more and more turbid. Thousands of logs and uprooted trees were floating everywhere, posing hazards never before seen on these waters. Planters (trees stuck solidly on the bottom but just at or below the surface where they could gash the belly of a boat) were everywhere in the shallower waters. Sawyers (floating trees or logs with one end fixed that undulated up and down with the waves in a sawing motion) were bobbing in great numbers from both banks, as well as from shallow shoals in the middle or the river.

Roosevelt's Steamboat Reaches New Madrid

When the *New Orleans* finally arrived at New Madrid on December 19, it was only to be greeted by the ghost of a town. A few boats were tied up in Chepoussea Creek (St. John's Bayou), but the bustling, busy river port that had been New Madrid was no more. It was in a shambles, partially burned and partially shaken down. Mostly, it was abandoned. As the *New Orleans* idled a few yards from the shore, the few stragglers left behind motioned from the bank for the steamer to dock and rescue them and take them away from this place of horror. They did not care to where. They just wanted a passage out.

The New Orleans needed supplies, but it did not appear that New Madrid would be in a position to offer them. While Lydia and Nicholas felt sorry for the pathetic people on the shore, they were reluctant to let the boat land for fear they would be flooded with refugees. So they passed on without docking or going ashore.

Because Lydia was breastfeeding little Henry, there was no problem with food for the baby. As for meat for the others, black bear, white tailed deer, wild turkey, and other game were plentiful and easy to obtain anywhere along the river—not to mention the bounty of fish available throughout these waters. At the speed they were now making, they could be in New Orleans in less than a month. Natchez was on the way. Surely the earthquakes had not destroyed Natchez. Besides, there were other villages along the way—Point Pleasant, Little Prairie, and Big Prairie. Surely they could get a few eggs, some cornmeal and flour, and a little produce somewhere.

The passengers on the *New Orleans* were grateful to be on board a boat, thinking that the brunt of the earthquake was being borne by those on land. Little did they know that the most hazardous place of all was the river. Most of the deaths from the earthquake were either on or near the water. Chances of their making it through alive were slim. But they did not know that.

During their voyage that day, they could see more and more signs of the earthquake and its devastating toll along the river. Whole groves of trees were snapped off. Others were under water with only the top limbs projecting above. Missing sections of river bank, some more than a mile long, had been observed with increasing frequency ever since they had entered the Mississippi. Things were definitely getting worse below New Madrid.

But the most disturbing signs were the empty vessels and drifting cargo. Abandoned flat boats, crewless keelboats, barrels, bales, boxes, splintered timbers, a dead horse, a bloated hog, floating cattle, drowned chickens, and most disturbing of all, the occasional sight of a hat or a jacket surfacing in those churning waters. Meanwhile, black buzzards roosted in the treetops along the bank, the sentinels of death. These were not good signs.

And there was something else they had already noticed, even before they left the waters of the Ohio: For the last three days, since December 16th, they had not met a single boat coming upstream.

With the evidence of wrecked boats here and there, would the *New Orleans* suffer a similar fate? Waterfalls. Indians. Fires. Earthquakes. What peril had they not faced already? So far they had prevailed. But things also seemed to be getting worse as they continued downriver.

With a channel altered by earthquakes, Andrew Jack could no longer follow Cramer's *Navigator.* He had piloted boats through this reach several times before, but nothing looked familiar anymore. All he could do was to follow the course of the current's swiftest flow as the best sign of the deepest channel. But such a practice was not always certain. One could be led into snags, whirling eddies, and other perils of those turbulent waters. Planters and sawyers were everywhere.

Twenty miles downstream from New Madrid they approached Point Pleasant on the water's edge. But no one on shore came to meet them. The tiny village was a ghost town, abandoned and awaiting its final destiny which, at that time, had not yet come. Its days were numbered. Unable to purchase any supplies there, they continued.

Twenty-five miles further they approached the site of Little Prairie. Perhaps they could stop here. But what they found was not a town. Sunken cabins, shattered trees, partially flooded, the settlement desolate and deserted. No sign of human life could be seen. Only the birds and the vultures were there. Little Prairie was gone, lost to the river and to the earthquakes.

New Madrid had been badly damaged, but this was much more. The effects of the earthquakes seemed to get visibly worse as they descended the river. How much worse would it get before they could extricate themselves from this "river of no return?" What would they find at the next village, Big Prairie? And what was the fate of Nachez? New Orleans? They did not know, and no boats were coming upstream to inform them.

It was late afternoon, and the sky was rapidly growing dark. It looked like a winter storm was brewing in the west. They had gone far enough for a day. Tying up just below Island #16, they spent a relatively uneventful night. By this time, the occasional shudders of another shake did not even wake them. Island #16 is below Caruthersville, today, where Interstate #155 crosses over the Mississippi River.

Logjam in Long Reach

The next morning a light snow was falling. They passed Island #20, which is where the Missouri and Arkansas state lines touch the Mississippi River. When they reached Island #25 they were shocked to see many acres of land under water, sunk by the earthquakes until only the treetops were showing. Even part of Island #25 had sunk below the water while its trees were broken and

tilted in every direction, some laying on the ground.

The stretch below this island was called "Long Reach." Normally, a clear course without any navigational problems at all, today it was clogged with newly created sandbars and an impassable mass of roots and trees. The passengers and crew aboard the *New Orleans* counted the wreckage of three boats smashed into the log jam. They were to learn later that this was part of the Davis party where at least one man had perished in the crash. The trees formed a great raft that completely blocked the channel. In order to pass through, four of the crew launched the rowboat and set out to clear a passageway with muscle power and axes.

As they hacked away, the *New Orleans* shut down. Only the soft shush of the flowing waters could be heard. In the still of the waiting ship, the thunder of more temblors periodically interrupted the calm, slapping the hull of the boat with shock waves and rippling the surface of the river. Several times the stream boiled nearby bringing sticks, sand, and red mud to the surface, giving the waters the appearance of dark blood. Meanwhile, noxious gases, the odors of sulfur and rotting vegetation, permeated the atmosphere.

It took them several hours to form a narrow corridor through the logs through which Andrew Jack was able to thread the long blue ark of the *New Orleans* with precision. They were free again and on their way.

Zadoc Cramer's next edition of the *Navigator* was to contain these comments: "Island #25 is about a mile long. It has been severely handled by the earthquake. From this island you have a fine view of The Long Reach, about ten miles in length. At the lower end is now a dangerous bar in the middle of the river. The pass is difficult, the river being filled here with snags. The best channel is on the right side of the bar, two-thirds over from the right shore. Since the earthquakes this has become one of the most dangerous places in low water between the Ohio and New Orleans."

Tied Up On Island #32

The temperature was falling and it was still snowing. The wind was beginning to pick up. Not wishing to find themselves caught in a winter storm on open waters, they did not try to go much further that day. It was mid-afternoon when they arrived at Island #32 not too far below the logjam. It seemed like a good time and place to stop.

Again, they noticed some strange craters in the sandy shores of the Island, like the ones they had seen on Island #16 the previous day and on Wolf Island two days before. They eventually realized that these giant pockmarks in the land surface had been caused by earthquakes, but it would be more than a century later before scientists and engineers would come to understand that these were liquefaction features—places where temporary quicksand conditions had been induced by seismic ground motion. Island #32 was about three miles long, with a heavy growth of timber. Slowly drifting along the east side, they slipped around the southern toe and tied up on the downstream end so they would not be

struck by the trees and floating debris swept by the swift current.

Island #32 is close to the site of present-day Osceola, Arkansas. An Indian camp was there at the time of the earthquakes. Nicholas and Lydia did not know this fact, but they would not have to worry about Indian attacks from that village tonight. The right bank along that stretch had been inundated during the quakes earlier in the week—drowning the encampment of Indians. It was Friday, December the 20th.

The crew took the rowboat to the Island to tie the heavy hawser of the steamboat securely to a large tree. They then set about to gather wood for the next day and haul it back on board. For the first time in days, there was a sense of hope and tranquility among the crew and passengers of the *New Orleans*. Perhaps they were through the worst of it.

Again, they slept through what they had thought was another uneventful night—except for a few thumps from earthquakes. They had not paid much attention during the night as they were getting used to them by this time. About 4:30 in the morning, however, Lydia was awakened by an unusually strong tugging of the boat that lasted for more than a minute and made the boat bounce up and down. There also seemed to be a pulling sensation from upstream. It was still dark. Lydia rolled over and went back to sleep.

At daylight, the next morning, Nicholas Baker, the engineer, was the first on deck. Gazing upstream, Island #32 was nowhere to be seen. It first flashed into his mind that the boat had broken loose during the night and they were drifting with the current. But a glance toward the far shore showed that they were stationary. But how could that be? They were in the middle of the river, hundreds of feet from the nearest land.

The boat seemed to be listing slightly to the north. Baker leaned over the bow to see the mooring rope taut and pulled almost straight down into the murky depths of the river. The top of the tree to which it was tied was barely visible beneath the swirling waters. Island #32 had sunk during the 4:30 A.M. temblor, pulling the anchor rope with it. Luckily, Captain Roosevelt had allowed plenty of slack the night before, or the vessel could have been drawn under and sunk with the island. Lucky, too, that the quake had occurred when everyone was on ship and not while the men were on the island wooding up with fuel.

Cutting the taut line and leaving it behind, the *New Orleans* turned into the current and continued its southward journey. Zadoc Cramer lived at Natchez. They would have to tell him to take Island #32 off of his map in the next edition of *The Navigator*.

By this time everyone on the boat was beginning to conclude that Providence was on their side, after all. Their survival to this point was nothing short of miraculous. Truly, as they had anticipated, the worst was over. By this time, they could even anticipate some of the shocks before they hit. Tiger would move toward Lydia, moaning and trembling, and lay his head on her lap—a sure sign of a tremor about to begin.

On December 22nd they reached the mouth of the St. Francis River and spent the night. There they met John Bradbury, the British naturalist. They were glad to see another boat with living people on it. Bradbury was the first human contact they had made outside their own vessel for days.

It was there that they learned of the disappearance of Big Prairie, Arkansas. They were also told by Bradbury that a day or two before, on December 21st at half past four in the morning, a good shaker had toppled some trappers' cabins. Nicholas had an even better story to tell on that same quake.

"We were tied up on Island #32," he told John, "and the whole island disappeared during the night. It nearly pulled us under. We're lucky to be alive!"

Zadoc Cramer's next edition would note the following concerning Islands #31, #32, and #33: "At the lower end of No. 31 are now a number of snags and sawyers. Opposite, on the left side, is a sand bar, of No. 32, (Destroyed by the earthquake.) This large bar begins two miles above where used to stand No. 32 and extends three miles down. Keep in with the left shore passing No. 31 until you get near the point, then strike over for the right hand shore, leaving the sand bar of No. 32 on your left. The river here is much filled with snags and sawyers.

"No. 33, Flour Island, is near the middle of the river, main channel now right side, keeping as close to the right hand point as the water will admit of . . . This island takes its name from having had flour boats wrecked upon it."

Maiden Voyage of the
THE NEW ORLEANS
First Steamboat to Enter the Ohio & Mississippi Rivers
October 20, 1811, to January 10, 1812
from Pittsburgh to New Orleans
Under the Command of
Captain Nicholas Roosevelt

KEY TO
NEW ORLEANS STEAMBOAT TRIP MAP

1. **Sunday, Oct. 20, 1811.** Leave Pittsburgh, Pennsylvania.
2. **Oct. 22-23.** First Stop. Spend night anchored at Wheeling, Virginia.
3. **Oct. 24-25.** Stop to purchase fire wood. Point Pleasant, Virginia.
4. **Oct. 27.** Pass Cincinnati, Ohio..
5. **Oct. 29.** Arrive at Louisville, Kentucky, around midnight. Henry Latrobe Roosevelt born October 30 on board New Orleans. First steamboat birth in history. Boat remains at Louisville next five weeks.
6. **Sunday, Dec. 8.** Leave Louisville. Pass over the Falls of the Ohio.
7. **Dec. 8-12.** Layover at Shippingport, Kentucky.
8. **Dec. 14-16.** Layover at Yellow Bank, Indiana to rest and take on coal. New Madrid earthquakes begin on 16th.
9. **Dec. 16.** Stop at Henderson, Kentucky, to see John & Lucy Audubon and survey earthquake damage.
10. **Dec. 16-17.** Spend night at Hurricane Island just below Cave-In-Rock, Illinois.
11. **Dec. 18.** Pass Smithland and reach mouth of Ohio. Chased by Indians from Illinois side.
12. **Dec. 18-19.** First night on Mississippi. Tied up on Wolf Island. Fire on board during night watch.
13. **Dec. 19.** Pass New Madrid, Point Pleasant, and Little Prairie.
14. **Dec. 19-20.** Tied up on Island #16 just below remains of Little Prairie.
15. **Dec. 20.** Logjam on Long Reach.

16. **Dec. 20-21.** Tied up on Island #32, which disappeared during the night, nearly pulling the New Orleans under.
17. **Dec. 21-22.** Stopped to cut fuel wood on President Island, just below Fort Pickering.
18. **Dec. 22-23.** Spend night near mouth of St. Francis, and learn about disappearance of Big Prairie from John Bradbury party.
19. **Dec. 23-24.** Spend night tied up on Island #66 and gather more wood for fuel.
20. **Dec. 24-27.** Spend three days relaxing, hunting, and fishing at Ozark Island, just below mouth of Arkansas River. Wild goose and fresh venison for Christmas Dinner.
21. **Dec, 27-28.** Spent night tied to Seary's Island (Is. #90) across from boundary between Upper and Lower Louisiana. (33º latitude)
22. **Dec. 28.** Pass through Nine Mile Reach and notice that Island #94 is missing.
23. **Dec. 28-30.** Tied up on Island #99, a few miles upstream from the mouth of the Yazoo River and high bluff where Vicksburg, Mississippi would some day be founded.
24. **Dec. 29-30.** Island #111 near mouth of Big Black River.
25. **Dec. 30.** Arrive at Natchez, Mississippi, On December 31, Nicholas Baker, the engineer, marries Missy, Lydia's maid, on board New Orleans. First steamboat marriage in history.
26. **Jan. 1.** Leave Natchez.
27. **Friday, Jan 10, 1812.** Arrive at New Orleans.

On to Natchez

The *New Orleans* was now 400 miles from Natchez and 600 from New Orleans. On Christmas Eve they arrived at the mouth of the Arkansas River and decided to land at Ozark Island and rest. They stayed three days fishing, hunting, relaxing, and fixing up the boat. For Christmas dinner they had a feast of wild goose and fresh venison. Since the early morning temblor of December 21 that sank Island #32 had nearly sunk their boat, they had felt no more earthquakes. They were all relieved to realize that, at last, they were moving further from the source, not closer. On December 27 they loosed anchor and continued their trip, reaching the northern boundary of the Orleans Territory on the evening of December 28.

The next day they passed through Nine Mile Reach where Island #94 should have been plainly visible in the middle of the river. On clear days the Island could be easily spotted in the distance a good four miles away. But today is was nowhere to be seen. Where the Island should have been there was nothing but snags, a sand bar, and swirling water. Andrew Jack made a note to tell Cramer that two islands, not just one, were now missing. Not until they reached Natchez would they learn of Captain Sarpy's narrow escape and the fate of the pirates on Stack Island. That night they tied up on Island #99, a few miles upstream from the mouth of the Yazoo River and the high bluff where Vicksburg would later be established.

On December 30th they arrived at Natchez, first capital of the Mississippi Territory, cotton center, health resort, a hub of southern commerce, and boom town. Founded in 1716, it was the oldest town on the Mississippi, older even than New Orleans. Towering two hundred feet above the river, it boasted itself to be the most beautiful, most prosperous, the wildest, roughest, most sinful, and most exciting town along the river.

News of the strange new boat had already reached them. Hundreds gathered on the bluff to see the *New Orleans* glide in. The Roosevelts were relieved to find Natchez intact after the damages they had seen to less fortunate settlements up the river. The people at Natchez had felt four strong shocks on the morning of December 16th and a number of lesser ones since. According to Myron Fuller, "Many houses were shaken, suspended objects swung to and fro, some plastered walls were cracked, a few articles fell from shelves, and several clocks were stopped. The surface of the river was agitated, and parts of the banks fell in. The tops of the trees waved from side to side but there seems to have been little or no noise at Natchez." Natchez suffered only minor losses from the earthquakes.

City officials were on hand, as was Zadoc Cramer, anxious to receive the latest reports of river conditions. Sam and Jane Davis were also there with their youngest boy, Jeff. Although he was too young to appreciate it at the time, later, when he would become a successful plantation owner, his ability to market his cotton and, therefore, his profits would depend, to a great extent, on the invention of the steamboat which he was seeing for the first time at the age of three. Neither could little Jefferson Davis know that 50 years later he would be the President of the Confederate States of America who would use steamboats to fight a Civil War.

Meanwhile, the engineer, Nicholas Baker, had popped the question to Lydia's maid. With the birth of Henry Labtrobe Roosevelt on October 30th, the *New Orleans* had been cradle to the world's first childbirth on a steamboat. Today, on December 31st, 1811, it would be host and witness to the first steamboat wedding ceremony. There would be many to follow.

The 30th of December marked the ninth day since the passengers of the New Orleans had felt an earthquake. Then, at 4:05 A.M. on December 31, the City of Natchez was awakened again by the passing of a tremor.

The next morning, on New Year's Day, 1812, the Roosevelts left Natchez. Ten days later, on Friday, January 10, the steamboat *New Orleans* made its triumphal entry into the metropolis of New Orleans. A motley multilingual throng of excited observers waved to them along the banks of the river city—including Daniel Bedinger and Dr. Foster who had arrived only a few days before.

Edward Livingston, Robert's youngest brother, was on hand to step aboard and congratulate Nicholas, Lydia, and their crew for a successful maiden voyage. Not once in their long and perilous Odyssey did they have to resort to sails or oars. The era of steam-powered boats had been launched. Life along the Mississippi would never be the same again for two reasons: steamboats and earthquakes.

The Unpleasant Fate of Point Pleasant

The earthquake ordeal was over for the Roosevelts and their companions on the steamboat. But for those they left behind in New Madrid and the surrounding territories, the worst was yet to come.

Thursday, January 23, 1812, was less than two weeks after the *New Orleans* had safely harbored a thousand river miles distance—outside the damaging grip of the New Madrid Fault, but not outside of its touch. On that day, about 9:00 in the morning, another massive shock burst forth. It was clearly felt in New Orleans, but no harm resulted to the city.

This earthquake has been estimated at 8.4 on the Richter scale. It is thought to have been centered about ten miles south of the riverside settlement of Point Pleasant, Missouri. Although few details were recorded, it is known that the entire community was destroyed and thrown into the river. In fact, the entire point that had projected into the river and which had given the town its name was gone. Whether any deaths or injuries resulted is not known. None were recorded. So far as is known, the settlement had been abandoned shortly after the onset of the disturbances. No one was there on December 19th to witness the passing of the *New Orleans*. And no one appears to have been there a month later when the entire town collapsed into the river.

Apparently, everyone had evacuated to New Madrid. The residents of

Point Pleasant Today. The top view shows Point Pleasant from the air, with the Mississippi River in the foreground and the levee curving around the town a mile from the water's edge. The light colored streaks are seismic sand fissures from the earthquakes of 1811-12. On the bottom left is the road into town with a sign saying POINT PLEASANT and a corner of the levee visible behind. The right photo is a view from the levee of the town, itself.

Point Pleasant did not know the fate of their tiny town until late February when several went back to find that it had vanished without a trace. Until after 1900, the river occupied the site. Today, the river has migrated to the west such that the the original location of Point Pleasant now lies in Tennessee, over two miles from the river.

A more recently organized community of the same name now occupies a location across the river and five miles to the northwest of the original site. This time the founders wisely avoided the river bank. It sets about one mile inland from the water's edge.

Twentieth century Point Pleasant is directly over one of the presently most active portions of the New Madrid fault. People there experience microtremors on a regular basis. Point Pleasant is about fifteen miles south of New Madrid, seven miles northeast of Portageville, and eight miles northwest and across the river from Tiptonville, Tennessee, and Reelfoot Lake. Neither of these last two towns existed at the time of the earthquakes, of course. Six miles downstream from Point Pleasant, at the river's edge on Highway 162, there used to be a regular ferry that took passengers between Missouri and Tennessee in the Reelfoot Lake area. It still operates from time to time when river conditions are favorable. One can check at Portageville or Tiptonville for this information.

Death Strikes the Crist Family

The family of George and Besy Crist in Kentucky had been shaken almost daily since the beginning of the earthquakes in December. George had vowed to leave and resettle in Pigeon Roost, Indiana, some 250 miles further east than the source of the temblors. However, when the massive 8.4 magnitude earthquake of January 23 struck the territory, they were still living on their Kentucky homestead. George made the following entry in the Crist Journal dated January 23, 1812:

"What are we gonna do? You cannot fight it cause you do not know how. It is not something that you can see. In a storm you can see the sky and it shows dark clouds and you know that you might get strong winds but this you can not see anything but a house that just lays in a pile on the ground—not scattered around and trees that just falls over with the roots still on it.

"The earth quake or what ever it is come again today. It was as bad or worse than the one in December. We lost our Amandy Jane in this one—a log fell on her. We will bury her upon the hill under a clump of trees where Besy's Ma and Pa is buried. A lot of people thinks that the devil has come here. Some thinks that this is the beginning of the world coming to an end."

Amandy Jane was their youngest child. She was fifteen.

John Audubon and
the Birth of Reelfoot

The famous naturalist and artist, John Audubon, and his wife, Lucy, lived along the banks of the Ohio River in Henderson, Kentucky, at the time. When he could get away from his responsibilities as a small shop owner, he kept busy making a study of the birds, plants, and animals of the region, describing them in meticulous detail by words and by carefully-drawn colored pictures. A Frenchman by birth, a scientist by nature, and an artist at heart—Audubon was among the first to catalogue and document the wildlife of the New World. He self-published all of his books, which were very popular throughout the eastern United States at the time.

On January 23, he appears to have been about 18 miles due east of New Madrid on a prominent bluff overlooking Mississippi River Island

View from Chicken Point, Hickman, KY.
Looking west, the Mississippi River and Missouri side can be seen in the distance. Island #6 is seen just beyond the buildings on the right. On a really clear day one can see the smokestack of the Associated Electric Plant at New Madrid on the horizon at the center of this picture, 18 miles away. Audubon used to come here because of the abundance of birds for his studies. The slope below, with streets and buildings, is a landslide from the quakes of 1811-12, which is still unstable. The castle-like structure is Fulton County Court House, a National Historic Landmark more than 100 years old. See closer view to the left.

#6. The bluff, called "Chicken Point" by the Indians, was a gathering area for thousands of wild birds and other game, an ideal location for Audubon's research. The scenic town of Hickman, Kentucky, founded in 1819, has been built on and around that point today.

About 8:45A.M., on the morning of January 23, 1812, Audubon was enjoying the view from the crest of Chicken Point—looking west across the river toward the skyline in the direction of New Madrid. A few minutes before the quake struck, Audubon's horse stopped suddenly, hung his head, began to moan, spread out his four legs, and refused to move. "I saw a sudden and strange darkness rising from the western horizon," Audubon wrote in his journal. "I heard what I imagined to be the distant rumbling of a violent tornado," he continued. "I thought my horse was about to die and would have sprung from his back had a minute more elapsed, but at that instant all the shrubs and trees began to move from their very roots. The ground rose and fell in successive furrows like the ruffled waters of a lake."

The January 23 event caused two huge sand boils that dammed up Reelfoot Creek located less than twenty miles south of Audubon's position on Chicken Point. The stream flows out of the Chickasaw Bluffs near the Kentucky-Tennessee Line and crosses the floodplain of the Obion and Mississippi Rivers. This started the impondment that subsequent seismic and tectonic events in February were to make into an enormous, permanent lake.

Reelfoot Lake was originally nearly twenty miles long, five or six miles wide, and twenty feet deep in some places. Sixty-five square miles in surface area when formed, it has now gradually silted in to a fraction of its original size. As the crow flies, the lake is less than fifteen miles southeast of New Madrid on the opposite side of the river.

Still there today, Reelfoot Lake is a very scenic resort area with excellent fishing, beautiful boating, and a fascinating history— both culturally and geologically. The restaurants, the visitors center and museum, the boating and good fishing, the opportunity to see bald eagles and an abundance of water fowl all make Reelfoot Lake a wonderful place to visit and spend some time. There you can still see the stumps of dead cypress beneath the surface where a large forest was submerged in 1812. Some of the submerged cypress are still alive and can be seen in deep water where they could not have taken root but did survive the quakes and the subsidence. Other cypress, now 200 to 300 years old, are on high ground where they were uplifted at the same time the lake bed sank.

Zadoc Cramer
Reports from Natchez

Zadoc Cramer, author of the *Navigator*, had eagerly listened to the stories of Nicholas and Lydia Roosevelt, as well as everyone else coming down the river to dock at Natchez. Even though he was only 39 at the time, he was in poor health and had moved to Natchez because of the mild resort-like climate. His popular, self-published river guide had been through nine editions since its first one in 1801. An avid reporter and meticulous note taker, he wrote the following letter to a friend in Nashville, Tennessee, which was published on February 21, 1812, in the *Pittsburgh Gazette*.

"January 23, 1812, serves to corroborate the remarkable phenomena in nature, with which we have not before become acquainted." Cramer wrote. "This morning another pretty severe shock of an earthquake was felt here. Those shocks on the 16th ultimo and since did much damage on the Mississippi River, from the mouth of the Ohio to Little Prairie, particularly.

"Many boats have been lost, and much property sunk. The banks of the river, in many places, sunk hundreds of acres together leaving the tops of the trees to be seen above the water. The earth opened in many places from one to three feet wide, through whose fissures stone coal

Aerial View of Reelfoot Lake Museum and Visitors Center (top photo). The Museum is in the bottom-center portion of the photo—the large building with the light-colored roof. Note how the trees seem to protrude into the lake in an unnatural way, as if there were high water conditions. That's actually what happened to these trees, only the flood happened in 1811-12 because of an earthquake. The town seen surrounding the Visitor's Center is Blue Bank, Tennessee.

Sand Boils on South End of Reelfoot Lake (bottom photo). These boils are thought to be some of those that formed on January 23, 1812, and dammed up Reelfoot Creek, which started the permanent Lake we see beyond the trees in this photo

Ground Waves in Mississippi County. According to John Audubon, during the earthquakes "the ground rose and fell in successive furrows like the ruffled waters of a lake." Eliza Bryan described the earth as "visibly waving," like the surface of the sea. Several other New Madrid residents, including Francois LeSieur, also described the ground motion to be like waves on water. According to one witness, the amplitude of the ground swells "was about twelve inches to and fro," while others said they were even larger. It is clear from the testimony of first-person accounts that the earth's surface did, in fact, ripple with visible waves. No one had a camera to film the phenomenon then, but the picture above may be approximately how it would have looked. This photo was taken in 1990 on a late afternoon between East Prarie and Charleston, Missouri, in Mississippi County—about 15 miles northeast of New Madrid. While this may be similar to what the eye witnesses saw in 1811-12—there is at least one big difference. The ripples in the ground surface seen above are frozen and motionless. Those seen during the shaking of the great earthquakes were moving rapidly—up and down, sideways, and sweeping at high speed across the landscape.

was thrown up in pieces as large as a man's hand. The earth rocked, and trees lashed their tops together. The whole seemed in convulsions, throwing up sand bars here, there sinking others, trees jumping from the bed of the river, roots uppermost, forming a most serious impediment to navigation, where before there was no obstruction,"

"Boats rocked like cradles," Cramer's narrative continues, "Men, women, and children confused, running to and fro and hallooing for safety. Those on land pleading to get into the boats. Those in boats willing (almost) to be on land.

"This damning and distressing scene has continued for several days, particularly at and above Flour Island (Island #30). The Long Reach, though formerly the best part of the river, is now said to be the worst, being filled with innumerable planters and sawyers which have been thrown up from the bed by the extraordinary convulsions of the river.

"Little Prairie, and the country about it, suffered much. New Lakes have been formed and the beds of old ones raised to the elevation of the surface of the adjacent country.

"All accounts of those who have descended the river since the shocks began give the most alarming and terrific picture of this desolating and horrible scene."

Cramer was to live only one more year, dying at the age of 40. However, he did finish another edition of the *Navigator* before he died. The tenth and last edition was published posthumously in Pittsburgh in 1818. It contained descriptions of the earthquakes and the permanent changes they had made on the river, including comments on the missing islands and destroyed villages.

Eastern Earthquakes Are More Destructive

The 8.4 magnitude quake of January 23, 1812, illustrates an important point. The great San Francisco earthquake of April, 1906, was measured at 8.3 and, for practical purposes, was the same size as the January 23 New Madrid event. The 1906 earthquake is the largest in California History. But the New Madrid sequence had at least three quakes this large or larger.

There is a distinct difference between earthquakes that occur east of the Rocky Mountains and those in the West. From the Rockies west the rocks that comprise the crust of the earth are recently faulted, extensively fractured, and relatively warm. There are active volcanoes in California, Oregon, and Washington, along with geothermal areas such as Yellowstone Park and Imperial Valley, California. The rocks of the west are geologically young, hot, and broken

up. These are not conditions that enable the efficient propagation of seismic waves through the crust. Hence, when an earthquake occurs in the western United States, the energy of the seismic waves is dissipated and used up as it traverses many cracks and faults. In relatively short distances quake vibrations do no damage and cease to be felt—their motions having been spent and absorbed in the bedrock.

East of the Rockies the rocks that make up the crust are relatively old, and cold, and do not have many recent faults. In the Ozark Mountains some of the rocks exposed at the surface are almost two billion years old. Old, cold, unfractured rock are conditions that enable very efficient propagation of seismic waves. When the rocks of the Midwestern and Eastern United States are struck with the hammer of an earthquake, they ring like a bell. The ripples can travel hundreds of miles with almost undiminished amplitudes—posing risks at a distance unheard of in the west.

The San Francisco quake of 1906 did damage for a hundred miles up and down the San Andreas fault and for fifty miles to either side. It was only barely felt in southern Oregon, western Nevada, and southernmost California. No damage occurred outside the state of California.

By way of comparison, the greatest of the New Madrid quakes were felt over two-thirds of the United States—from trappers in Yellowstone to fishermen in south Florida, from the Rockies to the entire Atlantic seaboard. Eighteen of them were felt in Washington, D.C. People also felt them in three other countries—Canada, Cuba, and Mexico. Hundreds of chimneys were thrown down in Cincinnati nearly 400 miles away. Acres of land subsided several inches near Charleston, South Carolina, in response to the vibrations originating hundreds of miles to the west. These quakes cracked plastered walls in homes in Atlanta, Georgia, and Richmond, Virginia, buckled sidewalks in Baltimore, rang church bells in Boston, and the scaffolding that had been erected to construct the dome of the nation's capitol in Washington, D.C., was said to have been thrown down by these earthquakes more than 800 miles away.

Such a thing will never happen west of the Rocky Mountains. It would be geologically impossible. The properties of western bedrock won't permit it.

Given the same size earthquake, the same amount of energy released, the same value on the Richter scale—such a quake east of the Rockies will do damage over 10-20 times the area as one in the West.

What this means is that you could live within fifty miles of the notorious San Andreas Fault of California, experience a major earthquake, and actually be safer than if you lived 150 miles from the New Madrid Fault.

What saves the East from a much greater earthquake risk is frequency. For every destructive quake east of the Rockies there will be 10-20 in the west. But the one experienced in the east will do 10-20 times the damage. Hence, over a long period of time, measured in centuries, there will be as many earthquake losses east of the Rocky Mountains as west. The difference will be that the people of California, Washington, Idaho, and Utah will experience their damages in many smaller disasters distributed over time and touching every generation. The people of the East will suffer their losses in a few big ones, experiencing large spans of time with no earthquake disasters—skipping whole generations without a single major event.

The last strong earthquake in the eastern United States was a 6.5 magnitude quake near Charleston, Missouri, on October 31, 1895. It was Halloween. The source of the quake was the New Madrid fault. The next large one before that was nine years earlier in Charleston, South Carolina, in 1886. It was a magnitude 7.4 on a distant fault system unrelated to the New Madrid Seismic Zone.

As of the publishing of this book (1995) it has been one hundred years since a 6.0 or greater earthquake has struck anywhere in the United States east of the Great Plains. Are we overdue? Who knows? Chapter Six issues a forecast and prognosis about this while Chapter Seven tells you what can be done about it.

Meanwhile, it is January, 1812, and back at New Madrid there's a lot more to come. The siege has only begun.

Intensity Map of the Great New Madrid Earthquakes 1811-12

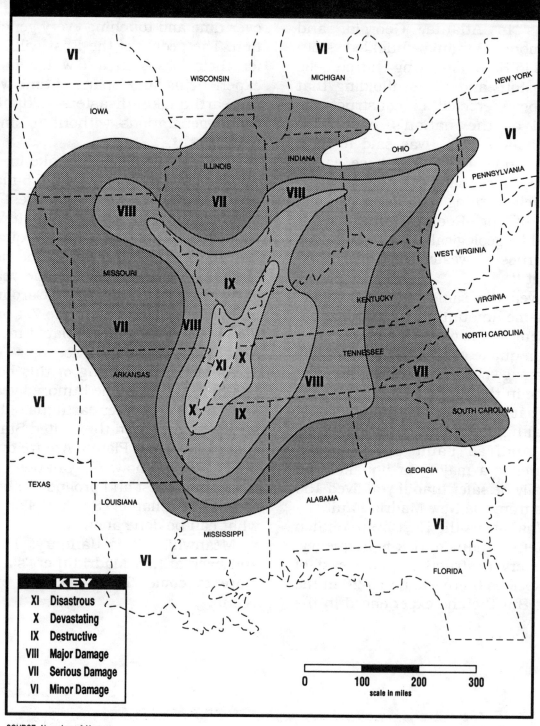

KEY

XI	Disastrous
X	Devastating
IX	Destructive
VIII	Major Damage
VII	Serious Damage
VI	Minor Damage

scale in miles
0   100   200   300

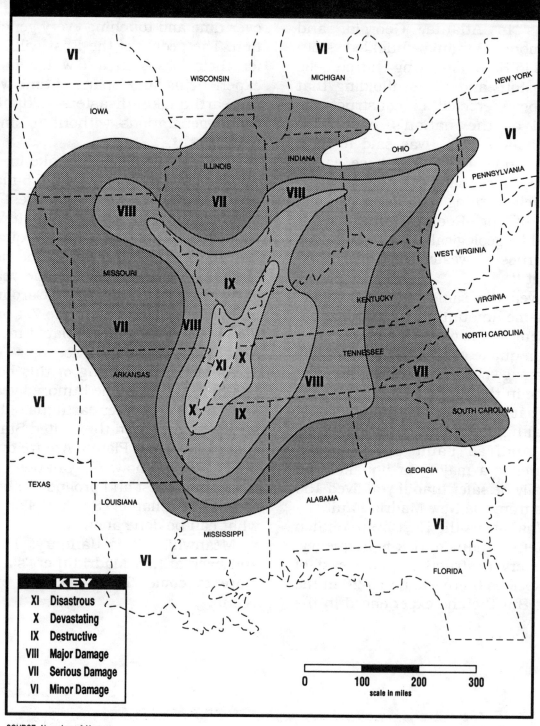SOURCE: Algermissen & Hopper

Chapter Four

THE BIG ONE

The exodus started within hours after the quakes began on December 16. In panic, certain that the quakes would spell their doom if they stayed, hundreds abandoned their homesteads and moved out of the fault zone. Several men disappeared, leaving their wives and children behind, never to be heard from again. The New Madrid residents who remained had moved to tent encampments on or shortly after December 16 and stayed there, fearing to return to their damaged houses by the river. By mid-January most of them had constructed light wooden structures more adapted to the cold weather and yet seismically designed, safe from the hazards of falling log walls or a heavy collapsing roof.

After the January 23 quake at Point Pleasant, many aftershocks followed. At Ste. Genevieve, Missouri, 115 miles north of New Madrid, a Dr. Robertson, who practiced there, meticulously counted the tremors he had experienced. By February he had tabulated more than 500.

Then, on Tuesday, February 4, the people at New Madrid began to experience something different. They said that the earth began to twitch and "quiver like a side of freshly killed beef." Eliza Bryan reported that the earth "was in continual agitation, vis-ibly waving as a gentle sea." Nothing violent—just little jerks and spasms throughout the day and all night, throughout Wednesday, and the next day. The disturbances continued without ceasing for yet another night and another day—accompanied by faint thumps and rumbles from deep under the ground.

By Thursday evening it was a tired and apprehensive town that tried to find some sleep amid the tremblings and groanings of the earth. The moon was in its last quarter, high in the sky and beaming brightly at 3:15 in the morning when, suddenly, the residents of New Madrid were again violently jarred from their slumbers. It was Friday, February 7, 1812. On the east side of New Madrid, along St. John's Harbor, the earthquake hurled a huge wave from the river, a fluvial tsunami, inundating that part of town, splintering cottonwood trees, smashing boats, and killing an untold number of people.

Thirty-four years later, in 1846, Sir Charles Lyell, a British geologist, explored the area and "saw a fault produced by the earthquake near Bayou St. John east of New Madrid where the descent was eight to ten feet." It was the sudden upthrust of this fault, he reasoned, that caused the Mississippi River to respond so

Tywappity Hill Today. The view on the left is on Interstate Highway 55 headed north toward Cape Girardeau, 12 miles away. The hill before you was called Tywappity Hill in 1811-12. These are the first true hills north of New Madrid. A few miles further north the Ozark highlands begin. According to John Shaw, approximately 2,000 people congregated here on February 7, 1812, on their way out of the New Madrid Fault Zone—fleeing in terror. The spot where the Interstate is seen climbing the hills is almost exactly where John Shaw described this throng to have assembled and prayed together that fateful Friday. Today these are called the "Benton Hills," after the town of Benton located about two miles to the west of here. Just to the right of where the Interstate ascends the hills is a cleared area with a few buildings. This piece of bare hillside is actually the scarp of a landslide from the earthquakes of 1811-12 and would have been freshly broken at the time the pilgrims were moving northward out of the fault zone. The photo on the right is from Tyappity Hill at the top of the landslide looking south. The hummocky surface of the slide is in the foreground. Interstate 55 traverses the distant corner on the right. We are looking out over the New Madrid Fault Zone which begins at the base of these hills. New Madrid is 42 miles away in the distance, just over the horizon, in the center of the picture. The bright spot near the center of this photo is a seven-acre sand boil from the earthquakes. It is clearly visible from a mile away. The refugees pausing on this hilltop during their exodus in 1812 would have seen the same view as seen here, except that most of the landscape would have been forested instead of cleared, as it is today.

violently that fateful night.

A New Orleans journalist in the area reported that "the ravages of this terrible convulsion has nearly depopulated the district of New Madrid. Few remain to tell the sad tale. The inhabitants have fled in every direction."

Col. John Shaw, of Marquette County, Wisconsin, was visiting the area when the great shock hit. He wrote a report for the Wisconsin Historical Society published in 1855, wherein he said:

"On the morning of the 7th of February I was in New Madrid when people of all ages fled in terror from their falling dwellings in that place and the surrounding country." According to Shaw, approximately 2,000 people from the region converged about 40 miles north "to Tywappity Hill, on the western bank of the Mississippi and about seven miles back from the river."

This would have been in the vicinity of present-day Benton, Missouri, or where Interstate Highway 55 leaves the Mississippi Lowlands and climbs the Benton Hills near Milepost #81. The 2,000 refugees estimated by Shaw would have represented about half the population in the area of what would later become northeastern Arkansas and southeastern Missouri.

Shaw's report continues: "This was the first high ground above New Madrid, and here the fugitives formed an encampment. It was proposed that all should kneel and engage in supplicating God's mercy." Then, according to Shaw, who had migrated with the multitude, "Catholic and Protestant alike knelt simultaneously and offered solemn prayer to their Creator."

The Ripples Sweep the Country

Like ripples on the surface of a pond when disturbed by a pebble cast into the water, the seismic waves originating at 3:15 A.M. near New Madrid spread out in concentric curves on the surface of the earth at speeds of four to six miles a second.

Less than thirty seconds after they were released, Daniel Boone's home near St. Louis began to rock.

One minute after the fault ruptured at New Madrid, Thomas Lincoln's cabin started shaking near Louisville.

About twenty seconds after the Lincolns sensed the disturbance in Kentucky, the Indians started receiving tremors at Fort Osage near the future site of Kansas City. The ground pitched and tossed for more than a minute.

Two minutes after ground zero at New Madrid, Judge James Witherall in Detroit, who happened to be awake at that hour, took note of the time—3:17 A.M.—and recorded the duration of the vibrations which he felt for approximately 90 seconds.

At 4:18 A.M., eastern time, three minutes after the quake had begun in New Madrid, the waves raced across the eastern seaboard, ringing church bells from South Carolina to New York City.

In Canada. at Montreal, Quebec, people were awakened at 4:19 in the morning (eastern time) by the passing of the earthquake as windows and chinaware rattled for more than two minutes.

If seismographs would have existed in that day, Australian seismologists would have recorded the surface waves of the New Madrid earthquake on their side of the planet at about 3:48 in the afternoon their time—thirty-three minutes after the fault had ruptured in Missouri. Most of the world would not feel the quake. But had a global network of sensitive seismic stations been in place, as they are today, it would have been recorded everywhere. The ripples would travel around the world and back again before they would gradually fade away. Their effects, however, would never fade away.

Fifty-five miles to the north, in Cape Girardeau, where damages had occurred from a number of the previous shocks—"many brick homes were shattered" with this most recent shake. A reporter for the *Louisiana Gazette* who was in Cape Girardeau wrote the following: "The shock of the 7th was more violent than any preceding and lasted longer, perhaps, than any on record, from 10 to 15 minutes. The earth was not at rest for an hour. . . It has done considerable damage in this place by demolishing chimneys and cracking cellar walls."

One hundred miles due south was

Fort Pickering on the southernmost of the Chickasaw Bluffs, where "the land is strong and high." Nevertheless, "the earth was extremely agitated, and the block-house of the fort, which is almost a solid mass of hewn timber, trembled like an aspen leaf." Fort Pickering was the only white settlement on the Mississippi River in Tennessee. Memphis would later be founded on that site. While the solid bluffs were "extremely agitated," the same report pointed out the contrast with the experience of the lowlands and islands around the Fort which were "shattered and devastated." This eyewitness reported that large areas of land adjacent to the river "had been cleft from the main shore and tumbled into the water, leaving their growth waving above the surface." This does not bode well for the future of Mud Island nor the location of The Pyramid at Memphis today.

Located 145 miles north of New Madrid was Herculaneum, Missouri, a lead smelter and ore depot on the river. Much of the lead shot fired in the War of 1812 was made here. Herculaneum had already been reported as "wrecked" by the previous quakes of December and January. This one nearly finished it off.

Meanwhile, 180 miles to the north, just west of St. Louis, Daniel Boone and his wife, Rebecca, were jarred from their bed as their house shook violently. They had just completed their dream home in 1810, a four-story mansion of timber and limestone. It had already been cracked and weakened by the earthquakes of December and January. This shock almost knocked it down. The massive two-foot-thick walls shifted and buckled. Solid oak beams and floor joists were wrenched apart, leaving permanent gaps and straining the house within inches of collapse. One of the main supports on the ground floor, a huge ten-inch-thick oaken post, was shoved out of perpendicular, and its base moved more than four inches from its original setting, where it remains today. In all, the house, which stood on a slope, shifted almost a foot. Miraculously, no one was injured. The house remained standing and was repaired, but not before its mistress passed away. Rebecca died on March 18, 1813. Daniel lived for seven more years.

In St. Louis, almost 200 miles to the north, chimneys were thrown down, brick and stone houses were split, floors fell, and roofs collapsed while sand boiled in the Mississippi and Missouri River flood plains to the north (Columbia Bottoms) and west (Earth City). Jesuit Priests reported seismic explosion craters that erupted and blasted holes in the bottom ground across the river in Illinois.

In Louisville, more than 250 miles to the east, Jared Brooks, an engineer, had set up several pendulums rigged up with pens (crude seismographs) in late December by which he was carefully tabulating times and intensities of the New Madrid earthquakes as they occurred. He labeled the February 7 event as "Tremendous!" Brick buildings in Louisville, already weakened by the previous quakes, caved in and collapsed.

Twenty-five miles east of Elizabethtown, Kentucky, 40 miles south of Louisville on their farm at Knob Creek, the log cabin of Tom and

Ste. Genevieve Houses that Survived the Earthquakes. The house on the left was built in 1790 by Pierre Dorlac. Many homes were damaged, and many chimneys were thrown off in Ste. Genevieve, Missouri, 115 miles north of New Madrid. The Dorlac chimney was probably one that was damaged. Inside the attic of the Dorlac house the rafters have been racked out of square, possibly due to the earthquakes. It is the motion of the roof and gabled portion of a house during quakes that throws off chimneys. This chimney was repaired with brick, rather than the native limestone that forms its base. The flood of 1993 was over the base of the chimney and covered the basement windows in front of the Dorlac house— water was within 1.5 feet of the first floor. The house on the right is the oldest brick building west of the Mississippi, built in 1785. The upper portion appears to have been added later. It has several cracks, and the bricks below the windows appear patched and uneven. It may have been damaged during the earthquakes, but if so it was repaired and still stands today. The first American court was held here.

Earthquake Damage at Boone's House, Defiance, Missouri. The upper left photo shows Daniel Boone's house from the back where all four stories can be clearly seen, including the dormers of the top floor ballroom and the ground floor with kitchen and dining room. The top right view shows the east wall which, like the west wall, is solid limestone masonry—two feet thick. The absence of windows on both ends of the house (except for the small ones on the top floor) added considerable strength and helped prevent collapse during the quakes. The thickness of the walls can be seen in the lower left at the ground floor doorway to the dining room. Note that this stone wall is out of plumb. In the bottom right photo we are standing in the dining room looking through a corridor into the kitchen. The heavy supporting masonry has been bowed out of vertical, probably from the earthquake. Note the sagging wooden beam over the doorway. Boone's home was 180 miles from the epicenters and of very rugged construction. The principal reason it was so damaged is because it was not on level ground but built into a hillside which shifted during the shaking.

Earthquake Damage to Boone's House, cont'd. The top left view is in the dining room. Note the heavy beams and joists that bear the weight of the floor above. The joists have been pulled away from the beams. (See close-up on top right.) The earthquakes did this and came close to pulling the joists completely off of the beams. If you add up the inches these joists were pulled from the front of the house to the back, it comes to nearly a foot of displacement. Boone's house came within inches of collapse. The lower left photo is of one of the stone walls in the ground floor. It has been buckled. The dark cabinet is vertical, but the wall behind it is not. On the middle right we see Boone's long rifle over his mantle. Look carefully, and you will see a piece of wood embedded in the stonework of the fireplace to which the mounts for the rifle have been attached. This board was originally laid level but was put out of level during the quakes when the stone fireplace shifted. In the lower right we see the base of a dark 10-inch square oak support column that has been scooted four inches to the left from its original location visible as the light area by the man's finger.

Earthquake Damage to the Kibby House, St. Charles, Missouri. Col. Timothy Kibby built this house in 1805. During the earthquakes this house was badly damaged. Several cracks formed in the brick masonry, and one of the dormers is said to have been shaken down. The photos above show a front view, and a side (back) view. Note the cracked and patched up brick in the other three photos. Especially note the crack from the limestone foundation wall to the roof, the entire height of the house (top right photo). The bottom left photo is a close-up of this same crack, which can be seen not only along the mortar line, but across the bricks, themselves. Why would this brick house be so damaged 185 miles from New Madrid when an older brick house at Ste. Genevieve, only 115 miles from the epicenters, appears to have had less damage? Part of the answer probably lies in the fact that the Ste. Genevieve house was built on firm rock while this one was built on soft river deposits.

Nancy Lincoln was severely shaken, but it stood. Some dishes and utensils were knocked down, and their only table was moved. There was some damage to their stick and clay chimney, but Tom could fix that. This was not the first shock they had felt since mid-December, but it was the strongest. Sleeping under bearskins and blankets on a bed of cornhusks and hen feathers, the Lincoln family, like thousands of others in the Midwest, was awakened that night by the rolling of the earth. Three days later, on Monday, February 10, 1812, the Lincolns would celebrate the fifth birthday of their daughter, Sarah. Two days after that, on Wednesday, February 12, they would celebrate the third birthday of their son, Abraham, whose life would eventually have far greater impact on the lives of Americans than even the great New Madrid earthquakes.

At Fort Osage, 330 miles to the northwest, on the Missouri River near present-day Kansas City, the February 7 shock was clearly felt. The oscillations lasted for more than a minute, but there was no major damage. Metal pots and implements on the shelves of the trading post crashed to the floor. Several stone chimneys formed new cracks, but none were toppled. During the shaking, however, it was difficult for people to stand. Heavy cannon mounted on iron wheels grated and rumbled on the wooden floors of the second story lookouts. The sturdy log fortress groaned, creaked, and swayed with the gyrations of the ground for more than sixty seconds.

The noises and movements awakened American soldiers quartered in the stockade. At first, some thought they were being attacked by Indians. The men in the Fort and the Indians around it had experienced several of the earlier temblors, but this one was definitely the strongest.

Several thousand friendly Osage villagers lived around the Fort at that time, and many became alarmed. Some had been with Tecumseh in Arkansas and southern Missouri the previous spring and had heard his prophesies first hand. Did the Mississippi River really swallow up the white man's villages, as he had said it would? They were already aware of reports of Indian villages being drowned along the river from the earthquakes in December and January. Was this a sign of displeasure of the Great Spirit? And if so, was Wakonda displeased with them or the Long Knives? They weren't sure.

Fort Osage was the westernmost outpost of the United States during the earthquakes. Although the February 7 earthquake was alarming to the Indians and soldiers living there, it incurred no appreciable losses.

When the big quake hit, George Sibley, the man in charge of the trading post, was 470 miles due south of Fort Osage in Nacogdoches, Texas, visiting relatives. Thus, Sibley was only 390 miles southwest of the epicenter; yet the quake was barely noticed in Nacogdoches.

The mild experience of the earthquakes at Nacogdoches and Fort Osage represents one of the unexplained paradoxes of these earthquakes: Settlements to the west and south of New Madrid (like Fort Osage,

Natchez, and New Orleans) were not as strongly affected as those at equal distances to the east and north—like Louisville, Vincennes, Pittsburgh, Detroit, Cincinnati, and Charleston, South Carolina.

In Cincinnati, almost 400 miles east of the epicenter, the February 7 shock caused considerable damage. Fissures formed and split open the ground. Sand deposits liquefied, and groundwater flowed onto the surface. Houses were moved on their foundations. What few chimneys had remained upright following the former shocks were finally thrown down with this one.

By contrast, in New Orleans, 500 miles to the south, a February 8 news report said simply, "There was another shock of an earthquake felt in this city yesterday morning about half past 3 o'clock . . . more strong than the one felt some time ago." There was no damage.

In Detroit, 550 miles northeast, Judge A.B. Woodward reported that the February 7th event was the ninth shock to be felt there. In June of 1812 Woodward returned from a trip to upper Canada, more than 1,000 miles from New Madrid, where he learned that residents there had also felt nine shocks. The intensity of the vibrations in Detroit was similar to that experienced at Fort Osage except that the Fort was 220 miles closer.

In Pittsburgh, 600 miles east, glassware was broken, furniture moved, and brick walls cracked. People leapt from their beds running into the streets in panic.

Charleston, South Carolina, 700 miles east of New Madrid, was more than twice the distance from the epi-center as Fort Osage, yet it experienced almost the same intensity of shaking. The February 10, 1812, issue of the *Charleston Courier* reported experiencing "a severe shock" that lasted more than two minutes, caused some of the clocks to stop, the bells to ring, moved houses on their foundations, and caused walls to crack.

In Washington, D.C., nearly 800 miles to the east, President James and First Lady Dolly Madison were abruptly awakened by the New Madrid earthquakes once again. Some residents of the city rose from their beds and grabbed their weapons, believing that their houses were being burglarized by robbers. According to one correspondent, "The shaking continued upwards of two minutes." The scaffolding erected to build the dome of the nation's capitol was said to have toppled.

In Norfolk, Virginia, 150 miles south of Washington and 800 miles from New Madrid, a 126 gallon cask of wine was thrown off its mount, crashing to the floor and spilling its contents.

Church bells rang in Boston, 1,000 miles from New Madrid. The ground motion lasted several minutes. Water sloshed from ponds, ducks squawked, waterfowl took to flight, and tall steeples rocked. Almost everyone was awake in Boston that night, frightened and unable to go back to sleep.

In Canada, the February 8 issue of the *Montreal Herald* contained this report: "Another shock of an earthquake was felt in this city by most of the inhabitants. It appears to have affected some parts of the city more

Epicentral Area of Largest Earthquake in American History—Magnitude 8.8. Beneath the St. Jude Industrial Park sign in the distance is seen the Associated Electric Power Plant and its two smoke stacks, the tallest of which is 812 feet. The grove of cypress trees in the distance to the right of the St. Jude sign is a fragment of what used to be Bayou Portage. Spanish, American, and French boats used to pass through here between New Madrid on the Mississippi River and Spanish Mill on the Little River. Bayou Portage was destroyed by the earthquakes. On the right we see Associated Electric and Noranda Aluminum Company on the river's edge. Downtown New Madrid is six miles distance around the river bend. Note the curved line of sand boils along the fissure in the foreground—a scar in the landscape from the eartuquakes of 1811-12.

than others, for whilst some were seriously alarmed by it, there are many who did not perceive it. The cups and saucers on breakfast tables were heard to rattle, and picture frames, etc., hanging on the walls were seen to vibrate." Another report from Montreal stated that the quake "had force enough to shake furniture and move doors on their hinges." Some pendulum clocks were stopped.

The "Hard Shock"

This one was called "The Hard Shock" by Eliza Bryan and others who experienced it near the epicenter. It was the greatest earthquake of the entire series. Scientists estimate it to have been 8.8 on the Richter scale. It was centered near present-day Marston, Missouri, and St. Jude Industrial Park. The tall 812-foot smokestack of the Associated Electric Company, six miles south of New Madrid, is a marker for this epicentral region—easily visible from Interstate 55 and which can be seen for up to thirty miles in four states.

When you visit or drive through and see the Associated Smoke Stack, realize that you are passing through the focal region of the largest earthquake in American history. The New Madrid-Marston Welcome Center on Interstate 55 is in the epicentral zone of this monster quake.

A magnitude 6.0 earthquake releases about as much energy as one of the atomic bombs dropped on Hiroshima and Nagasaki in 1945. A magnitude 8.8 earthquake would release 8,000 times more energy than a 6.0. But how can one visualize the energy in 8,000 A-bombs?

To gain some perspective on such a gigantic temblor, consider Hurricane Hugo that ravaged the coast of South Carolina in the fall of 1989 and

Hurricane Andrew that devastated Florida in 1992. These horrific hurricanes blasted their fury against the earth for eight to ten days and were among the largest of the twentieth century.

Consider now the fury of an 8.8 magnitude earthquake. Such a quake will release, in less than five minutes, more energy than did Hurricanes Hugo and Andrew, combined, over a period of days. Earthquakes can loose more energy in less time than any other force of nature.

The River Runs Backwards

Vertigo. That's what airplane pilots call it when they temporarily lose their sense of which way is up, down, left or right. Only a trust in their instruments can save them from disaster when they experience such disorientation.

No doubt, many boatmen on the Mississippi River experienced vertigo during the earthquakes of 1811-12. Unfortunately, they had neither the instruments to guide them, nor the power to control their fates. Some survived to tell of their horrors. Many did not.

The February 7, 1812, earthquake produced some of the most spectacular geologic and hydrologic phenomena ever recorded anywhere at any time in the course of history. There appears to have been a combination of tectonic faulting along the Reelfoot scarp, uplift on the west with downwarping and massive subsidence on the east which dammed off Reelfoot Creek and provided a permanent basin for the lake. Reelfoot Scarp is a normal fault about 10-20 feet higher on the west than on the Reelfoot Lake

side. It is quite visible as an abrupt, linear change in elevation running north and south between Tiptonville and Cates, Tennessee. It extends along the west side of Donaldson Point.

The most amazing effects were on the river itself. For several hours the Mississippi ran backwards. This happened between Islands #10 and #8 on the east side of Donaldson Point. Boatmen who survived reported the retrograde motion on the morning of February 7.

Between Islands #8 and #9, violent waves were thrown over the river banks with such force that thousands of acres of virgin forest were shattered into stumps and splinters. As the vast volumes of water then rushed back into the channel, thousands of limbs and logs were dumped into the river posing additional hazards for boatmen. Planters and sawyers were everywhere, waiting to snag every boat that drifted by.

For decades boat pilots would pass through this stretch and see only the skeletal remains of a former forest, where stately stands of oak, cottonwood, tupelo, and cypress had once stood. As annual floods inundated these desolated regions, the stumps acted as strainers to capture the muds and sands suspended by the swollen waters. After several decades they were all buried in a vast tree cemetery. Today, fertile farm lands over these stumps produce abundant crops of corn, soybeans and cotton. As the steep muddy banks erode, these giant stumps reappear into the water's edge. Some can be seen today. Dead trees. Victims of the earthquakes of 1811-

12. Their gaunt bony roots and splintered tops bear mute, yet eloquent, testimony to the violent upwellings that caused their demise nearly two centuries ago.

Waterfalls on the Mississippi

Two temporary waterfalls formed that day spanning the entire breadth of the Mississippi. One was located eight to ten miles south of New Madrid between Bessie's Neck and Donaldson Point, the other only a mile or two upstream from town. They lasted no more than two or three days. They were described as being "like the Falls of the Ohio," about six feet of vertical drop at the head with a series of smaller step-downs and a reach of shallow shoal stretching for about two miles, yielding a total drop of about twenty feet.

A boatman, Captain Mathias Speed, and his crew were coming down the river on a pair of rafts lashed together. They were tied up near Island #9 during the night of February 6—some fifteen miles upstream from New Madrid on the east side of Donaldson Point. In a communication Speed wrote on March 3, 1812, he described his experience: "In descending the Mississippi, on the night of the 6th of February, we tied our boat to a willow bar on the west bank of the river opposite the head of the 9th Island. We were lashed to another boat. About 3 o'clock, on the morning of the 7th, we were waked by the violent agitation of the boat, attended with a noise more tremendous and terrific than I can describe or anyone can conceive, who was not present or near to such a scene. The constant discharge of heavy cannon might give some idea of the noise for loudness, but this was infinitely more terrible on account of its origin appearing to be subterraneous.

"As soon as we waked," Speed continued, "we discovered that the bar to which we were tied was sinking. We cut loose and moved our boats for the middle of the river. After getting out so far as to be out of danger from the trees that were falling in from the bank, the swells in the river were so great as to threaten the sinking of the boat every moment. We stopped the outholes in our cabin with blankets to keep out the water."

After a horrifying night on the river they found themselves at daybreak drifting backwards, towards Island #8. This retrograde motion lasted several hours. As the currents finally began to turn back to their normal direction (toward New Madrid), Speed and his men witnessed tons of water cascading into the channel from the temporarily flooded lands on either side. "The water of the river, after it was fairly light, appeared to be almost black, with something like the dust of stone coal," Speed said.

Later in the morning, as they were drifting around the bend at Donaldson Point near Island #10, they noticed that the trees of the island were leaning chaotically in every direction, with some sunk and others split to their tops. The island appeared to have been rent in two by the earthquakes. Realizing that this was not a good sign they were apprehensive about what they might encounter next. Nevertheless, they continued drifting around the bend.

Then suddenly they were confronted with sight of the first of the two falls. Caught in the suck of the swift current, it was too late to turn back. Abandoning all hope of surviving the crew drifted inexorably toward what they believed to be certain destruction.

They managed to keep their two flatboats bound together and their bow pointed downstream. This enabled them to pass over the cataract without injury.

Meanwhile, the occupants of another vessel a mile upstream watched in horror as they witnessed the disappearance of Speed's boat over the falls. They became so alarmed that the men abandoned ship and immediately put to shore in a canoe. They watched helplessly as their boat with all of its cargo crashed over the cataract and was destroyed. The survivors had to make their way to town over land on foot, ten miles away.

As Speed and his crew approached the ruins of New Madrid they encountered a second falls which, again, they miraculously survived. The town was all but deserted. Not a house was left standing. Only a few Frenchmen in camps remained. The wreckage of boats was strewn along the banks, including "a large barge, loaded with flour and other articles, which was split from end to end and turned upside down at the bank." They had not planned to stop, but upon docking their raft, they decided to spend a few days in New Madrid. After all, what was the hurry?

Another boatman was five to six miles south of, and upstream from,

New Madrid that night. He and his crew had been caught between the two waterfalls, although he did not know this until he had shared stories with Speed and his crewmen.

"We were just downstream from Island #10," the man told Speed, "when a tremendous jolt nearly overturned our boat. We immediately cut our cable and put off into the middle of the river where we soon found the current changed. The boat hurried up for about the space of a minute with the velocity of the swiftest horse. I was obliged to hold my hand to my head to keep my hat on. We continued to proceed down the river when, at about daylight, we came to a most terrific fall which I think was at least six feet perpendicular, extending across the river, and about half a mile wide. The whirls and ripplings of this rapid were such that our vessel was altogether unmanageable, and destruction seemed inevitable. Some of the whirlpools appeared to be as much as thirty feet deep and seemed to be formed by the waters being violently sucked into some chasm in the river's bottom. My men and I were constantly employed in pumping and bailing, by which, and the aid of Providence, we got safe through. We then landed and found New Madrid a complete wreck and sunk down about twelve feet from its former height."

The death toll from this great wave was never tallied. Those who survived simply fled for their lives.

Eliza Bryan, described the behavior of the river during the quake. "At first the Mississippi seemed to recede from its bank. Its waters gathered up like mountains, leaving boats high upon the sands. The waters then moved inward with a front wall 15 to 20 feet perpendicular and tore many boats from their moorings and carried them up Chepoussea Creek (St. John's Bayou) just east of the town, leaving them closely packed for a quarter of a mile and stranded on dry land. Then the river fell as rapidly as it had risen, receding within its banks with such violence that it took with it a grove of cottonwood trees. A great many fish were also left on the banks. The river was literally covered with the wrecks of boats."

During the next two or three days Mathias Speed and his companions watched thirty boats come around New Madrid Bend and get caught in the falls. Twenty-eight of them capsized with almost total loss of life. The desperate cries of the drowning men could be heard on the shores at New Madrid amidst the roar of the turbulent waters.

Five days after he had landed, Mathias Speed traded his boat and cargo for a pittance, abandoned his plan to continue downstream, and decided to walk back to St. Louis. He'd had enough of the river. He had seen too many men die and was afraid for his life. It was obvious to him that the earthquakes were not yet over. For all he knew, there could be even worse events yet to come. He turned north and started walking, following the trace of El Camino Real. A few days later he reached Cape Girardeau, a distance on foot of about 70 miles. By the first of March, he was in Herculaneum in St. Louis County (now Jefferson County) where he rested for a few days and wrote down his account of the earthquake.

Stumps of Trees Broken during the Quakes of 1811-12. From the top of the bank you can see some of these stumps. Part of Island #8 is visible in the top photo across the river on the right. The river ran backwards from here down to Island #10. The stumps in the middle photo are the same as in the top photo, but taken from a boat when the water was lower. To get an idea of the size of these shattered stumps, Ray Knox, seen in the photo, is six feet two inches tall. The cypress stumps in the bottom photo are in the "Stump Hole," a pit not far from the other stumps above, dug for dirt to build the levee.

Pages 156-157 From

The Navigator
by Zadoc Cramer

10th Edition
1818

Concerning
Island No. 5
(Wolf Island)
to
Island No. 10
south of
New Madrid

●

The numbers on the right of the page are distances from the mouth of the Ohio and from the last island. Island No. 10 has the numbers 6/57 which means it is 6 miles downstream from the head of No. 9 and 57 miles below the mouth of the Ohio. The fine white lines drawn through the map of the channel show which side (left, right, or either) is the safest course past each island.

NAVIGATOR.

157

This island is six miles long on its left side, while the right is ten, and 5 miles broad, containing 15000 acres of the first rate land, well timbered, having near its middle a beautiful prairie, high and dry, producing the finest grass for cattle. Grapes grow on the island in great abundance. A Mr. James Hunter, the only man I ever knew who seemed to take a pride in letting it be known that he was a professed gambler, is the only occupant of Wolf island at present. He says he has on it 100 head of hogs, and a large stock of cattle, with whose beef and pork he supplies boats, barges, keels, &c. passing up and down the river, together with butter, milk, &c. I saw at his house a pair of wild geese tamed, running with the common geese, without any wish to leave them; I observed, however, they always kept close together, and generally, in the rear of the others; they were caught when goslins. This kind of wild and tame goose will not breed beyond the first generation. [b 2]

A good landing can be made at the foot of the bar near the island.

Chalk Banks, another high falling in bluff, begins near the head of Wolf island, on the left side of the river.

Sand bar, with some willows on it.

It is two miles below No. 5, about 300 yards from the left shore, a mile long, and in high water it is covered—channel to the right of it.

Island No. 6,

Joins the above bar,—channel right shore. Opposite this island on the left shore.

Bayou De Sie puts in, immediately above a point of high land on the left, and which runs back from the river a considerable distance into the country.

Island No. 7, four miles below No. 6.

Lies close to the right shore in the upper part of a bend; it is a large willow island, three miles long, at its head there is a large willow bar—channel left shore; in all situations of the water.

Island No. 8, a mile below No. 7,

Lies near the middle of the river, and opposite a point of the left shore; it is about 4 miles long. Best channel on the right side of it, the left side is good in high water, and as the nearest.

Island No. 9, three miles below No. 8,

Is close to the left shore, and about three miles long—the channel is on the right of the island in all stages of the river.

Island No. 10, three miles below No. 9,

Lies nearest the left shore, river turns to the right. At the head of No. 10 is an ugly sand bar covered with willows. Best channel is to the right of both. First left hand point below No. 10 there is a sand bar at the middle of the river, channel to the right of it.—In passing No. 10, specially in high water, keep pretty close to the right hand point just above the head of the island. No. 10 is about a mile in length.

This island and the right bank opposite it, shew the first evident marks of the effects of the earthquake which commenced December 16, 1811. The right bank for several miles above and below the island, appears to be several feet about three or four, as near as I could judge from the adjoining land, lower

O

NAVIGATOR.

MAP I.

Ft. Jefferson
Mayfield C.
Iron B.
5 Wolf Is.
Chalk B
Bayou de She

156

Zadoc Cramer's Post Earthquake Commentary on Island No. 10 from THE NAVIGATOR

(page 157 of the adjoining figure)

"Island No. 10, three miles below No. 9, Lies nearest the left shore, river turns to the right. At the head of No. 10 is an ugly sand bar covered with willows. Best channel is to the right of both. First left hand point below No. 10 there is a sand bar in the middle of the river, channel to the right of it— In passing No. 10, especially in high water, keep pretty close to the right hand point just above the head of the island. No. 10 is about a mile in length.

"This island and the right bank opposite it, shew evident marks of the effects of the earthquake which commenced December 16, 1811. The right bank, for several miles above and below the island, appears to be several feet, about three or four, as near as I could judge from the adjoining land, lower (cont'd from p. 158) than it formerly was. Many of the trees standing in all directions on the island, and particularly the willows on the willow point opposite it, clearly evince the concussions of the earth. This island is said to have cracked to that degree that several large trees, standing on the cracks, were split from the roots up to their tops.

"Two miles above No. 10, a bayou runs out from the right side, and comes in again three miles below the island. A few years may make this a safe pass and form another island. From the entrance, or mouth, of this pass, or bayou, you have a fine view of New Madrid six or seven miles ahead."

More Perils Downstream

Boats on the Ohio River at Louisville and Shippingport had been trapped by the onset of winter ice. Thus, there was a period of time between the first and last week of January when no boat traffic could pass. This prevented many vessels from finding themselves near new Madrid during the worst of the January earthquakes. However, a mid-month warming trend caused the ice to break up on the twenty-second. There was some hazard to taking the Falls of the Ohio alongside huge chunks of crashing ice, but the boatmen were growing impatient to get on with their business.

According to Louisville engineer, Jared Brooks—weather-watcher and ardent statistician of the New Madrid events—the morning of January 23, 1812, was "hazy with a south wind. . . At 8:50 A.M. a very violent earthquake occurred much the same character as the first" [on December 16th]. According to Brooks' meticulous records, two more "considerable" shocks struck Louisville again the same day, one at 1:00 P.M., the other at 10:30 that evening. They were followed by another "considerable" shock the next morning and several others during the day. Furthermore, according to Brooks, after the largest shock on January 23, it began to "rain, hail, and snow" at Louisville.

None of this daunted the fearless boatmen. Over the Falls they went and on their way to New Madrid and other points beyond. The departure of a large number of boats from Shippingport at this time placed them at, or near, New Madrid at the time of "The Hard Shock." Thus, the weather conditions at Louisville, which prevented many boats from being near New Madrid during the shock of January 23, doomed them to be there in large numbers on the eve of February 7 to endure the worst upheaval of them all. Many would not survive.

Among those who had departed from Shippingport on, or shortly after, January 23rd was Vincent Nolte, a New Orleans merchant with a small fleet of twenty boats. Nolte had met the Emperor Napoleon, had tea with Queen Victoria, had consulted with General Lafayette, advised an Austrian premier, arranged loans for the Pope, was a friend of James John Audubon, and had won (and lost) several fortunes. As fate would have it, on the evening of February 6, 1812, he and his flotilla were anchored just below New Madrid.

Nolte's head was full of politics and concerns over the impending war with Great Britain. He could not sleep. At 3:15 A.M., when the great earthquake struck, Vincent Nolte was in his cabin drawing a cartoon of President Madison by candlelight. While the captains and crews of all nineteen of his other boats cut their moorings in panic and cast off down the river, Nolte kept his head.

Perhaps in their confusion they thought it would be safer to quickly leave the area. They did not know that they were only six miles upstream from the epicenter so that when they headed downstream they were drifting into what was probably one of the most troubled, treacherous, and violent reaches of the river at the time of its maximum turbulence.

Nolte later wrote, "I at once reflected that if, under the usual circumstances, it was dangerous, and, therefore, by no means advisable, to trust to the stream in the night, it must now be much more so, when the danger was greatly increased . . . and that consequently it would be a better plan to remain where we were until daylight."

Since there were no survivors to describe what happened, we can only surmise that at that hour that stretch of river was probably a murderous, raging body of impassable water, rising and falling in colossal waves, opening up into chasms, whirlpools seething, full of large trees, stumps, and other hazards that would largely clear themselves by daylight on February 7. Any boat venturing into those waters at that time could have found itself shooting down some towering wave, like a surfboard on a sea wave out of control, tossed like a piece of drift, capsized, smashed in the roaring billows, and sunk in pieces. Such things had already been described by witnesses on the Mississippi from lesser earthquakes of December and January. The descent downriver of those nineteen hapless vessels was, no doubt, a descent into a maelstrom of no return.

When Nolte eventually reached Natchez, Mississippi, he inquired about the boats that had preceded him. But "nothing afterwards was ever heard of the boats that had been so hastily cast off." Today the Associated Electric Plant and the Noranda Aluminum Company occupy the banks of the river along the stretch where these and many other, boats disappeared.

How Many Died?

Ten people were reported dead at New Madrid on December 16. On the same date a man drowned in Arkansas when the White River, near present-day Newport, suddenly rose during the tremors and swept him away. The squeezing action of seismic waves on underground aquifers can cause sudden large discharges of groundwater into streams causing earthquake-induced flash flooding. A boy in the St. Francis River bottoms near present-day Kennett, Missouri, was also counted as dead from the quakes. He was looking for lost cattle on January 23 and never returned. He was probably drowned in a sunk land, washed away by a seismic flash flood, or caught in the quicksand of a sand boil. At least one elderly person is known to have died of exposure when the populace of New Madrid evacuated and camped in tents and lean-tos at the start of the series, which was during the coldest months of winter. No doubt there were many others. A number of people died at New Madrid during the dark hours of February 7th when the waters of the Mississippi rushed over the land in a giant wave at the mouth of St. John's Bayou, but no one knows how many. Also killed were a couple of dozen pirates on Island #94.

The Crist family living in Kentucky, approximately 80 miles due east of New Madrid, lost one daughter on January 23, but they were not alone. Many of their neighbors had been injured and had also lost loved ones. On February 8, 1812, the day after "The Hard Shock," George Crist, Sr., made the following entry in the Crist Log Book:

"If we do not get away from here the ground is going to eat us alive. We had another one of them earth quakes yesterday and today the ground still shakes at times. We are all about to go crazy from pain and fright. We can not do anything until we can find our animals or get some more. We have not found enough to pull the wagons."

In Cape Girardeau no deaths were reported but many homes were severely damaged, and two brick buildings were said to have collapsed. For a village of only 200 people, these may have been the only two non-residential brick buildings in town. Most of Cape rests upon solid limestone which experiences only a fraction of the ground wave intensities experienced on sand, clay, and flood plain sediments which are characteristic of the soil conditions south of Cape and across the river in Illinois.

According to some accounts less than twenty deaths were documented on land but this is extremely misleading. No systematic effort was ever made to compile all the reports and obtain a true count. Since communications were so poor and many families and communities lived in isolation, most deaths on land, like those on the river, probably went unrecorded. Reasonable estimates would be at least a hundred deaths on land, if not double or triple that figure. These casualties would have been from a variety of earthquake phenomena, including landslides, earthquake flooding, caving river banks, crevasses, and collapsing cabins.

According to the traditions of the Indians, there were more redskins killed than white men. This would make sense, for the Native Americans outnumbered the settlers at least two to one throughout the zone of the greatest disturbances. Since they often camped on the river's edge, they would have been particularly vulnerable to the threat of earthquake-induced flooding and failing banks that pushed many of their camps into deadly waters There were probably many Indian villages that were sunk and flooded like Little Prairie, but where the people were not so fortunate to have escaped as did George Roddell and his neighbors.

For example, in the formation of Reelfoot Lake, Indians say that a village was drowned and everyone killed. We should probably take them at their word on this instead of considering such a report as "legend." It is also highly probable that one or more Indian villages were drowned in the formation of Big Lake. And when the town of Big Prairie disappeared in Arkansas, Indians along the river there also reported the submergence of one or more Indian villages with complete loss of life.

In totaling deaths from the New Madrid earthquakes, those of the Native Americans have never been really considered. One reason for this was that there was no mechanism by which red man's losses were tallied into white man's records. Hence, these data were just not available.

One thing is certain. Hundreds of Native Americans died who were never counted. Many were lost in their camps and villages, and many were lost from their canoes, as testified by the large numbers of empty ones seen drifting downstream during the five months of the siege.

The River of Death

As for the Mississippi River, untold hundreds lost their lives. A crude accounting could be made for some. For example, at least a hundred lives were probably lost over the second waterfall at New Madrid between February 7 and 10, as witnessed by those on shore. There were also the nineteen lost boats of the Vincent Nolte convoy, which could account for another 100 lives lost. And Nolte's boats weren't the only ones to disappear below New Madrid that day. These, plus scattered records of other boats lost, might add up to another 100-200. No one knows how many died over the first waterfall ten miles above New Madrid and while Mathias Speed and his crew survived the violence of the river's retrograde motion, no one knows how many others did not. Most deaths on the river could never be accounted for. Only the battered debris of their broken, empty vessels were available to tell the tale.

Surviving passengers, and those fortunate enough to preserve their lives while witnessing events from the shores, reported seeing numerous enormous river bank cave-ins. Sometimes a mile or more of land would collapse at once. Boats tied up to slumping banks were buried, swamped and sunk, often with everyone still aboard. These massive cave-ins also caused huge waves that rapidly swept across the channel, bashing the other side and bouncing back. Many boats caught in the middle were capsized by this process.

During the five months of the earthquakes, from December to May, boatmen became so afraid of being sunk and killed by a failing bank that many preferred to drift in the middle of the river at night rather than take a chance by tying up on the edge. Stories of sinking islands deterred many from tying up there, as well. Some reported seeing chasms opening up in the river where turbid waters rushed in—sucking boats and their occupants into the abyss, never to be seen again. At other times the waters would suddenly rise or suddenly fall several feet. The river was a very dangerous place to be.

The safe passage of the steamboat, *New Orleans*, was nothing short of a miracle. The wreckages of many boats were strewn up and down the river during those months. It was a busy artery of traffic, the main interstate highway of its day. Thousands of people ordinarily passed along the Mississippi waterway each month. There can be no doubt that, at the very least, hundreds died on the river.

In total, then, by our manner of reckoning, deaths of all races from the New Madrid earthquakes of 1811-12 would definitely be in excess of 500. That would be the low estimate. It would not be unreasonable to postulate that the number of deaths was greater than 1,000. Most would not have been residents of the area, but travelers passing through on the river. Any way you figure it, 500 to 1,000 is a significant percent of the sparse population of the region in that time, which numbered no more than 15,000—including every white settler, black slave, and redskin.

Many previous publications have remarked on the low number of fatal-

ities attributable to the New Madrid earthquakes. Some sources have placed the number of deaths on land at less than a dozen and have not added to this any estimate of deaths on the river. As for Native Americans, it does not appear that anyone has included these mortalities, which were considerable. By attempting to account for everyone, as we have done here, an entirely different picture emerges. It does not bode well for the future.

Today, in the same zone between St. Louis, Evansville, Memphis, and Little Rock, there are approximately 5,000,000 people. This is over 300 times the population living there then. If we were to have another series of earthquakes equal in magnitude, intensity, and duration as those of 1811-12, with the same rate of casualties, the death toll could be well in excess of 20,000. That would be, by far, the greatest calamity in North American history. For probabilities of this happening in your lifetime, see Chapter Six.

The End of Old New Madrid

While the shocks previous to February 7 had devastated the homes of New Madrid, many were still standing in some condition, although none had chimneys. The gravity of the damages from the February 7 earthquake left no doubt that it was the strongest. Boatmen described the town on the morning of February 7 as "destroyed, the houses all thrown down, some unroofed, some prostrated, not a house left entire, not a chimney left standing."

As for the townspeople, those few remaining had all fled before day-

NEW MADRID BEND
in 1810

Before the earthquakes of 1811-12 there were two towns on New Madrid Bend, New Madrid and Point Pleasant. There were also three inlets to the Mississippi: St. John's Bayou, Bayou Fourche (which connected with Gut Ste. Anne) and Bayou Portage (which connected with Portage Open Bay). Gut Ste. Anne and Portage Open Bay both connected with the Little River which, in turn, was connected with the St. Francis River.

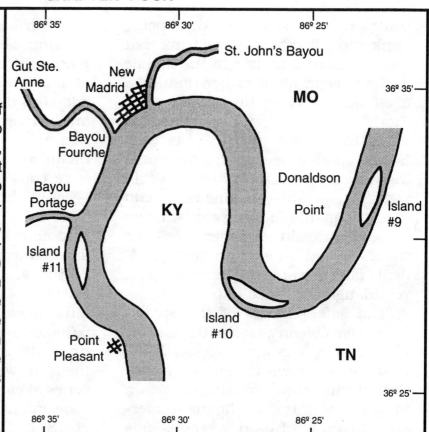

NEW MADRID BEND
in 1905

The earthquakes destroyed Gut Ste. Anne, Bayou Fourche, and the mouth of Bayou Portage. The original site of Point Pleasant was thrown into the river as was part of old New Madrid. By 1905 the Mississippi River had completely occupied the sites of both towns. Islands #9 and #11 were almost completely incorporated into the bank by this time while Island #10, which had been on the left bank was now on the right. Donaldson Point had moved west and south.

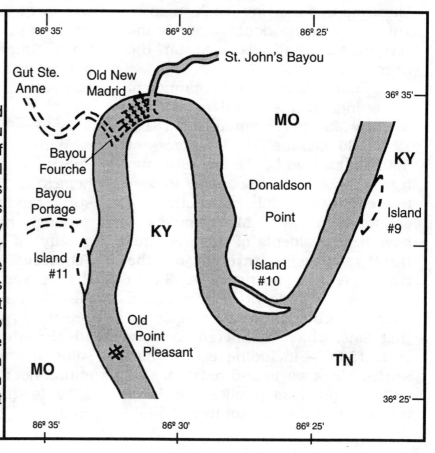

NEW MADRID BEND in 1990

By the late 20th century, the Mississippi River had migrated a mile northward at New Madrid. The waterfront of the original town is now a river bank in Kentucky. The site of Old Point Pleasant is now in Tennessee. Island #9 has been absorbed into the Kentucky mainland while Island #11 has been absorbed into the Missouri side, as has been the mouth of Bayou Portage. Island #10 is now half missing while the remaining half is absorbed into Donaldson Point.

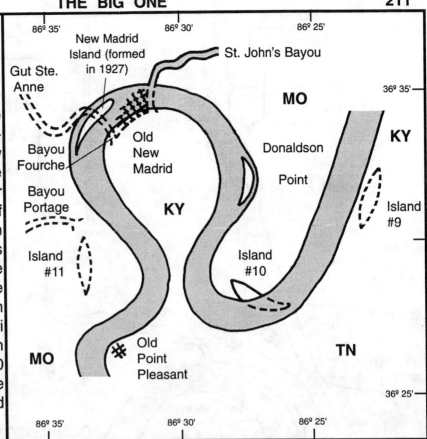

SUPERPOSED VIEWS OF NEW MADRID BEND 1810, 1905 & 1990

This composite view of the Mississippi River at New Madrid Bend shows the course of the river in 1810 (shaded), in 1905 (solid line), and in 1990 (dashed line). You can see how Donaldson Point has moved to the southwest and how the neck of the bend has narrowed to where it is less than a mile wide today. Some places, such as the original site of Point Pleasant, have actually changed to the other side of the river.

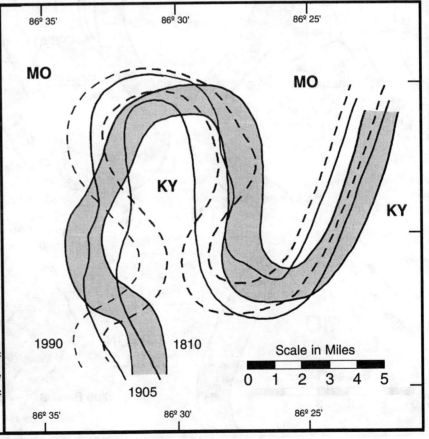

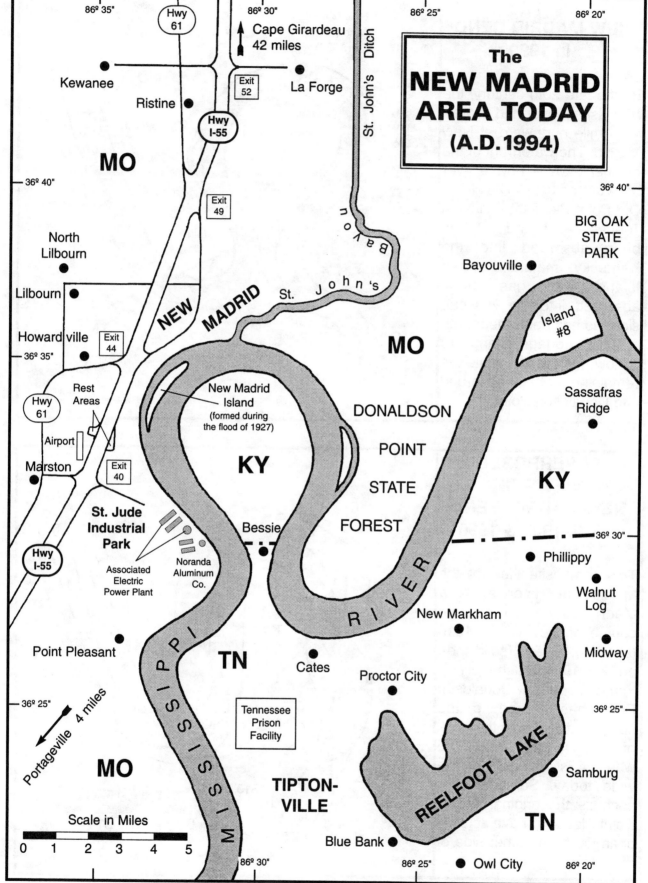

86º 35"
Hwy 61
86º 30"
↑ Cape Girardeau 42 miles
86º 25"
86º 20"

The
NEW MADRID
AREA TODAY
(A.D. 1994)

Kewanee
Ristine
Exit 52
La Forge

St. John's Ditch

Hwy I-55

MO

36º 40"   36º 40"

Exit 49

Bayou

BIG OAK
STATE
PARK

North Lilbourn

Bayouville

St.   John's

Lilbourn

NEW   MADRID

MO

Island #8

Howardville
Exit 44
36º 35"

New Madrid Island
(formed during
the flood of 1927)

Sassafras Ridge

Hwy 61
Rest Areas

DONALDSON

Airport

KY

POINT

KY

Marston
Exit 40

STATE

St. Jude
Industrial
Park

FOREST

Bessie

36º 30"

Hwy I-55

Associated
Electric
Power Plant

Noranda
Aluminum
Co.

RIVER

Phillippy

Walnut Log

New Markham

Midway

Point Pleasant

MISSISSIPPI

TN

Cates

Proctor City

36º 25"   36º 25"

36º 25"
↙ Portageville 4 miles

Tennessee
Prison
Facility

REELFOOT   LAKE

MO

Samburg

TIPTON-
VILLE

TN

Scale in Miles

0 1 2 3 4 5

Blue Bank

86º 30"
86º 25"
● Owl City
86º 20"

New Madrid Area Today

The adjoining figure shows some of the towns and highways around New Madrid in 1994. In 1810 this map would have shown only two towns, New Madrid and Point Pleasant, both of which were destroyed by the quakes and whose original locations are now both on the other side of the river. An 1810 map would also not have shown Reelfoot Lake, which was created by the earthquakes of 1811-12.

Island #11 is now incorporated into the mainland between St. Jude Industrial Park and Point Pleasant. The location of the mouth of Bayou Portage, destroyed by the earthquakes, is to the west of the Associated Electric Company plant within the St. Jude Industrial Park. Today a remnant of the old bayou can still be seen as a grove of cypress trees in the industrial complex.

The St. Jude Industrial Park is the approximate location of the largest of the epicenters, the 8.8 magnitude event of February 7, 1812. The 812 foot tall smokestack of the Associated Electric Plant, which is visible for more then 30 miles in all directions, is a good marker for this quake's location .

"Gut" is an old French word meaning "gutter," "ditch," or "creek." Gut Ste. Anne was a small stream that connected the Mississippi and the Little Rivers. It had a mouth (Bayou Fourche) just below the original site of New Madrid. It was destroyed by the earthquakes. Today its former course can be traced by a discontinuous series of channels that no longer flow, including Lake Ste. Anne near Howardville. A trace of the old Gut crosses Interstate Highway 55 between Exit 44 and the Rest Area. It can be seen as a sand-filled channel with willows growing on the west end. Where modern trucks and cars speed by at 65 mph, Spanish and French boats once passed through carrying out the commerce of the times.

light. The flight from the New Madrid area had begun for some in December and January. On February 7th there was a mass exodus. Only a few Frenchmen living in camps by the riverside remained. Panic prevailed that night. During that precipitous evacuation, some had the presence of mind to hitch teams and load provisions. Many left at daybreak with only a few things they could carry by hand, never to return.

Moreover, the high banks that supported what was left of the town were shaken so violently on February 7 that they slumped 15-20 feet downward into the edge of the river. The remains of New Madrid were washed away in the spring floods of 1812—never to be seen again.

Since 1812 the river has continued to undercut the bank, migrating northward. Today the present town sets a full mile north of the original site. The place where New Madrid used to be can be seen from the observation deck outside the New Madrid Museum. When standing there, look due south toward Kentucky. The river is a mile wide here. From the middle of the river to the Kentucky shore is where the original town used to be. Beneath that river lies the site of a city. Not a trace is left. What used to be the bustling riverfront of old New Madrid is now a sand bar and willow grove in Kentucky. What used to be Missouri is now another state.

For several weeks after the February 7 megaquake, dozens of strong shocks continued to hammer the countryside around New Madrid. Several of these were major earthquakes—well in excess of 7.0 on the

Richter scale.

A few people stayed to rebuild another New Madrid where the new banks had been established after the quakes. Those who stayed were of two types: Those too stubborn to leave and those so poor they couldn't afford to leave. Almost everyone with the means to relocate had done so.

The Land, Itself, was Destroyed

Five settlements and two large islands are gone because of these earthquakes, as well as Fort Jefferson, Kentucky. They were literally wiped from the face of the earth, without a sign of their former existence. Every map of the area had to be revised. No one even tried to count the small Indian villages along the river that disappeared in those violent cataclysms.

Wiping out towns, islands, and settlements was not the only permanent destruction done by these earthquakes. They destroyed the land, itself. Thousands of fissures, sand boils, explosion craters, crevasses, and surface faults now criss-cross and dot the land surface for more than 5,000 square miles. Former dry land was sunk into swamp while former wet land was uplifted high-and-dry. Streams that once flowed into the Mississippi now drained away from the river while other stream beds were so disrupted that there was no stream left at all—only a string of ponds and sand features going nowhere.

At least ten earthquake lakes were formed, either by subsidence, damming of former channels, or a combination of both processes. Shortly after the quakes, A.N. Dillard,

a woodsman and trapper, described his experience on some of the newly formed lakes in the Missouri Bootheel: "There is a great deal of sunken land caused by the earthquake of 1811. There are large trees of walnut, white oak, and mulberry, such as grown on high land which are now seen submerged ten and twenty feet beneath the water. In some of the lakes I have seen cypresses so far beneath the surface that with a canoe I have paddled among the branches."

Of the ten known quake lakes of 1811-12, only Reelfoot and Big Lake still exist today. The rest were drained during the 1920's for agriculture and/or for mosquito control. The biggest was forty-mile long Lake St. Francis, described earlier. Lake Ste. Anne (between New Madrid and Howardville) is all that is left of old Gut Ste. Anne (St. Ann's Creek), a stream that used to flow by a large Indian Mound which was there long before the earthquakes and is still there today. As for the lake, it is easy to find Lake Ste. Anne (also spelled St. Ann), but all you will see today is a large grove of willows in front of New Madrid Central High School which fills with water only during heavy rains.

There was also Lake Tyronza near present-day Tyronza, Arkansas; and Flag Lake, north of Kennett; as well as Lost Lake, a large shallow body of water ten miles long and two miles wide between present-day Bell City and Vanduser, Missouri.

Lake Nicormy, formed by the earthquakes, was quite large—about twelve miles long and six miles wide. Its former bed lies between Kennett and Hayti. It was a favorite resort place for hunters and fishermen, complete with vacation cabins, a hunting lodge and boat docks. It, too, was drained about 1924.

Lake St. John (between Benton and Sikeston) was there for more than a hundred years after the quakes but has been drained by St. John's ditch which diverts the runoff all the way to St. John's Bayou on the river at New Madrid.

You won't find water and scenic lakeshore at these locations any more. Only the rich, black lacustrine soils of a former lake bed will be seen at Lake Nicormy, Lost Lake, Cagle Lake, and Lake St. John. If you want to know exactly where these lakes are (or were), in order to visit the sites, you will find the maps and directions you need in the other two books of this trilogy.

Following the quakes, the natural drainage patterns of the Missouri Bootheel and northeast Arkansas were so disrupted that vast areas became unuseable swamp. One of the largest of these was the so-called, "East Swamp" that used to lie between Portageville and Malden, which was sixteen miles wide and twenty-five miles long. Even high ground held newly-formed swampland in many places because of clogged or truncated drainage channels that had destroyed the former patterns of runoff.

But the fault zone was not all turned to swampland. Eliza Bryan, a New Madrid resident at the time, reported that "the beds of some ponds were lifted up so that they were drained" and no longer held water. George Roddell, a resident of

Little Prairie, "was standing in his own yard situated on the bank of the Bayou of Big Lake," when a great shock occurred. "The surface on the opposite side of the Bayou, which before was swamp, became dry land while the side" on which he was standing "became lower" which, later that day, became submerged under several feet of water.

Regardless of whether dry land was made wet or wet land was made dry, there were so many cracks, craters, fissures, and downed trees, as well as other newly-created impediments to farming, that many people could no longer make a living by agriculture.

Disruption of Transportation

One of the "newly-created impediments" to commerce and agriculture was the destruction of the means of travel and transport. According to Zadoc Cramer's *Navigator*, before the earthquakes there were "two water courses from the Mississippi below New Madrid to the St. Francis." He commented that it was difficult to tell "whether they run from the latter to the former, or from the former to the latter." Actually, they could flow either direction depending on which of the two rivers they connected was the higher at any given time.

Francois and Joseph LeSieur were founders of New Madrid (L'anse Ala Graisse) and had lived in the area since 1783. Around 1803, Francois founded another town on the river he named "Little Prairie." Almost all of the bayous and other features of the landscape in that area had been named by the LeSieur brothers. A.N. Dillard was a trapper and a contemporary of the LeSeiurs who had worked most of his life along the streams and forests between New Madrid and the St. Francis River.

According to Dillard, "Previous to the earthquake keel boats would come up the St. Francois River and pass into the Mississippi River three miles below New Madrid. Now," Dillard said, "the bayou is dry land." The LeSieurs identified this as "Bayou Fourche."

Bayou Fourche was described by the LeSieur brothers as follows: "The Bayou left the Mississippi River, entered Lake St. Marie and Gut Ste. Anne, then flowed past La Grande Cote, or Big Mound (a Mississippian Indian settlement now called "The Lilbourn Site"), and entered Little River. In the early days a ferry across this stream was maintained near this mound." From the Little River there were several navigable channels to the St. Francis further to the west. Actually, before the earthquakes the St. Francis and Little Rivers formed a braided stream system where waters from one passed freely to the other, going both ways, across a distance of sixteen to twenty miles between the two streams. The communication between the Little and St. Francis Rivers was permanently destroyed by the earthquakes.

Today, at milepost #44, Interstate Highway 55 crosses the place where this channel was located, just inside the New Madrid city limits. Another portion of the channel is still visible today as "Lake Ste. Anne," just east of Howardville and in front of the New Madrid Central High School.

According to the LeSieurs, another place where boats could be passed

from the Mississippi inland to the Little River and the St. Francis was where Portageville, Missouri, is today. The earthquakes destroyed that passage, too. "Bayou Portage flowed out from the Mississippi River, running to the southwest and entering Little River one mile south of a Spanish Mill" (now Boekerton, Missouri). "This bayou was frequently used for the purposes of transportation. Barges and keel boats were accustomed to coming up or down the St. Francois, crossing over to the Little River, and then pass up through Bayou Portage to the Mississippi. In time of low water it was necessary to make a carry across the ridge which separated a part of the bayou from the Mississippi. This carry was usually made to a point on the river where there was originally an Indian Village." Around 1804 this place became the site of a white settlement called Point Pleasant.

Evidently, there were two openings on the Mississippi that connected with Portage Open Bay and, thus, the Little River. According to the LeSieurs, "Four miles south of Point Pleasant a low place in the banks of the river allowed the water to flow into a lake." Because of its grassy, mossy banks, which felt like a soft sponge when walked upon, it was called Cushion Lake. An outlet from Cushion Lake also connected with Portage Open Bay. The lake survived into the mid-twentieth century—even though its connections with the Mississippi and Portage Open Bay did not. A remnant of the old lake, choked with willow trees, is still visible today.

Since the 1920's most of what had

Cushion Lake Today. It is hard to imagine that this was once a sizeable lake. It is even more difficult to imagine that this was once an important commercial waterway, that Spanish keel boats, French pirogues, and Indian canoes once passed through here between the Mississippi River and Spanish Mill on the Little River. But the earthquakes changed that. Today it is little more than a willow thicket disconnected from the rivers it once served. Somewhere in the vicinity of the photo on the left a Spanish boat is buried in the mud, sunk more than 200 years ago during a different era.

been Portage Open Bay has been kept dug out to keep the land drained for agricultural purposes, but it does not carry the quantity of water it used to carry before the earthquakes. Interstate Highway 55 crosses this Bay just east of Portageville today. This waterway became impassible after the earthquakes, its flow checked by caved in banks, and its channel broken and filled with trees, sand, and mud.

At the same time some channels were plugged, some wetlands were made dry. The disruption of natural drainages caused a vast amount of permanent flooding which submerged all or portions of many of the main roads. In a government report compiled in 1837-38 the impediments to transportation posed by the newly-formed swamps were described as "being a complete barrier against an approach to the Mississippi River from the west."

According to the report, "The people on the slip or tongue next to the Mississippi are, by this line of swamps, entirely separated from the other portions of Missouri and Arkansas, while the people in the interior sections are entirely cut off from a market for their goods by being cut off from the navigable waters that lead to the points of sale." The report continued, "West Prairie," which would be near present-day Malden, Missouri, "one of the most beautiful and productive portions of the State," is about 26 miles in a straight line from New Madrid. There used to be a road between the two, but several feet of water cover that area since the earthquakes. According to the government document, "The distance that must necessarily be traveled to obtain that point is now about 130 miles." To get there from New Madrid "one must either go around the head of the delta or swamp," almost to Cape Girardeau, "or else go south nearly to the Arkansas line to a place where the swamp can be waded on horseback, but not with any vehicle."

Portage Open Bay Today. Portage Open Bay marks the line between New Madrid and Pemiscot Counties. The top two photos are where Interstate Highway 55 crosses the Bay. The bottom view is several miles east near the site of an old Indian village. What appears to be a brush-clogged ditch today was once a major thoroughfare flowing between Cushion Lake and the Little River where it connected with distributaries of the St. Francis River. The earthquakes permanently destroyed this once busy commercial waterway.

Another Town's Future Destroyed

Spanish Mill was a small port on the Little River seventeen miles southwest of New Madrid and five miles west of present-day Portageville. It was established in the late 1700's. It was strategically located for passing commerce across the Bootheel between the St. Francis River and the Mississippi River. There were two places a boat could leave the Mississippi and pass over to the Little River at Spanish Mill. One was just north of Point Pleasant via Bayou Portage. The other was eight river miles south of Point Pleasant at Stewart Landing. Keel boats on the Mississippi could enter an inlet there that flowed into Cushion Lake and from there to a point where it joined with Bayou Portage to form Portage Open Bay, which went all the way to the Little River at the Spanish Mill. From there boats could work up and down the Little River or take a distributary west and work up and down the St. Francis River. In addition to the mill, which was powered by the flow of the Little River, the Spanish settlement was also a center for trade, there being a store and market for exchange of goods at the site. Being positioned at the intersection of the commercial waterways of the area, the future of that settlement appeared excellent—a good place to invest and build a business. That was before the earthquakes.

When the quakes began, the residents of Spanish Mill were among those who evacuated to New Madrid and, from there, to the north. The earthquakes devastated the buildings at Spanish Mill, but they could have been rebuilt. What really spelled the end of the settlement was the permanent alteration of the land, itself.

By the time the earthquakes had finished reforming the landscape, Little River no longer flowed with sufficient current to run the mill. The mill's access to the Mississippi via Bayou Portage and Portage Open Bay had also been cut off. Furthermore, the clear channels that had once carried traffic by the mill, to and from the St. Francis River, were no longer navigable. The St. Francis, itself, was also blocked with permanent logjams and congested channels—a result of the quakes. Furthermore, just west of Spanish Mill a perennial swamp had formed sixteen miles wide and two to four feet deep, flooding the road that used to run westward across the Bootheel. The settlement was almost completely isolated by the seismic reshaping of the land. Its advantage and purpose in being there no longer existed. So it was abandoned.

In 1840 a man by the name of John Weaver bought the land that had once been the site of Spanish Mill and named it Weaverville. About the same time a "pole road" was constructed across the swamp between Weaverville and Clarkton, sixteen miles to the west near the St. Francis River. The road consisted of a line of earthen mounds three or four feet high with wooden bridges in between. There were 146 such bridges that made up that stretch across the swamp.

Weaver built the bridge over the Little River that comprised the eastern end of the pole road. He charged a small toll. One day a traveler tried to cross the bridge without paying.

He and Weaver became caught up in a heated argument. The dispute was settled when the stranger pulled a gun. John Weaver was shot and killed—all because of a nickel toll.

The pole road lasted until the Civil War when it was burned by the Confederates. The road was eventually rebuilt, but the swamp was also eventually drained. That took place around 1924. About the same time Weaverville was renamed Boekerton, the name by which the site is known today.

Thus, Boekerton, Missouri, marks the spot where a promising settlement once lay—its hopes destroyed forever by the earthquake. The old waterways across the Bootheel that passed the Spanish Mill have never been re-established. Today the Little River is little more than a ditch through which very little water flows. It is no longer the vital stream it used to be—swift, clear, full of fish, and busy with boats carrying commercial cargo. Thus, neither Weaverville nor Boekerton ever had the potential for growth that Spanish Mill did in its day.

Boekerton has a population of 30 people today with no apparent prospects for future expansion. Its only businesses are a used car lot, a catering service, and a hair dresser, the Boekerton Beauty Shed. There is one church, the Boekerton Baptist. There is also a federally funded school for preschool children, the Delta Headstart Program.

Perhaps the Boekerton residents like it that way, small and quiet. Growth is not always a good thing. But things could change. They did for Spanish Mill. In less than three months, it's promising future was destroyed, cut off from the world, and its site rendered commercially useless by an earthquake. The only evidence that a thriving enterprise once flourished there are a few Spanish coins found at the location of the Boekerton School.

Spanish Mill Today. A mill and trading post once flourished along the banks of the Little River near the junction of Portage Open Bay and the distributaries of the St. Francis River. Spanish Mill was a busy crossroads for commerce in the late 1700's. The earthquakes changed that forever. Today, the Boekerton Head Start School stands on the site where the mill used to be. The trees behind the school mark the banks of the Little River. The town there today, founded in 1840, has only 30 residents. The recent photos of Boekerton above show the sign to the Boekerton Beauty Shed, the Boekerton Baptist Church, and a curious cow in someone's yard. The two bottom views are of the Little River today as seen from the Boekerton Bridge looking upstream (right) and downstream (left). Once brim full of clear flowing water, teeming with fish, and laden with the goods and boat traffic of the day, it is now not much more than a ditch full of weeds that only carries water when it rains hard.

Big Lake, Missouri. Big Lake was created by an 8.6 quake on Dec. 16, 1811. The Lake was in the epicentral area on the Missouri-Arkansas line. In the 1920's the Missouri end of the lake was drained and renamed as the Hornersville Swampland, but the Arkansas half remains a lake. The photos above show the drained bottom of the Missouri portion of Big Lake just east of Hornersville—photographed in 1974 by the U.S. Geological Survey. These and the other USGS photos on the next 3 pages present visual evidence of how the earthquakes "destroyed the land itself" and how that evidence is still visible almost 200 years later. The white stripes are seismic fissures that filled with quicksand. Note the large fracture zone on the left of the upper photo. Also note the pair of concentric ring fractures on the left of the bottom photo—surface expressions of seismic liquefaction ring dikes. The numerous light dots that look like measles on the landscape are earthquake sand boils—each 30-60 feet in diameter. These boils are the pores of the earth through which millions of gallons of groundwater were extruded in 1811 to fill the lake. There are about 2,000 boils per square mile here or approximately 8.000 boils visible in the lower photo. There were no known survivors from this area in 1811-12.   Scale: 3.25 inches equals 1 mile

PEMISCOT
BAYOU

STEELE
AIRPORT

STEELE

I-55

Pemiscot Bayou & Culbertson's Farm. Pemiscot Bayou was a River before the earthquakes broke it up into discountinuous pieces. The old channel meanders from the right, to center, to upper right, off to the left, and loops back in view in the lower left corner. Earthquake sand fissures (light streaks) are seen throughout this view, including Steele, Missouri, and across Interstate 55 (lower right corner). The grey portion of the Bayou in the upper left is thought to be the new channel formed December 16, 1811, that put the Culbertson's smokehouse across the river from their house. Note the curved trace of the former bend of the river above the bayou. It looks like streaks of quicksand were squeezed out here during the quakes. Photo 1974. Scale: 2.25 inches - 1 mile.

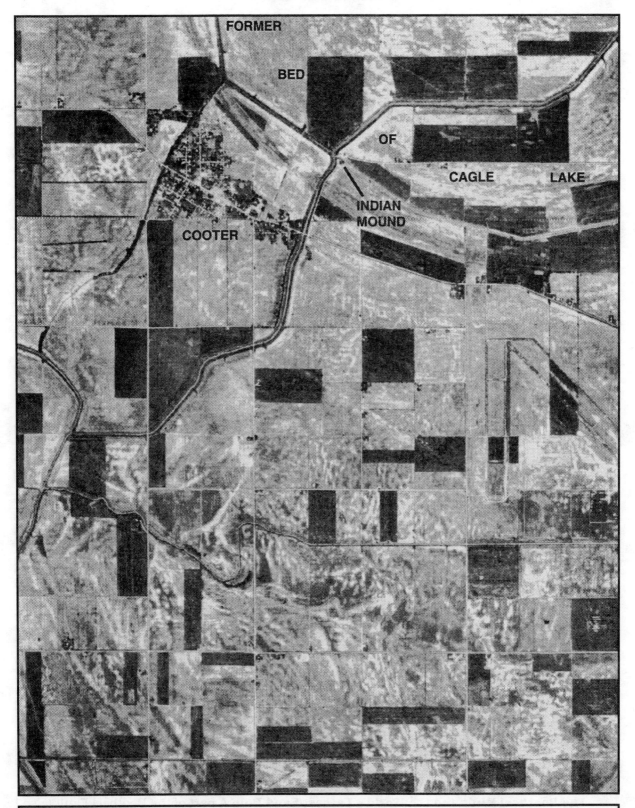

FORMER

BED

OF

CAGLE LAKE

INDIAN MOUND

COOTER

Cagle Lake & Epicentral Area of 8.0 Quake, December 16, 1811. Cooter, Missouri, is the small town in the upper left. In the upper right is the southern part of the former bed of Cagle Lake, created by the earthquakes. Mr. Cagle's Indian Mound is the dot at top center on the edge of the curved shoreline visible here. The white patches and stripes are seismic sand boils or sand fissures from 1811-12. The surface of the earth was completely fractured to pieces here. Photo by U.S. Geological Survey, 1974.   Scale: 3 inches = 1 mile.

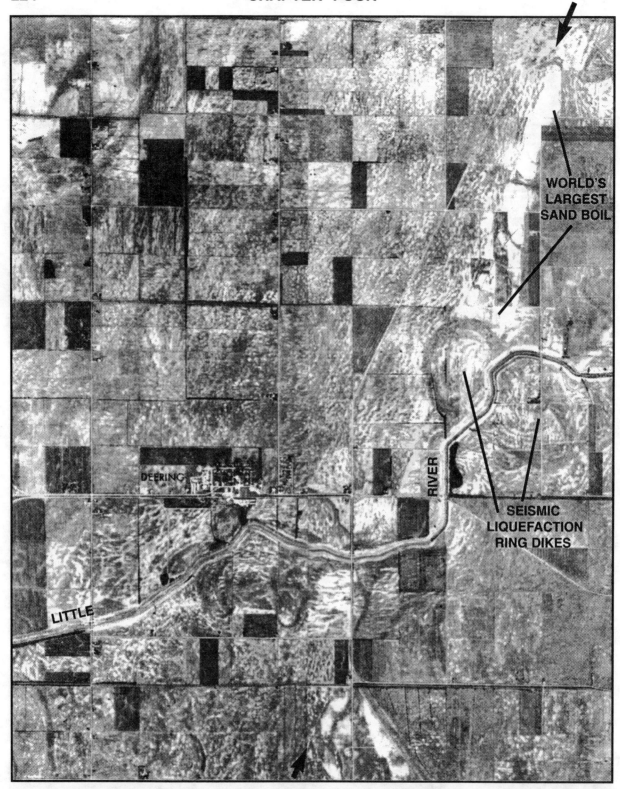

WORLD'S
LARGEST
SAND BOIL

RIVER

DEERING

SEISMIC
LIQUEFACTION
RING DIKES

LITTLE

The Bootheel Fault and the World's Largest Sand Boil. A part of the Bootheel Fault (also Bootheel Lineament) is denoted by the pair of black arrows above. It can be traced visibly in the land surface for about 80 miles—between Marked Tree, AR, and Lilbourn, MO. Notice that the sand boils on the west side are numerous and small while those on the east are fewer but large. The huge white patch along the east side of the fault at the top is the world's largest sand boil—almost 1.5 miles long and 136 acres in size. The town in the center is Deering, MO, and the stream meandering across the photo is the Little River. Notice the series of seismic ring fissures on the right which the Little River bends around. This 1974 view is about 8 miles west of Hayti, MO   Scale: 2 inches = 1 mile.

Redeeming Ruined Real Estate

More than a hundred years ago southeast Missouri had been nick-named as "swampeast" Missouri. People living there were accused of having webbed feet. But the Bootheel had not always been a wetland.

On February 20, 1850, the 31st Congress of the United States published Report No. 108 addressing the question of whether or not it would be financially feasible for the lands destroyed by the earthquakes to be reclaimed. The data and conclusions had been authored by a member of the U.S. Corps of Engineers, Captain W.B. Guion, who made a reconnaissance of southeast Missouri and northeast Arkansas in 1836-37. The report was in support of H.R. #44, a bill to reclaim parts of Missouri and Arkansas from the devastation of the earthquakes.

Guion noted that there were more than 2.3 million acres of land in Missouri and Arkansas that were now "a continuous sheet of water and situated on both sides of the line dividing those two States . . . The water over this land is generally from one to two feet deep and remains nearly the same the year round. And as the water has deadened the trees, it presents the appearance of a lake studded with a forest of snags, and forms a picture of desolation not easily surpassed. The character of the timber in these stumps is peculiar to dry land only. Their perishing condition amidst the waste of waters, tell the history of the past, and that at no remote period, more eloquently than language could portray. At the period of the growth of that timber the land was dry, which demonstrates its original formation, and the perfect susceptibility of the soil for reclamation. These immense overflows, or shallow lakes, are, unquestionably, the result of the earthquakes of New Madrid in the years 1811 and 1812, whose terrible history is familiar to all, and whose awful ravages have left their impress upon the whole face of the country," the Captain wrote, "but not so indelibly as to be beyond the reach of improvement." Guion believed the lands could be salvaged, that it was economically feasible to do so, and that the U.S. Congress should pass a bill to allocate the resources and authorize the Corps of Engineers to do the work.

Guion explained that the cause of the submergence was not that the lands had all sunk. It was mainly because of the clogging of the natural streams that once drained the area. The courses had been filled in by the collapse of their banks, the upheaval of their beds, and the formation of "rafts" or huge logjams that acted like dams, blocking the flow and causing the waters to overflow their channels and spread out over the land. The streams most affected were the Little River, which flows down the middle of the Bootheel, and the St. Francis, which forms the western boundary of the Bootheel.

Between December 24, 1836, and January 17, 1837, Captain Guion navigated the St. Francis River from Greenville, Missouri, to its mouth at Helena, Arkansas, a distance of 419 miles. He described seven gigantic rafts (floating logjams) that spanned the entire width of the River from a point a few miles north of Fisk,

Missouri, to a point between Campbell, Missouri, and Piggott, Arkansas. Some of them were as much as 200 feet wide and 600 feet long. Guion, whose report was heard by Congress in 1850, argued that these government lands were useless in their present state and, as a result, had not been purchased by anyone even though they had been up for sale for more than thirty years since the earthquakes.

The price of clearing logjams and widening the natural channels he estimated to be around $5,000. "To retain it in its present condition adds not one dollar to the treasury, either now or in prospective," Guion said. The government would get its money back in increased sales of the land, whose value had been improved, as well as in the potential for more taxes and a greater flow of commercial traffic along the St. Francis River. The St. Francis connected the Mississippi River with the rich mineral district around Potosi and Iron Mountain, Missouri, where lead, silver and zinc has been mined since the 1700's. After the earthquake, large boats could no longer reach the mineral area by way of the St. Francis.

Guion informed Congress that not only had the lands drowned by the earthquakes been rendered unproductive and that the clogged streams raised barriers to trade and commerce, but that the "miasmic" waters also posed a serious health problem to anyone who lived near these areas "where conditions were so difficult the land could not even be surveyed." The vast mosquito breeding grounds created by the quakes supported ferocious hoards of the stinging, blood-sucking insects that not only made life unbearable, but spread many diseases, some lethal.

Congress rejected Guion's proposal. H.R. Bill #44 did not pass. Seventy years later the State of Missouri, in cooperation with Arkansas, formed the Little River Drainage District to deal with the problem. The final price tag to restore the land to "pre-earthquake" conditions was nearly 1,000 times Guion's estimate of $5,000, but the investment has been paid back many times over. Today, the Bootheel of Missouri contains the richest soils in the state and produces almost half of its agricultural produce, mainly cotton, soy beans, corn, and rice. In fact, many of the families that ventured to invest in the lands reclaimed from the quakes became quite wealthy. There are a number of millionaire farmers who live in that area today. They can thank the earthquakes for the richness of the land that has produced their fortunes.

Fear of Being Swallowed Alive

The crevasses had been one of the most horrifying experiences of the quakes. Everyone was afraid the ground would open up and swallow them alive.

The morning after the "Hard Shock," a boatman found himself stranded on Island #10, ten miles from New Madrid. He had abandoned his flatboat to avoid "the rapids" created by the quake. "During my stay on the island," he said, "there were frequent eruptions in which sand and stone, coal and water were thrown up. The violent agitation of the ground was such at one time as induced me to hold to a tree to support myself. But the earth gave way at that place, and I, with the tree, sunk down. I got wounded in the fall," he said. "The fissure was so deep as to put it out of my power to get out at that place. I made my way along the fissure until a sloping slide offered me an opportunity of crawling out." At another point during that experience, the ground became so agitated and broken up that the boatman had to run and jump in the river, swimming and treading water to save himself from being swallowed up on the land. He was later rescued by a canoe dispatched from a raft on the river.

Sir Charles Lyell, a geologist from England, found many fissures still visible during his visit in 1846. He noted them particularly near Caruthersville and Campbell, Missouri, and Blytheville, Arkansas. He also noted their presence east of the river in Tennessee. "Many," Lyell noted, "had been partly, if not entirely, filled." In some cases, he observed, the fissures were "filled by the pushing up of material from below. As the walls of the fissure opened, sand and water below the alluvium were pushed up and, in some cases, overflowed the walls of the fissure." These latter fissures can be seen today as linear stripes of sand. Thousands of them can still be observed today throughout the Missouri Bootheel as well as all of northeast Arkansas.

A red man near Little Prairie during the disturbances described how "seven Indians were swallowed up" in one of these chasms. Only one of them (himself) escaped to tell about it. The surviving redskin said "he was taken into the ground" by a deep crack "100 trees in length." It was too deep for him to climb out. The trench immediately began filling with water from the bottom up. Soon it was over his head. Swimming desperately for his life, he was lifted by the rising fluid to the brim of the abyss where the water "threw him out." He had to swim and wade four miles before finding dry land. "The Shawnee Prophet," the Indian said, "had caused the earthquake to destroy the whites."

George Roddell describes how, on the morning of December 16, his house sank suddenly "during the tenth shock." His wife and children started to run into an open field when a huge crevasse opened, blocking their way and forcing them to run for the woods instead. Just as Roddell and his family had reassembled, "the eleventh shock came on after which there was not perhaps a square acre of ground unbroken in the neighborhood." Cracks and crevasses were everywhere, and water was coming out of them. "In about fifteen minutes after the shock the water rose round them waist deep." As they tried to wade to higher ground, many times they fell "headlong into cracks in the earth, which were concealed from the eye by the muddy water." Each time they swam across until they could gain footing on the opposite side.

The size of these cracks varied from inches in width and a few feet in length to tens of feet wide and a mile or more long. Some were V-shaped while others were wide with a flat bottom. Some were as much as twenty feet deep.

Godfrey LeSieur was a young boy at the time of the quakes and a member of the band that fled from Little

Earthquake Fissures from 1811-12. The top two photos show an aerial and a ground view of a fissure near Kewanee, Missouri—more than 1,000 feet long, 100 feet wide, and 15 feet deep. Seen in aerial view, it starts where Interstate 55 bends and continues off the corner of the picture. About one-third of its length holds water. The V-shaped crevasse is in a Tennessee hillside near Obion that split during the quakes. This crack is more than 30 feet deep. The last photo is a view of the Sikeston Power Plant with two white streaks which are seismic sand fissures—places where the earth cracked open and filled with liquid sand during the quakes.

Prairie with George Roddell. He was a son of Francois LeSieur who had co-founded New Madrid in 1783 and established Little Prairie in 1803. Godfrey described how some crevasses were formed. "The earth rolled in waves several feet high with visible depressions between the swells, finally bursting and leaving parallel fissures extending in a north-south direction for distances as great as five miles in some cases."

Another observer reported many fissures 600 to 700 feet in length and 20 to 30 feet wide. Some were sufficiently wide to swallow horses or cattle, which they did and where some

livestock died.

Today, most of these cracks have filled in by erosion or have been smoothed over by heavy agricultural equipment. But some can still be seen. The other two books of this trilogy tell you where you can still experience falling into one of these openings today if you wish.

With more than 2,000 earthquakes in five months, the residents of the area got lots of practice reacting to ground motion. It didn't take them long to observe that, for any given area, the crevasses always seemed to form in preferred directions, often north-south. By felling

Dry Bayou, Earthquake Fissure from 1811-12. This fissure has sloping sides and a flat bottom (called a "graben fissure") like the one shown at the top of page 228. It is one quarter of a mile long. The Dry Bayou Missionary Baptist Church is on one side and a cemetery on the other. This stand of cypress trees have been dated to be post-1812 in age—which is what one would expect since this crack, that collects water in the winter, did not exist prior to 1811. In the last photo, the head and shoulders of Ray Knox can be seen in barely protruding above the rim of the fissure. He is 6 ft 2 inches. This view is behind the church in the cemetery.

large trees in an east-west direction, a man, his wife, and his children could run for the nearest downed tree when the ground began to move, riding out the quake. Then if the ground should split open beneath them, they would already have a bridge in place. Several families reported that such efforts had saved their lives when, in fact, the ground actually did open up beneath their fallen logs as they sat and held on in safety.

As far as deaths of people "swallowed alive" in the jaws of a fissure, only the six Native Americans mentioned earlier are known to have been killed in this way. Some received minor injuries by falling into such cracks. Others required help to be rescued. Some cattle and some buffalo were caught and perished in these crevasses. But there were no reported deaths of other people outside of the Indian race.

The lack of such reports does not mean no such incidents happened. The probability is high that a number of people did die in this way—buried alive without a trace. Without witnesses, such deaths would be noted as "missing persons," and there were many missing after these quakes whose whereabouts were never determined.

How the Bootheel was Formed

If you look at a map of Missouri, most of the southern boundary corresponds exactly with the latitude of 36.5 degrees north, except for the region between the St. Francis and Mississippi Rivers in southeast Missouri. There the boundary drops south to the 36th parallel. The resulting shape was flat on the bottom and curvilinear on the east and west, conforming to the meanders of the two rivers that define it. It looks like the outline of a bootheel.

The boundaries of Missouri as a state were not established until after 1820, several years after the earthquakes. Missouri did not become a state until August 10, 1821. In 1811-12, the Missouri Territory included a large region from the Orleans Territory to the Canadian border. The survey to establish a state line between Missouri and Arkansas was not completed until after the earthquakes had considerably altered the landscape in this region, making it difficult to travel there.

This fact has caused some to speculate that, perhaps, the surveyors who had marked out the 36.5 line from the western corner of Missouri toward the east found the passage too difficult to continue further eastward at that latitude when they arrived at the St. Francis River—because of the swampy conditions and disrupted terrain left by the earthquakes. Therefore, the speculation goes, they must have dropped down 30 or 40 miles to the 36th parallel and continued their survey to the Mississippi River where the work would be easier. This would have made the Bootheel a consequence of the earthquakes. It is an interesting hypothesis, but not true.

Another explanation has it that when the surveyors, coming from the west, got to the St. Francis River, they got drunk and fell asleep in their boat. By the time they had sobered up, they had drifted 30-40 miles downstream to the 36th parallel. So, when they resumed their survey, they just went due east from where they were instead of going back up to the other latitude at 36.5 degrees north.

The true story is this. Col. John Hardiman Walker was a resident of Little Prairie during the earthquakes and one of those who survived the trek from there to New Madrid with George Roddell between December 16 and December 24, 1811. He was also one of those determined individuals who returned to what was left of the devastated site of Little Prairie and attempted to organize another town there—the so-called "Lost Village," which struggled on for a few years after the earthquakes before it, too, was washed away by the Mississippi. He was also a cattle rancher and an influential owner of some large tracts of land between Little Prairie and Pemiscot Bayou.

When authorities were deciding where to place the southern boundary of Missouri, they had chosen to make it at the 36.5 latitude all the way across from Oklahoma to the Mississippi River. This would have made the northern and southern boundaries of Missouri perfectly parallel. That line passes about eight miles south of New Madrid but almost 20 miles north of present-day Caruthersville, near where Little

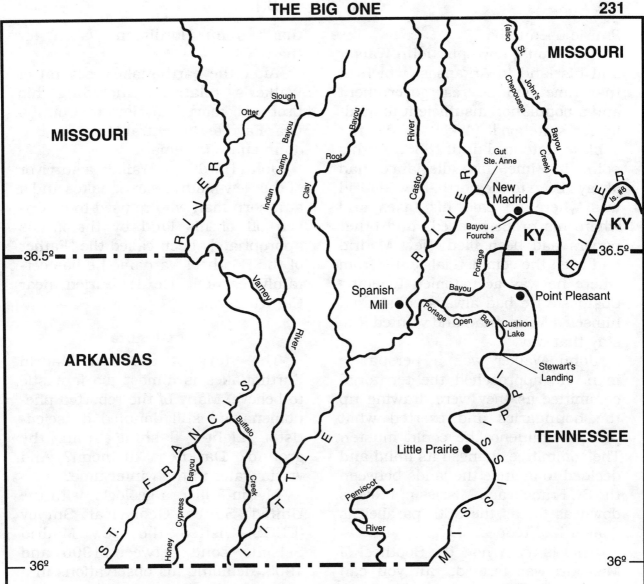

Map of the
MISSOURI BOOTHEEL
SHOWING STREAMS AND
SETTLEMENTS PRIOR TO THE
EARTHQUAKES
OF 1811-12

SCALE: 1 inch = 10 miles

0   4   8   12   16   20 miles

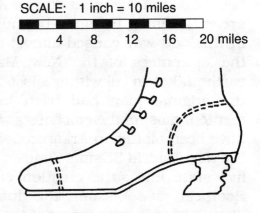

NOTE: Before the earthquakes of 1811-12, boats could freely pass across the Bootheel via a variety of routes from the Mississippi, to the Little River, to the St. Francis and back. The earthquakes destroyed the connections between these three main rivers, broke up the channels of the St. Francis and Little Rivers, and flooded most of the the Bootheel with perennial lakes and swamps. Thus, many commercial waterways were permanently destroyed. This wetland condition was not corrected until the creation of the Little River Drainage District in the 1920's, by which time railroads had taken over most of the transportation that had formerly been by boat and water.

Prairie used to be.

This would have put John Walker and his land in Arkansas, which at that time had no real government and a population insufficient to qualify for statehood. (Arkansas did not achieve statehood until 1836.) To this point in time, his allegiance had always been to the north. New Madrid was where he paid his taxes and where his property deeds and other papers had been filed. New Madrid had been the commercial center from where he was accustomed to doing business. He had always considered himself a Missourian and wanted it to stay that way.

John Walker was a persuasive man. He approached the territorial committee as they were drawing up the boundaries and exerted what political influence he could muster. The committee changed its mind and decided to include the lands between the St. Francis and Mississippi Rivers down as far as the 36th parallel as Walker had requested.

That is really how the Bootheel of Missouri was formed. But you can believe one of the other stories if you prefer. Defining the state boundaries in this odd way caused almost all of the epicenters of the New Madrid earthquakes to fall within Missouri. If the original plan had been implemented, most of the epicenters would have been plotted in Arkansas. While the New Madrid Seismic Zone crosses five state lines, the creation of the Bootheel gave Missouri the dubious distinction of owning most of the New Madrid fault. It would have been Arkansas's fault, but, as history would have it, it belongs mostly to the Show Me State. Missourians can

thank John Hardiman Walker for that.

After the earthquakes, several of Walker's relatives, including his brothers, moved to Howard County, near Fayette, in central Missouri. But John chose to remain.

John Hardiman Walker, a survivor of the New Madrid earthquakes and a stubborn man who refused to be driven off of his land by them, has appropriately been called the "Father of the Bootheel," a name he has certainly earned. He is buried near Caruthersville.

Night Lights

The story of the New Madrid Earthquakes is almost too fantastic to believe. Many of the reported phenomena are still doubted by scientists. Lights flashing from the ground? Darkness at noon? And warm water in the winter time?

Myron Fuller, a geologist with the United States Geological Survey (USGS) visited the New Madrid Seismic Zone between 1900 and 1905, detailing his observations in a classic book entitled *The New Madrid Earthquake*, USGS Bulletin 494, published in 1912. (This publication is still in print; see end of this book for details of its availability.) In addition to this field work, Fuller compiled every written source he could find at the time. He noted the numerous sightings of light flashing from the ground, but, not seeing any physical explanation for such, like most scientists of the time, he doubted the reliability of such reports. This was the position of most seismologists and geologists until the middle of the twentieth century when "piezoluminescence" was produced in a laboratory and came to be understood as an electrical phenomena.

When quartz crystals are squeezed, they produce voltages and can emit visible light. Quartz is the most abundant mineral on earth, composing the sandy beaches of the world, present in most soils, and a constituent of most rocks. Hence, when a big earthquake occurs, lots of quartz gets squeezed many times, once with each cycle of the seismic waves that pass.

When an earthquake is large enough to squeeze the quartz, light can and does emit from the ground. Just as electric light fixtures pulse rapidly at the rate of alternating current (sixty cycles per second) to produce what appears to be a continuous light source, the earth can pulse at the rate of seismic waves to produce either brief flashes or periods of continuous light—depending on the frequencies of the ground vibrations.

In Fuller's day "earthquake lights" were discounted by authorities as "products of the imagination" or "hallucinations induced by fear." The phenomenon now has a scientific name: Seismoluminescence. It has not only been seen by countless people the world over, it has also been photographed and videotaped. The colors can be almost anything including white, pink, green, blue, and yellow. They can flash in a instant or glow for ten, twenty, thirty seconds or more.

During the New Madrid earthquakes they were not only seen in the central Mississippi Valley but as far away as Georgia and South Carolina. The boatman described earlier, who was caught in the crevasse on Island #10 stated that "frequent lights appeared" while he was on the island and while he was caught in the crevasse.

The same boatman is also quoted as having said, "in one instance, after one of the explosions near where I stood, I approached the hole from which the coal and sand had been thrown up, which was now filled with water, and on putting my hand into it I found it was warm."

Warm Water

Warm water from an earthquake is something the geologist, Myron Fuller, did not seem to believe when he wrote his New Madrid earthquake report at the turn of the century and which many seismic experts don't believe even yet. Like the scientists of Fuller's day who could not accept seismoluminescence because they could not explain it, some seismologists and geologists today do not accept the reports of warm groundwater during the New Madrid earthquakes because they cannot explain it. We think the time has come to accept these reports at face value and find an explanation.

At least one modern earthquake is reported to have produced warm groundwater. The Hebgen Lake earthquake in Montana, a magnitude 7.5 on August 17, 1959, caused some normally cool springs to become temporarily warm. Natural springs are sites where groundwater flows to the surface. This example may not be comparable with the New Madrid Fault Zone, however. Lake Hebgen is near Yellowstone Park, a natural hot spot in the earth's crust where thermal springs are common. There is no igneous, voclanic, or geothermal activity in the New Madrid Fault Zone.

Groundwater normally has a temperature that reflects the mean annual temperature of the region. For the New Madrid area at that time, the mean temperature would have been about 55° Fahrenheit. This would have been the normal temperature of the groundwater there.

It has been proposed that the "warm water" reported by so many during the earthquakes was merely a subjective experience of the contrast between frigid air temperatures and the warmer groundwaters that percolated upwards, filling fissures, flowing out of sand boils, and flooding the ground. But 50°-60° is the temperature of spring water and spring water, independent of earthquakes, is groundwater flowing to the surface under normal hydrologic conditions. Anyone who has drunk or waded in spring water in the winter in Missouri can tell you, conclusively, that such waters do not feel warm at all. Spring water may be warmer than the winter air, but it is a lot cooler than your body temperature and feels sharply cold to the touch.

Another problem with this explanation is that several sources emphasized that the water was not just "warm," but "lukewarm." Fifty-five degree water does not feel warm unless your hands or body surface temperature are near frost-bite degrees. The people reporting the "warm water" were not that cold. Besides, the weather during the earthquakes was not freezing all the time. There were many days around

New Madrid during December, January, and February that the temperatures never dipped below freezing. There were some days with highs in the fifties and lows in the forties.

Godfrey LeSieur is considered a reliable source of information on the quakes. According to him, "The water thrown up during the eruption of the land" when fissures formed "was lukewarm, so warm, indeed, as to produce no chilly sensation while wading and swimming through it." Samuel L. Mitchell, whose account is also considered reliable, also reported the extruded waters as "lukewarm." Another who experienced the quakes described the waters to be "at blood temperature."

Enough people experienced the "lukewarm" waters that there was widespread speculation that the quakes were of volcanic origin, that somewhere deep in the earth, molten rock was moving around causing the quakes and the warm water. This, of course, was not true, but even the men of science at that time gave credibility to the volcanic hypothesis and took it very seriously. It was to be more than half a century later, after the invention of the seismograph in the late 1800's, before earthquakes were understood well enough to replace the "volcanic theory" with "tectonics."

There are people living in New Madrid today who have gone swimming in earthquake ponds left by the New Madrid earthquakes of 1811-12. These are explosion craters which fill from the bottom up with groundwater. These sandy depressions were described by everyone who remembered them as being filled with very cold spring water the year round.

Therefore, it is not likely that the reports of "warm" groundwater extrusions during the New Madrid earthquakes are merely due to a subjective sensation of contrasting temperatures between the air and the water. It seems more likely that the extruded groundwaters were, at least in some instances, warmer than normal. What could raise the temperature like this?

Friction, Geothermal Energy, or Light?

There are three explanations we shall explore here. One has to do with the geothermal gradient. Another has to do with friction. The other has to do with seismoluminescence.

The interior of the earth is hot. The deeper you go the hotter it gets. At some depth, it is hot enough to melt rock, which is the source of magma for volcanos. If you measure temperatures in a well or in a deep mine, you find that the temperature increases with depth. This is called the "geothermal gradient." The average gradient for the world at large is about one degree Fahrenheit per 70 feet. Hence, the rock (and the groundwater) in the bottom of a 700-foot hole should be about ten degrees warmer than at the surface. In areas of tectonic activity (active faulting), such as the New Madrid Seismic Zone, the geothermal gradient is greater than the average. In some areas it has been measured as high as one degree Fahrenheit per 20 feet. Studies in the New Madrid area do show a thermal anomaly. The measurements show that the subterranean temperatures are slightly

higher in the fault zone than in the surrounding country rock. However, these data do not indicate enough temperature difference to produce "warm" groundwater.

To feel warm, water needs to be at a higher temperature than the surface temperature of your body. Eighty-five degree water feels lukewarm most of the time. Ninety-five degree water would definitely feel warm. Any temperature much over 110° F. would start feeling hot.

If we assume a higher than average geothermal gradient of one degree F. per 50 feet for New Madrid, the groundwater would have to come from over 1,500 feet in depth to be perceived as "warm." For water to have risen rapidly through the ground to the surface from over 1,000 feet deep is unbelievable, if not physically impossible. The source of the water extrusions during the New Madrid earthquakes may have risen from 100 feet down, maybe even 200 feet down— but even these extraordinary depths would not produce groundwater any warmer than the 60's. This would not be felt as "warm." Therefore, we conclude that if truly warm water was extruded during the New Madrid earthquakes, it was not due to the geothermal gradient.

So much for that hypothesis. But we have another. Shaking produces friction and friction produces heat. Strong shaking that lasts a long time can produce tremendous heat.

For example, in earthquake engineering one method of protecting buildings from shaking damage is to isolate the building from the ground so that when the earth shakes, the building does not. One successful method of accomplishing this is to mount buildings on "springs." These are not ordinary, everyday springs, however.

San Bernardino County, California, is the largest county in the United States. It is bigger than some states. The county courthouse is huge, with more than a dozen court rooms that can all conduct legal proceedings simultaneously. The building, which is several stories tall, takes the area of an entire city block. It is mounted on "springs" consisting of alternate layers of rubber and lead. Inside the "spring" is a solid core of lead. When an earthquake shakes, the ground moves, but the building does not. Rather than the seismic ground motion being transferred to the building, it is dissipated in these lead and rubber shock absorbers.

How is this energy dissipated? By friction. The friction produces heat which is rapidly conducted by the lead. However, if the shaking is strong enough or long enough, the lead core inside the "springs" melts. Hence, for a few seconds, during the shaking, the building can actually be floating on liquid lead.

The system works. On February 28, 1990, at 3:43 in the afternoon an earthquake measuring 5.5 on the Richter scale occurred at Upland, California, less than five miles away. The building and its contents suffered no damage whatsoever. And what is even more amazing, it was a working day. The courts were in session. Yet they were able to continue their proceedings without interruption, scarcely aware that a quake had occurred.

Meanwhile, outside the courthouse and in the towns that surrounded the epicenter, there was mayhem. Windows broke, ceilings fell in, shelves and filing cabinets were overturned, hillsides failed, foundations cracked, and some people were thrown down, unable to stand. Before the shaking had stopped, thirty persons were injured and 12.7 million dollars in earthquake damages had occurred.

The melting point of lead is over 500 degrees Fahrenheit. The 1990 event may or may not have melted the lead-base isolators beneath the San Bernardino County Courthouse, but it surely made it very hot, perhaps 300 degrees or more. If a few seconds of shaking can produce hot or molten lead from the weight of a building less than 50 feet tall—shaking from a moderate earthquake that lasted only a few seconds—what would happen 50 feet below the ground from the weight of a loose overburden shaken by a great earthquake lasting several minutes? All that has to be done is to raise the temperature 30°-40° and truly warm groundwater would result.

We think those conditions were probably met on more than one occasion during the shaking of the great New Madrid earthquakes, which would explain the "luke-warm water" that people claimed to experience.

But we have one more theory. Earthquake lights were seen repeatedly during the New Madrid earthquakes. When quartz crystals are squeezed, they can produce light. But only the quartz near the ground surface has the opportunity for this light to shine into the atmosphere and be seen. The vast majority of the volumes of quartz squeezed during the compressions of the quakes would be too deep for their light to be seen. What happened to all of this light?

There is only one way for this buried light to go. It had to be absorbed into the rock, into the ground, and into the groundwater as heat. Now if you have a hard time visualizing light transforming into heat, consider that virtually all of the energy we use and live by on earth came to the planet as light—sunlight. When bright sunlight falls on your face or arm, it feels warm. Even on a cold winter day, it feels warm.

Therefore, we suggest that there may be two mechanisms whereby the mechanical energy of seismic vibrations can be transformed into heat—friction and the absorption of seismoluminescence. They are just theories. Perhaps there is yet another and better explanation. But as for the warm water, itself, we believe it actually happened in 1811-12 and that the people who experienced it were not imagining it.

Earthquake Smog

During the duration of the disturbances and throughout the New Madrid region, people reported the darkening of the skies following the largest shocks. Clear nights became overcast while clear days became dark and gloomy. Eliza Bryan described her family's experience on December 16 when the first shock struck: "My maw tried to light the lamps, but the darkness was so dense they didn't help at all." She also spoke of "the awful darkness of the atmosphere" during some of the daylight shocks. Godfrey LeSieur said that following the severest shocks, "a dense black cloud of vapor overshadowed the land." Another resident of New Madrid said that when a large shock occurred, "the air would be clear at first, but in five minutes it would become very black, and this darkness returned at each successive shock." Another New Madrid observer noted that "a vapor seemed to impregnate the atmosphere, had a disagreeable smell, and produce difficulty of respiration."

According to the recollection of Ben Chartier, who was at Little Prarie when the earthquakes began, the sky changed color with one of the shocks. "We felt a little earthquake," he said, "the sky turned green and then it shook hard."

A minister living near Cape Girardeau reported that from December 16 until December 19, "the sun, moon, and stars were concealed by a mist and fog which dropped like a heavy dew."

Another man at Herculaneum, more than 100 miles up the river from New Madrid, said that, following a shock, "the air was filled with smoke or fog so that a boat could not be seen at twenty paces nor a house fifty feet away. The air did not clear until the middle of the day after the shocks that morning." Other examples of such reports have been given elsewhere in this book.

The naturalist, John James Audubon, also observed what may have been the same phenomenon from a distance. As told in the previous chapter, Audubon was on a bluff near present-day Hickman, Kentucky, on the morning of January 23, 1812, when one of the largest of the New Madrid earthquakes hit. At this location he would have been about eighteen miles due east of New Madrid and about 25 miles from the epicenter between Point Pleasant and Little Prairie, Missouri. The bluffs are 150 to 200 feet above the river at that location, and the visibility on a clear day is at least forty miles. Audubon was looking toward the west, in the direction of New Madrid and Point Pleasant, at the time. He wrote, "I saw a sudden and strange darkness rising from the western horizon and heard what I imagined to be the distant rumbling of a violent tornado." It wasn't until a few seconds later that the seismic waves traveled to where he and his horse were standing, and the ground began to shake. Is it possible that what Audubon saw in the distance was the same "fog," "mist," or "smoke" described by others?

Scientists do not doubt this phenomenon to have been real, but are not in agreement as to its cause. Several explanations have been proposed. Some geologists ascribe it to the projection of dust into the air by the agitation of the ground. Dust could be discharged into the atmosphere by the opening and closing of crevasses in dry soil, as well as by landslides and falling buildings or chimneys. But this explanation is not satisfactory. Much of the time the soil was wet, not dry. Furthermore, this phenomenon did not require the juxtaposition of landslides or collapsing structures. Besides, clouds of dust generated from these last only minutes, not hours.

Besides the dust hypothesis, it has also been proposed that "vapors coming from the warm water sent up from the cracks and small craters was condensed and helped to make the air foggy." If warm water was, indeed, present, and we believe it was, then this hypothesis makes the most sense. In fact, warm water vapors rising from the ground into cold air containing dust particles would be a perfect environment for the condensation of cloud droplets, a form of natural "smog." In fact, we propose the term, "earthquake smog" for this phenomenon. If our theory is right, then the presence of earthquake smog would be proof of the presence of warm groundwater.

Seismic Tar Balls

One other unusual item is worthy of note. In addition to lignite and coal extruded with the quicksand during liquefaction, there were also "black balls" of a substance unknown to the people at that time. These ranged in size from small pellets, less than a quarter of an inch wide, to spheroidal nodules as big as hickory nuts to the size of golf balls. Godfrey LeSieur, who picked up some of these nodules as a young boy during the quakes, thought of them as "a charcoal substance with the odor of bituminous coal impregnated with sulphur," but later, when he became familiar with the odor of petroleum, which was unknown in 1811-12, he described them as "solidified asphaltum."

When crevasses and sand boils discharged their contents of sand and water, Col. John Shaw observed that "through the fissures were forced up vast quantities of a hard, jet black substance which appeared very smooth, as though worn by friction."

According to Shaw, "It seemed a very different substance from either anthracite or bituminous coal."

Samuel Mitchell gave the most thorough description of these oddities. "I found the substance very inflammable," he noted. "It consumed with a bright and vivid blaze. A copious smoke was emitted from it. . . Taken out of the fire in its ignited and burning state, it did not immediately become extinct but continued to burn until it was consumed. While blowed upon, instead of being deadened, it became brighter by the blast. Ashes formed during the combustion were of a whitish color."

These hardened tar balls are not found in every sand boil or sand fissure. However, we have found them in scattered locations many miles apart. We have collected them in sand boils in Arkansas close to Newport. We have also found them in sand boils between Charleston and Dorena, Missouri. We have seen them between Point Pleasant and Portageville. We have found handfulls of them at the site of the world's largest sand boil about eight miles west of Hayti, Missouri. "Petroliferous nodules," is the technical name we have chosen to call them, but you can call them "seismic tar balls" if you would rather.

Upon first finding them, the initial reaction is to say they are probably of human origin—leftovers from the asphalting of the highway department, or the railroad, or a pipeline company. But upon closer inspection, one realizes that these items are unusual and are found in places where human sources of asphalt have never been. Since they were first

World's Biggest Sand Boil. 1.4 miles long, 136 acres in extent, this huge earthquake feature lies along the Bootheel Fault about eight miles west of Hayti, Missouri. Seismic tar balls are very numerous here. The boil has been nicknamed, "The Beach."

described by eyewitnesses during the earthquakes long before the first oil wells were drilled, it is safe to assume that they are natural. But their origin remains a mystery.

Natural oil deposits often accumulate in fault zones. Are there pools of petroleum hidden in the subsurface of the New Madrid Seismic Zone—as yet undiscovered and untapped? Several oil companies have explored the area and have drilled test holes, but none, to date, have drilled producing oil wells. None of the residents of the area know if they found oil or not. Their information is proprietary and top secret.

In any event, you may visit the New Madrid area some day, and you may find some of these enigmatic nodules. Now you will know that they are natural and related to the earthquakes. *The New Madrid Fault Finders Guide* tells where they can be found. Seismic tar balls (*petroliferous nodules*) look like smooth irregularly-shaped lumps of hard asphalt ranging in size from the size of a pea to an inch or more in diameter. If you find one, use your pocket knife or fingernail file and "scratch and sniff." It will emit a smell like highway tar. But it isn't. These tar balls at land surface are related to the earthquakes somehow. Maybe you have a theory.

Not a Simple Earthquake

When the shocks began on December 16th and continued through the end of January, people kept thinking the worst was surely behind them. But it wasn't. Not only did February bring the greatest shock, it also brought the largest number. During the five-month attack, there were more earthquakes in February than any other month. March came in a close second. Things didn't taper off until April and May.

Even a year later earthquakes, though less frequent and less severe, were still occurring, some of them felt hundreds of miles away. Daniel Drake, a statistician, historian, and resident of Ohio, noted that even two years later, on December 12, 1813, two shocks originating in the New Madrid region were felt in Cincinnati.

Most major earthquakes follow a simple pattern. There may be one or more small foreshocks, followed by one big event which, in turn, is followed by many smaller aftershocks which die off in frequency and size until there are no more.

The New Madrid sequence was an anomaly in many ways. There were no foreshocks. There was a definite beginning of a sudden event of incredible magnitude. But instead of tapering off, the number and intensi-

ties of the aftershocks seemed to increase, reaching a peak in February and slacking off after that. They continue to this day.

Some seismologists have suggested that the hundreds of small events recorded on the New Madrid fault each year are the continuing aftershocks of "The Big One" that happened two hundred years ago. If this is so, when will it ever end?

The Final Tally

In terms of human life, no less than 500 people died as a direct result of these earthquakes. These fatalities occurred in parts of at least six states: Arkansas, Illinois, Kentucky, Missouri, Mississippi, and Tennessee. However, this is probably a gross underestimate. The true number of mortalities from these events is probably well over 1,000—mostly transients on the Mississippi River and Indians along the banks. The significance of this number lies in the fact that no more than 15,000 people, including visitors and all races—red, white, and black—were present in the New Madrid Seismic Zone during the disturbances. Hence, 500 to 1,000 lost lives represents 3-6% of those present. As many as one in twenty people there at the time died. Take those percents in consideration with the number living in this same zone today, and you find yourself in the five figures.

As for property damages, the residents of New Madrid, Point Pleasant, Big Prairie, and Little Prairie lost everything—including their means of livelihood and the land, itself. There were also considerable losses in Cape Girardeau, Ste. Genevieve, St. Louis,

Henderson, Vincennes, Louisville, Cincinnati, and virtually every other city, town, and settlement within three hundred miles of the epicenters. No one knows how much was lost in boats and cargo, but, considering that the Mississippi was the only thoroughfare between America's interior and the Gulf of Mexico, these losses would have been staggering.

In terms of the value of today's goods and commerce, a repeat of the great New Madrid earthquakes now would permanently break many businesses and bankrupt the insurance industry. Considering how intimately the banking and monetary systems of the world are linked today—to some extent such a loss would financially impact every developed country in the world. The economic ripples would encompass the globe, extending much farther than the physical waves of the quakes, themselves.

Such an event would be a calamity exceeding all natural disasters in American history. The probability of this happening in the near future is the topic of the next chapter.

An example of economic destruction from the New Madrid earthquakes (as opposed to physical) is Spanish Mill. Although it was directly and seriously damaged by the strong ground motion, that could have been fixed. What was unfixable was the fact that the commercial value of its location was irrevocably destroyed. Isolated by newly-created, impassable swamps, its access by land cut off, the river that ran the mill and the navigable waterways that brought its trade were also obliterated by the earthquakes. Its reason to exist had been taken away, as was its will to live. Hence, the settlement died, never to be rebuilt as the center of commerce it had formerly been.

Fort Jefferson in Kentucky was unoccupied during the earthquakes and it is well that no one was there since the site was destroyed by earthquake-induced landslides. Although rebuilt after 1818 and occupied until after the Civil War, the second Fort Jefferson was located about a mile from the first one. The original site had been made permanently unstable by the earthquakes and undesirable as the location for a settlement. The site is now a tree farm operated by the Westvaco Company who grows them for pulpwood for paper.

From Cape Girardeau, Missouri, to Natchez, Mississippi, there were a total of seven occupied white settlements on the river during the earthquakes. Four of them vanished. Only Cape, Natchez, and Fort Pickering made it. Three out of seven. That's a survival rate for river towns of 43%. If Fort Jefferson had been occupied, the survival rate would have been three out of eight, or only 37% Apply those percents to the number of settlements on the river today, including the gambling boats and their onshore complexes, and see what you get. The odds are not good.

To summarize, it can be said that at least five towns, two islands, and one fort, representing portions of five states, were totally destroyed by these earthquakes, several completely wiped off the map. Not a trace of any of these settlements can be found today. If they had not been written about and remembered, no one would ever know they had even existed. Their obituaries are as follows:

EARTHQUAKE OBITUARIES

1. Big Prairie, Arkansas. Destroyed on December 16, 1811, lost to liquefaction and subsidence. The Mississippi River occupies the site today. Helena, Arkansas, was established nearby in 1820.

2. Little Prairie, Missouri. Destroyed on December 16, 1811, lost to liquefaction and subsidence. The Mississippi river occupies the site today. Caruthersville, Missouri, was established nearby in 1857.

3. Island #94, Mississippi (also known as Stack Island or Crows Nest Island). Destroyed on December 16, 1811, lost to liquefaction and subsidence, drowning everyone there. One hundred years later a new sand bar was deposited near this site by the Mississippi River. It has been given the old name of Stack Island, along with the old number—#94.

4. Island #32, Tennessee. Destroyed December 21, 1811, lost to liquefaction and subsidence. The Mississippi River still flows over that site today.

5. Point Pleasant, Missouri. Destroyed on January 23, 1812, lost to bank slides into the Mississippi. Another town of the same name was established years later west of the original site (now in Tennessee) and a mile inland from the river bank.

6. Fort Jefferson, Kentucky. The site of which was destroyed in January and February, 1812, lost to landslides. The town of Wickliffe, Kentucky, was incorporated in 1882, just north of the original location of the Fort. The instability induced by the earthquakes has made it impossible to build on the original site of the Fort, even to this day.

7. Spanish Mill, Missouri. Its access to navigable streams destroyed between December and February, 1811-12, lost to liquefaction, lateral spreading, and permanent alterations in surface drainage patterns. Another settlement was established there in 1840 originally called "Weaverville," but now known as Boekerton, Missouri.

8. New Madrid, Missouri Destroyed by shaking, river tsunamis, and subsidence from December through February, washed away by floods in April and May of 1812. The Mississippi River and a Kentucky sandbar occupy the site today. The modern town by that name is a mile north of the original location. Today's New Madrid overlooks the place where it used to be—now beneath the water on the Kentucky side of the river.

This requiem litany is not complete. Lost Indian villages are not included because we do not have the information to tabulate them. Other white settlements may have also disappeared, as yet unnoted by historians. But the real question isn't "What did happen?" The question is "What will happen?" What epitaphs will comprise such a list after the next great New Madrid earthquake?

Chapter Five

AFTERSHOCKS

As for these things that you see, "the days will come when not one stone will be left upon another; all will be thrown down." Then they asked him, "Teacher, when will this be, and what will be the sign that this is about to take place?"

And Jesus said, "When you hear of wars and insurrections, do not be terrified; for these things must take place first, but the end will not follow immediately." Then he said to them, "Nation will rise against nation, and kingdom against kingdom; There will be great earthquakes, and in various places famines and plagues; and there will be dreadful portents and great signs from heaven." (Luke 21:6-11)

Throughout history earthquakes have often carried religious significance. Earthquakes are associated with Mount Sinai and the delivery of the Ten Commandments to Moses (Exodus 19:18). Throughout the Old Testament, they are associated with "the wrath of God" (II Samuel 27:7-8; Psalm 18:6-7; Psalm 60:2; Isaiah 29:6; Jeremiah 10:10; Amos 1:1; Zechariah 14:5); To Christians they are associated with the crucifixion (Matthew 27:54) and with the resurrection (Matthew 28:2). They are also associated with the end of the world (Matthew 24:7; Mark 13:8; Revelation 6:12-13; 8:5; 16:18). During, and preceding, the five-month swarm of earthquakes that struck the central United States in 1811-12 everything listed in the scriptures quoted above seemed to be taking place.

There were, in fact, threats of war, insurrections, nations rising against nations, famines, plagues, and great signs from heaven, including an eclipse that had been viewed by most Americans, and all of this taking place to the accompaniment of terrestrial temblors on a daily basis for weeks and weeks. Devout Christians of that time also noted Revelation 6:12 which warned that after the "great earthquake" the sun will become black as sackcloth, the full moon like blood, and the stars of the sky will fall to the earth. A solar eclipse had darkened the midwestern sky in September, but three months later, when the quakes began, the dust and vapors that rose from the ground during the shaking repeatedly blackened the sun and caused the moon to take on a reddish hue. And as for "stars falling," the Great Comet of 1811 certainly fit that description close enough to be convincing.

Another scripture, Revelation 16:18, refers to "a violent earthquake, such as had not occurred since people were upon the earth," accompanied by "flashes of lightning, rumblings, and peals of thunder." To the people living in or near the Central Mississippi River Valley these passages from the New Testament sounded like an exact prophecy of what they were seeing and hearing:

"Flashes of lightning?" Bursts of light did accompany these earthquakes but not necessarily from heaven. Most of these eerie manifestations were probably from the ground, itself. Seismoluminescence is the scientific term. The source of this luminosity is the presence of quartz in rocks and soil. Flickering earthquake lights and the phosphorescence of glowing ground were repeatedly witnessed in 1811-12 as far away as the East Coast.

The earthquake of Biblical proportions mentioned in Revelation 16:18 also associates "rumbles and peals of thunder" with the event. "Isn't that exactly what we hear when the ground shakes?," people were saying. And it was true. When many of the shocks took possession of the earth during that fateful five months, they roared and thundered with deafening decibels, just like the Bible said. But there was another phenomenon even more alarming than that.

Earthquakes can produce light in at least two ways. Besides seismoluminescence, it is possible that people also saw discharges of electricity, actual "flashes of lightning," during or just prior to some of the major events. The ubiquitous presence of quartz in the rocks of the earth, subjected to the alternating stresses of seismic vibrations, can generate not only light, but also powerful electric fields that attract lightning to strike the earth from the sky above, sometimes even when there are no clouds. "Piezoelectricity" is the technical term for this phenomenon. Many witnesses said they heard thunder-like rumblings and even saw flashes of light just prior to the sensation of shaking. Seismic waves travel twenty to thirty times faster than sound waves. Rumbling noises can be generated by earthquakes during the shaking by the coupling of the vibratory ground motion with the air. But the fact that people repeatedly heard the "thunder" before they felt the shaking can only mean that the precursory rumble was caused by something other than the coupling of ground with air. In other words, there actually could have been "earthquake lightning" just before the shock waves arrived and even several minutes before the shaking started.

The phenomenon of earthquake lightning is well documented in other parts of the world, especially in China. In that country, which has been visited by numerous killer quakes throughout its history, the citizens are trained in how to recognize the types of anomalous animal behavior and other signs known to preceed earthquakes. Children, even in elementary school, are taught to note and report the occurrence of lightning when there are no clouds. Sometimes earthquake lightning can preceed a major quake by several hours or even a day.

Bolts of lightning from a clear sky? Ghostly luminescence flashing from the ground? Strange signs in the heavens? Political unrest? Wars between nations in America, and in Europe, as well? Innumerable earthquakes in the states and then, the killer quake that hit Caracas, Venezuela, in March of 1812? It did not take much imagination or initiative for preachers to recognize and seize upon this unprecedented opportunity to evangelize.

The Elder Wilson Thompson

Elder Wilson Thompson was a Baptist minister from Campbell County, Kentucky, located a few miles upstream from Cincinnati on the Kentucky side of the Ohio River. He and his parents owned land there. Just as Daniel Boone had been swindled out of many of his holdings in Kentucky, so the Thompsons found themselves in similar disputes over property titles. In January, 1811, when he was 23 years old, Wilson, his wife, his two children, and his parents moved to Cape Girardeau County, Missouri. They settled on some land owned by his Uncle Benjamin Thompson on a fork of Bird's Creek just south of the city limits of present-day Jackson. (The town of Jackson, named after General Andrew Jackson, later to become the Seventh President, was not laid out until 1815.)

The only Baptist Church for thirty miles around was Bethel Meetinghouse located near his Uncle's property. It was formally constituted on July 19, 1806. Bethel was the first Baptist Church established west of the Mississippi River. It was also the first permanent Protestant Church west of the river as well.

Elder Thompson had felt called to this part of Missouri to administer the gospel. When he arrived in Cape County he wrote, "I soon found that I

Elder Wilson Thompson, 1788-1866

was surrounded with a very rough class of society. The Lord's Day was devoted to hunting, sporting, and shooting at marks, horseracing, jumping, and foot-racing. Shooting matches and all wild sports were principally set for Sunday. It was common for hatters to bring hats, blacksmiths their hoes, axes, etc., while others would bring turkey, geese, ducks, chickens, deer-skins, etc., to the place of assembly (Hubbe's Mill) where all things were there shot for. I had to pass by that mill going to and coming from church. As I would go in the morning, the crowd, with their guns, and the articles for which they were going to shoot, would be gathering; and by the afternoon, on my return, they would be pretty well inebriated, for these festivities were generally attended by plenty of whisky. Some would be quarrelling, some fighting, some swearing, and some playing tricks, such as knocking off each others hats, and cutting bridles and saddles. I, therefore, would expect nothing less than abuse from such outlaws. Oaths and vulgarity, and all that bad words and threats could do to annoy, were hurled at me. My course was to pass on my way, without either making any reply or seeming to notice them. All this was so very different from anything that I had ever seen before. I sometimes felt awful bad to see so much wickedness, dissipation, and immorality among the people."

The first week of December, 1811, Elder Wilson Thompson moved to a fifty-acre plot "in the green woods" which they had purchased for $3.00 per acre. It was only one mile and a half from the Bethel Church. The property had an old abandoned log cabin with the back wall missing. Elder Thompson rebuilt the wall and made other repairs so that he and his wife and children could move in.

On Sunday, December 8, 1811, Thompson selected a scripture he felt was appropriate to the kinds of "wicked, dissipated, and immoral people" that seemed to occupy the countryside around Bethel Church. The passage was from the eighteenth Psalm, a text also found in II Samuel, chapter 27. It is a prayer of King David and a description of God's response. It reads as follows:

"I will love thee, O Lord, my strength. The Lord is my rock, and my fortress and my deliverer: my God, my strength in whom I will trust; my buckler, and the horn of my salvation, and my high tower. I will call upon the Lord, who is worthy to be praised: So shall I be saved from mine enemies.

"The sorrows of death compassed me, and the floods of ungodly men made me afraid. The sorrows of hell compassed me about: the snares of death prevented me.

"In my distress I called upon the Lord and cried unto my God. He heard my voice out of his temple, and my cry came before him, even into his ears.

"Then the earth shook and trembled; the foundations also of the hills moved and were shaken, because he was wroth."

To Elder Thompson, this prayer of David's had become his own personal prayer, and God was about to answer. Thompson's autobiography relates this account: "The next Sunday night (actually early Monday morning) occurred those notable earthquakes that produced such eruptions on the Mississippi River, about New Madrid, and which rent the earth with deep chasms in many parts of southern Missouri. Even where I lived, large trees were broken down, fences and brick buildings were prostrated or much injured. My door-hinges were loosened, and the back wall which I had just put up was shaken down. For three days and nights the sun, moon, and stars were concealed by a mist and fog which dropped like a heavy dew, while ever and anon, a hard shock would seem to threaten the world with destruction."

Elder Thompson considered the quakes an act of Providence and a God given opportunity for winning souls. "I viewed the phenomena as a matter of God's wise arrangement," he said, "and I pursued my daily business with a composed and contented mind. The next day, after the first shock, I was building up my chimney of sticks and clay. Sometimes I would be upon it when a heavy shock would come. To keep from being shaken down, I would have to throw my arms around a log of the house until the violence of the shock was over. All these things never moved me nor caused me to doubt for one moment but that the Lord would speedily make bare His arm and almighty power, revive his saints, and gather in His redeemed children."

The next Sunday, December 22, 1811, witnessed a record turnout at the Bethel Meetinghouse. The Elder reported, "That day was a day never to be forgotten by me, and many others have reason to remember it as a day of days to them. It was a new country, our roads were mere traces and paths, the thick woods of the forest and underbrush were still in their natural state. The people lived in settlements or patches here and there along the creeks, with frequently some twenty miles of unbroken forest between these small settlements. This day the crowds of strangers from different settlements, for twenty or thirty miles around, were thronging every trace and path. Solemnity, deep as death, was depicted on most of the countenances, while joy and comfort sat with a heavenly smile and serene peace on the lips and brows of the saints. It was soon found that the church would hold but a small part of the gathering crowd, and, although it was now the middle of winter, yet, as there had been a rain and a thaw, the ground was very muddy. This day, however, was pleasant for the season. The seats were all carried out of the house and placed where there were a number of logs. A stand was arranged for the minister, and the services commenced."

The earthquake had been so severe at New Madrid that the Baptist preacher there, Elder John Tanner, had left. Virtually every member of his flock had fled from the quakes. There were not enough people remaining to make up a congregation. So he came to the highlands of Cape Girardeau County. For a time, Tanner, Thompson, and the other Baptist pastor in the district, Elder Steven Stilley, all three ministered to Bethel Church.

During the next year, Elder Thompson was constantly busy. "I baptized four or five hundred subjects," he wrote, "some old and some young, and some white and some black, but all professed to be sinners, and to trust in Christ as their Savior."

Bethel Church grew so rapidly following the earthquakes that its meeting house was no longer adequate. On September 12, 1812, a committee was appointed "to build a meeting house for this church of the size of 30 by 24 feet of hewed logs." It was completed in 1813 and stood until about 1867. The sanctuary could hold up to 150 people. You can visit the site today, located just 1.5 miles south of Jackson near the end of Lee Street. The location is marked by some 200-year-old cedars and the broken stones of old Bethel Cemetery.

Following the earthquakes, the congregation at Bethel not only grew, but it reached out as a missionary to

Bethel Baptist Church and Cemetery. The top two photos show a scale model of the Bethel Meetinghouse as it was rebuilt in 1813 following the earthquakes. This model can be seen at the Cape Girardeau Baptist Association in Jackson, Missouri, located about four miles from the actual location of Bethel Church. Today a granite monument, shown in the two middle photos, marks the location of the log meetinghouse where it stood until about 1867. The top of the grey stone marker reads: "HERE STOOD BETHEL BAPTIST CHURCH. THE FIRST PERMANENT NON-CATHOLIC CHURCH WEST OF THE MISSISSIPPI RIVER, CONSTITUTED JULY 19, 1806." The two bottom photos are views of the cemetery that surrounds the church site. The granite marker can be seen in the distance of both photos. The tombstone at bottom right says: "IN Memory of ELIZABETH MORISON, BORN Nov. 8, 1792. DIED Sep. 4, 1846. AGED 53 yrs. 10 ms. & 25 ds."

organize and support at least three sister churches: one at Johnson's Settlement on Turkey Creek, twenty miles southwest of Bethel (between present-day Chaffee and Advance); One at Caldwell's Settlement on the St. Francis River sixty miles from Bethel (near present-day Fisk); and another church at Saline Settlement, forty miles north (between present-day Perryville and St. Mary). The Rev. Thompson was one of the great evangelists of that era and recognized the unique window of opportunity afforded by the aftermath of the earthquakes. He regularly visited all three sister churches on foot or on horseback—traveling a total distance of 240 miles every month. He continued to baptize newcomers tirelessly.

In one instance, a black slave, whose name was Dick, wanted to be baptized. His master, Judge Robert Green, an avowed atheist, would not permit it. He threatened to take legal action against Elder Thompson if he carried out the sacrament. "I forbid you to lay hands on my property and put it in the water. You will be liable under the law if you do," said the wealthy Judge. But Dick did not give up his hope for baptism. A few weeks later he came to the church with an extra set of clothes and asked again, before the whole congregation, if Elder Thompson would baptize him.

Thompson asked him, "Has your master given you liberty?"

"No, sir."

"Do you wish to disobey your master? The good Book says: 'Servants, obey your masters.'"

"I got two masters, sir," Dick replied. "One is greater than the other. My great Master says to me, 'be baptized.' But my other master says, 'you shall not be baptized.' Now, sir, I cannot obey both. And I wish to obey my greatest Master and also to obey Master Green in all things when his commands do not forbid the commands of my greater Master."

As Dick stood at the front of the crowded hall, Thompson asked, "Dick, do you not expect that your Master Green will whip you, if you are baptized?"

"Yes, sir, but my great Master says, 'Fear not him that can kill the body, but fear him that can destroy both soul and body in hell.'"

"Have you concluded, Dick, to lay your back bare to your master's lash, rather than disobey your Master in heaven?"

"Yes, sir."

"Well, Dick, the church will receive you for baptism. You are not afraid of your Master Green's whip, and I am not afraid of his law. I will baptize you."

Dick was baptized then and there in the small creek that flowed by the church. All passed quietly for several weeks.

One evening the judge came home in a good mood and began speaking in very high terms of Dick:

"Dick has always been one of my best servants," Green said, "but for some weeks past he has been better than usual."

His wife and daughters, who had known of the baptism and had kept it secret from the Judge, took this as an opportune time to tell about Dick.

"Father, we can tell you what has made Dick so much better of late," one of his daughters volunteered. "A few weeks ago we were at Bethel at a meeting, and Mr. Thompson baptized Dick. Dick seemed so happy when they all gave him their hand and called him brother."

"Did you see Mr. Thompson baptize him?" asked the judge.

"Yes, sir, we saw it all."

"Well," said the judge, "I wish to God he would baptize all my negroes if it would make them all as good as Dick."

And that was the end of the judge's threatening of a lawsuit, the prospects for a whipping, and the complaints about the dipping. As the earthquakes continued, and more and more people joined the church, even the good Judge was seen attending the Bethel Meetinghouse from time to time.

The old Bethel Church Book contains this entry: "Robert Green Esq.'s negro, Dick, was received by experience June 18, 1813." Dick was 52 years of age at the time of his baptism, but that was only the mid-point of his long life. Half-a-century later Abraham Lincoln issued the *Emancipation Proclamation,* which took effect on January 1, 1863. The church records show that "Brother Dick Green departed this life" as a free man "in 1864 at the age of 103."

As for Elder Thompson, the Church Book notes that he served at Bethel only one more year. In September, 1814, he and his wife were dismissed by letter. Four months later his father, mother, and brother were also dismissed from the Bethel congregation. The whole family then moved to Ohio where the dauntless elder continued in his calling.

There is no doubt that hundreds confessed their conversions in response to the persuasive Elder Thompson—which was no small accomplishment on such a difficult and sparsely settled frontier. To him, the temblors had been an answer to his fervent prayers. There was no doubt in his mind that Providence had manifested itself in the form of the earthquakes for the purpose of saving souls. But there is no record of how many remained converted once the earth quit shaking.

Earthquake Christians

The New Madrid earthquakes did, in fact, stimulate a dramatic increase in church attendance. "Earthquake Christians," they were called. Ministers of all denominations took quick advantage of the situation, flocking to the region from afar—missionaries in a disaster zone. Many of them noted that when a tremor passed "people raised their voices in grateful thanks to the Supreme Ruler of Nature for their preservation."

"It was a time of great terror to sinners," as one preacher remarked. "Many hardened sinners fell like those slain in battle."

The flamboyant Reverend James B. Finely was in Zanesville, Ohio, during December of 1811. Zanesville is 525 miles from New Madrid. Yet the earthquakes caused serious damage throughout that area. People could not walk, and some were injured when violently thrown to the ground. Most masonry buildings were damaged, including the toppling of many chimneys. Plaster cracked. Parapets came down. Glass windows shattered. Waves splashed from ponds and creeks. Stream banks caved in. Church bells rang, and tombstones moved and fell over causing some to conclude that the end of the world was at hand and the dead were beginning to resurrect from their graves.

During one of the daylight shocks of December 16, Rev. Finely observed (with some delight) that "consternation sat on every countenance, especially upon the wicked." Transporting his evangelism into western Kentucky during the earthquakes, Rev. Finely leaped upon a table during one ground shaking event and shouted, "For the great day of His wrath is come, and who shall be able to stand?" Finely reported that many Kentucky youth had given up dancing and drinking in favor of prayer meetings. This trend did not last long after the earthquakes ceased.

Shortly after the tremors began, a group of tattered, unshaven fanatics appeared in New Madrid. With solemn faces they marched about town, in and out of houses, chanting "Praise God and Repent." The citizens of New Madrid were not impressed, referring to them as "repulsive" and their visitations as "ill-timed."

The main Midwestern denominations at the time were Baptist, Catholic, Methodist, and Presbyterian. Membership in the Baptist and Methodist Churches grew by 50% in 1812. Significant increases were also noted on the church rolls of the Shakers and the Quakers of Kentucky.

Religious revivals were also rampant among the Indians, who carried out innumerable purifying ceremonies to appease an angry Great Spirit. To the Indians, who had been valiantly trying to hold their ground against the encroachment of the white men, the earthquakes were Armageddon.

In Louisville a group of Christians concluded that God must be angry with them to smite their city with such fearful shaking and damage. Louisville was not known for its churches nor for the piety of its citizenry, except for Presbytcrianism, which was strong there. After the December 16 shock, a group of businessmen took up a collection to build a new church. $1000 was received. After the January 23 event, they took up another collection, and another $1000 was received. Following the great shock of February 7, another collection netted yet another $1000. Then the frequency and the intensity of the earthquakes tapered off. So did the zeal of the would-be church builders. God's wrath seemed to have been placated. The next year the custodians of the collection built a theater with the money.

Government Relief and Fraud

Because of the destruction of the land, itself, and because of the lingering fears and nightmares people carried indelibly in their memories after the winter of 1811-12, most residents of the New Madrid Seismic Zone left. The human tragedy of these events eventually led the United States Congress to enact the very first Disaster Relief Act in U.S. History in 1815. It was three years late, but at least Congress did something. Today the government tries to respond to natural disasters a little more quickly.

Part of the delay in responding to the plight of the New Madrid earthquake victims was because effective news-gathering mechanisms were not in place for the Midwest at that time. And what sketchy news was written up took a long time to reach the East. And there were no photographs to convey the horror. It would be another forty years before the science of photography was to be invented and developed. It has taken more than a century to piece together what really happened.

People didn't expect disaster support from their government in that time, either. They were used to tending to their own troubles. Today, in such a disaster, victims would be inclined to first turn to the government for help. Back then they relied upon themselves first, the government last. Congress was also preoccupied with fighting the War of 1812, which continued until 1815.

The disaster relief act of 1815 was prompted in an odd way. On March 26, 1812, a terrible temblor destroyed most of the city of Caracas, Venezuela. More than 20,000 died. Most were crushed in collapsing churches. It was Holy Thursday, just before what would have been the celebration of Easter Sunday.

Although there is no geologic connection between this earthquake and those that were simultaneously taking place near New Madrid, a German scientist actually published a technical paper in a scientific journal a few years later linking the two events by a common fault he projected to extend from New Madrid, down the Mississippi River, across the floor of the Gulf of Mexico, and into Venezuela.

During the Caracas Earthquake,

freedom fighter, Simon Bolivar, was engaged in a war for liberation against Spain. The shock became a temporary setback for his campaign for independence. The Catholic priests of the country interpreted the earthquake to be "the wrath of God," a sign that their rebellion against Spain, their mother country, was unholy and should be discontinued. Spain was quick to take advantage of this lapse in committment to the revolution and began recapturing lost territories in the months following the quake. Meanwhile, the devastated populace of Caracas was suffering.

In an act of sympathy Congress passed a bill in 1815 to send $50,000 in aid for the recovery of the stricken Venezuelans. Some Congressmen objected. "We had a devastating earthquake in our own country the same year, and we have done nothing for our own American countrymen," they pointed out. "Why not help them recover, too? Should foreign aid take priority over domestic aid," they asked."

Thus Congress passed a bill authorizing all land owners who had possessed property in the earthquake-devastated region to acquire equal parcels of unclaimed land anywhere in the Missouri Territory up to, but not to exceed, 640 acres (one square mile) by any one party. Thus, certificates were issued, redeemable in new land in what are now the states of Missouri and Arkansas. Hence, if you had 500 acres destroyed by the quakes, you could trade them for 500 acres of government land elsewhere away from the earthquake zone.

The 640-acre limit had the effect

of encouraging the largest land holders in the New Madrid area to stay there. Why would you trade, say, 2,000 acres for only 640, even it it was outside of earthquake country? John Hardimon Walker, "Father of the Bootheel," was one of these large landowners. The area of his property was over the limit by several times. So he stayed, and because he stayed, the shape of Missouri was forever altered.

Because there were no telegraphs, telephones, radios, or televisions, and because many people did not even have access to a newspaper, it was weeks before many New Madrid landowners were to learn about the offer. The New Madrid Certificates, as they were called, were issued from St. Louis.

Meanwhile, real estate dealers from the city and the East, who were among the first to hear of the plan, hastened to New Madrid. Before rural residents knew what was going on, many had sold what they had considered to be their "worthless" property to the eager buyers. Hence, it was land speculators and real estate opportunists who cashed in on many of the New Madrid Certificates. This is not what Congress had in mind.

That isn't all of the story. Some New Madrid property owners got smart. If there were so many people interested in buying their property, why not sell to all of them? In some cases the same piece of property was sold to several buyers, each attempting to apply for a New Madrid Certificate with their purchase.

To make matters even worse, some owners of the Certificates made as many as ten duplicates, selling

them to others. The term, "New Madrid Certificate" soon came to be synonymous with "fraud." So many New Madrid claims were filed that the total acreage applied for was more than the area of the entire county, which, at that time, extended from the river all the way to Kansas and Oklahoma. The ensuing lawsuits tied up the federal courts for more than twenty years following the quakes.

Congress had good intentions, but its first disaster relief act turned out to be something of a disaster, itself. It wasn't Congress's fault. The fault was to be found in the greed of those who corrupted a well-meant process. But this book deals with another kind of fault.

Bankruptcy and Counterfeiting

Counterfeiting was nothing new to New Madrid. False copies of property deeds and New Madrid Certificates were not the first instances.

Judge Goah Watson operated a shipping and trading business out of that town from 1809 until several years after the earthquakes. He said that it was very common for "some innocent man, owner of some flatboat loaded with produce, to be imposed upon by a gang, who purchased supplies and in return gave the basest kind of counterfeit money. The whole country, from Evansville, Indiana, to Natchez, was full of these counterfeiters," he added. "And as the good honest people were in the minority, our lives and property were placed in a great danger."

While no people from New Madrid were reported as having been swallowed up by the fissures that split the land in and around the town, one counterfeiter had a close call. A large chest of counterfeit castings (copper pieces) had been hidden in an out-building behind his house. It was sucked into the ground when a fissure, several feet wide, opened beneath the structure, and quicksand gushed in to fill the void. If the town of New Madrid, itself, had not been washed into the river, that chest of counterfeit treasure might still be buried there.

Judge Watson was nearly bankrupt by the earthquakes because so many left, abandoning not only their property, but also their debts, many of which were owed to him. He had extended a great deal of credit, not only to the white settlers, but to the Indians, as well. "What little was left to me, I had to subsist on and divide with those who remained and could not get away," he wrote.

But the good Judge was one of those daring ones who did not leave nor claim a New Madrid Certificate to resettle elsewhere, as most did. "We had a trying time," he wrote, "with most of the population gone, no business taking place, and no capital with which to do business. Heavy losses at different times, including the earthquake period, robbed me of nearly $30,000 and left me practically destitute with a small family to support. However, together with a small number of residents, we remained in New Madrid hoping for a comeback. Eventually we were rewarded for our perseverance."

All the Way to the Supreme Court

Among the numerous legal battles that ensued over the New Madrid Certificates, one is particularly out-standing. It is the case of DeLisle vs. the State of Missouri.

The brothers, John and Eustache DeLisle, moved to New Madrid from Detroit in 1795. Their sister was the wife of one of the town's founders, Francois LeSeiur. John left New Madrid for a visit with his sister, Mrs. Gremar, who lived in Vincennes, Indiana. There he became interested in the impending war with Great Britain and enlisted under General William Henry Harrison. He served until the War of 1812 ended.

During this time the earthquakes struck. The report that John DeLisle received was that the town of New Madrid had been totally destroyed and almost everyone killed. Since he had not heard anything from his relatives back in New Madrid following the disturbances, he assumed that his brother, Eustache, and his sister and brother-in-law, Mr. and Mrs. Francios LeSeiur, had all died in the earthquakes.

After the War of 1812 John settled in New York, married, and raised a family. In 1839 a cholera epidemic killed his wife and all of his children.

Grieved and bereft of his family, he returned to Vincennes to live with his sister. He was astonished when she informed him that his brother, sister and brother-in-law were all still alive and well in New Madrid.

He communicated with them at once. They, too, were astonished. Since they had not heard from him in many years they presumed that he had been killed in the War of 1812. In fact, they had actually received a military report that he was dead, killed in battle.

John had owned a 160-acre tract

near New Madrid. Upon receiving the notice of his demise, his brother and sister had sold the parcel for a very small sum. This land had, then, passed into the hands of persons who had speculated in land grants from the New Madrid Certificates. The 160-acre claim that had been associated with his New Madrid property turned out to be a choice site on a bluff overlooking the Missouri River. The site was none other than the grounds of the Missouri State Capitol Building in Jefferson City.

Upon discovering how valuable a grant had come from his modest property holding at New Madrid, DeLisle brought a suit against the State of Missouri to have the title of the land, thus granted, changed to his name.

The case was appealed to the United States Supreme Court. There the case continued from 1844 to 1862 when a decision was finally handed down. The claim that DeLisle had made to the grounds of the State Capitol was denied.

Thus it happened that the Capitol of the State of Missouri came to be located on a New Madrid Land Grant.

How Many Aftershocks?

Early in the series of events a Louisville engineer, Jared Brooks, had devised an ensemble of springs and pendulums with pens that would record tremors in a continuous manner twenty-four hours a day—a set of crude seismographs. From December 16, 1811, to March 15, 1812, he meticulously noted 1,874 tremors. Eight of these he had classified as "violent," ten as "severe," and thirty-five as "moderate, but alarming." The rest he classified as between "generally perceptible" in the Louisville area and "barely perceptible."

Of course, the 1,874 tremors noted by Jared Brooks were not a complete count of the temblors released by the New Madrid fault but only of those that could be perceived 250 miles east of their source. There were other shakes felt in Louisville after March 15, but Brooks quit counting every event after that date, although a partial record was continued.

To the Crist family, who lived 180 miles closer to the source than Brooks at Louisville, and to those living in the immediate New Madrid area, their experience would have probably been double Brooks' number—at least.

Hence, to say that the New Madrid earthquakes consisted of "more than 2,000 earthquakes in five months," is an understatement. For every tremor felt in Louisville, three to five would have been experienced in and around New Madrid. The true number of sensible aftershocks would have been at least 6,000 and, probably, more than 10,000. And they did not end in five months.

During a five-week period in April and May of 1812, Jared Brooks was registered at least 37 events, an average of more than one a day. He described several of these as "moderate," "strong," or "severe." Perceptible tremors were still occurring several times a month through December of 1812.

Eliza Bryan, who survived the earthquakes at New Madrid and stayed there afterwards, was to write in 1816, "It is now four years since the big quake, and we still feel slight jarrings now and then."

Even ten years later, occasional aftershocks continued to startle residents, although by that time most had become insensitive to such disturbances, accepting them as normal for the area. Those who never got used to them had eventually moved away, and all were gone by 1818.

A group of men and ladies were passengers on a steamboat ascending the Mississippi in 1820. They went ashore at New Madrid to shop and browse. They entered a house where they found a small collection of books and knick knacks. One of the travelers, Edwin James, tells the story. "As we were amusing ourselves with the examination of these items, we felt the whole house so violently shaken we were scarcely able to stand upon our feet. Some consternation was, of course, felt, and much terror expressed."

"Don't be alarmed," said the lady of the house. "It is nothing but an earthquake."

The Crist Family in Indiana

The family of George and Besy Crist of Livingston County, Kentucky, had suffered great losses and injuries from the earthquakes. Among other things, their teenage daughter, Amandy Jane, had been crushed to death when their cabin collapsed in January. They desperately wanted to leave and move to Pigeon Roost, Indiana, where they had relatives and where they had heard that the intensities of the shocks were considerably less.

During the first ten days of March, 1812, the Crist family had experienced more than thirty earthquakes ranging from "faint tremors" to "powerful shocks." Not only had the family members been rattled by these events, but their horses and oxen had been spooked and scattered, lost in the woods, and strayed onto neighboring properties. On March 10, 1812, George Heinrich Crist, Sr., recorded the following on page 178 of their family journal:

"I do not know if our minds have got bad or what. But everybody says it. I swear you can still feel the ground move and shake some. We still have not found enough animals to pull the wagons, and you can not find any to buy or trade."

One year and one month later, on April 14, 1813, George, Sr., wrote the following on pages 179-180:

"We lived to make it to Pigeon Roost. We did not lose any lives, but we had aplenty troubles. As much as I love my place in Kentucky—I never want to go back. From December to April last year no man, woman or animal, if they could talk, would dare to believe what we lived through. From what people say, it was not that bad here. They felt the ground move and shake, but it did not destroy cabins and trees like it did in Kentucky. I guess that things was as bad here, but at least they could see the enemy.

"On 3 September 1812 the Shawnees that William thought was friendly went crazy, and them savages killed twenty-four people. Most of them was just little children. William says they was all drunked up and that there was some bad blood between them and two of the settlers over a white elk that the Indians claimed these two settlers stole. I don't know how one elk could cause this—so many little innocent ones gone because of greed and hate, I guess. Me and Besy have decided to live out our lives here. These people need help. It is bad. William lost his son, Henry, and his wife. Henry lived to tell that Little Kill Buck shot him. William thought the Indian was his friend. His son Richard's wife was killed and nine of his grandchildren was killed. they dug a big hole under the big sassafras tree and buried all the dead together. It is all so very sad. We all have bad nightmares amongst us and we will most likely always have them."

Massacre at Pigeon Roost

The "William" referred to above was William E. Collings, Besy Crist's brother, who had founded the village of Pigeon Roost only three years before, in 1809. The massacre had been mostly by the Shawnees, but members of the Delaware and Miami tribes had also participated. In fact, the brave, "Little Killbuck," who shot Henry Collings, was a Delaware and the leader of the war party. This was not an isolated Indian incident. It was actually part of the War of 1812 where the British had armed Native Americans and directed them to attack the pioneers of the western frontier (i.e. anyone east of the Appalachians at that time).

William Collings had fought in the Revolutionary War and was known for his expert marksmanship with the rifle. The name he had given to the settlement came from the thousands of passenger pigeons that nested around the area, which provided a plentiful food supply for the settlers.

The birds were slaughtered and sold for 25 cents per bushel to residents at nearby Jeffersonville. The total population of the Pigeon Roost community at the time of the tragedy was less than 100, with only a few families—mostly the Collings and their in-laws.

With the outbreak of the War of 1812, several men from Pigeon Roost went to join General William Henry Harrison. Realizing that the British were stirring up the Native Americans against the Indiana settlers, three small watchtowers, or blockhouses, were constructed in Scott County to protect the settlers: one six miles north of Pigeon Roost near Vienna, one eight miles southeast of Pigeon Roost at Silver Creek, and another at the Zebulon Collings farm five miles south. In August of 1812 the British had captured Fort Detroit and Fort Dearborn (at the site of present-day Chicago) which gave them command over the old "Northwest Territory," which consisted of present-day Wisconsin, Michigan, northern Illinois and northern Indiana. Several Indian tribes in the area rushed to join the British. Chief Tecumseh had already been fighting with the British since the Spring of 1812. After a disappointing attempt by the redskins to take Fort Harrison in northwestern Indiana, a small band rode southeast to vent their frustrations on the innocent populace—burning cabins and slaughtering livestock as they came.

The first victims at Pigeon Roost on the afternoon of September 3 were the wife and seven children of Elias Payne—all of whom were killed within a few minutes. The raiding war party then scattered the family's household goods in the yard and burned the cabin. Proceeding on they came upon Elias Payne and Isaac Coffman who were hunting bee trees and were unarmed. They were both shot and killed.

Continuing south, they next spotted Mrs. Henry Collings, who was returning from a visit to Mrs. Jeremiah Payne on horseback. She was murdered instantly and her body horribly mutilated.

Next was the home of Richard Collings, a son of the settlement's founder, who was with General Harrison's Militia near Vincennes, leaving his family unprotected. The Indians then attacked and killed Richard's wife and seven children, after which they proceeded to the cabin of Henry Collings.

Henry was behind the house pulling flax when he was shot and wounded. He lay motionless under a pile of flax until the next day when he died, but not before he had identified Little Killbuck.

Finally, the warriors found the cabin of William E. Collings where old Captain John Norris also lived. Norris had fought with Harrison in the Battle of Tippecanoe in November of 1811, which had been the final defeat of Tecumseh's tribal confederation. He had been wounded in the shoulder and disabled from that combat.

At the first sight of the Indians, Captain Norris, who had been working outside, charged one of the Indians to protect William's children—Lydia (fifteen) and John (thirteen). Fortunately, William had his rifle nearby and was able to shoot the Indian just as he was about to tomahawk the boy. William and Norris then rushed into the house with the two children. Norris could not handle a rifle because of his injuries at Tippecanoe, but William was a crack shot. Aiming from a window, he killed three more red men in quick succession. The band then retreated. William Collings was the only resistance the Indians met in their raid on Pigeon Roost.

Realizing that the warriors could return in the darkness of night to attack again and burn their cabin, the foursome slipped out after dusk and tried to get to the blockhouse stockade on Zebulon Collings' place. In the darkness William became separated from Norris and the two children. They wandered, lost, in the woods all night. The next morning William and Norris had found their way to Zebulon's house, but the children were nowhere to be seen. Fearing the worst, William and Norris walked the five miles back to Pigeon Roost where, happily, the Indians were nowhere to be seen, and the children were found safe and alive.

Their numbers diminished by the encounter with William Collings, the Indian party then turned west, away from Pigeon Roost. They found the home of John Morris, who was serving in the military with General Harrison. They immediately broke into the cabin and killed Morris's mother, wife, and child.

John Biggs was also away with the U.S. army at Vincennes. His house was just west of Morris's. Mrs. Biggs was the daughter of William Collings. She saw the red men coming and escaped into the woods with her children. One of them was a small baby. In attempting to keep the infant from crying and giving away their hiding place to the Indians, she accidentally smothered the child with her shawl. The mother and her other two children were to survive.

The cabins of John Ritchie, William Colling's son-in-law, and those of Ben Yount, Betty Johnson, and Mrs. Beals were also raided by the marauders, but these settlers all succeeded in escaping to safety.

In addition to those who were killed, one child was kidnapped and carried off. Little three-year-old Ginsey McCoy was living with her aunt, Mrs. Elias Payne. Ginsey grew to womanhood with the Indians and migrated with them to Kansas when they were forced to leave Indiana. She never returned to her white heritage.

A posse of more than 200 armed men under Major John McCoy Ginsey's father) were quickly organized to pursue the murderous tribesmen and kidnappers, but they were unsuccessful in capturing even one of the guilty parties. On October of 1812, General Harrison sent a letter to the Secretary of War stating that he was holding a Miami warrior as a prisoner, who admitted to participating in the Pigeon Roost massacre and that he also had the name of one Little Killbuck—a Delaware, who had been identified as another of the assaulting band.

On Thanksgiving Day, November 23, 1813, George Heinrich Crist Sr. made his last entry in the Crist log book before handing it over to his oldest son, George Heinrich Crist Jr. That entry, on pages 181-182, contained the following closing remarks:

"We go out under the sassafras tree ever day and hold prayer. It is a cool calm feeling under this tree that I can not put into words. It kind of feels like that something just wants to hold you there, but you are not afraid. We all feel it, even the children. It is the biggest tree that I have ever seen in my life.

"I am gonna put the account book up and give it to George Jr., my oldest son, when I see him. My pa and his pa always wanted to let their grandchildren and the ones that followed them to know a little something about them. Maybe, just maybe, that we have done a little something to help the ones that will follow us in the years to come. All me and Besy ask for is to be able to worship our God—a place to lay our bodies and a little food to eat and to see our children and grandchildren and for them to have an easier life then we have had. I was borne a long time ago.

"Today that old sassafras tree just seems to keep on drawing a body to it just before the sun goes down. Even in the hot summer it is a cool calm feeling under it—I wish that I could understand it enough to tell about it."

Consider a visit to Scottsburg, Indiana, county seat of Scott County, just 25 miles north of Louisville, Kentucky. From the courthouse there, proceed 4.7 miles south on U.S. Highway 31, parallel to Interstate Highway 65. Watch for the marker indicating the location of the Pigeon Roost State Historic Site, just over the railroad tracks and 0.3 miles east of U.S. 31. The town has long vanished, its post office closed in 1862. There you will find an obelisk and a tribute inscribed to pioneers that first came there and to the victims of the massacre of September 3, 1812. The monument, dedicated by the State of Indiana in 1929, is a state memorial owned by the Indiana Department of Natural Resources. The stone marks the location of three mass graves beside the sassafras tree where the twenty-four victims were buried.

George Junior Visits His Parents

George Crist, Sr., and his wife, Besy, had arrived at Pigeon Roost in April of 1813. It had been a long and difficult trip by wagon, over 250 miles by dirt trails and muddy roads, punctuated by numerous fords and ferry crossings.

One-and-a-half years later, his oldest son, George, Jr., came for a visit with his thirteen-year-old son, Reason. His wife, Elizabeth, and their other six children had remained on the Crist homestead in Kentucky. Upon his arrival, responsibility for keeping up the Crist Account Book was handed down to George, Jr. George's first entry on page 183 reads as follows:

"Me and my son, Reason, got to Pigeon Roost two days ago. The wars and savage indian attacks and them earth quakes has took its toll on Pa and Ma. It is about the same with Uncle William and Aunt Phebe. I don't think that none of them will ever be the same. The Indian raids and attacks has been bad on all of us never knowen when they would attack or how many it would be. If Captain John Norris had not been at Uncle Williams him and John and Lydia would most likely been killed. Aunt Phebe was at Zebs helpen tend the sick, and I am thankful for that

cause what she had to go through burying the dead was hard on her. (10 October 1814)"

Four days later George, Jr., made another entry:

"Some more kin got here today. We are goin to help build back the cabins that was burned. Ma don't much like the dogs I brought—says she is as scared of them as a savage. One will stay inside the cabin at night and one outside to warn them of danger. The dogs they have is old. (14 October 1814)"

On October 28, 1814, George Crist, Jr., wrote a final comment on the impact of the New Madrid earthquakes on his family:

"I thought when I come here that Pa and Ma would go back home with me, but they won't hear of it. They say they want to live out the rest of their years here. They feel that these people need them. Some of the other children has moved into Indiana Territory from Kentucky on account of them earth quakes."

Where Did the New Madrid Refugees Go?

Besides Indiana, many New Madrid earthquake refugees settled in central Arkansas. Others headed north. Callaway, Boone, Randolph, Carrol, Chariton, Cole, Livingston, and Howard Counties along the Missouri River in north central Missouri all have a history of immigrants from New Madrid following the earthquakes. Others obtained valuable properties near St. Louis. One man, Francois Langlois, attempted to secure the Hot Springs of Arkansas with a New Madrid Certificate. He was not successful in his bid. There were some limitations on what land could be claimed by these deeds.

Many New Madrid Certificate bearers were not refugees of the earthquakes and had never lived in or near New Madrid. These included settlers from North Carolina, Kentucky, Illinois, and other states who had legitimately purchased the certificates from property owners who did live in the New Madrid region during the earthquakes.

One town whose early settlers were holders of New Madrid Certificates was Fayette, Missouri, the seat of Howard County. Almost 100 New Madrid Grants were issued in that county, including portions of the land within the city limits of Fayette, itself. Laid out in 1823, Fayette was not incorporated until 1855. It is best known for Central Methodist College established there in 1854.

Marion County, Missouri, bordering the Mississippi River 100 miles north of St. Louis, was another area that attracted many New Madrid Certificate holders. Eighteen New Madrid land grants were issued there, totaling more than 7,000 acres. The parcels ranged in size from 107 to 640 acres. One of these was granted to Francis Langlois, the man who had tried to claim Hot Springs, Arkansas. Langlois's grant in Marion County was for 150 acres on the South River with Certificate #470.

Marion County's seat, Hannibal, has a history related to the New Madrid earthquakes. It seems that an Abraham Bird owned land in the earthquake zone and, thus, qualified for a Certificate (#379) for 640 acres. Actually, Abraham never lived in New

Madrid. He was in Kentucky during the earthquakes and died in Baton Rouge, Louisiana, in 1816, before his Certificate had been cashed in for land. His son, Thompson Bird, who lived in St. Louis, inherited the certificate.

Thompson Bird joined forces with several other entrepreneurs, including Moses Bates, former Sheriff of St. Louis County. Bates bought Certificate #379 from Bird. Bird and Bates then teamed up with Baptiste Grimard, a former resident of the New Madrid area who held Certificate #425 for 200 acres which he had staked near the mouth of Bear Creek. This site provided a natural landing and harbor on the Mississippi, protected by towering bluffs to the north and to the south which became known as Cardiff Hill and Lovers Leap. By situating the Bird/Bates land claim adjacent to Grimard's land, the valley and mouth of Bear Creek were consolidated to form a perfect townsite more than a square mile in size.

In the late fall of 1818, Moses Bates brought eleven people to visit the site who were interested in moving there to establish businesses that would benefit by the river location. During that trip, an Indian was killed in December, but that did not deter the developers who recognized the natural advantages of this location. An ad in the *St. Louis Gazette*, published on St. Patrick's day, March 17, 1819, promoted the sale of lots in a new town that was to be called "Hannibal."

Hannibal was later to gain fame as the fictional home of Tom Sawyer, Huckleberry Finn, and Becky

Thatcher. Hannibal, of course, is the real home of Samuel Clemens, "Mark Twain," who was to write so much about the river, including some mention of the New Madrid earthquakes.

Other refugees of the New Madrid earthquakes resettled in Illinois, a few as far north as Chicago. Still others went back east. Only a few families stayed to rebuild New Madrid again. According to some accounts, of the 1,000 people living there when the quakes struck, less than two dozen remained. Many simply abandoned their holdings, never to return again, not even to claim a Certificate

The Year Without a Summer

1815 was the year in which the War of 1812 was ended. It was also the year the New Madrid Certificates were issued. But there was another natural event that took place in 1815 that was to have an impact around the world , including the New Madrid Seismic Zone.

Half-way around the globe, in the Pacific Ocean, just east of Java in the Republic of Indonesia, is the tropical island of Sumbawa. Its highest elevation today is the top of Mt. Tambora, 9,354 feet above sea level. Prior to December of 1815, the mountain had been more than 13,000 feet in elevation. A violent volcanic eruption in late 1815 blasted 25 cubic miles of rock from the top of Mt. Tambora, reducing it to its present height. The sound of the explosion was heard as far as Australia, 1,000 miles away. A giant sea wave was generated that killed several thousand residents on neighboring islands and was measured by ocean gauges as far as the British Channel.

The billions of tons of debris spewed into the atmosphere from that eruption were largely reduced to ashes and fine dust. The heavier particles fell into the surrounding oceans, forming a slush on the sea floor several feet thick. The finest particles blanketed the skies over most of the northern hemisphere, circling the globe and causing red sunsets for the next three years. But the immediate impact on the year that followed was a great deal more than rosy sunsets. The solar energy that normally warmed the northern hemisphere, ushering the winter out and escorting the summer in, was effectively blocked.

Oddly, the months of January and February of 1816 were so mild that many people let their fires go out. Then came March and April, which were to be the harbingers of Spring and warm weather. By the end of April, it was becoming clear that the weather was taking a turn for the worse. According to Missouri historian, Ralph A. Weinel, the weather reports for southern Missouri and Illinois were "cold and stormy" for March and April. During the month of May, 1816, the same people who had survived earthquakes four years before were now being called upon to survive the weather. May brought "seventeen days of snow or sleet while young birds froze in their nests." The month of June had snow or frost almost every day in the New Madrid Fault Zone, and repeated plantings of crops froze to death. July, in the New Madrid area, was reported as cold and frosty while an early freeze in August left an inch of ice everywhere killing almost everything green.

In New England, thick layers of ice formed in May and were still accumulating on the ground in July. In addition to the ice, there was seven to ten inches of snow. It continued to get worse through August and September. By the spring of 1817, starvation was driving New Englanders to move south and west.

In Virginia, Thomas Jefferson applied for an emergency bank loan to tide him over from his crop failures.

England and Europe were also hard hit. A typhus epidemic killed more than 65,000 people in the British Isles in 1816 and was blamed on the famine that had been induced by the cold.

1816 became known as "The Year Without a Summer." Meanwhile, throughout the year, aftershocks continued to rattle the residents of the New Madrid region. But in 1816, earthquakes were the least of their worries.

Tecumseh's Second Prophecy

When Chief Tecumseh toured the South and Midwest in 1810-1811, trying to rally supporters to resist the white man, he uttered a veiled prophecy in early 1811 to the Osage Indians of Missouri and Arkansas. "Brothers," he said, "The Great Spirit is angry with our enemies. He speaks in thunder, and the earth swallows up villages and drinks up the Mississippi." That was his first prophecy.

That speech was made from one of Tecumseh's winter camps on the White River near the Missouri-Arkansas line. Today a small town, whose name is "Tecumseh," can be found near the site of the chief's 1810-11 encampment—on the upper end of Norfolk Lake, thirty-five miles west of West Plains, Missouri. Where redskins once gathered around their campfires to discuss how they were going to stop the white man, you now find a gas station and convenience store—"Daugherty's One Stop." If you stop there to fill up your tank, perhaps Jack Daugherty or his daughter will share some of the lore they have assembled on Tecumseh and the Indians that once roamed that region.

Later in 1811, in October, Tecumseh uttered a second prophecy amidst a gathering of more than a thousand Creek Indians at Tuckhabatchee, near Montgomery, Alabama. The location of this speech held symbolic significance for Tecumseh. It was the childhood home of his mother, Methoataske. Although she had abandoned her family when Tecumseh was eleven, she had instilled in him certain values—an implacable hatred of the whites and a drive for vengeance that had set the course for his life. Ironically it was that very drive, stemming from early childhood, that had led him back to his mother's ancestral home to recruit warriors to stand against the Long Knives. His mother would have been about seventy and was apparently dead by this time. She was born in Tuckhabtchee and probably died there. While Tecumseh was there in the fall of 1811, his words were meticulously recorded by government scribes, commissioned by Congress to follow and take down his every word.

On October 5, two months and

eleven days before the first New Madrid earthquake, Tecumseh slowly and deliberately made his way to the lodge of the Chief of Tuckhabatchee. He was followed by a vast crowd who anticipated that something significant was about to happen. The Chief of the Indian town was known by the name of "Big Warrior," but he was only half red. His father had been a Scot and his Christian name was William Weatherford.

Tecumseh arrived with great dignity, explained his object to Big Warrior, delivered his war talk, presented a bundle of red medicine sticks (symbols carried by those pledged to follow Tecumseh), gave a piece of wampum (Indian money consisting of a belt of beads), and presented a war hatchet. Acceptance of these items would be symbolic of the acceptance by the Creek Warrior of Tecumseh's leadership and Tecumseh's cause.

When Big Warrior accepted all of the items, Tecumseh stood silently with piercing eyes, "reading the spirit and intentions" of the Creek Chief. Looking him steadily in the eye without blinking, suddenly Tecumseh pointed his finger toward the Chief's face and said in a loud voice, "Your blood is white! You have taken my talk and the sticks and the wampum and the hatchet, but you do not mean to fight. I know the reason. You do not believe the Great Spirit has sent me."

Tecumseh was angry. There he stood, surrounded by the members of his own mother's village, a native people who had not yet committed themselves to stop the Long Knives. Too bad Methoataske could not have

lived to be there to see her son at this moment, standing on the soil of her homeland, addressing her own kinsfolk, eloquent, magnificent, and still burning with the mission that she had ignited in him so many years before when Tecumseh was yet a small boy. She would have been proud. She would have thought her life was well spent to have had such a son.

Tecumseh concluded with a threat. "You will know that the Great Spirit has sent me. I leave and go directly to Detroit. When I arrive there, I will stamp on the ground with my foot and shake down every house in Tuckhabatchee."

So saying, he turned, left, and pursued his journey. Big Warrior stood in stunned silence. Everyone was struck with amazement at both the words and the manner of Tecumseh's threat. Big Warrior and the Creeks at Tuckhabatchee began to dread the day of Tecumseh's arrival in Detroit. They met and often talked over this matter, carefully counting the days when they thought Tecumseh should arrive in Detroit. The Shawnees, Choctaws, and Chickasaws also believed. The word spread rapidly, and, before December, even the Osage in the remote west had heard the prophecy.

According to legend the time the Creeks had fixed upon for Tecumseh's arrival in Detroit was mid-December, 1811. Exactly within the time-frame anticipated, in the dark hours of an early morning, the ground in Alabama suddenly rumbled and convulsed, the Indians ran outside in fear, and all the houses of Tuckhabatchee fell down. It was the first day of the New Madrid earthquakes.

Many redskins took up their rifles to follow Tecumseh after that, including William Weatherford, the half-Scot war chief of the Creeks. They were convinced that the earthquake had been a sign from the Great Spirit, just as Tecumseh had said. But it was too late for Tecumseh's cause.

The truth was that he never made it to Detroit. Instead, when the quakes first struck in December, he was near Cape Girardeau, Missouri, seeking the support of the Shawnees and the Delawares encamped throughout the area. He experienced many of the subsequent quakes as he crossed Illinois in January.

He reached his headquarters at Prophet's Town on the Tippecanoe in February as some of the greatest of the New Madrid quakes were sending their ripples across the continent. There he found that what he had heard rumored, and had feared the most, was true—the vast alliance of tribes he and his brother had gathered to fight the white men had been defeated and dispersed by the army of General William Henry Harrison. In his absence, his dream and his life work had been destroyed forever.

Tenskwatawa and the Earthquakes

With the defeat of the Indian confederacy at Tippecanoe, Tecumseh's brother, the Shawnee Prophet, was held to blame.

During the Battle of Tippecanoe, Tenskwatawa was in his lodge engaging in prayers of intercession with the Master of Life to grant victory to his followers. His disciples believed that Tenskwatawa's supplications would make them invincible, that his mystical medicine was more powerful than the weapons of the Long Knives.

When it became evident that the battle was being lost by the Indians, leaders of the warring tribes ran back to Prophet's Town to ask what had gone wrong and what should be done to turn the tide against Harrison's troops. This was Tenskwatawa's first news of the impending disaster. Searching for words to appease and uplift the anxious chiefs, he suddenly exclaimed that the problem was his wife. "You see," he said, "my wife is in her menstrual period and did not tell me! When she handed me the medicine fire sticks and other sacred instruments of worship, they had been defiled and rendered impotent. I have now cleansed them and will continue my appeals to the Great Spirit." This explanation made sense to the warriors who then returned to battle—only to lose.

After the humiliating defeat on November 7, 1811, the angry Winnebagos tied Tenskwatawa with a rope and forced him to live in bondage at a temporary camp on Wildcat Creek, about twenty miles from Prophet's Town. There he was publicly taunted and ridiculed. When the earthquakes struck a month later, Tenskwatawa tried to persuade his captors that the Master of Life had summoned the quakes to punish the palefaces and destroy them. But his detractors did not agree. "The Great Spirit has shaken the ground because the Shawnee is an imposter," they said.

Tenskwatawa was then blamed not only for their military and political defeat, but for the earthquakes, as well.

The New Madrid Earthquakes in World Perspective

The world has seen earthquakes of larger magnitudes than the 8.8 Richter of New Madrid. Quakes in excess of 9.0 have been experienced at least twice in this century: Chile in 1960 (Richter 9.6) and Alaska in 1964 (Richter 9.3). The Chilean quake was the largest in the twentieth century and caused the entire world to ring as a unit like a bell. These global oscillations lasted more than a week.

Many quakes have killed more people. During every century of Chinese history there have been monster quakes that have killed 100,000, 200,000, and even more in a single event. The Xiansi Province quake in China in 1556 killed more than 800,000. The cause of such massive death was a combination of loess liquefaction which caused mudflows and loess failure which caused landslides from the hills and plateaus that buried many towns and villages. Loess is a fine grained, light tan soil deposited by the wind.

Loess blankets the tops of the Chickasaw Bluffs that line the eastern side of the Mississippi River. Loess also covers the top of much of Crowley's Ridge in Arkansas, as well as the Benton Hills, in Missouri. Loess also covers the highlands of southern Illinois.

The New Madrid earthquakes caused more than 200 landslides in the loess deposits of Arkansas, Kentucky, Missouri, Tennessee, and Illinois. Some Indian camps were crushed or carried away. But fortunately, no white settlements were on the brinks of the hills that broke during the quakes nor were any located at the bases of the loess bluffs where they would have been buried. That is not true today. A number of towns, farms, and homes are now situated along these vulnerable loess features that could be destroyed in a future major earthquake.

The greatest earthquake disaster in human history, as measured by lives lost, was the Xiansi Province quake, mentioned above. The cause was loess landsliding in a densely populated area. The central Mississippi Valley was not densely populated in 1811-12, and it is a good thing that it was not.

Some earthquakes have been felt over areas as large or larger than the New Madrid series. The Lisbon, Portugal, earthquake of 1755 was felt throughout Europe and much of northern Africa. It caused large waves in lakes and streams as far away as Norway and Finland. Some even reported it to have been felt across the Atlantic on the east coast of North America. The 1897 earthquake in Assam Province, India, was also felt over a very large area, including the entire eastern half of the Indian subcontinent, all of Nepal, Burma, Thailand, southern Tibet, and parts of several other countries. It damaged every brick or stone building for 170 miles in every direction from its epicenter.

Many earthquakes have changed the course of history. The Lisbon quake occurred on All Saints Day (the day after Halloween) when the city's churches were filled with the faithful. The cathedrals collapsed, killing tens of thousands of worshippers, while the brothels and drinking halls of the city survived intact. This caused many to doubt, if not renounce, their faith. The age of blind religious belief was dealt a blow from which it would never fully recover.

But even in spite of all these facts about other earthquakes, the New Madrid earthquakes are unique in all the world. No earthquake sequence in history has ever lasted so long, produced so many major shocks, nor created such spectacular phenomena on land and water as the New Madrid earthquakes. New lakes, waterfalls, rivers running backwards, whole towns disappearing, whole forests reduced to stumps and log piles, thousands of square miles put to ruin—stories like these are not heard in such magnitudes and numbers for any other earthquake recorded in history. No other quake in the world is known to have left so much permanent and widespread visible evidence for future generations to visit. It is not surprising that so many of those who actually lived through the quakes mistook them for the "violent quake, such as has not occurred since people were upon the earth" mentioned in the sixteenth chapter of Revelation that was supposed to mark the end of time.

There is no other earthquake in the world for which one could write a book like this almost two centuries after the fact and still have thousands of seismic features preserved to see, to touch, and to experience. What other earthquake has so many fascinating stories to tell? This book is only a sample of what could be and what has been written

In these ways, the New Madrid

earthquakes have no equal and are truly among the greatest in world history.

December 16, 1812

It is an irony that the first anniversary of the beginning of the New Madrid earthquakes marked another historic date. This was the day that Napoleon crossed over the Niemen River in retreat. The river was the boundary between Russia and Eastern Europe in what is now Lithuania.

Five months before, on June 24th, as the New Madrid aftershocks continued, an optimistic Emperor Napoleon had charged over the river with 600,000 troops to do battle with an outnumbered, ill-trained, and poorly-equipped Russian Army assembled to defend their homeland. But instead of fighting, they retreated. As Napoleon followed in pursuit, deeper and deeper into Mother Russia, the Muscovites continued to retreat, striking by surprise, suddenly disappearing, and burning everything behind them. Eventually they drew Napoleon's Legions within sight of Moscow, itself. Then they drew a line and stood their ground.

Napoleon was not used to fighting like this. The Muscovites fought more like the American Indians than their European neighbors. Napoleon did not know how to deal with the "ambush, vanish, retreat, and burn" tactics of the Russian peasantry. He was used to clashing with trained troops who staged their attacks in more predictable ways. Napoleon should have studied the experience of American colonists who had learned about these forms of warfare and defense from the Indians.

By this time, Napoleon was 600 miles into hostile territory. Although he was able to occupy Moscow for one month, it was an empty victory. The citizens had abandoned the city and set it afire. Napoleon had suffered fearful losses in his conquest, and his supply line had been cut off. When the Czar, Alexander I, refused to surrender and the Russian winter had begun to set in, Napoleon began his retreat on October 19, 1812.

When he finally reached safety on the western bank of the Niemen on December 16, 1812, he was a broken ruler with fewer than 100,000 surviving troops. Those who had not been killed in battle or by the incessant harassment of the Cossacks during their retreat either starved or froze to death, along with their horses. The Emperor would never recover from this defeat. Less than three years later on June 18, 1815, at Waterloo, Belgium, he was defeated for the last time and exiled to a lonely island in the Mid-Atlantic—half-way between the New World and the Old. There he remained until his death six years later.

History Changed for Both Red Men and White

The earthquakes brought an era to a close for the white settlers of New Madrid. The dreams of a "Queen City" on the Mississippi were forever destroyed by those events.

At the same time an other era also came to a close for the American Indians. The earthquakes had engendered a widespread belief among red men that the Great Spirit was displeased with them and was about to destroy the world or at least the part of the world that included their settlements in the Midwest. Although no reliable count was ever compiled, the Indians believed that the earthquakes had killed large numbers of their tribesmen.

In fact, they had the impression that considerably more of their people were killed than were white men. This was an important point to them. It implied that God favored the white man. It meant that, perhaps, the Great Spirit was siding with the settlers and telling Native Americans to move west.

It could have been that during the chaos of the quakes many Indians simply ran away in fear, disappearing from the area, and when discovered missing were counted as dead, victims of the earthquakes. On the other hand, more red men probably were killed than white or black because there were more of them and many of them lived in vulnerable locations, subject to earthquake flooding. At the time of the earthquakes, the Indian population of Missouri, Arkansas, Illinois, Mississippi, and western Tennessee and Kentucky was at least double the population of the African/European settlers. Regardless of whether more red men died than white is true or not, this was their belief and they acted upon it.

Reelfoot and The Legend of Kalopin

According to a legend circulated among Native Americans, Reelfoot Lake was another result of the wrath of the Great Spirit directed specifically against Indians. The man, "Reelfoot" (Kalopin), was a Chickasaw chief with a club foot. His name came from his lumbering gait. Against the traditions of the tribe, he stole a princess from the Choctaws for his wife. Her name was "Laughing Eyes."

He had been warned in a dream that if he carried out his plan, the earth would tremble with the rage of the Great One. Such a threat did not diminish the love and the yearning Reelfoot held for his beautiful Laughing Eyes. "As soon as the maize has been gathered, the leaves have found their rest upon the ground, and the winter ice begins to paint the surface of the waters, I will to take my bride from the Choctaws," Reelfoot vowed.

"But your dream," his friends reminded him. "The Great One has warned you if you take this maiden the earth will rock and the great waters will swallow our village. Take another wife, a woman from our own tribe," they urged him. Their pleas were to no avail.

The story goes that Chief Kalopin, his bride, and his wedding party were all drowned in Reelfoot Lake during the earthquakes that formed it. Whether true or not, this was believed by thousands of Indians who took it as yet another sign of the Great Spirit's displeasure.

Dying Comets

The Great Comet of 1811 gradually faded from view after the greatest of the New Madrid earthquakes. This strange sign crossing the heavens was witnessed throughout the duration of the disturbances. Many thought there was a link between the two natural events—one celestial, the other terrestrial. Others considered the appearance of the comet as an omen of inevitable war. The comet was last seen on August 17, 1812, just twenty-nine days after the United States had declared war against Britain and only twenty-three days after Napoleon had invaded Russia.

If Napoleon had not been blinded by his ego, he and his advisors might have interpreted the comet's meaning differently and saved themselves the disaster they brought upon themselves in Russia. The comet was first spotted in France in 1811 and was taken by Napoleon as a good omen for his country, a good time to begin the move to invade Russia. However, it was last seen in Russia when Napoleon was only three-and-a-half weeks into his doomed campaign. Applying the same logic as before, he could have concluded that this was a good omen for Russia and a bad one for him. The disappearance of the comet came in plenty of time for Napoleon to reconsider and turn back. Thus, he could have saved the lives of over half a million of his troops. As it turned out, what had been regarded as "Napoleon's Comet" in Europe and as "Tecumseh's Comet" in America could be interpreted as "The Czar's Comet" in light of the outcome of Napoleon's tragic Russian campaign.

After the Comet of 1811 had faded from view, the Great Native American "Comet," Chief Tecumseh, "The Shooting Star" of the Shawnees, was to blaze across the skies of history for yet another thirteen months and eighteen days. Then, like his astronomical analogue, he, too, would disappear.

Tecumseh as British Officer in the War of 1812. This portrait of Tecumseh is based on a pencil sketch made about 1808 by a fur trader named Pierre Le Dru. The original sketch, which has been lost, showed Tecumseh in his native Indian garb. The rendition above is based on a revision of the original sketch that appeared in Benson Lossing's *Pictoral Field Book of the War of 1812* published in 1868. The large medal shown around Tecumseh's neck displays a profile of King George III and is of a kind distributed to the Indians by the British during the Revolutionary War. Tecumseh is known to have worn such a medal during his service to the British in the War of 1812, and one is said to have been taken from his body following his death in the Battle of the Thames near Detroit on October 5, 1813.

Illustration by Anthony Stewart

Judged by his followers and his enemies alike, Tecumseh was rightly considered the equal in nobility, charisma and natural leadership to the greatest statesmen of his day. Though committed to fight the Long Knives with every sinew of his being for as long as his body could draw breath, his death was mourned by every race, including those against whom he had fought the most. No warrior can gain a finer tribute than to be admired by his enemy.

Tecumseh's Last Prophecy

After the quakes Tecumseh went to Canada where he fought against the United States as an officer with the British in the War of 1812. During the conflict he inspired thousands of Indian warriors to fight with him and the English. Never a subject to the Crown, he considered himself a "superior ally." At least some of what the Indians had lost from the Americans, he hoped they could regain from the British. When Tecumseh volunteered his service to General Isaac Brock, he made the following indictment of the American settlers: "We gave them forest-clad mountains and valleys full of game. And, in return, what did they give to our warriors and to our women? Rum and trinkets and a grave."

When the Americans won a decisive battle on Lake Erie on September 10, 1812, it became apparent to Tecumseh that the British were going to retreat and eventually abandon that campaign. Tecumseh's loyalty to his redskin troops, who had come to fight at his behest, caused him to remain while many royalists were withdrawing. Because of his fidelity,

he continued to fight in a battle that was already lost.

The night before his last battle he had a premonition. William Henry Harrison, the nemesis of the Shawnees at Tippecanoe, had dug entrenchments around his camp along the Thames River. After nightfall, Tecumseh and his scouts had inspected Harrison's base undetected and had concluded that their only hope would be an early dawn surprise. But General Henry Proctor, commanding officer for the British, refused to accept Tecumseh's plan.

After his conference with Proctor, Tecumseh spent the remainder of the night with five of his closest friends, men who had been his companions on many journeys and who had shared in many battles: Shabbona, Naw Kaw, Four Legs, Wasabagoa, his brother-in-law, and Billy Caldwell. Billy was an Irishman who had originally settled with the colonists in Pennsylvania. However, he had fought for the King of England during the revolution. He had never accepted United States citizenship. After the revolution he married a Shawnee and lived with the Indians. For years he had been a close companion of Tecumseh and served as his personal secretary. Caldwell is responsible for preserving many of the Chief's sayings.

As was the Indian custom, the six men sat in stone silence around the embers of their fire awaiting the dawn that would bring them another battle. It was a chilly October night. The five men considered it to be an honor and a privilege to sit up with their leader whom they idolized and revered. Suddenly Tecumseh broke the silence and lurched back with an abrupt groan, as if he had been hit in the windpipe. His brothers thought he had been struck. Another period of silence followed. Then Tecumseh began to speak, calmly and with certainty:

"Brother warriors," he said, "we are about to enter an engagement from which I shall not return. My body will remain on the field of battle."

He was killed on October 5, 1813, in the Battle of the Thames just east of Detroit, shot in the throat. Though slain on the battlefield, as he had predicted, the whereabout of his body is unkown to this very day.

Paradoxically, Tecumseh's death was mourned by both redskins and white. Daniel Boone's death was similarly mourned by the peoples of all races. Boone, the Indian fighter, and Tecumseh, the chief enemy of the Long Knives, were both men who evoked the respect of all sides, pro and con. It is only fitting that a portion of the lives of these two pivotal characters had been spent together thirty-five years before in the camp of their mutual adopted father, Chief Blackfish. The brothers, Big Turtle (Boone) and Shooting Star (Tecumseh), both Shawnees, one by birth the other by rite, had came to earth as men of equal genius whom the lottery of fate had placed on opposite sides of a historic drama whose outcome had been predetermined before either of them entered in.

Although Tecumseh had not reached Detroit in December of 1811 to kick off the New Madrid earthquakes as he had prophesied in Alabama on October 5, 1811, it is a strange twist of fate that when he did reach the vicinity of Detroit, it was to die, two years later to the exact day. With his death the Indian movement ended. The strange words he had uttered in Alabama contain a chilling ring of truth. Perhaps his prophecy was true in a larger sense than even he could comprehend. "When I get to Detroit," he had said, "I will stamp on the ground with my foot and shake down every house in Tuckhabatchee."

Tuckhabatchee had fallen to the earthquakes. But, with Tecumseh's fall, the houses of every Native American east of the Mississippi, whose house had not already succumbed to the quakes, would soon fall to the onslaught of the white man. Tuckhabatchee was a place in Alabama, but, within the context of Tecumseh's prophecy, it may also have been an allegory for much more.

Tenskwatawa Fades Away

As for Tenskwatawa, he, too, had been at the Battle of the Thames when his brother had fallen. But once the fighting began, he fled. The rest of his life he moved from place to place trying to regain his former status as a leader of his people. Most of these years he lived in abject poverty on the edge of starvation, sitting around campfires on cold winter nights, barely surviving.

At one point he even signed an agreement with William Clark, of the Lewis and Clark Expedition, who was then the Federal Superintendent of Indian Affairs in St. Louis. The agreement pledged Tenskwatawa to assist in the moving of Native Americans westward into the reservations of Oklahoma and Kansas, which he did.

Tenskwatawa in Exile. This portrait is based on a painting made by George Catlin in 1832 when the Shawnee Prophet had been forced to move to an Indian Reservation in Kansas. In posing for the artist, he attired himself in the same ear bobs, nose ring, silver scalplock tube, and wide armbands he had worn in his younger days as a powerful leader. He also held in his right hand his "medicine fire stick" and a string of sacred beans—like those distributed to his followers by the thousands when he was revered as the "One Who Opens the Door." The beans and the stick were among the sacred intruments employed by the Prophet to evoke the power of the Great Spirit on behalf of his brothers at the Battle of Tippecanoe. He is 57 years old in this picture. Four years later he died forsaken and forgotten.

Illustration by Anthony Stewart

He was a leader, again, but a leader of what?

The fate to which he led others was to become his own. On May 14, 1828, Tenskwatawa, his family, and other Indian emigrants arrived in Kansas, compelled to take residence on the Shawnee Reservation there. This man had been one of the most powerful Indian leaders in America. This was the man who had unified the redskins, solidified the resistance against the white migration, and provided the basis for Tecumseh's campaign. Now he had been reduced to the status of an exile, driven away in disgrace and poverty from the land of his birth forever. He died of natural causes, impotent and forgotten, at age 61 in November of 1836. His body lies unmarked somewhere under the streets and buildings of modern Kansas City, Kansas, near the Shawnee Mission.

And, as for Tecumseh's final resting place, after the "Indian Armageddon" on the River Thames, his body was never found. Some say it was carried away and buried secretly by his followers. Others have proposed more mystical explanations. One thing is certain, in the hearts of everyone, both red and white, Tecumseh has been inducted into the Hall of American Folk Heroes. His legend will live on, but the ancient lifestyle of his people was already a thing of the past, even as he was born.

Tecumseh's Sister

According to the records of the Immaculate Conception Church in New Madrid, there was a wedding on September 4, 1838. Tecumseh's sister, Teciekeapease, was there. At this time, however, she was known by a European name, Genevieve Marie Maisonville. She was accompanied at the nuptial festivities by her husband, Francois Maisonville. They were the parents of the bride whose name was Modest Maisonville. The groom was Edouard Myette (which was later spelled as "Edward Meatte"). He was twenty-two. She was twenty-four.

Unlike most of the residents of New Madrid, Genevieve and Francois had chosen to remain after the earthquakes. Between 1814 and 1830 they had twelve children, all half Shawnee and all born and raised in New Madrid. Modest was their oldest.

Less than a year after Modest's marriage Genevieve (Teceikeapease) died and was laid to rest in a New Madrid cemetery.

A few years later another wedding took place in New Madrid. This time Angelica, the youngest of the Maisonville children, married Franciscus Meatte, one of Edward's younger brothers.

In 1848 Edward Meatte, his wife, Modest, and his partner, Charles Davis, organized a trading post called "Shinbone" where Bayou Portage meets Portage Open Bay, twelve miles south of New Madrid. In 1872 Shinbone was renamed to become the town we know today as Portageville, Missouri.

Thus, the blood of the Shawnees still lives in the central United States through the descendants of Puckeshinwa and Methoataske—great nieces and great nephews of the Shawnee Prophet, Tenskwatawa, and the Shawnee Chief, Tecumseh.

The Last of the Shawnees

The large Shawnee town of Chillicothe, north of Cape Girardeau, Missouri, was a victum of the fear generated by the earthquakes. Before the tremors had even stopped, the residents completely abandoned their "Big Town" in 1812—leaving behind only their burial grounds.

Besides Chillicothe, more than a dozen other villages of the Shawnee and the Delaware in Cape, Stoddard, and Scott Counties were similarly abandoned. A few months after the Indians left, Rev. Joab Peck, a historian, passed through Chillicothe and wrote, "I saw only a herd of deer browsing among the empty huts. A lone redbird whistled from the top of a peach tree—a strange contrast to the once bustling village." Thus, the "City of the Wilderness" had vanished—like dust in the wind. Within the next fifty years, virtually all traces were covered over except the graves. Eventually, even those were to disappear. By the turn of the century farmers clearing the woods, plowing the fields, and excavating for their homes and barns, hauled away dozens of wagon loads of skeletons and grave rocks.

One prominent living remnant of the Shawnees still remains, however. If you take the north Cape Girardeau exit from Interstate Highway 55 (Exit 99) you will be turning onto a portion of the old Spanish Highway, El Camino Real established in 1789 to link all the river towns from New Madrid to St. Louis. El Camino Real had been established along an existing set of trails called the Shawnee Path. After you exit from the interstate, turn toward Jackson only three miles to the west. When you get to the second stop light, you will be at the intersection of East Jackson Boulevard and Shawnee Avenue. On your left is the entrance to a subdivision called "Indian Hills" whose name is inscribed on an ornamental brick wall. Just behind the wall, and less than ten feet from the curb, is a large, strangely twisted oak tree with ivy wrapped around its trunk—almost four feet in diameter at its base. At the time of the earthquakes it was a young sapling about an inch or so in diameter—a teenager less than fifteen years of age. A small white sign facing the highway, installed by the Federated Garden Clubs of Missouri, says—"Thong Tree and Indian Trail."

When the Indians marked their trails, they selected small trees which they bent and bound with leather thongs so that they would grow in a characteristic crooked shape. This tree had been thonged by the Shawnees a few years before the earthquakes to mark this portion of the Shawnee Path. Shortly after the quakes, they all left the area, but the marked tree remained and lives to this day. During its 200 year-old life, literally millions have passed that tree. It is a living bridge between our time and that of the people of 1811-12.

Tecumseh passed here in 1811 when he sought to enlist the Shawnees and the Delewares for his cause against the Long Knives. His very hands may have touched the bark of this ancient oak when it was young. Tecumsleh's sister, Teceikeapease and her husband, Francis Maisonville also passed by here, as did Tecumseh's mother, Methoataske. In

Indian Thong Tree, Jackson, Missouri. Four views of a 200-year-old oak tree bent by Indians around 1800 (before the earthquakes) to mark the Shawnee Path and El Camino Real. The small white sign of the Missouri Garden Club that identifies the tree can be seen in the two lower photos.

addition to countless Indians, hundreds of settlers passed this tree in flight from New Madrid County during and following the earthquakes—Mathias Speed, Col. John Shaw, Elder John Tanner, and many others—some on foot, others on horseback, others pulling wagons with all their possessions. Elder Thompson's house and the Bethel Baptist Meetinghouse were only two miles from this tree. The Reverend passed it many times, as did his family and parishioners—including a baptized black named Dick.

Today the intersection of Shawnee Avenue and East Jackson Boulevard has a busy four-way stop light. What was once an Indian trail and Spanish roadway is now a metropolitan thoroughfare where three main highways combine. Missouri Highways 61 and 34, as well as Business Interstate 55, all use this route. Thousands pass daily, but few realize the poweerful history that emanates from the lone oak that shades the southeast corner of that busy intersection.

The centuried giant watches in silence as the throngs pass by. It has witnessed much, but says nothing. It has survived fires, high winds, the assault of urbanization, the impact of car crashes, and the New Madrid earthquakes of 1811-12. This tree has has seen Spanish coaches and French horsemen, travelers from an era gone by. It has seen the evolution of transportation from mule-drawn wagons to Stanley Steamers. It was witness to the first model A Fords. Today hundreds of sleek aerodynamicly designed vehicles zoom by along with thundering eighteen-wheelers and buses loaded with people who would be amazed at the history buried beneath the bark of that old bent oak. Touched by Indians so long ago, it reaches across the centuries into our present lives of rush and bustle to touch us, too, if we will allow. If only that tree could talk, what tales it could tell. We can thank the Shawnees for that tree. Here is a living creation that has survived not only earthquakes and the forces of nature, but also the encroachment of civilization. May the Master of Life bless it with health, and strength, and continued longivity.

After 1812, the next time large numbers of Native Americans were to pass through this area was in the winter of 1838-39 during the forced march of the Cherokees from North Carolina to Oklahoma. The compulsory evacuation of the Native Americans east of the Mississippi had been first ordered by President Andrew Jackson but actually took place under the direction of his successor, Martin Van Buren.

The Trail of Tears State Park is near Jackson, Missouri. Princess Otahki died there, not far from old Chillicothe, abandoned a quarter of a century before. Her tomb in the park is a place of pilgrimage for visitors today. Thousands of brother and sister Cherokees, Chickasaws, Choctaws, Creeks and Seminoles died along the way during those cruel relocations. Some froze to death. Others died from exhaustion and starvation. Others committed suicide. Before these enforced migrations were over in 1840, the "Five Civilized Tribes" of the East had been completely uprooted, their properties confiscated, their life styles destroyed, compelled to leave their ancestral land, never to return again.

Twenty six years earlier, in 1812, the Shawnees from Cape Girardeau County had migrated en masse to northwest Missouri in what was then Howard County. There they resettled a day's distance ahead of the homesteads of westward migrating white men. The area abounded with elk, deer, buffalo, pheasant, and black bear, as well as with wolves, lynx, fox and bobcat. The Shawnees established another set of towns and villages and lived among the Chippewas, Iowas, Sacs, Fox, Kickapoos, and Pottawatomies, many of whom had also been displaced from the east. The largest new Shawnee settlement, located in the Grand River valley, was established between 1812 and 1815. They called it "Chil-li-co-a-thee" like their previous home near Cape Girardeau and their home before that in Ohio. But it was to be short-lived.

In 1833 the settlers struck a treaty with the tribes that nullified the title to their land and required that they move out of Missouri onto the Great Plains of Kansas. Why would the Indians agree to such terms? One reason was that they knew that Congress was in the process of drafting legislation that would force all Native Americans to relocate west of Missouri and Arkansas. They understood the handwriting on the wall and knew they could do nothing about it. They could leave voluntarily or by a "Trail of Tears." Those were their choices. Another significant reason the tribes were willing to move westward again wasn't any threat of military force from the U.S. calvary, nor was it because they had been offered better parcels of land elsewhere. It was because of small pox. An epidemic had begun to sweep Missouri, but the deadly microbes were selective in their choice of victims.

When the white men moved in, so did their diseases. The Native American races had no immunities to European viruses. In some cases, whole villages had died to a person. The spread of some of these plagues had been deliberate by some early settlers back East who had given contaminated blankets to the natives. But, at this time, in the early 1800's, it was a simple matter of nature carrying out its predestined course. The Indians were fleeing westward to save their lives from the white man's pestilence, against which they had no defense but retreat.

The migration of Indians westward had actually begun in the East within a century after the landings of the Dutch and British in the 1600's. It was the only way many tribes had survived into the nineteenth century, when they were finally trapped and confined on reservations.

Honey was not a food consumed by Native Americans prior to the voyage of Columbus. When bees were first introduced along the eastern seaboard of North America, they, like the people, migrated inland and westward. The Indians, fearful of the white man's diseases, learned to interpret the meaning of the bees. "White man's flies," they called them. The sight of the insects made red men angry. When the bees would first appear, the Indians knew it was time they needed to break camp again and move further westward. They knew that within a few years, not far behind the bees, there would follow an invasion of white men and their deadly disease.

In 1837, the pioneer settlers of Howard County formed a new county where Indians had once raised families, fished the streams, and hunted for game. They borrowed its name from Kentucky, a state from which many of the new settlers had come. Robert R. Livingston was the namesake for the Kentucky county whose name the Missourians had chosen. His brother, Edward Livingston, was a popular member of Andrew Jackson's Cabinet at the time. Thus, Livingston County, Missouri, was named in honor of two American statesmen—the brothers, Robert R. and Edward, whom we have met in previous chapters of this book.

After the treaty of 1833, the Shawnees were the last tribe to leave Livingston County and Missouri. But the red men left a permanent legacy. The name of the county seat is Chillicothe.

An Arch with a Double Meaning

The Jefferson National Expansion Memorial in St. Louis celebrates the westward migration of the early settlers. The colossal archway that dominates the Mississippi Riverfront at the Memorial site is a proud symbol with a double meaning.

To those of white or black ancestry, the monument stands for the triumph of freedom, prosperity, and the birth of a world power. To those whose ancestors are red, it also stands for defeat, poverty, and the death of many native nations. Thus, the very same monument—who for most is a symbol of promise and new glory, both realized and yet to be—is to others a symbol of broken promises and former glory that is no more.

For the pioneers, St. Louis and the Mississippi River were the Gateway to the West beyond which lay the a promised land of unlimited opporutnity. But to the Indians, it was not a gateway, but a prison door. Thus, the St. Louis Arch symbolizes both life and death, the birth of a new American Dream and the death of the Native American Dream.

Even though Tennessee achieved statehood in 1796, by the time of the earthquakes in 1811-12 only the eastern portion was populated with settlers. The western lands of Tennessee still remained largely under Indian control. Except for Fort Pickering at the site of present-day Memphis, there were almost no white settlements. To non-tribesmen passing through, it was a dangerous and hostile territory.

In the early 1800's the residents of eastern Tennessee had for years unsuccessfully tried to bargain with the Indians to buy the rest of the state. The Native Americans wouldn't sell. However, after the earthquakes they changed their minds. They sold what they could, abandoned the rest, and moved to the west, far beyond the waters of the Mississippi.

By 1818 there were virtually no Native Americans left on either side of the river for three hundred miles up and down the New Madrid Fault Zone. Heading west, they had all turned their heads toward "the Land of the Setting Sun"—never to return.

The white men had been trying to drive them out of that territory for a long time. But what ultimately compelled their exodus was not the white man's might—but an earthquake.

Jefferson National Expansion Memorial, The Gateway Arch at Sunset

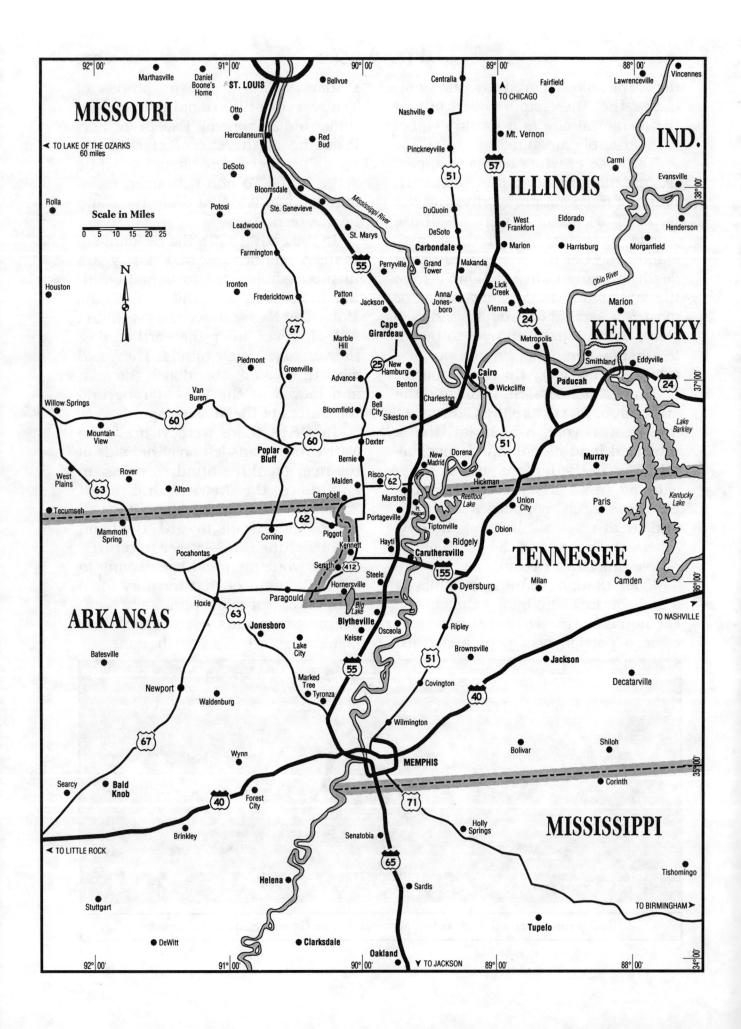

Chapter Six

FUTURESHOCKS

It is a little known fact that earthquakes do damages in the Midwestern United States every year. Thousands of dollars in insurance claims are filed annually. Yet, in this century, at least so far, such losses have never been due to large earthquakes. They have all been from earthquakes less than 5.5 on the Richter scale. In many instances damages resulted from quakes less than magnitude 4.5. While in a few documented cases, serious damages resulted from events even less than 3.5 in magnitude.

This chapter could be the most important one in this whole book for you. It will be informative, and we hope it will be interesting. It is meant to be practical and useful to you, whether you read it as an individual, a business owner, a community leader, administrator, scientist or engineer.

Understanding the Richter Scale

You have probably read or heard that each one-unit increment on the Richter scale of earthquake measurement represents a ten-fold increase in the size of the quake. This is wrong. Each change of one unit actually represents a 32-fold increase in energy released at the source. Hence, a magnitude 6.5 earthquake is actu-

ally 32 times larger than a magnitude 5.5. Here are two easy rules you can use to compare earthquake sizes: (1) The Two Unit Rule; and (2) The Two Tenths Rule.

The Two Unit Rule states that every two units change on the Richter scale represents a change in energy released of 1,000 times. That means that a 5.0 magnitude is 1,000 times larger than a 3.0. A 5.7 would be 1,000 times larger than a 3.7. And a 7.7 would be 1,000 times larter than a 5.7, etc. The factor multiplies so that if you compare a 3.7 with a 7.7, that would be 1,000 times 1,000 or a difference of a million times.

The Two Tenths Rule states that every two tenths change on the Richter scale is double the energy released. Hence, a 5.2 is double the size of a 5.0. A 5.4 is double a 5.2 and 2x2 or four times larger than a 5.0. A 5.6 event would be double the size of a 5.4, four times the size of a 5.2 and eight times the size of a 5.0. If you carry this up to the next unit, you find that a 6.0 is 32 times the size of a 5.0.

The Richter scale value, or magnitude, of an earthquake is obtained by a fairly complicated procedure usually involving the interpretation of data from seismographs. In cases of extremely large earthquakes, magnitudes can also be calculated by taking into consideration the length, depth, and amount of movement on a fault. The manner by which seismologists obtain these figures is beyond the scope of this book, but it is not an easy process and not a very accurate one.

In fact, at this time it is impossible for seismologists to measure an earthquake with any more certainty than within two tenths of a unit, at best. This is why when an earthquake has just happened, different news sources will report different magnitudes for the same event when, in theory, there should be only one value for any given quake. What has happened is that different journalists have contacted different seismographic installations, each of which will report a different value. After a few days, seismologists compare notes and agree, by concensus (not by science), which value should be the "official magnitude."

More often than not, the official value is the one determined by the United States Geological Survey (USGS), not because they necessarily have more accurate instruments, but because most of the funding for earthquake research comes through that agency, and seismologists are

Table One
REPEAT INTERVALS FOR EARTHQUAKES IN THE LARGE NEW MADRID FAULT ZONE

EQ Size	Richter Range	Repeat Interval	Comments
Tiny	1.0 - 1.9	Once every 2 days	Not felt; Detected by Instruments Only
Very Minor	2.0 - 2.9	Once every 2 weeks	Some felt locally if 2.5 or more
Minor	3.0 - 3.9	Once every 4 months	Almost always felt, little or no damage
Light	4.0 - 4.9	Once every 4 years	Minor damage; last ones 87, 89, 90, 91
Moderate	5.0 - 5.9	Once every 4 decades	Damaging; 1843, 1865, 1968, 76, 87
Strong	6.0 - 6.9	Once every 8 decades	Destructive; last one in 1895
Major	7.0 - 7.9	Once every 2 centuries	Devastating; last ones in 1811-12
Great	8.0 - 8.9	Once every 5 centuries	Disastrous; last ones in 1811-12

Modified from Nuttli & Stewart (1989) *Effects of Earthquakes in the Central United States*, Center for Earthquake Studies, SE Missouri State University, 50 pages.

reluctant to contradict the source of their grant money. Hence, in the end, the final values of Richter magnitudes often become a political decision, not an objective or a scientific one.

The fact that, at this time, the accuracy of a Richter magnitude is no better than plus or minus two tenths of a unit is significant. As you have just learned on page 281, a difference of two tenths is double the energy. That is a very large range for error. If you were to measure a peppermint stick with a ruler and reported that it was approximately four inches, but could be half that length (two inches) or possible double (eight inches), we would have to conclude that your measurement of "4 inches ± 2 inches" was pretty approximate. A range of two to eight inches for such a measurement would be unacceptable. We would probably say to go back and measure again because, with a simple ruler, you can get a lot better accuracy than that. But with seismographs and the complexities of earthquakes, such as they are, scientists just can't do any better with Richter magnitudes at this time.

For example, on October 17, 1989, an earthquake occurred on the San Andreas Fault 60 miles south of San Francisco during the Baseball World Series. That particular area is probably one of the most densly instrumented places on earth. Millions of dollars in seismographic installations monitor the fault zone continuously. If it were possible to get accurate Richter scale readings anywhere, it should be there. Shortly after the earthquake, scientists announced that it was a strong quake measuring

6.9. A few days later they announced that they had reconsidered their measurements and that it was actually a major event measuring 7.1. That is an adjustment of two tenths. Although few in the public realized it, what the seismologists were really saying is "we now believe that this quake is twice as large as our instruments first seemed to indicate."

Geophysicists wish that more reliable measurements were possible, but, for the time being, magnitude measurements for earthquakes are only sophisticated approximations—extremely useful, but not accurate.

Basic Truths About Earthquakes

Regions where large earthquakes have occurred in the past will experience them again and again in the future. With few exceptions, that is a basic maxim of geophysics. Occasionally, a zone with a history of past earthquakes will become quiet and produce no more for centuries. Other areas with no known history of large earthquakes can suddenly produce a destructive temblor and continue with seismic activity thereafter. But these are exceptions to the rule.

The New Madrid Fault Zone is no exception. It has been active for thousands of years, continues to be active today, and will produce strong earthquakes again and again in the future. No seismologist is going to be surprised when the New Madrid Fault causes a major earthquake. It can do so at any time. It is the most active North American earthquake zone east of the Rocky Mountains.

Seismic experts agree on this: The New Madrid Fault is a threat and a hazard to the Midwest at all times.

What remains to be determined is when, how large, how many, and how much damage to expect.

Faults move in geologic time, not human time. What may seem like a long time to us, is only a blink in the eye of geology. From the perspective of people, whose life spans are measured in decades, a fault may seem erratic and episodic in its movements, skipping whole generations without consequence. But from the perspective of the earth, whose age is measured in millenniums, the motions of a fault may seem quite regular, even though sprinkled with years of quiescence between periods of rapid movement. All this makes earthquake forecasting difficult from a human frame of reference. A practical method of precise prediction is the dream of many earthquake specialists, which may some day become a reality, but, thus far, it has been impossible.

Another law of geophysics is that small earthquakes happen more frequently than large ones. The southern end of the New Madrid Seismic Zone (Marked Tree, Arkansas, to Metropolis, Illinois) averages more than 200 earthquakes a year measured by seismographs in the area. That's about three or four a week. During a typical year these will range from less than 1.0 on the Richter scale to no more than 3.5. These usually do no damage. Normally, only those greater than 2.5 are even felt.

With hundreds of small quakes emanating from the New Madrid Fault every year, one might conclude that this was healthy. "If enough small quakes occur," so the logic goes, "then perhaps they will relieve the stresses and prevent a big one." The problem with this is that the difference in the energy released from a small quake compared to a destructive quake is astronomical. You can prove this to yourself by application of the two rules given at the beginning of this chapter.

A magnitude 3.9 event is minor. It would take 1,000 of them to equal one moderate 5.9 event and a million to equal one major 7.9 event. A 3.9 event in the Midwest would be felt over at least a 10,000 square mile area. That would include parts of several states. A million 3.9 events would be one every thirty-one seconds for a whole year, or one every five and a half minutes for ten years. Small quakes happen more often than large ones, but not that much more often.

The late Dr. Otto Nuttli of St. Louis University said it best: "Minor chest pains do not prevent a major heart attack. They are warnings. Likewise, minor earthquakes do not prevent major ones. We must take them as warnings."

Repeat Times for Midwestern Earthquakes

Seismologists have a set of adjectives they use to describe different sizes of earthquakes. Table One lists these designations from "Tiny" to "Great" and tabulates their average repeat intervals in the New Madrid Fault Zone, an extended region stretching from Marked Tree, Arkansas, through New Madrid, Missouri, through Metropolis, Illinois, to Terra Haute, Indiana.

Light earthquakes in the New Madrid Seismic Zone in the 4.0-4.9

range will occur every four years, on an average, but they seem to come in bunches. On June 10, 1987, a magnitude 5.2 earthquake occured near Lawrenceville, Illinois, followed by a 4.1 on June 13 near Catron, Missouri, and a 4.3 in September near Wyatt, Missouri. In 1989 there was a 4.2 near Steele, Missouri. In 1990 there was a 4.6 near New Hamburg, Missouri, and in 1991 there was another 4.6 quake near Risco, Missouri. These events had been preceded by eleven years of no quakes in the Extended New Madrid Seismic Zone larger than 3.9. The last ones exceeding that magnitude were a 4.5 and a 5.0 near Marked Tree, Arkansas, in 1976.

What to Expect in Future Earthquakes

The three most important points to realize about earthquakes from the New Madrid Fault are these:

(1) Great earthquakes (8.0 and larger) like those that occurred in 1811-12 are not expected to happen again for at least 200 years. Their repeat interval is thought to be 400-700 years. It has been less than 200 years since the last one.

(2) Strong and major earthquakes (6.0-7.9 in magnitude) could occur at any time. You can expect one of these about once a century. That's about one every three generations. The last one in this range was in 1895.

(3) Light to moderate earthquakes (4.0-5.9 in magnitude) are the most common causes of earth-

quake damage originating from the New Madrid fault. These are usually not life-threatening. If you live within 100 miles of the New Madrid fault, you will probably feel at least a dozen quakes in this range during your lifetime.

There you have it in a nutshell. So far as you and I and our generation are concerned here are the three most important points to take from this:

> **1. We are not going to have any great New Madrid earthquakes (8.0-9.0) during our lifetimes or even during our grandchildren's lifetimes.**
>
> **2. We will probably have one strong or major quake (6.0-7.9) in our lifetime which has the potential of being the disaster of the century.**
>
> **3. We will most certainly experience a number of light to moderate tremors (4.0-5.9) which, to a few people, will be quite expensive but will pose no significant threat of injury.**

Our great-grandchildren will have to worry about the really big ones, 8.0 and larger. But we, of this generation, need to prepare for the 6.0-7.9 sized quakes now, in our lifetimes.

The 5.0 magnitude quake in 1976 near Marked Tree, Arkansas, is the largest on the New Madrid Fault during the 20th century so far. It is also the only moderate quake (5.0-5.9) on that fault to occur in more than a hundred years. The last earthquake on the fault in this range of magnitudes was a 5.3 near Portageville, Missouri, in 1865. As of 1995, the New Madrid Fault is decades overdue for more shocks 5.0 or greater in Richter magnitude. While moderate earthquakes rarely result in deaths or serious injuries—property damages from such quakes can tally in the tens of millions of dollars when they do occur.

For a more complete presentation of recurrence intervals for earthquakes on the New Madrid Fault, obtain a copy of the publication, *Effects of Earthquakes in the Central U.S.*, by Nuttli with appendices by Stewart. (See Bibliography) Included there are several catalogs of past earthquakes in the midwest, giving magnitudes, dates and locations. Also given in that publication is a list of 350 towns and places nearest the fault which would be the most likely to experience severe damage from future quakes.

Earthquake Probabilities for the Midwest

Table One and the preceding discussion give recurrence intervals for New Madrid earthquakes. The data from which such information is compiled comes from four sources:

(1) History. Written and oral history since the 1500's and the first European explorers, including a prevalent Indian Legend of a series of earthquakes that must have been as great as those of 1811-12, but occurring about 100-200 years before Columbus.

(2) Instrumental Records. Seismograms since 1974 obtained from a network of about sixty seismographs within and around the New Madrid region administrated by St. Louis and Memphis State Universities.

(3) Paleoseismic Evidence. Surface faults, sand boils, and other geologic features still recognizable today whose ages predate 1811-12.

(4) Archeology. Evidence of past disappearances of Native American culture in the central Mississippi Valley that may have been compelled by episodes of great earthquakes such as those of 1811-12.

The publishing of recurrence rates for earthquakes on a given fault is basically a way of summarizing its past history. By making some assumptions about the way earthquakes occur, seismologists can mathematically manipulate recurrence rate data into probabilities. Probability figures are more useful in some ways than recurrence data, provided they are valid. The problem is that the probabilities obtained by such mathematical analyses depend upon the assumptions made. The making of assumptions is a subjective exercise, not an entirely scientific one.

As of the writing of this book, only two sets of probabilities for the New Madrid have been published. One set of probabilities by Johnston and Nava (Table Two) was published in 1985. The other, by Nishenko and Bollinger (Table Three), was published in 1990. (See bibliography for complete citations.) They all used the same data, but their assumptions were different. As you can see in

Tables Two and Three, their calculated percent probabilities are also quite different. The question will be, "Which probabilities are the right ones?" Or you may rightfully ask, "Is either of them correct?"

The difference between these two is the result of subjective choices on the parts of the seismologists who did the calculations. Therefore, you, as a reader of this book, are just as entitled to make a personal choice of what to assume as anyone else, whether you are scientifically trained or not. That's why we have listed both sets of data here.

A technically detailed discussion of the differences, limitations, and similarities between these two sets of probability figures is given in lay terms in the manual, *Damages and Losses from Future New Madrid Earthquakes*, (4th printing), by Stewart, published in 1994. (See Bibliography) Read that if you want a more thorough and rigorous treatment of the subject. For purposes of this book, let the following three points suffice:

First: The data base for both is identically the same. There has been some confusion about this in the past. To most people, the term, New Madrid Seismic Zone or New Madrid Fault implies a region centered around New Madrid, Missouri. In the case of these calculated probabilities, both pairs of scientists used a data base that includes earthquake data from the so called "Large New Madrid Source Zone," a complex of faults that stretch from Marked Tree, Arkansas, to Terra Haute, Indiana, and from Ste. Genevieve, Missouri to central Kentucky. Metropolis, Illinois, which is the location of a large riverboat gambling complex, would be close to the center of this system of faults. The point is this: The probabilities of Tables Two and Three actu-

Table Two TIME DEPENDENT PROBABILITY ESTIMATES FOR EARTHQUAKES IN THE CENTRAL U.S.		
Magnitude (surface wave)	Percent Probability Next 15 Years	Next 50 Years
6.3	50%	90%
7.1	33%	66%
7.6	10%	25%
8.3	1%	3%
Modified from Johnston & Nava (1986) *Journal of Geophysical Research,* Vol. 90, pp. 6737-6753.		

Table Three TIME INDEPENDENT PROBABILITY ESTIMATES FOR EARTHQUAKES IN THE CENTRAL U.S.		
Magnitudes (surface wave)	Percent Probability Next 15 Years	Next 50 Years
6.3	20%	50%
7.1	15%	33%
7.6	5%	20%
8.3	3%	10%
Modified from Nishenko & Bollinger (1990) *Science,* Vol. 249, Sept. 21, pp. 1412-1416.		

ally apply to a much larger area of the Midwest than has been stated in most news sources. In other words, Indianpolis, Chicago, St. Louis and Cincinnati may be closer to a source of strong earthquakes in the near future than the general public has been aware of.

Second: Table Two assumes that the probability of an earthquake happening now depends on what the fault system has done in its recent past. It is, therefore, "Time Dependent."

Third: Table Three assumes that the probability of an earthquake happening now is not related to recent past history. It is, therefore, "Time Independent."

In order to better understand the difference between "Time Dependent" and "Time Independent," consider the two illustrations that follow:

(1) A familiar time independent situation is that of flipping a simple coin for heads or tails. The probability is always the same—50% for either a head or a tail. It makes no difference how many times you may have flipped heads in a row, the probability for head or tail in the next toss is still 50%. Future tosses are totally unaffected by previous history. This would be analogous to Table Three.

(2) An illustrative time dependent situation would be like a blindfold drawing from a box of coins, half of which were Jefferson nickels and half of which were buffalo nickels. On the first draw the chances of picking either a Jefferson or a buffalo would be 50% for either possibility. However, for each Jefferson nickel removed, the likelihood of the next draw being a buffalo increases. If one

were to remove a whole string of Jefferson nickels, the probability of the next blind draw being a buffalo would be increased considerably. Previous history would have a great influence on the future probabilities of the draw. This would be analogous to Table Two.

Before you make your decision as to which table to believe, consider the way earthquakes happen. Earthquakes are the result of the slow build-up of stresses in the deep rocks of the earth's crust. When the stresses reach a point that exceeds the strength of the rocks, they suddenly snap and move along a fault rupture. It is this sudden movement that generates shock waves that propagate away from the fractured zone which we feel at ground surface as the earth shaking.

The longer the period of stress build-up, the larger the eventual quake will be when the rocks do rupture. It is generally thought that it takes centuries for the potential forces to reach levels capable of producing a great earthquake, 8.0 in magnitude or more. Decades are required to accumulate enough strain for a strong quake, magnitude 6.0 or more.

When the stress has built up to a breaking point and then released by fault motion and seismic wave generation, it takes time for the stresses to build up again for another quake. The strain energy, accumulated before the earthquake, is gone or reduced afterwards.

The Big Bang Balloon Theory

The build-up of stress on a fault and the sudden release of energy in an earthquake is analogous to the gradual blowing up of a balloon. If one blows air into a rubber balloon a puff at a time and continues to do so, the inevitable consequence is a sudden rupture. One can predict with a certainty that a "break" or "quake" will occur sometime. The only unpredictables are the exact instant and the exact size it will be when it snaps. The longer you blow and the larger the balloon becomes before it breaks, the bigger the bang. When you experience the sudden noise of a breaking balloon as a spectator remote from the location of the balloon, it is not that the pieces of broken rubber have flown across the room to hit you. What you experience is the sound of the shock wave generated at a point some distance away but which propagates through the air to where you are as a sonic disturbance in the atmosphere.

It is the same with earthquakes. If a faulted portion of the earth's crust is under growing stresses that continue to mount week after week, year after year, the inevitable consequence is a sudden rupture. Just like the balloon, a pressure that builds up slowly over a long time will eventually be released in a split second or very short time. As for prediction, one can say with a certainty that a "break" or "quake" will occur sometime. The only unpredictables are the exact date and the exact magnitude of the earthquake when the rock snaps. The longer the stress mounts and the larger portion of the fault zone affected, the bigger the resulting earthquake. When you experience the sudden ground motion of a breaking fault remote from the location of the epicenter, it is not that the fault has jumped a hundred miles across the country to hit you. What you experience are the shock waves generated at a point some distance away but which propagate to where you are as a disturbance in the ground.

As for the New Madrid fault, it has been well documented that the midwestern United States is under a continuous compressional stress and has been for as long as measurements have been taken. It is reasonable to assume that this mounting stress condition has been working on central North America for many centuries and will continue indefinitely for centuries into the future. It is also reasonable to assume that during the 1811-12 sequence a great deal of strain energy was released from the fault that will take a long time to rebuild.

Now you are ready to choose which set of probabilities you consider to be the more valid of the two:

OPTION A: If you believe that recent past seismic activity on the fault makes no difference in today's probabilities, then choose Table Three—the Time Independent set of percentages.

OPTION B: If you believe that recent past seismicity does have a bearing on what might happen today—then choose Table Two.

OPTION C: If you have doubts about both or can't decide—then you may choose Table One, the set of recurrence intervals which involves fewer subjective assumptions, being essentially a summary of the historic, seismographic, and geologic data for the region.

TYPES OF FAULTS

STRIKE SLIP FAULTS

LEFT LATERAL

RIGHT LATERAL

DIP SLIP FAULTS

REVERSE

NORMAL

FAULT BLOCKS

HORST

HORST

GRABEN

• **FAULT (def..).** A fracture or zone of fractures along which there has been displacement of the two sides relative to one another parallel to the plane of the fracture. The displacement may be a few inches or many miles. Faults are classified by their relative displacements according to the diagrams above. The term normally refers to breaks in rocks but may also refer to fractures in soils. Seismologically, there are two kinds of faults: (1) Those that cause earthquakes (Primary); and (2) Those that are caused by earthquakes (Secondary). Primary faults are often miles deep and unseen at the surface. Secondary faults are often visible and are sometimes called "surface faults."

THE NEW MADRID RIFT COMPLEX

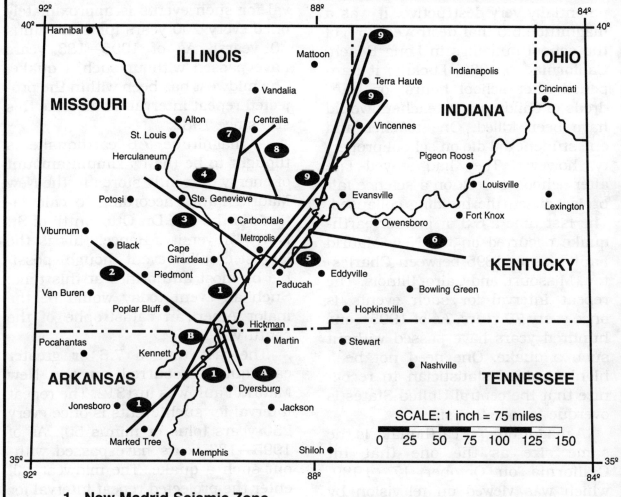

1. New Madrid Seismic Zone
    A. Reelfoot Fault
    B. Bootheel Lineament
2. Black Fault
3. Ste. Genevieve Fault Zone
4. Cottage Grove Fault System

5. Shawneetown Fault Zone
6. Rough Creek Fault System
7. Centralia Fault
8. Rend Lake Fault System
9. Wabash Valley Fault Zone

• There are many faults in the central United States, but those shown above are the major ones. As you can see, all of these faults are interconnected as a single complex system. The term "New Madrid Seismic Zone" or "New Madrid Fault" usually refers to the southern end of this complex which generated the events of 1811-12. The two largest events of the 20th century, however, were on the northern or Wabash Valley end of the system. Braile, et al. (1984 & 1986) refer to the entire midwestern fault system shown above as "The New Madrid Rift Complex." Johnston & Nava (1985) and Nishenko & Bollinger (1990) refer to the southern end of the rift complex as "The Small New Madrid Source Zone" and entire region of faults shown above as "The Large New Madrid Source Zone." Probabilities and recurrence intervals for future "New Madrid" earthquakes given in this book apply to the entire rift complex and not just to the southern end or "Small Source Zone." Hence, when we say there is a 50% chance of a 6.0-6.9 magnitude earthquake in the next 15 years in the "New Madrid Fault System," this could be for an epicenter anywhere from Marked Tree, Arkansas, to Terra Haute, Indiana. This is important in determining how close you actually are to a potentially destructive earthquake source.

What do Probabilities Mean?

A magnitude 6.3 earthquake is potentially very destructive. It was a magnitude 6.3 that destroyed 75% of the school buildings in Long Beach, California, in 1933. Luckily, it happened after school hours, or hundreds of children and teachers would have been killed. One teacher and one student did die on school property, however. They had stayed late after school to work on a science fair project when the building collapsed. The last time a 6.3 or greater earthquake occurred on the New Madrid Fault was in 1895 between Charleston, Missouri, and Cairo, Illinois. The repeat interval for such events is once every 70 years. As of 1995—one hundred years have passed without such a quake. One need not be a highly trained statistician to recognize that the central United States is overdue for one this size.

A magnitude 7.1 earthquake is the same size as the one that hit California on October 17, 1989, which was viewed on television by millions watching the baseball World Series at Candlestick Park in San Francisco. The scientific name for this event is "The Loma Prieta Earthquake," because that was the obscure mountain located at the epicenter. A 7.1 is a major earthquake. The damage levels seen in San Francisco sixty miles north of the epicenter can be expected from a 7.1 quake originating near New Madrid as far as St. Louis and Indianapolis, with even greater destruction in Memphis, Tennessee, Paducah, Kentucky, and Evansville, Indiana. The last time a 7.1 or greater earth-quake occurred on the New Madrid Fault was in 1812. The repeat interval for such events is approximately once every 200 years (plus or minus 30 years). As of 1995—183 years have passed without such a quake. The midwest has been within the projected repeat interval for a quake this size since 1982.

A magnitude 7.6 earthquake is thought to be the maximum amount of energy currently stored in the New Madrid Fault, according to calculations of the late Dr. Otto Nuttli of St. Louis University. Hence, this is the largest credible event thought possible by most authorities at this time. Such an event today would be the major American catastrophe of the century.

The last time a 7.6 or greater earthquake occurred on the New Madrid Fault was in 1812. The repeat interval for such events is once every 250 years (plus or minus 50). As of 1995—183 years have passed without such a quake. The midwest will enter the projected repeat interval for an event this size in the year 2012 A.D.

You will notice that the probabilities of a major 7.6 event during the next 15 years is given by Tables Two and Three in the range of 5-10%. This may seem small, but consider this: If you were given the opportunity to purchase a lottery ticket with a 5-10% chance of winning $10 million, would you buy it? Most people would not pass up odds like that. Neither should we ignore such odds for a 7.6 earthquake.

A magnitude 8.3 earthquake would approximate the largest of those of 1811-12. If such a great magnitude quake should occur, it would be the greatest human disaster in American history, exceeding all natural calamities of the past. The last time an 8.3 or greater earthquake occurred on the New Madrid Fault was in 1812. The repeat interval for such events is once every 550 years (plus or minus 100). As of 1995—183 years have passed without such a quake. The midwest will enter the projected repeat interval for a quake this size in the year 2262. Therefore, it is reasonable to assume that this one can be ignored at this time for purposes of emergency planning and mitigation. Our great, great grandchildren will have to worry about this one, but not us. Seismologists are not 100% certain of this, however, which is why the two tables do not assign zero probabilities, but small probabilities of 10% or less. It is a matter of subjective choice, not science, as to whether or not such a prospect should be considered or ignored at this time. All we can do is accept the fact that the scientific record to date (1995) has not provided any compelling evidence that we should be concerned about Richter 8.0 or greater quakes at this time nor in the immediate future.

Now that you have two tables of probabilities and have the information by which to choose the one you think is more likely to be correct, "What, exactly, does 'percent probability' really mean?"

Literally, a 50% probability of a 6.3 magnitude quake occurring in the next fifteen years (as given in Table Two) means that there is "one chance in two" of it happening within this time span. But what does this mean in the real world?

Consider this. In 1988 a body of scientists, called "The Working Group on California Earthquake Probabilities," published a report through the United States Geological Survey. This report stated, among other things, that the Santa Cruz portion of the San Andreas Fault had a 30% chance of a 6.5 magnitude earthquake during the thirty-year interval of 1988-2018. One would think that, given such a forecast, the area would have plenty of time to prepare.

One year later, in October of 1989, the Santa Cruz fault segment slipped, producing a 7.1 magnitude quake. Scientists may call it "Loma Prieta," but most will remember it as "The World Series Earthquake." The event that occurred was considerably bigger than the one forecast. The Richter scale is logarithmic to a base 32 which means that the energy released by a 7.1 is eight times more than would have been released by a 6.5. Moreover, it occurred at the beginning of the projected thirty-year window of probability. California did not have thirty years to prepare, as one might have been tempted to think.

Your Risk May Not Be What You Think

If you live anywhere in the Midwest, you are probably within the reach of the New Madrid Fault to cause you at least minor damages sometime. If you live in the Midwest, you are also within the reach of at least one or more other potentially damaging faults.

For example, the Wabash Valley Fault can be considered as the northeastern extension of the New Madrid Fault Complex, starting near Metropolis, Illinois, and extending up the Illinois-Indiana state line for at least a hundred miles. The two largest Midwestern earthquakes in the 20th century have not been on the so called "New Madrid Fault" but on the Wabash Valley Fault. (A 5.3 magnitude quake on November 9, 1968, near Eldorado, Illinois; and a 5.1 event on June 10, 1987, near Lawrenceville, Illinois.) The probabilities given in Tables Two and Three of this Chapter actually apply to the combined region of both the New Madrid and Wabash Valley Faults.

Recently discovered paleoseismic evidence of ancient sand boils and other large features from earthquakes centuries ago in the Wabash Valley prove that this fault has produced magnitude 6.0, 7.0 and even 8.0 disturbances during the last 8,000-12,000 years and can do so again. The area showing the largest concentrations of these fossil remnants of former great earthquakes covers an area in Indiana and Illinois, as big as the region defined as the New Madrid Seismic Zone. This means that, at some future time, hopefully many centuries from now, the Chicago and Gary, Indiana, areas may find themselves devastated by a great earthquake epicentered less than 80 miles away. The relative silence of this fault zone in terms of major activity during the past 500 years or more could be a bad sign, not a good one.

According to the Seismic Gap Theory, active faults with no major activity in recent times are more likely release large earthquakes in the near future than faults that have already done so in the recent past. Hence, the high level of minor earthquake activity on the New Madrid fault today could be a good sign, not a bad one. Its release of energy in 1811-12 plus the subsequent aftershocks and activity may mean that this fault is less ready for another big one than the Wabash.

Therefore, the next strong or major earthquake in the Midwest may or may not come from the New Madrid Fault, as some seismologists have defined it. It is just as likely to come from the Wabash Valley. This is of considerable significance to states like Ohio and Michigan and cities like Chicago, Indianapolis, Cincinnati, and Louisville which are much closer to the Wabash Valley than they are to the Central Mississippi Valley, not to mention cities like Terre Haute, Vincennes, and Evansville, Indiana, which are actually in or adjacent to the Wabash Valley.

Near the beginning of this chapter we stated, categorically, that for those of us living today there will be no great earthquakes on the New Madrid fault. We also said that you can expect one strong to major quake in your lifetime and that for this it would be wise to prepare, a subject we shall discuss in the next chapter. We also said that you can expect to experience a number of light to moderate events.

The topic of small earthquakes is what we want to address in the paragraphs that follow because these events do considerably more damage than is commonly recognized, even by earthquake professionals and insurance companies.

If you live east of the Rocky Mountains, your greater risk may be from a small earthquake than a big one because they are so much more frequent and can reach out so far in the Eastern U.S. In California, a small earthquake would probably do no damage at all because the physical properties of the underlying bed rock are different. In the Midwest and Eastern United States, the earth's crust propagates seismic energy much more efficiently than out West. This means that a small quake, such as a 4.0 or 4.5, that may do no damage in the West could reach out and produce significant damage even a hundred miles away in the Eastern and Central United States.

Almost all earthquake preparation publications address the larger events where shaking is severe and the potential for injury is high. But in the Midwest, such events are not likely to happen more than once in a lifetime, if that. We should still prepare for such major events because probabilities have now grown very high that they could occur at any time. But what is more certain to happen, and more certain to happen repeatedly, are numerous smaller events, earthquakes in the range of 4.0 to 5.9. While seldom life-threatening, they can do millions of dollars in property damages. They are also not entirely without risk to human life and limb. Your preparedness efforts for "The Big One" could pay off even in a relatively small one.

So read on with careful attention. If you are a property owner, you may find that the situations described below apply to you some day, and, if you recognize it, you could be tens of thousands of dollars better off and also be spared a lot of grief. If you are an insurance representative, you should really read this chapter carefully. Your liability may be much greater than you know, or can afford. Here, again, the information here could save you many thousands of dollars in a variety of ways.

Serious Damages from Small Quakes

Every time a light earthquake occurs in the Midwest, there are damages. These are usually not serious, in the sense of affecting large numbers of people, but to the people suffering the losses they are quite serious and quite expensive to repair.

The subject of serious damages from small earthquakes comprises a gap in the technical literature and in the education of seismic specialists. Earthquake researchers and engineers are usually more interested in the larger events where damages are widespread, massive, and dramatic. These are the ones they study in school, make field trips to, write reports on, publish papers about, and discuss at professional meetings.

The media has the same bias. Everyone takes note when a major earthquake kills people or causes damages measured in millions or billions. But when a minor quake damages only one or two homes and does bodily harm to no one, it rarely makes the prime time news. Seismologists may record it on their instruments, but to them it is only a statistic, another data point to add in with hundreds of others. They virtually never go out into the field on small events to canvass the area for damages. Hence, if one or two or half a dozen people have serious damages adding up to tens of thousands of dollars each, the professionals never hear about it, neither first hand, nor in school, nor at a technical meeting where case studies are presented.

A February, 1988, Special Report of the Earthquake Engineering Research Institute acknowledged the dearth of published information in this area. Commenting on the moderate earthquake of June, 1987, near Lawrenceville, Illinois, they said: "It appears to us that there is a need to gather data on the excitation that takes place in the central states from events of this nature, which are occurring rather regularly."

Big damages from small earthquakes have been a well-kept secret, even from many who have spent a lifetime in the earthquake field. Another reason for this, other than those given above, is the fact that it is not easy to find out about isolated or scattered cases of damage. If only one or two people in a neighborhood have damage to their homes from an earthquake, they will sometimes keep it to themselves for fear that it might affect the resale value of their home. Odd as it may seem, they don't want anyone to find out. Many times, such property owners even have earthquake insurance but prefer to make the repairs at their own expense rather than let it be known that their house was damaged by an earthquake.

To do research in this specialized field, one must also be a detective and learn how to canvass an area to find the damages. This is time consuming, and few are willing to do it,

especially when they are already busy studying bigger events. Thus, for a variety of reasons, the seismic community remains largely unaware of the fact that small, seemingly insignificant, earthquakes can sometimes cause major losses to isolated individuals. Because of this lack of knowledge among earthquake professionals, insurance companies offering quake coverage are at greater exposure to claims than they realize.

One consequence of a lack of awareness is this: When you file a significant earthquake damage claim with your insurance company subsequent to a light quake they may reject your application without even coming to inspect your property. What they will do is to contact one of their "experts" who "knows about earthquakes." But that expert, well schooled, experienced, and knowledgeable as he or she may be, could be completely unfamiliar with the possibility of serious damages from small quakes. The insurance company claims department may call a civil engineer, structural engineer, seismologist, geophysicist, geologist, or geotechnical engineer. They would then ask a question like this: "We have a party 50 miles away from a 4.4 magnitude earthquake who says that their house moved two inches and their foundation was cracked. Is this possible?"

At this time at least 90% of earthquake authorities would answer that question with a definite "No." The insurance company would then reject your claim, believing it was on solid scientific grounds for doing so. At this point you might be forced to take them to court, at which time conclusive evidence of your earthquake damages would be presented, and you would win the case. In the meantime, everyone loses. The insurance company is out legal expenses and consultant fees it would not have had to pay if their claims adjusters had recognized the validity of your claim in the beginning and simply paid it. And you are out legal and consultant fees, too, not to mention the delays, grief and troubles you have suffered.

The problem is that the vast majority of professionals schooled in earthquake-related fields have no experience or training in evaluating serious damages from small earthquakes. It is difficult for insurance companies to find a real authority in this area of earthquake knowledge because most experts have never seen it nor heard of it. They have not encountered it being discussed in professional meetings. They have never read a technical paper on it in a scientific journal. They never saw any such thing in the textbooks they studied in college. And they have never read about such things in a newspaper or magazine. Furthermore, a large percent of American-trained seismologists and earthquake enigneers receive their education and experience in California where small earthquakes almost never do significant damage, even at the epicenter, and never do damage at a distance—as happens fairly frequently in the Eastern and Central United States. Therefore, most earthquake specialists think serious damages from small earthquakes virtually never happen and certainly never happen very far from the epicenter.

But this impression is false. It is only an artifact of the tendency for researchers and writers about earthquakes to concentrate almost entirely on the larger, more dramatic events. Hence, information on the smaller ones never makes it into the journals and textbooks. The only way an earthquake authority can become knowledgeable in this specific area at this time is to have concentrated on it themselves, gathering first hand information by their own consulting and their own field work. As far as written sources of information, there just aren't any, except for this book. So far as we know, this is the first and the only published source on the subject at this time.

Therefore, if you find yourself with earthquake damages and your insurance company and their "experts" say it was impossible because the quake was too small or too far away, you should bring this book to their attention.

The title of this chapter is "Futureshocks." To most people, that title would cause them to think of potential damages from a large earthquake. Your insurance ccompany is much more likely to pay your claim in a big quake when not only you, but all of your neighbors are filing claims, too. The problem arises when you are the only one, or there are only a few of you, and the ground motion was not strong.

The following examples are all true, all from the Midwest, all since 1987, and all compiled from the direct experience of Stewart—one of the authors who has made it a point to seek out, find, and study the damages from small earthquakes for a number of years, both as an independent researcher and as a private consultant to both property owners and the insurance industry.

The Lawrenceville Earthquake

On June 10, 1987, at 6:48 P.M. local time, a magnitude 5.1 earthquake occurred with its epicenter near Lawrenceville, Illinois, ten miles west of Vincennes, Indiana. It was felt over a twenty-one state area and parts of Canada.

There was one injury in a mobile home in Lawrenceville. A small girl was struck by a bunk bed being assembled by her parents when the quake struck. She required several stitches.

Merchandise falling from shelves and breakage of jars and bottles in grocery stores were reported within a twenty-mile radius of Lawrenceville.

Damage occurred to a cell block ceiling in the Lawrence County Jail, but there were no escapes. In Bridgeport, nearby, electrical service was disrupted, and a brick belfry in a local church was split.

Twenty miles west, at Olney, a large slab of stone fell from the chimney of the Zirkle Funeral Home and fell through the roof, damaging the ceiling inside.

Paul Willis, graphics editor for the *Sun-Commercial Newspaper* at Vincennes, said, "I was in my back yard, and I could see my broccoli swaying for about twenty seconds."

In Indiana about 100 bricks fell when an iron lintel collapsed over a window in the Greene County Courthouse at Bloomfield 56 miles away. At the Madison County Courthouse at Anderson, 150 miles away, a glass facade was cracked. The Indiana State Patrol reported limited damage to some highway overpasses.

A two-story building at New Albany, Indiana, 116 miles away and just across the river from Louisville, was seriously damaged. Used as a hospital during the Civil War, it is listed on the National Register of Historic Places. It is now a school administration building. Fortunately, the earthquake occurred in the evening when no one was at work. When school officials returned the next morning, they found that two hidden chimneys had collapsed, leaving two feet of brick and plaster on the floor of an office, crushing the furniture.

In an eighty-foot tall control tower at the Capital Airport near Springfield, Illinois, 140 miles west, windows were rattled on all four sides while the tower swayed enough to alarm personnel and cause them to think that they were on the verge of being buried in a shower of shattered glass. However, there were no injuries, only jangled nerves.

Tall buildings in St. Louis, Chicago, and Indianapolis swayed, but there were no damages. However, in Columbia, South Carolina, 520 miles southeast of the epicenter, residents of a twelve-story apartment complex were evacuated due to the strong oscillations of the building.

The distant experiences of this quake illustrate the difference in seismic wave propagation east and west of the Rockies. In California and other western states no buildings would ever sway and no one would ever feel a magnitude 5.1 earthquake 520 miles away as was this moderate quake centered in Illinois.

The Case of the Broken Basement

One of the most astonishing incidents of damage from the Lawrenceville quake involved five residences that were 175 miles to the west, near Advance, Missouri. The area is sparsely populated, consisting of scattered dwellings in the midst of large tracts of cultivated land. The region is flat, the remnants of the Mississippi River flood plain when it held a different course to the west thousands of years ago. Projecting through the river sediments are several rocky outcrops of limestone, erosional remnants of the Ozark Mountain foothills. The northern end of Crowley's Ridge begins near here.

It was also noted, in our field work, that this area is the site of an earthquake lake created by the New Madrid earthquakes. This area of several square miles had subsided in 1811-12, forming a shallow lake (called "Lost Lake") that existed until about 1924 when it was drained for agriculture. Hence, a variety of geologic conditions contributed to the earthquake vulnerability of this area.

Beyond 25 miles west of Lawrenceville no damage was reported in that direction, even minor damage. That is, there was no damage until you went another 150 miles to the area around Advance, described above. In this isolated region, remote from the quake, the basement of one single story house was literally broken in two. No steel reinforcement had been used in pouring the concrete. The east end sank down four inches, cracking the concrete completely down one wall, across the floor, and up the opposite side. The gaps were several inches wide, and, according to the hapless owners, snakes had actually crawled through to infest their cellar.

Just as amazing as the damages were the presence of fissures in the yard, two to four inches wide, in concentric patterns about the house. It was a clear case of liquefaction. But how could this be? According to one of the dogmas of earthquake science, liquefaction never occurs for earthquakes less than 5.4 or 5.2, and, when it does, it is always close to the epicenter where ground motion intensities are the highest.

When the retired couple living there filed a claim for earthquake damages from their insurance company, they were refused. The extent of the damages had been established to be in excess of $35,000.

In this case, the insurance company had hired a reputable consulting firm from St. Louis to look into the matter. The engineers made a site visit on August 14, 1987, and concluded the following: "Damage to this residence was not caused by earthquake disturbance. The distance of the structure from the earthquake epicenter and the absence of structural damage commonly characteristic of earthquake disturbance further substantiate the above opinion."

The engineering report did, however, note that all of the cracks were very recent. The engineer who authored the report stated, "Although the damage does not display signs of earthquake disturbance, it is clear that the residence has been subjected to recent and an extraordinary amount of settlement. Since a typical residential structure experiences the greatest amount of settlement during the first five to seven years of its life, a house of this age should only be affected primarily by expansion and contraction due to daily or seasonal temperature change." The house was twenty-three years old at the time and according to the engineering report, "was in very well maintained condition."

The problem here was not lack of competence on the part of the inspecting engineer. It was lack of training and experience in this specialized field. As an engineer, he had been trained to look for shaking damages which are related to the amplitudes and accelerations of ground motion. The intensity of the ground motions in this area were not sufficient to produce shaking damage, and he had not observed any, as noted in his report.

What he had failed to consider was ground failure damage. This is where the ground, itself, becomes unstable as in a landslide, the formation of fissures, lateral spreading, or liquefaction when the ground becomes temporarily fluid like quick sand. Because of his focus on "the distance from the earthquake" (175 miles from a 5.1) and "the absence of damage commonly characteristic of earthquakes" (shaking damage), he had unwittingly closed his mind to the possibility of ground failure, even when the signs were obvious at first glance to anyone who has seen the signs of liquefaction before.

Up close to an earthquake's epicenter, most of the damage is directly related to shaking. But at a distance, ground failure becomes a greater threat. In fact, when the distance is so great that seismic ground motion is no longer a hazard, the risk of ground failure is still present. Ground failure can actually be worse at great distances than up close. This is a paradox not widely understood among earthquake professionals. But there are good physical reasons for this to be true.

For one, the nature of an earthquake changes with distance. Earthquake energy is transmitted by waves. All wave motions have amplitudes. (How big are the vibrations?) They have frequencies (How fast are the vibrations?) And they have duration. (how long do the vibrations last?) Up close to the epicenter, amplitudes are usually at a maximum, frequencies are high (very fast), and the duration of the quake relatively short. As the waves travel away from the source, the amplitudes diminish, but the frequencies become low (much slower), and the duration is longer.

In general, the further you are from an earthquake the longer it lasts. This is because of the fact that at the source there are many types of waves released. They travel at many speeds. They are like a pack of runners in a race. When the gun goes off at the starting line, all runners are together in a clump. If you are standing a few feet down the track, they will all pass you by in a few seconds. However, as you watch them go around the track, they begin to spread out, the faster runners pulling ahead and the slower ones falling behind. The longer the race the more they spread out. If it is a long race, like one or two miles, it may take several minutes for all the runners to pass the finish line. The same is true for earthquake waves. This is why the further you are from the quake, the longer it takes for the packet of waves to pass through where you are.

Another thing also happens to earthquake waves as they travel. The higher frequency waves (the fastest vibrations) tend to dissipate more easily with distance than the low frequency waves. This would be analogous to runners who tire out more easily than others. Energetic runners may be very fast for a while, but they don't finish a long race. Neither do high energy, high frequency waves. But the slow pacers, like low frequency waves, can keep going for hundreds of miles.

Here is the significance of all of this. Up close to an earthquake you expect to see shaking damages which are primarily due to the high amplitudes of the waves up close. At some distance from the epicenter you stop finding shaking damages. However, you can then start looking for other types of damage sensitive to low frequencies and long durations.

It turns out that large buildings are very sensitive to low frequencies so that at a distance, large buildings may be at greater risk from an earthquake than up close. Furthermore, ground failure is very sensitive to long durations and to low frequencies.

This is why the house near Advance was so badly broken while thousands of houses much closer to the quake remained intact and unharmed. A test hole was drilled, and it was found that the house was underlain by thirteen feet of clay beneath which was 75 feet of water-saturated, relatively loose sand. The geologic conditions beneath and around that home were such that there was a high probability of liquefaction. All it would take is for the vibrations to be just the right frequency to match the deposits beneath the house and for them to last long enough.

It doesn't take a large force to induce liquefaction if soil and groundwater conditions are right and the duration of the vibrations is long enough. The effect of successive earthquake motions is cumulative. Enough small forces can add together to make a large one. Inducing liquefaction by an earthquake is like pumping up a tire. With each plunge of the cylinder, you only add a small amount of pressure. But if you pump long enough, you could even burst the tire. If a passing wave train from an earthquake vibrates one or two times a second and lasts several minutes, hundreds of pulses can add up sufficient to induce liquefaction. People in the area may not notice anything but the initial pulse of the first and largest waves, but the ground is responding to all of the waves. The ground can fail from earthquake forces with no shaking damages at all. It can fail through liquefaction, ground fissuring, hillside creep, or landsliding.

In this case history, the insurance company eventually had to pay an amount considerably in excess of the $35,000 in actual damages. Because they failed to recognize the legitimicy of the claim at the outset, they ended up having to also pay for their policy holder's consultant and attorney as well as the fees of their own consultants and attorneys. All of this could have been avoided if the insurance company had been able to find a knowledgeable consultant to advise them correctly when the claim was first filed. The company would have been time and money ahead, and so would have been the property owner.

In doing the investigative field work to prove this case for settlement in court, five other examples of remote damage from a moderate earthquake were also discovered.

Within a five mile radius of the home with the broken basement the following were found, damages all attributed to the Lawrenceville Earthquake, 175 miles away:

(1) Two partially full grain bins were buckled at the level of the corn inside while the concrete pads on which they stood were cracked. There was no steel reinforcement in the pads.

(2) A beam at an inside corner of an L-shaped house was pulled loose, ripping the wallpaper.

(3) A carport sank one inch while the back yard, a few feet away, which had always had a low spot, was raised up level with the rest of the ground. Nails popped through the sheet rock on the carport end of this same house.

(4) A house on a hillside shifted slightly downgrade causing cracks in the ceilings. It was later determined that the slope was actually an old landslide, probably from the New Madrid earthquakes of 1811-12.

(5) A below-ground swimming pool in sandy soil was thrust upwards four inches on one corner, breaking the concrete patio.

These five properties represented almost every neighbor of the party with the broken basement. The area was rural and sparcely settled with one's nearest neighbors often two miles or more away. Had this been the site of a city, damages would have been tremendous.

None of the other five property owners had earthquake insurance or they, too, could have filed successful claims. Because they did not have insurance, they had told no one about their damage until we persisted in our investigation and discovered them.

There may have been even more damage. One neighbor, about a mile from the property with the broken basement, refused to talk to us. He, too, may have suffered damages and just didn't want anyone to know. This secrecy on the part of property owners suffering earthquake damages has created a false impression that such losses rarely occur.

The New Hamburg Earthquake

On September 26, 1990, at 8:19 A.M. local time, a light earthquake measuring 4.6 on the Richter scale occurred near New Hamburg, Missouri. It was felt in six states and as far east as Cincinnati, 325 miles away.

More than half a million dollars in damages is known to have occurred inspected by co-author, Stewart. The epicenter was about twelve miles south of Cape Girardeau, a city of approximately 35,000, and eighteen miles north of Sikeston, with a population of 15,000. One two-story concrete and masonry building within twenty miles of the epicenter suffered a horizontal crack from front to back between the first and second floors.

Numerous homes and buildings suffered cracks to foundations and brickwork in Cape Girardeau and Sikeston, including damage to chimneys. These varied from a few hundred to as much 10,000 dollars per damaged structure. Several concrete lampposts on the campus of Southeast Missouri State University in Cape were cracked. The University replaced them with metal posts in consideration of future quakes.

The six property owners near Advance who sustained losses from the Lawrenceville Earthquake in 1987 pose a paradox. The Illinois quake of 1987 was 175 miles away and damaged them all while the New Hamburg Quake was only 20 miles away and caused no damage to any of them. Furthermore, a 5.0 earthquake in 1976, 120 miles south near Marked Tree, Arkansas, also caused no damages in this area. How could this be?

A thorough canvass of Advance and surrounding country uncovered only one case of significant damages in the whole area from the New Hamburg quake. This was to a two-story building constructed of concrete blocks. It was split from the top down, with diagonal cracks at the upper corners of the door frames, a classic example of earthquake shaking damage. A leak also formed in the roof where a building addition had been attached—other evidence of shaking damage. No ground failure was found anywhere near Advance, in contrast to the experience three years before from the distant event originating in eastern Illinois.

However, there were many ground failures elsewhere as a result of this quake. One mile from the epicenter, a hillside cracked and began to slump, a translational block slide. At another location in the woods, another landslide was found, triggered by the same quake, another block slide. There were no human constructions in the vicinities of these two landslides and, thus, no damages.

Two miles away from the epicenter, west of Benton, Missouri, fissures opened transverse to a hillside behind a house, at the location of a septic leach field. A few months later a massive landslide broke loose, moving land and large trees more than twenty feet, pushing several into deep water in a pond below. It was at 3:00 A.M. on Easter Sunday morning. The sliding of tons of earth behind the house had awakened the whole family with the sound and the vibrations, causing them to think another earthquake had occurred. When they looked out the back window at daylight, their back yard was missing. A large earthquake insurance claim was eventually paid for this damage.

Six miles away, near Oran, Missouri, fissures also opened transversing a hillside below a brick house, also at the location of a septic leach field. A few months later, within three days of the catastropic landslide near Benton, a huge rotational slump broke loose here, also. Severe damages resulted to the brick house whose owners also collected a large insurance settlement for earthquake damages.

Near Wolf Lake and Grand Tower, Illinois, 28 and 37 miles away, respectively, two water wells in the flood plain of the Mississippi River were destroyed. The one at Wolf Lake simply collapsed and provided water no more. The other near Grand Tower suddenly changed quality and became so mineralized it was undrinkable. The owner had to drill a new well on the other side of his property, about 1,000 feet from the first well, at considerable personal expense.

Remote Damages
from Light Earthquakes

The most dramatic damages from the New Hamburg earthquake were not close to the epicenter.

At Desoto, Illinois, 50 miles northwest of New Hamburg, three basements were cracked. They were all neighbors. All had the same type of construction, built at the same time, and all resting on wet clay soils. In all three instances, the houses had been built first without a basement back in the 1950's. Later they all had a contractor excavate beneath their existing houses and add basements lined with concrete block walls. This was probably a case of weak construction combined with clay amplification from the earthquake

Only one of the three property owners filed an insurance claim in this instance, which amounted to tens of thousands of dollars. However, before they received their just claim, the insured couple had to battle with the company who had issued the policy. The insurance company had first called the Illinois State Geologist who told them that such damages were impossible from a 4.6 earthquake that far away. The company then hired a geologist who wrote them a report alleging that the cracks

were either settling or hydrostatic pressure but certainly not from an earthquake.

After hiring a lawyer, retaining some consultants, drilling several test holes, and persisting for more than three years, the company finally agreed that the damages were, in fact, due to the earthquake as originally claimed. The claim was paid in full. But this family had been put through a lot of unnecessary grief simply because the community of earthquake experts, in general, were uninformed of the fact that light earthquakes can do damages of this scale and at this distance.

Your Soil Type
May Increase Your Risk

Among the most important factors in whether or not a particular house or building suffers earthquake damage are the soil conditions underneath. The best foundations are level ground on bedrock or on dry, dense soils within 50-100 feet of bedrock and a deep water table. The worst conditions are slopes (which can fail as slumps or slides) and over loose sediments with a high water table. If the soils are water-saturated clays, then they will amplify the seismic ground motion by factors of 10, 20, and even 50 times compared to bedrock sites nearby. That is called "clay amplification." If the deposits consist of water-saturated sand, they can liquefy during an earthquake. Just remember: "Clay amplifies. Sand liquefies."

Thus, there are two good reasons not to build on a flood plain. One is that you can be caught in a flood, even if there are levees. The second reason is that flood plains are mostly composed of layers of sand and clay saturated with groundwater, which are the worst possible soil conditions for earthquake risk.

Differences in slope and soil conditions are the main reasons why earthquakes seem to choose some areas for worse damages than others. Slope and soil conditions are also the main factor in explaining why many areas close to an epicenter may have no damage while at considerable distances scattered pockets of serious damages can occur.

For example, in the World Series Earthquake of October 17, 1989, San Francisco was about 60 miles away. This was a major quake, 7.1 Richter. But most of San Francisco escaped damages. The collapsed buildings and totally devastated sections of San Francisco (the Marina District) were all near the edge of the bay on filled land—soil consisting of either liquefiable sands or amplifying clays saturated with water. (They were less than 15 feet above sea level.) Abruptly, a few blocks away, there were no damages at all, but these dwellings were on bedrock.

During the New Hamburg earthquake in 1990, Piggott, Arkansas, was 67 miles to the southwest of the epicenter. The quake measured a light 4.6, yet a hillside of clay failed, tearing apart two homes and damaging a third. The hillside was unusually saturated with water and a lake existed at the bottom of the slope. The combined losses on this hillside, alone, approached $100,000.

At Pocahantas, Arkansas, 101 miles from the New Hamburg epicenter, a frame house with brick facing was damaged in the amount of about $10,000. It was a long house on a sharp hillside which had one story on the uphill side and two stories on the downhill end. The foundation at the middle of the house, where the one story and two story halves of the house came together, was cracked. This caused the downhill end of the house to move slightly, pulling the roof, buckling the soffits, and warping windows and door frames. After deductibles, the insurance company paid $8,000 on this claim.

In addition to the damages listed above, the New Hamburg earthquake also caused minor damages in Arkansas at Corning (72 miles away), Halliday (82 miles), Reyno (85 miles), and Lake City (103 miles). It also caused minor damages in Kentucky in Paducah (52 miles) and at Fancy Farm (49 miles). In all of these cases of remote damages from a light earthquake, the factors that created the vulnerability involved soil and slope conditions.

The Risco Earthquake

On May 3, 1991, at 7:18 Central Standard Time, an earthquake measuring 4.6 on the Richter scale occurred near Risco, Missouri. Risco is in southeast Missouri, halfway between New Madrid and Malden. The quake was felt in a six-state area including Arkansas, Illinois, Indiana, Kentucky, Ohio, and Tennessee.

A driveway was reported to have been cracked at Gideon, eight miles south, while several hundred bricks were thrown down from a parapet in Malden just over the entrance to a pool hall. It was a Friday evening, and several people were inside playing on the billiard tables. Fortunately, no one was leaving, entering, or standing in the doorway when the bricks came raining down. Otherwise, a fatality or serious injury would surely have happened.

Except for these two instances close to the epicenter, remarkably little damage resulted from this event, especially when compared to the New Hamburg quake less than eight months earlier. The energy, as measured by the Richter scale, was the same for both quakes. The two events were only 45 miles apart. For some reason, the Risco quake did not produce the same level of damage over such large distances as did the New Hamburg event. This illustrates an important point. Earthquakes of equal magnitude do not imply equal levels of damage at the same distances.

Nevertheless, the Risco event was not without its remarkable consequences. Here, again, is an example of remote damage from a light earthquake. Even more remarkable is the fact that this 4.6 event caused liquefaction, a violation of one of the common beliefs of geoscientists and geotechnical engineers, namely, that "liquefaction cannot occur from quakes less than 5.2 on the Richter scale."

Liquefaction from a Light Quake

In the small town of Keiser, Arkansas, just west of Osceola, 65 miles to the south of Risco and 27 miles southwest of Blytheville, perhaps as many as 15 or 16 houses were damaged, several of them severely so. In one case, on the south side of town, a house with a concrete slab foundation suddenly settled on three corners, cracking the brick facing on both the front and back of the house. In the back yard, a shed sank down several inches and was left in a dishpan-shaped depression about thirty feet in diameter. Several other "sink holes," as the owner called them, formed in her yard shortly after the quake, which she subsequently filled in with dirt. The shifting of her floor and foundation had caused a break in her water pipes which she hired a plumber to fix right after the quake.

Although the insurance claims adjuster's initial conclusion was against the idea of quake damage and in favor of "normal settlement," an engineer from Little Rock later made an inspection for the insurance company and concluded the following: "I believe the cracks observed in the brick veneer and garage slab were caused by a recent earthquake. Although the brick veneer cracks are typical settlement cracks, the house was built in 1973, and normal settlement would have all taken place before 1980. These are recent and, in my opinion, were primarily caused by earthquake forces. The crack on the south side of the house was pre-existing but widened during the tremor, causing additional settlement to take place. One of the primary earthquake indicators here is the type of settlement beneath the shed (which appears to have been induced by liquefaction) and the recent occurrence of several veneer and garage floor cracks."

The engineer had noted that the yard was composed entirely of sand (except where the lady had hauled in dirt to fill the sink holes) and that the materials observed beneath the house, when it was jacked up for repairs, were also pure sand.

The damages were definitely not from shaking. They were from ground failure. But liquefaction from a 4.6 quake 65 miles away? How could that be? Nevertheless, the insurance company paid the lady's claim and fixed her house.

On the north side of Keiser the damage was worse. In a subdivision containing about 90 homes, there were three cases of definite earthquake damages and possibly a dozen more. Two of the houses were next-door neighbors. Both faced west. Both were single-story frame residences on a concrete slab foundation with brick facade. They were about twenty feet apart. During the earthquake the north end of one house and the south end of the other both sank two to four inches. Meanwhile, a small ridge of raised ground surface formed between the two residences.

This is a classic liquefaction scenario quickly recognized once it has been seen several times in the field. A clayey or silty top soil 10-25 feet thick with liquefiable sands beneath with the water table close to the surface, is a common setting for liquefaction. When the layer of sand liquefies below the clay and beneath a house, the weight of the structure presses down on the fluid deposit below. This puts pressure on the slurry of sand and squeezes it like toothpaste in a tube. The quicksand will move away from beneath the house, causing one end or one side of the house to sink down while pushing up the ground nearby.

A test hole was drilled between the two houses which showed that the silty clay only extended to a depth of 23 feet below which sand was found to a depth of 60 feet, where they stopped drilling. The water table was approximately 20 feet down. The most remarkable finding of the test hole was the presence of an interface zone between the sand and the clay where the two were mixed. This was proof of the movement of quicksand below which plucks nodules of clay from the adjacent layers.

The sand at this level was also incredibly loose. A standard penetration test (SPT) was made where a two-inch diameter rod was driven into the ground with a standard weight. When the rod reached the depth of the sand, it took only three blows to drive it one foot, which indicated a very soft soil. One measure for liquefaction potential is where twice the depth (2D) is divided by the number of blows (N) and, if the result is greater than five, you have a definite liquefaction problem. In this case N=3 and the depth was 30 feet. This gave a value of 20 for the test parameter, which is considerably higher than 5. Hence, all the necessary conditions for liquefaction potential were there.

Further evidence for liquefaction potential was provided by observing that the Keiser, Arkansas, area is surrounded with sand boils and sand fissures from the New Madrid earthquakes of 1811-12. The lady on the south side of Keiser had evidently built directly in the center of a large sand boil from 200 years ago.

Once liquefaction features are formed, they can liquefy again and again in future earthquakes. It is not

HOW LIQUEFACTION AT DEPTH CAUSES DAMAGE

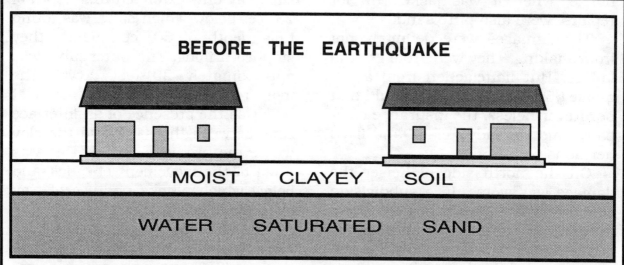

BEFORE THE EARTHQUAKE

MOIST   CLAYEY   SOIL

WATER   SATURATED   SAND

• Given two houses on a layer of damp clayey soil 5 to 30 feet thick underlain by saturated sand below the water table. The houses are of wood frame construction with a brick facade. The foundations are unreinforced concrete slabs. The weight of the houses is not distributed evenly, the heaviest end usually being the one opposite the garage unless one or more cars are parked there. • During the quake the shaking may be only slight, insufficient to cause shaking damage to the house or its contents. However, if the seismic ground motion lasts a minute or more, which can be the case for even a moderate earthquake 50-100 miles away, then liquefaction ground failure is possible even though the intensity of the shaking is mild. • When the layer of sand below the clay soil liquifies, it may stay in a quicksand condition for several hours, even days. During this time the house above will settle. Because the weight of the house is unevenly distributed, the settling will be uneven. The heaviest part of the house will sink first and most. If heavy vehicles are parked in the garage during and immediately following the quake, the heaviest end could be the garage. If not, then the opposite end of the house will sink first, breaking (or bending) the concrete slab foundation. • The front and back walls will crack through the windows (as shown) since this is the weakest part of the wall. The rear wall will lean outward from the top, damaging the soffit. This sinking and cracking may take place over a period of minutes, hours, or days following the quake until the sand returns to a solid state. If the bending of the clay layer is sufficient, a fissure can form as shown. If the fissure extends deep enough to reach the quicksand, it will flow to the surface forming a sand boil. • This example shows two houses with the quicksand being squeezed between them. However, even one isolated house can be damaged by liquefaction if it is built over soil and groundwater conditions like these. In fact, both ends of the same house can sag and break If a house is built over an unreinforced concrete basement, the entire basement can be broken. If your house or business rests on liquefiable sands, there are ways to reduce such risks.

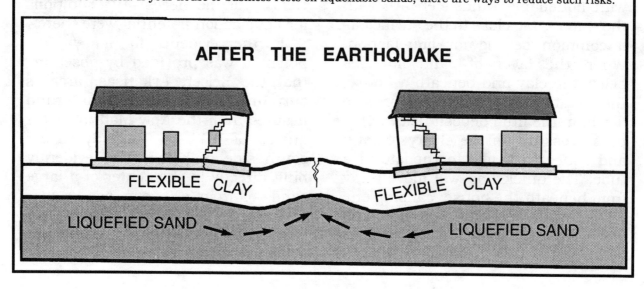

AFTER THE EARTHQUAKE

FLEXIBLE CLAY   FLEXIBLE CLAY

LIQUEFIED SAND   LIQUEFIED SAND

wise to build over them. In this example, the lady was lucky. Her sand boil only partially liquefied during the moderate Risco quake. In a much larger event, her whole house could sink several feet under—filling with sand and water like the houses at Little Prairie on December 16, 1811.

Insurance Company Reluctant to Pay

The lady on the south side of town, who was the first Keiser resident to file a claim, was quickly paid by her insurance company. The people whose homes were damaged by the Risco quake on the north end of town also carried insurance with the same company as the first lady. However, when they filed their claims, they did not find the company so cooperative.

The physical evidence of an earthquake origin for their damage was overwhelming, not to mention the fact that the owners all testified that the time of occurrence was May 3, 1991, during the Risco event. The first engineer hired by the insurance company had been asked only to inspect the first house. He advised them that it truly was, in fact, a case of earthquake damage, and that the claim should be paid.

However, for the second claim received by the company, which was on a house in north Keiser, the insurance carrier hired a different engineer who drew a different conclusion. The second engineer stated, "The damage observed and noted in this report is a result of moisture variations and expansive clays—and is not due to earthquake forces."

His justification was as follows: (1)

A larger event in 1976, a 5.0 magnitude event only 20 miles away at Marked Tree, had not damaged any of these houses, which were all there at that time, and so how could a smaller event more than three times further away cause the damages he had seen? (2) The possibility of shaking damage can definitely be ruled out since the intensity of the ground motion at this distance from a 4.6 would be insufficient. And (3) The possibility of liquefaction can be ruled out because "no site has been observed for an earthquake with a magnitude of less than 5.0."

This consultant was right on one point. Shaking was not the problem. But as for structures being damaged from a distant event and not damaged from one up close, it happens all the time. Earthquakes are like that. So while it is surprising that these houses were not damaged by a 5.0 quake 20 miles away, such experiences are not without precedent. In fact, such examples are so common they can be found with virtually every earthquake that causes damages.

As for his point on there being "no observations of liquefaction for magnitudes less than 5.0," this statement is only a reflection of the dearth of published information on significant damages from small earthquakes. The consultant, in this case, had mistaken a factoid for a fact; that is, he had mistaken something widely believed as something true.

We (the authors) have made the same mistake many times ourselves, including this specific example. We, too, used to believe, and even taught, the above factoid on the limits of liquefaction. Now we know better. We have seen the evidence with our own eyes. We have learned that just because no scientific literature yet exists on a phenomenon does not mean that phenomenon cannot happen. Instead of relying on the existence or nonexistence of published information on this type of liquefaction, one needs to look at the actual situation, the type of damage, the soils, the water table conditions, etc., and made a determination based on the data, and observations at hand. Had this consultant done so, as did the first engineer, he would have drawn the same conclusion, remarkable as it may be—liquefaction really did occur here. Geotechnical engineers and other geoscientists need to revise their maxims.

One bit of information not mentioned by the second engineer, and of which he may not have been aware, is this: At Memphis State University, 91 miles from the earthquake and only 30 miles from Keiser, seismologists measured the vibrations to be at frequencies between one cycle every two seconds to a very slow one cycle every five seconds. Low frequencies like this would probably not be felt by people but can be especially prone to induce liquefaction. The most significant finding of the Memphis group was that the vibrations were recorded for six minutes. That is a very long time—long enough to induce liquefaction where the conditions are ideal for quick conditions, as the test hole at Keiser indicated.

Earthquake at Rover

On July 7, 1991, a Sunday afternoon, an earthquake occurred near Rover, Missouri at 4:24 P.M. It was 4.0 in size. It was felt for about 100 miles in all directions, which includes southcentral Missouri and northcentral Arkansas. Rover (population 23) is in Oregon County, 15 miles west of Alton, the county seat (population 715), and 15 miles east of West Plains (population 7,200). Rover is 20 miles north of Thayer, Missouri, and the Arkansas State line at Mammouth Springs.

Damage to three homes and to the county courthouse was inspected by a co-author. The Courthouse is a three-story structure. Damage there was in the form of cracks in the walls, which were greatest near the ceiling on the top floor. This is typical shaking damage. One single-story brick house a few miles east of Alton had fresh fragments of brick shattered near the carport and some cracks around a large window on the front. Another single story brick house west of Alton and close to Rover had numerous cracks in the chimney and on two sides of the house, as well as some split beams in the attic and a sagging roof. A third house ten miles south of Alton and 20 miles from the epicenter was a split level home on a hillside. A large living room area with a cathedral ceiling had overhead beams that had been visibly dislodged as well as damage to a large fireplace. Preliminary news accounts reported damages in Hardy, Arkansas, 35 miles south of Rover, but no inquiries there were able to locate or confirm the report.

The Rover earthquake had no examples of ground failure or remote damage. Every case of confirmed earthquake damage was within 20 miles of the epicenter. The tremor is remarkable only in that it was a mere 4.0 on the Richter scale—which is not a very big earthquake. But to each of the property owners affected, thousands of dollars in damages were the result. Only one, the house near Rover, had earthquake insurance. When a claim was filed, the company first balked at the idea of damage from such a small quake. It later reconsidered.

Earthquake at Lick Creek

At 8:56 A.M., February 5, 1994, on a Saturday, an earthquake measuring 4.2 on the Richter scale occurred in Southern Illinois near the small town of Lick Creek. Its epicenter was 15 miles southwest of Marion on Interstate Highway 57. Lick Creek is 35 miles northeast of Cape Girardeau, Missouri.

One home near Makanda, Illinois, only eight miles north of the epicenter, was severely damaged. The two-story frame structure with brick veneer suffered a cracked basement floor, cracked walls, brick facing which pulled away from the window and door frames, a cracked fireplace, cracks in the sheetrock, damage to the sidewalk next to the house, and one broken window. Costs of repair were estimated by an engineering firm at $20,000. This was an example of shaking damage near the epicenter.

In Jackson, Missouri, 30 miles southwest, residents reported pictures falling from walls and objects knocked off of shelves and tables. A concrete swimming pool patio was cracked throughout its entire length at Longtown, Missouri, 32 miles due west of the epicenter. This was an example of ground failure damage.

The most amazing damage from the Lick Creek quake was 52 miles to the west near Fredericktown, Missouri. A double-wide mobile home, on the concrete walls of a full basement, was twisted on its foundation. The chimney was cracked at ground level and at the roof line. There were also large fresh cracks through the basement walls and floor indicating that the south end of the foundation had subsided, which had pulled the mobile unit and caused it to twist. In addition, the back door frame was warped so that the hasp no longer lined up with the loop for the lock. A fissure was noted on the uphill side of the house while a recently formed unevenness of the ground was noted on the downhill side near the septic tank. The damages were measured in the tens of thousands of dollars. This turned out to be an example of ground failure damage remote from the epicenter.

When the insurance adjuster came to inspect the property, he got out of his car, saying, "I know this isn't earthquake damage. It can't be. The quake wasn't big enough, and it was too far away."

A week later the claims representative wrote to the property owner refusing the claim and stating the following: "My inspection and photos taken were reviewed with my manager. Based on the angles of the cracking and position of those cracks, it would seem to be more consistent with settling rather than that of an earthquake situation. Settling is specifically excluded in your policy. We regret that we are unable to afford you coverage for this loss."

The property owner was outraged. He wrote to the supervisor of the adjuster who had refused his claim and reiterated his assertion of earthquake damages from the Lick Creek earthquake. One month later the District Claims Manager replied, "At the epicenter of a quake 4.2 on the Richter scale, an earthquake of this magnitude would create a vibration like that due to the passing of a heavy or heavily-loaded truck. There would be rattling of dishes, windows, doors, glassware and crockery. Hanging objects would swing, and liquids in open vessels would be slightly disturbed. But no damage would occur." He went on to conclude that since no damage could occur from such a light event even at the epicenter, the probability of damages 52 miles away "would be considerably less."

"Again," the letter concluded, "We regret we are unable to afford you coverage for this loss."

The District Claims Manager was correct in his description of the earthquake at the epicenter. Indeed, everything he described was confirmed by interviewing several residents of the epicentral area. The manager was right. There was no damage in the immediate epicentral area. The fallacy of his reasoning is to assume that whatever the levels of damage are at the epicenter, the damage levels will always be less the farther you get from the source. Nothing could be further from the truth, as the case histories described above have proven.

Septic System Slope Failure

The insurance company and its experts were right in one thing. The levels of ground shaking 52 miles away were not sufficient to be the direct cause of the damages to the Fredericktown property. What they missed was the high probability of ground failure, which is often worse at a distance than close to the epicenter. As discussed earlier, earthquake waves change as they travel with distance.

Up close they are high amplitude, high frequency, and short duration. This can cause shaking damage but usually not ground failure damage. Residents at Lick Creek described the vibrations like the passing of a heavy truck lasting no more than five seconds. No damage was reported at Lick Creek, but there was one case of serious shaking damage seven miles away near Makanda.

At a distance (with some exceptions) seismic waves become low amplitude, low frequency, and long duration. People around Fredericktown described the earthquake ground motion as "lasting a long time, twenty seconds at least," and longer by some accounts. While this type of seismic wave motion does not usually cause shaking damage, it is exactly the kind of motion that can cause ground failure when conditions are just right. Throughout the hundreds of square miles of area over which this earthquake was felt, there was bound to be one or two places with just the right conditions for ground failure damage.

One of these was the swimming pool patio at Longtown, Missouri, 32 miles from the source. In this case, the pool, which appeared to be below ground, was actually only partially so, the surrounding soils on three sides being mostly poorly compacted fill. It was a relatively new house and pool—less than five years old. When the waters of the pool resonated with the vibrations of the quake, the surrounding ground was not strong enough to support such stress so the supporting soils shifted, causing the concrete patio to crack for its entire length. Hence, this isolated case of damage was due to the peculiar combination of the east-west orientation of the pool, the resonance of the water inside, and the weakness of the confining soils. Had the quake been closer or farther or from a different direction, the patio would probably not have cracked. But somebody else's might have.

In the case near Fredericktown, the house had its long axis oriented north-south and was on a south facing clay slope with many visible seepage areas, indicative of its high water content. Furthermore, 40 feet below the house, where the basement wall had sagged, was a septic leach field, a long trench transverse to the slope 40 feet wide and 4 feet deep, a definite zone of weakness. (Remember the cases at Benton and Oran during the New Hamburg earthquake discussed above.)

To make matters worse, a ravine 18 feet deep had formerly existed below the septic drain field which, in 1991, had been dammed up to create a three acre lake. This further weakened the slope by saturating the soils and infiltrating back under the foundation of the home. The creep of the hillside between the house and the lake was evident by the many large leaning trees, evidence that the ground had moved recently.

All that was needed to cause this hillside to shift toward the pond, pulling the house with it, was an earthquake from the right direction and at the right distance to deliver just the right frequency and duration of ground motion. Apparently, the Lick Creek earthquake, coming directly from the east at 52 miles distance, was just right. Had it been closer or farther or from another direction, it probably would not have damaged this specific property, but others that escaped this time may have been damaged.

The property owner at Fredericktown is fortunate that the Lick Creek quake was not stronger. The ground had only shifted slightly, producing some subsidence of part of his basement, shifting his mobile home slightly, producing many cracks in the foundation, but leaving his house pretty much intact. The real loss will come at the time for him to sell the property. He had bought it without any cracks in the basement walls whatsoever. Now it was obviously broken apart in several places.

A worse scenario is now possible with this dwelling. The damages to this house were limited because the earthquake was small. Now that the integrity of the ground and house have been weakened and compromised, another quake of equal or larger magnitude has the potential for causing a cataclysmic landslide, pushing the home down slope and into the pond.

The owner could reduce his vulnerability to such a catastrophe by draining the three-acre lake, but then much of the charm of the woodland setting would be lost. In any event,

SEPTIC SYSTEM SLOPE FAILURE

BEFORE
THE
QUAKE

• Given a home on a soil slope with a septic system buried downhill from the house. At the bottom of the slope is a pond, lake, or stream. The presence of the water at the bottom of the slope keeps the toe of the slope saturated and the water table high below the house. This weakens the strength of the hillside. Excavation for the septic drain field has also weakened the slope, which is perennially wet with the wastewater which weakens the slope further. If a quake is intense enough, the hillside will fail catastrophically at the time of the seismic ground motion, breaking away as a landslide at the weakest part (i.e. the septic drain field).

• If the quake is less intense, fissures may form across the slope over the drainfield area. During the next few weeks or months, rain run-off flowing down the slope will enter the fissures, infiltrate into the ground, gradually saturating and weakening the slope. When the strength of the slope has been reduced to the point that it cannot support its own weight, it will break away and slide suddenly. This can be as much as six months or more after the quake. Once it has failed, the hillside is permanently unstable. It will creep for a few weeks, or months, as the blocks of displaced earth gradually move into a more stable position. Meanwhile, the head scarp of the landslide may start breaking away threatening the house. At first the house's foundation will start cracking. In extreme cases, the entire house, itself, may eventually slide down the hill. This is a form of earthquake damage from ground failure as opposed to damage directly caused by shaking at the time of the quake.

AFTER
THE
QUAKE

this was another case of significant remote damage from a light earthquake. The losses were not due to ground shaking, but ground failure induced by just the right combination of factors. It was one of those situations where insurance companies and their experts needed further education in order to understand that a legitimate claim had truly been filed and ought to be paid.

Big Damage from Really Small Tremors

On January 21, 1992, at 5:36 A.M., a minor quake, 3.1 in magnitude, occurred near Camdenton, Missouri. One earthquake damage claim was filed with an insurance company. A thorough canvass of the insurance companies that cover properties in the area was unable to discover any other claims of earthquake damage. Although the quake was felt over several counties, news sources had reported no damages anywhere.

Still, there was this one claim. The residence was single story and fairly large, with general dimensions of 60 feet by 75. The orignal part of the house had been built in 1950. The couple who owned the house had lived there for twenty-two years and had raised a large family who were now all grown and living elsewhere. The house was very oddly shaped, owing to several additions that had been made as the family's needs expanded. At one time there had been at least five bedrooms, a huge family room, a dining area, a kitchen, a laundry room, and a large attached double garage. The walls of the house rested on concrete footings with poured concrete floors through-

out and no steel reinforcements.

When the house was located, it was found to be right over the epicentral area, which was in a rural, wooded area on a ridge above the Lake of the Ozarks. The damages were extensive. Large cracks traversed the family room floor in several places. It appeared that a gap had formed under one end of the cracked slab so that it actually rocked slightly. There were skewed cabinet and closet doors, racked out of parallel. The stone chimney was separated from the house. Cracks in the kitchen floor ran under the stove and caused it to shift out of level. Fried eggs now ran to one side of the skillet. There were cracks in the wallboards and ceilings in several places, and all of them appeared fresh. Estimated costs of repair were well in excess of $25,000.

The house had no basement, and for good reason. Limestone bedrock outcropped several places in the yard. However, in limestone the bedrock surface can be extremely irregular so that the house, with its large square footage on one level, was probably built over a variety of bedrock/soil conditions. In some places the footing and floor may have been resting on actual bedrock while in others, it could have been on soils tens of feet thick. It could even have been built over a filled sink hole. There was no way to tell since there was no way to inspect under the house. All one could see was the damage and wonder how it could have happened from such a small quake.

Three months later, on April 29, 1992, at 7:01 in the evening, a magnitude 3.0 earthquake occurred near York Village, Missouri, twenty miles north of Poplar Bluff. People at Lake Wapapello, five miles east of the epicenter, reported seeing waves ripple across the lake during the quake. Like the Camdenton quake in January, only one house claimed damages from the York Village quake.

The damaged residence was isolated in a rural area directly over the epicentral area as in the Camdenton case. This time, the house was relatively small, single story, with only two small bedrooms, a kitchen, and a living room. It was constructed where a level place had been graded from the back of the house with fill for the front portion. The floor of the house was a simple concrete slab without steel reinforcements. A concrete porch, about two feet high, had been poured along the width of the front of the house, which also contained no reinforcement. The back wall and west side of the house, with a side door, was also of unreinforced poured concrete. The rest was frame.

The owner of the house and her teenage son were in the dwelling when the quake struck. "The whole house shook," they said, "floor and all. The stove shook like a washing machine out of balance. Window panes rattled. Everything rattled. The cabinet doors opened, and several plastic bowls fell out." The boy, who was on the couch watching television, said he tried to get up during the shake and was knocked back down onto the couch. "It lasted about ten seconds," they said.

The damages consisted of cracks on the west side about the top corners of the door, cracks in a stone fireplace in the kitchen/dining area, and cracks throughout the length of the concrete front porch.

Most of the examples cited in this chapter are for light to moderate earthquakes that produced serious damages at a distance or which produced ground failures not previously thought to have been possible from such small events. These last two examples of extremely small quakes (a 3.1 at Camdenton and a 3.0 near York Village) show that even for tiny events, if one happens to be so unlucky as to be right over the epicenter, considerable losses can occur.

The point is that you may suffer earthquake damages some day, and it may or may not be from "The Big One." If you happen to be one of those unlucky ones to suffer from a really small quake right under your house, or if you are the victim of serious damages from a light earthquake dozens of miles away, you may have a challenge convincing your insurance company to pay what it owes. The information in this chapter may help you collect your claim.

You may have noted another important point that becomes apparent in reading these case histories. Unreinforced concrete walls, floors, and porches are not very strong during earthquakes. If you live in an earthquake zone, like the Midwest, be sure to imbed adequate steel reinforcements in any masonry or poured concrete. You may have good insurance that will pay promptly in the event of earthquake damage, but wouldn't it be better to have no damages at all? Besides, insurance policies have exemptions and deductibles. They won't pay for all of your damages no matter how good your policy may be. As old Ben Franklin once said, "An ounce of prevention is better than a pound of cure."

When The Big One Hits What'll Happen Where You Live?

A book has been written entitled, "*Damages and Loses from Future New Madrid Earthquakes*" by Stewart (4th printing, 1994). It was commissioned by the Missouri State Emergency Management Agency (SEMA) and the Federal Emergency Management Agency (FEMA) in 1991. The underlying assumption of the book (which may or may not be correct) is that the most likely source zone for a strong, major or great earthquake in the central United States is the "Small New Madrid Source Zone" between Metropolis, Illinois, and Marked Tree, Arkansas.

The book presents a simple method by which anyone with a command of simple arithmetic can choose any county in the Central United States, conjecture any magnitude of an earthquake on the New Madrid Fault between 6.0 and 9.0, and then calculate the number of fatalities, serious injuries, displaced persons, collapsed buildings, bridges out of commission, broken water and gas lines, and whether or not there will be losses in electric power and telephone service.

Such information is essential for planning purposes to city, county, and state government officials, emergency management agencies, police departments, fire departments, hospitals, American Red Cross chapters, Salvation Army Units, Army National Guard Units, regional planners, earthquake engineers, architects, electric utilities, telephone companies, gas companies, water supply and waste water disposal facilities, highway department planners, state patrol officers, industrial complexes, large businesses, and anyone who has a reason for, or an interest in, knowing what to expect from future earthquakes. The beauty of this method is that it is quantitative. You get actual numbers. And it is simple.

If you are really serious about this, we recommend that you get the whole book. It is free. Only a small fee for shipping and handling is charged. Instructions on where and how to get a copy are in the back of this book. In addition to giving step by step instructions for using the method for your county, the book was written on the assumption that most readers would have no training in geology, engineering, or seismology. Written for the technically untrained, it makes an excellent primer and introduction to basic earthquake concepts. And, of course, the price is right. Federal funding makes it available to anyone on request.

If you just want to use the algorithm without reading all of the text that goes with it, then all you need is given here in what follows. The system is called "CUSEIS," pronounced "Q-Size." The acronym stands for "Central United States Earthquake Intensity Scale." Here is how it works.

How to Use CUSEIS

CUSEIS is the condensation of several engineering and geophysical documents put into a form that anyone can use—not just engineers and geophysicists. To determine the damages in any chosen county in the Midwest, just follow these five simple steps:

> **1. Choose any county shown on the maps at the end of this chapter (pages 327-330), and make note of the Roman numeral corresponding to that county.**
>
> **2. Obtain a current population figure for that county.**
>
> **3. Obtain a current count of buildings, bridges, and miles of pipeline in the county. (See estimation formulas on page 320 if you don't have ready access to such data.)**
>
> **4. Go to the CUSEIS Charts on pages 324-326 and find the row that corresponds to that Roman numeral.**
>
> **5. Using the numbers in that row and the population and other data or estimates that you have, calculate the people, building, bridge, and utility effects for the county you have chosen.**

What you will have computed are estimates of damages and losses for a major earthquake (7.0-7.9 in magnitude). To determine the level of damages to your county from a great earthquake on the New Madrid fault (8.0-8.9), simply raise the Roman numeral taken from the maps by one unit, go back to Step Four above, and recompute the losses. To determine the level of damages from a strong earthquake (6.0-6.9), simply reduce the Roman numeral given on the maps by one unit, and redo the calculations.

Note that in the columns for fatalities and serious injuries on the CUSEIS Chart (page 323) there is a range of figures. The safest time for an earthquake to occur is when everyone is home asleep. The worst time is during those hours when most people are at work and children are in school. An earthquake at 2:00 A.M. would have only one tenth the casualties as one at 2:00 P.M. on a school day. This is because homes are almost always safer than working environments. Homes are usually less than three stories while working environments and school buildings tend to be large, often multi-storied, and, many times, made of unreinforced brick, concrete block, or stone. If you have chosen for your earthquake to occur outside of working hours and school times, then use the lowest figures. If you want the worst case scenario, use the highest figures. For holidays and weekends, apply a numerical value in between the extremes.

Understanding Earthquake Forces

Note that all of the terminology used on the CUSEIS Charts is defined, word for word, on page 323, with one exception. The column with the heading, "Associated Horizontal Acceleration as % of Gravity" needs to be explained. Seismologists and earthquake engineers normally assume that the most destructive forces in an earthquake are those that are horizontal. Since we live in a continuously acting vertical gravitational field, everything we build is already designed to resist vertical forces. But horizontal forces are another matter altogether. A building that supports thousands of tons vertically could be caused to topple with a lateral force only a fraction that size. Hence, seismic building codes are intended to increase the lateral strength of a building.

To understand this better, consider that you easily support the weight of your body so long as you are standing upright and vertical. But if you are pushed sideways and lose your balance, you can be knocked over easily by even a small horizontal force.

The lateral forces of an earthquake are expressed in terms of "percent gravity" which is abbreviated "% g." Here is what this means. If you weigh, say, 100 pounds, that means that the force of gravity is exerting a vertical force on your body of 100 pounds. If an earthquake were to suddenly shift you sideways with a force of, say, 50 pounds, that would be half of your weight, or 50% of the force of gravity. We would then say that the lateral force of the earthquake was 50% g. It doesn't take 50% g from an earthquake to make it impossible for you to walk. 10% to 20% g would suffice and can even cause a building to collapse.

To further understand this concept, consider what it would mean for an earthquake to exert a lateral force of 100% g. This would mean that if you weigh 100 pounds, the earthquake would push you sideways with the same force of 100 pounds. Of course, such a force would throw you down violently, probably resulting in bodily injury. If you weigh, say, 200 pounds, then a force of 100% g would be 200 pounds. In other words, the heavier an object is, the greater the earthquake force. Therefore, don't conclude, erroneously, that because

something is heavy it won't move during an earthquake. In fact, it may be even more likely to move than something light. Take a 50 gallon water heater. Its weight, when full, would be around 400 pounds. An earthquake exerting a force of 50% g would exert a lateral force of 200 pounds on the heater. This would be more than enough to push it over.

Earthquakes exert vertical forces, too. If the upward force of an earthquake is greater than 100% g, then objects are thrown up into the air. This happened repeatedly during the New Madrid quakes of 1811-12.

The column in the CUSEIS chart giving the percent gravity figures is something useful to engineers for building design but can also be useful to you. If you are going to bolt down anything, like a book case or heavy appliance to secure it in place from earthquake forces, these figures will enable you to determine how strong the bolts and anchors need to be to resist any level of earthquake motion your county could experience from a large New Madrid earthquake.

In order to use CUSEIS you will need the population data. Statistics on population, buildings, bridges, pipelines, etc., are available from your county government offices. It is always better to use these data when possible. However, if you know the population, or a reasonable estimate of it, you can estimate all the other parameters you need from the following. Note, however, that using these formulas can yield estimates that are considerably in error. The only truly valid figures to use would be those obtained directly from your county offices or other published sources.

Estimation Formulas for Use with CUSEIS When Only Population is Known

A. Approx. **No. of Buildings** in a County = 400 per 1000 people = 0.40 x pop.

B. Approx. **No. of Bridges** in Rural County = 5 per 1000 people = .005 x pop.

C. Approx. **No. of Bridges** in Urban County = 1 per 1000 people = .001 x pop.

D. Approx. **Miles of Road** (Rural) = 100 mi per 1000 people = 0.10 x pop.

E. Approx. **Miles of Street** (Urban) = 6 mi per 1000 people = .006 x pop.

F. Approx **Miles of Pipeline*** (Rural) = miles of Commercial Line traversing county.

G. Approx. **Miles of Pipeline*** (Urban) = 18 mi per 1000 people = .018 x pop.

H. Approx. **Miles of Pipeline*** in County = Miles Commercial + Miles Urban = Formula F + Formula G.

*Note that the term "Pipeline" is meant to denote all types, including water, gas, petroleum, and/or sewer.

Impact of a Major Quake at Jonesboro, Arkansas

To show you how easy it is to use CUSEIS, we will work an example. Let's take Craighead County, Arkansas, whose seat of government and largest town is Jonesboro. Jonesboro is 90 miles southwest of New Madrid and 27 miles northwest of Marked Tree, Arkansas. It is located on the edge of the New Madrid Seismic Zone. Let's postulate the occurrence of a major earthquake (7.0-7.9 in magnitude) in the "Small New Madrid Source Zone." We then find the intensity of ground motion for Craighead County to be represented on Ground Intensity Map Two (page 328). The level of shaking will be VIII. We then turn to the three charts designated as "People and Land Effects," "Building Effects," and "Bridge and Utility Effects" (pages 324-326). Note the row of figures designated by Roman numeral VIII in these charts. These values apply to Craighead County for a major quake.

The total population of Craighead County is 68,956 (1990 census). Most of the residents live in Jonesboro, (population 46,535). There are approximately 27,583 buildings in the county and 150 bridges. Several major gas and petroleum product pipelines pass through the county so that there is approximately 1,000 miles of pipeline to consider.

Notice the range of numbers on CUSEIS Chart One (People and Land Effects) listed under the columns for Serious Injury and Fatalities. This is because earthquakes during school times or working hours harm more people than quakes during evenings, week-ends, or holidays. The higher figures apply to the worst times. Let's choose the worst case scenario, between 11 A.M. and 2 P.M. on a week day during school time. For this we will use the highest figures.

Now the rest is easy. All we do is to apply the percents given in the chart for intensity VIII to the population, miles of pipeline, and number of buildings and bridges in Craighead County to see what the impact would be from a 7.0-7.9 magnitude event. Here are the results:

• Serious injuries = 1% x 68,956 = 690 people.
• Fatalities = .2% x 68,956 = 138 people.
• Displaced persons = 33% x 68,956 = 22,755 people.
• Cracks, fissures and surface faulting: Probably.
• Landslides and/or liquefaction: Yes.
• At least some damage to contents of every building in the county, 100%.
• Number of buildings with at least architectural damages = 95% x 27,582 = 26,202 buildings.
• Number of buildings with moderate structural damage = 30% x 27,582 = 8,275 buildings.
• Number of buildings that will collapse = 1% x 27,582 = 286.
• Bridges with at least slight damage = 25% x 150 = 38.
• Number of bridges severely damages = 5% x 150 = 8.
• Number of bridges collapsed = 2% x 150 = 3.
• Breaks in sewar, water, and gas pipelines = 1.6 x 1,000 = 1,600.

• Will there be electric power outages—definitely, yes.
• Loss of telephone communications—also definitely, yes.

As you can see, when you run out the numbers through CUSEIS, the impact of a potential earthquake on a given area suddenly takes on reality. It is one thing to say "a lot of people" will be unable or unwilling to stay in their houses immediately following the quake, but quite another to say the number will be "22,755." Use of an actual figure removes the vagueness of what must be prepared for in the event of such a quake.

While this exercise reveals how devastating the property losses would be in Jonesboro and the surrounding county following a major earthquake, the figures are also encouraging in some ways. When you look at the death and injury categories, you can see that one's odds are very good not to be seriously hurt or critically injured. While chances of property loss are high, chances of bodily harm are very low, even in a major earthquake. By following the suggestions in the next chapter, you can eliminate your chances of significant injury almost entirely. That's good news.

These results are for a postulated 7.0-7.9 magnitude quake. If we want to know the impact of a strong, but lesser, quake in the range 6.0-6.9 all we have to do is use a Roman numeral value of VII and redo the calculations. If we want to know what a great earthquake on the New Madrid fault would do to Craighead County, we need only to apply the figures in the CUSEIS chart for the row indicated by Roman numeral IX.

Earthquake Mitigation Doesn't Cost, It Pays

The bottom line is this: Every earthquake listed in Tables Two and Three will happen sometime. That is a certainty. The 6.3 magnitude event could happen anytime, even tomorrow. On the other hand, there is a 10% chance it won't happen even in the next fifty years, but that is highly unlikely. Regardless of when they do eventually occur, every day is a day closer to the next destructive New Madrid earthquake.

It makes good sense to make reasonable preparations. You don't have to go overboard. Earthquakes are only one of many prospects our country must face now and in the years to come. Therefore, we must prioritize our resources and weigh earthquake risk against other social problems and challenges. It should be realized, however, that even a little earthquake mitigation and planning can save you from dire consequences and colossal sufferings. Such effort has been proven to be extremely cost effective.

The hundreds of millions of dollars California has spent on seismic engineering, emergency planning, and public education over the years was all returned a hundred times over in one earthquake, the World Series event of 1989. Because the Soviet Union did not invest in such engineering, planning, and education, the Armenian earthquake of 1988, half the size of the California event, did more than double the damages. Furthermore, California lost only 67 people to its quake while in Armenia between 25,000 and 50,000 died. The final figure will never be known because so many buildings full of people collapsed so completely that the bodies could never be counted amid the debris

So earthquake preparation does pay. In a known earthquake zone, such as the central Mississippi Valley, every dollar invested wisely in earthquake preparation will return a hundredfold at some future time. We know there will be major quakes in the Midwest. There will probably be one in your lifetime. It would be wise for us to adopt safe building practices and maintain an appropriate level of preparedness, now. The next chapter tells you how.

DEFINITIONS TO BE USED WITH CUSEIS CHARTS

A. EFFECTS ON PEOPLE
1. Percent of people feeling ground motion.
2. Percent of people injured and requiring professional care or hospitalization (low figures are for night; high figures for day).
3. Percent of people killed (low figures are for night; high figures for day).
4. Percent of displaced persons requiring temporary shelter.

B. EFFECTS ON LAND
1. Ground cracks, fissures, faulting, uplift.
2. Landslides, slumping, subsidence, liquefaction (temporary quicksand conditions).

C. EFFECTS IN OR ON BUILDINGS
1. Damage to contents (glassware, furniture thrown down, bookcases toppled, pictures fall off walls, equipment moved, etc.).
2. Architectural damage (damage to non-supporting aspects of building such as plaster, windows, stucco finish, brick siding, ceilings, light fixtures, chimneys, etc.).
3. Slight structural damage (structural damage refers to supporting members such as foundations, beams, columns, frames, joists, floors, roofs, and weight-bearing walls such as brick or concrete block. "Slight" means fixable—no need to evacuate during repairs).
4. Moderate structural damage (fixable—buildings must be evacuated during repairs for safety's sake).
5. Severe structural damage (not fixable—building must be demolished and rebuilt).
6. Collapse (significant portions of beams, floors and columns have fallen).

D. EFFECTS ON BRIDGES
1. Slight to moderate damage (can be used with caution, but inspection required to ascertain safety).
2. Severe damage (must be repaired before use).
3. Collapse (one or more members of bridge fallen).

E. EFFECTS ON UTILITY LIFELINES
1. Pipelines broken (water, sewage, gas, liquid fuel, etc., measured in repairs per mile of pipeline).
2. Electric power outage.
3. Loss of telephone communication.

CUSEIS Chart One • PEOPLE AND LAND EFFECTS

CUSEIS Intensity Levels	Associated Horizontal Acceleration as % of Gravity	A. People Effects				B. Land Effects	
		1. % of People Feeling Quake	2.** % Receiving Serious Injury	3.** % Fatalities	4. % Displaced Persons	1. Cracks, Fissures, Faults	2. Land-slides, Lique-faction
I	Less than 1% g	0-2%	0	0	0	0	0
II	Less than 2% g	2-15%	0	0	0	0	0
III	Less than 3% g	15-30%	0	0	0	0	0
IV	1-5% g	30-60%	0	0	0	0	Possible but unlikely
V	3-10% g	60-90%	0	0	0	0	Possible but unlikely
VI	5-15% g	90-100%	0-.02%	0	0-1%	Possible but unlikely	Possible
VII	10-30% g	100%	0-.1%	0-.02%	10%	Possible	Probable
VIII	20-50% g	100%	.1-1%	.02-2%	33%	Probable	Yes
IX	30-70% g	100%	0.5-5%	.1-1%	50%	Yes	Yes
X	50-100% g	100%	1-10%	.2-2%	65%	Yes	Yes
XI	70-150% g	100%	1.5-15%	.3-3%	80%	Yes	Yes
XII	100-200% g	100%	2-20%	.5-5%	100%	Yes	Yes

*Note: To properly use this chart one must be familiar with the associated CUSEIS definitions and discussion. The figures contained in the above table are rounded averages. Counties or cities with more recent, refined or specific figures should use those data.

**Low figures are for a nighttime earthquake; high figures are for a daytime earthquake.

CUSEIS Chart Two • BUILDING EFFECTS

CUSEIS Intensity Levels	Associated Horizontal Acceleration as % of Gravity	C. Effects On And In Buildings					
		1.** Damage to Contents	2. Architech-ural Damage	3. Slight Structural Damage	4. Moderate Structural Damage	5. Severe Structural Damage	6. Collapse
I	Less than 1% g	0	0	0	0	0	0
II	Less than 2% g	0	0	0	0	0	0
III	Less than 3% g	0	0	0	0	0	0
IV	1-5% g	1%	0	0	0	0	0
V	3-10% g	10%	3%	0.1%	0	0	0
VI	5-15% g	50%	25%	5%	0.1%	0	0
VII	10-30% g	80%	70%	45%	5%	0.1%	0
VIII	20-50% g	100%	95%	90%	30%	10%	1%
IX	30-70% g	100%	100%	95%	50%	20%	5%
X	50-100% g	100%	100%	100%	70%	30%	10%
XI	70-150% g	100%	100%	100%	90%	50%	20%
XII	100-200% g	100%	100%	100%	100%	70%	30%

*Note: To properly use this chart one must be familiar with the associated CUSEIS definitions and discussion. The figures contained in the above table are rounded averages. Counties or cities with more recent, refined or specific figures should use those data.

**Figures refer to percent of buildings with some damage to contents.

CUSEIS Chart Three • BRIDGE AND UTILITY EFFECTS

CUSEIS Intensity Levels	Associated Horizontal Acceleration as % of Gravity	D. Bridge Effects			E. Utility Lifeline Effects		
		1. Slight to Damage	2. Severe Damage	3. Collapse	1.** Pipeline Repairs Per Mile	2. Electric Power Outage	3. Loss of Telephone Communi-cation
I	Less than 1% g	0	0	0	0	0	0
II	Less than 2% g	0	0	0	0	0	0
III	Less than 3% g	0	0	0	0	0	0
IV	1-5% g	0	0	0	0	0	0
V	3-10% g	0	0	0	0	0	0
VI	5-15% g	2%	0	0	.016	Possible	Possible
VII	10-30% g	5%	2%	0	0.16	Probable	Probable
VIII	20-50% g	25%	5%	2%	1.6	Yes	Yes
IX	30-70% g	50%	30%	10%	16	Yes	Yes
X	50-100% g	100%	65%	30%	160	Yes	Yes
XI	70-150% g	100%	100%	45%	more than 200	Yes	Yes
XII	100-200% g	100%	100%	60%	more than 200	Yes	Yes

*Note: To properly use this chart one must be familiar with the associated CUSEIS definitions and discussion. The figures contained in the above table are rounded averages. Counties or cities with more recent, refined or specific figures should use those data.

**Numbers given in this column refer to repairs per mile (R/Mi) of pipeline. To convert to repairs per kilometer (R/Km), 1.0 Km = 1.61 miles, so that for intensities VI through X the figures become .01, 0.1, 1.0, 10, and 100 R/Km respectively (see O'Rourke, et al, 1991) This category is meant to be applied to buried pipelines of all types—gas, petroleum, water, sewer, and others.

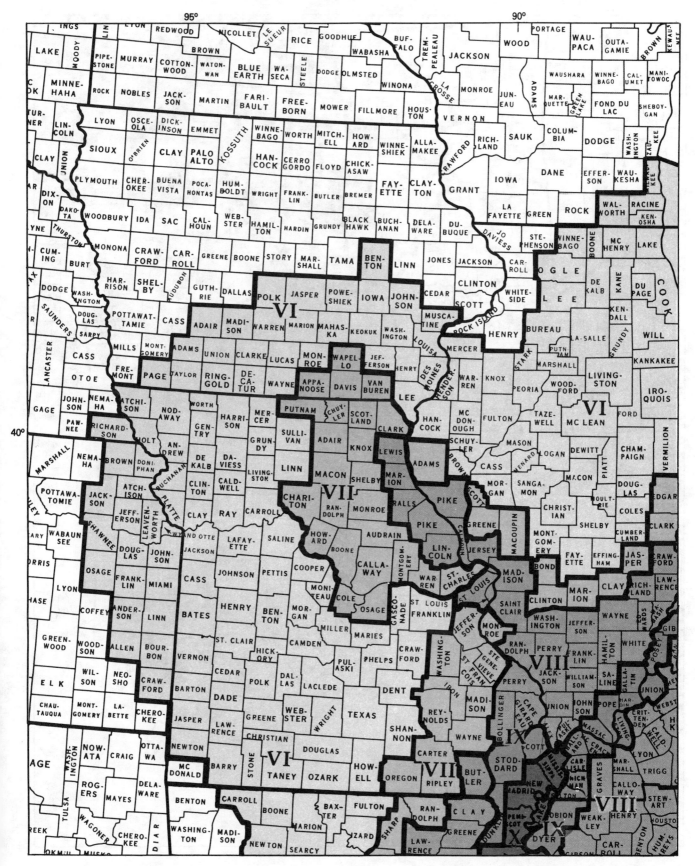

CHAPTER SIX
Central U.S. Major Earthquake Ground Intensity Map Two

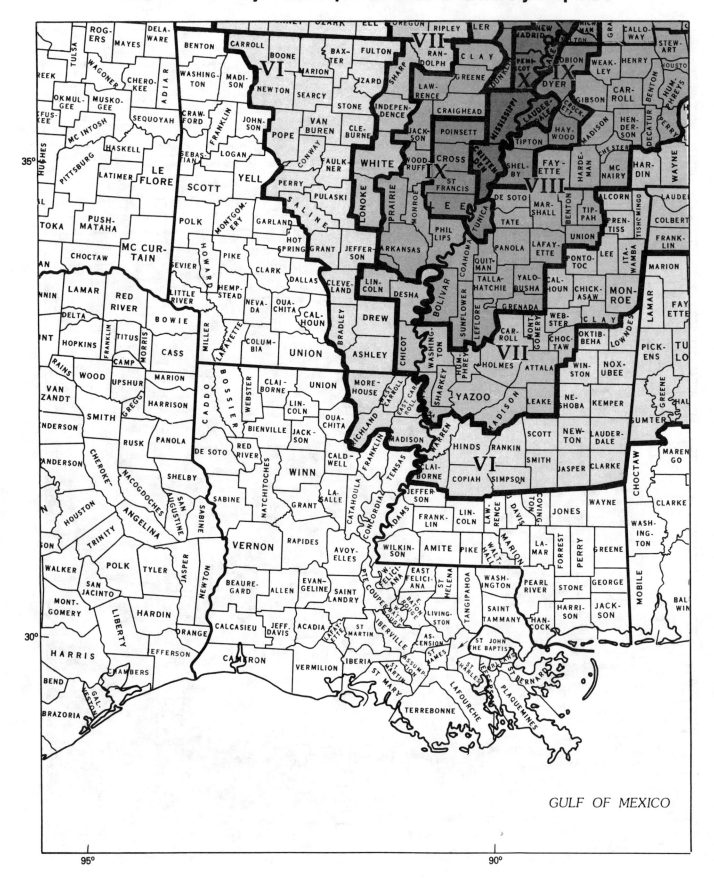

GULF OF MEXICO

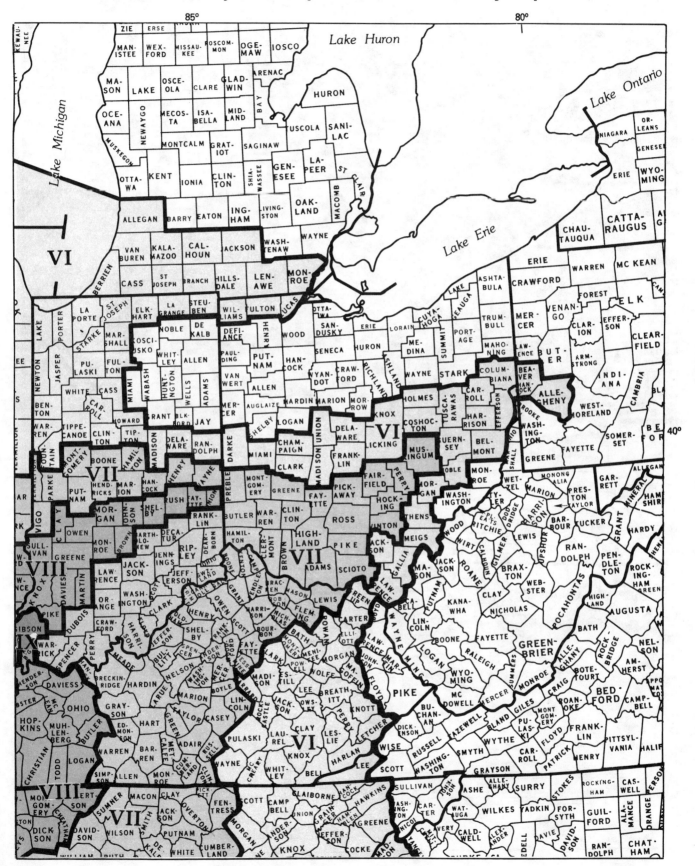

Central U.S. Major Earthquake Ground Intensity Map Four

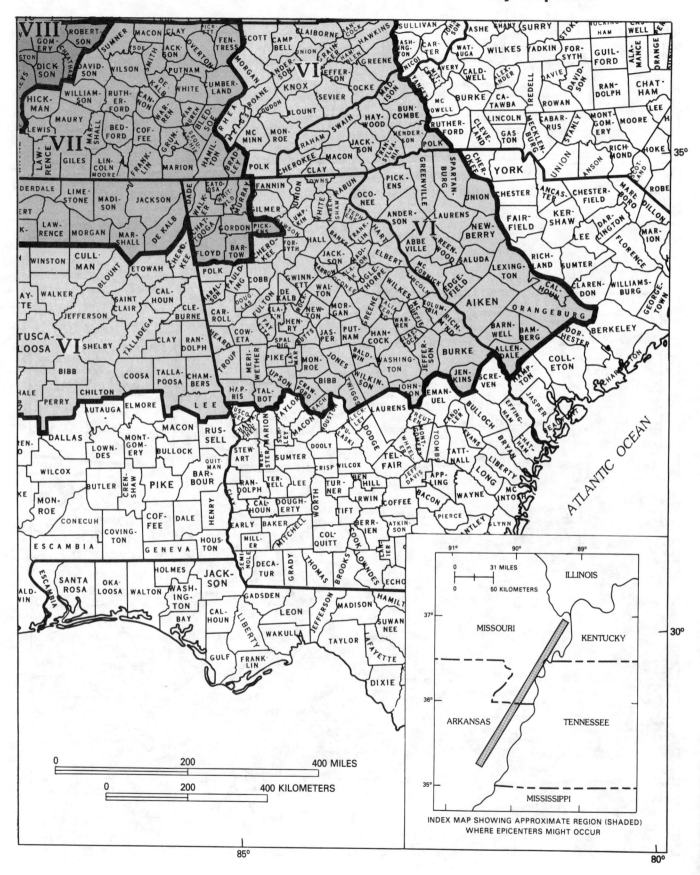

INDEX MAP SHOWING APPROXIMATE REGION (SHADED)
WHERE EPICENTERS MIGHT OCCUR

Chapter Seven

PROTECTING SELF AND FAMILY

Earthquakes pose risks, but they may not be quite what you think. Even in a major earthquake the statistical odds of being killed are very small. The chance of serious injury is four to five times higher. However, the most likely loss you could suffer from an earthquake is property damage. Fortunately, a little knowledge and effort on your part can almost eliminate the risk to your person as well as reduce significantly the potential loss of property.

Most earthquake hazards do not come directly from nature. They come from the failure of human constructions: falling objects, collapsing buildings, broken dams, failing bridges, spills of hazardous materials, and fire started by electric sparks from severed wires and fueled by broken gas lines. The good thing about it is this: Because people have created these hazards, people can reduce or eliminate them. We may not be able to control the hazards that nature may pose, but we can control our vulnerability and risk.

This will be a short chapter. Hundreds of publications exist that cover every aspect of earthquake preparation. There are publications for homes, for hospitals, for nursing homes, for schools, for businesses, for utilities, for museums, for high rise buildings, for apartment complexes, for mobile homes, and more. There are publications for senior citizens, for children, for parents, for teachers, for policemen, for firemen, for engineers, for architects, for building contractors, for bus drivers, for the news media, for the handicapped, for medical personnel, for psychologists, for business leaders, as well as for government officials and emergency responders at all levels. There are even publications for pets. Therefore, there is no need to repeat here what is already available. We shall, instead, provide only a brief summary of information and direct you to the sources.

Four Phases of Earthquake Preparation

There are hundreds of roles to be played in earthquake preparation depending on whether you are acting as an individual, a parent, an employer, a professional, an administrator, a community leader, or in another function. Regardless of the specific demands of the role, earthquake protection consists of four states:

(1) MITIGATION: What you do before an earthquake that reduces or eliminates a risk.

(2) SAFETY: What you do during the earthquake that protects you from injury.

(3) RESPONSE: What you do immediately after—in the first minutes, hours, and days—to reduce the impact of what has happened.

(4) RECOVERY: What you do over the long term following the quake to restore and rebuild your life and the lives of your family, your business, and your community back to normal.

Because earthquakes occur without warning, it is important to take steps to prepare now, so that you will know what you can do and how to respond.

Before the Quake

It is a good idea to have certain emergency supplies on hand both at home as well as in your car or place of work. Consider the following items: flashlights, portable radios, first aid kits (and first aid knowledge), fire extinguishers, non-perishable food, bottled water, tools (such as pipe or crescent wrenches), and special items such as necessary medications or special foods for those on limited diets. Even if you never use such items in an earthquake, you may find them to be invaluable resources at other times, such as during power outages, floods, wind storms, and other emergency situations.

At home, all family members need to know how to turn off electricity, gas, and water if necessary. However, do not turn off the gas following an earthquake unless a leak or the odor of gas has been detected. In most areas, the gas company will be required to turn it back on and relight all pilot lights. If you turn off your gas when it is not necessary, you may create an unnecessary inconvenience for yourself and your family. But do turn off the gas is you think there is leakage.

Before the quake, look for potential hazards around the house. Tall, heavy furniture that could topple over should be bolted to the wall. Hot water heaters can easily be thrown over by an earthquake, but can be secured by metal or nylon straps. A toppled water heater may not only cause water damage to your house, but could also be the cause of a fire. Make a note of all appliances that could move and break electric or gas lines. Remove heavy pictures, mirrors, and other weighty objects from over your bed.

Brick chimneys can fall, crashing through a roof onto occupants below. They can also pose a subsequent fire hazard. Consider bracing your chimney. If you are building, put steel reinforcement in your chimney. Also take an inventory of flammable liquids in the house. You may want to remove them to an outside storage area.

Another thing worth checking is to see if your house has been firmly bolted to its foundation. Thousands of homes are simply sitting on their foundations, which is fine if the only external force is gravity, which is always vertical. However, the sideways forces of an earthquake can scoot your house right off its foundation not only causing serious structural damages, but can also sever gas and electric lines that start a fire. If your residence is not secured to its foundation, you might look into what it would take to do so. It may be relatively inexpensive, considering the value of your home.

You don't have to do all of the above. On the other hand, you could do even more. The point is this: Even if you do only one or two of these things, your risk from earthquakes has been reduced accordingly. Mitgation is a smart thing to do.

During the Shaking

Before the quake take note of the safest places to be during the shaking at home and at work. These would be places away from windows and the possibility of flying glass, as well as places that avoid the risk of falling objects and overturning furniture.

During the shaking don't try to run out of the building. If the earthquake is strong enough to knock down objects, it will be strong enough to knock you down, too. Countless individuals have been injured or have lost their lives in earthquakes while running out the door where falling debris can strike.

Find the nearest place to duck under something—like a chair, desk or table—and ride it out. Then leave the building cautiously and stay out-of-doors. There can be aftershocks that do more damage than the original shake.

There are no guarantees during a major earthquake, but, in general, the following are the safest options:

• **If indoors**, duck and cover. If you have only a chair or small desk that won't totally cover your body,

put your head and shoulders in the most protected place. Don't try to leave until the shaking is over. Then carefully go outside to a safe place.

• **If in the kitchen**, turn off the stove at the first sign of shaking and then quickly take cover under a counter or table, if you can. Watch for flying cans, falling appliances, crashing dishes, and food items spilling from the refrigerator. The kitchen poses more risks than any other room in your house. It is the one place where running into another room might be safer than it would be to "duck and cover" where you are.

• **If out-of-doors**, stay there. Get in an open area away from buildings, trees, walls, and power lines.

• **If in a crowded public place**, do not rush for the nearest exit. You could be trampled. Move away from display shelves containing objects. In a supermarket you can quickly sweep the merchandise from the bottom shelf and lie there protected. You can even partially duck under your shopping cart.

• **If in a high rise building**, duck and cover. Stay away from windows. Stay on the same floor. Expect power to go out, fire alarms to sound, and sprinkler systems to turn on. Expect elevators to fail. Use stairways to exit the building—very cautiously. Don't run.

• **If in a car**, pull to the side of the road and stop. Do not park under or on bridges or overpasses. Stay away from overhead powerlines. Stay in the car. If quake has been severe, do not attempt to cross bridges that appear damaged.

The above suggestions for earthquake safety are not intended to be a comprehensive list. The most important thing you can do to protect yourself during a quake is keep your head. Think and observe.

The best protective actions may include things not mentioned here or things you may not think of until the instant the quake hits. Keep calm, and you will know what to do when the time comes.

Your First Response

Research has shown that during a sudden emergency, like an earthquake, people will look after themselves in the first few seconds or minutes. Then the natural impulse for most persons is to look after those nearby. Don't expect the usual help to be there when an earthquake hits. If it has destroyed your area, it has also damaged all surrounding areas for, perhaps, a hundred miles or more.

The first responders to an earthquake disaster, so far as you are concerned, will be you and the people in your vicinity at the time. In a public place these people may all be strangers whom you have never met before. Most people rescued from a collapsed building or other hazardous situations are saved, not by professionals, but rather by relatives, neighbors, or co-workers—persons at the scene when the disaster struck. It can take hours, even days, for professionals to arrive. This is what makes earthquakes different from almost all other hazards: The fact that victims are isolated from remote assistance because surrounding areas face the same situation and are, thus, unable to respond to their neighbors.

A Family Reunion Plan

If you are caught in an earthquake disaster and separated from your family, take care of yourself and those around you first. Realize that wherever your spouse, your children, or other loved ones may be, they, too, will probably be near others who will help them, just as you are helping those near you. Communication will probably be impossible for a while and even transportation may be limited. As you look after yourself and those nearby, know that probabilities are good that your family members are also similarly cared for.

Don't leave all this to chance, however. Make sure that your children all have some training in what to do in the event of an earthquake. Devise a family reunion plan—how you will all get together if separated during an earthquake (or any other disaster). Give your children instructions regarding neighbors they can contact, relatives they can call, places they can leave messages, alternative places they can stay in an emergency situation, etc. You can't think of everything or anticipate every situation, but even if you and your family just go through the exercise of thinking about it, things will be much better for you when an actual disaster occurs.

Learn CPR and first aid now. The more members of your family that have this training, the better for all of you in the event of an earthquake or any other disaster. If you are a school teacher or office building administrator with others for whom you are responsible, learn how to use fire extinguishers and acquire other skills you may need during such an emergency. Earthquake response is what you do immediately afterwards, but you must train for that response ahead of time. Assume that most of what you will immediately need at that time you will have to provide for yourself.

Long Term Recovery

Utilities, businesses, municipalities, hospitals, universities, and other institutions need to think in terms of a plan to restore their functions and facilities back to normal in an expeditious and economical manner. The costs of lost commerce and industrial productivity can often exceed the direct property losses of the earthquake.

Earthquake insurance should be classified under "recovery." Insurance is not mitigation. It does not prevent a loss. It only offers some partial compensation after the fact. Insurance is neither safety nor response, either. It is a factor in recovery.

Some prefer to invest in mitigation rather than insurance. Many utilities have made this decision. When an electric company may lose millions of dollars a day during downtime, their best option is to try to prevent or minimize downtime by investing in mitigation measures.

Insurance is no substitute for mitigation and safety. Mitigation saves lives. No amount of insurance can compensate for a life. Whether or not you should have earthquake insurance on your home or business is a decision you'll have to make.

Sources of Earthquake Information

You could fill a library with earthquake publications. Many are for sale. However, many agencies offer free information, including many government-published books, maps, brochures, and pamphlets. Given below are several places for you to make inquiries for such information. In making your request, specify in which role you are asking for material: individual, parent, home owner, teacher, builder, health care provider, employer, business owner, building superintendent, regional planner, administrator, legislator, etc.

The following is not intended to be a complete list. No such list probably exists. Since this publication focuses on the midwestern United States, most of the sources given are for this part of the country. In California, sources of earthquake information are easy to locate. Even shopping bags in some California supermarkets contain earthquake safety tips.

Some of the following sources are specific. Others are general, and you will have to find the specific address or contact in your state or area. In addition to literature, some of these sources provide earthquake videos, sets of earthquake slides, and, in some cases, they will provide speakers to come to your area and give a talk on earthquakes and earthquake preparedness.

The Central United States Earthquake Consortium (CUSEC) is funded by the Federal Emergency

Management Agency (FEMA) with its headquarters in Memphis, Tennessee. It is an association of fifteen southeastern and midwestern state emergency service agencies for the purpose of developing and coordinating earthquake programs across state lines. Every one of these state agencies has earthquake preparation and safety literature which they distribute free upon request.

Another source of information for earthquakes on the New Madrid Fault and other faults throughout the Midwest is the Center for Earthquake Studies (CES) at Southeast Missouri State University in Cape Girardeau. The address is given below.

The publisher of this book, Gutenburg-Richter Publications, is also a source of earthquake information. (See pages 361-367.) Available resources include books, as well as a set of 35mm color slides with a written narration about the New Madrid Seismic Zone. This set includes some of the photographs in this book, but in color. With this set of slides, anyone can make an interesting presentation on the New Madrid Fault. Write for a catalogue. The address and phone number are given on page 336 as well as on pages 374 and 376. Gutenberg-Richter's *"Earthquake Hazard Warranty and Money Back Guarantee"* are detailed on page 374, and there's a convenient Order Form on page 376.

The authors of this book are also available for earthquake presentations as well as for consulting and earthquake damage assessment. They may be contacted through the publisher. Sources noted with an asterisk (*) are members of CUSEC:

Specific Sources of Earthquake Information

*Alabama Emergency Management
    Agency
P.O. Box 2160
Clanton, AL 35045-5160

American Red Cross,
    St. Louis Bi-State Chapter
4050 Lindell Boulevard
St. Louis, MO 63108

*Arkansas Office of Emergency Services
P.O. Box 758
Conway, AR 72032

Center for Earthquake Research
    & Information (CERI)
Memphis State University
3890 Central Avenue
Memphis, TN 38152

Center for Earthquake Studies (CES)
Southeast Missouri State University
One University Plaza
Cape Girardeau, MO 63701

*Central United States Earthquake
    Consortium (CUSEC)
2630 Holmes Road East
Memphis, TN 38118

Earthquake Engineering Research
    Institute (EERI)
499 Fourteenth Street, Suite 320
Oakland, CA 94612

Federal Emergency Management
    Agency (FEMA-Region VII)
911 Walnut Street, Room 300
Kansas City, MO 64106

Federal Emergency Management
    Agency (FEMA-Region V)
300 South Walker Drive
Chicago, IL 60606

*Georgia Emergency Management Agency
P.O. Box 10055
Atlanta, GA 39316-0055

Gutenburg-Richter Publications
Route 1, Box 646
Marble Hill, MO 63764
1-800-758-8629

*Illinois Emergency Management Agency
110 East Adams Street
Springfield, IL 62706

*Indiana Emergency Management Agency
302 W. Washington St., E-208
Indianapolis, IN 46204

*Iowa Emergency Management Division
Hoover State Office Building, Level A
Des Moines, IA 50319

*Kentucky Disaster & Emergncy Services
Boone Center
Frankfort, KY 40601-6168

*Louisiana Office of Emergency
  Preparedness
P.O. Box 44217
Baton Rouge, LA 70804

*Mississippi Emergency Management
  Agency
P.O. Box 4501
Jackson, MS 39296-4501

*Missouri State Emergency
  Management Agency (SEMA)
P.O. Box 116
Jefferson City, MO 63119

*North Carolina Division of Emergency
  Management
116 W. Jones St.
Raleigh, NC 27603-1335

National Center for Earthquake
  Engineering Research (NCEER)
Red Jacket Quadrangle
State University of New York
Buffalo, NY 14261

National Earthquake Information Center
United States Geological Survey
Denver Federal Center
Box 25046
Denver, CO 80225

New Madrid Historical Museum
Main Street
New Madrid, MO 63869

*Ohio Emergency Management Agency
2825 W. Granville Road
Columbus, OH 43235-2712

*Oklahoma Civil Emergency Management
  Agency
P.O. Box 53365
Oklahoma City, OK 73152

*South Carolina Emergency
  Preparedness Division
1429 Senate Street
Columbia, SC 29201

St. Louis University
  Seismological Observatory
Department of Earth Sciences
3507 Laclede Avenue
St. Louis, MO 63103

*Tennessee Emergency Management
  Agency
P.O. Box 41502
Nashville, TN 37204

General Sources

The following may also be sources of earthquake information:

• Your local chapter of the American Red Cross.

• Your state, county, or city emergency management agency.

• Your state geological survey or department of natural resources.

• Other offices of the Federal Emergency Management Agency (FEMA) than the two given above.

• Your local college or university department of geology, earth sciences, geophysics, or geosciences.

• Your local hospital or county health department.

• Your local telephone, gas or electric company.

• Your insurance company
• Your local television station or newspaper
• Your local library
• Your employer (Some companies have literature for their employees.)

Conclusion

Earthquakes cannot be prevented, but damages and casualties can. At least such losses can be significantly reduced. The New Madrid Fault will move again. It has the potential to cause damages in more than twenty states. A quarter of the American people could be adversely affected. If you live within five hundred miles of New Madrid, you could be one of them. If you live within 1,000 miles of New Madrid, you would be within the felt area of a great earthquake. For any reasonable preparations you make now, you will some day be glad. Everything you need to know can be found through the sources given here.

BIBLIOGRAPHY

NOTE: REFERENCES IN BOLD FACE PRINT ARE ESPECIALLY RECOMMENDED

1. Algermissen, S.T., and Hopper, M., 1984, *Estimated maximum regional seismic intensities associated with an ensemble of great earthquakes that might occur along the New Madrid seismic zone:* U.S. Geological Survey, Reston, Virginia, Map MF-1712, Reprinted 1986.

2. Amick, D., Maurath, G., and Gelinas, R., 1990, *Characteristics of seismically induced liquefaction sites and features located in the vicinity of the 1886 Charleston, SC earthquake:* Seismology Research Letters, v. 6l, p.ll7-130.

3. Anonymous, 1888, *History of Southeast Missouri.* Goodspeed Publishing Co., Chicago. 1215 pages.

4. Anonymous, 1975, *History and travel guide to southeast Missouri region.* SE Missouri Regional Planning and Economic Development Commission, Perryville, MO. folded map with notations.

5. Anonymous, 1991, *The other (?) Missouri earthquake: American History.* Illustrated, v. 25, January.

6. Anthony, A., 1987, *River at the door:* River Micro Studies Publishers, Ft. Davis, Texas. 145 pp.

7. Ashe, T., 1808, *Travels in America performed in 1806,* Wm. Sawyer & Co., London. 345 pp.

8. Atkinson, W., 1989, *The next New Madrid earthquake: a survival guide for the midwest.* Southern Illinois Press, Carbondale and Edwardsville.

9. Audubon, J.J., 1951, *The Favorite Animals of America.* (Original edition, 1848, published by author), Grosset & Dunlap, New York. 40 pp.

10. Audubon, J.J., 1946, *The birds of America.* (Original edition, 1830, published by author), MacMillan Co., New York, 455 pp.

11. Bagnall, N., 1995, *The big one.* Missouri Heritage Series, University of Missouri Press, Columbia. 96 pp.

12. Balesi, C.J., 1992, *The time of the French in the heart of North America* (1673-1818): Alliance Francais, Chicago, 346 pp.

13. Bennett, M.J., et al., 1979, *Subsurface investigation of liquefaction, Imperial Valley earthquake, California*, 14. October 15, 1979: USGS Open File Report 81-502.

14. Blythe, E., et al., 1981, *Earthquakes and related features of the Mississippi River Valley:* Proceedings of symposium and field trip, U. Tennessee Martin, 28 pp.

15. **Bolt, B., 1988, *Earthquakes.* W.H. Freeman & Co., New York, 282 pp. A good primer on earthquakes.**

16. Boyd, J.N., 1878, *History of Livingston County,* Missouri.

17. Braile, L.W., et al., 1984, *Tectonic development of the New Madrid Seismic Zone:* In proceedings of the symposium on the New Madrid Seismic Zone. USGS Open File Report 84-770. p. 204-233.

18. Braile, L.W., et al., 1986, *Tectonic development of the New Madrid rift complex, MississippiEembayment, North America:* Tectonophysics, v. 131, p. 1-21

19. Brinkman, G., 1986, *The Year Without a Summer.* Republic Times Shopper, Republic, Missouri. December 22, page 8.

20. Chapman, C.H., Anderson, L.O., and Spier, R.F., 1955, *The Campbell Site: A late Mississippi town site and cemetery in southeast Missouri:* Missouri Archaeologist, v. 17, nos. 2-3, pp. 3-140.

21. Clendenin, C.W., et al., 1989, *Reinterpretation of faulting in southeast Missouri:* Geology, v. 17, p. 217-220.

22. Cochran, K.J.H., 1992, *The world discovered the region in 1811:* Southeast Missourian Newspaper, February 5, 1992, page 7A.

23. Coffman, J., Von Hake, C., and Stover, C., 1982, *Earthquake history of the United States.* U.S. Dept. of Commerce (NOAA) and U.S. Dept. of Interior (USGS), Boulder, Colo., Publication 41-1, Revised.

24. Cramer, Zadok, 1818, *The Navigator,* Tenth Edition, Cramer & Spear, Pittsburgh. 270 p.

25. Crist, G.H. Sr. & Jr., 1811-14, *Crist family account book,* a weekly diary over 200 pages long of notes kept by Crist family members for generations, since the mid-1700's. The notes quoted here had been preserved by Eloyce Noel of Wright City, Missouri, the great great granddaughter of

one of the diary writers, George Heinrich Crist, Sr.

26. Chrone, A.J., et al., 1985, *Structure of the New Madrid Seismic Zone in Missouri and Arkansas:* Geology, v. 13, p. 547-555.

27. Daniels, J., 1972, *The Randolphs of Virginia:* Doubleday and Company, New York., 362 pp.

28. Dohan, M.H., 1981, *Mr. Roosevelt's Steamboa: The First Steamboat to Travel the Mississippi:* Dodd, Mead Co., NYC, 194 pp.

29. Douglas, R.S., 1912, *History of Southeast Missouri:* Lewis Publishing Co., New York. 1298 pp.

30. Dyhrkopp, F., 1994, *Letter referring to Gallatin County records regarding the New Madrid earthquake, Cave-In-Rock, Rev. Wilson Thompson, and other historical information,* Shawneetown, IL.

31. **Edmunds, R.D., 1983, *The Shawnee Prophet:* University of Nebraska Press, Lincoln, 260 pp.**

32. **Edmunds, R.D., 1984, *Tecumseh and the quest for Indian leadership:* Little, Brown and Company, Boston, 245 pp.**

33. EERI, 1988, *Illinois Earthquake of June 10, 1987.* Earthquake Engineering Research Institute, Berkeley, CA, Spec. Report, 4 pp.

34. Ervin, C.P., and McGinnis, L.D., 1975, *Reelfoot Rift: reactivated precursor to the Mississippi Embayment:* GSA Bulletin, v.86, p 1287-1295

35. Fisk, H.N., 1944, *Geological investigations of the alluvial valley of the lower Mississippi River:* US Army Corp of Engineers, Vicksburg, MS. 78 pp. Many maps and cross sections.

36. Flint, R.F., 1957, *Glacial and Pleistocene Geology,* Wiley, p.170

37. **Fuller, M., 1912, *The New Madrid Earthquake:* USGS Bulletin 494. 120 pp. Illustrated. Republished in 1990 with foreword and cover story by David Stewart by Center for Earthquake Studies, Southeast Missouri State University, Cape Girardeau, Missouri. 120 pp. Photographs. Figures. Maps. The earliest systematic research publication on the New Madrid earthquakes from a geologic point of view. Available from Gutenberg-Richter Publications, Rt. 1, Bo 646,Marble Hill, MO 63764. $12.95 plus $3 shipping.**

38. Funk, A.L., 1965, *Tales of our Hoosier heritage,* Adams Press, Chicago, 101 pp.

39. Garrett, J.S., 1954, *Bountiful bootheel borning,* Hayti, MO, pp. 172-184.

40. Gillespie, M.L., 1992, *Fort Osage: a history of its first occupation, 1808-1813:* Michael L. Gillespie, Sibley, MO. 42 pp.

41. Gerhardt, J.W., 1975, *Traces remain of villages,* article in Thilenius, et al.,1975, pp. 11-12, Bicentenial Commission, Cape Girardeau. 72 pp.

42. Gomberg, J., 1991, *Tectonic deformation in the New Madrid Seismic Zone:*(abstract), Seismological Research Letters, v. 62, p.

43. Gori, P., Hays, W., et al., 1984, Proceedings of symposium on New Madrid Seismic Zone: USGS Open File Report 84-770, 468 pp. With map.

44. Grohskopf, J.G., 1955, *Subsurface geology of the Mississippi Embayment of southeast Missouri:* Missouri Geological Survey and Water Resources, v. 37, Structure maps and cross sections.

45. Guccione, M., and Hehr, L., 1991, *Origin of the "sunklands" in the New Madrid Seismic Zone: tectonic or alluvial,* Seismological Research Letters, v. 62, p. 171.

46. Hagood, J.H., and Hagood, R., 1990, *Mirror of Hannibal,* Revised Ed. (from 1905 edition by T. Bacon), Jostens Publications, Marceline, MO. Indexed

47. Guion, W.B., 1850, *Reclaiming swamp lands or submerged lands occasioned by the New Madrid earthquake:* Report from the Commission on Public Lands, 31st U.S. Congress report No. 108, February 20, 1850, 45 pp.

48. Hamilton, R., and Johnson, A., 1990, *Tecumseh's prophecy: preparing for the next New Madrid Earthquake:* USGS Circular 1066, 30 pp.

49. Hildenbrand, T.G., 1984, *Rift structure of the northern Mississippi Embayment from the analysis of gravity and magnetic data:* In proceedings of the symposium on New Madrid seismic zone. USGS Open File Report 84-770p. 168-203.

50. Holcombe, R.K., 1979, *History of Marion County,* (Reprint of 1884 edition), Walsworth Publishing Co.

51. Hopper, M., et al., 1985, *Estimation of earthquake effects associated with large earthquakes in the New Madrid seismic zone:* USGS Open File Report, #85-457. 185 pp. Fold-out map.

52. Houck, L., 1908, *A History of Missouri:*

Donnelly & Sons, Chicago. 2 vols. 720 pp.

53. Howard, J.H., 1981, *Shawnee! The ceremonialism of a Native Indian Tribe and its cultural background.* Ohio Univ. Press, Athens, Ohio, 454 pp.

54. Howard, L.D., *Pages from the past:* Compilation of notes, short historical accounts, and letters. 10 pp.

55. Jackson, K.C., 1979, *Earthquakes and earthquake history of Arkansas*: Information Circular 26, Arkansas Geological Commission, 70 p.

56. Jacob, K.H., editor, 1987, *Seismic hazards, ground motions, soil liquefaction and engineering practice in eastern North America*: National Center for Earthquake Engineering, Buffalo, New York, Proceedings of Symposium, Tuxedo, NY, October 1987, 521 pp.

57. Jibson, R.W., 1991, *Static and dynamic analysis of landslides in the New Madrid Seismic Zone: (*abstract), Seismological Research Letters, v. 62, p. 175.

58. Jibson, R.W., and Keefer, D.K., 1988, *Landslides triggered by earthquakes in the central Mississippi Valley, Tennessee and Kentucky:* USGS Professional Paper 1336-c, 24 pp. Fold-out map.

59. Johnston, A.C., 1982, *A major earthquake zone on the Mississippi:* Scientific American, v. 246, p. 60-68.

60. Johnston, A.C., 1991, *An overview of the New Madrid Seismic Zone*: (abstract), Seismological Research Letters, v. 62, p. 175.

61. Johnston, A.C., and Nava, S., 1985, *Recurrence rates and probability estimates for the New Madrid seismic zone:* Journal of Geophysical Research, v. 90, p. 6737-6753.

62. Johnston, A.C., and Kanter, L.R., 1990, *Earthquakes in stable continental crust*: Scientific American, v. 95, March, pp. 68-75

63. Kane, J.N., 1972, *The American counties,* 3rd ed., Scarecrow Press, Metuchen, NJ. 582 pp.

64. Kane, M.F., et al., 1981, *Model for the tectonic evolution of the Mississippi Embayment and its contemporary seismicity*: Geology, v. 9, p. 563-568.

65. Keefer, D.K., 1984, *Landslides caused by earthquakes*: GSA Bulletin, v. 95, p. 406-421.

66. Lemos, L., and Coelho, P., 1991, *Displacements of slopes under earthquake loading:* Proceedings of Second International Conference on Recent Advances in Geotechnical Engineering and Soil Dynamics, St. Louis, p. 1051-1056

67. Lewis, Arthur A., et al., 1958, *History of the Lewis family—1635-195*8: Published by Lewis Family, Franklin County, Missouri. 49 pp.

68. Lewis, Mildred., et al., *Lewis geneology:* Loose leaf compilation distributed by Lewis family, New Madrid, Missouri. 58 pp.

69. Logsdon, D., 1990, *I was there! In the New Madrid earthquakes of 1811-12*(Eyewitness accounts by survivors of the worst earthquake in Amerian History): Kettle Mills Press, Nashville, Tn.

70. Marple, R.T., and Schweig, E.S., 1992, *Remote sensing of alluvial terrain in a humid, tectonically actively setting: The New Madrid seismic zone*: Photogrammetric Engineering and Remote Sensing, v. 58, pp. 209-219.

71. Mathews, J.J., 1961, *The Osages: children of the middle waters.* University Oklahoma Press, Norman, 826 pp.

72. McCracken, M., 1971, *Structural features of Missouri:* Missouri Geological Survey and Water Resources, Rolla, MO., 99 pp. Fold-out map.

73. McFarlane, James, 1883, *The "earthquake" at New Madrid, Missouri, in 1811, probably not an earthquake*: Proceedings of the American the Advancement of Science, v. 32, pp. 247-248.

74. McGee, W.J., 1892, *A fossil earthquake*: Bulletin of the Geological Society of America, v. 4, p.411-414.

75. McKeown, F.A., and Pakiser, L.C., 1982, *Investigations of the New Madrid, Missouri, earthquake region*: USGS Professional Paper 1236, 201 pp.

76. Meatte, M., 1994, *Letter and Geneaology charts on Meatte, Maisonville, and Puckeshinwa families:* Jacksonville, FL.

77. Merrill, Boynton, Jr., 1976, *Jefferson's Nephews: A Frontier Tragedy:* Princeton Press, New Jersey. 462 pp. An excellent scholarly work with a great deal of historic information about late 18th and early 19th century America.

78. Nishenko, S.P., and Bollinger, G.A., 1990, *Forecasting damaging earthquakes in the central and eastern United States.* Science, v. 249, September 21, p. 1412-1416.

79. Nuttli, O., 1973, *The Mississippi Valley Earthquakes of 1811-12: Intensities, ground motion, and magnitudes.* Bulletin of the seismological Society of America. v. 63, pp. 227-248. (Includes microfiche appendix of numerous newspaper accounts throughout U.S. during the time of the earthquakes.)

80. Nuttli, O., 1990, *Effects of Earthquakes in the Central United States*: 2nd edition with foreword and appendices by David Stewart, Center for Earthquake Studies, Southeast Missouri State University, Cape Girardeau, Missouri. 50 pp. Photographs. Figures. Maps. Excellent summary of all of the active earthqua faults in the Midwest. Available from Gutenberg-Richter Publications, Rt. 1,Box 646, Marble Hill, MO 63764. $7.95 plus $3 shipping.

81. Obermeier, S., 1984, Liquefaction potential in the central Mississippi Valley: USGS Open File Report 84-515.

82. Obermeier, S., 1989, Earthquake-induced liquefaction features in the coasta lsetting of South Carolina and in the fluvial setting of the New Madrid seismic zone: USGS Professional Paper 1504.

83. Penick, J., 1981, *The New Madrid earthquakes:* University of Missouri Press, Columbia, MO. 130 pp. Illustrated. A fascinating scholarly account of the New Madrid earthquakes from a historian's point of view. Available from Gutenberg-Richter Pubications, Rt. 1, Box 646, Marble Hill, MO 63764. $13.95plus $3 shipping.

84. Peterson, C.E., *Early Ste. Genevieve and its architecture*: Missouri Historica lReview, pp. 207-233.

85. Purcell, M.G., *Lucy Jefferson Lewis: Sister of President Thomas Jefferson*, Virginia 1752; Kentucky 1811, 12 pp.

86. Qualkinbush, R., 1970, *Qualkinbush-Lewis geneology.* Published by Ross Qualkinbush, compilation of loose sheets, 21 pp.

87. Quinn, J.H., 1961, *Prairie mounds of Arkansas:* Arkansas Archaeological Society Newsletter, v. 2, p. 1-8.

88. Ramsey, Robert L., 1952, *Our storehouse of Missouri place names*, University of Missouri Bulletin, Mo. Handbook No. 2.

89. Raymond, E.T., 1920, *Tecumseh: A Chronicle of the last Great Leader of his People:* Glasgow, Brook & Co., Toronto, Canada, 212 pp.

90. Reagor, G., and Brewer, L., 1987, *Preliminary isoseismal map and intensity distribu tion for the southeast Illinois earthquake of June 10, 1987.* U.S. Geological Survey, Open File Report 87-578, 3 pp.

91. Rofs, Lieut., 1775, *Course of the river Mississippi:* Rob Saver Publisher, London, large map.

92. Royall, P.D., et al., 1991, *Late quaternary paleoecology and paleoenvironments of the central Mississippi alluvial valley:* GSA Bulletin, v. 103, p. 157-170.

93. Russ, D.P., 1979, *Late Holocene faulting and earthquake recurrence in the Reelfoot Lake area, northwestern Tennessee*: GSA Bulletin, v. 90, p. 1013-1018.

94. Russ, D. 1982, *Style and significance of surface deformation in the vicinity of New Madrid, Missouri*, in Investigations of the New Madrid, Missouri earthquake region: U.S. Geological Survey Professional Paper 1236.

95. Sandburg, C., 1954, *Abraham Lincoln: the prairie years*, Dell Publishing Co.,New York, 320 pp.

96. Sanders, T.E. and Peek, W.W., 1973, *Literature of the American Indian*, Glencoe Press, New York, 534 pp.

97. Saucier, R.T., 1974, *Quaternary geology of the lower Mississippi Valley:*Arkansas Archaeological Survey Research Series 6.

98. Saucier, R.T., 1977, *Sand dunes and related eolian features of the lower Mississippi River alluvial valley:* Geoscience and Man, v. 19, p. 23-40.

99. Saucier, R.T., 1987, *Geomorphological interpretations of late Quaternary terraces in western Tennessee and their regional tectonic implications:* USGS Professional Paper 1336-A, 19 pp.

100. Saucier, R., 1989, *Evidence for episodic sand-blow activity during the 1811-12 New Madrid (Missouri) earthquake series*: Geology, v. 17, pp. 103-106.

101. Saucier, R.T., 1991, *Geoarchaeological evidence of strong prehistoric earthquakes in the New Madrid, Missouri, Seismic Zone:* Geology, v. 19, pp. 296-298.

102. Schachner, N., 1951, *Thomas Jefferson: A Biography.* Appleton-Century-Crofts, Inc., New York, 2 vols, 1070 pp.

103. Schneider, S., 1989, *Historic St. Charles*, Nutwood Publishing Co., St. Louis, 52 pp..

104. Schweig, E., 1991, *The bootheel lineament: results of trenching and shallow seismic reflection studies:* (abstract), Seismological Research Letters, v. 62, p. 183.

105. Schweig, E., and Marple, R.T., 1991, *Bootheel Lineament: A possible coseismic fault of the great New Madrid Earthquakes:* Geology, v. 19, p. 1025-1028.

106. Schweig, E., and Jibson, R., 1989, *Surface effects of the 1811-12 New Madrid earthquake sequence and seismotectonics of the New Madrid seismic zone:* GSA Field Trip Guidebook, p. 47-67.

107. Seed, H.B., 1968, *Landslides during earthquakes due to soil liquefaction:* American Society of Civil Engineers; Journal of Soil Mechanics and Foundation Division. v. 94 p. 1055-1122.

108. Shrum, E.E., and Mates, M., 1980, *The slaves and slave owners of Cape Girardeau County,* Edison E. Shrum, Scott City, MO. 152 pp.

109. Shrum, E.E., 1989, *The real New Madrid earthquakes,* Scott County historical Society, Scott City, MO. 154 pp.

110. Smalley, R., and Dorman, J., 1991, *Long-duration seismic surface wave motion at Memphis from the Risco earthquake of May 3, 1991.* Seismological Research Letters, Vol. 62, Nos. 3-4, pp. 184-185.

111. Snyder, G.S., 1970, *In the footsteps of Lewis and Clark.* National Geographic Society, Illustrated, 216 pp.

112. **Stewart, David, 1994, *Damages and Losses from Future New Madrid Earthquakes*: (4th Printing) Published by the Missouri State Emergency Management Agency (SEMA) and the Federal Emergency Management Agency (FEMA) . 68 pages with charts and fold-out maps. Written with assumption that reader knows nothing about earthquakes, it is an excellent primer. Enables reader to choose any county in the Midwest, postulate any size of earthquake on the New Madrid fault, and calculate numbers of resulting casualties, displaced persons, collapsed buildings, etc. for that county. Available free from Gutenberg-Richter Publications, Rt. 1, Box 646, Marble Hill, MO 63764. Enclose $3.00 for shipping & handling**

113. Stewart, David, and Knox, Ray, 1992, *Representative earthquake features in*

theNew Madrid Seismic Zone: Second Printing. Center for Earthquake Studies, Southeast Missouri State University, Cape Girardeau 63701. 62 pp.

114. **Stewart, David, and Knox, Ray, 1993. *The earthquake that never went away:* Gutenberg-Richter Publications, Rt. 1, Box 646, Marble Hill, MO 63764. 240 pages, 150 photos, figures, maps and tables. Shows permanent effects on landscape from the quakes of 1811-12 and how they impact industry and agriculture today. $17.95 plus $3.00 shipping.**

115. **Stewart, David, and Knox, Ray, 1995. *The New Madrid Fault Finders Guide*: Gutenberg-Richter Publications, Rt. 1, Box 646, Marble Hill, MO 63764. $12.95 plus $3.00 shipping. Contains photos, figures, maps, milages, directions, road logs—a set of self-guided tours of the New Madrid Fault Zone. You can take short tours of an hour or two around New Madrid, or tours of a day or more in four states. You will see the sand boils, exlosion craters, landslides, fissures, earthquake lakes, where the river formed water falls, sites of lost towns, and other features impressed on the landscape by the New Madrid earthquakes of 1811-12.**

116. Stickney, M. C., and Musselman, R., 1993, *Earthquakes: history and seismic safety in Montana.* Info. Pamphlet 2, Montana Bureau of Mines and Geology and Montana Division of Disaster and Emergency Services, Butte. 17 pp.

117. Sugden, J., 1947, *Tecumseh's last stand.* Univ. Oklahoma Press, Norman, 298 pp.

118. Swanberg, C.A., Mitchell, B.J., Lohse, R.I., and Blackwell, D.D., 1982, *Heat flow in the upper Mississippi Embayment:* U.S. Geological Survey, Washington, DC, Professional Paper 1236-M, in McKeown & Pakiser, 1982, op cit., p. 183- 189.

119. Taylor, K.B., et al., 1989, *The Southeastern Illinois earthquake of 10 June 1987.* Seismological Research LEtters, Vol. 60, No. 3, pp. 101-110.

120. Taylor, R., 1989, *Indiana: a new historical guide.* Indiana Historical Society, Indianapolis, 682 pp.

121. Thilenius, J.E., et al., 1975, *Biography of historic Cape Girardeau County:* Bicentenial Commission, Cape Girardeau, 72 pp.

122. Thompson, J., and Stewart, D., 1992, *Landslides subsequent to a 4.7 magnitude earthquake in the Benton Hills of Missouri.* Trans. Missouri Academy of Science, Vol. 26, pp. 91-104.

123. Thompson, W., 1867, *The Autobiography of Elder Wilson Thompson.* Reprinted in 1978, Old School Hymnal Co, Conley, Georgia, 363 pp.

124. Tributsch, H., 1984, *When the snakes awake:* MIT Press, Cambridge, Mass., 248 pp. This is the best book available on animal behavior prior to earthquakes. Provides data and anecdotes from many countries and time periods, dating even back as far as 411 B.C.

125. Tucker, G., 1956, *Tecumseh: A vision of glory:* Bobs-Merril Co., Indianapolis, Indiana, 399 pp.

126. Turner, W., 1990, *The War of 1812: The war that both sides won.* Dundurn Press, Toronto, Canada, 144 pp.

127. US Department of Agriculture, 1977, *Soil survey of New Madrid County, MO:* 120. US Department of Agriculture and Missouri Agricultural Experiment Station, 71 pp.

128. Vaughn, J., 1991, *Evidence for multiple generations of seismically induced liquefaction features in the western lowlands, southeast Missouri:* (abstract), Seismological Research Letters, v. 62, p. 189.

129. Watson, Judge Goah, 1815, *Early New Madrid History.* Newspaper reprint of un-8known origin.

130 Weinel, R.A., 1986, *Weather Report for Southern Illinois, 1816.* Collected notes. Unpublished.

131. Wuenscher, R., et al., 1991, *Attenuation of body waves in the New Madrid seismic zone:* (abstract), Seismological Research Letters, v. 62, p. 191

132. Yong, C, 1988, *The great Tangshan earthquake of 1975.* Pergamon Press, Oxford, New York, 210 pp.

133. Youd, T.L., 1973, *Liquefaction, flow and associated ground failure.* U.S. Geol. Survey, Circular 688, Reston, VA, 12 pp.

134. Zoback, M.D., 1979, *Recurrent faulting in the vicinity of Reelfoot Lake, northwestern Tennessee:* GSA Bulletin, v. 90, p. 1019-24.

NOTE: In addition to the above 134 references a number of old newspaper articles not cited here were also used—articles published in 1811-12 during the time of the earthquakes. Most of these old news accounts can be found in the microfiche appendix of Nuttli (1973).

A considerable amount of the information and facts contained in this book can also be found in three sets of encyclopedias that were heavily used throughout the research for this book. They are as follows:

1. *Colliers Encyclopedia*, 1954 edition, published by P.F. Collier & Son, New York.
2. *Encyclopedia Britannica*, 1958 edition, published by Encyclopedia Britannica, Inc., Chicago.
3. *New Standard Encyclopedia*, 1960 edition, published by Standard Education Society, Inc., Chicago.

INDEX

A

A-bomb 133, 199
Abraham 58, 115
abstinence from alcohol 65, 66
Abu Simbel, Temple at 55, 57
acceleration, earthquake 318-319
acetyl salicylic acid (aspirin) 105
act of God (see God's wrath)
Adams, John 76, 78
adultery 27, 65
Advance, MO 54, 132, 249, 280, 299-302, 303
Aegean Sea 115
Afganistan 89
Africa 89, 104, 105, 116, 266
African Americans 16, 17, 25, 27, 28-30, 31, 32-33, 35, 50, 98, 103, 150, 155, 240, 249-250, 279
aftershocks 240, 255-256
agriculture 104, 116, 215
air liquefaction 156
airplanes 90
Alabama Emergency Management Agency 336
Alaskan earthquake 266
alcohol & drinking 31-32, 37, 62, 63, 65, 68, 70, 80, 133, 151, 164, 198, 230, 245, 251, 256, 266-267, 271
Albemarle County, VA 27, 33
Allegheny River 75, 79, 82
Alexander, Czar 268
All Saints Day 266
alphabet, use of 104
Alton, IL 125
Alton, MO 280, 310
Amazon River 116
American Association for the Advancement of Science 8
American Dream, The 279
American elm 96, 97
American flag 21, 50, 79, 127
American Journal of Nursing 368
American Journal of Science & Arts 156
American Red Cross 5, 317, 336, 337

American Revolution (see Revolutionary War)
Amos, Book of 243
amplitude of seismic waves 300
Anderson, IN 298
Andrew, Hurricane 200
Anglican Church 47
animal behavior before earthquakes 7, 15, 55, 84-85, 90-91, 162, 175, 182, 244
Anna, IL 280
Annus Mirabilus 55
Antarctica 116
Anthem, U.S. National 127
antimony 35
Appalacian Mountains 53, 59, 111, 257
Arabia 89, 116
Arabian Plate 115
Arbyrd, MO 137
archeology 139-141, 223, 286
Arkansas Office of Emergency Services 336
Arkansas River 75, 108, 144, 169, 178
Arkansas statehood 232
Archbishop of Canterbury 46
Argentina 116
Armageddon 243-244, 251, 274 (also see end of the world)
arm bands 64, 71, 273
arm broken 155
Armenian earthquake 322
Ashe, Thomas 164-165
Asia 89, 104
asphalt (see petroleum)
aspirin 105
Assam Province, India 266
Assam earthquake 266
Assiniboine Indians 68
Associated Electric Plant 21, 22, 113, 199, 206, 212, 213
astrologers 86
Aswan Dam 56
athiest 249
Atlanta, GA 187
atmospheric electricity (see electricity, atmospheric)
atomic bomb 133, 199
Atwell, James 160, 162

Audubon, John James 19, 78, 81, 85, 90, 95, 97, 163, 181, 185, 206, 237
Audubon, Lucy Bakewell 78, 81, 85, 95, 163, 181
Audubon, Victor 81
Australia 104, 116, 118, 191
Austrian Premier 206

B

Babylon 65, 115
Bakewell, Benjamin 78
Bakewell Glassworks 78
Bakewell, Lucy (see Audubon, Lucy Bakewell)
B & O Railroad 11
backwards flow of Mississippi (see Mississippi River, retrograde motion)
Baker, Charles 15
Baker, Nicholas 80, 85, 166, 167, 174-175, 179
Baltimore, MD 11, 187
bananas 104, 105
banana splits 105
banks caving in 144, 159, 160, 161, 162, 163, 165, 172, 225, 179, 208-209, 213, 242, 251
bald eagles 137, 138, 183
balloon theory 288-289
baptism, Christian 247, 249-250
Baptist Church 133, 148, 220, 229, 245-250, 251
barges 79, 143-144, 158-162, 167, 216
Baseball World Series 13, 283, 292, 293, 305, 322
base-isolation of buildings 235-236
basement damage 299-302, 304, 322-313
Bates, Moses 261
Baton Rouge, LA 261
Battle of Blue Licks 92
Battle of Fallen Timbers 62, 68
Battle of New Orleans 30, 31, 38
Battle of Point Pleasant 59
Battle of the Thames 270-272, 274
Battle of Tippecanoe 87, 258, 265, 271, 273

Bayou Fourche 210-213, 231
Bayou of Big Lake 215
Bayou Portage 199, 210-213, 215-216, 218-220, 231, 274
bays and harbors created by earthquakes 114-115
Beach, The (world's largest sand boil) 239
Beals, Mrs. 259
beans as food 66, 104, 105
beans as prayer beads (see prayer beans)
bear 91, 111, 139, 171, 277
Bear Creek 261
beautiful scenery resulting from earthquakes 114-117
Becket, St. Thomas 46
Becktie, Capt. 158
Bedinger, Daniel 157-161, 179
Beechland, KY 94
beef 66, 189 (also see cattle)
beer 65, 80, 81
bees, honey 258, 278 (also see honey)
Belgium 30, 86, 268
Bell, Alexander Graham 12
Bell City, MO 54, 132, 214, 280
bells 187, 191, 198, 251
Ben (LaRoche's slave) 155
Benton Hills 266 (also see Tywappity Hill)
Benton, MO 132, 190, 215, 280, 303, 313
Benton, Thomas Hart 32
Bentonville, AR 369
Bernie, MO 280
Bessie Hotel 114
Bessie's Bend 112-114 (see New Madrid Bend)
Bessie's Neck 113-114, 201, 212
Bessie, TN 112-114, 212
Bethel Baptist Church 245-250, 276
Bethel Cemetery 248
Bethel Meetinghouse (see Bethel Baptist Church)
big bang baloon theory 288-289
Big Black River 169
Biggs, John 258

Biggs, Mrs. John Collings 258-259

Big Lake, AR-MO 132, 137-138, 208, 214, 221

Big Oak State Park 212

Big Prairie, AR 75, 129, 143-144, 168-169, 172, 173, 175, 208, 240-242

Big Turtle (Boone's Indian name) 92, 272

Big Warrior 264-265

billiards 305-306

Billy Goat (see Lewis, Lilbourn Anexamander)

Bird, Abraham 261

Bird, Thompson 261

birds 90, 91, 160, 182, 275

Bird's Creek 245

Birdsville, KY 28, 31

bird watching 369

birth (see childbirth)

birthdays (Sarah and Abe Lincoln's) 197

bison (see buffalo)

bituminous coal (see coal)

bizarre animal behavior (see animal behavior before earthquakes)

Black fault 291

Blackfish 60, 61, 92, 272

Blackhoof 72

Black, MO 291

blacks (see African Americans)

black sun 69, 86

bloodletting, therapeutic 34-35

Bloomfield, IN 298

Bloomsdale, MO 280

Blue Bank, TN 184, 212

blue denim jeans 105

Bequette, Jean Baptiste (house of) 109, 110

Blue Licks, Battle of 92

Blytheville, AR 100, 102, 132, 134, 137, 168, 227, 306

boats thrown up on land 189, 202-203

bobcat 277

Bock, Kathleen Newsom 50

Boekerton Beauty Shed 219-220

Boekerton Baptist Church 220

Boekerton, MO 168, 216, 219-220, 242

Boer Commandos 89

Bogota, Colombia 368

boils (see sand boils)

Bolduc, Louis (house of) 110

Bolivar, Simon 88, 252

Bolivia 88

Bollinger County, MO 369

Bollinger, G.A. 286-287, 291

Bolt, Bruce 7

bolts of lightening (see earthquake lightening)

Bonaparte, Joseph 88

Bonaparte, Napoleon (see Napoleon Bonaparte)

Book of the Year Award 368

Boone, Daniel 19, 92-98, 192, 245, 272

Boone County, MO 260

Boone, Fort 129

Boone, Jemima 92

Boone, Rebecca Bryan 92, 96, 98, 192

Boonesboro, KY 75

Boone's children 92, 96

Boone's grave 96, 98

Boone's Indian name (see Big Turtle)

Boone's Mansion 56, 95, 96, 97, 191, 192, 194-195, 280

Bootheel fault 132, 224, 291

Bootheel lineament (see Bootheel fault)

Bootheel of Missouri 117, 143, 214, 218-219, 225, 226, 227, 230-232

Boston, MA 4, 187, 198

Bowling Green, KY 291

Bowman, Col. John 61

Bowman's Battle 61

Bradbury, John 143-144, 175

Bradley, James 15

Braggadocio, MO 132

Braile, W.L. 291

Brazil 116

breastfeeding 171

Brick House, The (oldest west of Miss. R.) 193, 196

Bridgeport, IL 298

Brighton, AR 143

Bringier, Louis 156-157

British 15, 80, 86, 87-88, 89, 91, 103, 137, 257, 270, 278

British Channel 33, 262

broccoli 298

Brock, Gen. Isaac 271

broken arm 155

broken cypress trees, stumps of 200-201, 203

broken nose 150

broken leg 155

broken stream channels (see discoutinuous channels)

Brooks, Jared 192, 205, 255

brothels 266-267

Broughton 40, 45

Broughton, Elizabeth Ann Lewis 45

Broughton, Lilbourn Lewis "Libba" Hunter 40, 45

Browning, Iben 4-6, 14

Bryan Cemetery 96, 98

Bryan, Eliza 55, 135, 185, 189, 199, 202, 215, 237, 255-256

Bucks County, PA 92, 98

buffalo 63, 92, 111, 139, 229, 277

buffalo nickels 288

building codes, sesimic 5, 322

Bunge Grain Elevator 152, 153

bunk bed 298

Burma 266

burning at the stake 66-67, 100

Burr, Aaron 32

buzzards 172, 173

C

Caanan, Land of 57

Caesar, Julius 120

Cafe Beignet 125

Cagle Lake 139-141, 223

Cairo, IL 102, 132, 142, 147, 280, 292

Caldwell, Billie 271

Caldwell County, KY 28

Caldwell's Settlement 249

California 3, 12, 15, 17, 116, 186, 295, 297, 322

Callaway County, MO 260

calomel 35

Camdenton, MO 315-316

Campbell County, KY 245

Campbell, Dr. Arthur 34-35, 36

Campbell Indian Mound 139-141, 223

Campbell, MO 226, 227, 280

camphor 35

Canada 75, 87, 106, 116, 119, 128, 187, 198, 230, 298

Candlestick Park 13, 292

canoes 122, 144, 166-167, 208, 214, 217, 227

cantelope 104

Cape Girardeau Baptist Association 248

Cape Girardeau, MO 61, 73, 75, 91, 98-101, 102, 109, 130-131, 132, 147, 190, 191, 203, 207, 237, 240, 241, 265, 275, 280, 302-303, 368, 369

Cape Girardeau County, MO 129, 245, 247, 275, 277

Cape Hatteras 55

Capitol Building, Missouri State 255

Capitol Building, U.S. national 187, 198

Caracas, Venezuela 244-245, 252

Carbondale, IL 99, 102, 280, 291

carbonized wood 156 (also see seismic tar balls and coal)

Cardiff Hill 261

Cardwell, AR 143

Carlson, Virginia LaValle 2, 50, 51

Carolina earthquake 137

Carolina parrot (paroquet) 19, 90

Carr, Dabney 45, 50

Carr, Martha Jefferson 45, 50, 51

Carrol County, MO 260

Caruthersville, MO 8, 132, 134, 144, 151-152, 153, 168, 173, 227, 230, 242, 280

caskets, cherrywood 96, 98

castor oil 35, 126

castor oil factory 126

casualties (see earthquake injuries and earthquake deaths)

Cates, TN 200, 212

Catholic Church 41, 42, 95, 99, 106, 107, 119, 133, 191, 206, 251, 252, 266-267, 274

Catlin, George 273

Catron, MO 285

cats 91

catsup 105

cat tails 148

cattle 91, 167, 172, 228, 229, 230, 256

caving banks (see banks caving in)

Cave-In-Rock 163-165, 166

cedar of Lebanon 105

Celestial Tiger, as name for Tecumseh 59

Center for Earthquake Research and Information 336
Center for Earthquake Studies 336, 368
Central America 104, 106
Centralia fault 291
Centralia, IL 280, 291
Central Methodist College 261, 368
Central Missouri State University 368
Central U.S. Earthquake Consortium (CUSEC) 5, 335, 336, 368
Central U.S. Earthquake Intensity Scale (CUSEIS) 317-330
city parks as part of urban planning 119
Chaffee, MO 249
Chalk Bluffs 204
Chariton County, MO 260
Charlemagne 45, 47, 86
Charlemine, John 146
Charles the Great 45, 47, 86
Charleston Courier, The 198
Charleston, MO 1,102, 132, 148, 185, 187, 239, 280, 292
Charleston, MO earthquake (1895) 1, 187, 292
Charleston, SC 4, 187, 198
Charleston, SC earthquake (1886) 187
Chapel Hill, NC 368
Chartier, Auguste 150
Chartier, Ben 144, 146, 150, 237
Chepoussea Creek 171, 203 (also see St. John's Bayou and St. John's Ditch)
Cherokee Indians 68, 103, 277, 369
cherrywood caskets 96, 98
chest pains 284
Chicago 5, 71, 267, 262, 288, 294, 298
Chicago Museum of Natural History 71
Chiksika 58, 59, 61, 62
childbed fever 35
childbirth 35, 36, 60, 80, 81, 149, 179
Chile 266
Chilean earthquake 266
chili 105
chillicothe, meaning of the word 99

Chillicothe, MO (Cape Girardeau County) 61, 73, 99-100, 275, 277
Chillicothe, MO (Livingston County) 100, 277, 278
Chillicothe, OH 60, 61, 75, 92, 100
chimney damage 29, 30, 163, 187, 193, 198, 209, 238, 247, 250, 298, 311, 315, 332
China 6-8, 89, 91, 105, 114-115, 244, 266
Chinese food 105
Chickasaw Bluffs 161, 182-183, 192, 204, 266
Chickasaw Indians 53, 72, 88, 103, 264, 268-269, 277
chicken 66, 245
Chicken Point 182, 183
Chippewa Indians 68, 277
chocolate 104-105
Choctaw Indians 72, 88, 103, 264, 269, 277
cholera epidemic 254
Chosen People, God's 56-57, 67
Christ, Jesus 243
Christianity 58, 66, 250-251 (also see Anglican, Baptist, Catholic, Methodist, Moldavian, Presbyterian, protestant, Quaker, Shaker, and Jesus)
Christmas Eve 150, 178
church bells 187, 191, 198, 251
Church of England 47
Cincinnati, OH 68, 75, 80, 130, 198, 240, 241, 245, 288, 291, 294, 302
civil engineers 296
Civilized Tribes, The 102, 103, 277
Civil War, American 2, 20 27, 32, 40, 94, 127, 179, 219, 241, 298
Clark, Donette 14
Clark, George Rogers 52, 53, 71, 122
Clark, William 48, 71, 73, 79, 82, 122-123, 272
Clarksdale, MS 169, 280
Clarksville, IN 83
Clarkton, MO 219
clay amplification 304-305
clay expansion 309
Clay, Henry 87
Clemens, Samuel 262
Clemson, Capt. Eli B. 123

Clermont, The 76
Cleveland, MS 169
climatologist 4
Clinton, KY 54
club foot 268
coaches, horse-drawn 277
coal 85, 147, 151, 161, 185, 226, 238-239 (also see carbonized wood and seismic tar balls)
Cochran, K.J.H. 90
Coffman, Isaac 258
Coil, Oscar T. 148
coins 254, 288
Cole County, MO 260
Cole, Fred 1, 2
Coles Fort 129
collapsing banks (see banks caving in)
Collings, Henry 257
Collings, John 258, 260
Collings, Lydia 258, 260
Collings, Mrs. Henry 258
Collings, Phebe 260
Collings, Richard 257, 258
Collings, William E. 256-259
Collings, Zebulon 257, 258, 260
Colombia 88, 368
Colonies, Thirteen Original 127-128
Columbia Bottoms, MO 192
Columbia, PA 11
Columbia River 82
Columbia, SC 298
Columbus, Christopher 104, 164, 278, 286
comet, as a name for Tecumseh 59, 269, 272
Comet of 1811 55-58, 59, 74, 86-87, 243, 269
Commerce, MO 149
compass, magnetic 91
Confederacy of the Five Civilized Tribes 102, 103, 277
Confederacy of the Rhine 86
Confederate flag 21
Confederate States of America 21, 179, 219
Confederation of Native Americans 68, 70, 72, 258, 265
Congress (see U.S. Congress)
Connecticut statehood 127
Constitution (see U.S. Constitution)
consanguinity (see intermarriage)
consumption 70

continuous ground motion lasting more than a day 189
Coosa River 58, 75
Cooter, MO 134, 140, 223
corn 66, 74, 90, 104, 105, 118, 200, 226, 302
Corning, AR 54, 132, 280, 305
corn-on-the-cob 105
corn whiskey 66
Corpse Maker, The 81
Corps of Engineers (see U.S. Army Corps of Engineers)
Cottage Grove fault 291
cotton 104, 118, 178, 200, 226
Council Island (see Island #53)
counterfieiting 253-254
Cove of Grease 111
cows (see cattle)
coyotes 147
CPR 334
crab, the ugly 67
Craighead County, AR 320-321
Cramer, Zadoc 82, 83, 84, 130-131, 141-142, 167, 168-169, 175, 178, 183, 185-186, 204-205
Cramer & Spear Publishers 82
cranberries 104, 105
cranberry sauce 105
Cree Indians 68
Creek Indians 58, 72, 103, 263-265, 277
Creoles 80, 166
Crespellani, Teresa 23
crevasses (see earthquake fissures)
Crisler, Lilbourn Lewis "Libba" Hunter 40, 41, 45
Crist, Amandy Jane 136, 181, 256
Crist, Benjamin 136
Crist, Besy Collings 136, 181, 256-257, 259, 260
Crist, Catherine 136
Crist, Elizabeth 136, 260
Crist, Elizabeth Gerard 136
Crist family 136-137, 207, 255, 256-260
Crist, George Heinrich Jr. 136, 259, 260
Crist, George Heinrich Sr. 136, 181, 207, 256-257, 259, 260
Crist, Hanna 136

Crist, Henry Phillip 136
Crist, James Martin 136
Crist, Nicholas George 136
Crist, Nicholas Heinrich 136
Crist, Rachael 136
Crist, Reason 136, 260
Crist, Sarah 136
Crist, Stephen 136
Criittenden County, KY 27
Criittenden Press, The 27
Crowley's Ridge 266,299
Crows Nest (see Island #94)
Crystal City, MO 368
Cuautla, Mexico 88
Cuba 187
cucumbers 104, 105
Culbertson family 152-154, 222
Cumberland Gap 92
Cumberland River 28, 31, 75
Cumberland Trail 33, 92
cursing (see swearing)
CUSEC (see Central U.S. Earthquake Consortium)
CUSEIS (Central U.S. Earthquake Intensity Scale) 317-330
Cushion Lake 216-217, 218, 231
Cyclone, MO 369
cypress stumps (see broken cypress trees, stumps of)
Czar Alexander 268
Czar's Comet, The 269

D

Daguerre, Jaques Maude 12
Daguerreotype 12
darkness following earth-quakes (see earthquake smog)
darkening of sky (see earth-quake smog)
Daughters of the American Revolution (DAR) 31, 98
David, King 246
Davis, Charles 274
Davis, Jane Cook 94, 178
Davis, Jefferson 94, 178, 179
Davis, John 161-162
Davis Party, The 161-162
Davis, Samuel 94, 178
Dead Sea Rift 115
Dearborn, Fort 75, 257
death (see earthquake deaths, murder, and near-death experience)
death canoe 166

death march (see Trail of Tears)
deckhands 80, 155, 170
Declaration of Ihdepen-dence for Bolivia, Colombia, Ecuador, Mexico, Panama, Peru, and Venezuela 88
Declaration of Indepen-dence, U.S.A. 24, 28, 47, 60, 67
deer 84, 91, 139, 171, 245, 275, 277
Deering, MO 224
Defiance, MO 95,195-196
deficiencies in professional earthquake education 295-297
DeLisle, Eustache254-255
DeLisle, John 254-255
DeLisle vs. State of Missouri 254-255
Deleware Indians 63, 66, 67, 68, 99, 257, 259, 275
Deleware statehood 127
Delta Headstart Program 219
democracy as a form of government 99
Democrat 78
Denmark 86
Des Cyprie 12
desertion of families by fathers 136, 189
Desoto, Hernando 106, 107, 164
Desoto, IL 280,304
Detie, John 146
Detroit, MI 75, 191, 198, 257, 264-265, 270, 272
Deuteronomy, Book of 57
Devil's Channel 143
Devil's Elbow 143, 168
Dexter, MO 102, 132, 280
Dick (Judge Green's slave) 249-250, 276
Dillard, A.N. 214, 215
disaster relief, government 251-253
discontinuous channels 152-154, 214, 215-217, 219, 231, 241
diseases transmitted to Indians from whites 63, 70, 123, 278
dismemberment (see mutilation)
divide and conquer strategy 68, 99
dog 30, 91, 260 (also see Tiger)

Dome of Capitol, scaffolding collapse 187, 198
Donaldson Point 112-113, 114, 142, 200, 201-202, 210-213
Dorlac, Pierre (house of) 193
Dorena, MO 132, 239, 280
draining of lakes or ponds 159
Drake, Daniel 240
drinking (see alcohol)
drought 55, 74
drownings (see earthquake-related drownings)
drunkeness (see alcohol)
Dry Bayou fissure 229
Dry Bayou Missionary Baptist Church 229
ducks 91, 160, 245
dueling 32
dugouts (see canoes)
Duke of Normandy, William 45
duration of shaking 300, 312
dust clouds from earth quakes 238 (also see earthquake smog)
Dutch 89, 278 (also see Holland)
duties (see taxes)
Dyersburg, TN 54, 102, 114, 132, 280, 291

E

eagles (see bald eagles)
ear bobs 64, 273
Earth City, MO 192
earthquake acceleration 318-319
Earthquake Alley (see Interstate Highway 55)
earthquake Christians 250-251
earthquake darkness (see earthquake smog)
earthquake deaths 7, 16, 155, 172, 181, 189, 202-203, 208-209, 227-229, 240, 266, 292, 318, 324, 322
earthquake drownings 155, 189, 202-203, 208-209
earthquake engineering 322
Earthquake Engineering Journal 369
Earthquake Engineering Research Institute (EERI) 5, 296, 336

earthquake experts, limits of knowledge 295-297
earthquake explosions (see explosion sand blow craters)
earthquake fear 136, 155, 260
earthquake fissures 138, 145-147, 150, 151, 152-154, 159, 180, 198, 199, 205, 209, 214, 215, 221-224, 226-230, 238-239, 254, 299-302, 303
earthquake flooding 116, 139, 141, 145-147, 151, 153, 159, 162, 174, 183, 184, 186, 201-202, 207, 208, 209, 217, 221, 223, 225-226, 227, 231, 234, 268
earthquake, forcasting the future 317-330
earthquake forces 318-319
earthquake-free countries 116
earthquake geysers 145, 159, 162, 226, 306-309
earthquakes, great, magni-tude 8+ (see great earth-quakes)
earthquake ground motion, continuous for more than a day 189
earthquake hazard warranty 361
earthquake heat 145, 233-237, 238
earthquakes, how they hap-pen 288-289
earthquake injuries 150, 155, 226-229, 298, 318, 324
earthquake insurance (see insurance)
earthquake intensities for the New Madrid events 188, 327-330
earthquake lakes 139, 144, 186, 214-215, 231, 267, 299, (also see Big Lake, Cagle Lake, Flag Lake, Lake Nicormy, Lake St. Francis, Lake St. John, Lake Ste. Anne, Lake Tyronza, Lost Lake, and Reelfoot Lake)
earthquake landslides 137, 167, 207, 236, 238, 266, 300, 302, 303, 305
earthquake lightning 91, 243-244

earthquake lights (see seismoluminescence)
earthquake liquefaction (see liquefaction)
earthquake magnitude (Richter) explained 282-283
earthquake mitigation 322, 331, 332
earthquake noises 135, 145, 149, 151, 156, 159-160, 162, 182, 201-202 (also see earthquake thunder)
earthquake ponds 153, 155, 156-157, 161, 170, 174, 234
earthquake precursors 7, 15, 55, 90-92, 244
earthquake prediction 4-8, 90-92, 284, 289
earthquake recovery 332, 334
earthquake research, funding for 282-283
earthquake response 332, 335
earthquake safety 332, 333-334
earthquake sand boils (see sand boils and liquefaction)
earthquake smells 145, 173, 237
earthquake smog 135, 144, 237-238, 243-244, 246
Earthquake Spectra, Journal 368
earthquake subsidence 116, 139, 144, 145-147, 150, 156, 159, 175, 183, 185-186, 187, 207, 214, 215
earthquake thunder 7, 149, 159, 162, 170, 182, 201, 243-244 (also see earthquake noises)
earthquake uplift 151, 183, 186, 214, 215, 225
earthquake stream flow disruption, permanent (see discontinuous channels)
earthquake swamps (see earthquake flooding and swamplands)
earthquake tree damage (see trees, destruction of)
Eastern U.S. quakes vs. Western 186-187, 298
Easter Sunday 252, 303
East Florida 127-128
Easton, Mary 123
East Prairie, MO 102, 185

East Swamp 215
Eckert's Tavern 125
eclipse, solar 55, 69, 86, 243
Ecuador 88
Eddyville, KY 28, 280, 291
Edmonds, R.D. 20
Egypt 55-57, 58, 65, 86, 89, 115
eighteen-wheelers 277
eight-magnitude earthquakes, how many happened? 17-18 (also see great earthquakes)
El Camino Real 99, 101, 102, 275-277
El Camino Trailer Park 102
electricity, atmospheric 55, 91
Eldorado, IL 280, 294
electric power 101,102
Elizabethtown, KY 33, 192
Elm, Judgement 96, 97
El Rio del Espirito Santo 106
Emancipation Proclamation 33, 250
emetics 34-35
emotional trauma (see post traumatic stress disorder)
empty boats 144, 172, 173, 183
Empty Quarter, The 116
end of the world 243, 250-251, 267, 268
engineers 296, 299, 306-307, 317
England 33, 45, 46, 48, 87, 89, 111, 116, 120, 206, 254, 263 (also see British)
English Channel 33, 263
engulfment of buildings (see houses engulfed)
epilepsy 49
Eppes, Francis W. 49
epicenters of New Madrid earthquakes 132, 221-224
Equatorial Africa 116
Espirito Santo, Spanish name for Mississippi River 106
Estonia 116
Euphrates River 115
Europe 4, 15, 86, 88, 104, 120, 263
Evansville, IN 162, 253, 280, 291, 292, 294
Evergreen Cemetery (see New Madrid Cemetery)
Evil One, The 66, 67
Exodus, Book of 243
exodus, from Egypt 57

exodus, from Little Prairie 150-152, 228-229, 230
exodus, from New Madrid 189-191, 209, 213
exodus of Native Americans 279
experts, limitations of knowledge 295-297
explosion sand blow craters 145, 150 151, 155, 156-157, 161, 170, 174, 192, 214, 215, 226
exposure to the elements following quake 155, 207
Extended New Madrid Fault Zone (see Large New Madrid Source Zone and Small New Madrid Source Zone)
extinctions 90
eye injury, to Lalawethika 62, 64, 68

F

factoids 16-17, 309-310
Fallen Timbers, Battle of 62, 68
falls (see Falls of the Ohio and Mississippi River, falls of)
Falls of the Ohio 81-84, 85, 172, 201, 205
Falls of the Mississippi (see Mississippi River, falls of)
family reunion plan 334
famine 55, 243, 263
Fancy Farm, KY 54, 305
Farmers Friend, The 49
Father Joseph 155
Father of the Bootheel 232
fathers deserting their families 136, 189
faultless countries 116
faults 284, 286, 290, 291
Fayette, MO 232, 261, 368
Fayetteville, AR 369
Federal Emergency Management Agency (FEMA) 5, 317, 335, 336-337
Federated Garden Clubs of Missouri 275, 276
Femme Osage Creek 95
Femme Osage District 96
Ferdinand VII 88
Fertile Crescent, The 115
fertility of soil increased by earthquakes 116, 226
Finely, Rev. James B. 250-251

Finland 116, 266
Finn, Huckleberry 80, 262
fire 55, 144, 156, 170-171, 172, 276, 331, 332-333
fire canoe (Penelore) 166
firemen 322, 331
fire sticks (see medicine fire sticks)
firewater (see alcohol)
first aid training 334
First World War (see World War I, World War II, and Real First World War)
fish 139, 151, 172, 219
fishing 215, 369
Fisk, MO 54, 132, 226, 249
fissures (see earthquake fissures)
Fitler, MS 169
Five Civilized Tribes, The 102, 277
flag, American 21,50, 79,127
flag, Confederate 21
flag, French 21
Flag Lake 214
flag, Missouri State 21
flag, Spanish 21
flag, (see wild iris)
flammable materials 332
flatboats 27, 79, 151, 202, 226
flax 258
Fletcher, James 145
Flint, Timothy 10, 151-152
Flood of 1993, The 108, 109, 110, 193
floods, earthquake-related (see earthquake floods)
floods, non-earthquake-related 55, 74, 84, 108, 109, 110, 193, 213
flood plain, risks of 304-305
Florence, Italy 23
Florida 58, 127-128
flour 151, 202
Flour Island (see Island #33)
flu (see influenze)
fluvial tsunami 189, 202-203, 207, 242
fog from earthquakes (see earthquake smog)
food, Indian (see Native American food)
forced march (see Trail of Tears)
Ford, Model A 277
forecasting future losses, how to do it 317-330
foreshocks 134, 240
Fort Boone 129
Fort Cole 129

Fort Dearborn 75, 257
Fort Detroit 257 (see Detroit, MI)
Fort Jefferson 52, 132, 142, 167, 168, 204, 241-242
Fort Miamis 62
Fort Osage 73, 75, 122-124, 129, 191, 197, 198
Fort Pickering 26, 75, 102, 161, 168, 192, 241, 279
Fort Point 122
Fort Washington 68, 80
Foster, Dr. 157-160, 179
Foster, Stephen 58
four-leaf clovers 369
Four Legs 271
Fountainbleau, Treaty of 111
fox 91
Fox Indians 68, 277
fractures (see earthquake fissures)
France 31, 33, 48, 55, 76, 86, 89, 99, 103, 105, 108, 111, 120-122, 269
Frankfort, KY 98
Franklin, Benjamin 317
Franklin Lake 139
fraud 251-253, 254-255
Fredericktown, MO 280, 311-315
Freedom of the Press 125
French & Indian War 72, 111
French Revolution 88
French vanilla ice cream 105
frequencies of seismic waves 300
frequency spectra of earthquakes 300
freshly killed beef 189
friction as source of groundwater heat 235-236
Friday the Thirteenth 133
frightened to death 155
Frisco Railway 39
Fuller, Myron 20, 178, 232, 233
Fulton, Robert 74, 76, 77, 78
Fulton's Folly 76
funding for earthquake research 282-283
fur trading 108, 155
future New Madrid earthquakes 209, 241, 282-288, 291, 292-293, 317-330

G

gambling 133, 165, 241, 245, 287, 292
game preserves 118-119, 137

Garden Grove, CA 368
Garfield, James A. 27
Gary, IN 294
gates of hell 145
Gateway Arch (see Jefferson National Expansion Memorial)
Gateway to the West 25, 279
geese 91, 160, 167, 245
Geological Survey (see U.S. Geological Survey)
geologists 296, 304
geophysicists 283, 296, 317
George III, King 270
George (Lilbourn's slave) 28-29, 32, 33, 37-38, 47, 50
George's murder 28-29, 32, 33, 47
Georgia Emergency Management Agency 336
Georgia (Russian province) 89
Georgia statehood 127
Georgia (U.S. state) 51, 58
geotechnical engineers 296, 306, 310
geothermal energy 186, 234, 235
geothermal gradient 235
German research paper connecting New Madrid and Caracas earthquakes 252
German potatoes 105
Germany 86, 105, 115
germ theory 34
Ghent, Treaty of 30
Gideon, MO 305
Girardeau, Jean Baptiste 99
Girardo (see Girardeau)
Girardot (see Girardeau)
God 73, 80, 175, 191, 197, 243-247, 250, 251, 259, 268, 269 (also see Master of Life)
God's Chosen People 56-57, 67, 73
God's wrath 80, 83, 87, 171, 243, 246, 251, 252, 268, 269
Goellner Printing Co. 125
gold 108
Gospels, New Testament 243
government relief 251-253
grain bins buckled 302
Grand Gulf, MS 169
Grand River valley 277
Grand Tower, IL 280, 303-304

granny (see midwife)
graves disturbed by earthquakes 140-141, 151, 251
graves, Native American 107, 140-141, 272, 275, 277 (also see skeletons)
gravitational forces of sun and moon 4-5
gravity, earth's 318-319
gravy 105
Greaseport (New Madrid) 111
Greasy Bent 112-113 (also see New Madrid Bend)
Great Britian (see England)
great earthquakes 134, 186, 188, 199, 213, 266, 282, 284-285
great earthquakes, definition of 282, 284-285
great earthquakes at New Madrid, how many? 17-18
Great Father (see Master of Life)
Great Lakes, The 87, 108, 111
Great Plains 187, 277
Great Salt Lake 115
Great Spirit, The (see Master of Life)
Greece 86, 105, 115
Greeley, Horace 12
Greene County Courthouse 298
Green, Judge Robert 249-250
Greenland 115
green sky 146, 237
Greenwood, Don 19
Greenwoods, The 246
Greenville, MO 225, 280
Greenville, OH 62, 69, 75
Greenville, Treaty of 62
Gremar, Mrs. Delisle 254
Grimard, Baptiste 261
Grinder, Mr. 49
ground failure (see earthquake fissures, landslides, liquefaction, subsidence, etc.)
ground failure damage (see shaking damage vs. ground failure)
groundwater flooding (see earthquake flooding)
groundwater, superheated 133
groundwater, warm 145, 233-237, 238
ground waves 183, 185, 191-198, 228, 244

Gulf of Mexico 75, 85, 108, 167, 241, 252
Guion, Capt. W.B. 225-226
Gut Ste. Anne 10, 108, 210-213, 214, 216, 231 (also see Lake Ste. Anne)

H

Haicheng, China 7
hail 205
Halliday, AR 132, 305
Halloween 1, 187, 266
Hamilton, Alexander 32
Hannibal, MO 261-262, 291
happy hunting ground 63
Hardin County, KY 33
Hardy, AR 310
Harrison, Benjamin (father of Wm Henry) 67
Harrison, Benjamin (grandson of Wm Henry) 68
Harrison, William Henry 19, 66, 67-69, 70, 80, 87, 254, 257, 258, 259, 265, 271
hatchet (see tomahawk)
Hayti, MO 132, 150, 215, 224, 239
hazardous materials 101, 331, 332
hazards of infrastructure (see modern infrastructure, hazards of)
hazmats (see hazardous materials)
headache remedies 105
Headstart Program 219
heart attack 155, 284
heat produced by earthquakes (see earthquake heat)
heaven (see happy hunting ground)
Hebgen Lake earthquake 233
Hebgen Lake, MT 233
Hedington, Capt. 158
heiroglyphics 164
Helena, AR 143, 168, 169, 225, 242, 280
hell 148, 246
hemorrhage 34-35
Henderson, KY 75, 78, 81, 85, 95, 162, 163, 166, 181, 241, 280
Henry I, King 45
Henry II, King 46
Herculaneum, MO 143, 147, 192, 203, 237, 280
Herschel, Willian 55
Hibbs, Jonah 30

Hickman, KY 54, 102, 132, 142, 182-183, 237, 280, 291
high rise buildings 101
Hiroshima, Japan 199
Hog Lake 144, 146
hogs 90, 146
holidays, earthquakes during 318, 320
Holland 76, 86, 136 (also see Dutch)
Holloman, Allen 90
Hollywood, CA 14
Holy Ghost, River of the 106
Holy Land, The 58
Holy Spirit, River of the 106
Holy Thursday 252
Homicide (see murder)
honey 66, 278
Hong Kong 4
Hopkinsville, KY 94, 291
Hornersville, MO 137, 221, 280
Hornersville Swampland 221
horses 91, 148-150, 156-157, 172, 182, 228, 238, 256, 277
hospitals 35, 331
Hot Springs, AR 260, 261
houses engulfed by quicksand 145-147, 151, 173, 227
Howard County, MO 129, 32, 260-261, 277, 278
Howard, Lena E. (see Lewis, Lena elizabeth Howard)
Howardville, MO 132, 212, 13, 216
how earthquakes happen 288-289
how to forcast future earthquake losses 317-330
H.R. Bill #44 225-226
Huckleberry Finn 80, 262
Huckleberry Ridge 369
Hudson River 75, 76
Hugo, Hurricane 200
Huguenots 33
Hunter 40, 45
Hunter, James 167
Hunter, Lilbourn Lewis Broughton "Libba" 40, 45
Hunter, Mary Ann Lewis 45
Hunter, Tom 14
Hurley, Dickson 30
Huron Indians 68
Hurricane Andres 200
Hurricane Hugo 199-200
Hurricane Island 165
hurricanes 55, 116, 199-200
hypocondriac 49

I

iatrogenia 35, 36
ice across rivers 147, 148, 205-206
Ice Age (see Little Ice Age)
ice cream 105
ignorance among earthquqke professionals 295-297, 304, 309-310
Illinois Emergency Management Agency 337
Illinois Indians 68, 163-164, 166
Illinois State Geologist 304
Illinois Territory 127-128, 130, 163
Illmo United Methodist Church 369
Immaculate Conception Church 41, 42, 274
Immaculate Conception School 22
Imperial Valley, CA 186
Inca Indians 104
incest 48
India 89, 266
Indiana Department of Natural Resources 260
Indiana Emergency Management Agency 337
Indianapolis, IN 288, 291, 292, 294, 298
Indiana State Patrol 298
Indiana Territory 70, 127-128, 137, 162, 260
Indian burial grounds (see graves, Native American
Indian food (see Native American food)
Indian Hills Subdivision 275, 276
Indian money (see wampum)
Indian Park 100,101
Indian reservations (272, 273, 274, 278
Indians (see Native Americans)
Indonesia 262
influenza 70
infrastructure, hazards of (see modern infrastructure)
insanity 48, 49, 50
insurance, earthquake 241, 281, 294, 296-298, 299, 301-302, 303, 304, 306-307, 309-310, 311-312, 315-316, 335, 338, 368
interior of the earth 235

intermarriage between cousins 45-49, 78, 94
Interstate Highway 55 10, 113, 212, 213, 218, 222, 228, 275
Interstate Highway 65 259
Interstate Highway 155 173, 190
Iowa City, IA 369
Iowa Emergency Management Agency 337
Iowa Indians 68, 72
Iraq 115
Ircland 105, 116
Irish potatoes 105
Iron Age, The 104
Iron Mountain, Mo 226
Ironsides, George 73
Ironton, MO 280
Isaiah, Book of 243
Isham, Henry 45
Isham, Mary 45
Islam 58, 89
Islands of the Mississippi 84, 132, 142, 168-169, 209
Island #1 132, 167, 168, 204
Island #2 168, 204
Island #3 168, 204
Island #4 167, 168, 204
Island #5 (Wolf Island) 167, 168, 204
Island #6 142, 168
Island #8 132, 142, 168, 171, 200 201, 203, 204, 212, 231
Island #9 168, 171, 200, 201, 204, 210-211, 213
Island #10 142, 155, 168, 200, 201, 202, 203, 204, 205, 210-211, 213, 226, 233
Island #11 168, 210-211
Island #13 157-160, 168
Island #16 144, 151, 168, 173
Island #20 168, 173
Island #23 161, 168
Island #25 161, 168, 173-174
Island #31 143, 168, 175
Island #32 143, 168, 174-175, 241-242
Island #33 (Flour Island) 143, 162, 168, 175, 185
Island #35 143, 168
Island #46 (President Island) 168
Island #53 (Council Island) 168

Island #59 (St. Francis Island 168
Island #60 143, 168-169
Island #82 (Ozark Island) 169, 178
Island #94 (Crows Nest or Stack Island) 142-143, 169, 178, 207, 241-242
Island #99 169, 178
Island #127 142, 169
Islands of the Ohio 81, 83, 84, 142
Islands #61-#64 (Ohio River) 81, 83
Israel 89
Israelites 57
Italian food 105
Italy 23, 86, 105, 115

J

Jack, Andrew 80, 83-85, 163, 166, 167, 172, 173, 178
Jackson, Andrew 30, 31, 76, 78, 245, 277, 278
Jackson, MO 54, 132, 150, 245, 248, 275-277, 280, 311
Jackson Purchase 53
Jake (slave owned by Fr. LeSier) 150
jalapeno peppers 104
James, Edwin 256
Jamestown 33, 45, 46, 47
Japan 6, 8, 115, 199
Jarvis, Mrs. 155
Java 262
Jean Baptiste Bequette House 109
jeans, blue 105
Jefferson, Anna Lewis 45
Jefferson, Anna Scott 49
Jefferson City, MO 255, 368
Jefferson County, MO 203
Jefferson, Elizabeth 49
Jefferson, Fort 52, 132, 142, 167, 168, 240-242
Jefferson, Jane Randolph 45, 46
Jefferson, Jane W. Lewis 45, 48
Jefferson, Lucy (see Lewis, Lucy Jefferson)
Jefferson, Martha (see Randolph, Martha Jefferson)
Jefferson, Martha, sister to Thomas (see Carr, Martha Jefferson)
Jefferson, Martha Wayles Skelton 45, 49

Jefferson, Mary R. Lewis 45, 48
Jefferson National Expansion Memorial 25, 26, 278-279
Jefferson nickels 288
Jefferson, Peter 45, 46
Jefferson, Peter Field 45
Jefferson, Randolph 45, 48
Jefferson, Thomas 19, 24, 25-28, 31, 32, 34, 36, 39, 40, 46, 47, 48, 49, 50, 51, 53, 73, 76, 78, 87, 94, 103, 104, 120-123, 263
Jefferson, Thomas Jr. 45
Jeremiah, Book of 243
Jericho 115
Jesuit priests 106, 192
Jesuit Seismological Society 106
Jesus Christ 243, 247
John, King (Magna Charta) 45, 46
Johnson, Betty 259
Johnson's Settlement 249
Johnston, A.C. 286-287, 291
Jolliet, Louis 106, 108
Jonesboro, AR 54, 102, 132, 280, 291, 320-321
Jonesboro, IL 280
Joseph, Father 155
Joshua 115
Judaism 57-58
Judgement Elm, The 96, 97

K

Kaintucks 80
Kalopin, Chief 268-269
Kansas City, KS 274
Kansas City, MO 122, 191
Kansas Territory 73, 253, 259, 273, 274, 277
Kanto Plain, Japan 115
Karnak, Temple at 56
Kaskaskia, IL 53, 99
Kaskaskia Indians 68
keelboats 79, 108, 122, 144, 216, 217
Keiser, AR 280, 306-310
Kennett, MO 54, 132, 139, 215, 291
Kentucky 25, 32-33, 34, 92, 94, 98, 111, 127, 213
Kentucky Bend 112-113 (see New Madrid Bend)
Kentucky Disaster & Emergency Services 337
Kentucky Lake 280
Kentucky militia 34
Kentucky statehood 127

Kentucky, University of 98
ketchup 105
Kewanee, MO 132, 212, 228
Key, Francis Scott 127
KFVS-TV 1
Kibbey, Col. Timothy 194
Kibbey House 196
Kickapoo Indians 68, 277
kidnapping 92
kidney beans 105
Killbuck, Little 257, 258, 259
Kingshighway 99, 101, 102 (also see El Camino Real)
Kiskopoke Clan of the Shawnee Tribe 58, 59
Knob Creek 33, 192
Knox, Karen Twell xvii, 369
Knox, Ray 203, 229, 369
Kumskauskau 60, 61, 62

L

Labrador retriever 80
LaFayette, Gen. Marie Joseph Paul Montier 206
Lafayette, IN 69
LaFont, Mrs. 155
LaForge, Emma C. (see Lewis, Emma C. LaForge)
LaForge, MO 41, 212
Lake Barkley 280
Lake City, AR 132, 139, 280, 305
Lake Erie, 271
Lake Nicormy 132, 214, 215
Lake of the Ozarks 280, 315
Lake Providence 169
lakes (see earthquake lakes)
Lake Ste. Anne 108, 113, 213, 214 (also see Gut Ste. Anne)
Lake St. Francis 137, 139
Lake St. John 132, 215
Lake Ste. Marie 216
Lake Superior 104
Lake Tyronza 214
Lalawethika 60, 61-63, 65 (also see Tenskwatawa)
lamb 66
landslides (see earthquake landslides)
Land of Nothing, The 116
landslides (see earthquake landslides)
Langlois, Francois 260, 261
L'Anse a la Graisse (New Madrid) 111, 112, 215
Large New Madrid Source Zone 282, 287-288, 293-294 (also see Small New Madrid Source Zone)

LaRoche, Firmin 155
LaSalle, Robert Cavalier de 108
Last Chance Saloon 21
lateral spreading (see earthquake fissures and earthquake landslides)
Latin America 88, 89
LaTrobe, Benjamin 78
LaTrobe, Mary Hazelhurst 78
Latvia 116
Laughing Eyes, Princess 269
LaValle, Jean Baptiste 50
lawsuits 249-250, 253, 254-255, 296-297, 301-302, 304
Lawrence County Jail 298
Lawrenceville, IL 280, 285, 294, 296, 298-302, 303
laxatives 34-35
Leachville, AR 54, 137, 138
lead (Pb) 143, 192, 226 236
Lebanon 89, 105
LeDru, Pierre 270
leg broken 155
Lenox, TN 132
LeSieur, Francois 111, 144, 150, 185, 215-216, 254-255
LeSieur, Godfrey 227-228, 234, 237, 238
LeSieur, Joseph 111, 215-216
Lewis and Clark Expedition 48, 73, 79, 82, 122-123, 126, 272
Lewis, Anna Jefferson 45
Lewis, "Billy Goat" (see Lewis, Anexamander)
Lewis, Carol C. 42
Lewis, Charles "Byrd" 33, 45, 47
Lewis, Charles 27, 45
Lewis, Charles "Buck Island" 45
Lewis, Charles Lilbourn 26, 28, 31, 36, 38, 45, 46, 47, 74
Lewis, Charles Lilbourn Jr. (son of Randolph) 40, 45
Lewis, Charlotte (see Riley, Charlotte Lewis)
Lewis County, TN 36
Lewis, Elizabeth (see Phillips, Elizabeth Lewis)
Lewis, Eizabeth Ann (see Broughton, Elizabeth Ann Lewis)

Lewis, Elizabeth "Betsy" Jane Woodson 28, 31, 36, 39, 45, 49
Lewis, Elizabeth Warner 45
Lewis, Emma C. LaForge 40, 41, 42, 43, 45
Lewis, Francis 47
Lewis, George, slave of Lilbourn (see George)
Lewis, Hannah Ramsey Hayden 39, 40, 43, 44, 45
Lewis, Isabella Warner 33, 45, 47
Lewis, Isham 25, 28-31, 33, 36, 38, 45, 47, 49, 50
Lewis, James Randolph 38, 50
Lewis, Jane Meriwether 45
Lewis, Jane W. (see Jefferson, Jane W. Lewis)
Lewis, Jane Woodson 45
Lewis, John I (Major) 33, 45, 47
Lewis, John II "Councillor" 33, 45, 47
Lewis, "L.A." (see Lewis, Lilbourn Anexamander)
Lewis, "L.A. Jr." (see Lewis, Lilbourn Alexander)
Lewis, Lena Elizabeth Howard 45
Lewis, Letitia Griffen Rutter 29, 37, 50
Lewis, Lilbourn 25, 27, 28-31, 33, 34, 36, 38, 39-45, 46, 47, 49, 50, 165
Lewis, Lilbourn (as a name) 39-45, 46
Lewis, Lilbourn Alexander 40, 45
Lewis, Lilbourn Anexamander 39, 40, 41, 42, 43, 45, 47
Lewis, Lilbourn G. 40, 44, 45
Lewis, Lilbourn Livingston 26, 39, 40, 43, 44, 45, 47
Lewis, Lilbourn Mitchell 40, 45
Lewis, Lucy Jefferson 26, 28, 31, 36, 38, 45, 46, 74
Lewis, Lucy Meriwether 45
Lewis, Mary Ann (see Hunter, Mary Ann Lewis)
Lewis, Mary Howell (wife of Charles "Byrd") 45
Lewis, Mary Howell (wife of Randolph) 38, 40, 45, 49
Lewis, Mary R. (see Jefferson, Mary R. Lewis)
Lewis, Mary Randolph 45

Lewis, Matilda (see Matilda Threlkeld)
Lewis, Meriwether 36, 45, 47-48, 49-50, 73, 79, 82, 122
Lewis, origen of name 33
Lewis Plantations in KY 28, 31, 94, 165 (also see Rocky Hill and Randolph Plantation)
Lewis Plantation in VA (see Monteagle)
Lewis Prairie 40
Lewis, Randolph 27, 28, 34, 36, 40, 45, 49, 165
Lewis, Robert "Belvoir" 45. 47
Lewis, Robert "Byrd" 45. 49
Lewis, Robert (General) 33, 45, 46
Lewis, Sarah C. Meriwether 40, 41, 44, 45
Lewis Street 41, 42
Lewis Township 39
Lewis, Warner 40, 45
Lewis, William 45
Lewis, Winston P. 40, 45
Lexington, KY 74, 86, 134, 136
Lexington Gazette, The 86
Liaoning Province, China 7
Libya 116
Lick Creek, IL 280, 311-312
light earthquake, definition of 282, 284-285
light earthquakes, damage from 295-316
light earthquakes, liquefaction from 306-307
lightening (see earthquake ightening)
lignite (see coal)
Lilbourn, alternate spellings 41
Lilbourn Lewis, as a name 39-45, 46
Lilbourn, meaning of 40
Lilbourn, MO 12, 39, 40, 42, 43, 47, 51, 224
Lilbourn Mound 104, 106, 107-108, 113, 214, 216
Lilburn 41 (see Lilbourn)
Lilburne 41 (see Lilbourn)
lima beans 104
Lima, Peru 368
Lincoln, Abraham, grandfather of President 94
Lincoln, Abraham, President 19, 32-33, 94, 197, 250
Lincoln, Bathsheba 94

Lincoln, Josiah
Lincoln, Mary 94
Lincoln, Mordecai 94
Lincoln, Nancy 94
Lincoln, Nancy Hanks 32-33, 94, 197
Lincoln, Sarah 33, 197
Lincoln, Thomas 32-33, 94, 191, 192, 197
liquefaction 9, 10, 14, 116, 145-147, 150, 152, 156-157, 162, 174, 221-224, 226-230, 238, 266, 286, 294, 299-302, 304-304, 306-309 (also see air liquefaction)
liquor (see alcohol)
Lisbon earthquake 266
Lisbon, Portugal 266
Lithuania 116, 267
litigation 368 (also see law suits)
Little Ice Age, The 147-148
Little Killbuck 257, 258, 259
Little Prairie, MO 75, 129, 132, 144-147, 150-152, 155, 159, 160, 168, 172, 183, 185, 208, 215, 227, 228, 230, 231, 237, 238, 240-242, 309
Little River 40, 108, 199, 210-213, 216, 218-220, 224, 225, 231
Little River Drainage District 139, 226, 231
Little Rock, AR 99, 306
Livingston County, KY 27, 31, 38, 50, 76, 90, 94, 136, 256, 278
Livingston County, MO 260, 278
Livingston, Edward 31, 76, 179, 278
Livingston, Robert R. 28, 39, 76, 77, 78, 120-121, 179, 278
loess 266
logarithmic scale (Richter) 293
logjams 173-174, 219, 225-226
logs in the river, hazards of 160, 162, 167, 171, 172, 173-174, 185, 200
Loma Prieta earthquake 13, 283, 292, 293, 305
London, England 164
Long Beach, CA 292
Long Beach earthquake 292
Long Knives, origin of name 59

Long Reach 143, 162, 173-174, 185
Longtown, MO 311, 312
Lord ((see God, Jesus Christ, and Master of Life)
Lorimier, Don Louis 99, 100, 101, 109
Los Angeles Trade Technical College 368
Lossing, Benjamin 270
lost islands 242
Lost Lake 132, 214, 215, 299
lost towns & settlements 242, 267
Lost Village 151, 230
lottery ticket 292
Louis XIV, King 108
Louis Bolduc House 110
Louisiana Gazette, The 191, 261 (also see St. Louis Gazette)
Louisiana Office of Emergency 337
Louisiana Purchase 120-122
Louisiana statehood 130
Louisiana Territory 36, 48, 82, 108, 111, 112, 120-122, 127-128 (also see Missouri Terriitory and Orleans Territory)
Louisville, The (barge) 158-161
Louisville, KY 30, 33, 74, 75, 81-84, 94, 111, 191, 192, 198, 205, 241, 251, 259, 294
Lovejoy, Dr. Elijah 125
Lower Louisiana Territory (see Orleans Territory)
Lovers Leap 261
Lucy Jefferson (see Lewis, Lucy Jefferson)
Lucy Jefferson Lewis Memorial Bridge 31
Luke, Gospel of 243
Lydia Roosevelt's maid (see Missy)
Lyell, Sir Charles 152, 189, 227
lynch mob 125
lynx (see panther)
Lyon County, Ky 28

M

MacFarlane, James 8
Madison County courthouse 298
Madison, Dolly 78, 137, 198

Madison, James 78, 87, 89, 137, 198, 206
Mad River 59, 60
Magna Charta 45, 46
magnetic field changes 91
magnitude (see earthquake magnitude)
magnitude-eight earthquakes (see great earthquakes)
Maine, District of 127-128
Maisonville, Angelica 274
Maisonville, Francois 73, 274, 275
Maisonville, Genevieve Marie 73, 274, 175 (also see Teceikeapease)
Maisonville, Modest 274
major earthquake, definition of 282, 284-285
Makanda, IL 280, 311, 312
Malden, MO 54, 132, 215, 217, 280, 305=306
malt liquor 65 (also see alcohol)
Mammouth Springs, AR 280, 310
Manchu Dynasty 89
Manete 62
Manhattan Island 76
Manila, AR 138
Manifest Destiny, Doctrine of 73
manna 58
maple sugar 66, 104
maple suryp 105
Marble Hill, MO 54, 280, 369
Marconi, Guglielmo 12
Marina District 305
Marion County, MO 261
Marion, IL 280, 311, 368
Marion, KY 27, 280
Marked Tree, AR 54, 102, 139, 224, 280, 284, 285, 287, 291, 303, 309, 317
Mark, Gospel of 243
Mark Twain 262
Marquette, Father Jacques 106, 108
marriage (see wedding)
Marston, MO 10, 132, 199, 212, 280
Marston-New Madrid Welcome Center 10, 199, 212
Marthasville, MO 96, 280
Martin Lake 139
martyr for the free press 125
Maryland statehood 127
Massachusetts statehood 127

Mass, Catholic 106, 107
massacres by Indians 53, 164, 257-260
Master of Life 65, 66, 67, 69, 72, 73, 74, 86, 197, 251, 264, 265, 269, 270, 273, 277 (also see God)
Masters, Betsy 155
mathematics 104
Mather, Thomas 125
Matthew, Gospel of 243
Matthews, MO 132
Matilda, Aunt (see Threlkeld, Matilda)
Mayfield Creek 205
McBride, James 151
McCoy, Ginsey 259
McCoy, John 258
McGhehee, AR 169
measles 70
Meatte, Angelica Maisonville 274
Meatte, Edward 274
Meatte, Franciscus 274
Meatte, Modest Maisonville 274
Mecca, Muslim 89
Mecca, Native American 69 (also see Prophet's Town)
medicine fire sticks 264, 265, 273
medicine men 62, 63
Medina, Arabia 89
Mediterranean Culture 58, 115
Memphis State University 4, 286, 310, 336
Memphis, TN 17, 26, 54, 99, 102, 131, 168, 192, 279, 292, 336
menstrual period 265
mental retardation 48, 49
Meriwether, Jane (see Lewis, Jane Meriwether)
Meriwether, Lucy (see Lewis, Lucy Meriwether)
Merrill, Boynton 19
Mesopotamia 58
messboy 171
Methoataske 58-61, 73, 92, 100, 263, 264, 274, 275
Methodist Church 119, 133, 251, 261, 369
Metropolis, IL 54, 108, 280, 284, 287, 294, 317
Mexican Revolution 88, 127
Mexico 55, 88, 106, 127, 187
Miami Indians 68, 257, 259
Miamis, Fort 62
Michigan Territory 127-128

Middle East 89, 104
midwife 33, 35, 81, 149
Millin, Jeanne 5
Millington, Dr. Jeremiah 126
Millington, Dr. Seth 125, 126
millionaire farmers 226
milo 118
mineral deposits in earthquake zones 118
Mingo Indians 68
Minominee Indians 68
minor earthquake, definition of 282, 284-285
missionaries 67, 68, 106, 107, 155, 247, 249, 250-251
Mississippian Indians 103-104, 107, 216
Mississippi County, MO 185
Mississippi Emergency Management Agency 337
Mississippi River 74, 75, 82, 84, 103, 108, 142, 192, 208-209, 210-213, 279, 299
Mississippi River, ancient course of 299
Mississippi River, falls of 21, 132, 201-203, 208-209, 226. 267
Mississippi River, origin of name 104, 106
Mississippi River, retrograde motion 2, 8, 14, 132, 200-201, 203, 267
Mississippi Steamboat Navigation Co. 70
Mississippi Territory 127-128, 178
Missouri (name of Ray Knox's great grandmother) 369
Missouri Archeologist 141
Missouri Bootheel (see Bootheel of Missouri)
Missouri capitol building 255
Missouri Indians 104
Missouri River 75, 82, 103, 122-124, 192, 255
Missouri State boundaries established 230-232
Missouri State Capital, St. Charles 126
Missouri statehood 130, 230
Missouri State Emergency Mangement Agency 3, 317, 337
Missouri State Third District Normal School 148 (also see Southeast Missouri State University)

Missouri Territory 36, 48, 95, 96, 101, 121-122, 127-128, 129, 130-131, 230-232, 252
Missy (Lydia's maid) 80, 85, 167, 179
Mitchell, Samuel L. 234, 239
mitigation (see earthquake mitigation)
Moab 57
mobile homes 311-313, 331
Model A Ford 277
moderate earthquake, definition of 282, 284-285
modern infrastructure, hazards of 99, 101-102, 106, 156
Moldavians 67
monarchy as a form of government 99, 120
money, Native American (see wampum)
Monkey's Eyebrow 132
Monongehela River 75, 79, 82
Monroe, James 78, 120-121
Monteagle 34, 48
Montgomery, AL 58, 263
Monticello 24, 27, 28, 34, 36, 48, 51, 53
Monticello Cemetery 50
Montreal Herald, The 198
Montreal, Quebec 3, 75, 191, 198-199
moon 4, 29, 134, 144, 189, 237, 243, 246
moors of Scotland 105
Morgan, Col. George 19, 111-112, 118-120
Morelos, Gen. Jose Maria 88
Morison, Elizabeth 248
morphoseismic features (see discontinuous channels, explosion sand blow craters, earthquake land slides, earthquake fis-sures, earthquake lakes, earthquake ponds, earth-quake subsidence, earth-quake uplift, sand boils, iquefaction, etc. A morpho-seismic feature is any land form created or modified by an earthquake).
morphoseismology 369
Morris, John 258
Morse, Samuel 12
mortalities (see earthquake deaths)
Moscow, Russia 267-268

Moses 56-57, 243
mosquitos 214, 226
mound, Indian (see Camp-bell Mound, Lilbourn Mound, and Towosaghy)
mountain goat watching 369
mountain lion (see panther)
mountains created by earth-quakes 114-116
Mount Nebo 57
Mount Sinai 58
Mount Tambora 262
Mr. Roosevelt's Steamboat 78 (alsop see New Orleans, The)
mudflows (see earthquake landslides and loess)
Mud Island 192
mule killed 1
murder 28-29, 32, 33, 38, 47, 48, 125, 164=165
murder of George Lewis 28-29, 32, 33, 38, 47
Muscogee Indians 58
museums 331
Muslims (see Islam)
mutilation of bodies 70, 100, 258
Myette, Edouard (see Meatte, Edward)

N

Nacodoches, TX 75, 197
Nagasaki, Japan 199
nakedness of Shawnees 65
nail pop-ups 302
Nantes, Edict of 33
Napoleon Bonaparte 15, 55, 86-87, 88, 89, 120-122, 206, 267-268, 269
Napoleon's comet 86, 269 (also see Tecumseh's comet)
Nashville, TN 183, 291
Natchez, MS 32, 75, 84, 94, 130, 161, 165, 169, 172, 173, 175, 176, 177, 178-179, 198, 206, 241
National Center for Earth-quake Engineering Research (NCEER) 337
National Earthquake Infor-mation Center 337
National Guard 5, 317
National Intelligencer, The 144, 150, 158
National Register of Historic Places 110, 298
Native American Dream, The 279

Native American food 66, 104-105

Native American graves (see graves, Native American)

Native Americans 17, 25, 47, 48, 53, 58-74, 84, 86, 87-88, 89, 91, 94, 96, 99, 102-106, 119, 123, 139-141,144, 152, 155, 156, 163-164, 166-167, 172, 174, 191, 197, 208, 216, 218, 227-229, 240, 242, 251, 256-259, 261, 263-265, 266, 268, 269-279, 286, 369

Navigator, The 82-84, 130-131, 141-142, 167, 172, 173-174, 183, 186, 204-205, 215

Naw Kaw 271

Nava, S. 286-287, 291

near-death experience 63, 68

Nebo, Mount 57

Nefertari, Queen 56

negro (see African Americans)

Nehaaeemo 59, 61, 73

Neiman River 87, 267, 268

Nepal 89, 266

Netherlands (see Holland)

Neu Tscherkask, Russia 55

New Albany, IN 298

New Amsterdam 76

New England 76, 119, 121, 263

Newfoundland 55

New Hamburg, MO 132, 280, 285, 302-305, 306, 313

New Hampshire statehood 127

New Jersey statehood 127

New Madrid Airport 10, 212

New Madrid Bend 9, 112-114, 210-213

New Madrid Cemetery 43-44

New Madrid Central High-school 10, 107, 214, 216

New Madrid Certificates 252-253, 254-255, 260-262

New Madrid County 129, 130, 131, 253, 276

New Madrid County Health Department 15

New Madrid earthquake epi centers 132

New Madrid Electric Power Plant (see Associated Electric Plant)

New Madrid Elementary School 9

New Madrid fault (see New Madrid Seismic Zone)

New Madrid Garrison 50

New Madrid Golf Course 12, 23

New Madrid Historical Museum 2, 3, 20-21, 50, 107, 213, 337

New Madrid Island 9, 21, 211, 212

New Madrid Land Grant (see New Madrid Certificate)

New Madrid-Marston Rest Stop 10, 199, 212

New Madrid, MO 2, 3, 9, 10, 12, 14, 17, 20-23, 28, 39, 40, 41-45, 46, 50, 51, 73, 75, 102, 106, 111, 113, 118-120, 122, 127-131, 155-156, 171-172, 199, 202, 205, 209-214, 231, 232, 240-242, 247, 251, 253-254, 268, 274, 287

New Madrid Museum 2, 3, 20-21, 50, 107, 213, 337

New Madrid Nursing Home 9

New Madrid, original name of 111, 112

New Madrid Rift Complex 291 (also see Large New Madrid Source Zone)

New Madrid Seismic Zone 9, 13, 16, 23, 54, 96, 98, 99, 100, 103, 106, 116, 122, 187, 209, 232, 239, 267, 279, 282-288, 291-293 (also see Large and Small New Madrid Source Zone)

New Mexico 4, 124

New Netherland 76

New Orleans, Battle of 30, 31, 38

New Orleans, LA 4, 25, 30, 51, 75, 78, 111, 120-121, 130, 142, 161, 165, 172, 173, 178, 198

New Orleans, The (steamboat) 19, 74-85, 162-179, 209

New Orleans, The, description of steamboat 79-80

New Orleans, The, summary of voyage 178-179

Newport, AR 207, 239, 280

New Spain 106, 112

newspapers 12, 252, 253, 282, 368-369

New Testament 66, 243, 244, 249

New Year's Day 179

New York, NY 4, 13, 51, 75, 76, 191, 254

New York statehood 127

New York Tribune 12

Nile River 55

Nine-Mile Reach 142, 169, 178

Nishenko, S.P. 286-287, 291

niter, spirits of 35

Noah's Ark 27

Noisemaker (see Lalawe-thika)

Nolin Creek, KY 33

Nolte, Vincent 206, 208

Noranda Aluminum Co. 113, 199, 206, 212

Norfolk Lake 263

Norfolk, VA 198

Normal School (see Missouri State Third District Normal School and Southeast Missouri State University)

Norris, Capt. John 258, 260

North Carolina Division of Emergency Management 337

North Carolina statehood 127

Northern Louisiana Territory (see Missouri Territory)

North Lilbourn, MO 39, 212

Northwest Ordinance 24, 68

Northwest Territory 68, 87, 257

Norway 33, 86, 116, 266

nose broken 150

nose rings 64, 273

nuclear reactors 101

nursing (breastfeeding) 171

nursing homes 9, 331

Nuttli, Otto 282, 284, 286, 292

O

oarsmen 80

Obion, TN 54, 132, 228, 280

odors (see earthquake smells)

oil deposits trapped in earthquake zones 118 (also see petroleum)

opium 35

Old Brick House, The 193, 196

Old Chillicothe (see Chillicothe, OH)

Old Hickory (see Jackson, Andrew)

Old Jake (slave of LeSier) 150

Old Kingshighway (see El Camino Real)

Old Piqua, OH 59, 60, 75

Old Testament 56, 66, 115, 243

Ohio Emergency Management Agency 337

Ohio River 74, 75, 79, 81-84, 103

Ohio River, Falls of (see Falls of the Ohio)

Ohio statehood 127

Ohio, The (barge) 158-159

Ojibway Indians 72, 103

Oklahoma Civil Emergency Management Agency 337

Olney, IL 298

Oneida Indians 68

Onondaga Indians 68

Oregon County, MO 311

Orleans Territory 127-128, 130, 178, 230

Original Thirteen Colonies 27-128

Osage, Fort 73, 75, 105, 122-124, 129, 191, 197, 198

Osage Indians 72, 73, 74, 96, 99, 104, 105-106, 123, 155, 264

Osceola, AR 143, 168, 174, 280, 306

Otahki, Princess 277

Owensboro, KY 162, 291

Ozark Island (see Island #82)

Ozark Mountains 186, 190, 299, 369

P

Pacific Ocean 25, 108, 122

Paducah, KY 28, 99, 102, 131, 280, 291, 292, 305

Palace of the President 137

paleoseismic evidence of past quakes 286, 294

Palestine 89

Palestinian desert 115

Panama 88

Pan American Health Organization (PAHO) 368

panther 59, 91, 139, 277

paragoric 35

Paraguay 1160

Paragould, AR 102, 280

Paris, France 120

Paris, Treaty of 25
Parkfield, CA 6
Parkfield earthquake prediction 6
paroquet (see Carolina parrot)
parrot (see Carolina parrot)
passenger pigeons 90, 257
Paw Paw Junction, MO 39
Payne, Elias 257-258
Payne, Mrs. Elias 259
Payne, Mrs. Jeremiah 258
Peck, Rev. Joab 275
Pemiscot Bayou 154, 222, 230
Pemiscot County 152, 218
Pemiscot, meaning of name 152, 153
Pemiscot River 152-154
Penalore (Fire Canoe) 166, 167
pendulums 192
Penick, James 18
Pennsylvania statehood 127
period, menstrual 265
Persia 89
Perryville, MO 249
Peru 88, 368
petroleum 238, 239
petroliferous nodules (see seismic tar balls)
pharoah 55-57
pheasant 277
Philadelphia, PA 4, 11, 13, 17
Philadelphia Gazette, The 134
Phillips family 39
Phillips, Elizabeth Lewis 39, 45, 51
Phillips, Mayor Dick 51
Phillips, Richard 39, 45, 51
photography 12, 252, 368
Piankashaw Indians 68
piano 368, 369
Pierre Dorlac House 193
Pickering, Fort 26, 75, 102, 192, 241, 279
pickles 105
Pictoral Gield Book of the War of 1812   270
Piedmont, MO 1, 280, 291
Pierce, William Leigh 91
piezoluminescence 233 (see seismoluminescence)
Pigeon Creek, IN 33
Pigeon Roost, IN 137, 181, 256, 257-260, 290
Pigeon Roost Historical Site 259-260

Piggot, AR 102, 132, 226, 280, 305
pillar of fire 57
pillory 31
pineapple 104
pinto beans 104, 105
Pineville, MO 369
pirates 141-143, 163-165
pirogues (see canoes)
Pittsburg Gazette, The 183
Pittsburg, PA 27, 74, 75, 76, 80, 82, 85, 112, 198
pizza 104
Plantegenet line of kings 45, 46, 47
planters 171 (also see logs in the river, hazards of)
plate tectonics 115
plow, Native American 63
plow, white man 66
Pocahantas, AR 74, 102, 132, 280, 291, 316
Pocahantas, Princess 47
Point, Fort 123
Point Pleasant, Battle of 59
Point Pleasant, MO 132, 159, 168, 172, 179-181, 189, 210-213, 216, 218, 231, 238, 239, 240-242, 280
poison 48, 66
politics in science 7, 282-283 (also see subjectivity in science)
Poland 86, 105, 116
pole road 219
police 322, 331
Polish pickles 105
polygamy 65
Pomeroy, Lee 369
Pony Express, The 12
pool hall 305-306
pop corn 105
Pope, The 206
Poplar Bluff, MO 54, 74, 102, 132, 280, 291, 316
Portage Open Bay 168, 215-217, 218-220, 231, 274
Portageville, MO 1, 159, 181, 212, 215, 216, 218, 239, 274, 280, 286
Portageville-Tiptonville Ferry 1, 2
Portugal 86, 266
posse 92, 164, 259
possum 147
Postal Service, U.S. 12, 123, 126
postmaster 123, 126
postpartum depression 60

post traumatic stress disorder 136, 260
potato chips 105
potatoes 66, 104, 105
Potawatomi Indians 68, 277
Potosi, MO 226, 291
prayer beans 65, 265, 273
prayer sticks 65, 264, 265, 273
precursors of earthquakes 7, 15, 55, 91, 244
prediction, earthquake 4-8, 90-92, 284, 289
preferred directions for fissures 228-229
pregnancy 60, 76, 80
premonition 91, 271-272
preparation (see earthquake mitigation, earthquake recovery, earthquake response, and earthquake safety)
Presbyterian Church 38, 47, 251
President Island (see Island #46)
President's Palace, The 137
preventive medicine 35
prices, early 19th century 37
primary faults 290
Printerboyer, Uncle 144
probabilities for future quakes 23, 241, 282-288, 291, 292-293
Proctor, Gen Henry 271
prohibition against slave importation 32
Promised Land, The 56-57, 67, 73
prophecy 74, 86, 243-244, 263-265, 271-272
prophet (see Tenskwatawa)
Prophet's Town, IN 69, 73, 75, 86, 265
protestants 33, 119, 191, 245, 248
Provo, UT 115
Prussia 86
Psalms, Book of 243, 246
psychological disorders (see insanity, mental retardation, and post traumatic stress disorder)
public schools 119
Puckeshinwa 58-60, 92, 274
Pugeshashenwa 62
puma (see panther)
pumping up a tire 301
pumpkin 104, 105
pumpkin pie 105
puncheon floor 146

pyramids of MIssissippian Indians 104, 164
Pyramid, The (at Memphis) 192

Q
Q-size (see CUSEIS)
quake burger 14
Quakers 67, 92, 251
quartz 29, 145, 233, 236, 244 (see piezoelectricity and seismoluminescence)
quick conditions (see liquefaction and sand boils)
quicksand (see liquefaction and sand boils)
quinine 35

R
rabbits 91
raccoons 91, 147
racers compared to seismic waves 300-301
radio 12, 91, 253
Radio Corporation of America (RCA) 13
radio transmission disrupted 91
raft, as flatboat (see flatboat)
raft, floating logjam (see logjam)
rail fences of walnut 139
railroads 11, 90, 101, 120, 231
Ramses II, Pharoah 55-57
Randolph County, MO 260
Randolph, Isham 45, 46
Randolph, Jane 45
Randolph, Jane Lilbourn Rogers 40, 45
Randolph, John of Roanoke 46, 87, 88
Randolph, Martha Jefferson 48
Randolph Plantation 28, 31, 33, 36
Randolph, Richard 48
Randolph, Thomas Mann 48
Randolph, William 45
raspberry briars 149
real estate dealers 253
Real First World War, The 90
recovery (see earthquake recovery)
recurrence rates (see repeat intervals for Midwestern earthquakes)

Red Cross, American (see American Red Cross)
Red Sea 58
red sticks (see medicine fire sticks)
Reelfoot, Chief 268-269
Reelfoot Creek 183, 184, 200
Reelfoot Fault 113, 132, 189. 200, 291
Reelfoot Lake 1, 2, 8, 102, 113, 114, 117, 118, 132, 181, 183, 184, 200, 208, 212-213, 214, 268-269, 280
Reelfoot Lake Museum and Visitors Center 184
Reelfoot Scarp (see Reelfoot Fault)
Reeves, Benjamin 125
refried beans 105
regional planning 118-120
relief, government 251-253
religion, Shawnee 65
religious freedom 33, 47, 48
remote damage from small earthquakes 299-302, 304-307, 309
Rend Lake fault system 291
repeat intervals for Mid-western earthquakes 282, 284-287, 292
Republican 78
reservation, Indian (see Indian reservation)
resort on Lake Nicormy 215
response (see earthquake response)
resurrection from the dead 63, 68, 251
retardation, mental 48, 49
retrofitting, seismic 5, 22
retrograde flow of Missis-sippi (see Mississippi River, retrograde flow)
Revelation, Book of 243, 244, 267
Revolutionary War, American 25, 47, 48, 51, 60-61, 87, 88, 111, 122, 257, 270, 271, 273
Revolutionary War, French (see French Revolution)
Revolutionary War, Mexican (see Mexican Revolution)
Revolutionary War, Vene-zuelan (see Venezuelan Revolution)
Reyno, AR 305
Rhine, Confederacy of 86
Rhode Island statehood 127

rice 118, 226
Richard I, King 45, 46
Richard the Lion Hearted 45
Richmond, VA 55, 187
Richter scale explained 281-283
Ridgely, TN 280
Riley, Charlotte Lewis 45
Riley, Howard Edwin 45
Riley, Lilbourn Lewis "Pud" 40, 45
ring dikes from liquefaction 221, 224
ring fissures (see ring dikes)
Rio del Espirlto Santo 106
Ripley, TN 54, 132, 280
Risco, MO 280, 285, 305-306, 309
Ristine, MO 212
Ritchie, John 259
ritual, Shawnee 65
river banks falling (see banks caving in)
river pirates (see pirates)
river tsunamis (see fluvial tsunamis)
roast beef 105
Robertson, Dr. 189
Rocking Cave (see Cave-In-Rock)
Rocky Hill 25, 28, 30, 31, 35, 46, 47, 50
Rocky Hill Cemetery 31, 36
Rocky Mountains 51, 186, 187, 283
Roddell, George 147, 150, 208, 215, 228-229
Rogers, Jane Lilbourn 40, 45, 46
Rogue's Rest (see Island #94)
Rolfe, John 46
Rolla, MO 368
Rolling Fork, MS 169
Romans 89
Rome, Italy 31, 120
Rosie's Diner 51
Roosevelt, Eleanor 78
Roosevelt, Franklin 78
Roosevelt, Henry Latrobe 81, 162, 163, 167, 171
Roosevelt, Klaes Martensen van 76
Roosevelt, Lydia Latrobe 19, 76, 77, 78, 80-85, 162-179, 183
Roosevelt, Nicholas J. 76, 77, 78, 79-85, 163-179, 183
Roosevelt, Rosetta 80, 162

Roosevelt's Steamboat 78 (also see New Orleans, The)
Roosevelt, Theodore 78
Roosevelt, Tiger (see Tiger, Roosevelt's dog)
Rough Creek fault system 291
Rover, MO 280, 310-311
Royal, Catherine 45
Rub Al Kahli 116
rubber springs 236
runners in a race 300-301
Russelville, KY 49
Russia 6, 8, 15, 55, 86-87, 89, 267-268, 269, 322

S

Sac Indians 68, 277
safety (see earthquake safety)
St. Charles County, MO 98, 129
St. Charles, MO 75, 95, 123, 125-126, 130
St. Francis Island (see Island #59)
St. Francis River 75, 137, 143, 168, 175, 207, 210, 215-216, 217, 218-220, 225-226, 230, 231, 240, 249
St. John's Bayou 112, 133, 171, 189, 203, 207, 210-213, 215, 231
St. John's Ditch 212, 215
St. Jude Industrial Park 113, 199, 212-213
St. Lawrence River 75, 108
St. Louis County, MO 129, 261
St. Louis Gazette 191, 261 (also see Louisiana Gazette)
St. Louis, MO 4, 17, 25, 32, 36, 49, 75, 95, 99, 102, 106, 130, 131, 142, 191, 192, 203, 240, 253, 261, 278-279, 288, 292, 298
St. Louis Newspaper & Freedom of the Press 125
St. Louis University 4, 284, 286, 292, 337
St. Marys, MO 249, 280
St. Patrick's Day 261
St. Thomas a Becket 46
Ste. Genevieve County, MO 129
Ste. Genevieve fault zone 108, 291

Ste. Genevieve, MO 75, 102, 108-110, 130, 189, 193, 196, 287, 291
Sahara Desert 116
Saline Settlement 249
Salt Lake City, UT 115
Salt River, KY 160
Salvation Army 5, 317, 337
Samuel, Book of 243, 246
San Andreas fault 186, 187, 283, 293
San Bernardino County, CA 236
sand blow craters (see explosion sand blow craters)
sand blows (see explosion sand blow craters)
sand boils 9, 10, 11, 12, 13, 14, 23, 116, 145, 151, 183, 184, 192, 198, 199, 207, 214, 221-224, 234, 238-239, 286, 294, 307, 309
sand boil, world's largest 224, 239
sand traps 12, 23
San Francisco, CA 13, 114, 186, 283, 292, 305
San Francisco earthquake of 1906 186
San Ildenfonso, Treaty of 120
Santa Cruz, CA 13, 293
Santa Fe Trail 124, 125
Sarah, wife of Abraham 115
Sarpy, Capt. Paul 142-143
Sauk Indians 68
Sauvanogee, AL 58
Sauwauseekau 59, 61, 62
savages 100-101
Savannah, GA 4
sawyers 171 (also see logs in the river, hazards of)
Sawyer, Tom 80, 261
scaffolding of capitol dome 187, 198
scalping 70, 100
scalplock tube 64, 273
school hours, earthquakes during 320
science fair project 292
Scientific American, The 15
Scott City, MO 9, 149, 369
Scott County, MO 275
Scotland 105
Scottsburg, IN 259
scratch and sniff 240
secondary faults 290 (also see Bootheel fault and Reelfoot fault)

Second World War (see World War II)

secrecy of property owners with earthquake damage 296, 302

seismically altered streams (see discontinuous channels)

seismic building codes 5, 322

seismic building design 109-110, 189, 235-236 (also see retrofitting, seismic)

seismic gap theory 294

seismic retrofitting (see retrofitting)

seismic tar balls 238-240

seismic wave propagation 300-301 (also see ground waves)

seismographs 191, 192, 234, 255, 281, 283, 286

seismologists 4, 6, 282-283, 286-289, 294, 296

seismoluminescence 14, 29, 145, 232-233, 235, 236-237, 244

Semetic people 58

Seminole Indians 103, 277

Senath, MO 280

Seneca Indians 68, 72

septic systems & increased risk of ground failure 303, 313, 314

serpent of evil 67

Sethi I, Pharoah 56

settlement damage, normal 299-300, 304, 306, 309, 311-312

Shabbona 271

Shain, Mike 1

Shakers 67, 251

shaking damage vs. ground failure damage 300, 303, 306-307, 309-310, 311-315 (also see ground waves)

shaving heads, Shawnee custom 65

Shaw, Col. John 135, 155, 190, 238-239, 276

Shawnee Avenue 275-277

Shawnee Indians 58-74, 92, 94, 99, 103, 256-259, 263-265, 269-279 (also see Tecumseh and Tenskwatawa)

Shawnee Mission, KS 274

Shawnee Path, The (see El Camino Real)

Shawnee Prophet, The (see Tenskwatawa)

Shawnee Reservation 274

Shawnee thong tree 275-277

Shawneetown, MO 100

Shawneetown fault zone 291

Shawtunte 59, 61, 62

sheet rock 302, 311

Sheriff of St. Louis County 261

Shinbone, MO 274

Shippingport, KY 83, 84, 205, 206

shock waves 244 (also see ground waves)

Shooting Star (as name for Tecumseh) 59, 269, 272

shopping bags with earthquake information 335

Show Me State 232

Shrum, Edison 9

Siberia, Russia 116

Sibley, Maj. George 105, 123-124, 125, 197

Sibley, Mary Easton 123

sidewalks buckled 187

Sikeston, MO 1, 54, 102, 132, 135, 215, 280, 302

Sikeston Power Plant 228

silver 226

Silver Creek 257

Sinclair sand boil 11

Sinai, Mount 58, 243

Sinai plate 115

skeletons broken by earthquakes 140-141

skeletons, Native American 107, 140-141, 275

Skelton, Martha Wayles (see Jefferson, Martha Wayles)

slavery 29, 31, 32-33, 125, 127 (also see African Americans)

slavery in Kentucky 29, 31, 32-33

slavery, prohibition against importation of 32

slaves owned by Native Americans 103

sleet 262-263

slope conditions as risk factors 304-305, 311-314

small earthquakes, damage from 281, 294-317

Small New Madrid Source Zone 291, 317, 320

smallpox 70, 123, 278

smells (see earthquake smells)

Smithland, KY 28, 30, 31, 32, 75, 165, 166, 168, 280

Smithland Neighborhood 28

smog (see earthquake smog)

smokehouse 152-154, 222

smoking tobacco 63, 74, 104, 146

smothered child 259

snakes 7, 37, 91, 147

snow 173, 174, 205, 262-263

soil conditions as risk factors 304-305, 311-314

soil fertility increased by earthquakes 116, 226

solar eclipse 55, 69, 86, 243

solar heat 237

sounds (see earthquake noises)

sound waves 244

South Africa 89

South America 55, 58, 88, 104, 106

South Carolina Emergency Preparedness Division 337

South Carolina statehood 127

Southeast Missourian, The 91

Southeast Missouri State University 148, 303, 336, 368, 369

South River 261

Soviet Union 6, 8, 322 (see Russia)

soy beans 118, 226

Spain 25, 86, 88, 95, 99, 103, 106, 111, 115, 119-120, 121, 127, 252

Spanish Mill, MO 168, 199, 216, 217, 218-220, 231, 241-242

Sparks, Richard 59, 62

Speed, Mathias 201-203, 276

spirits of niter 35

Springfield Airport 298

Springfield, IL 298

springs as results of seismic activity 114, 115

springwater 233-234

SPT test for liquefaction potential 307

squash 66, 104

squirrels 85, 90

Stack Island (see Island #94)

Standard Penetration Test (SPT) 307

Stanley Steamer 277

Star Spangled Banner, national anthem 127

Steele, MO 132, 134, 137, 153, 222, 280, 285

Steeleville, MO 17

steel reinforced concrete 299, 302, 304, 315, 316

Stewart, Anthony 19

Stewart, David 282, 286, 287, 297, 302, 317, 368-369

Stewart Island 28

Stewart, Lee Pomeroy xvii, 369

Stewart's Landing 218, 231

Stewart Towhead 159

Stilley, Elder Steven 247

Stoddard, Amos 121

Stoddard County, MO 275

strange animal behavior (see animal behavior before earthquakes)

strawberries 104, 105

stress (see insanity and post traumatic stress disorder)

strong earthquakes, definition of 282, 284-285

structural engineers 296

Stuart, John 92

stumps, broken cypress (see broken cypress trees)

subjectivity in science 4, 6, 287, 289 (also see politics in science)

subsidence (see earthquake subsidence)

suffocated child 259

suicide 36, 38, 48, 49-50, 277

Sumbawa 262

sun as earthquake trigger 4

Sun Commercial News 298

sunlight converted to heat 237

sunken houses (see houses engulfed by quicksand)

sunklands (see earthquake subsidence)

superheated groundwater 133

Supreme Court, U.S. 255

surface faults 290 (also see Bootheel fault and Reelfoot fault)

surface waves 183, 185, 191-198, 228, 244

Susquehannock Indians 72

Suwanee River (see Swanee River)

swallowed alive by earthquake crevasses 226-230

swallowed up (see houses engulfed by quicksand)
Swampeast Missouri 225
swamplands 144, 150, 153, 215-226, 231, 241
Swanee River 58, 75
swearing 246
Sweden 86, 116
Sweet Springs, VA 161
swimming pool damage 302, 311, 312
Swiss cocoa 105
Switzerland 86, 105
Syria 86

T

taco shells 105
Tai Ping Rebellion 89
Tallapoosa River 58
Tamboro, Mount 262
Tangshan, China 7
Tangshan earthquake 7
Tanner, Elder John 247, 276
tar balls 238-240
taxes 119, 120, 226, 232
Teceikeapease 59, 61, 73, 100, 274, 275
Tecumpease 59, 61
Tecumseh 15, 20, 58-74, 86, 88, 92, 99-100, 103, 197, 257, 258, 263-265, 269-272, 274, 275
Tecumseh, MO 263, 280
Tecumseh's comet 59, 86, 269 (also see Napoleon's comet)
telegraph 12, 253
telephone 12, 101, 253
television 12-13, 253, 292, 369
Temple at Abu Simbel 55-57
Temple at Karnak 56
Ten Commandments, The 243
Tennessee Emergency Management Agency 337
Tennessee Prison Facility 113, 212
Tennessee River 75
Tenskwatawa 19, 20, 65-70, 86, 88, 100, 227, 265-266, 272-274 (also see Lala-wethika)
Terra Haute, IN 284, 287, 291, 294
Terra Rouge 152
test holes 301, 307, 310
Texas 127
Thailand 266

Thames, Battle of the 270, 271-272, 274
Thames River 75, 270, 271, 274
Thanksgiving Day 259
Thatcher, Becky 262
Thayer, MO 310
theater 55, 251
Thirteen Original Colonies 127-128
Threlkeld, Aaron 27
Threlkeld, Matilda 27, 35, 45
Thompson, Benjamin 245
Thompson, Elder Wilson 148-150, 245-250, 276
thong tree, Shawnee 275-277
thunder, absence of prior to New Madrid quakes 55, 84
thunder associated with earthquakes (see earth-quake thunder)
Tibet 266
tidal forces of sun and moon as earthquake triggers 4-5
tidal wave (see tsunami, fluvial)
Tiger, Celestial, as name for Tecumseh 59
Tiger, Roosevelt's dog 80, 84, 162, 175
Tigris River 115
time dependent probability 288-289
time independent probability 288-289
tiny earthquakes, definition of 282
Tiptonville, TN 1, 114, 159, 181, 200, 212, 280
Tiptonville Horst 132, 189
Tippecanoe, Battle of 87, 258, 265, 271, 273
Tippecanoe River 69, 75, 265
tire, pumping up 301
tobacco 104, 105
Todd County, Ky 94
Tokyo, Japan 115
toll bridge, Weaverville 219
tomahawk 66, 94, 164, 258, 264
tomatoes 104
tombstones moved 251
Tom Sawyer 80, 261
Tom's Grill 14
toothpaste 307
tornado 62, 90, 125, 182, 238
torture 92

Towosaghy Indian Mound 104
toxic fumes 102
Trail of Tears 103, 277, 278
Trail of Tears State Park 277
transcontinental railroad 11
treason 32, 111
Treaty of Fountainbleau 111
Treaty of Ghent 30
Treaty of Greenville 62
Treaty of Ildefonso 120
Treaty of Paris 25
trees, destruction of by earthquakes 139, 145, 146, 149, 150, 155, 156, 159, 162, 165, 172, 173, 181, 185, 200-201, 203, 205, 214, 215, 225, 227, 246, 267
Tributsch, Helmut 7, 91
triplets 60, 62
tsunami, fluvial 189, 202-203, 207 242
Tuckhabatchee, AL 58, 73, 74, 75, 263-265, 272
turkey, as a bird 115, 171, 245
Turkey, as a country 86, 89
Turkey Creek 249
Turtle, Big (Boone's Indian name) 92, 272
Turtle Laying Eggs (see Methoataske)
Twell, Karen 369
twins 62, 68, 136
Two Tenths Rule (for Richter scale) 281
Two Unit Rule (for Richter scale) 281
typhoid fever 263
typhus epidemic 263
Tyronza, Ar 214, 280
Tywappity Hill 190, (also see Benton Hills)

U

Union City, TN 8, 54, 102, 132, 280
U.S. Army Corps of Engineers 142, 225-226
U.S. Congress 12, 74, 121, 123, 225-226, 251-253, 263, 277
U.S. Constitution 103
U.S. Geological Survey 4, 6, 221, 222, 223, 224, 232, 282, 293, 368
U.S. National Park Service 25, 110
U.S. Naval Observatory 4

U.S. Navy 76
U.S. Postal Service 12
U.S. Supreme Court 255
United Kingdom (see England)
United Methodist Church (see Methodist Church)
United Nations Disaster Relief Organization (UNDRO) 368
University of Arkansas 369
University of Iowa 369
University of Kentucky 98
University of Missouri, Rolla 368
University of North Carolina, Chapel Hill 368
unreinforced concrete 299, 302, 304, 315, 316
Upland, CA 236
Upper Louisiana Territory (see Missouri Territory)
UPS van 102
Uranus 55
urban planning 118-120

V

Vanduser, MO 214
vanilla 104, 105
Van Buren, Martin 277
van Roosevelt (see Roosevelt)
vapors (see earthquake smog)
Varney River 231
Venezuela 88, 244-245, 252
Venezuelan Revolution 88, 252
Venus, The (barge) 158-159
Vermont statehood 127
vertical forces of an earth-quake 318-319
vertigo 200
very minor earthquakes, definition of 282
Vibernum, MO 291
Vicksburg, MS 142, 169, 178
Victoria, Queen 206
videos, free, where to get 336
Vienna, IN 257
Vincinnes, IN 70, 75, 198, 241, 254, 258, 280, 291, 294, 298
Virginia statehood 127
Viviers, France 55
volcanos 55, 186, 234, 235, 262-263
vulgarity 246
vultures 172, 173

W

Wabash River 69, 70, 75, 87, 291, 293-294
Wabash Valley fault zone 291, 293-294
Wakonda (see Master of Life)
Wales 47
Walker, John Hardiman 151, 230, 232, 253
Walmart 369
walnut logs and rail fences 139
Walton, Sam 369
wampum 264
war hatchet (see toma hawk)
War of 1812 15, 30, 87-88, 89, 123, 127, 137, 192, 206, 252, 254, 257, 262, 269, 270
warm groundwater 145, 233-237, 238
Warren County, MO 98
Warrensburg, MO 369
Warsaw, Duchy of 86
Wasabagoa 61, 271
Wasatch fault 115
Washington, DC 4, 36, 49, 74, 75, 106, 111, 121, 144, 150, 158, 186, 187, 198
Washington, Fort 68, 80
Washington, George 27, 28, 35, 72, 88, 122
waterfalls (see Falls of the Ohio, and Mississippi River, falls of)
waterfowl 160 (also see birds, geese, and ducks)

water heaters 332
Waterloo, Belgium 268
watermelon 104, 118
Waters, The Year Of 74
waterwell anomalies prior to earthquakes 7
waterwell damage from earthquakes 303-304
Watson, Judge Goah 253-254
waves (see groundwaves, seismic waves, shock waves, sound waves, surface waves, fluvial tsunamis, and waves on the Mississippi)
waves on the Mississippi 143, 144, 159, 189, 200, 201-203, 207, 242
Wea Indians 68
Weatherford, William 264-265
Weaver, John 219
Weaverville, MO 219, 242
webbed feet or toes 225
week-end earthquakes 318, 320
wedding 78, 179, 274
Weinel, Ralph A. 262
West Florida Territory 127-128
Westo Indians 68
West Plains, MO 217, 263, 280, 310
Westvaco Paper Mill 52, 53, 241
West Virginia statehood 127, 128
wheat 66, 90
wheel, invention of 104
whipping post 31
whirlpools 202, 206

whiskey 66, 151 (also see alcohol)
White House, The 137
White Lotus Rebellion 89
white man's flies 278
White River 207, 263
Whizbang, MO 369
Wickliffe, KY 52, 132, 142, 242, 280
Wildcat Creek 265
Wilderness Trail, The 92 (see Cumberland Trail)
wild iris 148
Wilkinson County, MS 94
William I, King 45, 47
William the Conquerer 45, 47
Willis, Paul 298
willow leaves or bark, as medicine 105
Wilson Gang 164-165
wine 65, 66, 198 (also see alcohol)
wine cask broken 198
Winnebago Indians 68, 265
Wireless Telegraph and Signal Company 12
Wisconsin Historical Society 190
witchcraft 66-67, 100
Witherall, Judge James 191
Wolf Lake, IL 303-304
wolves 91, 147, 277
Woodward, Judge A.B. 198
working-day earthquakes 318, 320
Working Group on California Earthquake Probabilities 293

World Series earthquake 13, 283, 292, 293, 305, 322
world's largest sand boil 224, 239
World War I 89
World War II 2, 8, 15, 89
World War, forerunner of 90
wrath of God 80, 83, 87, 171, 243, 246, 251, 252, 268, 269
written language 104
Wyandot Indians 68, 369
Wyatt, MO 285
Wyoming Territory 51

X

Xiansi Province, China 266
Xiansi earthquake 266

Y

yams 104
Yazoo River 169, 178
Year of Waters, The 74
Yellow Bank, IN 85, 162, 166
yellow fever 121
Yellowstone Park 186, 233
Yingchow, China 7
Yong, Chien 8
York Village, MO 316
Yount, Ben 259

Z

Zanesville, OH 250
Zechariah, Book of 243
zinc 226
Zirkle Funeral Home 298

GUTENBERG-RICHTER PUBLICATIONS

THE EARTHQUAKE AMERICA FORGOT

2,000 Temblors in Five Months . . .
And it Will Happen Again

by Dr. David Stewart & Dr. Ray Knox
Cover by Don Greenwood, Illustrations by Anthony Stewart

You'll be an eye witness. An experience you'll never forget. This book will take you back to the times and places of the greatest sequence of earthquakes in the last 2,000 years of World History—the New Madrid earthquakes of 1811–12. From the safety of your favorite reading chair, you'll encounter River Pirates, Indians, Romance, War, Peace, Good Times, Tough Times, Slavery, Corruption, Heroes, Scoundrels, Bizarre Animal Behavior, Murder, Mystery—Political, Social and Geologic Upheavals all at the same time. Famous people were there—President Thomas Jefferson; Artist and Naturalist, John James Audubon; Explorer and Governor, Meriwether Lewis; Abraham Lincoln (age three at the time); Teddy Roosevelt's Grandfather, the fiery, charismatic Shawnee Chief Tecumseh, and his brother, the Shawnee Prophet Tenskwatawa. This is the most complete account of these earthquakes ever published. Dozens of incredible stories, fascinating first-person accounts, and here-to-fore unpublished facts—plus more than two-hundred photographs, figures, maps and illustrations, including pictures of seismic features still visible in the landscape of the New Madrid Fault Zone today. The definitive work on the Great New Madrid earthquakes. Reads like a novel. But this is not fiction. These fantastic events actually happened. Once you start you won't want to put it down. When you read this book you'll feel like you were there . . . and are glad you survived.

(EAF) First Edition 1995
376 pages, 8.5x11, 252 illustrations, index, bibliography, hardcover
LCCN 91-91492
ISBN 0-934426-45-7 $29.95

GUTENBERG-RICHTER PUBLICATIONS

THE EARTHQUAKE THAT NEVER WENT AWAY

The Shaking Stopped in 1812 . . . But the Impact Goes On

by Dr. David Stewart & Dr. Ray Knox

Get comfortable and take an armchair field trip to the greatest display of earthquake features in the world. See how a sequence of massive earthquakes long ago still effect the live and times of people living in and around the New Madrid Fault Zone now. When the shaking is over, the impact of a great earthquake is not. It's lasting effects can reach down through the centuries to touch people today—influencing engineering, agriculture, transportation, and the way people live and think. You will see seismic sand boils formed two centuries ago where farmers still get stuck with their tractors. You'll see 200-year-old seismic sand fissures under railroad tracks that cause train derailments today. You'll see modern houses built over old earthquake landslides whose foundations are cracking up and creeping down hill—a process started by seismic forces long before the town was settled. This book gives you a "vicarious visual tour," complete with the narrative you would hear from two leading world authorities as your personal guides. 138 original photos, 5 figures, and 3 maps of faults, fissures, and scars in the landscape still visible today from the great New Madrid earthquakes of 1811–12. (These same illustrations are also available as 35 mm color slides, see page 357). Carefully researched and scientifically rigorous, yet written with wit and entertainment for the enlightenment of the public. You will be amazed at what you can still see of these earthquakes—evidence permanently impressed upon the landscape of the unbelievable churning, boiling, cracking and splintering of the earth's surface from the unimaginable violence of the cataclysms that caused these lasting landforms that people must still deal with today.

(NWA) First Edition 1993
222 pages, 8.5xll, 138 photos, 5 figures, 4 tables, 3 maps, index, bibliography, quality paperback
LCCN 92-75133
ISBN 0-934426-54-6

$19.95

GUTENBERG-RICHTER PUBLICATIONS

The New Madrid Fault Finders Guide

by Dr. David Stewart & Dr. Ray Knox

Fault finding is fun. And the New Madrid Seismic Zone is the place to do it. This book has maps, road logs, directions and commentary—a set of exciting and educational self-guided field trips. Shows you where to visit and see for yourself some of the thousands of faults, fissures, crevasses, sand boils, and other scars in the landscape still seen today—200 years after the great New Madrid earthquakes of 1811–12. Step into an explosion crater. Climb into an earthquake crevasse. Walk barefoot on the world's largest sand boil. Go boating on an earthquake lake. Talk with a living witness —a giant 300-year-old oak caught in a sand boil in 1812. See where the Mississippi River ran backwards and waterfalls formed. See where whole towns disappeared. Visit the epicenter of the largest earthquake (8.8) in the history of the lower 48 states—a place where a factory, a power plant, and an airport are located today. See city streets slowly sinking and cracking because they were built over earthquake landslides from 1811-12. Look out over the Mississippi River where the original site of New Madrid, Missouri, is now under water on the Kentucky side. You will learn how to recognize sand boils, explosion craters and other earthquake features that dot the farm fields and line the highways throughout this fascinating region—features you may have passed many times before, but did not recognize as seismic in origin. Interstate Highway 55, between Blytheville, Arkansas, and Benton, Missouri, is a 101-mile stretch that should be called "Earthquake Alley." There is at least one chance in four that a measurable earthquake will happen on the New Madrid Fault on any day you should drive the Interstate through here. This is the greatest outdoor earthquake laboratory in the world. Numerous photos and figures. Great vacation guide. One trip with this book and you'll never look at a landscape the same again. It'll change your outlook on earth.

(FFG) First Edition 1995
154 pages, 8/5x11, maps and figures, index, bibliography, quality paperback
LCCN 91-91374
ISBN 0-934426-42-2 $14.95

GR
GUTENBERG-RICHTER
PUBLICATIONS

150 EARTHQUAKE SLIDES
ON THE NEW MADRID SEISMIC ZONE
by Dr. David Stewart & Dr. Ray Knox

It has been said that "an expert is someone more than twenty miles from home with a tray of slides." Now you can become an expert on the Great New Madrid Earthquakes of 1811-12—taking friends, civic groups, professional peers, and students of all ages on a fascinating picture-tour of the fault zone and its thousands of earthquake features. The New Madrid Fault Zone is the most extensive and outstanding display of landforms sculptured by earthquakes known on earth. Scientists, engineers, and visitors from all over the world come to see what is there and marvel. There are more sand boils, fissures, landslides, broken stream channels, seismic ponds, explosion craters, and earthquake lakes in this region than anywhere on earth. See the world's largest sand boil—over a mile long and 136 acres in size. (Most sand boils are less than 10 feet in diameter.) These slides will take you and your audience on a tour where you fly over, drive by, and walk on some of the world's greatest morphoseismic features. Step into a graben crevasse. Fly along the Bootheel fault. Climb up an earthquake landslide. Photos from five states—Arkansas, Illinois, Kentucky, Missouri and Tennessee. 150 color slides, 35 mm, two carousel trays full. Complete set of narrative notes, a glossary of definitions, and instructions for a smashing presentation to any group. The New Madrid Seismic Zone has a story to tell and you can be the one to tell it. All you need is this set of slides and the book that accompanies it. You will be awed by what you see—and so will your audiences.

Slide set comes in an attractive 3-D-ring binder with archival plastic sleeves for storage and easy previewing. Delivered shrunk-wrapped and ready to use. Binder contains a 3-hole punched copy of *The Earthquake that Never Went Away* (see p. 355) which serves as the narrative notes for the set.

(SET) First Edition 1993
150 color slides, 35mm, D-ring binder, 222 page book of notes with index, bibliography
ISBN 0-934426-51-1 $180.00 for complete set with book
Slides from set also available individually $4.00 each ppd

OTHER BOOKS Available from Gutenberg-Richter

DAMAGE & LOSSES FROM FUTURE NEW MADRID EARTHQUAKES
Dr. David Stewart

The New Madrid Fault has the capability of causing damage in 22 states. Do you live in one of them? What will happen in your area when the next major New Madrid quake hits? What is the probability in your lifetime? With this easy-to-use manual you can find out how many buildings will collapse, how many will be injured, how many will die, how many bridges will be out, and a host of other valuable information about the county where you live. Ideal for medical personnel, emergency planners, business owners, insurance personnel, school officials, government leaders, national guard units, Red Cross chapters, or anyone who wants to know what will happen during the next destructive New Madrid earthquake. Published jointly by Missouri State Emergency Management Agency and Federal Emergency Management Agency. (DAL) Fourth Printing 1994. 74 pp, 8.5x11, 16 maps, softcover
ISBN 0-934426-53-8   FREE ON REQUEST (postage & handling $3.00)

THE NEW MADRID EARTHQUAKE
by Myron Fuller (Foreword by Dr. David Stewart)

This is the book all researchers and serious students start with in studying the great New Madrid earthquakes of 1811-12. Originally released in 1912 as a U.S. Geological Survey publication, Written by a geologist, this is the first serious scientific study of these events to be put into print. Many photos and figures. Published by Center for Earthquake Studies, SE MO State University. (NMF) 1990 edition. 120 pages, 8.5x5.5, quality paperback
ISBN 0-934426-49-X $13.95

THE NEW MADRID EARTHQUAKES
by Dr. James Lal Penick Jr. (Foreword by Dr. Otto Nuttli)

A scholarly and authoritative account of the New Madrid earthquakes written by a historian. Meticulously documented. Photos and line drawings. Well written. Published by University of Missouri Press, Columbia. (NMP) Revised Edition 1981. 176 pages, 5x7, quality paperback.
ISBN 0-8262-0344-2 $13.95

EFFECTS OF EARTHQUAKES IN THE CENTRAL UNITED STATES
by Dr. Otto Nuttli (Foreword by Dr. David Stewart)

Dr. Nuttli was the leading world authority on this subject in his life-time. This was his last published work. Maps, figures, and photos. Considers all active faults in the Midwest. Clearly articulated. The perfect primer on central U.S. earthquake risk. (CUS) 1990 edition. 50 pages, 6x9, quality softcover.
ISBN 0-934426-50-3 $8.95

OTHER ITEMS Available from Gutenberg-Richter

NEW MADRID FAULT TOURS

Take a tour of the New Madrid Fault Zone with Dr. David Stewart and/or Dr. Ray Knox. If interested, send name, address and phone number to Dr. Stewart in care of Gutenberg-Richter Publications.

GUEST LECTURERS

David Stewart is available for a variety of public lectures or seminars suitable for any audience, profession, or age group. Address inquiries to Gutenberg-Richter Publications, address and phone given on page 361.

T-SHIRTS AVAILABLE WITH EAF COVER ART

Don Greenwood's exquisite artwork displayed on the cover of this book is available on a T-shirt. For information on prices and available sizes, contact Gutenberg-Richter Publications, address and phone given on page 361.

HOW TO MAKE YOUR OWN LIQUEFACTION MODEL
Free Booklet by Dr. David Stewart

Complete and simple instructions on how to make an earthquake liquefaction model. Make an earthquake (hit the table or stomp on floor) and watch the soil turn to quicksand. A great science fair project. Copies are free with book order. Otherwise, send $1.00 for postage and handling.

EARTHQUAKE GUIDE FOR HOME AND OFFICE
Free Booklet by Maria Dillard and Dr. David Stewart

Published in 1990 by Southwestern Bell Telephone Company and the Center for Earthquake Studies at Southeast Missouri State University, this excellent illustrated twelve-page booklet summarizes the hazards, what you should expect, and what you should do during an earthquake whether you are at home or at the office, in a vehicle, in an elevator or on the street. Also contains advice on earthquake preparation and what phone numbers you should post prior to an earthquake emergency. Copies are free with book orders. Otherwise send $1.00 for postage and handling. Available in bulk quantities to schools, civic organization, and others for cost of shipping.

G̶R̶
GUTENBERG-RICHTER
PUBLICATIONS

ORDERING INFORMATION

You may order Gutenberg-Richter Publications by directly from the publisher by remitting check or money order. A convenient order form is given at the end of this book on page 369 which may be photocopied, completed, and sent with your order. You may also use your VISA or Master Card, either by mail (see the order form on page 369) or by telephone via the toll free number given on the next page. You may also inquire at your local bookstore who can special-order these books for you should they not have them in stock. If your library does not have copies of Gutenberg-Richter publications, encourage them to order copies directly from the publisher.

MISSOURI SALES TAX: Missouri residents must pay 6% sales tax on all orders. For non-Missouri residents there is no tax.

SHIPPING INSTRUCTIONS

BOOK ORDERS: Please remit appropriate total for books desired plus shipping and handling as follows: For U.S.A., Mexico and Canada, add $3.00 for first book, plus $1.50 for second book, plus $1.00 per book thereafter. Other countries: Surface Parcel Post is $8.00 for first book, plus $4.00 for second book, plus $2.00 per book thereafter; Air Parcel Post is $15.00 for first book, plus $8.00 for second book, plus $3.00 per book thereafter.

SLIDE ORDERS: Complete set of 150 Colored Slides including book of narrative notes, $8.00 for Priority Mail within the U.S.A., $10.00 for Canada, and $35.00 for International Air Parcel Post in all other countries. Individual slides retail for $4.00 each which includes First Class Postage for U.S.A., Mexico, and Canada. All other countries include an additional $1.00 per slide for International Air Mail. Specify slides by numbers given in the book, *The Earthquake that Never Went Away.*

COMPLETE LIBRARIES: Books only, $8.00 (N. America), $15.00 (Other countries). Books plus Slide Set, $15.00 (N. America), $50.00 (Other countries)

✌ SPECIAL DISCOUNTS ✌

COMPLETE NEW MADRID EARTHQUAKE LIBRARY at SPECIAL PRICE
All seven books listed on Order Form on page 369 ($102 value) — Only $82
All seven books plus full set of 150 colored slides ($282 value) — Only $242
• **SAVE $20.00 ON BOOKS** • **SAVE $40.00 ON BOOKS & SLIDES** •

ABOUT THE AUTHORS
Dr. David Stewart

David Mack Stewart was born September 20, 1937, in St. Louis, raised in Crystal City, Missouri, graduated from high school in Jefferson City (1955), attended Central Methodist College in Fayette, Missouri, 1955-58 (majoring in philosophy, religion and English) and went to Los Angeles Trade Technical College, 1959 (to study photography). He was the photographer for Self Realization Fellowship, Inc., 1959-1962. He went to Central Missouri State University in Warrensburg, 1962-63 (majoring in social and life sciences), transferred to the University of Missouri at Rolla where he worked his way through college as a piano teacher, and received a B.S. in Math and Physics (1965), graduating as Salutatorian of his class. After two years as a hydrologist and hydraulic engineer with the U.S. Geological Survey in Garden Grove, California, he returned to Rolla to earn an M.S. and Ph.D. in Geophysics in 1971.

Former Director of the Central U.S. Earthquake Consortium, Marion, Illinois. Former Director of MacCarthy Geophysics Laboratory and Assistant Professor at the University of North Carolina, Chapel Hill. Founder and former Director, Center for Earthquake Studies and Associate Professor at Southeast Missouri State University, Cape Girardeau. He is an Adjunct Instructor at the Emergency Management Institute, Emmitsburg, Maryland. He is a private consultant on seismic risk and damage assessment to government, insurance, and industry. He has given expert testimony for earthquake legislation on state and federal levels and has been an expert witness in many litigations.

He has given lectures, presented seminars, led field trips, or taught courses to thousands of people on virtually every aspect of earthquake seismology, mitigation and engineering. He has given international seminars on earthquake preparation for hospitals in Lima, Peru,

and Bogota, Colombia, at the invitation of the Pan American Health Organization and the United Nations Disaster Relief Organization. He has been invited to conduct tours of the New Madrid Seismic Zone attended by scientists and engineers from many countries.

Dr. Stewart is author or coauthor of more than 200 publications, in eight languages, including more than eleven books. Two of his works received the "Books of

the Year" Award from the *American Journal of Nursing*. Two of his papers won national awards for larity in technical writing. Two other publications have sold or circulated over a million copies each. In 1990-93 he served on the Editorial Board of *Earthquake Spectra*—the International Journal of Earthquake Engineering.

Dr. Stewart has been quoted in many journals and magazines, as well as by virtually every newspaper in the United

States. He has appeared on national television in forty-four countries.

He and his wife, the former Lee Pomeroy, have five children ages 18 to 31 (as of January 1, 1995), two married. They have two grandchildren. and a third on the way. David cannot claim any Native American blood, but Lee and his children are all part Cherokee. David and Lee celebrated their thirty-second wedding anniversary on September 1, 1994.

Dr. Stewart is a former licensed United Methodist Pastor who served the Illmo United Methodist Church at Scott City, Missouri, in 1993 and 1994. David and Lee are both members of the First United Methodist Church of Marble Hill, Missouri, where Lee is a choir director. David enjoys playing the piano, loves hiking and raises four-leaf-clovers for a hobby. David and Lee live on a farm in Bollinger County, Missouri.

Dr. Ray Knox

Burnal Ray Knox was born March 29, 1931, at Whizbang, Missouri, a country store and a post office and not much else. It no longer exists. Whizbang was in the Ozark hills of southwestern Missouri, "Not too far from Cyclone," he likes to say, "and actually not too far from Pineville and Huckleberry Ridge, either." He attended high school and "did most of his growing up" in Bentonville, Arkansas—better known as home of the late Sam Walton, founder of the Walmart Chain.

Dr. Knox is also part Native American. His great grandmother was a full-blooded Indian of the Wyandot Tribe. Her native name was "Missouri."

Presently, Dr. Knox is a Professor of Geosciences at Southeast Missouri State University and former Chairman of that Department. His major research interest is geomorphology, the scientific study of landforms and how they got that way. He earned his bachelors and masters degrees in geology from the University of Arkansas at Fayetteville and his doctorate from the University of Iowa in Iowa City.

In recent years he has become quite interested in morphoseismology—the study of how earthquakes mold and alter the landscape. Prior research had focused on the formation of the Ozark Mountains—especially its streams and caves. He is author of fifteen professional presentations and sixteen professional publications. He is coauthor of four books on the New Madrid Seismic Zone.

Dr. Knox is an avid fisherman and backpacker. He loves to involve his students in hiking trips that usually combine geology with such things as trail building and maintenance, wildflower admiring, bird watching, mountain goat observing, and fishing.

He is married to the former Karen Twell, his "bride" of 39 years, with whom he lives in Cape Girardeau, Missouri. Karen and Ray have three kids and two "extraordinary" granddaughters.

What People Say about this book . . .

"An aged enigma asks, "When a tree falls in a forest, can there be a noise if no one is there to hear it?"

"Similarly we ask, "When the earth is violently shaken, can it be an earthquake if no one is there to experience it?"

"The New Madrid earthquakes of 1811-12, the greatest series in world history, came very near to being this country's greatest non-event—it being experienced only by a few frontiersmen and Indians, the record of it being buried away in obscure archives. To leave it so would have been a great loss. We desperately need all the knowledge we can get about earthquakes and their effects upon us.

"Now, at last, Doctors Stewart and Knox have rescued the quake from obscurity. They give a detailed, highly readable account of this fearsome event, an exciting narrative indeed! Scientifically correct—yet not weighted down with technical jargon. But more than that, they cast this account into its human setting. They describe the people (red, white and black) who experienced it—their forebears and their descendants still living in the area. They examine the profound effects that this quake had, not only on its immediate victims, but also in shaping the course of the nation.

"Just as we expect the authors to begin winding the book down, in Chapter Six they create another temblor of no small magnitude of their very own. In the chapter called *Futureshocks*, they describe their field observations of the very destructive effects of minor quakes every year along the New Madrid fault. This chapter, alone, is worth far more than the price of the book.

"The sketches of the human setting would, alone, have made this an outstanding book, but it contains much more. I thought the section on 'Forerunners to World War' was particularly insightful. There are several essays and stories here that could stand alone, yet they have been brilliantly tied together. Beautifully written."

John Bormuth, Professor Emeritus
Department of Behavioral Sciences
Lombard, Illinois

"A magnificent book. The stories seem to ground in reality the actual events. A book of warning as well as a book of historical documentation. Descriptions of the quake zone bring the reader right into the present and right into Mid-America. A most comprehensive and informative volume.

"'A strong magnitude 6.0 earthquake will reach out and touch at least 25 states of the Midwest and Eastern seaboard.' This was one of the most stunning statements to me. Of those 25 states, at least 19 are fairly ignorant of almost everything you have written in this book. The time to awaken them is NOW!

"Thank you. I enjoyed it immensely!"

Gayle Watts
Clarkston Publishing Group
Clarkston, Michigan

"What a story! I can personally relate to the experiences of many described in the book because I was only ten miles from the 7.1 magnitude earthquake in California of October 17, 1989. I know the fear felt at the moment of a major earthquake, the fear of uncertainty.

"One aspect of the book that shines throughout is human survivability in the face of desperate uncertainty. One can survive a major earthquake if one is prepared mentally and materialistically. We who live in the midst of the threat of earthquakes all the time know how important is it to have accurate information from books like this—information that can rise in our minds and become useful at the moment the shaking starts. Such knowledge helps us to endure the hardships of the following days and subsequent aftershocks—so vividly described in this book.

"A Fantastic work. My partner saw my copy before I was finished and I nearly had to break his arm to get it back. 'I gotta read this when you're through," he said. I really like the way it has been written.

"It ties everything together so well. The most important message I got from the book is 'What was true then, is still true today.' A great book!"

Keith Morin, Electronics Technician
Advanced GeoMagnetic Technology , Inc.
Santa Cruz, California

What People Say about this book . . .

"A most remarkable book Stewart and Knox have put together. First they take you on a journey in time where you feel the pulse of the communities on the frontier—a land where the lives of Native Americans, whites, and blacks are all intertwined.

"Then it happens! An earthquake so massive that President James Madison is awakened in the White House, 800 miles away. Tremors from New York to New Orleans, from Georgia to the Wyoming Territory. Landslides in North Carolina, the Mississippi River running backwards, and more violent quakes yet to come!

"The reality of the disaster becomes all the more vivid with the realization that the New Madrid Seismic Zone is still very active today. This book allows the reader to grasp the seriousness of impending future shocks. Stewart and Knox have given us the information we need to prepare for the inevitable.

"I can't tell you how much I enjoyed the book. It was an experience! It was great!"

David Janczek
Free Lance Photographer
Makanda, Illinois

"What a great movie this would make! Fast and easy reading. After I started I didn't want to stop till I finished. Very informative. Historically, scientifically, and geographically. Lets you live the 1911-12 earthquakes. Tells you what to expect and what to do when an earthquake occurs today."

Vera Hennemann
Benton, Missouri

"FASCINATING from cover to cover! A true story, yet read like a novel. I learned some of the precursor signs of an eminent earthquake and got a real feeling of how it would be to go through a serious devastating quake. Our home sits right on the Wasatch fault and the possibility of our being affected by an earthquake is very high. This book gives good suggestions on how to prepare and protect ourselves. Important reading for everyone! Very enjoyable."

Dianne Bjarnson, Director
Utah School of Midwifery
Pleasant Grove, Utah

"Engaging. Interesting. Fun to read. Not only a book about earthquakes, but the development of the country and the whole history of the people of the time. It was fascinating how the earthquake was woven through many little stories, each of which could stand alone, and yet were related to one another.

"Action, adventure, and honesty characterize this book. Usually there are 'good guys and bad guys' but in this book people were presented honestly, as they were and in the context of their time. The authors made the people so real. Indians, white settlers, slaves, politicians, the rich and the poor—A compassionate treatment of everyone, both victims and perpetrators. The truth is that all people are both good and bad.

"This book looks back at that time in history, not with a traditional mainstream perspective—but with a wholistic perspective. Has the readability of a novel, a historical novel—but this is no novel. It is historical truth. A rewarding book."

Justine Clegg, CNM, Director
Midwifery Program, Medical Center Campus
Miami-Dade Community College
South Miami, Florida

"Dramatic. Reads like a good novel. As engaging as a film documentary. Today we have television and other media coverage of earthquakes, but such coverage was not available back in 1811-12.

"This book has woven together the people, places and events of that era so vividly that the New Madrid earthquakes are brought back to life—like the live coverage of a California quake today that keeps you glued to the tube. An experience. A walk through history.

"The Native American history and stories of Chief Tecumseh make this relevant reading for everyone in the country. The chapter describing recent quakes in the Midwest serves as a useful warning that they could shake again.

"Overall, a very good book."

James Comienski
High School Earth Science Teacher
Bay Village, Ohio

What People Say about this book . . .

"What an enlightening book! Very well done. So easy to read. So well written. So good! A thorough chronological presentation of the history of the New Madrid earthquakes presented from a professional standpoint. It's hard to state complex things so simply, yet this is a book each of us can understand and enjoy. Fabulous! A delight to read!"

Dr. Grant Hedgpeth, Optometrist
Amway Crown Direct Distributor
Rancho Cucamonga, California

"A masterful job of research and communication. I wish to endorse this book warmly to future readers. All Americans should be better informed on this subject. All Midwesterners, in particular, should have a vital interest in this book.

"Fascinating. Very readable language. Deals with much more than just the New Madrid earthquakes. Lives of the settlers are vividly portrayed—the trials, hardships, isolation, and disease. Almost unimaginable. And the lives of the slaves were even worse. The place of Native Americans, their relationships with the settlers, and their ultimate surrender are well told.

"It was particularly interesting to learn how familiar historical figures were connected with this cataclysmic event—men like Thomas Jefferson, Meriwether Lewis, William Clark, Daniel Boone, William Henry Harrison, Abraham Lincoln, John Audubon, Chief Tecumseh, and others.

"The earthquakes are pictured in clear detail. It is hard to conceive of a mile of river bank collapsing at one time, a whole island disappearing, or the Mississippi river running backwards.

"It is interesting to read of the damage that can be done by even small earthquakes, sometimes at considerable distance from the epicenter. The need and means of mitigation and family safety are appropriate conclusions to a fine publication.

" Congratulations! *The Earthquake America Forgot* is Intriguing! Delightful! Well done!"

James P. Thogmorton, Dean Emeritus
Central Methodist College
Fayette, Missouri

"What an ambitious effort! These authors, scientists by profession, have turned the true story of a series of little-remembered 19th century earthquakes into an adventure beyond what any history book could give us.

"With painstaking research, they have unearthed (no pun intended) the details of life in the old Midwest, from Rebecca and Daniel Boone's dream house (nearly destroyed by the earthquakes) to the incestuous family tree of Presidents—linking these details by a narrative replete with birth, murder, Native American heroes, and steamboat rides down the Mississippi. The common thread that ties is the New Madrid fault whose 1811-12 earthquakes ripple through Mid-America—and our hearts—like the main character in a novel. A marvelous tale!"

Alice Gilgoff, Author of Home Birth Book
(Bergin & Garvey Publishers)
Douglaston, New York

"Outstanding! A Great book! This volume goes much further than any previous publication on the New Madrid earthquakes. Filled with information—An encyclopedic historical narrative that not only recounts the great quakes, but also places them in the context of 19th century American history.

"Although both scientists, one of the authors must also be a historian! It is wonderful how they have taken the great comet of 1811, thrown in a little astronomy and Egyptian history, Tecumseh's wonderful prophecies, President James Madison, Thomas Jefferson's nephews, the *Steamship New Orleans*, animal behavior, the Legend of Chief Reelfoot, and a myriad array of other materials that are seemingly unfathomable. Your bibliography is extremely valuable.

"The New Madrid Seismic Zone is 'the world's greatest earthquake laboratory' and is as seismically important as Los Angeles, San Francisco or Tokyo. This book will be a primary source of information for all future presentations on the New Madrid earthquakes. I greatly value this work. It has been extremely useful to me in my field. Comprehensive. Helpful. Inspiring. Eloquent!"

Tim Keel, Professional Speaker & Historian
TMK Illustrated Lectures
Osceola, Indiana

What People Say about this book . . .

"An uplifting book! A good read! A real page-turner.

"I am a Californian, and we Californians do love our land surfing. (That's what we like to call it when we ride out a wave-maker.) This book is a must-read, in part because of the fascinating information about the New Madrid quakes . . . but also because of the detailed living history of the 1800's. The seismic events are all the more interesting because of the human dimensions detailed by Dr. Stewart and Dr. Knox.

"What did Thomas Jefferson, Chief Tecumseh, Daniel Boone, and Abraham Lincoln have in common? All their lives were touched by a virtually unremembered series of seismic events that occurred in a place most of us never heard of. We are talking BIG here. The largest single event was more powerful than ANY of our puny California quakes. The whole seismic sequence was unparalleled anywhere on earth for at least two thousand years!

"This is a book about history, genealogy, medicine, American Indians, geography, economics, steamboats, European royalty, land deals, expansionism, river pirates, disappearing islands, birth, death, destruction, survival, and life itself . . . Don't Miss It!

"Yes, it is an earthquake book, but it is also much, much more. I couldn't put it down. It reads like a techno-thriller, but with historical fact and modern science thrown in. Give this book a chance. It will reward you richly."

Jay Hathaway, Executive Director
Natural Childbirth Academy
Sherman Oaks, California

"Wonderful Imagery. The book makes it easy to visualize what was happening. Colorful use of adjectives. I could picture everything in my mind."

Laurie Koenig, College Student
Jackson, Missouri

"My husband and I both greatly enjoyed *The Earthquake America Forgot*. The research involved has clearly occupied many years of the authors' lives. You might wonder why a person living in the Hawaiian Islands, so far from the New Madrid fault, would like such a book. The answer is that it reads like a good novel.

"Hawaii is a place frequented by earthquakes, hurricanes, tropical storms and tsunamis. Those who live in the path of such potential disasters revere the earth and it's power. It is fascinating to read how others have coped with the loss of life and land, like those who endured the New Madrid earthquakes. These experiences hold many lessons for all people.

"The authors have woven a wonderful narrative, rich with the fabric of everyday people and their lives. Thoroughly enjoyable. I was caught up in the story. This book will surely capture the interest of many everywhere, including the people of the Hawaiian Islands."

Jahaan Martin, Wife and Mother
Honolulu, Hawaii

"This book is great. The kind you can't put down. Anyone would enjoy this book regardless of where they live."

Melanie Ice
New Madrid, Missouri

"Reference books usually treat the New Madrid earthquakes as a footnote of history, but David Stewart and Ray Knox bring these earthquakes vividly to life in their book *The Earthquake America Forgot*.

"They carefully document not only the quakes, damage, and aftermath, but also the historical, cultural, and religious background of the region and era. The chapters about earthquake damage patterns and earthquake survival are valuable reading for all of us.

"One of the most fascinating books I have read in a long time."

Rick Soulier, Adjunct Faculty
Department of English
Utah Valley State College
Orem, Utah

G·R
GUTENBERG-RICHTER
PUBLICATIONS

What People Say about this book . . .

"At last, a treatment of the New Madrid earthquakes that places them into human and historical perspective. Authors Stewart and Knox have provided us with information with which we readily identify, and, at the same time, we gain an understanding of what the inhabitants experienced at the time—considering them as humans rather than statistics.

"This book graphically brings home the very important message that victims of the next large New Madrid earthquake can suffer greatly unless they start preparedness measures now.

"Dr. Stewart and Dr. Knox are to be complimented for their pioneering scientific treatment of the damaging effects of small earthquakes—which are more common than major ones in the Midwest.

"This text provides key information, not only to inhabitants of the New Madrid Fault Zone, but to earthquake program managers and emergency response personnel everywhere."

Daniel J. Cicirello
Earthquake Program Manager
State of Arkansas

"Geology, history, geography, and genealogy, all in one book—but with a personal touch. It gave me an 'everyday' view of what the people went through during this time. I especially enjoyed the Native American stories. Good work!"

Ginnie Felch, Midwife
Cascade, Wisconsin

"*The Earthquake America Forgot* is anything but a boring scientific journal. While the authors went to great length to make sure the book was as scientifically and historically correct as possible, they captivate their audience by entertwining true stories told as tales—stories involving Thomas Jefferson, Chief Tecumseh, Daniel Boone, and many other colorful American figures of the time.

"This book really should be made into a Hollywood movie. The natural disasters occasioned by this great earthquake would even make Hollywood tremble.

"Besides the spell-binding story told by the authors, they also show a sincere desire to warn and make us aware that it could happen again. Readiness and preparedness are the keys to survival.

"Take this book, sit back, and enjoy a truly tantalizing tale of American history."

Mike Pender,, Landscape Artist
Classic Gardens & Landscape
Birmingham, Alabama

"I only meant to read a little bit, but once I started I was hooked. I had work to do for my classes the next day, but instead there I sat reading this book sitting, literally, on the edge of my seat for hours late into the night. I couldn't seem to put it down. It is really good.

"The next day I could hardly pass the coffee table without picking it up for another snatch, and then another, and another. It is hard to read in snatches. You want to devour it all right now!

"I can hardly wait to introduce this book to my fifth graders. It contains so many fascinating tidbits, and it ties together that time in America in such an interesting and unforgettable way. This is history presented in a style that students will never forget. It would behoove any teacher to use this book."

Barbara Wallace Stevens
Elementary Teacher
Seattle, Washington

"A great case study filled with fascinating historical references and rich descriptive details. Informative. Scientific. Practical.

"Planners, decision-makers, scientists, lay-persons, and curious readers everywhere should find this book both entertaining and thought provoking."

J.E. Martin, M.P.H.
Honolulu, Hawaii

"Easy readability. The words of common sense seemed to leap out of the pages of the chapter on protecting yourself and family. Not a book you could put down very readily."

Judy Sellers
Caruthersville, Missouri

GR GUTENBERG-RICHTER PUBLICATIONS

Money-Back Guarantee   **ORDER FORM**   Earthquake Hazard Warranty

ISBN	Code	Title	Author(s)	Price	Qty	Total

BOOKS:

ISBN	Code	Title	Author(s)	Price	Qty	Total
0-934426-45-7	(EAF)	The Earthquake America Forgot	Stewart/Knox	$ 29.95	___	___
0-934426-54-6	(NWA)	The Earthquake that Never Went Away	Stewart/Knox	19.95	___	___
0-934426-42-2	(FFG)	The New Madrid Fault Finders Guide	Stewart/Knox	14.95	___	___
0-934426-49-X	(NMF)	The New Madrid Earthquake	Fuller	13.95	___	___
0-8262-0344-2	(NMP)	The New Madrid Earthquakes	Penick	13.95	___	___
0-934426-50-3	(CUS)	Effects of Earthquakes in Central U.S.	Nuttli	8.95	___	___
0-934426-53-8	(DAL)	Damages & Losses from Future Quakes	Stewart	FREE*	___	___

* The book DAL is FREE, but Please enclose $3.00 shipping.

35 mm COLOR SLIDES:

ISBN	Code	Title	Author(s)	Price	Qty	Total
0-934426-51-1	(SET)	150 EQ Slides on the New Madrid Fault	Stewart/Knox	$180.00	___	___
	(SGL)	Single Slides (Specify by numbers given in NWA)		4.00 ea	___	___

OTHER ITEMS:

Code	Title	Author(s)	Price	Qty	Total
(EQG)	Earthquake Guide for Home and Office	Dillard/Stewart	FREE**	___	___
(LIQ)	How to Make Your Own Liquefaction Model	Stewart	FREE**	___	___

**Please enclose $1.00 shipping unless request is accompanied with purchase.

GET A COMPLETE NEW MADRID EARTHQUAKE LIBRARY & SAVE $20–$40

All seven books listed above (A $102 Value) • Save $20   ONLY $ 82.00 ___ ___

All seven books plus full set of 150 slides ($282 Value) • Save $40   ONLY 242.00 ___ ___

SUBTOTAL _____

SHIPPING CHARGES: (complete international shipping info on p. 360 of EAF)

Books: (for USA , Mexico & Canada) $3 for first book, $1.50 for 2nd book, $1.00 per book thereafter.
150 Slide Set: (for USA) $8.00. (For Mexico & Canada) $10.00 (Other Countries) $35.00 for Air Parcel Post.
Single Slides: (for USA, Mexico & Canada) No additional charge. (Other Countries) Add $1.00 per slide.
Complete Libraries: (for USA, Mexico & Canada) Books only, $8.00.   Books and Slide Set, $15.00.

SHIPPING _____

6% SALES TAX (MO Residents Only) _____

NOTE: Prices Subject to Change Without Notice   **TOTAL** _____

NAME _____

COMPANY _____

CITY _____ STATE _____ ZIP _____

COUNTRY (if outside the U.S.A.) _____

❑ Enclosed is Check, Cash or Money Order in Amount of _____
❑ Please Charge to my VISA or MASTER CARD
❑ VISA   ❑ MASTER CARD   Expiration Date _____

VISA   **MasterCard**

Card Number _____ Signature _____

• Please Make Checks or Money Orders to: Gutenberg-Richter. Enclose with Order and Send To: •
Gutenberg-Richter, Rt. 1, Box 646, Marble Hill, MO 63764 USA
☎ **For Telephone Orders Use Toll Free Number: 1-800-758-8629** ☎

What People Say about this book . . .

"The best book I have ever read on the New Madrid earthquakes. It is in a class of its own. No comparison to any other publication. Other books are so deadly dull—factual and statistical, but this one is colorful, fascinating, and exciting—yet factual, too.

Fun to read. But scary, too. Horrible when you realize it is not fiction. A real horror story. Like a Stephen King Novel. I couldn't put it down.

"This is the book we have all been waiting for."

Virginia Carlson, Director Emeritus
New Madrid Historical Museum
New Madrid, Missouri

"This book puts it all together. Descriptions of the New Madrid area are so realistic I immediately wanted to take a tour."

Alberta Hardin, Elementary Teacher
Qulin, Missouri

"The book is appropriately titled since the New Madrid earthquakes have left so much evidence yet have received so little attention compared to more recent earthquakes.

"I thoroughly enjoyed the book—cover to cover. Having visited some of the sites mentioned in the book has given me a greater appreciation of what people at that time in that area went through. The book has effectively combined historical facts and paleoseismic evidences into an easy-to-read, non-technical and lively story book for the public. It is an important document on the impact of the New Madrid earthquakes, as well as an excellent historical book.

"The vivid stories of Chapters Three, Four and Five, made me feel like part of the action during the siege, the big one, and the aftershocks.

"I congratulate Dr. Stewart and Dr. Knox for making such a valuable contribution, including their other two books of the trilogy, which will help to increase public earthquake awareness and preparedness."

Dr. Alex Sy, Professional Engineer
Klohn-Crippen Consultants, Ltd.
Richmond, British Columbia, Canada

"I relished every word! I enjoyed this book not only for the geological information, but also for the local history, plus the reactions of the population to a literal ground shaking event. The reactions of people involved in natural disasters are a puzzle to me. However, Dr. Stewart and Dr. Knox outline the aftermath of one of the greatest natural, social, and historical disasters in this country with compelling and interesting detail."

William Hopkins
Circuit Court Judge
Bollinger County, Missourii

"These two geologist-authors have given us a fascinating work that not only describes historical figures we've heard about, but puts them right in the middle of the most powerful series of earthquakes ever recorded in the United States. 2,000 tremblers in five months, several measuring 8.0 or more on the Richter scale!

"Growing up in Southern Illinois, I feared tornados but never earthquakes. Perhaps those who live in the area now should give some thought to the potential for earthquakes. According to the authors, the area is due for a devastating major earthquake any time.

"But this is not a book about fear. It is a book jam packed with details of people and places during those anxious five months and how those people came to be there. I learned details about Daniel Boone I'd never read anywhere else. Did you know the Boone and Lincoln families intermarried for several generations? Daniel Boone was a blood relative of Abraham Lincoln.

"The book is full of remarkable nuggets of information. There is easily enough material for a mini-series on television. Enough stories for the writing of several novels.

"Making history personal and interesting, the authors have given us a wealth of information about a geological phenomenon that will repeat itself. The only question is when."

Roberta Scaer, M.S.S.
Co-author of "A Good Birth, A Safe Birth"
Boulder, Colorado